Accountability for Criminal Justice

Selected Essays

Accountability, the idea that people, governments, and business should be held publicly answerable, is a central preoccupation of our time. The criminal justice system, already a system for achieving public accountability for illegal and antisocial activities, has been the focus of much attention, and accountability *for* criminal justice therefore takes on a special significance. These eighteen original essays, most commissioned for this volume, summarize and assess what has been happening during the past fifteen years in the area of accountability for criminal justice in English-speaking democracies with common law traditions. Looking at the issue from a variety of disciplines, the authors explore accountability with respect to all phases of the criminal justice system, from policing to parole.

Philip C. Stenning is a professor with the Centre of Criminology, University of Toronto.

Accountability for Criminal Justice

Selected Essays

Edited by
Philip C. Stenning

UNIVERSITY OF TORONTO PRESS
Toronto Buffalo London

© University of Toronto Press Incorporated 1995
Toronto Buffalo London
Printed in Canada

ISBN 0-8020-0647-7
ISBN 0-8020-7601-7

Printed on acid-free paper

Canadian Cataloguing in Publication Data

Main entry under title:

Accountability for criminal justice

ISBN 0-8020-0647-7 (bound). ISBN 0-8020-7601-7 (pbk.)

1. Criminal justice, Administration of – Canada.

I. Stenning, Philip C.

HV7405.A3 1995   345.71   C95-931405-9

This book was published with the help of a grant from the Centre of
Criminology, University of Toronto.

University of Toronto Press acknowledges the financial assistance to its
publishing program of the Canada Council and the Ontario Arts Council.

This volume is respectfully dedicated to the memory of

Professor John Ll.J. Edwards
(1918–1994)

Emeritus Professor of Law and
Founding Director, Centre of Criminology,
at the University of Toronto,
whose great humanity, and whose life's
commitment to accountability for criminal justice,
was a source of inspiration and encouragement
to so many of us.

Contents

Foreword

The idea of accountability in government has a long history. It played an important role, for example, in the political and constitutional history of early modern England. Accountability was at the centre of the conflict between the king and Parliament in the seventeenth century, continued to shape their changing relationships well into the eighteenth, and emerged most clearly in the fundamental structure of the government of the newly independent United States in the Constitution of 1787. In seventeenth- and eighteenth-century England the social elite confronted an increasingly powerful central state that they feared would ultimately threaten their rights and liberties, their property and religion. The survival and the strengthening of Parliament as a representative body – and in particular its control over taxation – provided the vehicle by which the governing classes could bring monarchs and their ministers to account for their policies and programs and to bring the king's powers under the law. Much of the political history of the eighteenth century in England turned on efforts to preserve the independence of the House of Commons from the corrupting power of the executive and thus to preserve the ability of Parliament to hold the government accountable. Nor did members of the House of Commons themselves escape scrutiny by those they represented. The accountability of the British Parliament to the electorate was significantly advanced when newspapers won the right in 1771 for the first time to publish debates. And at various times in the eighteenth century radical groups in several constituencies attempted to make their members directly accountable by issuing instructions as to how they should vote on crucial issues in

Parliament – a radical attitude towards the relationships of members and electors that has been recently revived in Canada by the Reform party and has given rise to much discussion in Ottawa of Edmund Burke's famous speech in 1774 in support of the independence of members of Parliament once elected.

The institutions of criminal justice also came under radical scrutiny in the eighteenth century – and with the same intention: to make those who administered the law more accountable, in particular the justices of the peace who were at the centre of the system of law enforcement. The preliminary hearing into criminal charges by magistrates was gradually exposed to public scrutiny in the eighteenth century. At the same time, the power of trial judges was limited and their accountability for decisions in court significantly increased (and those accused of criminal offences given the possibility of mounting a more effective defence) when defence lawyers were allowed to take part in criminal trials for the first time. In addition, the possibility of bringing officials to account and of scrutinizing the work of those who administered the law, constables, jurors, judges, jailers, and the like, was considerably increased in the eighteenth century by the phenomenal growth of the press and by the public's evident hunger for accounts of trials and execution scenes and for biographies of notorious criminals – indeed by the creation and rapid expansion of a popular literature of crime and criminal justice.

Accountability is thus not a new idea. There is no doubt, however, that, as Philip Stenning says in his Introduction to this volume, the past twenty years have seen an increasing anxiety to bring to public account a wide range of institutions that have been hitherto impervious to such scrutiny, including institutions of criminal justice. Indeed, so extensive and pressing have such ideas become over these two decades that it seemed to my colleagues at the Centre of Criminology that it would be valuable to invite scholars whose work has touched on issues surrounding accountability in the criminal justice system to contribute to a volume of essays that might capture something of the range and character of what is clearly a rapidly unfolding process. The volume which has resulted, bringing together, as it does, essays written by scholars from a variety of academic disciplines, reflects the Centre's long-standing commitment to multidisciplinary research as the strongest basis for gaining a better understanding of complex criminological issues. We at the Centre are extremely grateful to Philip Stenning for taking on the task of organizing the project, editing this volume, and writing the Introduction.

We are also grateful to the Ministry of the Solicitor General of Canada for the financial support that made the project possible in the first place. For twenty years now the ministry has provided support for criminological research in Canada through its financial contributions to the eight centres and institutes across the country at which such research is carried on. At the University of Toronto we are conscious of the debt we owe to this enlightened support. It has immensely strengthened our ability to train students and to carry on a wide range of research projects. One of the conditions of the contributions program has been an obligation on the recipients to devote a portion of the grant to a piece of 'focused' research on a subject of our own choosing but one that would be of value to the ministry itself or to one of the agencies within its purview. It was under that rubric that we carried out this project. In some senses the essays that have resulted are our account to the public for their support. We hope that they will prove to be of value to a wide audience.

John Beattie
Director, Centre of Criminology, University of Toronto, 1989–92

Contributors

David Bayley is a professor at the School of Criminal Justice at the State University of New York, at Albany.

John Beattie is a professor in the Department of History and the Centre of Criminology at the University of Toronto.

Jean-Paul Brodeur is a professor and director of the Centre International de Criminologie Comparée at the Université de Montréal.

Mary Condon is an assistant professor at the Osgoode Hall Law School at York University.

Anthony N. Doob is a professor in the Centre of Criminology and the Department of Psychology at the University of Toronto.

The late **John LL. J. Edwards** was an emeritus professor in the Faculty of Law, and the founding director of the Centre of Criminology, at the University of Toronto.

Richard V. Ericson is principal of Green College and a professor in the Faculty of Law and the Department of Sociology, at the University of British Columbia.

Stuart Farson is a consultant and a sessional lecturer in the Department of Political Science at Simon Fraser University.

Andrew Goldsmith is a senior lecturer in the Faculty of Law at Monash University.

Ian Greene is an associate professor in the Department of Political Science at York University.

Laurence Lustgarten is a professor at the School of Law, Southampton University.

Mike Maguire is a lecturer at the School of Social and Administrative Studies, University of Wales.

Allan Manson is a professor in the Faculty of Law, Queen's University.

Roger F. McDonnell is a principal consultant with Parallax Ethnographic Research in Ottawa.

Rod Morgan is a professor of Criminal Justice in the Faculty of Law, Bristol University, and director of the Bristol Centre for Criminal Justice.

Frank Pearce is a professor in the Department of Sociology, Queen's University.

Robert Reiner is a professor of Criminology in the Law Department, London School of Economics.

Kent Roach is an assistant professor in the Faculty of Law and Centre of Criminology, University of Toronto.

Philip C. Stenning is an associate professor at the Centre of Criminology, University of Toronto.

Don Stuart is a professor in the Faculty of Law, Queen's University.

Philip Tetlock is a professor in the Department of Psychology, and director of the Institute of Personality Assessment and Research, at the University of California at Berkeley.

Accountability for Criminal Justice

Selected Essays

Introduction

PHILIP C. STENNING

If the decade of the 1960s is thought of, in the Western world-view, as a decade of 'liberation,' and the decade of the 1970s as one of conspicuous consumption and material consolidation, there is surely a case to be made for thinking of the decade of the 1980s as a decade of accountability. During those years, accountability became a cental preoccupation not just at the level of public and state institutions (Day and Klein, 1987) – whole systems of government were 'brought to account' during the 1980s, most dramatically symbolized by the tearing down of the Berlin Wall – but also at the level of private institutions (with a focus on the 'bottom line') and personal relationships (with growing attention to such issues as 'date rape,' domestic violence, and gender equity more generally). The notion that people and governments should be held publicly accountable for matters that have hitherto been thought of as falling exclusively within the private domain, or within the realm of government privilege, 'national security' or 'cabinet confidentiality,' has become a hallmark of recent history.

The arena of 'criminal justice' has been no exception in this regard (Matthews, 1993; *Optimum*, 1993). Indeed, because the 'criminal justice system' itself is ostensibly a system for achieving public accountability for illegal and antisocial activities, accountability *for* criminal justice inevitably takes on a special significance. The 'trial' and execution of the Romanian president and his wife on Christmas Day in 1989 shocked even many of those who thought their fate was deserved, not just because it was so swift and brutal, but also because it seemed to lack even those minimal vestiges of accountability that we regard as essential to legitimate criminal justice. As the saying goes, it is not enough that justice is done; it must be seen to be done. 'Seeing,' in this case, involves not just visibility, but accountability.

In this volume, eighteen original essays have been collected together in an attempt to summarize and assess what has been happening in the area of accountability for criminal justice in English-speaking democracies with common law traditions during the last fifteen years. With three exceptions, the essays were commissioned for this volume. The intent was to assemble in one accessible form a collection of writings by established scholars that would explore the issue of the accountability of all phases of the criminal justice system, from policing to parole. Surprisingly, given the modern preoccupation with accountability in the arena of criminal justice, such a comprehensive examination of the topic appears never to have been attempted before.

Although all of the contributors to this volume are academic scholars with a variety of disciplinary perspectives, these questions are, of course, of much more than purely academic interest. Of all the institutions of government, the institutions of criminal justice are the ones that most explicitly and self-consciously affect people's freedom and privacy, and this generates heightened expectations with respect to accountability – to the public generally as well as to affected individuals – for criminal justice decisions. In societies that purport to value liberty, deprivation of it without visibility and accountability is generally not considered acceptable.

The integrated approach to the issue of accountability for criminal justice that is developed in this volume allows linkages and comparisons to be made which are not so obvious from the more isolated literatures concerning, say, police, prosecutors, courts, or corrections, and provides the opportunity for some more general questions to be addressed. Have the political, social, and technological changes of recent years resulted in more or less accountability for decisions made in the name of 'criminal justice'? What changes have occurred in the nature and implications of this accountability, and are such changes evident throughout the criminal justice system, or more so in some parts of it than others? Has there been any discernible improvement in the quality or integrity of criminal justice as a result of changes in its accountability? Or, to put it more bluntly, do we know any more about what is done and accomplished in the name of criminal justice than we did ten or fifteen years ago, and are things any better (or different) as a result? Or is 'accountability' in this context no more than an illusion, a game of smoke and mirrors, which conceals more than it reveals?

At the heart of much of the discussion in many of the essays in this volume is an ongoing debate about the very meaning of accountability and its implications for the controllability and responsiveness of institutions. Fundamentally, accountability is about no more nor less than requirements to give accounts. It entails a set of normative prescriptions about who should be required to give accounts, to whom, when, how, and about what. But accountability also involves a set of practices, often rooted more in custom and power than in the formal law or rules. Much of the debate in which many of the authors of the chapters of this book are engaged has to do with the relationships between the prescriptions and the practices of accountability.

Not unexpectedly, legal scholars often see this relationship as a more or less direct one, in which the normative prescriptions dictate and determine the relationships and practices of accountability. If these are not as we might wish them to be, amending or clarifying the legal prescriptions, or inventing new ones, is commonly suggested as the principal solution. Social scientists, however, tend to focus on the relationships and practices as of primary interest, arguing for the most part that these reflect fundamental structures and relations of power and authority in society, and are only tenuously, problematically, and indirectly related to the corpus of relevant normative prescriptions.

Doreen McBarnett was perhaps the first scholar in recent times to clarify the precise nature of this problematic. In an influential essay published in 1979, she argued that the conventional socio-legal model of this relationship – in which laws govern and determine relationships and practices – was in fact a distorted inversion of the empirical reality. Through an examination of the rules themselves (in this case the rules 'governing' police powers to arrest and detain suspects) and how they are interpreted and applied in practice, she raised the possibility that the laws themselves are framed in such a way that they effectively undermine the rhetoric of due process of the law and enable the police, in day-to-day practice, to effectively determine the content and application of the very rules which are supposed to govern their conduct and by which they are held 'accountable' in the courts. Drawing on this important insight, Richard Ericson (1981a) later coined the expression 'account ability' to describe this enabling process, through which normative requirements designed to achieve accountability in the traditional sense of the word are used by powerful officials as 'resources' to 'construct,' explain, and justify their actions in ways that often preclude effective scrutiny and control by outsiders. As Philip Tetlock points out, in his essay in this volume, the distinction between a requirement to explain and a requirement to justify one's actions can be critical in terms of the different coping strategies that may be adopted by those being held to account, which in turn have different implications for individual behaviour and organizational goals.

Several of the essays in this volume draw on this critical approach to accountability. Ericson's chapter applies this perspective to the role of the media in criminal justice accountability. Tetlock draws attention to the 'corruptibility' of accountability standards, the ways this can in practice undermine the intent of norms of accountability, and the critical importance of the timing of demands for accountability in this regard. In a similar vein, Mary Condon points to the ability of powerful players in financial markets not only to shape the content of the very standards of accountability which are to apply to them, but to apply such rules in an enabling rather than a constraining way.

The relationship between accountability and control is a related theme that surfaces in many of the essays. As I have pointed out in my contribution to the volume, this relationship is especially problematic in the area of criminal justice because peculiarities that pose particular challenges to more general conceptions of accountability for government acts and decisions are claimed with respect to most of the traditional institutions of criminal justice. In the first place, despite the expectation that 'justice must be seen to be done,' many of the most critically important institutions of criminal justice (especially police, security, and correctional agencies) have long been noted for their 'low visibility' and for claims that at least some (and in some cases, a great deal of) secrecy is vital to their effectiveness. Yet, as Laurence Lustgarten and Stuart Farson both point out in their chapters, supposed needs for secrecy are frequently invoked in questionable ways as means to avoid or frustrate legitimate demands for accountability and control.

Even in the domain of the courts, where the values of openness and publicity have been most consistently emphasized in the traditional rhetoric of legitimacy, the so-called *sub judice* rule and apparent trends in some countries towards closing hearings to the public and the media for a variety of reasons involve implicit claims that openness and accountability must yield, either temporarily or more permanently, to the requirements of efficiency and effectiveness, and sometimes even to those of justice itself. Have these and other such balances in criminal justice been shifting in recent years? And if so, why? What has been the role of technology, and especially of the media, in influencing such changes?

Another major challenge to conventional notions of public account-ability for governmental decision-making comes from claims to political and other forms of 'independence,' which are routinely to be heard from key players in criminal justice, such as police, prosecutors, judges, and members of parole boards. While such claims are of course not unique to criminal justice, they certainly represent a very significant feature of it (Marshall, 1984: ch. 7) and raise important questions about traditional assumptions regarding the relationship between accountabil-ity and control. Yet they, too, as the essays by John Edwards, Don Stuart, Ian Greene, Anthony Doob and Jean-Paul Brodeur, and Allan Manson all illustrate, are now being challenged in ways that were largely unthinkable only a generation ago.

A related pair of themes that is featured in many of the essays in this volume involves the relationships between 'internal' and 'external' ac-countability, and the factors that facilitate or inhibit effective resistance to the latter. Here, two countervailing trends appear to have been pres-ent in criminal justice in recent years. On the one hand, as most of the essays emphasize, there has been a remarkable proliferation of external review and accountability mechanisms during recent years, whether they be civilian review boards, judicial councils, correctional investiga-tors or ombudsmen, inspectorates, or other administrative agencies such as human rights commissions, equal opportunities commissions, or government auditors. On the other hand, as the chapters by David Bayley, Andrew Goldsmith, Laurence Lustgarten, and Stuart Farson in particular illustrate, this very trend has raised significant new questions about the relationship between such external accountability mechanisms and the effectiveness of structures of accountability within the organiza-tions which are to be held accountable.

The suggestion, which David Bayley and others have raised, that undue reliance on mechanisms of external accountability and control may actually weaken both accountability and control, by fostering resistance and indifference within organizations, and by undermining internal mechanisms of accountability and control that might be more effective if nurtured and supported, is a troubling one which poses a significant challenge to prevailing policies and institutions of ac-countability for criminal justice. Equally troubling, however, is that the internal structures and social organization that Bayley sees as having so much potential for effective accountability and control are portrayed by others (such as Ian Greene and Stuart Farson, in their chapters) as providing the means through which some organizations resist almost any effective accountability and control at all. Together, the essays suggest that achieving the right balance and relationships between 'internal' and 'external' mechanisms of accountability and control in criminal justice will continue to pose one of the greatest challenges in the future.

Related to these last themes is another one that appears in many essays in the volume and that concerns the focus of accountability within criminal justice. The debate here revolves around whether specific individual actions, decisions, or incidents (for example, a complaint about the conduct of an individual police officer), or more structural, institutional patterns of behaviour and contexts (for example, discriminatory management policies in a correctional system), should be the principal focus of accountability for criminal justice. Many contributors have argued that the incident-orientation – which, perhaps not coincidentally, has always been one of the defining characteristics of criminal justice itself – of much accountability for criminal justice, has constituted one of its principal weaknesses, encouraging scapegoating of 'rotten apples' while at the same time deflecting attention from broader, systemic problems. The chapters by Kent Roach, David Bayley, Andrew Goldsmith, Stuart Farson, Laurence Lustgarten, Frank Pearce, and Mary Condon in particular emphasize how the institutional forms of accountability can be critical in determining the effectiveness of accountability for structural rather than individual problems. In a more general vein, Philip Tetlock shows, in his chapter, how modes of accountability can trigger coping mechanisms that may be either beneficial or detrimental to broader organizational interests and goals.

As Richard Ericson has pointed out elsewhere (1981b), in a discussion of internal police disciplinary systems, there are reasons to think that the predominant focus on individual rather than institutional accountability in the area of criminal justice may not be accidental. David Bayley's suggestion, in his chapter in this volume, that 'bottom-up' models of police accountability may be ineffective because they overemphasize the 'bottom' and underemphasize the 'up' (that is, they relieve managers from accountability for their own management policies, styles, and practices, which provide the context for the actions of their subordinates), is one that undoubtedly has relevance for accountability in other institutions of criminal justice. As Ericson would have it, there is reason to suspect that such systems foster forms of institutional (or at least managerial) 'account ability' that, in practice, all too often undermine the intent of formal accountability norms and processes. Such results often remain unacknowledged; whether this is because they are intended or because they are simply not adequately appreciated remains very much a matter of debate among scholars in this area.

Some of the essays included in the volume deal with areas not traditionally included under the rubric of 'criminal justice.' Philip Tetlock's chapter, for instance, explores aspects of the psychology of accountability that have been almost completely neglected in the various literatures on accountability for criminal justice; yet, as he illustrates, these aspects are just as important for understanding the dimensions of accountability in the context of criminal justice as they are for understanding it in any other context. Richard Ericson's chapter on the role of the media in providing accountability for criminal justice similarly addresses aspects of the topic that until very recently have received very little attention in the relevant literatures, which have tended to focus exclusively on the roles and relationships of the traditional principal players in criminal justice (police, prosecutors, judges, government ministers, and parole board chairpersons), rather than on the main purveyors of public information about the system. We may well ask, however, how our understanding of accountability for criminal justice can be adequate if we ignore the role of the media, knowing as we do that most public understanding (and misunderstanding) of criminal justice is derived directly from the accounts of it that are mediated and disseminated by the media.

Another inescapable feature of the context of criminal justice during the past two decades, which has significant implications for accountability in this area, has been the growing 'fiscal crises' of the state. For administrators of criminal justice the result has been that accountability, in the 1980s and 1990s, has come more and more to mean showing how to do 'more with less' (or at least maintaining levels of service without any increase in resources; see, for example, Doob 1993). Yet the demands for criminal justice 'services' have, if anything, increased rather than diminished in recent years, for a complex variety of reasons. Faced with these dilemmas, administrators and scholars alike have been forced to re-examine some assumptions about criminal justice that were previously taken for granted. Not least of these have been the supposed monopoly that the state should maintain over the provision of such services and the idea that, even within the structures of the state, criminal justice institutions have a 'proper' sphere, which is exclusively theirs and must be kept distanced, and be treated separately and differently (from the point of view of accountability and control), from other institutions of the state.

Recent re-examinations of these 'sacred cows' of criminal justice have produced some surprising – and to some, troubling – new insights. Policing, even of crime, is not done exclusively by the public police (Shearing and Stenning, 1987; Johnston, 1992); prosecutors do not have exclusive control over decisions about whether, and in what forums, formal proceedings will be pursued against those involved in criminal conduct (Levi, 1987); the separation between law and politics is not as clear as was once suggested – judges are engaged in making what can often fairly be described as 'political' rather than purely 'legal' decisions (Griffith, 1977: Kairys, 1982; Harden and Lewis, 1986: ch. 3); the private sector, whether through private policing, private justice, or private sanctioning or correctional systems, has much more influence in shaping 'criminal justice' than had hitherto been acknowledged (Matthews, 1989).

What is more, as Rod Morgan and Mike Maguire point out in their chapter, conservative governments, dominated and preoccupied by the interests of private business and capital, have been seen to be increasingly turning to 'alternatives' for solutions to the problems of criminal justice. Not only were terms such as 'downloading' and 'privatization' frequently heard on the lips of criminal justice administrators and policymakers during the 1980s, but the language of corporate boardrooms and management gurus began to infuse and dominate the discourse of accountability for state criminal justice institutions (Johnston, 1992: ch. 2). In the process, the taken-for-granted assumptions about the unique character and accountability of public criminal justice have been increasingly challenged and, in some cases, largely debunked. New players, such as public auditors (Canada, Auditor General, 1990: ch. 26 and 27; United Kingdom, Audit Commission, 1991; Andrews, 1992), entered the arena of criminal justice accountability. And it became clear not only that criminal justice policy and implementation is not the exclusive preserve of a limited and readily identifiable set of state institutions of criminal justice, but also that it is not, probably has never been, and probably never will be, the exclusive preserve of the state.

As Rod Morgan and Mike Maguire point out, the rethinking about accountability that has accompanied the advent of privatization in criminal justice is having an impact not only on the new 'private' institutions in this field, but also on the traditional state institutions, which now find themselves in market competition with the newcomers. The market imperatives come with a language of accountability that is quite unfamiliar to traditional criminal justice practitioners.

The implications of all of this for public accountability for criminal justice have barely begun to be explored, even in the context of particular sectors of criminal justice, let alone in any more systematic way. In this volume, an attempt has been made to stretch the boundaries of inquiry into accountability for criminal justice in a way that allows some of these new developments to be addressed. Thus, in her essay on accountability within the Ontario Securities Commission, Mary Condon examines a state agency that is not traditionally thought of as an agency of criminal justice, but which most certainly has major responsibility for responding to some very serious criminality. And in his essay on accountability for corporate crime, Frank Pearce reveals the very different conceptions of this phenomenon that activate private corporations, and he sets criminal justice within the context of a much wider range of options for achieving accountability for corporate criminality. In both essays, the focus shifts from traditional institutions of criminal justice and accountability to alternative conceptions based on fundamentally different assumptions, not only about what crime is and how to respond to it, but also about how the responsibility for such matters is best shared between the state and privately controlled interests and how these responses are to be accounted for.

The growing demands for 'self-determination' by indigenous peoples in many of the Western democracies have posed other challenges to conventional systems of criminal justice. In his provocative and insightful chapter on the quest for accountability for justice in Aboriginal communities in Canada, Roger McDonnell makes clear the ethnocentricity not only of law and legal institutions (including criminal justice institutions), but also of the concepts of the state, and of the relationship between the state and the individual, which underpin conventional mainstream understanding of accountability. While the nature of possible alternatives in this context is still very unclear – partly because the place of Aboriginal peoples within the wider society is still so unclear – this issue provides another illustration of why it is important to re-examine some of the assumptions about accountability for criminal justice that we most take for granted.

The cultural context of accountability is not only of importance in the kinds of contexts discussed by McDonnell, however. As Laurence Lustgarten, Robert Reiner, and John Edwards have all made clear in their chapters, institutions and traditions of accountability for state criminal justice and security agencies can only be properly understood in the broader context of the constitutional rules and conventions applicable to government in general in a particular jurisdiction. Comparative scholarship on the accountability of such agencies is bound to be misleading if it does not take the variability of these more general traditions of governance and accountability into account.

From many of the essays in this volume there can be little doubt that at the heart of most of our difficulties in achieving effective accountability for criminal justice are some very fundamental features of the official ideology about crime and criminal justice, and of the public discourse about them which it informs. These features are perhaps nowhere more eloquently captured than in that most enduring symbol of criminal justice, the blindfolded maid with the sword and scales, and the hallowed rhetoric – a 'cloistered virtue' as it was once famously described – used in referring to it. Implicit here are the characteristics attributed to criminal justice – remoteness, aloofness, awe, and unquestionable incorruptibility and purity – which have perhaps made it so difficult to achieve real honesty about, and effective public accountability for, criminal justice decisions. In the process, criminal *in*justices (such as abuses of power, corruption, discrimination, and wrongful convictions and imprisonments) have been protected, to an unconscionable degree on occasion, from effective scrutiny and timely correction. For many, the fact that such an overtly female symbol continues to be invoked to represent such a patently male-dominated set of institutions, has merely added insult to injury. The concerns expressed here involve not simply the male dominance of criminal justice staffing – which in most jurisdictions is also white male dominance – but also the 'masculinity' of the language of criminal justice and its accountability, which, it is claimed, effectively excludes the voices and experiences of whole segments of society (Finley, 1989).

While these symbols, and the ideology which supports them, may have constituted significant obstacles to the achievement of democratic accountability for criminal justice, it can also be recognized that in recent years they have been exposed to questioning and challenge as never before. Movements towards 'democratic' and 'community' policing, 'popular justice,' and 'community corrections' (Abel, 1982; Duffee and McGarrell, 1990), and towards gender and cultural sensitivity in criminal justice, have represented the principal vehicles for such challenges, and can be seen growing in the cracks in the official structures all over the English-speaking world. While their meaning, impact, and implications remain very unclear and much in dispute, their potential for transforming the nature of accountability for 'criminal justice' is not hard to see. And even those – including some of the contributors to this book – who harbour scepticism or outright pessimism about (or opposition to) such developments, might nevertheless concede that the very fact that they have been thought about and publicly discussed in recent years has had some perceptible impact on the ways in which we think about accountability within the traditional and official institutions of criminal justice.

One of the more powerful ideas that has emerged from these discussions in recent years is the idea that modes and mechanisms of accountability for criminal justice need to be devised whereby public accountability is more directly to the public, rather than always mediated by politicians, courts, bureaucracies, and the media. While 'communities' have often been identified as the appropriate level for such 'direct public accountability,' questions about how these are to be defined (geographically, politically, culturally, or according to some other commonalities) and what mechanisms might achieve the desired results remain very much matters of discussion and do not yet appear to have engendered much consensus. Technological advances, especially in the area of communications, would seem to open the door to a lot of new options in this regard. In particular, the development of so-called freedom of information laws, and of innovative strategies to 'empower' communities, would seem to be the ones to watch in this regard, although, of course, neither has been without its sceptics and critics.

Because the contributors to this volume were encouraged to work independently in preparing their chapters – with a view to broadening, as much as possible, the range of viewpoints and perspectives brought to the topic – the chapters are not focused around any single overarching intellectual or theoretical agenda. Indeed, if there is any single theme that can be drawn from the book as a whole, it is the rather familiar one that what we so carelessly call a 'criminal justice system' is hardly a system at all, but rather, as Hagan, Hewitt, and Alwin (1979) once described it, a set of 'loosely-coupled' institutions whose evolution is as often contradictory as it is systematic. While similar trends can be seen in the development of accountability across many of these institutions in recent years, change in this area has been neither uniform nor in a single identifiable direction. The nature and implications of such change are as often the subject of dispute as of agreement among observers and critics.

As might be expected, the post-modern penchant for 'deconstruction' can be glimpsed in some of the chapters in this volume. In the editor's view, however, it is the deconstruction of narrow and monolithic perspectives and conceptual understandings of accountability for criminal justice, which is accomplished by the collection of essays as a whole, that constitutes the most important contribution of the volume. The collection represents an important beginning in this regard that, if the trends highlighted in the book and in this Introduction are indeed occurring, is long overdue and much needed as a basis for developing new prescriptions, practices, and understandings of accountability (and 'account ability') for criminal justice in the future. We hope that others will be encouraged to take up these challenges from where the contributors of this volume have left off.

Mechanisms of accountability for the criminal justice institutions in the various countries that are considered by the authors of this volume are constantly changing, with innovative practices in one jurisdiction often being imitated shortly thereafter, with or without variations, by others. The eruption of scandals can sometimes prompt feverish legislative or policy reforms that for years previously have been either resisted or simply not seen as important enough to warrant action. Under these circumstances, it is almost impossible to produce a collection of essays as expansive in their scope as these that will remain totally up-to-date in matters of detail even at the time of publication. Readers are cautioned, therefore, that in some cases, descriptions of specific accountability arrangements that appear in the volume may have been overtaken by events and reforms occurring during the publication process. Such unavoidable difficulties of timeliness, however, do not, I think, detract from the contribution the volume as a whole makes to our understandings of the major concerns, preoccupations, trends, and shifts in thinking about accountability for criminal justice that now characterize the last decade of the twentieth century, and that seem likely to shape developments in this area in the early decades of the twenty-first.

Accountability in Social Systems: A Psychological Perspective

PHILIP TETLOCK

It is a truism of social psychology that, when things go wrong, people look for someone to blame. This 'need to blame' is deeply rooted in human nature (Semin and Manstead, 1983) and may even be adaptive, at least to a point. If we can identify a culprit to whom we can attach moral responsibility, we may be able to prevent recurrence of the undesired outcome. If parole boards release dangerous criminals who subsequently commit violent crimes, we can hold the parole boards (or their political patrons) accountable. If police officers fail to intervene in suspected cases of domestic violence, we can hold the police chief accountable who, in turn, can 'turn up the heat' on the officers on the beat.

Accountability is, however, no panacea. Cranking up the social pressure to minimize or maximize one outcome (violent crimes per parolee, arrests for domestic violence) invariably has a host of spin-off effects. If parole boards become too conservative, our expensive prisons may soon be overflowing; if police officers set too low a threshold for intervention in domestic disputes, they will arrest too many innocent spouses. Demands for accountability in one policy direction will usually produce an equally heartfelt demand for accountability in the opposite direction. To paraphrase one of William Blake's Proverbs of Hell: We never know we have had enough until we have had more than enough (Blake, 1793/1965: 36). The history of social reform is, in this pessimistic view, a dialectical progression from one type of error to another, with no point of equilibrium.

This essay takes no formal position on the transitoriness or perfectibility of accountability systems. The chapter does argue, however, that designers of accountability systems should be alert to the evidence on how individual human beings respond to pressures to justify their views or conduct to others. Decision-makers cope with demands for accountability in diverse ways. Much hinges on the ground rules of the accountability relationship. Who must answer to whom and for what purpose? Is the decision-maker accountable to a single constituency or to multiple constituencies? Are the views of the relevant constituency known or unknown? Is the decision-maker accountable for acts performed in the past or for acts that might be performed in the future? Do decision-makers have the option of escaping making any decision at all by procrastinating or passing the buck?

In what follows, I present a social contingency model of judgment and choice that predicts how people are likely to cope with various types of accountability. I sketch the key cognitive and motivational assumptions of the model (all well grounded in the psychological literature) and identify the conditions under which people will respond to accountability in each of three qualitatively distinct ways: strategic attitude shifts, preemptive self-criticism, or defensive bolstering. I also consider the conditions under which each strategy is likely to prove adaptive or maladaptive to both individual decision-makers and the institutions for which they work.

The Social Contingency Model of Judgment and Choice

Psychological research on judgment and choice has traditionally been dominated by theories that isolate individual decision-makers from their social context. Subjects in laboratory experiments typically work in a social vacuum (or as close an approximation as the investigators can create) in which they do not need to worry about the social consequences of the preferences they express or the choices they make. Subjects believe they are anonymous and that they will never be called upon to explain or justify what they have done. If one accepts certain assumptions about human nature, this methodological strategy is not altogether unreasonable. Many investigators, for example, assume that people can be viewed as 'intuitive scientists' (whose major goal in life is to understand the world around them) or as 'intuitive economists' (whose major goal is to maximize subjective expected utility). If people are 'good scientists,' they should refrain from jumping to conclusions from fragmentary evidence, change their minds when confronted with contradictory evidence, and consider arguments both pro and con in gauging their confidence in their beliefs. If people are 'good economists,' they should acknowledge difficult value trade-offs, ignore sunk costs in deciding whether to stick with the status quo, and factor in opportunity costs in evaluating options. There is little place in either theoretical framework for exploring the social content, context, or functions of judgment.

Such issues are absolutely central, however, to the social contingency model (SCM), which is anchored in a very different metaphor for understanding human nature: the person as politician, whose primary goal in life is to maintain the positive regard of the constituencies to whom he or she feels accountable. The SCM begins where the traditional cognitive programs leave off. The starting point for analysis is the thinker – with whatever cognitive limitations he or she may possess – in an environment structured by institutions to which the individual belongs and with which the individual may identify. Whereas traditional research attempts to identify fundamental laws of human thought, the central objective of the SCM is to identify the behavioural strategies that people have developed for coping with fundamental features of the social world such as the ubiquity of accountability. The key research questions become: What cognitive and social strategies do people use in coping with demands for accountability? When do these strategies prove productive or counter-productive – from both the standpoint of the individual decision-makers and the institutions they are supposed to represent? In short, how effective are people as intuitive politicians?[1]

UNDERLYING ASSUMPTIONS OF THE SOCIAL CONTINGENCY MODEL

Given the crucial role that underlying assumptions play in guiding empirical work – especially in the early stages of a research program – these assumptions deserve to be spelled out in detail. The first assumption deals with the nature of the social world in which people make up their minds; the second, with the goals and motives that drive the decision-making process.

Assumption 1: Accountability of Conduct as a Universal Feature of the Social Life

Attribution theorists have long noted that in everyday life people are presumed to be responsible for their own actions (Jones and Davis,

1965). It makes sense to ask others for the reasons underlying their actions because people can monitor and control their conduct in accord with self-generated plans of action (another once heretical idea that is now widely accepted – Bandura, 1977).

The accountability of conduct is a societal adaptation to the problem of how to coordinate relationships among individuals who can observe, comment on, and plan their own actions. As such, accountability is a key component of the solution to the primal sociological riddle of how society is possible (see Scott and Lyman, 1968). Organized social life cannot exist without some regularity. This regularity is provided by shared rules, norms, and social practices (Weick, 1979). Accountability is a critical rule- and norm-enforcement mechanism – the social-psychological link between individual decision-makers and social systems. Failure to offer acceptable accounts leads to varying degrees of censure, depending on the gravity of the offence and the norms of the society (see Pfeffer, 1981; Tetlock, 1985).

Although accountability is a fundamental prerequisite for social order (Semin and Manstead, 1983), the specific norms and values to which people are held accountable vary dramatically from one culture or time to another. When people leave groups and join new ones, they must learn new rules for generating acceptable explanations of behaviour (see Day and Klein, 1987). These 'vocabularies of motives' (Mills, 1940) vary with both the micro- and the macro-context. The micro-context includes ideologies and values that characterize distinctive organizations within societies (such as street gangs, penitentiaries, police forces) and rules within organizations (such as prosecutors who are accountable to both the district attorney and the courts). The macro-context refers to cultural ideologies and values (should the goals of imprisonment be retribution or specific deterrence or general deterrence or rehabilitation?).

Assumption 2: People as Approval-and-Status Seekers

People seek approval and respect for many reasons, including both symbolic and tangible rewards and punishments. Theories of impression management and self-esteem maintenance have emphasized symbolic motives (see Baumeister, 1982; Greenwald, 1980; Schlenker, 1982). Especially important here are:

1 The motivation to protect and enhance one's social image or identity. One of the most influential motivational assumptions in social science

is that people seek approval and respect as ends in themselves. In the words of Linton (1945: 9), 'The need for eliciting favorable responses from others is an almost constant component of personality. Indeed it is not too much to say that there is very little organized human behaviour which is not directed toward its satisfaction in at least some degree.' Zetterberg (1957: 189) has even proposed that 'the maximization of favorable attitudes from others is the counterpart in sociological theory to the maximization of profit in economic theory.' A warehouse of findings in experimental social psychology attests to the influence of this view of human nature, including work on ingratiation (Jones and Wortman, 1973), conformity (Hare, 1976), and strategic attitude shifts (Cialdini, Petty, and Cacioppo, 1981).

2 The motivation to protect and enhance one's self image. This assumption has an equally venerable status in social and personality psychology (Allport, 1937; Sherif and Cantril, 1947). People seek approval not as an end in itself, but rather as a means of bolstering their own self-worth on important dimensions of evaluation (such as whether one is intelligent, conscientious, or likeable). There is a substantial literature on the ego-defensive tactics that people use to dissociate themselves from negative outcomes and to associate themselves with positive outcomes (Greenwald, 1980; Schlenker, 1982; Tetlock and Levi, 1982).

3 The motivation to acquire power and wealth. Social exchange theorists (such as Blau, 1964) have emphasized a third motive for seeking approval and respect: the desire to control desirable material resources. Researchers in organizational behaviour have been most sensitive to this motivational dimension of human nature: decision-makers in organizations can be fruitfully viewed as actors in competition for scarce resources within a rule-governed political contest for power (Pfeffer and Salancik, 1978). Much of what people in organizations do can be understood as tactical manoeuvres to legitimize their claims on scarce resources.

Any complete analysis of the decision-maker as politician should take account of all three of these sources of motivation. Unfortunately, we know little about the relative importance of these motives or about when one or another becomes dominant. Attempts to disentangle motives have, moreover, proven frustrating (Tetlock and Manstead, 1985). In most situations the three motives are closely intertwined; for example, impressing others will boost not only one's social image but also one's self-image (as advocates of the looking-glass self hypothesis would argue) and one's material standing in the world (one's social image largely determines one's interpersonal market value – Blau, 1964). Conversely, improvements in one's material standing will tend to enhance both one's self- and social image (as observers of conspicuous consumption have long been aware – Veblen, 1889).

STRATEGIES FOR COPING WITH ACCOUNTABILITY

The SCM thus rests on two hard-core assumptions: the first posits that accountability of conduct is a universal problem of social life; the second posits that people seek the approval and respect of those to whom they are accountable. These hard-core postulates raise a host of empirical questions: What type of politician is the average person? What strategies do people use to cope with demands concerning accountability from important constituencies? What are the consequences of these strategies?

The SCM developed here is an eclectic creation that borrows from a number of theoretical traditions. The model posits, for instance, that the cognitive-miser image of the thinker provides a useful first approximation for predicting how people cope with accountability. All other things being equal, people prefer solutions that require minimal cognitive effort. They adopt positions likely to gain the favour of those to whom they feel accountable (a coping strategy labeled here as the acceptability heuristic). The SCM also posits, however, that the solutions to accountability predicaments are not always so straightforward. In some situations, it is not obvious what the most acceptable option is. The model predicts that, when people do not know the views of the prospective audience and are under no pressure to justify past actions, accountability will motivate people to abandon their cognitive-miserly ways to become self-critical and multidimensional thinkers. Finally, the model identifies a third major coping strategy. When people have irrevocably committed themselves to a course of action, accountability will again motivate cognitive effort. The result will not, however, be self-critical thought. Rather, the result will be rigid, defensive, and evaluatively consistent thought. Accountability will prompt people to generate as many reasons as they can for why they are right and potential critics are wrong.

We should be careful, however, in making normative judgments of these three coping strategies. Many scholars emphasize the adaptiveness

of 'pre-emptive self-criticism' and the maladaptiveness of the 'acceptability heuristic' and of 'defensive bolstering' (see Janis, 1989). From the
standpoint of the SCM, however, there are strong normative cases for
and against each coping strategy. The theoretical challenge is to identify
the conditions under which each strategy is likely to prove adaptive –
a challenge to which we shall return after reviewing the activating
conditions for each coping strategy.

The Acceptability Heuristic: The Cognitive Miser in Social Context

The simplest coping strategy is to make decisions that one is confident
others will accept. This strategy is compatible with a view of people as
cognitive misers. Often the socially acceptable option is obvious, likely
to come to mind quickly, and likely to be bolstered by supportive
arguments readily available in the environment (especially true in group
polarization and 'groupthink' situations). The acceptability heuristic
allows one to avoid 'unnecessary' cognitive work (analysing the pros
and cons of alternative courses of actions, interpreting complex, often
contradictory, patterns of information, making difficult trade-offs). All
one needs to do is to adopt the salient acceptable option.

   Laboratory and field studies suggest that people frequently do exactly
that: they choose the most clearly defensible action open to them. For
instance, several experiments have found that negotiators who expect
to justify bargaining outcomes to the groups they represent have much
more difficulty arriving at mutually beneficial compromises than do
negotiators who are not under such pressure (Klimoski, 1971; Pruitt,
1981). The most plausible explanation is that accountability to constituents (who presumably favour tough negotiation stands) induces concern
for appearing strong by refusing to make concessions. Negotiators
respond by employing competitive bargaining tactics that, while
obstacles to resolving conflicts of interest, are effective in protecting
their images in the eyes of constituents (Carnevale, 1985). In a similar
vein, experimental work on ingratiation reveals the willingness of
people to tailor their opinions to those of others – especially high-status
others (Jones and Wortman, 1973).

   In experimental work, this author and others have documented that,
when subjects know the views of the audience and are not locked into
any prior commitment, they shift their views towards the prospective
audience (Tetlock, 1983a and b; Tetlock, Skitka, and Boettger 1989).
Subjects accountable to a liberal audience report substantially more

liberal attitudes (such as pro-affirmative action or anti-capital punishment) than do subjects accountable to a conservative audience. Moreover, most subjects do not internalize these attitude shifts. When we analyse the contents of confidential protocols of thought, accountability to a known audience affects neither the number nor the self-rated importance of the liberal and conservative thoughts reported. When attitudes were assessed in a later follow-up interview, there was virtually no evidence that these strategic attitude shifts had persisted over time. Consistent with the 'elastic-band' findings of Cialdini, Levy, Herman, Kozlowski, and Petty (1976), most people quickly snap back to their original attitudinal positions. In these studies, people (intuitive politicians) look more like opportunists than ideologues.

The acceptability heuristic is not limited to laboratory experiments; it also operates in high-level policy-making settings. The political necessity of defending one's conduct is a key constraint on how policy-makers choose among options. In the words of Snyder, Bruck, and Sapin (1962), 'The decision to perform or not to perform a given act may be taken on the basis of available answers to the question, "What will be said?"' Consistent with these propositions, historical case studies of government decisions abound with references to policy-makers assessing the possible lines of defence against critics and opponents (Anderson, 1981; Goldmann, 1971; Graber, 1976; Snyder, et al., 1962).

Over time, the search for courses of action that can be readily justified may become scripted or ritualized, thus requiring even less cognitive effort. For instance, Meyer and Rowan (1977) have argued that the formal structures of many bureaucratic organizations reflect the 'justificatory myths' of the political environment, not the rational demands of the work. In this view, it often becomes more important to institutionalize practices that appease political observers than it is to get the job done. Accountability requirements (filing the right forms, going through the right procedural motions) are primary; actual performance, secondary.

In overview, the acceptability heuristic complements and fleshes out the cognitive-miser characterization of the decision-maker. The most salient consideration in many decisions is the justifiability of policy options to others. The cognitive research program tells us that people often use only a few items of information in making up their minds; the social contingency model tells us that decision-makers' estimates of the probable reactions of others will be prominent among the few items considered. The cognitive research program focuses on process (how people think), the SCM focuses on content (what people think). Although this may seem a congenial division of labour, the distinction is far from airtight. Demands for accountability not only affect what people think; they also affect how people think.

Pre-emptive Self-criticism

Although the acceptability heuristic can be cognitively economical and socially adaptive, its usefulness is limited to settings in which one can easily figure out what others want. What happens, however, when people do not know the audience wants, and they are not constrained by prior commitments? Under these conditions, accountability can motivate cognitive misers to think in vigilant, complex, and self-critical ways.

Tetlock (1983a) and Tetlock et al. (1989) hypothesized that when people know the views of the audience, they rely on the acceptability heuristic and simply shift their views towards the audience. By contrast, when people know nothing about the prospective audience, they need to think through the issue much more carefully to arrive at a defensible position. Accountability to unknown others motivates people to consider arguments on both sides to prepare themselves for a variety of critical reactions to their views. To test these hypotheses, we conducted experiments in which subjects took stands on controversial policy issues (capital punishment, affirmative action) under one of four conditions: expecting the positions they took to be confidential or expecting to justify their positions to a liberal, conservative, or unknown audience. In addition, subjects reported their thoughts (confidentiality was always guaranteed) on each issue prior to committing themselves to positions. These 'thought protocols' were then subjected to detailed content and structural analysis designed to assess the 'integrative complexity' of subjects' thinking on the issues: How many aspects or dimensions of each issue did they distinguish? Did they interpret issues in dichotomous, good– bad terms, or did they recognize positive and negative features of stands on both sides of the issues?

Subjects coped with accountability in two qualitatively distinct ways: strategically shifting their public positions on the issues (thus making the task of justification easier) and thinking about issues in more multi-dimensional ways (thus preparing themselves for possible counter-arguments). They relied on strategic attitude shifts (the acceptability heuristic) when they felt accountable to an audience with known liberal or conservative views. Not surprisingly, subjects accountable to a liberal audience expressed more liberal views, whereas subjects accountable to a conservative one expressed more conservative views. Accountability to a known audience had no impact, however, on the complexity of private thoughts on the policy issues. The reverse pattern emerged among subjects who felt accountable to an unknown audience. Here accountability had no impact on the liberalism–conservatism of the public stands, but had a pronounced impact on the complexity of private thoughts. Subjects were more tolerant of evaluative inconsistency (recognizing good features of rejected policies and bad features of accepted ones) and aware of difficult value trade-offs (for example, the need to deter crime and protect the lives of the innocent, the need to remedy past racial injustices without creating new ones). Subjects accountable to the unknown audience engaged in pre-emptive self-criticism. They attempted to anticipate arguments that critics could raise against their positions. This cognitive reaction can be viewed as an adaptive strategy to protect both one's self- and social image. Expecting to justify one's views to an unknown audience raised the prospect of failure: the other person might find serious flaws in one's position. To reduce the likelihood of such an esteem-threatening and embarrassing event, subjects demonstrated their awareness of alternative perspectives. The implicit message was, 'You can see I'm no fool. I may believe this, but I understand the arguments on the other side.'

The Rationalization Heuristic: The Cognitive Miser on the Defensive

The previous section focused on situations in which the desire for approval and respect motivated complex patterns of thinking. In all these situations, people had no basis for inferring the policy preferences of the audience, thus greatly reducing the usefulness of the low-effort acceptability heuristic. Another critical ingredient was also present. People realized that they would need to explain their conduct before they had committed themselves to a course of action. Pre-decisional accountability – combined with normative ambiguity – promoted vigilant analysis of options.

Other combinations of circumstances can trigger very different coping responses. For instance, imagine that people are accountable not for decisions they have yet to make, but for decisions they have already made. Imagine, moreover, that these decisions have led to undesirable consequences (say, lower profits, bad publicity, or employee dissatisfaction). Here, the same basic motive – the desire for approval and respect – will lead not to a forward-looking rationality, but rather to a backward-looking rationality – a defensive search for ways of rationalizing past conduct. The primary concern of decision-makers will be to portray earlier actions in the best possible light.

Tetlock et al. (1989) illustrated how a seemingly minor variation in the timing of an accountability manipulation can dramatically influence the coping strategies activated. In this study, subjects reported their thoughts on four controversial issues either *before* or *after* they had made a commitment to attitudinal stands on those issues. Some subjects believed their stands were private; others believed that they would later be asked to justify their stands to an audience with unknown, liberal, or conservative views. There was a strong interaction between when subjects reported their thoughts and the manipulation of accountability. Subjects who felt accountable and reported their thoughts after making attitudinal commitments reasoned in more integratively complex ways than both unaccountable subjects who reported their thoughts after making commitments and unaccountable or accountable subjects who reported their thoughts prior to taking a stand. Once accountable subjects had publicly committed themselves to positions, the major function of thought became generating as many justifications for those positions as they could. As a result, the integrative complexity of thoughts plunged (subjects were far less likely to concede legitimacy to other points of view) and the number of pro-attitudinal thoughts increased (subjects generated more reasons for why they were right).

It might be tempting to downplay the importance of these post-decisional cognitive defences. Post-decisional accounting, however, goes far beyond mere verbal posturing (Brockner and Rubin, 1985; Staw, 1980; Teger, Cary, Katcher, and Hillis, 1980). In a variety of experimental paradigms investigators have demonstrated that the need to justify policies that have worked out badly places great pressure on decision-makers to increase their commitments to these failing policies. This prediction follows from both cognitive dissonance and impression management theories; see Schlenker (1982) and Wicklund and Brehm (1976). For instance, in a series of business simulation experiments, Staw (1976) found that pressures to account for poor past decisions increased the rigidity of the policy-making process. One group of subjects (the personally responsible group) was instructed to allocate research and development funds to one of two operating divisions of a company. They then learned that their initial decision was successful or unsuccessful, and they were asked to make a second allocation decision. Another group of subjects received the same information, but they did not make the initial allocation themselves (this decision had supposedly been made earlier by a financial officer of the firm). The results revealed that subjects allocated the most money to the failing division of the company only when they felt personally responsible for having directed funds to that division in the initial allocation. Subjects apparently sought to justify a poor decision by escalating their commitment to it.

Staw's earlier work – inspired by the cognitive dissonance theory – treated justification as an intrapsychic process (people want to protect their self-images as competent and rational beings). A later simulation experiment by Fox and Staw (1979) focused on the political dimensions of accountability. In this simulation, subjects were placed in an administrative situation in which they believed that the board of directors (to whom they were accountable) was receptive or unreceptive to the policies they had pursued. Fox and Staw hypothesized that decision-makers would escalate their commitment to a failing policy when they were most vulnerable (low job security and a sceptical board of directors). The results supported these hypotheses. Decision-makers who were worried about keeping their jobs and fending off high-level critics within the organization were most likely to escalate their commitment to their initial decision and were most inflexible in defending their original positions.

There are many reasons to suppose, then, that post-decisional accountability – far from encouraging complex, self-critical thought – actually exacerbates many judgmental biases and defects of the cognitive miser. Demands for accountability sometimes motivate people to 'bolster' previous decisions, to be overconfident in those decisions, to over-assimilate new evidence, and to deny difficult value trade-offs, particularly when the trade-offs require acknowledging flaws in one's past decisions (see Festinger, 1964; Kiesler, 1971).

Hybrid Responses to Accountability.

We have identified an assortment of coping strategies, including strategic attitude shifts, mindless endorsement or organizational rituals and myths, thoughtful analysis of available evidence and options, and the rigid defence of earlier choices. The antecedent conditions for activating each coping strategy rarely, however, appear in pure form, but rather in varying degrees and combinations in any given situation. The coping strategies are thus not as mutually exclusive as presented here. In many situations, the views of those to whom one is accountable are neither perfectly obvious nor completely unknown. We have suspicions (held with varying degrees of confidence) about what others want to hear. In other situations, we are accountable not to one but to many individuals whose views may be in harmony or in conflict. Preliminary evidence from our experimental work suggests that these forms of accountability will trigger a variety of coping responses, including both the search for a least common denominator as acceptable policy and vigilant information processing to anticipate objections to that policy (see also Carnevale, 1985). In still other situations, we may be called upon to account both for actions we have already performed and for decisions we have yet to make. The views of those to whom we are accountable may be only partly known. Again, multiple coping responses will probably be activated; for instance, a search for a policy acceptable to key constituencies in conjunction with complex thought and the development of rationalizations that render new decisions consistent with previous commitments.

Normative Assessments of Coping Strategies

A widely held misconception is that accountability is a fail-safe cure to a wide range of social ills (Day and Klein, 1987). If the graduates of our schools cannot read, then we should mandate compulsory testing and link funding to performance on those tests. If prison crime escalates, then we should link promotions of prison officials to tangible indicators of success, such as a reduced incidence of violence. If professors are aloof and indifferent towards undergraduates, then we should link promotions to undergraduate course evaluations. From government bureaucracies to academia to the military to corporate capitalism, the clarion call can be heard: 'Hold the rascals accountable.'

Although one may sympathize with the frustration behind such calls, this simplistic view fails for a number of reasons. One problem is that most social indicators of performance (to which we hold people accountable) are easily corrupted. Teachers may teach the content of tests; prison officials may adopt new procedures for measuring violence that create spurious impressions of progress; professors might entertain rather than educate undergraduates. A second problem is that the criteria we use to measure progress are only probabilistically related to the objectives we are trying to achieve. The productivity of doctors is imperfectly captured by the number of patients they see or the number of procedures and drugs they prescribe; the long-term effectiveness of chief executive officers of corporations is weakly correlated with the latest quarterly profit figures; the long-term effectiveness of government leaders is only loosely connected to the most recent trends in crime, economic indicators, or international relations. By anointing the wrong standard of performance in our accountability system, we may wind up encouraging the wrong kinds of behaviour (e.g., rewarding doctors who examine many patients superficially or who overprescribe expensive procedures – in the process, increasing both patient mortality and the cost of health care). Or we may wind up holding people responsible for outcomes that are outside of their control (such as cyclical economic trends that increase or decrease profitability, or demographically induced trends in crime or unemployment) and fail to hold people responsible for outcomes that are under their control (for example, not rewarding doctors for practising preventive medicine that saves lives and money in the long run, not rewarding corporate leaders for investing in infrastructure and modernization programs that are critical for long-term competitiveness).

In designing systems of accountability we should, of course, be sensitive to both the corruptibility of our standards and the danger of anointing the wrong standards. The SCM underscores this point by highlighting the importance of characterizing precisely the incentives that accountability systems create. Each of the three major strategies for coping can be viewed as a reasonable response to accountability ground rules that affect the costs and benefits of the alternatives open to decision-makers. In addition, each coping strategy can be viewed as either adaptive or maladaptive for either the individual decision-maker or the institutions the decision-maker inhabits. In the next sections, the functional pros and cons of each coping strategy are summarized.

THE ACCEPTABILITY HEURISTIC

The acceptability heuristic is, perhaps, the least inspiring strategy for coping with accountability. This strategy does, however, have obvious adaptive value for the individual decision-maker. People, quite correctly, view conformity of opinion as a reliable means of gaining the approval and respect of others. Although limiting conditions exist (one should not be too sycophantic), we generally evaluate others more positively to the degree that their attitudes are similar to our own. We see similar others as more likeable and intelligent than dissimilar others (Byrne, Nelson, and Reeves, 1966), as well as more deserving of promotion (Baskett, 1973).

The acceptability heuristic may also have adaptive value for the groups or organizations to which the individual belongs. To the degree that group members practise this heuristic, it will be relatively easy to reach consensus and unanimity. And to the degree that group members feel accountable to constituencies who have a good understanding of the issues, decision-makers who take the views of these constituencies into account are likely to do a better job than decision-makers who ignore these constituencies. Indeed, under such conditions, the acceptability heuristic may check a wide range of judgmental fallacies that decision-makers never would have corrected on their own.

The acceptability heuristic can, of course, also have highly dysfunctional effects, from both an individual and an organizational perspective. From the standpoint of maximizing individual career prospects, a decision-maker who relies solely on the acceptability heuristic runs the risk of appearing uncreative, unnecessary, or spineless. From an organizational standpoint, decision-making groups that consist solely of practitioners of the acceptability heuristic are likely candidates for 'groupthink' (Janis, 1982, 1989). If no one is willing to voice unpopular doubts or misgivings, the likelihood of serious miscalculations may increase dramatically. Finally, just as it is possible for decision-makers to recommend the right solution because they are accountable to a wise audience, it is equally possible for them to recommend the wrong solution because they are accountable to a short-sighted audience. The acceptability heuristic may cause doctors to overprescribe drugs and tests for their patients (because they expect to be accountable to judges and juries who are susceptible to the effect of the certainty of hindsight) or it may cause the chief financial officers or corporations to argue against costly long-term restructuring that will adversely affect immediate cash flow and profitability (because they expect to be accountable to an investment community that focuses on maximizing quarterly returns). The acceptability heuristic implies that decision-makers can be no better, as well as no worse, than the constituencies to whom they are accountable.

Several experiments have illustrated the dysfunctional effects of the acceptability heuristic. For instance, Adelberg and Batson (1978) found that accountability impaired effective helping whenever the resources of the agency were inadequate to assist everyone in need and difficult choices were necessary. Accountability did so by distracting help-givers from the problems they were supposed to be solving and focusing their attention on the need to justify what they were doing. Accountable help-givers were more likely to avoid hard-to-justify, but necessary decisions concerning which applicants for aid (in this case, student loans) would receive assistance. They made a much higher proportion of wasteful decisions – giving ineffectively small amounts of money to large numbers of students.

In an experimental simulation of decisions of the United States Food and Drug Administration to permit drugs into the United States pharmaceuticals market, Tetlock and Boettger (1991) asked both accountable and unaccountable subjects to judge the acceptability of an anticlotting drug that (a) was or was not already on the market (the status quo manipulation) and that (b) according to initial research would save 300, 600, or 900 lives but at the cost of side-effects (hemorrhaging) that would claim zero, 100, or 300 lives. We found a significant three-way interaction between accountability, the status quo manipulation, and the magnitude of the expected risk. Relative to unaccountable subjects, accountable ones were especially reluctant to accept a drug that would impose suffering on an identifiable population of patients even if the number of lives saved greatly exceeded the number of lives lost. Moreover, this differential response of accountable and unaccountable decision-makers was much more pronounced when judging a drug not yet on the market than when judging a drug already on the market. Accountable decision-makers were also more likely than their unaccountable counterparts to try to escape the decisional dilemma that had been created for them (cf. Janis and Mann, 1977, on defensive avoidance). Accountable subjects confronted by close-call, cost–benefit decisions on a drug not yet on the market were more likely to procrastinate (by deferring the decision until further research had been done, although many people would die in the interim and there was little prospect of more conclusive evidence from the further work) and to pass the buck (to refer the decision to another government agency).

Reasonable observers can, of course, judge those effects differently. From a harsh perspective, accountability encourages moral and political cowardice; from a more charitable perspective, accountable subjects were appropriately circumspect about their qualifications to make decisions that would profoundly affect the well-being of others. Defenders of the judgment policies of accountable subjects may, however, have the more difficult assignment. When confronted by a drug already on the market, accountable subjects were almost as willing as unaccountable subjects to trade off lives saved from prescribing the drug for blood clots against lives lost from side-effects. Accountable subjects found the trade-off especially aversive only when they believed the drug was not on the market. The key difference between accountable and unaccountable subjects does not lie in moral objections to utilitarian cost–benefit reasoning; rather, it resides in the asymmetrical treatment of both omissions versus commissions and losses versus gains (Spranca, Minsk, and Baron, 1991; Tversky and Kahneman, 1982). Most accountable subjects were willing to save 600 lives at the cost of 100 when the drug was on the market, but they baulked at the same cost–benefit ratio when the drug was not yet on the market. The losses one imposes by changing the status quo loom larger than the gains one confers. As the evidence of the thought protocol indicated, accountable subjects were primarily concerned about the patients who would die from banning an available drug or about the patients who would die from side-effects from introducing a currently unavailable drug. This pattern of focus of attention is what one would expect from decision-makers who were preoccupied with justifying their choices and anticipating the cohesiveness, size, and anger of the relevant audiences. It is not hard to imagine the furor from patients whose lives have been saved (and might again be) by a drug that the FDA now wants to withdraw from the market (although that protest will be offset by support from the victims of side-effects). It is also not hard to imagine the protests of those who will suffer the side-effects from a newly introduced drug. When those who would have benefited from the drug do not know who they are (as is generally the case when the drug is not yet on the market), the safest political strategy is to procrastinate and defer responsibility. Only when this normally quiescent interest group is mobilized (for example, the recent surge of action among people with AIDS who seek out risky, unapproved drugs to forestall what is currently the certainty of painful death) is it possible to highlight the opportunity costs of procrastination and buckpassing (Graham, 1991).

In short, simple normative generalizations about the acceptability heuristic fail us. Whether one applauds the results of the heuristic depends on whether one approves or disapproves of the priorities of the relevant audience. Focusing on the heuristic as decision-making procedure, one's normative assessment is coloured by one's assumptions about whether the decision-making benefits (savings in cognitive effort, emotional strain, social controversy, and time) are outweighed by the potential liabilities (would decision-makers have done a better job if they had disregarded the views of the relevant constituencies and thought through the issues on their own?).

PRE-EMPTIVE SELF-CRITICISM

Pre-decisional accountability to unknown audiences often motivates people to anticipate objections that others might raise and to incorporate those objections into their own positions. The result is more evaluatively inconsistent, flexible, and multidimensional thinking. The normative question is: Does motivating integrative complexity increase, decrease, or have no effect on well-replicated biases in human judgment?

Once again, a highly conditional assessment is in order. Pre-emptive self-criticism attenuates, even eliminates, certain biases (belief persever-ance, the fundamental attribution error, and overconfidence), but mag-nifies others (the dilution effect, the tendency to pay undue attention to worst-case scenarios, and the tendency to take weak initial negotiating stands). From one normative perspective, pre-emptive self-criticism represents flexibility, open-mindedness, the sophistication; from another, it looks like confusion, vacillation, and weakness.

THE BENEFITS OF COMPLEXITY

Inducing pre-emptive self-criticism has proven to be a powerful method of eliminating judgmental biases that are resistant to other types of experimental manipulations and incentives.[2] I consider three examples here: belief perseverance, the fundamental attribution error, and over-confidence.

Reducing Belief Perseverance

The prevailing view of the person within the cognitive research pro-gram has been that of a theory-driven thinker who relies heavily on preconceptions in interpreting new information. Considerable evidence buttresses this view that people are sometimes slow to revise their initial impressions of events, even in the face of directly contradictory evidence (see Nisbett and Ross, 1980; Ross, 1977).

Belief perseverance is not, however, an immutable law of thought. Tetlock (1983b) found that accountability can, under certain conditions, prevent first impressions from dominating final judgments (although it cannot reverse the effect once it has occurred). He presented subjects with a long list of arguments from a murder trial; half of these cast doubt on the defendant's guilt and half suggested that the defendant was indeed guilty. He also varied the order in which subjects received the evidence: an exonerating/incriminating, an incriminating/exonerating, and a randomly alternating order of presentation. Subjects who did not expect to justify their judgment of the defendant's guilt showed a substantial primacy effect: early evidence had greater impact on subjective probability ratings of guilt than later evidence. Subjects who expected to justify their judgment of the defendant's guilt before viewing the evidence were, however, immune to the primacy effect. Order of presentation made no difference. Moreover, accountability did not eliminate the primacy effect by merely affecting the types of judgments subjects were willing to express (e.g., accountability did not turn people into fence-sitters who were unwilling to commit themselves to any position). Two lines of evidence argued strongly against such an artefact of response bias. First, accountability *per se* was not sufficient to eliminate the primacy effect. Subjects who realized they were accountable only after exposure to the evidence displayed primacy effects comparable in magnitude to those of unaccountable subjects. Only accountability prior to the evidence destroyed the primacy effect. Second, subjects who realized they had to justify their views prior to the evidence recalled significantly more information about the case than did subjects who felt unaccountable or accountable only after exposure to the evidence. A response-bias interpretation cannot explain these effects on memory. Taken as a whole, the data strongly suggest that pre-exposure accountability induced people to become more vigilant information processors who were willing to revise initial impressions in response to changing evidence.

A SOCIAL CHECK ON THE FUNDAMENTAL ATTRIBUTION ERROR

Many social psychologists believe there is a systematic bias in the process of perceiving persons: a pervasive tendency among observers to overestimate personality or dispositional causes of behaviour and to underestimate the situational constraints on behaviour (Jones, 1979; Nisbett and Ross, 1980; Ross, 1977). Indeed, Ross (1977) was sufficiently confident in the robustness of the phenomenon to label it the fundamental attribution error. One widely accepted explanation for the effect emphasizes people's reliance on simple, highly overlearned, judgmental heuristics in social-perception tasks. Heider (1958), for instance, argued that 'behaviour engulfs the perceptual field.' The person and his or her behaviour form a natural perceptual–cognitive gestalt. And what could be simpler than to ascribe behavioural dispositions to the actor that render the actor–act linkage intelligible (aggressive people behave aggressively, intelligent ones intelligently)? Nisbett and Ross (1980) noted the compatibility of this explanation with recent work on heuristics. Personality traits are generally the most cognitively available and representative explanations for behaviour. People prefer dispositional explanations because such explanations are typically the first ones to come to mind, and people rarely bother to consider less obvious situational ones. People are content with top-of-the-head causal interpretations of behaviour (Fiske and Taylor, 1991).

The most widely cited evidence for the fundamental attribution error comes from the attitude–attribution paradigm (Jones, 1979). In a typical experiment, subjects are presented with written or spoken statements of opinion that someone allegedly made freely or under situational pressure. The tasks of observers is to infer the 'true' attitude of the target person who expressed these opinions.

Tetlock (1985) conducted an essay attribution experiment that explicitly manipulated whether subjects felt accountable for their attributional judgments and when they learned of being accountable. The essay topic in this case concerned minority quota systems in college admissions. Subjects were sometimes confronted by an essay that advocated a quota system and sometimes by an essay that opposed such a system. In addition, subjects learned either that the essay writer had little choice concerning the position advocated (a requirement for participating in an experiment) or that the writer had freely chosen to take the position advocated. The final independent variable was accountability. Subjects either did not feel accountable for their causal attributions, learned they were accountable prior to exposure to the evidence on which they would be basing their judgments, or learned of being accountable only after exposure to the evidence.

The classic overattribution effect was replicated when subjects did not feel accountable for their attributional judgments or when subjects learned of being accountable only after exposure to all the evidence. Although subjects in these conditions made less confident inferences about the essay writer's attitudes in the low choice than in the high choice conditions, they still made quite strong inferences about underlying attitudes in the low choice conditions. Second, subjects who learned of being accountable prior to exposure to the evidence successfully resisted the overattribution effect. When these subjects were informed that the essay writer did not choose the position advocated, they refrained from drawing correspondent inferences about the writer's underlying attitudes from the essay. It is also worth noting that pre-exposure accountability did not make subjects indiscriminately cautious. Pre-exposure accountability subjects drew every bit as extreme inferences about the essay writer's underlying attitudes in the high choice condition as did unaccountable or post-exposure accountability subjects.

These results are difficult to reconcile with a response-bias interpretation. If accountability merely transformed people into fence-sitters, it should not have mattered whether subjects learned of being accountable before or after exposure to the evidence. It should also not have mattered whether subjects made inferences about essay writers with low or high choice. The specificity of the effects suggests that the accountability manipulation did not just shift some general response threshold; rather, it encouraged people to become more differentiated and circumspect thinkers about the causes of behaviour.

INDUCING APPROPRIATE CONFIDENCE

A substantial literature indicates that people are often excessively confident in the correctness of their factual judgments and predictions (Fischhoff, 1982). Tetlock and Kim (1987) investigated the impact of accountability demands on cognitive processing in a personality prediction task. We presented subjects with the responses of actual test-takers to sixteen items drawn from Jackson's Personality Research Form and then asked subjects to perform three tasks: (a) to form written impressions of each test-taker; (b) to predict how each of these individuals responded to an additional sixteen items drawn from the same tests; (c) to assign confidence ratings to their predictions.

Three experimental conditions were of special interest: no accountability (subjects learned all of their responses would be anonymous), pre-exposure accountability (subjects learned of the need to justify their predictions prior to forming impressions of any of the test-takers), and post-exposure accountability (subjects learned of being accountable only after forming impressions and reporting them, but not before making predictions and assigning confidence ratings to those predictions). The rationale for the pre- and post-exposure accountability manipulations was the same as in the belief perseverance and over-attribution studies. If accountability affects how people think about the evidence, then it should matter when they learn of being accountable. If accountability merely affects response thresholds, then it should not.

Several effects emerged. First, pre-exposure accountability subjects were more likely to recognize contradictory evidence on the test-taker's standing on personality dimensions and to offer multidimensional characterizations of the test-takers. The following remarks are typical: 'This person is friendly and outgoing in some situations, but not in others'; or 'this person likes the company of others, but will give priority to his work when push comes to shove.' Second, pre-exposure accountability subjects made more accurate predictions of how test-takers responded to the remainder of the tests. Relatively few people have such extreme scores on the affiliation or achievement scales that one can do a good job predicting their responses to individual items from global, undifferentiated trait labels. It helps, in most cases, to be more integratively complex. Third, pre-exposure accountability subjects reported more realistic levels of confidence than subjects with no accountability or post-exposure accountability. Moreover, this was not just a matter of accountability making people more cautious. Three aspects of the evidence allowed us to eliminate this interpretation:

1 Post-exposure accountability subjects did not display a reduction in the overconfidence effect. Rather, they reported confidence ratings that were virtually identical to those of unaccountable subjects.
2 The confidence ratings of pre-exposure accountability subjects were not just lower, they were also better calibrated. It is possible to partition the covariance between accuracy scores and confidence ratings into three additive components (a knowledge component, a calibration component, and a resolution component). The calibration component is the weighted average of the mean square differences between the proportion of correct predictions in each category and the probability value of that category. The resolution component is a measure of the judge's ability to assign confidence ratings to predictions so that the proportions of correct answers in different categories are maximally different – it is the variance of correct predictions across the confidence categories.

3 The superior calibration was not achieved at a cost in resolution (another sign that subjects did not just indiscriminately bunch up all of their confidence ratings at the low end of the probability scale in response to accountability demands).

A final result is worth nothing. Analysis of covariance indicated that when we controlled for the effects of pre-exposure accountability on the complexity of the initial impressions that subjects formed of the test-takers, the improvements in both accuracy and calibration were substantially reduced (although still significant). This result suggests that pre-exposure accountability improved judgment, in part because it motivated complex, self-critical thought.

POTENTIAL DYSFUNCTIONAL EFFECTS OF MOTIVATING
INTEGRATIVE COMPLEXITY

One might conclude at this point that motivating integrative complexity and improving judgment and choice are synonymous. That conclusion would be premature. There are settings in which encouraging integrative complexity, far from removing bias in judgment, makes matters worse. Tetlock and Boettger (1989), for instance, have shown that pre-exposure accountability to an unknown audience motivates integrative complexity (replicating previous studies) but also increases bias – in this case, the tendency to make inappropriately regressive predictions when diagnostic evidence is accompanied by diverse bits of non-diagnostic information (what Nisbett, Zukier, and Lemley, 1981, and Zukier, 1982 have called the 'dilution effect'). In one scenario, Tetlock and Boettger asked subjects to predict the grade-point averages of target students. Subjects received either only diagnostic evidence (such as, 'a student studies three or thirty-one hours per week') or diagnostic evidence plus a host of irrelevant information (such as, 'the student is a cheerful person, plays tennis three or four times a month, and has never dated anyone for longer than two months'). This information had been carefully selected from pre-testing; pre-testing subjects were virtually unanimous that the information was useless. Nonetheless, this 'useless' information caused subjects to be substantially less confident in their predictions. Moreover, accountability exacerbated the dilution effect. Accountable subjects tried to be 'good' processors of complex information and to integrate both diagnostic and non-diagnostic evidence in making predictions about grade-point average. By motivating integrative complexity, the accountability manipulation sent our subjects off on inferential wild goose chases. One accountable subject concluded from the information that the student is cheerful, that the student is therefore well adjusted and likely to do well in school; another subject concluded from the fact that the student occasionally plays tennis that he is in reasonably good physical shape and likely to be successful. Another subject concluded from the fact that the student had never dated anyone longer than two months that the student is therefore emotionally unstable and likely to be doing poorly in school. In short, pre-exposure accountability to an unknown audience motivated subjects to be more integratively complex, but it did not make them wiser – it did not make them more discriminating consumers of the information at their disposal.

Another example of the arguably maladaptive effects of integrative complexity comes from the Tetlock and Boettger (1991) study that examined judgments of the acceptability of a drug on the United States pharmaceutical market. Accountable subjects were much more responsive to the level of risk posed by the drug, and especially so when they believed the drug had not yet been admitted into the market. Analysis of covariance indicated that subjects who thought about the issues in more complex ways were largely responsible for this three-way interaction between the status quo, accountability, and level of risk manipulations. Examination of the thoughts reported by these subjects revealed a preoccupation with worst cause scenarios and explicit concern for what they would say to those who would be injured by their decisions. There is, of course, nothing immoral or irrational about such concerns. It is noteworthy, however, that these subjects were much more tolerant of the risk created by a drug that was already on the market (the status quo condition). Removing a drug with a high benefit–cost ratio from the market would antagonize those constituencies who currently benefit from it. Introducing a drug with an equally positive benefit–cost ratio focuses attention on those constituencies who would be hurt. In short, accountability pressures that motivate integrative complexity make people reluctant to take stands on divisive trade-off issues. Tetlock and Boettger (1991), for instance, found that accountable subjects (especially in the non-status quo conditions) were not only more hesitant to accept risks from the new drug, they also searched for ways to pass responsibility onto others (buckpassing) and to defer the decision (procrastination). Integrative complexity can be a sign of confusion, vacillation, and even weakness.[3]

THE RATIONALIZATION HEURISTIC

Post-decisional accountability often triggers defensive bolstering – efforts to generate as many justifications as possible. The normative costs and benefits of this coping strategy look like mirror images of those for pre-emptive self-criticism. The danger of defensive bolstering is that one will rigidly persevere with a failing policy in a vain effort to recoup sunk costs. By generating supportive cognitions, decision-makers who practice defensive bolstering blind themselves to changing policy in ways that would better promote their own values and those of the institutions they represent. Of course, it is not always a good idea to abandon a policy at the first sign of trouble. Decision-makers who practice defensive bolstering as opposed to pre-emptive self-criticism are more likely to stick with a fundamentally good policy that has recently run into serious short-term difficulties. There is a fine, normative line between principled determination 'to stay the course' and stubborn refusal 'to acknowledge the facts.'

Conclusions

Accountability is often the centrepiece of reformist programs. Although the urge to hold someone responsible in byzantine bureaucracies is understandable (and who among us has not experienced it?), such simplistic remedies beg the difficult questions: Who should be accountable? Accountable to whom? Accountable for what outcomes? Accountable for what purpose? The SCM of judgment and choice reminds us that (a) there are many types of accountability (indeed, as many types as there are interpersonal and institutional relationships) and (b) these different types of accountability create incentives for thinking and acting in a variety of ways that, in turn, have a variety of social and political consequences.

The SCM leads us to expect that reformers who view accountability as an all-purpose cure for institutional ills will often be bitterly disappointed. A multitude of things can go wrong. Accountability can promote mindless conformity in which decision-makers minimize or maximize the specified criterion for 'good performance,' but ignore spin-off effects. Accountability can promote procrastination as decision-makers try too hard to anticipate objections others might raise to what they are doing. Accountability can promote buckpassing as decision-makers try to duck responsibility for trade-off decisions that require imposing losses or identifiable constituencies. Accountability can promote cognitive (and bureaucratic) rigidity as decision-makers try too hard to justify previous policies. Finally, there is always the possibility that people will find easy ways of circumventing or corrupting accountability systems. We can rarely obtain perfect measures of 'good performance.' So we must rely on proxies (for example, judging police officers by number of arrests or citations, judging district attorneys by conviction ratios, judging judges by caseloads) – proxies that create incentives for deceptive bookkeeping, and sometimes even misconduct.

This argument can, however, be easily misunderstood as a counsel of despair. Drawing on the social psychological evidence, one can make a strong prima facie case that, no matter how one designs an accountability system, one is likely to make serious mistakes. Accordingly, I should close this chapter on a more balanced note. To argue that all accountability systems are occasionally dysfunctional is not to argue that all accountability systems are equally dysfunctional. To take a dramatic example, the checks-and-balance system of accountability in constitutional democracies can be slow, inefficient, and wasteful, but it protects us from the gross abuses of power that characterize totalitarian systems.

The contrast, moreover, need not be so stark. There is room for incremental improvements in the ground rules of accountability even within reasonably well-functioning systems. Leaders can encourage self-critical thinking by being more discreet about their own policy preferences; they can discourage procrastination by building time in as a factor in the evaluation of performance; they can deter sloppy, quick-fix efforts to improve productivity by monitoring quality more carefully in performance evaluation. The key point to remember is not that efforts to enhance accountability are doomed to fail, it is that every effort by those in power to fine-tune or overhaul systems of accountability will provoke reactions that, in turn, solve some problems, but create others. There are no final solutions. Accountability is ultimately about the exercise of political power, and politics is, by one famous definition, the art of the possible.

Notes

1 There are, of course, costs as well as benefits in shifting from one metaphorical framework to another in the study of judgment and choice. The

major disadvantage is the opportunity cost of diverting talent from the pursuit of 'normal science' within an established metaphor to the development of a normal science tradition within a novel metaphorical framework. In this case, I would argue that the advantages substantially outweigh these costs. There are two major advantages: (a) The politician metaphor highlights psychological processes that other metaphors obscure. It turns out that many well-replicated judgmental biases interact in complex ways with accountability manipulations. Moreover, it is not just a simple matter of accountability making things better. Accountability can exacerbate bias, attenuate bias, or have no effect – depending on the type of accountability manipulation and the type of bias under investigation. (b) In addition to identifying boundary conditions on generalizations from research inspired by rival metaphors, the politician research program offers us an alternative set of normative criteria for judging effects to be errors or biases. Effects that look like judgmental flaws from one metaphorical perspective often look quite prudent, even reasonable, within another perspective (these normatively controversial effects include the fundamental attribution error, the dilution bias, and ambiguity aversion). To be sure, it is possible to take this line of argument too far and to become an apologist for virtually every judgmental shortcoming documented in the literature. One can extend Quine's 'principle of charity' to the point of implausibility. My goal here is to strike a reasonable balance between awareness of alternative (metaphorically grounded) conceptions of rationality.

2 It is important to distinguish carefully among independent variables that, on intuitive grounds, one might suppose have similar effects. As we have seen, accountability is not simply a generic motivator of cognitive work. Different types of accountability can have radically different effects. Predictions of contingency theory need to be based on detailed analyses of the situational incentives for particular kinds of cognitive processing. Three examples underscore this point.

Superficially, cognitive tuning and accountability manipulations are quite similar. Placing subjects in a transmissions set (leading them to expect to communicate their opinions to others) might not seem very different from making subjects accountable (leading them to expect to justify their opinions to others). The two manipulations, however, sometimes have very different effects (see Zajonc, 1960; Tetlock, 1985). Subjects in transmission sets, for example, form more extreme dispositional attributions in an essay attribution paradigm than do subjects in a no-set control condition (see Harvey, Hawkins, and Kagchiro, 1976). By contrast, subjects given accountability instructions make less extreme and more discriminating patterns of causal attributions (Tetlock, 1985). Expecting to communicate one's impressions of an event places a premium on one's ability to generate succinct and readily comprehensible descriptions of that event; expecting to justify one's impressions of an event places a premium on one's ability not only to communicate one's opinions, but also to defend those opinions against possible counter-arguments. The former manipulation encourages people to suppress ambiguity and to present issues in sharp, polarized terms. The latter manipulation encourages people to express complex, many-sided opinions that are difficult to refute and easy to justify.

One might also expect an accountability manipulation to have very similar effects to a manipulation of decision importance. Although these two independent variables do sometimes have similar effects (see, McAllister, Mitchell, and Beach 1979), they also sometimes have quite dissimilar effects. For instance, the effects of accountability on overconfidence are very different from the effects of decision importance on overconfidence, as reported by Siebert (1974). She found that increasing the importance of the decision-making task exacerbated the overconfidence effect – a result that she interpreted in terms of Hull–Spence theory (the tendency for arousal to increase the likelihood of dominant responses). Obviously, given the many differences between the two experimental manipulations, there are many possible explanations for the diverging results. Perhaps Siebert's manipulation (course grades were thought to be at stake) was more powerful than the Tetlock and Kim (1987) manipulation and produced levels of arousal that interfered with, rather than facilitated, self-critical, integratively complex thought. Arousal is related in a curvilinear fashion to integrative complexity, with moderate levels most conducive to complex functioning (Schroeder, Driver, and Strenfert, 1967; Streufert and Streufert, 1978). The Tetlock and Kim manipulation may have created an optimum level of arousal, and Siebert's, a superoptimal level. It is also possible, however, that the two manipulations differ in significant qualitative ways. More important than the general arousing properties of accountability may be the specific cognitive coping responses activated by the need to justify one's views. Accountability may serve as a signal to subjects to take the role of the other towards their own mental processes and to give serious weight to the possibility that their preferred answers might be wrong. In this view, accountability does not simply motivate thought; it functions as a social brake on judgmental biases that occur in our less reflective moments.

A third example is the superficial similarity between accountability and the personal involvement manipulations employed by Petty and Cacioppo (1986), in their experimental work on attitude change. The elaboration likelihood model predicts that personal involvement will amplify 'dominant cognitive responses' to a persuasive message. If the message contains strong arguments, personally involved subjects will be all the more persuaded; if the message contains weak arguments, personally involved subjects will be less persuaded. Petty and Cacioppo (1986) have obtained the predicted interactions between personal involvement and other independent variables in numerous studies. The SCM, by contrast, predicts that pre-decisional accountability to unknown audiences will act as a check on dominant cognitive responses by motivating pre-emptive self-criticism. This type of accountability may actually cancel out the effects of personal involvement. The SCM is not always, however, in tension with the elaboration-likelihood model. Post-decisional accountability – which appears to motivate defensive bolstering and the generation of pro-attitudinal thoughts – may have effects quite similar to personal involvement.

These examples suggest that contingency theories need to specify the limits on the flexibility of processes of judgment and choice. Equally critical, contingency theorists need to clarify distinctions among independent variables that are often loosely classified as motivators of cognitive work or effort – including personal involvement, decision importance, transmission–receiver set, monetary incentives, and reversibility of outcomes.

3   As difficult as the normative issues that surround judgment and choice are those that arise in assessing coping responses to accountability in negotiation settings. One simple hypothesis is that those forms of accountability that motivate integratively complex thought increase the likelihood of reaching mutually beneficial compromise solutions to mixed-motive conflicts (sec. Pruitt and Lewis, 1975). Although one can make a reasonable empirical and logical case for this hypothesis, the hypothesis oversimplifies the normative issues at stake. Motivating the negotiators for one's own side to be integratively complex (to appreciate the concerns of the other side and develop compromises that take those concerns into account) may be a poor idea when one confronts an implacably hostile opponent who cannot be appeased. The search for a viable integrative solution in such situations may be as quixotic as are attempts to integrate all the stimulus evidence at one's disposal in the 'dilution' conditions of Tetlock and Boettger (1989). There are some negotiation contexts in which one is better off relying on simple rules for decision that protect one from ruthless exploitation.

Accountability in the Ministry of the Solicitor General of Canada

PHILIP C. STENNING

The office of solicitor general of Canada is one which dates from the late nineteenth century. In its earliest incarnation it was associated with the office of attorney general of Canada. The solicitor general was the attorney general's 'second in command' and gradually came to assume responsibility for particular aspects of the attorney general's responsibilities (Edwards, 1980: ch. 4; Stenning, 1986: ch. 5). This remained the case until 1966, when the office was transformed from its original position of 'relative obscurity to its present day position of high political visibility' (Edwards, 1980: 25). Under the Government Organization Act [1966] the solicitor general became a minister of Cabinet rank with responsibility for a separate government department, now the Ministry of the Solicitor General. Included within this ministry were three operational agencies: the Royal Canadian Mounted Police (RCMP), the Canadian Penitentiary Service (now called the Correctional Service of Canada – CSC) and the National Parole Board (NPB). To assist the solicitor general in fulfilling his responsibilities with respect to these three agencies, a small secretariat was formed, headed by the deputy solicitor general.

Although the ministry has undergone significant changes, its essential configuration has not changed. The creation of a separate domestic security agency, the Canadian Security Intelligence Service (CSIS), as a result of the recommendations of the McDonald inquiry's 1981 report (Canada, Commission of Inquiry Concerning Certain Activities of the RCMP, henceforth the McDonald Commission 1981a, b), added a fourth operational agency to the ministry in 1984. Another significant development which has occurred during the past decade, however, has been the establishment, within the responsibility of the solicitor general, of a number of oversight, review, and quasi-judicial agencies with respect to the four operational agencies. Thus, the solicitor general now also answers in Parliament for the RCMP Public Complaints Commission (PCC), the RCMP External Review Committee (ERC), the Security Intelligence Review Committee (SIRC), the inspector general of CSIS, and the correctional investigator. Following decisions made around the 1992 federal budget, the first two of these bodies are now in the process of being amalgamated into one.

Each of these new oversight bodies has a unique and distinct constitutional identity and relationship with the ministry. Indeed, as will be illustrated, the relationship of some of these agencies to the ministry remains a matter of some disagreement and controversy. In a 'Mission Document' published by the solicitor general's secretariat, the ministry is described as including the four operational agencies (RCMP, CSC, NPB, and CSIS) and all of the oversight bodies except SIRC (Canada, Solicitor General, n.d.: 2). In its 1990–91 annual report, however, the RCMP Public Complaints Commission categorically asserts that it 'is not and must not be regarded as an integral part of the Ministry of the Solicitor General or its secretariat' (RCMP, PCC, 1991: 154). The commission's claim to 'independence' in this regard raises fundamental questions about the public accountability and control of its activities and about the role of the solicitor general and the ministry in this regard.

Among the various agencies associated with the solicitor general's mandate, however, such issues are not confined to the PCC. Similar, but distinct, issues are raised by the RCMP's well-known claims to 'independence' with respect to its operational law enforcement decisions, and similar, but again distinct, claims can be, and are made with respect to decisions of the National Parole Board. The credibility of the correctional investigator in the eyes of federal penitentiary inmates has also been seen as requiring for the office a measure of independence from the ministry and the Correctional Service of Canada, against which the complaints it receives are usually directed.

In this essay some of these critical questions concerning accountability and control with the solicitor general's ministry are addressed within the context of some general conceptual issues around the notion of accountability. The chapter also reviews some of the approaches and initiatives which the various agencies associated with the ministry, as well as the secretariat, have taken with respect to these issues in recent years.

Methodology

The study that provided the basis for this chapter was undertaken in 1991, as part of a more general research focus on accountability at the Centre of Criminology, University of Toronto. This part of the study was of quite modest proportions and was in no sense intended to be a comprehensive review of accountability within the ministry and its associated agencies. Such a review would constitute a very major undertaking indeed, requiring far more resources and time than were available. The study had the more modest goal of trying to determine what were the major strands of thinking about accountability within the ministry (or at least among its most senior officials), what initiatives around issues of accountability had recently been taken or were being contemplated, and what were thought to be the major concerns and problems in this area.

To achieve this, senior officials in the secretariat and in the various agencies associated with the ministry were interviewed. The interview format was loosely structured and quite open-ended. In addition, officials were asked to supply whatever recent documentation on the subject of accountability they thought might be of assistance for the study. A great deal of information was received in this way from the ministry and its agencies. The author has also drawn to some extent on his own previous experiences as a researcher who has both been engaged in research in areas relevant to the ministry's areas of responsibility and has had direct dealings with various parts of the ministry over a number of years.

Because the Canadian Security Intelligence Service, and the legislation establishing it, had very recently been the subject of review by a special committee of the House of Commons, officials of this agency were not interviewed. The report of the special committee (Canada, House of Commons, Special Committee, 1990), the government's official response to it (Canada, Solicitor General Canada, 1991), and other documentation (such as reports of the McDonald commission), provided considerable information about issues of accountability and concerns in this area, however.

Accountability – Some Conceptual Variations and Wordplay

Interviews quickly made it clear that officials within the ministry think about accountability in very different ways. At its most basic, of course, the word 'accountable' means liable or bound to give an account (*Concise Oxford Dictionary*). In the English language, however, the suffix '-able' has two different meanings (see *Webster's Dictionary*). In one sense, it means 'capable of being' (as in 'retrievable' and 'manageable'). In its other usage, however, '-able' connotes 'liable to' or 'bound to' (as, for instance, in 'a punishable office' and 'accounts receivable'). In the case of 'accountable' and 'accountability,' the suffix is usually used in this latter sense – that is, liable, or bound, to be accounted for.

Some scholars who have written in this area, however, have taken advantage of this quirk of the English language to suggest that 'accountability' is more usefully regarded as connoting an *ability* to give an account, rather than a *liability* to give an account. The argument here is that whatever may be the theory or intention, in practice accountability becomes reduced to a mechanism that can be manipulated by organizations and their members as a vehicle for justifying their actions and avoiding effective scrutiny (see Ericson, 1981a; McMahon, 1988). In this context the statement in a recent article by the secretary of the Treasury Board that 'accountability makes the actions of ministers and public servants legitimate' (Clark, 1991) is particularly revealing.

Even when it is agreed that 'accountability' refers to a liability or obligation to give an account, there is great variation in the way people think about and classify accountability. The word is frequently accompanied by a qualifying adjective. Thus, interviewees spoke to us of financial accountability, legal accountability, moral accountability, and public accountability. But even when the same phrases were used, they did not always mean the same thing to all who used them. 'Legal accountability' provides a good example. For some, this phrase refers to accountability to courts and judges; thus, 'legal accountability' is contrasted with 'political' or 'administrative' accountability, the basis for differentiation being the person or body to whom the account is owed (courts and judges rather than ministers or deputy ministers). Others, however, used the term 'legal accountability' to refer to accountability that is required by law (for example, a statute that requires an agency to submit a report to the minister or Parliament), and thus contrasted it with what they termed 'moral accountability' (one interviewee said that he felt the ministry's secretariat is accountable to academic criminologists in this latter sense). Here, the basis for differentiation is not to whom an account must be given (as in the previous example), but what is the source of the obligation (the law or something else).

For others still, the critical factor for differentiating types of accountability is what has to be accounted for, or how the account must be rendered. Thus, financial accountability is often differentiated from other kinds of accountability, either because the spending of money is what has to be accounted for, or because whatever has to be accounted for has to be accounted for in terms of its monetary value or budgetary implications.

Such diversity of usage is both healthy and potentially hazardous. If two people are talking about 'legal accountability' but mean completely different things by it, it will be fine if they both know this, but conducive to considerable misunderstandings if they do not. If useful discussions are to be had about this topic, there will be a need for conceptual clarity.

Accountability and Public Relations

Many of our interviewees made it clear to us that there is a fine line between accountability and public relations, and that much of what is discussed as increased accountability is in reality increased public relations or public 'education.' It will be as well, therefore, to clarify at the outset the difference between these two concepts.

As already noted, the key element of accountability is a requirement to give an account. The stronger, and more enforceable, this requirement is, the stronger is the accountability. The paradigmatic case in this regard in recent years has been the development of so-called freedom of information laws. What these laws have done, for the most part, has been to create legally enforceable accountability of governments to interested members of the general public. Access to information about governments' actions and decisions (accounts) can now be required by citizens under such legislation. It is an example of what has elsewhere been termed (Stenning, 1983: 55–6) 'direct public accountability' (as opposed to political, administrative, and legal accountability).

As the elements of obligation and enforceability are weakened, so is accountability itself. When information is disseminated purely at the whim, and under the control, of a government agency, rather than pursuant to some enforceable obligation to do so, it is more appropriate to speak of public relations (or, more pejoratively, propaganda), rather than accountability. The key here is that it is the agency itself, rather than its 'audience,' which is primarily or exclusively determining what information will be disseminated, how, when, and to whom.

Law is not the only source of obligation for accountability. The highest constitutional form of political accountability in our system of government – ministerial responsibility to Parliament – provides a good example of this. The basis for this accountability is not law but constitutional convention (Marshall, 1984) which, as has been frequently demonstrated in recent years in Canada, is variably enforceable in practice. With respect to internal administrative governmental accountability (as well as external administrative accountability of governmental departments to the central agencies of government), administrative policies rather than laws are frequently the source of obligation.

In these terms, the notion of 'moral accountability' – a term which was used by more than one interviewee – is somewhat problematic. While agencies (or their leaders) may feel obligated, by pressures from interest groups, the media, or the public generally, to give accounts, it is questionable whether such responses can be regarded as accountability in the usually accepted sense of the word. More commonly, as one interviewee pointed out, agencies engage in sometimes aggressive public relations or public education (or 'communications') exercises precisely (or at least partly) to avoid the imposition of more formal, enforceable requirements of accountability. Again, this is a question of maintaining control of one's agenda and of shaping one's public image. As will be discussed further below, many of the agencies associated with the solicitor general's ministry have adopted this as a key strategy in their attempts to manage their relationships with outside publics.

The Legal Framework for Accountability within the Ministry

While law is not the only source of obligations of accountability, it is undoubtedly a very important one. Each of the agencies associated with the ministry is now legally constituted by statute: the CSC, the NPB, and the Office of the Correctional Investigator by the Corrections and Conditional Release Act [1992]; CSIS, SIRC, and the inspector general of CSIS by the Canadian Security Intelligence Service Act [RSC 1985]; the RCMP, the RCMP Public Complaints Commission, and the RCMP External Review Committee by the RCMP Act [RSC 1985]; and the secretariat by the Department of the Solicitor General Act [RSC 1985]. Each of these statutes contains provisions establishing accountability for the agencies to which it relates. Most common among such provisions are those that require the submission of reports to the solicitor general and/or to Parliament and those that require dissemination of information about the agencies' activities or decisions to the public, to interested parties, or to other government officials.

These statutes are important as sources of many of the accountability requirements of the ministry and its associated agencies. They are not, however, the only source of such legal requirements. A host of other statutes, too numerous to mention here, relating to such government agencies as the Treasury Board, the auditor general, the Public Service Commission, or the Canadian Human Rights Commission, also contain provisions that impose accountability requirements on the ministry and its associated agencies. Numerous items of subsidiary legislation (such as regulations or Orders in Council) also impose such requirements, as do internal policies, departmental rules and procedures, and standing orders (although the precise legal status of these latter varies considerably and is not always as clear as might be wished). Finally, court decisions and judicially established rules of court are sometimes also the source of accountability requirements for the Ministry and its associated agencies, especially with respect to their legal accountability to the courts and judges, in the sense that they define the extent to which such agencies can be required to produce documents and other information for inspection and scrutiny.

The sheer number and pervasiveness of these requirements of legal accountability reflects a fundamental principle of constitutional government in this country, which is commonly referred to as 'the rule of law.' This principle – according to which all governmental actions and decisions much be authorized by (or at least be not in contravention of) duly established laws – can only be implemented and guaranteed through meaningful and enforceable requirements of accountability. This makes the link between accountability and legitimacy very transparent.

Accountability and Control

Both the literature in this area and the study interviews have displayed a lack of clarity and agreement about the relationship between accountability and control. These are mutually independent concepts that are nevertheless frequently confounded, both in theory and in practice. While 'accountability' refers to a requirement to give an account, control refers to the ability or authority to give directions or instructions, or to influence decisions or outcomes. The relationship between the two has been captured well by two Australian authors who have referred to accountability and control as 'two parallel and interlocking mechanisms': 'The first is the mechanism of control, which extends from the controlling person or institution to the controlled statutory authority. The second is the mechanism of answerability or accountability. The answerability mechanism provides information to the controller, and *may* indicate the occasions on which the control mechanism is to be brought into play' (Goldring and Wettenhall, 1980: 136; emphasis added).

Frequently, however, there is an assumption that accountability and control necessarily go hand in hand – that accountability will always and inevitably lead to control. Thus, police (including the RCMP) have often argued for limited political accountability because they fear that accountability will inevitably lead to undesirable political control over the exercise of their law enforcement functions (powers as peace officers). Chapter 10 of the RCMP Public Complaints Commission's 1990–91 annual report provides another example of the dangers of confounding these two concepts, in the context of the ministry. Stressing the importance of the independence of the commission from political control (or even administrative control by the secretariat), the commission wrote:

As an independent body the Commission is not and must not be regarded as an integral part of the Solicitor General's Ministry or Secretariat. The Commission Chairman does not 'report' (*in the sense of being subject to direction*) to the Solicitor General, unlike the heads of agencies over which the Solicitor General, by statute, has direction, such as the RCMP, CSIS and Correctional Service of Canada. The Commission and Chairman are required under Part VII to send reports dealing with complaints to the Solicitor General, since the Minister is responsible for, and directs the RCMP. The annual reports of the Chairman must be submitted to the Solicitor General (as are those of the Security Intelligence Review Committee, whose independent functioning parallels that of the Public Complaints Commission) for tabling in Parliament. (RCMP, PCC, 1991: 154; emphasis added)

This passage reveals a clear, if not expressly stated, concern that a requirement to submit reports (an accountability mechanism) will be interpreted to authorize the exercise of control. To reduce this risk, the commission seems to be arguing that, despite the legal requirements for submitting reports to the solicitor general, it should not be regarded as truly accountable to him. Rather, the statutory requirement that the commission submit reports to the solicitor general, and that the latter subsequently lay these before Parliament, should, according to this view, be strictly construed as prescribing direct accountability of the commission to Parliament via the solicitor general, rather than accountability to the solicitor general as such.

Obviously, the correctness of this proposition could only be determined by a careful legal analysis, in which principles of statutory interpretation would have to be reviewed and applied. Such an analysis will not be undertaken here. The point, however, is not an unimportant one in terms of defining the precise relationship between the commission and the solicitor general and its implications for the accountability of the commission. Because similar legislated reporting requirements exist for the RCMP External Review Committee and the Security Intelligence Review Committee and have recently been introduced for the correctional investigator (by Section 192 of the Corrections and Conditional Release Act [1992], some clarification of this matter would seem essential for a proper understanding of accountability within the ministry and its associated agencies. In this connection, the difference between this provision and Section 95 of the act, which requires the minister to submit an annual report to Parliament on the activities of the CSC, is worth noting, as is the fact there is apparently no legislated requirement for an annual report to Parliament on the activities of the NPB. Section 5 of the Department of the Solicitor General Act [RSC 1985], however, requires the minister to submit an annual report to Parliament 'on the operations of the Department.' This provision makes it all the more important to be clear as to which of the various agencies are properly to be regarded as part of the solicitor general's department for this purpose.

In parliamentary hearings on what is now Section 192 of the 1992 act (requiring his office to submit an annual report to the solicitor general, who must in turn lay it before Parliament), the correctional investigator made the following interesting observation:

The issues surrounding the reporting relationship of the Office have centred on the question of balancing the requirement that the Correctional Investigator be and be seen to be clearly independent of Ministerial control with the requirement of Ministerial accountability for the operation of the Correctional Service. The above noted provisions, with respect to the tabling of any Reports, attempts [*sic*] to address this balance and clarifies, short of having the Correctional Investigator report directly to Parliament, the independence of the correctional investigator from Ministerial control. (Stewart, 1991: 3)

It is worth noting that in this statement the correctional investigator clearly claims independence from ministerial control, while recognizing his accountability to the minister.

As Marshall pointed out several years ago, it is not inevitable (although it has traditionally been common in government) that accountability must always imply control. Marshall described two modes of governance (actually he called them 'styles of accountability'), one of which involves, and the other of which eschews, a direct link between accountability and control:

Other areas of British administration besides policing have shown a need for a form of accountability that differs from the familiar type of ministerial and political responsibility that might be dubbed the 'subordinate and obedient' mode in which the supervisor's responsibility is typically accompanied by administrative control and the ability to direct and veto. In contrast a style of accountability that might be called the 'explanatory and co-operative' mode has emerged in some areas such as the relationship between independent commercial or regulatory bodies on one hand and Ministers and the House of Commons on the other. Something like this style of accountability to Parliament is written into the 1964 Police Act provisions for parliamentary questioning. The Home Secretary's responsibility for policing throughout the country is one that rests not on an ability to issue orders but on the capacity to require information, answers and reasons that can then be analysed and debated in Parliament and in the press. (1978: 61–2)

While they have been criticized for overly and unrealistically dichotomizing styles of governance (Stenning, 1983: 25–6), Marshall's two 'styles of accountability' illustrate well the possibility of separating accountability from control.

It is probably the element of obligation in accountability (the *requirement* to give an account) that is the main source of the fear that accountability will necessarily lead to control. This concern may be expressed in two ways. One argument is that it is but a short step from being able to require someone to give an account to being able to require them to do other things; to prevent the latter it is therefore necessary to forgo the former. The other argument is that the very power to require the giving of an account, and its exercise, will itself exert an influence over the actions or decisions of the person who is required to give the account; the person required to give an account will consciously or unconsciously desire to please the person to whom he or she must give an account. Another version of this latter argument is that whether or not the person giving the account is actually influenced in this way, the very relationship of accountability will create the perception in others that he or she is being, or is capable of being, so influenced. Both versions of the argument easily lead to the conclusion that accountability should be foregone in the interests of preventing unwanted control or influence, or perceptions of it. Such reasoning is at the heart of arguments against any political accountability of the judiciary, at least with respect to the exercise of their 'judicial' functions. The 'perception' version of the argument is well illustrated in Chapter 10 of the RCMP PCC's 1990–91 annual report, in which the commission expressed concern about avoiding being 'captured' by (pp. 150–1) or having a 'too-intimate relationship' (p. 153) in its dealings with the RCMP, and it recommends that it be more distanced from the secretariat (pp. 157–8) with respect to the provision of support services.

The 'Doug Small Case' in 1989 provided another illustration of this thinking with respect to the 'independence' of the RCMP from political control. In this case, the RCMP were investigating an alleged leak of federal budget documents to and by a television journalist. The solicitor general's chief of staff testified in the case that between the time the force began its investigation and the time charges were laid (a period of thirty-four days) he had talked to the deputy commissioner of the RCMP about the case 'between 12 and 15 times.' Insisting that no instructions had been given, he was quoted as saying: 'Prefacing our remarks saying we did not want to interfere in any way in the investigation, (we said) we just wanted a status report' (*Globe and Mail*, 13 February 1990). As is now well known, the investigator in the case concluded that the decision to lay charges was politically influenced, in the sense that it was made under pressure from senior officers of the RCMP who were trying to 'please elected officials' (*Globe and Mail*, 7 November 1989) – a conclusion which was denied by the commissioner of the force and eventually rejected by the trial judge in the case. It will be recalled that similar issues arose with respect to the solicitor general's contacts with the commissioner of the RCMP during the investigation of criminal charges against the premier of New Brunswick in 1984 (Simmonds, 1985: Addendum). These cases illustrate how easily accountability can be perceived to be leading to control, even when this is not in fact the intent of the person demanding it. They indicate the need for judicious exercise of the right to call for accountability, even (or perhaps especially) in such circumstances.

It should be noted that something akin to Marshall's 'explanatory and co-operative' mode of accountability has been advocated for, and to some extent implemented in, at least one area of the ministry. In its report in 1981, the McDonald inquiry considered the relationship that should exist between the deputy solicitor general and the commissioner of the RCMP. The report noted that the deputy solicitor general was responsible for advising the solicitor general with respect to the fulfilment of his responsibilities *vis-à-vis* the RCMP. To be able to do this, the deputy must be able to get appropriate information from and about the force. There was never any intention, however, that the deputy should ever be able to give any directions to, or have any direct control over, the force (this being the responsibility of the commissioner, under the direction of the minister, as per Section 5 of the RCMP Act [RSC 1985]. The inquiry concluded, therefore, that a relationship of accountability without control would be appropriate between the commissioner and the deputy solicitor general:

The Commissioner of the RCMP should be legally *accountable* to the Deputy Solicitor General. Such a legal relationship is imperative to ensure that ministerial responsibility is effective. The Deputy Minister is the principal adviser of the Minister. The Deputy Minister must have *unimpeded access* to all matters being handled by the RCMP, to be able to advise the Minister properly. Any doubts about the Deputy Minister's right to be *kept informed and to look into all matters* must be removed. The Deputy Minister is not a member of the Force itself and thus should be able to give the Minister informed, independent advice on *policy matters* relating to the Force, something which has not been possible in the past. (Canada, McDonald Commission, 1981a: 1013–14; emphasis added)

These proposals of the commission emphasize the essential character of accountability as a mechanism that confers an authority to require the giving of information, as discussed earlier, rather than any authority to exercise direct control over the person or agency accountable. They stand in marked contrast to the commission's recommendations concerning the relationship between the minister and the force with respect to matters other than what the commission termed the 'quasi-judicial' functions of the force (that is, the functions of arrest, investigation, and the laying of charges in particular cases). These recommendations emphasized the responsibility of the solicitor general to give directions to the force, as well as to hold it accountable: 'The government must fulfill its democratic mandate by ensuring that in the final analysis it is the government that is in control of the police, and accountable for it' (Canada, McDonald Commission, 1981a: 1006). Similar recommendations were made by the Independent Advisory Team on the Canadian Security Intelligence Service with respect to political direction of CSIS, in its 1987 report (Solicitor General Canada, Independent Advisory Team on CSIS, 1987: 27–8). With respect to the 'quasi-judicial' functions of the RCMP, however, the McDonald inquiry recommended a relationship of accountability without direct control:

We believe that those functions of the RCMP which we have described as 'quasi-judicial' should not be subject to the direction of the Minister. To be more explicit, in any particular case, the Minister should have no right of direction with respect to the exercise by the RCMP of the powers of investigation, arrest and prosecution. To that extent, and to that extent only, should the English doctrine expounded in *Ex Parte Blackburn* [the doctrine of 'police independence'] be made applicable to the RCMP. Even though the Minister should have no power of direction in particular cases in relation to the exercise by the RCMP of these 'quasi-judicial' functions, the Minister should have the right to be, and should insist on being, informed of any operational matter, even one involving an individual case, if it raises an important question of public policy. In such cases he may give guidance to the Commissioner [of the RCMP] and express to the Commissioner the government's view of the matter, but he should have no power to give *direction* to the Commissioner (Canada, McDonald Commission, 1981a: 1013).

Given the quasi-judicial functions of many of the agencies associated with the ministry, and the consequent need that they enjoy a measure of independence from political and administrative control, influence, or interference with respect to the exercise of these functions, the 'explanatory and co-operative' style of accountability would seem to be particularly well suited to these agencies.

Accountability and Technology – Less Is More

The technological revolution that has been occurring in recent years has greatly enhanced the capacity of governments to be accountable. Information can now be generated in volume and detail that were unthinkable only ten years ago.

As many of the ministry interviewees pointed out, however, there are dangers in this. Information can only serve the end of accountability if it is intelligible and usable. In the early days of computers, the idea easily grew that the more information that could be generated, the greater would be the accountability, and that more accountability was necessarily better. While to a great extent this has proved to be the case, there is now a growing realization – especially in the current climate of fiscal restraint – that, at least with respect to administrative accountability, better accountability, rather than simply more accountability, is the preferred goal. Nowhere is this thinking more clearly evident than is the federal Treasury Board's 'Increased Ministerial Authority and Accountability' (IMAA) initiative.

It is clear from the Treasury Board's accounts of IMAA that one of the principal objectives of the initiative is to reduce the quantity, while enhancing the quality, of accounts generated by federal government departments and agencies (see Treasury Board of Canada, 1989: 12). This is to be achieved by (a) treating accountability as an integral element of management at all levels; (b) reducing the number of accounts required to be given; (c) relating accounts more clearly to specified missions, objectives, goals, and standards; and (d) delegating authority (hence accountability) as much as legal requirements will allow. It is evident that this thinking has permeated most, if not all, of the agencies associated with the solicitor general's ministry, and that some, such as the CSC and the NPB, through their initiatives with regard to the development of their 'mission documents' (Vantour, 1991), can rightly be regarded as leaders in this field. Since this is a relatively recent development, however, it is too early yet to assess what its actual impact has been in terms of such indicators as performance, productivity, morale, efficiency, or public image.

This trend is important for two reasons. In the first place, technology is notoriously seductive, and it can all too easily become the master rather than the servant. Recognition that accountability is a means to an end rather than an end in itself can therefore be important in countering this tendency. Second, and related to the previous point, accountability is costly and technology, because it enhances the capacity for it, is likely to make it more so. In times of fiscal restraint especially, therefore, there is added reason to make accountability efficient as well as effective.

Accountability, Secrecy, Confidentiality, and Privacy

Secrecy is the very antithesis of accountability. Secrecy involves the deliberate withholding of information, while accountability requires it to be made available (Bok, 1982). Yet the practice of secrecy is, to a greater or lesser extent, essential to the functioning of many of the agencies associated with the Ministry of the Solicitor General. The most extreme case in this regard is the Canadian Security Intelligence Service, but the objectives of the Royal Canadian Mounted Police also frequently require a high degree of secrecy, at least while particular investigations are going on, and often subsequently as well (for example, to protect the identity of informants or undercover officers).

For organizations such as CSIS, where secrecy tends to be the rule rather than the exception, meaningful public accountability presents a great challenge. As was stated in a recent paper tabled in Parliament by the solicitor general: 'The challenge is to achieve both effectiveness and confidence, by finding an acceptable trade-off between secrecy and openness' (Canada, Solicitor General, 1991: 78). The dimensions of this challenge are nowhere better illustrated than in the recent report of the special committee of the House of Commons established to review the CSIS Act [RSC 1985] and the Security Offences Act [RSC 1985] (Canada, House of Commons, 1990). In numerous places in its unanimous report, the special committee detailed how the requirements of secrecy, at least as they are currently interpreted by the solicitor general and senior officials within his ministry, prevented this parliamentary committee from being able to carry out its legislated mandate fully and effectively. The committee concluded that in these respects, CSIS, the solicitor general, and his ministry are effectively unaccountable to Parliament and the people of Canada. The committee made a series of recommendations designed to overcome this problem, while seeking to maintain safeguards to ensure the effectiveness of the agency in fulfilling its mandate.

The government rejected most of these recommendations (Canada, Solicitor General, 1991), indicating that in its view the present arrangements are generally satisfactory and the need to preserve the secrecy of the agency's operations outweighs any need for fuller internal or external accountability in this area. It is perhaps worth noting, however, that when they were in opposition, at the time the present legislation was enacted, the Progressive Conservatives adopted a more critical view of the arrangements for accountability that the legislation established.

What this illustrates is not any unique proclivity for inconsistency among Conservatives, but that perspectives on the nature and scope of accountability in government are in practice affected as much by political considerations as by abstract theoretical principles.

There is no disagreement – at least among those who accept the necessity for a state security intelligence function at all – that *some* secrecy is essential for any agency performing this function. As *The Economist* magazine pointed out in another context in 1991, however, the issue here is how much secrecy is enough, and how much is too much: 'In spying, secrecy is sometimes essential. But secrecy must not become a cloak for anything a security service does. Once that happens, the cloak is thrown ever wider, until it covers whatever a government (or some of its officials) does not want the public to know. ... And the habit of secrecy tends to be joined quite quickly by another variety, no less pernicious: That of justifying lawbreaking in the cause of a greater good, like the 'national interest' (3 August 1991: 4).

The key issue here, then, may be stated as follows: In a democracy such as ours, at what point does accountability impair the effectiveness of the activities of a security intelligence agency, and at what point does its absence encourage or permit unacceptable conduct with impunity? The answers to these questions will often depend, first, upon *to whom* accountability is proposed and, second, upon *when* it is to be required. For example, accountability which might cripple a security service's ability to function effectively if it were owed to the public at large, might not do so if it were owed to a more restricted group of trusted representatives of the public who are sworn to maintain confidentiality. Thinking along these lines almost certainly lay behind the decision to make CSIS accountable to the relatively secretive Security Intelligence Review Committee, rather than to the relatively more public Standing Committee of the House of Commons on Justice and the Solicitor General (although a subcommittee of the latter has now been established specifically for the purpose of increasing parliamentary oversight of national security matters). Similarly, accountability which might impair a security service's effectiveness if it were required *prior* to decisions being made or activities undertaken, might sometimes not have this consequence if it were only required sometime afterwards (*ex post facto* accountability).

The dilemma that the protection of 'national security' poses thus illustrates well the need to be quite specific about exactly what is contemplated by 'accountability' and that the relationship between accountability and secrecy need not always be what game theorists call 'zero sum.' The conflict between the views of the special committee and those of the government make it clear that there is little agreement at present as to how the two objectives of secrecy and accountability are most appropriately balanced in a democracy such as ours, both in terms of how much accountability there should be and what kind of account-ability would be appropriate (see the debate on this issue in the House of Commons, *Hansard*, 26 February 1991).

It is important that debate about the internal and external accountabil-ity of CSIS be kept in context. And in this case the context is one in which, in the space of a decade, the public accountability of at least this part of the government's security service has increased substantially and thinking about this issue has changed considerably. It is worth recalling that it was less than fifteen years ago that the prime minister declared 'as a matter of principle' that there should be *no* political accountability for the day-to-day operations and methods of the RCMP (including, as it did then, the security service; quoted in Canada, McDonald Commis-sion, 1981a: 1006). It is doubtful if such a position would attract much support in the 1990s. CSIS, however, is not the only agency associated with the ministry for which secrecy is an issue. Indeed, for almost any agency of government that deals directly with, or keeps records pertain-ing to, members of the public, secrecy is to some extent now an un-avoidable necessity. In this respect, it is no coincidence that 'freedom of information' legislation, so fundamentally important to the modern public accountability of governments, is always coupled with 'privacy' legislation. Such legislation represents an attempt to enshrine principles for balancing the need for public accountability, on the one hand, with the need to protect the legitimate expectations of privacy of individual citizens, on the other. Almost all of the agencies associated with the Ministry of the Solicitor General are faced with this issue in one way or another.

Examples of different approaches to achieving the balance – and even of conflict on this issue between agencies associated with the ministry – abound. In its 1990–91 annual report, for instance, the RCMP Public Complaints Commission outlined its ongoing disagreement with the RCMP over the issue of whether complainants and the public generally have a right to know what disciplinary measures, if any, have been taken against members of the RCMP against whom complaints have been upheld. The PCC has taken the position that public accountability for these decisions is essential for the credibility of the force, the PCC, and the complaints process generally, and is in any event required by the RCMP Act. The force, however, on the advice of the Department of Justice, has taken the position that the federal Privacy Act precludes any such public accountability (see RCMP, PCC, 1991: 115).

The National Parole Board has faced somewhat similar issues concerning the public accountability of its release decisions. Here, the issue has revolved around who is entitled to know about the precise details of an individual parolee's release. Victim advocacy groups, in particular, have argued there is a positive duty on the board to inform the victims of crimes (especially crimes of personal violence), as well as perhaps potential future victims, as to exactly when and where 'their' offenders are being released, so that they may take whatever further precautions they deem necessary against further victimization. Some have gone further and insisted that victims should have a right to be heard at the board's hearings at which such decisions are reached. The board, however, took the position that it is not formally accountable to individual victims, victim advocacy groups, or the public more generally on these particular matters, and that it is under a positive legal duty to protect the privacy of individual parolees.

Since 1987, however, a Use and Disclosure Code, developed through negotiations between the federal privacy commissioner, the NPB, and the CSC, and covering both agencies, has been in effect. The code sets out guidelines detailing the circumstances under which information about an offender under the jurisdiction of either agency may, at the agency's discretion, be released to victims and/or potential victims of the offender, on request. Officials at the NPB described these guidelines as fulfilling a 'moral accountability' of the board to victims of serious injury offences, because they have a 'direct interest' in decisions made by the board. In addition, the board now encourages victims to submit written representations to it, outlining their concerns and needs (National Parole Board, 1989b: 10–11). The Corrections and Conditional Release Act [1992] now enshrines these broad principles in legislation and makes them applicable to the Correctional Service of Canada as well as the National Parole Board; see Sections 4(c), 26, 98(2), 101(c), 142, and 144 of the act. The act also makes it possible for 'observers' (including, presumably, victims) to attend Parole Board hearings under certain circumstances; see Section 140(4)–(6).

Interviews with ministry officials conveyed the impression that virtually all of the agencies within the ministry, including the secretariat, face issues of this kind in one way or another, and regularly. As the Use and Disclosure Code illustrates, there has been considerable cooperation among agencies of the ministry in attempting to develop common approaches and policies with respect to these difficult aspects of accountability. The deliberations of the Daubney committee, the publication of its report (Canada, House of Commons, Standing Committee on Justice and the Solicitor General, 1988), the subsequent development of the consultation paper on *Corrections and Conditional Release – Directions for Reform* (Canada, Solicitor General, 1990), and now the new legislation, have all provided opportunities for agencies within the ministry to cooperate in developing appropriate policies on such issues. The result has been the creation of new instruments of accountability, such as the National Parole Board's Decision Registry and its *Decision Policies* (Canada, NPB, 1989a).

While policies on such matters obviously must be tailored to the particular circumstances and needs of individual agencies, the benefits of such a cooperative approach deserve recognition. First, agencies can benefit from learning how other agencies experience and address similar difficulties. Second, a greater degree of consistency of approach and principle can be developed, which can enhance the ministry's effectiveness and credibility. Interviews within the ministry indicated that the oversight bodies associated with the ministry, which regularly face similar issues, have not been as included in such ministry-wide discussions as the 'core' agencies (especially CSC and NPB). Greater involvement of them would likely be of benefit not only to them, but to the ministry as a whole.

Accountability and Legal Liability

Interviews revealed that there have been concerns that greater openness and accountability might expose individual staff members, as well as the agencies themselves, to greater risk of legal liability. Some highly publicized cases in the National Parole Boards's jurisdiction have particularly given rise to such concerns. The Canadian Charter of Rights and Freedoms [1982], and the opportunities it provides for litigation against the government and its employees, is another factor that has fuelled such concerns. Interviews with ministry officials, however, suggest that such concerns are exaggerated. Experience so far has generally not confirmed their validity. In fact, NPB officials told us that the publication of its Decision Policies (Canada, NPB, 1989a) has probably served as often to protect the board and its members from litigation as to expose them to it. Making standards clear, it is argued, takes some of the guesswork out of litigation, and may actually deter the capricious or speculative litigator, as well as providing the board and its members with a more solid basis on which to defend their decisions. There is a feeling that the quality of decision-making has been significantly enhanced as a result of this accountability, and that this improvement has also served to protect, rather than jeopardize, the board and its members.

This experience of the National Parole Board is important, as it illustrates the potential benefits to be derived by an agency from taking the initiative to devise and promulgate standards, rather than simply waiting for (perhaps less palatable or appropriate) standards to be imposed upon it by the courts as a result of unpredictable litigation. In this way, the agency can often secure a more effective voice in shaping the nature and scope of its legal accountability (in the sense of accountability to the courts) so that the accountability requirement does not unduly or unnecessarily impair the agency's operational effectiveness.

On a more cautionary note, some interviewees felt that it is still too early to be complacent about these concerns. Jurisprudence in this area has been evolving in a gradual and rather unpredictable way, and some senior ministry officials feel that some added legal protections for bona fide actions and decisions of staff should be considered. Proposals for such legal protections to be included in the Parole Act were included in the consultation paper, *Corrections and Conditional Release – Directions for Reform* (Canada, Solicitor General, 1990: 22–3), albeit without any substantial discussion of the issues at stake. Since then, Section 154 of the Corrections and Conditional Release Act [1992] has now established a statutory immunity for parole board members from criminal or civil liability 'for anything done or said in good faith in the exercise or purported exercise' of their functions as board members. Similar protections for the correctional investigator are also included in the act (Sections 187 and 188). Again, this is an issue which, in one way or another, is likely to be of consequence to many of the agencies associated with the ministry, and which might therefore justify some more detailed ministry-wide discussion and policy development.

Other Potential Dangers of Openness and Accountability

Interviewees within the ministry were almost unanimous about the desirability and benefits of greater openness and accountability. In one agency, however – the office of the correctional investigator – this enthusiasm was more qualified. Staff of this office pointed out to us that unlike other agencies associated with the ministry, the principal 'public' to whom it feels most accountable is its clients, inmates in federal penitentiaries. They are not, of course, a very popular constituency, and the correctional investigator's staff whom we interviewed expressed some concerns that the publicity and public discussion which so often accompany increased openness and accountability, might actually impair the office's ability to serve its clients as effectively as possible. This effectiveness, they felt, depended to a considerable extent on the office's ability to negotiate its cases in a cooperative way, with informality, low visibility, and without the glare of publicity. It was felt that a legislated mandate for the office, which up to that time it had never had, public clarification of standards and procedures, and other more formal forms of increased public accountability, might lead to a more adversarial and less flexible environment for responding to inmate complaints and concerns, which might make it harder for the office to achieve beneficial outcomes for its clients. Inherent in this concern seems to be a sense that the general public might not be as supportive or responsive to inmate concerns and objectives as is the Correctional Service of Canada.

It is difficult to assess the validity or acceptability of this approach to accountability. In light of pressures in recent years to replace the Office of Correctional Investigator with a more formal, publicly independent and accountable 'auditor general – prisons' (advocated by the Canadian Campaign for Prison System Improvement) or 'inspector general of penitentiaries' (as proposed in Bill C-317, 1991), these concerns of the correctional investigator's office merit careful consideration and discussion within the ministry. The significantly different roles proposed for such officers from that of the current office of the correctional investigator need to be kept very much in mind, because the role of such an office carries significant implications for what might be appropriate accountability arrangements for it. In particular, penitentiary inmates, who are viewed by the office of the Correctional Investigator as its main 'constituency,' would not necessarily be viewed in precisely the same light by either of the other proposed officers.

Since the ministry interviews were undertaken, the Office of Correctional Investigator has been given full statutory recognition, and the relationships between the correctional investigator and the minister, the ministry, the CSC, inmates, and the public is now largely governed by law (Part III of the Corrections and Conditional Release Act [1992]). These provisions substantially formalize, and perhaps change somewhat, the role and accountability of the correctional investigator. In a carefully worded statement to the Standing Committee on Justice and the Solicitor General on those provisions of the bill introducing this legislation that are pertinent to his office, the correctional investigator noted, 'The authority provided within the legislation is consistent with that established in most ombuds legislation and the discretion afforded the Office in terms of how and when investigations will be undertaken ... provides the Correctional Investigator with the flexibility necessary to bring resolution to matters within what is oftentimes a difficult environment' (Stewart, 1991: 4).

Recognizing that the mandate for the office would remain 'basically unchanged' (ibid.: 3) by the provisions of the bill, the correctional investigator concluded, 'In short, I feel the proposed legislation in the absence of a direct reporting relationship to Parliament, will provide the Office with the independence and authority necessary to fulfil the proposed legislated mandate set out in Bill C-36' (ibid.: 4).

Another related concern, raised by some of the quasi-judicial oversight bodies associated with the ministry, is that they might lose their credibility with their constituencies (those whose complaints or grievances they address) if they are perceived to be too closely associated with the ministry, its secretariat, or the agencies whose actions or decisions they are supposed to be reviewing. This argument, which was put by a number of interviewees, was not presented as an argument against any accountability at all; rather, it was presented in the form of a caveat. Accountability that is exercised too frequently or vigorously, it was felt, risks being perceived as undermining the necessary independence of these quasijudicial bodies. As we have noted already, this concern has also led to a preference for a strict interpretation of legislated reporting requirements, such that they will be construed as providing for accountability to Parliament via the solicitor general, rather than accountability to the solicitor general as such.

The Role of the Minister's Political Staff

It is noteworthy that public discussion of accountability within government almost never includes any serious examination of the role of political staff within ministers' offices. A recent article entitled 'Public

Service Accountability: The Basic Bargain,' recommended by one inter-viewee, provides a good example of this omission. Its author, the secre-tary of the Treasury Board, describes government accountability in the following terms:

The Accountability of Officials
The personal accountability of ministers to the elected House is the 'basic bar-gain' from which flow all the ethical obligations of those who work in govern-ment. For ministers, accountability is political, and so are the sanctions and rewards for behaviour – you maintain the confidence of the House or you don't; you win the next election or you don't.

Accountability for officials is different. The deputy minister is accountable to the minister; individual public servants are accountable through their supervi-sors to the deputy minister and through the deputy to the minister. For officials, then, accountability is institutional and is governed by institutional standards and sanctions.

The power of the government is exercised by officials acting on behalf of, and under the broad direction of, ministers. This, too, is part of the 'basic bargain' and it involves obligations to behave in certain ways. The chain extends to every employee in the institution in a sequence of reciprocal obligations built on this 'basic bargain' between the minister and the Public Service (Clark, 1991: 17).

The four-page article that follows this introduction contains no mention of ministerial political staff, let alone any serious discussion of their role in fulfilling the 'basic bargain' to which the author refers. The Treasury Board's account of its IMAA initiatives (see Canada, Treasury Board, 1989) is similarly silent on the subject of ministers' political staffs. In-deed, none of the materials provided during the interviews for this study and subsequently touches on this topic.

The interviews, as well as recent well publicized events in Toronto (the Gigantes resignation from the Ontario government) and Ottawa (the 'Mashat Affair') have made it abundantly clear that this is an aspect of government accountability that requires some serious thought and discussion. Because members of the solicitor general's political staff were not interviewed during the study, it is not possible to detail here the concerns in this area. Problems concerning the role of political ministerial staff have barely been articulated, let alone elaborated, in the literature on governmental accountability. Broadly, however, they in-volve the proposition that, within current government organizational structures – and more especially since the introduction of the position of chief of staff in the mid 1980s – the minister's political staff are in a position to interrupt, if not actually sever, the direct line of accountability between the public service and the minister, that they become the 'gatekeepers' of what information reaches the minister from the public service, and that they themselves are not adequately publicly accountable. Examples illustrating the validity of these propositions surfaced during the interviews, but in view of the study's limited exploration of this issue, it would not be appropriate to rehearse these examples here. The study made it clear, however, that the matter of accountability within the ministry will not be adequately addressed unless this particular issue is included within the topics for discussion.

A revealing discussion of this issue appeared in the 1992 report of the Royal Commission into Commercial Activities of Government and Other Matters in Western Australia (Western Australia, Royal Commission, 1992). Bemoaning the secrecy and lack of public accountability that surrounds the appointment, terms of service, and activities of members of ministerial staffs, the report noted that:

Primarily, ministerial staff will be accountable to the minister concerned. But in exceptional circumstances the engagement may have other dimensions. To the extent that a member of a minister's staff assumes a positive role in the conduct of the affairs of a department or agency in the exercise of its functions, whether or not on his or her own initiative, that person is exercising public power. There is every reason in principle why that person's official conduct should be open, like that of any other officer, to examination and review by the Parliament through its committees. There can be no retreat from the principle that those who assume to exercise public power, whether through command, the exercise of influence or otherwise, be held accountable for their actions. (Ibid.: part II, 6.10–6.11)

Laudable as these sentiments may seem, they are far from reflecting the present-day reality in most parliamentary democracies. That reality suggests that ministerial staff have been growing more influential but no more publicly accountable in recent years.

Strategies for Accountability

Accountability does not just happen, and a commitment to it, however sincere, will be worth little unless suitable structures and resources are put in place to facilitate and implement it. Evidently, there has been considerable thought given by the various agencies associated with the ministry in recent years as to what are the most effective strategies in this regard. The main ones which seem to have found favour (not necessarily in order of priority) are:

1 Public clarifications, through published statements, of the mission, core values, objectives, goals, strategies, standards, plans, policies, and procedures of the agencies as a whole, and of their constituent parts.

   The thinking here seems to be that accountability will be largely meaningless unless there is some identifiable yardstick against which what is being accounted for can be measured. An important question concerns the extent to which such yardsticks as have been adopted (a) are appropriate and realistic and (b) are sufficiently clear that performance can actually be assessed using them. It is noteworthy that purposes and principles have now been enacted in legislation covering the Correctional Service of Canada and the National Parole Board (see Sections 3, 4, 100, and 101 of the Corrections and Conditional Release Act [1992]).

2 Creating and improving more appropriate and functional information systems and databases.

   The emphasis here is on quality and usefulness of information rather than just quantity.

3 Identifying more clearly, and surveying the needs and concerns of, distinct 'publics' relevant for accountability and clarifying the expectations of these.

   This involves distinguishing between the demands of internal and external accountability and tailoring accountability resources and practices to the particular needs of those to whom it is owed.

4 Developing and maintaining communications strategies and systems which will allow the agency to maintain effective communication with its relevant 'publics'.

   Accountability cannot be meaningful and effective unless those to whom it is owed are aware that it is owed to them and know how to exercise their rights in this regard.

5 Developing and maintaining audit systems and cycles which are efficient without being unnecessarily intrusive or disruptive.

   Audit systems must be such that they generate only information that is useful for the proposes of accountability, they duplicate each other or overlap as little as possible, and they cause as little intrusion into, and disruption of, the lives of staff as is necessary for effective accountability.

6 Delegating decision-making authority to the greatest extent that organizational efficiency, effectiveness, and economy will allow.

The thinking here is that staff will perform better and (hence) will be more committed to accountability, the greater the stake they have in the organization is, and the more satisfying and challenging their work is. Also, decentralized authority (and hence accountability) systems are usually more efficient, effective, and economical.

7 Frequent and vocal support and encouragement of accountability by senior managers.

Like most organizational objectives, accountability will only attract the commitment of line staff if they see clearly that senior managers are fully committed to it. An important strategy to reduce the risk that accountability will become mere 'account ability.'

8 Strategic research on the agency and its environment.

Many of the agencies have done, or commissioned, and published research of direct relevance to their mandates, and the secretariat also, to some extent, provides this service to the agencies. The series of discussion papers put out by the RCMP External Review Committee provides a good example of research designed to inform interested publics about the wider environment within which this agency operates. Provisions of the Corrections and Conditional Release Act [1992] would seem to be designed to encourage such research with respect to the operations of the National Parole Board, for example, Section 144(3).

9 Involving relevant publics in the setting of policies and priorities.

'Community-based policing' and the consultative committees which the RCMP have established in detachments to achieve it, are perhaps the most obvious exemplars of this strategy of accountability. Many of the other agencies associated with the ministry, however, have adopted similar strategies (such as the citizens advisory committees that have been established by CSC with respect to particular penitentiaries).

10 Regular review of accountability needs, priorities and procedures.

As the 'environment' (both within government and outside) within which an agency must operate is continually changing, the demands on it for accountability also change. Accordingly, its 'accountability regime' needs to be reviewed at reasonably frequent intervals to ensure its continued relevance and suitability. 'Environmental scans' appear to be the preferred means of achieving such reviews.

Accountability and Geography

The national jurisdiction of the ministry and its associated agencies inevitably makes geography an important factor in effective accountability. This is especially true of those accountability mechanisms that involve the disposition of public complaints against ministry or agency staff. Such mechanisms are rendered virtually nugatory if they are not made practically (including economically) accessible to all who may wish to use them. Successful achievement of this goal requires considerable financial outlay and resource deployment and concern was expressed by some interviewees that the ministry's budget does not always reflect an adequate understanding of this reality. Attempts to achieve this goal, furthermore, can easily engender misunderstandings, leading to resentments or outright hostility in relationships that should be characterized by mutual support and cooperation. The experiences of the RCMP Public Complaints Commission provide a good illustration of this.

To reach the public more effectively, the commission had flyers printed which described its composition and functions and explained the procedure for making a complaint against a member of the force. These flyers were displayed in RCMP detachment offices across the country, as well as in other public facilities such as post offices and public libraries. This particular 'communications strategy' (RCMP, PCC, 1990: 10) elicited some unfortunate, if not entirely unpredictable, reactions from some members of the force, as well as from others. While giving a lecture to some newly promoted middle managers in the force, I was asked why the 'first thing members of the public have to see' when they walk into a detachment office is how to lay a complaint against members of the force. The question was quickly followed by the questioner's own opinion to the effect that this strategy could do nothing but damage to the force's image and relationship with the public. More recently, a similar criticism was voiced in an editorial in one of Canada's leading security trade magazines, in which the PCC's strategy was described as an 'affront': 'Only in Canada. In my wildest imagination I cannot conceive the possibility that any other government in the world, elected or otherwise, would go to this length and expense to instruct the public on how to complain about the members of an organization which exists to assist in maintaining the protection of persons and property and in preserving law and order' (Percival, 1991).

While reactions such as this cannot always be anticipated or averted, the incident serves as a reminder that the notion of accountability is not always universally supported or appreciated and that strategies for overcoming the geographical obstacles to effective accountability need to be devised with great care.

Strategies of decentralization to overcome these problems of access must also take into account other legitimate objectives of these national agencies. Of great moment here is the debate which is ongoing in many of the agencies regarding the relative merits of uniformity and variability in the programs, policies, and practices of national agencies that are administered through regional offices. Achieving the right balance between uniform standards (which have perhaps become of greater concern since the passage of the Charter of Rights [1982] with its guarantees of equality under the law) and sensitivity to differences in regional (or even more local) conditions, will always pose a challenge for such agencies.

Current thinking about management of public services favours decentralization to the 'point of impact' (Vantour, 1991: 60–1) in order to increase access, effectiveness, and accountability. As the commissioner of corrections has recently pointed out, however, it is important to bear in mind that such decentralization, for all its benefits, does not detract from the need for effective accountability to the senior management at headquarters (Vantour, 1991: 213). Recognizing the distinction and relationship between accountability and control may be important in finding the best solutions to these dilemmas.

Concluding Comments

Some of the issues concerning accountability within the Ministry of the Solicitor General and its associated agencies have been examined, without in any way attempting a comprehensive evaluation of this aspect of the ministry's work. The interviews undertaken for the study left no doubt that accountability has become a major preoccupation of the ministry and its associated agencies. This is not unique to this ministry. Although there is evidence that parts of the ministry have shown leadership in this area in recent years, there is little doubt that much of the activity now evident has been in response to external influences, such as the 'Public Service 2000,' IMAA, and similar initiatives.

The situation at present is that the initial enthusiasm about increased accountability – which seemed to be characterized by thinking along the lines of 'the more accountability the better' – is now being tempered by a realization that accountability, like any other government activity, must be measured by the standards of the 'three E's' – efficiency, effectiveness, and economy. This means an emphasis on quality, and if one trend seems to be clear, it is a trend towards trying to increase the quality and usefulness of accounts while reducing their volume.

There is no question that the very idea of what constitutes appropriate accountability for government agencies is an evolving one that is historically specific and susceptible to political transience. The party which loudly demands increased accountability while in opposition is as likely as not to see things differently when in power. In economic hard times, accountability is as likely to be the target of cut-backs as any other government activity. And, in the context of the Ministry of the Solicitor General, when threats are perceived to be high, the balance between accountability and secrecy is likely to be seen in a different light. These realities raise questions about how important we think accountability really is to effective democratic government and whether we pay enough attention to, and are realistic about, its costs.

The irony, however, is that the government, through its control and manipulation of relevant information, is often in a position to shape the very informational environment in which these judgments are made. Thus, the solicitor general and CSIS are able to tell a special parliamentary review committee what information its members may have access to in order to be able to assess whether they are performing effectively and in the public interest. When the committee's report is released, the same solicitor general (presumably on the advice of CSIS and the secretariat) announces which of its recommendations will be implemented and which will not. As Bok (1982: 179) has observed, 'if officials make public only what they want citizens to know, then publicity becomes a sham and accountability meaningless,' or, as others have suggested, mere 'account ability' (Ericson, 1981a; McMahon, 1988).

It is not being suggested here that accountability within the Ministry of the Solicitor General is either meaningless or a sham (or worse): merely that the particular character of some of the agencies associated with the ministry – and more especially the covert and coercive nature of much of their power – dictate constant vigilance against this possibility, as well as the perception of it. It is often said that accountability is a vital mechanism through which organizations can be held in check, to ensure that they are both doing things right and doing the right things. The implications here is that it is outside surveillance and review that plays the key role in achieving this goal. But as Clark (1991: 19) has pointed out, the creation of an internal corporate culture committed to ethical behaviour and accountability is likely to be far more effective: 'We are trying to create a working environment in which employees regulate themselves. We are encouraging the internalization of our collective values because we believe that public servants, like most people, are motivated more by values and objectives than by external rewards and sanctions.' This study uncovered plenty of evidence that major progress in this direction has been made within the ministry and its associated agencies during the preceding decade. What is needed now is to build on that progress, and ensure that the momentum remains in the right direction.

Acknowledgment. This essay was originally prepared as a discussion paper for the Solicitor General of Canada and, with the solicitor general's permission, was published in *Optimum* 24(2): 41–57 (Autumn 1993). The author gratefully acknowledges the ministry's financial support for the study on which the chapter is based, and the research assistance of Ms Tammy Landau in undertaking the study. The views expressed in the chapter are my own and do not necessarily reflect those of the solicitor general of Canada or the ministry.

Counting the Coppers: Antinomies of Accountability in Policing

ROBERT REINER

> The difficulty of being a chief constable really is that people place you in impossible positions. They ask you questions, if you fail to answer you're arrogant and unaccountable, if you do answer, you are political.
>
> (British chief constable, quoted in Reiner, 1991: 324)

Introduction: *Casus Belli*

Policing issues have moved into the political spotlight in most common law countries in the past quarter of a century. In the United States the 1960s were a decade of multiple social conflicts and changes, with the police in the cockpit of controversy. Similar turbulent currents engulfed Britain and its 'bobbies' in the 1980s. In Canada, Australia, and many other countries there has been concern about police abuse of powers, discrimination, and ineffectiveness. In all these cases, underlying the disparate dramas and debates, disquiet about policing practices has stimulated concern about the adequacy of channels for democratic accountability.

Police accountability in various forms became a hot political issue in the United States in the 1960s (Goldstein, 1977: ch. 6 and 7; Rumbaut and Bittner, 1979), in Canada and Australia in the 1980s (Shearing, 1981; Stenning, 1981b; Hann, McGinnis, Stenning, and Farson, 1985; Goldsmith, 1991c). In Britain it remained high on the political agenda throughout the 1980s (Jefferson and Grimshaw, 1984; Lustgarten, 1986;

Reiner, 1991 and 1992a; Reiner and Spencer, 1993). Concern about any specific aspects of policing inevitably leads ultimately to questions of accountability: who has the power to set the agenda for policing, and how can police officers be brought to account for their actions? Yet, no jurisdiction appears satisfied that it has achieved an adequate structure of accountability for policing. The issue remains essentially contested everywhere, torn between seemingly irresolvable antinomies. As the quotation from a chief constable that heads this chapter suggests, the police are caught in the dilemma of appearing unaccountable or politically controlled, arrogantly unresponsive to outside views, or subserviently partisan towards powerful vested interests. Where reforms do occur they have usually confounded the intentions that motivated them and prompted a dialectic leading to reverse changes (Goldstein, 1977: ch. 6).

This chapter will consider the problems of achieving police accountability, concentrating on recent British experience as a case study. The next section will analyze competing interpretations and models of accountability. The third part will chart the British experience in the past thirty years, contrasting changes in formal structures with substantive developments in practice. Finally, the conclusions will reflect on the significance of this for the project of achieving an acceptable accountability structure for policing.

Police Accountability and Control: Dimensions and Dilemmas

Debates about police accountability have focused on two distinct areas of government. The first concerns the determination and execution of police policy. What is the relationship between police chiefs and government (central and local), the courts, and other external agencies with an interest in policing? How faithfully and efficiently are policies set by the leadership levels of the police organization translated into effective action on the streets?

The second broad area of debate about police accountability concerns the mechanisms for ensuring that individual officers adhere to law and departmental policy in their concrete practices. How effective are channels for registering grievances and securing redress? This is the province of complaints systems and legal action against individual officers for abuses. These have been vexed issues in most jurisdictions for some time, and there has been a flurry of reform aimed at enhancing the mechanisms for handling grievances through complaints procedures and the courts (Goldsmith, 1991c is a valuable collection of papers on recent developments in the United Kingdom, the United States, Canada, and Australia; the British experience is covered in detail in Maguire and Corbett, 1991; Clayton and Tomlinson, 1987). Complaints systems are the specific focus of Andrew Goldsmith's contribution to this volume, while this chapter concentrates on the question of accountability for the formulation and administration of police policy.

It must be emphasized first that the two aspects of accountability overlap. The overall legitimacy of the police is undoubtedly a function of the adequacy of accountability in both respects. More specifically, particular developments in law or organization may either enhance or retard accountability along both dimensions. For example, the Police and Criminal Evidence Act [1984] (PACE) establishes more precise recording practices for all exercises of police power by individual officers (Zander, 1990; Reiner and Leigh, 1994). This has relevance for the viability both of managerial and external monitoring of the administration of policy and for the prospects of complaints or civil actions against individual officers. Ultimately the distinction between the accountability of organizational policy-making, and of individual officers, is an echo of the ill-fated attempts to distinguish between policy and operations, which will be considered further below (see also Hann, McGinnis, Stenning, and Farson, 1985; Lustgarten, 1986: 20–2).

STYLES OF ACCOUNTABILITY

An important distinction between two fundamentally different forms of accountability was developed some years ago by Geoffrey Marshall. He dubbed the two contrasting styles the 'subordinate and obedient' and the 'explanatory and co-operative' (Marshall, 1978: 61–3). The 'subordinate and obedient' mode was 'the familiar type of ministerial and political responsibility ... in which the supervisor's responsibility is typically accompanied by administrative control and the ability to direct and veto.' By contrast, the 'explanatory and co-operative' mode 'rests not on an ability to issue orders but on the capacity to require information, answers and reasons that can then be analysed and debated' in the legislature, the media, and other relevant forums for discussion. The key characteristic of explanatory styles of accountability is that 'without any power to bind or reverse executive decisions they provide an avenue for challenge, for the requiring of reasoned explanation and for advice and recommendation.'

These two interpretations of accountability neatly encapsulate the core aspect of the concept, as well as indicating the reasons for its elevation to being the key buzz-word in discussions of the governance not only of the police, but also of other public service bureaucracies (Day and Klein, 1987). The basic idea of accountability invokes the responsibility of those who exercise delegated or conferred powers and duties to render a reckoning of how they have performed. The general liability of agents to account for actions to those who have empowered and/or obliged them to carry out tasks occurs in any form of social organization, whether public or private, democratic or authoritarian. However, the term 'accountability' and such other buzz-words as 'community' have the quality of connoting bland and undeniable virtue, so that it is impossible to argue against their desirability, while at the same time they are capable of encompassing many different and conflicting meanings. Their attraction in political debate is that they offer the rhetorical advantage of gaining support for controversial and contested positions by invoking the aura of their unexceptionable meanings. Thus, the relatively innocuous and uncontentious literal idea of accountability as an obligation to provide accounts of how responsibilities have been carried out – Marshall's 'explanatory' mode – may be borrowed as a cloak for a stronger interpretation, the 'subordinate and obedient' style, equating accountability with control. Very cogent arguments may be advanced for subjecting the police to the latter type of accountability. Indeed, this is the interpretation that Marshall himself sought to justify in his celebrated critique of the Police Act [1964], which enacts what is basically an explanatory mode (Marshall, 1965). Marshall's previously cited 1978 paper is to a large extent an auto-critique of this earlier book.

THE 'SUBORDINATE AND OBEDIENT' ACCOUNTABILITY MODEL

The 'subordinate and obedient' model, seeking some sort of external democratic control over policing, underlies most radical and critical accounts. It was the goal of English Labour Party proposals and interventions in the policing debate throughout the Thatcherite decade (Reiner, 1992a: ch. 6 and 7) and remains part of Labour's policy, although accountability has now been eclipsed by crime prevention as the centre-piece of its 'law and order' program (Sheerman, 1991).

The most cogent and compelling defence of this case (which is very much the common currency of left and liberal thinking about policing) was advanced by Laurence Lustgarten in his book *The Governance of the*

Police (1986). The starting point of the argument is the demonstration that, contrary to the conventional wisdom of police practitioners (see Mark, 1977, 1978; Oliver, 1987), policing at all levels inescapably involves decision-making that is political in the broadest sense. This flows from the inevitable discretion about law enforcement exercised by the police in relation to both general policy and specific interventions, one of the key 'discoveries' of early police research (Rumbaut and Bittner, 1979: 241–4). 'Once it is accepted that strict law enforcement must give way to more important considerations, the idea that the police can somehow stand apart from politics and from the process of public choice becomes untenable ... Once it is admitted that discretion in policing is inevitable, and that the choices involved in police managerial discretion are political, there inevitably follows the question, who determines how the discretion shall be exercised?' (Lustgarten, 1986: 23).

Contrary to the established conservative view that policing should be (and in Britain is) insulated from politics, policing is necessarily a political process in that it operates to preserve a particular set of values that are prioritized by a particular structure of power. Policing decisions are not matters of neutral professional expertise, as the case law suggests, (for example, the Court of Appeal judgment in *R v Secretary of State for the Home Department, ex p. Northumbria Police Authority* [1988] especially per Purchas, LJ (at pp. 604–6). Policing decisions are questions of political choice and value, and in a democracy such matters must ultimately be decided by the elected representatives of the people.

To secure democratic accountability policing should be organized and controlled fundamentally on a local basis. This both facilitates responsiveness to local communities (and their varying priorities) and provides countervailing pressures against the dangers of a monolithic concentration of coercive state power. The role of national government in policing should be a limited one, providing uncontentious common services to which economies of scale apply, overseeing minimum standards of professionalism and organization, and directly dealing with a limited number of national policing functions (such as diplomatic protection).

Policing policy should thus flow primarily from elected local representatives, to whom police chiefs should in the last instance be 'subordinate and obedient' (as should all local government officials). Any attempt to demarcate separate spheres of influence is chimerical. Thus, the frequently suggested distinction between 'policy' decisions which are the prerogative of elected representatives and 'operational' ones which are the legitimate preserve of the professional chief is logically and practically untenable (Lustgarten, 1986: 20–2). Controversial operational interventions may be disguised as general policy matters, as when, during the 1984–5 miners' strike, the South Yorkshire Police Authority unsuccessfully sought to prevent the disliked use of horses in controlling pickets by instructing the chief constable to disband the mounted police unit on what were purported to be financial grounds (see Reiner, 1991: 194–5). Even decisions that are seemingly remote from controversy per se at the very least imply choices about priorities in the allocation of resources, which ought to be the decision of elected representatives (illustrated by another incident from the 1984–5 miners' strike when the Greater Manchester Police Authority instructed the chief constable to disband the police band in view of the personnel demands of dealing with the strike; McLaughlin, 1990).

Obviously, efficient management requires some day-to-day delegation of responsibility, and this creates dangers of the transfer of de facto power to the professionals. But this iron law of professional oligarchy must be melted as far as possible. The sine qua non for this is that at least de jure power must clearly lie with elected representatives, even though this will be eroded in practice.

The management problem of ensuring that individual officers adhere to policy guidelines and the rule of law involves a microscopic application of the 'subordinate and obedient' mode. Rules governing police powers must be formulated tightly, with a clear structuring of discretion by guidelines emanating from the legislature. At present the powers of the police are couched (by the legislature and the judiciary) in an unnecessarily elastic and permissive fashion, which has the effect of shielding these state elites from responsibility for policing decisions (McBarnet, 1981; Jefferson and Grimshaw, 1984). To back this up, there must be an independent, powerful, and vigorous body with the duty to investigate as well as adjudicate complaints against the police, and with the capacity and will to level adequate sanctions (Lustgarten, 1986: ch. 9).

The essence of this 'subordinate and obedient' model of accountability is 'to build a constitutional corral for the office of constable' (Uglow, 1988: 148). This borrows the rational deterrence model of classical criminology from its initial task of controlling crime (Roshier, 1989) and applies it to controlling the constable. With regard to matters of management efficiency rather than malpractice, there is a presumed rational management model of the police, as an organization capable of translating democratically decided policies into faithful implementation on the ground, provided the rules and remedies are right.

The 'subordinate and obedient' approach is difficult to fault at the level of constitutional principle. Attempts to oppose it on principle usually fail to take on board the initial premise of the inherently political character of policing decisions. They argue that it is possible and desirable to insulate police from politics. This argument is often found among police chiefs (see Oliver, 1987; and the views quoted in Reiner, 1991: 210, 250–61). Other arguments against the 'subordinate and obedient' mode tend to be more historically specific. They may question the representatives of elected members of local authorities at a certain time, because of the failings of the electoral system (see the views cited in Reiner, 1991: 250–61). Marshall's own rejection of his earlier defence of this approach rests explicitly on the *ad hominem* argument that at the time he was writing local councillors could not be trusted to observe principles of legality as faithfully as could chief police officers (Marshall, 1978: 60–1). However, while the ultimate control of policing by the expressed wishes of the electorate is hard to argue against in principle, insufficient attention has been paid to the problems of achieving it in practice. Above all, there is relatively little attention paid to the implications of the mainstream sociological corpus of research on police culture and organization (Holdaway, 1982; Bayley, 1983; Reiner, 1992a: ch. 6 and 7; Reiner, 1994). This suggests that the relationship between police policy and practice is tenuous and problematic.

Paradoxically, the limitations of 'rational deterrence' are well recognized when critical criminologists (or left-wing politicians) confront conservative 'law and order' approaches to controlling ordinary crime. However, this tends to be lost sight of when the deviants concerned wear blue uniforms. What this implies is not that the successful achievement of democratic accountability in the sense of control is undesirable, but that it is hard to achieve, and requires more than legal declaration of the formal superiority of elected representatives. This should not be taken to mean that the 'explanatory' model is more acceptable in practice. It too fails to achieve its purported objectives. As this is the model that is enshrined in the present structure of police accountability in Britain as defined primarily by the Police Act [1964], it will be examined in terms of experience of this concrete system.

Explanatory Accountability in Practice: The Police Act and Its Legacy

The 'explanatory' model underlies the constitutional status quo in England and Wales, the so-called tripartite structure, in which police accountability is divided between chief officers, local authorities, and the Home Secretary. The current statutory basis for this is the Police Act [1964]. While the 'subordinate and obedient' interpretation of democratic accountability is coherent in principle – although it confronts problems in practical implementation – the 'explanatory' model is hard to defend in principle.

Essentially, it is based on a literal rendering of the term 'accountabili-ty.' Those who are account-able and account-liable. Those who hold power, and thus have a capacity to give accounts of their exercise of it, have a duty to render such a reckoning to appropriate authorities, to tell stories about their use of power. Thus, the Police Act [1964] obliges chief constables (whose function is 'direction and control' of police forces under Section 1) to provide local police authorities with both regular annual and ad hoc special reports on any particular matters which concern them (Section 12). This is to enable the local police authority (a body consisting of two-thirds elected members, one-third justices of the peace) to carry out its responsibility of maintaining 'an adequate and efficient' force (Section 4). Chief constables also have to give reports to the Home Secretary, to allow him to accomplish his general duty to 'exercise his powers ... in such manner and to such extent as appears to him to be best calculated to promote the efficiency of the police' (Section 28).

However, while chief police officers have to account to these local and central state authorities, the act does not require them to take account in turn of any critical response to the stories they tell. They are account-givers not -takers. Even the obligation to provide accounts is limited with regard to local authorities by Section 12 of the Police Act, which permits the chief constable to refuse requests for special reports if he deems it not to be in the public interest to give such a report, or if he considers it is not 'needed for the discharge of the functions of the police authority.' In the event of such conflict, the Home Secretary arbi-trates between the police authority and the chief constable.

While the Police Act is silent about any duty of the chief officer to respond to reactions to his reports, the case law on police governance has articulated a strong doctrine of 'constabulary independence' (Mar-shall, 1965; Jefferson and Grimshaw, 1984; Lustgarten, 1986; Reiner, 1991: ch. 2). A long line of cases has declared that in his decisions about how to enforce the law, a constable (and a fortiori a chief constable) is not the servant of any unit of government, and must exercise a pro-fessional judgment of his own in these matters. In the oft-cited (not least by himself) words of Lord Denning, a chief officer of police 'like every constable in the land ... should be and is independent of the executive ... I hold it to be the duty of the Commissioner of Police, as it is of every chief constable, to enforce the law of the land ... but in all these things he is not the servant of anyone, save of the law itself. No Minister of the Crown can tell him that he must, or must not, keep observation on this place or that; or that he must, or must not, prosecute this man or that one. Nor can any police authority tell him so. The responsibility for law enforcement lies on him. He is answerable to the law and to the law along' (*R v Commissioner of Police of the Metropolis Ex Parte* [1968] (at p. 136).

This doctrine supposedly had its roots in such classic pre-Police Act, 1964 cases as *Fisher v Oldham* [1930]. However, *Blackburn* and a number of other cases since the 1964 act have articulated the doctrine ever more emphatically (for example, *R v Chief Constable of the Devon and Cornwall Constabulary, ex p. CEGB* [1981]; *R v Oxford, ex p. Levey* [1986].

In principle these cases do place the chief constable in a 'subordinate and obedient' mode with respect to the law, while denying any accountability to governmental authorities stronger than an explanatory style. However, in the string of cases that have developed the doctrine of constabulary independence, the courts have consistently found that the decisions not to enforce the law that were at the heart of these matters did fall within the chief's professional discretion. While maintaining that a decision not to enforce the law at all might be declared *ultra vires*, short of that the courts would not interfere in the chief's exercise of professional judgment about *how* to do so. This is true even when the judges clearly disapprove of the substance of the chief's decision-making (as they appear to have done in the CEGB case).

Marshall has argued cogently that in each of the cases supposedly establishing the strong doctrine of constabulary independence, the specific statements of general principle are in fact only *obiter dicta* (Marshall, 1978: 59). This remains true of more recent cases. In *Oxford*, for example, it was alleged that the pursuit of robbers into the Toxteth area of Merseyside (scene of fierce riots on several occasions) was called off because it was a 'no go' area for police. This could have amounted to the failure to enforce the law at all, which the courts have said they would declare *ultra vires* the chief constable's legitimate decision-making. However, Mr Levey failed to establish in fact that there was such a policy, and the court accepted that the chase for his stolen jewels had been abandoned because the pursuing police car came under attack from a stone-throwing mob endangering the driver's life. Thus, the issue whether or not a 'no go' policy could be seen as a failure in the policy duty to enforce the law was not in the event tested by the case.

Not only is the legal basis for the doctrine of constabulary independence strictly a series of *obiter dicta* upon *obiter dicta*, but it is hard to defend it in principle. Lustgarten has remarked of the passage from *Blackburn* [1968] cited above, 'Seldom have so many errors of law and logic been compressed into one paragraph' (1986: 64). In a witty and incisive analysis, he identifies no less than six such fallacies (ibid.: 65). However, regardless of its dubious basis in legal logic or authority, Lustgarten is surely right when he concludes that the doctrine of constabulary independence has 'embedded itself in the lore and learning of both judges and police, and it is inconceivable that, without parliamentary intervention, the courts would resile from the position they have reached' (ibid.: 67).

Thus, the legal position is that police authorities (local and national) are entitled only to an 'explanatory' style of accounting from the police. The courts, to which the police in principle must be 'subordinate and obedient,' have adopted the self-denying ordinance that they would not challenge the chief officer's exercise of judgment (whatever they might think of it), short of a complete abandonment of responsibilities to enforce the law – with which they never seem to be confronted.

THREE INTO TWO WILL GO: THE TRIPARTITE SYSTEM IN ACTION

Although they are not compelled to listen to the views of local police authorities, most chief constables see it as a matter of good practice to try their utmost to work cooperatively with the authorities, and they do their best to cultivate good relations. They are likely to take some account of the authority's views, albeit for Machiavellian reasons, as a means of maintaining consent. Most chief constables see it as the course of wisdom to allow the authority some influence (Reiner, 1991: ch. 11). As one chief constable put it, 'My relationship with my police authority, which is not unique, is based on not making secrets of things ... I share information with them, I have an enormously good relationship ... I am not hidebound about this business of I'm boss and they're providers of resources. I treat them always as representatives of my shareholders, the public ... I use them, and talk to them and share things with them and seek opinions from them ... they feel involved. There's a little Marxist on it, who is now my best friend ... But he says: "You're very clever, you kick our people from under us all pre-emptively by coming to all of us before we ask" ... If I do my job properly, I'm moulding my police authority, and they're moulding me' (quoted in Reiner, 1991: 254–6).

In practice the relationship between most police chiefs and local authorities consists of negotiated compromises. While chief constables usually seek to diplomatically 'mould' their police authorities, rather than brazenly 'boss' them, for their part local police authorities have tended to adopt a deferential stance towards the professional expertise they attribute to the chief and have been content to be moulded. This emerges as the consistent finding of research on the views of police authority members (Brogden, 1977; Morgan and Swift, 1987; Day and Klein, 1987).

It is true that following the election in 1981 of radical Labour authorities in several large cities, conflict developed between them and their chief constables, and these metropolitan authorities were the heartland of Labour's attempt in the early 1980s to empower elected bodies to control the police (Loveday, 1985; Reiner, 1992a: ch. 6 and 7; McLaughlin, 1990). However, the metropolitan authorities were abolished by the Local Government Act [1985] which decapitated the radical local challenge to Conservative central government policy in general and to police autonomy in particular. The militant metropolitan police authorities were replaced by a new system of joint boards drawn from local areas, which have proved much easier for chief constables to 'mould' to their view of things (Loveday, 1991). One observer concluded that 'the 1985 Local Government Act represents the most significant and overt shift in responsibility for the police service, from local to central government, since the passage of the 1964 Police Act' (Loveday, 1987: 211–12).

The local police authority leg of the tripartite structure has been further eroded by many other changes in the later 1980s (Reiner, 1991: 24–38). The courts underlined the impotence of local police authorities more clearly than ever before in the highly significant judgment *R v Secretary of State for the Home Department, ex p. Northumbria Police Authority* [1988]. In this case, the Northumbria police authority had sought a judicial review of the Home Secretary's decision in 1986 to make plastic bullets for riot control available to chief constables whose local police authorities would not permit their purchase. The authority argued that the Home Secretary's powers under Section 41 of the Police Act [1964] to supply equipment 'for promoting the efficiency of the force' did not permit him to override the primary responsibility of the police authority to maintain an efficient force, which stemmed from Section 4(1). Thus, they claimed the Home Secretary's policy was *ultra vires*. The Court of Appeal ruled against the authority, holding that the Home Secretary's general duty to use his powers so as to promote the efficiency of the police (Section 28), together with the power to supply common services (Section 41), allowed him to sidestep the opposition of the local authority, at least when professional police opinion agreed with the Home Office. In any event, argued the Court of Appeal (confirming the earlier ruling in the Divisional Court), the royal prerogative permitted the Home Secretary to do what he felt was necessary to maintain the Queen's Peace, whatever the correct interpretation of the tripartite allocation of roles under the Police Act [1964] was. This seems to amount to a definitive ruling that if local government views of efficiency clash with that of chief officers or the Home Office, the latter prevails, both under the Police Act and the royal prerogative. The tripartite structure is not one with three clearly independent partners, as counsel for the authority had argued, let alone one with three equal partners, as the label appears to imply, and certainly not the preponderance of local democratic control that the 'subordinate and obedient' model seeks to implement.

Thus, the *power* of local authorities, in the Weberian sense of the ability to achieve their objectives against those of others, is now virtually nil. Any influence they do exert is by grace and favour. It depends on thin skins, Machiavellian diplomacy, or the urge for a quiet life on the part of chief officers. It also rests on the apparent wish of the Home Office to maintain the myth of tripartism and local accountability, which increasingly seems to be a fig-leaf allowing it to exercise power without responsibility, the ancient prerogative of the oldest profession, but a decidedly un-royal one (Lustgarten, 1986: 125). The police have a large measure of formal autonomy, in effect saying 'trust us.' The bodies which have sought to reduce this have been either abolished or defeated. However, the bodies with formal power to determine aspects of policing policy, the courts and central government, have consolidated the self-denying ordinance of constabulary independence, sheltering them from acquiring responsibility for policing decisions.

A Centripetal Force: Police Governance in the Late 1980s

In practice this does not mean, however, that the police necessarily exercise a strong measure of independence. The critical cliché that the police are 'out of control' is largely true of both the formal constitutional position and the reality of the legal and political limits on the power of local police authorities. However, the culmination of a series of developments had by the late 1980s created a de facto national structure of policing, a form of national control lurking behind the facade of local organization and autonomy of chief officers.

It would be misleading to represent this as national government controlling the police in a directive way against their wishes. The power of national government rests not on its ability to overcome the opposition of chief constables, but on its power to mould the subjectivity of chief constables so as to prevent the appearance of disagreement in the first place. The relationship of central government to chief constables is best conceived of as what Lukes has analysed as three-dimensional power (Lukes, 1974; Reiner, 1991: 36–8). This refers not to the Weberian, zero-sum concept – the ability to overcome opposition – but the structural capacity to form and manipulate consciousness so as to avert the realization of conflicts. Post-Foucauldian analyses of power have gone beyond representing this as the effective achievement of false consciousness. They have argued that the contemporary power of government is exercised in a complex way by a series of strategies and discursive projects that form subjectivities, working through rather than over or against individual autonomy. As Rose and Miller have put it, 'Power is not so much a matter of imposing constraints upon citizens as of "making up" citizens capable of bearing a kind of regulated freedom. Personal autonomy is not the antithesis of political power, but a key term in its exercise' (1992).

If instead of 'citizens' the term 'chief constables' is inserted in the quotation above, it precisely captures the nature of the power relationship linking chief constables to central government. The formal powers of the Home Office over chief constables are far from insignificant. The Home Office in Britain effectively controls the crucial selection and socialization processes in the careers of chief constables. The Police Act [1964] explicitly gives the Home Secretary the power to approve the short-list of candidates for appointments as chief constable, prior to their interview by the local police authority. It also gives the Home Secretary the power to veto the choice then made by the authority, a second bite at the same cherry. This veto power has only recently been exercised for the first time, when the Derbyshire Police Authority proceeded to interview (and select) the serving deputy chief constable after the Home Secretary had not approved him for the short-list (Reiner,

1991: 35), supposedly because of his close relations to the local authority. The dispute was resolved by the deputy stepping down, and the authority chose a candidate acceptable to the Home Office. Ironically the new chief constable has gone on to be a stalwart ally of the local authority in a long-running dispute over the funding and efficiency of the force! Such independence is rare nowadays, however, as we will see below.

The main weapons of Home Office power, however, are not the formal ones. Once a chief is in post, the main tool overtly available to the Home Office is its control of finance: 51 per cent of local policing costs are directly paid by the central government, and a substantial proportion of the rest comes indirectly from central grants generally supporting local government revenue. Payment of the central government's contribution is dependent upon a certificate of efficiency issued annually following scrutiny by Her Majesty's Inspectorate of Constabulary (HMI), all of whom are former chief police officers. While in principle this gives the central government a formidable stick to sanction wayward chief constables, denying a certificate of efficiency (and hence effectively removing almost all of a force's finances) is so draconian a penalty that it has never been used and only infrequently threatened (most recently in the Derbyshire dispute mentioned above). The real power of the Home Office lies in a network of influence it brings to bear on the socialization of potential chief constables.

Entering the circle of senior police officers who are regarded as potential chief constable material (and who would gain Home Office approval for short-listing) depends upon successful completion of various *rites de passage* that are under the aegis of the Home Office. None of these is formally a necessary qualification for the post. But in practice it is only possible to become a chief constable without them in the most exceptional circumstances (Reiner, 1991: ch. 4 and 5). Thus, almost all chief constables have successfully completed the Senior Command Course at Bramshill, the national Police Staff College, run by the Home Office. The vast majority of the chiefs are successful alumni of the Bramshill Intermediate Command Course as well. Most of the younger chiefs are also products of the various Home Office initiatives mounted in the past thirty years to pinpoint and form potential high-flyers early in their careers, such as the Bramshill Special Course for a select few constables destined for high places, and the Bramshill scholarships to send prospective stars to university. Nearly all chief constables have also experienced a period of attachment to a central policing body, such as HMI, the Bramshill directing or teaching staff, a Home Office research unit, or a Scotland Yard specialist squad, at some crucial stage in their careers. These central attachments and training courses are evidently vital factors transforming an individual's career away from being oriented mainly to the local force to becoming part of a national policing elite. The upwardly mobile police officer's reference group ceases to be local force colleagues and becomes the cosmopolitan league of fellow high-flyers, a new breed of police 'yuppies.'

The Home Office is thus the crucial patron of aspiring chief constables, and they arrive in office with orientations moulded by their vital socialization experiences in national policing bodies and receptive to the views of their benefactor. Nevertheless, this system, which lacks immediate and direct central control of chief officer selection, it seen as too haphazard by centralist critics. A growing body of Conservative opinion has recently bewailed the 'lottery' element in the choice exercised by local authorities which, given the Home Office's reluctance to use its veto, is usually the final selection. The parliamentary Home Affairs Committee report on *Higher Police Training and the Police Staff College*, for example, concluded that a number of reforms were needed to achieve a rational and effective system, most radically that all senior police officers should cease to be locally appointed but would be a national cadre deployed by the Home Office to where it saw fit (United Kingdom, House of Commons, Home Affairs Committee, 1989; vol. 1, par. 92). This last measure of overt nationalization was rejected by the Home Office. However, it approved the other measures, such as formally requiring all appointees to complete the relevant Bramshill command courses. What neither the committee nor the Home Office acknowledged was that the recommendations largely corresponded to the present reality, in which the Home Office is already the key influence on who becomes a chief constable.

This is reflected in the ideologies of present-day chief officers. Their attitude to the Home Office, and to other elements of the national policing structure, notably HMI and the Association of Chief Police Officers (ACPO) is very different to the way they regard local authorities, supposedly the third partners in the tripartite system. It has already been seen that local authorities are viewed very much *de haut en bas*. The Home Office by contrast is seen as a body with both power and authority, whose views have to be responded to by chief constables because it has sanctions available to it and because it is regarded as the legitimate expression of democratic government (Reiner, 1991: ch. 11).

In my recent study of contemporary chief constables, 70 per cent felt the Home Office exercised a lot of influence over their decision-making, and the rest all saw it as having a fair amount of influence (Reiner, 1991: 267–8). Partly, this was because of the former sanctions available to it, notably the ultimate threat to withhold finance. Of even greater importance were the informal powers it had. Above all, any chiefs with further career ambitions might hope for honours like a knighthood, which the Head Office could influence, and the unambitious were likely to want a quiet life. What none could afford was to fall out with the Head Office. However, chief constables' acceptance of Home Office influence was not primarily a matter of sanctions, informal or formal. It was largely accepted as legitimate, partly because of the electoral mandate central (but not local) government was seen as having. In addition, Home Office policy circulars and other 'advice' were seen as being usually the product of prior consultation with HMI and ACPO. They were thus informed by the collective wisdom of senior professional police opinion in the first place. Home Office policy was not idiosyncratic but the outcome of a professional consensus that had to be respected. As one chief put what was a widely shared perspective, 'I largely feel bound by Home Office circulars because they are a regurgitation of what we've told them all anyway, through ACPO. So really the Home Office circulars are usually a consensus of views' (quoted in Reiner, 1991: 272).

There is a clear contrast between chief constables' views towards local and central government authorities. Local government is seen as often dubiously representative, easily captured by minorities, and almost always ill informed. It needs to be moulded and educated by the skilled professionalism of the police chief. The policies of central government are seen as expressing the authentic voice of the electoral process, the legitimate law of the land, and anyway as being duly informed by the collective wisdom of professional opinion by prior consultative processes. It is clear that chief constables, increasingly politically acute as a group, have their antennae tuned more and more to the wavelengths of central government, while their communications with local government are a one-way street. Within the symbiotic world of Home Office and the professional polite elite, the significance is growing of national police institutions – ACPO, HMI, new national specialist units for processing criminal and other intelligence which have proliferated recently – largely or entirely outside the tripartite structure, with at best a tenuous thread of accountability to any local bodies (Reiner, 1991: 28–33; Dorn, Murji, and South, 1991).

The grip of central government institutions over policing has tightened in the past decade, and the power of local authorities has been severely eroded. However, one element of government strategy has been to seek to repair the damage to public confidence in, and consent to, policing by a variety of apparently countervailing measures purporting to bring local opinion back into the picture. One key example is the stimulation of local consultative arrangements that followed the recommendations of Lord Scarman's report on the 1981 Brixton disorders (Scarman, 1981). The Police and Criminal Evidence Act, [1984] Section 106 requires police authorities to establish means of consulting local community opinion. Following much arm-twisting by central government in many cases, this eventually resulted in a network of formal police–community consultive committees which exist around the country. However, these operate more effectively as a channel of communication of police views to the (largely unrepresentative) community members than vice versa (Morgan, 1987). They are more important as a means of legitimating the lack of power of police authorities than as an additional vehicle for calling the police to account (Morgan, 1989). Paradoxically, this apparent measure of enhanced local consultation, which was forced upon many parts of the country by Home Office pressure, is itself testimony to the spread of central government influence.

What the above case study of developments in the structure of accountability in England and Wales since the Police Act [1964] suggests is the limited impact and indeed durability of a purely explanatory mode of accountability. The local police authority leg of the tripartite structure has atrophied to virtual impotence. This is partly as a result of further legal change by statute (the Local Government Act [1985]) and case law (the *Blackburn* [1968] and similar cases reinforcing constabulary independence, and the *Northumbria* case [1988] underlining Home Office dominance). It is at least as much the result of a network of processes of ideological formation and discipline, moulding deferential local police authorities, and chief constables who are calculatedly 'explanatory' to local authorities and 'subordinate and obedient' to the centre. At the same time, however, this network of central police power has had at best limited impact in getting its policies to bite on the culture and practice of routine police work. The gap between formal policy and concrete practice remains wide, as the history of such changes as the Police and Criminal Evidence Act [1984] shows (McConville, Sanders, and Leng, 1991; Reiner, 1992b).

Conclusion: The Subversion of Accountability

The practice of accountability departs in complex and unpredictable ways from the formal legal position. Accountability in action is not accountability in the books. Most discussions of accountability remain on a formal constitutional plane. But if accountability is to have an impact on the practice of policing, then the network of relations mediating constitutional theory and practical policing must be penetrated.

There are two fundamental issues in the achievement of democratic accountability that the above account of the British experience and debate suggests. One is the way that a merely explanatory model of accountability to particular institutions stands to be subverted by complex webs of political and ideological conflict. The tripartite system of the Police Act [1964] under which local police authorities were supposed to be significant, perhaps equal, partners with police chiefs and national government, has been transformed into a system effectively controlled from the centre, by a symbiotic alliance of the professional police elite (ACPO and HMI) and the Home Office. This has been accomplished by a combination of developments in statute and case law, and Home Office control of the purse-strings and of the processes of ideological formation of chief police officers. However, because this effective centralization of power is not acknowledged, and is hidden by the myth of locally organized forces, virtually no formal (and certainly no effective) channels of accountability exist for national police policy-making (Reiner, 1991: ch. 13).

The second problem in achieving accountability is the frequently discussed practical autonomy of street-level policing, the low visibility and high discretion of rank-and-file officers. This means that capturing the nominal commanding heights of the police organization does not ensure that the polices decided at the top will be carried out on the streets. The problem is to capture the rank-and-file culture and gain its support for reforms (Bayley, 1983; Reiner, 1992a; Goldsmith, 1990).

Throughout the 1980s, and especially in the later years of the decade, the Conservative government in Britain tried to tighten the reins of financial and managerial accountability within police organizations, as indeed throughout the criminal justice system and the public sector as a whole (United Kingdom, Audit Commission, 1990; Rawlings, 1991). In 1993 this culminated in a reform package emanating from the Conservative government, embodied in two reports published in July 1993, that of the Sheehy Inquiry into Police Responsibilities and Rewards

(United Kingdom, Inquiry into Police Responsibilities, and Rewards, 1993) and the White Paper on Police Reform (United Kingdom, Home Office, 1993), the essentials of which were introduced into Parliament in late December 1993 in the shape of the Police and Magistrates' Court Bill.

Together these proposals represent an explicit centralization of police accountability and an enhanced capacity for police authorities to influence policing practice through the market process (Reiner, 1994: 751–7). As originally proposed, there would be a new type of 'local' police authority, with the elected local element reduced to 50 per cent, and the balance consisting of justices of the peace and Home Office appointees, with a chair selected by the Home Secretary (this last element was in fact defeated by opposition from peers – including several former Tory Home Secretaries – in the House of Lords). Police authorities would have to implement a nationally determined police plan and objectives for their area, and this would be underpinned by the central government's financial powers. Senior officers (from superintendent to chief constable) would be on short-term contracts and performance-related pay. The overall package amounts to a third style of accountability, supplementing the two outlined by Marshall. This can be called the 'calculative' and 'contractual' and implies much tighter and more explicit central control using the levers of pay and contracts.

The question remains open, however, whether the icy forces of the market will achieve what traditional systems of public accountability could not. Even if they do, what is involved is the pursuit of a narrow form of managerial accountability to ensure efficiency in the achievement of goals determined by central government. How the process of goal setting can be renderable accountable remains unaddressed, apart from the fig-leaf of government-directed consultative mechanisms lacking either representative or power.

The key antinomy of the 1980s was the proliferation of critical demands for 'subordinate and obedient' accountability of police to elected local authorities, coupled with the practical achievement of tighter accountability to central government. Behind an apparent concern for community consultation, the real locus of decision-making is more distant from the democratic process than ever before.

Getting Serious about Police Brutality

DAVID BAYLEY

The now infamous videotape of Los Angeles police beating Rodney King has once again focused attention on the question of police account-ability. This is both good and bad. Good because abuse of power by police officers threatens the freedom of all citizens and undermines the legitimacy of government, as well as the institution of the police itself. Most close observers of policing would probably agree that brutality, as well as corruption, are recurring problems in the United States. As one experienced chief of police said when asked whether his force had a problem with brutality, 'Every force has a problem with brutality.' Certainly the public seems prepared to believe the worst. A *New York Times*–CBS poll showed that 67 per cent of the public thought that charges of police brutality were often justified. Cynicism was much more intense among black respondents, 82 per cent of whom thought brutality charges were often justified. Moreover, 51 per cent of the public, white or black, believed that police were tougher on blacks than whites in big cities (*New York Times*, 5 April 1991). So renewed attention to accountability is good, if only to remind the police that the public is sceptical and concerned.

But renewed attention to police accountability is also bad because it will probably generate angry discussion between police and commun-ities without solving the problem. The general public suffers from tunnel vision on this topic, in fact double tunnel vision. It believes that the solution to correcting police misconduct is to find and punish the individual officers responsible, and, since police forces do not seem to be able to prevent serious misconduct, to consider creating some civilian body outside the police that can step in and do the job for them. The problem of police misconduct is commonly viewed as a matter of 'rotten apples' and 'civilian review.' Critics of the police will argue that civilian review is necessary because police seem to be powerless to prevent repeated instances of misconduct; police themselves will argue that civilian review is unnecessary because the rotten apples are few (Chevigny, 1969; Goldsmith, 1991c; Goldstein, 1977).

The tragedy of this situation is that both sides are wrong. The elimination of police misbehaviour, whether excessive use of force or corruption, cannot be prevented by catching and disciplining misbehaving individuals. What needs to be done is to transform the organizational climate in which police work, a climate that facilitates abuses of authority. However, police organizations must not be let off the hook, with responsibility transferred to some group outside the police. They need to become more, rather than less, responsible for the behaviour of their members.

The standard policy response is wrong because it focuses on individuals rather than policies, and it shifts responsibility away from the police. Communities must create a system that forces police departments to become responsible for developing and implementing management policies that reduce the likelihood that misconduct will occur.

This essay will, first, explain why the current approach to police misbehaviour is wrong; second, explore what needs to be done instead; and, third, lay down several principles for achieving more accountable policing.

Getting It Wrong

To shape a better system for ensuring police discipline, it is important to understand exactly what is wrong with trying to root out officers who abuse power by setting up a group of individuals who are independent of the police to see that the job is done.

The major problem with the 'rotten applies' approach is that it is entirely reactive; it catches people after the damage is done (Goldsmith, 1991c). It operates on the assumption that prevention will come through deterrence. That is, would-be 'rotten apples' will be deterred from misconduct by seeing what happens to other people who are caught and punished. People take the same approach to reducing crime, believing that if criminals can be punished severely enough they will 'go straight' and others will be influenced by their fate (Walker, 1989). And they cling to this approach even though they recognize that many criminals, as well as many police officers, are very often not caught and that punishment does not deter others from committing similar acts or even prevent offenders from reoffending.

Research from a number of directions supports this diagnosis. Criminologists have consistently found that the general deterrent effects of criminal justice sanctions, meaning the lessons others draw from examples of punishment, are very weak (Walker, 1989; Currie, 1985; Braithwaite, 1989). Even the specific deterrent effects, meaning using punishment to stop particular individuals from committing further crimes, are weak, because so small a proportion of total offenders are found and punished in ways that prevent them from committing further crimes. In policing specifically, studies have shown that actions officers take 'on the street' are more powerfully influenced by organizational context than by matters of the officers' individual backgrounds, like race or education, or features of the situations they encounter (Friedrich, 1980; Reiss, 1971; Bayley, 1985; Sherman, 1980). During the past twenty years American forces have produced remarkable changes in the tactical behaviour of officers through enactment of general guidelines for certain sorts of actions. Even in the controversial area of police shootings, where it was often thought action would have to be instinctive and instantaneous, research has shown that departmental action can reduce shootings, as well as injuries and fatalities to the public, without placing officers at greater risk (Sherman 1983, Fyfe 1988, Scharf and Binder, 1983). Police executives are learning rapidly what social scientists have often argued – roles determine behaviour. What people do is more powerfully shaped by what their associates expect of them than by their personal character or social background. For police officers, their role and behaviour is most powerfully influenced by the police organization, including its occupational atmosphere.

Deterrence through investigation and punishment of erring officers touches only the symptom of the problem of police misconduct. The untouched root of the problem is an occupational culture the excuses and encourages abuses of power (Reuss-Ianni and Ianni, 1983). The solution is to develop policies for the management of police forces that shape collective and individual attitudes in ways that support adherence to high moral and legal standards. Discipline involves more than established procedures for punishing the behaviour by individuals that has already taken place (Bayley, 1983, 1991). Discipline begins with the creation of an organization that does not accept, in any circumstances, thoughtless and demeaning behaviour, whether it is corner-cutting, verbal slights, demeaning gestures, sexual putdowns, or physical brutality. The solution to rotten apples is to fix the police barrel.

The general misunderstanding of what has to be done in order to prevent police misconduct is not surprising; it is wholly congruent with the approach to crime prevention more generally. In this view, the best way to prevent crime is through deterrent punishment. So there are calls for more jails, re-establishment of the death penalty, harsher fines, more mandatory sentences, and stricter conditions for parole. At the same time, however, many people are beginning to have serious doubts about the customary approach. Faith in the usefulness of the criminal justice system does not seem to be high. Moreover, many people understand that criminals are often made rather than born. As criminologists have demonstrated time and again, aggressive crime is not randomly distributed among people; it is carried out by, and affects most heavily, those who are poor, uneducated, unemployed, non-white, and products of broken homes (Braithwaite, 1989; Hagan, 1988). In other words, the social circumstances in which people live and work have an enormous influence on whether people will behave well or badly. This view is caught in the often-heard remark, 'There but for the grace of God, go I.'

Yet communities have trouble acting on this insight, whether in the case of criminals or errant police officers. All too often, discussions of crime become polarized between people who blame individuals and those who blame social circumstances. For the first group, the solution is punishment; for the other, improvement of circumstances. These are the 'conservative' and 'liberal' positions respectively (Walker, 1989).

With respect to the problem of misconduct by the police, this polarization produces a delicious irony. Conservatives, who want swift and sure punishment of criminals, tend to be the ones who excuse police misdeeds on the ground that their work is dangerous, dirty, and stressful. Liberals, who want to change the conditions in which criminals live, tend to be the ones who want police to be held strictly and individually accountable. People who want to punish police tend to want to understand criminals, while people who want to understand police tend to want to punish criminals.

The error of relying too heavily on deterrence for changing police behaviour is compounded by looking for some agency outside the police to do it. It is understandable that revelations about police misconduct weaken public trust in the ability of police forces to prevent misconduct, but it does not follow that an outside agency can do better. Indeed, there are several reasons for thinking it will do worse (Bayley, 1983).

First, outside agencies will know much less about wrongful actions than a police force collectively. Outside agencies, whether a civilian review board, district attorney, or judge, are always dependent on others to bring forward information about misconduct. If the informant is a member of the public, the allegation will be their word against a police officer's. It was sheer luck that someone videotaped the beating of Rodney King. There is, however, almost always a police witness to police abuses, or at least strong suspicions on the part of colleagues, such as patrol car partners, booking officers, jail custodians, and supervisors. Officers size up their colleagues all the time and word quickly gets around if an officer tends to act hastily or excessively. Officers with such reputations are often shunned by colleagues, who do not want to be put at risk of a civil suit or departmental censure. Research has shown, in fact, that appraisals officers make about the skills colleagues possess on the job conform to independent assessments of job performance, as well as to the evaluations made by supervisors (Bayley and Garofalo, 1988). If the subtleties of initiative, command presence, activity, and skill are generally known by members of the work group, it is a safe bet that brutality and other improprieties are too.

Second, outside investigation and review of discipline can actually be counterproductive, because it undermines the willingness of a police force to discipline itself. Outside intervention is invariably and instantly resented by police. It threatens the image of the police, undermining the self-esteem of its members. Police officers tell sad stories of their children being taunted for having fathers or mothers who are cops. Are you rich or is your father a cop? Notice that Chief Gates's immediate response to the Rodney King tape was to minimize the frequency of such events. When people point fingers at the police, police 'circle the wagons,' creating a conspiracy of silence so as not to tarnish the badge any further. Detectives assigned to internal investigations of complaints get the same subtle message from senior officers that they would prefer to get figures showing how many complaints are unfounded rather than how many turned out to be true (Sparrow, Moore, and Kennedy, 1990).

Third, outside intervention may also be counter-productive because it threatens the image of police officers as being skilled professionals. Civilians are seen by police as being inexpert and uninformed, unable to appreciate the operational imperatives of being a 'street cop.' Concerned with being viewed as the manual labourers of the criminal justice system, police have sought to enhance their status by stressing the scientific nature of their work, the subtleties of making decisions on the spur of the moment in dangerous and complex situations, the legal expertise required, and the stressful and dangerous nature of their work (Vollmer, 1936; Fogelson, 1977; Kelling and Moore, 1988). These features, they believe, make their work special, accessible only to experts like themselves. Civilian review, therefore, threatens this status, suggesting not only that the police cannot be trusted, but that inexperienced outsiders can evaluate the propriety of operational decisions as well as or better than they can.

Fourth, civilian review raises important political questions about the autonomy of police agencies. Ever since the Reform Era in American politics, it has been an article of faith in the United States that police are accountable to law, not to politicians. Both the police and the public are deeply distrustful of either partisan or 'special' interests deflecting the operations of law enforcement. Operational and personnel decisions particularly are supposed to be off-limits to any kind of partisanship. So whenever the idea of civilian review arises, police raise the banner of improper influence, arguing that law enforcement must not become political and amateur, but must be professional and expert.

During the 1980s the police sought to raise their image as self-regulating professionals by enacting 'value statements' which publicized the normative goals for all police actions. The Houston Police Department (1988), for example, committed itself (a) to involving the community in all police activities affecting the quality of life, (b) to preserving and enhancing democratic values, (c) to strengthening the city's neighbourhoods, (d) to improving the quality of neighbourhood life, and (e) to maintaining the highest levels of integrity and professionalism. The philosophies of community- and problem-oriented policing, developed during the 1980s, stress the development of front-line officers who can make decisions about priorities and programs that have previously been reserved for senior officers (Goldstein, 1990). Thus, renewed efforts to second-guess police officers run counter to what is regarded as innovative police management. Proponents of community-policing fear that the Rodney King incident will reinforce the traditional top-down, quasimilitaristic, highly centralized model of police discipline at the expense of the development of genuine self-guiding and responsible professionalism.

Outside intervention in police discipline puts supervisors, particularly, in a very awkward situation. It obliges them to choose between cooperating with angry outsiders or standing shoulder-to-shoulder with lifelong colleagues (Kelling and Wycoff, 1991). More is involved in this than group loyalty. To lead, one must earn respect. Police supervisors cannot be effective leaders if they are regarded as traitors to the organization. Thus, outside intervention in police discipline can undermine command authority, weakening rather than strengthening whatever disciplinary controls exist.

Fifth, civilian review is also likely to be more cumbersome and costly than internal disciplinary procedures. Police feel the need to erect procedural defences against the inexpert intrusions of outsiders. They may insist on a higher standard of proof in disciplinary decisions made by outsiders rather than by departmental colleagues. Internally, departments often act on a preponderance of evidence, like civil courts, rather than on the basis of proof beyond a reasonable doubt, like criminal courts (Goldsmith, 1991c). It is worth noting in passing, however, that the disciplinary procedures in police departments are already in the process of becoming less flexible and more formal. Several cities have recently enacted police officers' 'bills of rights' and the Congress is considering a similar bill that would apply nationwide. The net effect will be to reduce the flexibility and speed of internal disciplinary proceedings, making them more like full-fledged criminal trials.

Sixth, the ability of an outside group to affect the behaviour of individual officers is much more limited than that of the police organization itself. A civilian review board can punish, maybe admonish, but it cannot inspire, encourage, counsel, or lead by example. Outside leverage is limited; it cannot be as pervasive or as subtle as the informal controls exercised by trusted workmates.

The tragedy of the standard approach to police misconduct is that it misdiagnoses both the problem and the solution. It treats the problem almost exclusively in terms of deterring misguided individuals rather than transforming the lax management of an organization. And it finds the solution in transferring power away from the police organization to outside agencies that have even less influence over individual officers. Clinging to the belief that deterrence is the problem, the stock solution is to abandon the one institution that truly has power over the serving police officer, namely, the office organization itself. This is like saving the bath water after throwing out the baby.

Getting It Right

The police need to shape with care and forethought the social climate in which police officers work so as to encourage exemplary rather than abusive behaviour. This means that police forces must pay attention to the unintentional messages they send about what is permissible. For example, do supervisors tolerate, and sometimes participate in, telling demeaning racial and ethnic jokes? Do officers send belittling messages about the people they deal with on their computers? Do they routinely use degrading language in referring to minorities? Is locker-room humour commonly used in the presence of female officers? Are calendars and centrefolds of nude women posted on the walls in work areas? Such actions may seem small, but they set the tone of an organization. More insidiously, they legitimate a social pecking order, a hierarchy of respect, that can influence how police officers act. Because police forces are made up predominantly of white, middle class, heterosexual men, these unnoticed messages can lead to thoughtless and abusive actions particularly towards African-Americans, homosexuals, the homeless, and women.

Police forces are in an especially powerful position to influence behaviour because they deal with an impressionable group of people, namely, young, inexperienced men and women. The people who join the police are exactly the same kind who join college fraternities and sororities, compete in sports, hang out with friends, become gung-ho marines or high school cheerleaders, and join street gangs (Bayley, 1994; Carter, Sapp, Stephens, 1989). They have a tremendous need to fit in, to belong, to demonstrate that they are a reliable part of the group.

But the problem is not simply that police forces have become careless about what they tolerate. Several attitudes, which are almost articles of faith among police, strongly predispose officers to take liberties with the tremendous power they are given. Rather than being criticized, these beliefs are considered 'smart,' part of the lore that all police officers must learn (Skolnick and Fyfe, 1993).

First, police officers believe that unless criminals are caught and punished, crime and disorder will escalate until communities become unlivable. Faced with an avalanche of crime and a frightened public, they think of themselves as a 'thin blue line' standing between order and chaos (Bouza, 1990; Manning, 1977). Like the public, police too feel desperate and beleaguered. Unlike the rest of us, however, they are given the power to do something about it. They have the authority, backed up by a licence to use force, to find and punish people who commit criminal acts. Their tools are arrest and force. In these circumstances, overreaction is all but inevitable. As the saying goes, 'If you give someone a hammer, everything begins to look like a nail.'

Second, because police believe that they are the last best hope for order in a disintegrating society, it is only a short step to the view that people who treat them with disrespect constitute a serious threat to order. If not exactly criminal, such people are at least pre-criminal, displaying the kind of attitude that breeds disrespect for law and morality. Therefore, police often shape their actions according to the demeanour of citizens towards themselves – rude or polite, aggressive or acquiescent, sassy or restrained, demanding or passive, foul-mouthed or refined (Reiss, 1971; Friedrich, 1980; Bayley and Bittner, 1984). The disrespectful ones need 'to be taught a lesson', they 'can't be allowed to get away it.' This is particularly true if such people fit the stereotype of the chronic offender – young, black, and male. Police talk quite openly about people who 'flunk the Big A,' meaning the attitude test. People with a 'bad attitude' are seen not only as threatening to police individually, but as constituting a symbolic attack on law itself (Brown, 1981).

Despite this attitude on the part of police, they are undoubtedly more restrained most of the time than members of the public would be in similar circumstances. Most of the time they ignore what would be regarded as 'fighting words' by most of us. Indeed, given the frequency with which police encounter anger and aggression, the wonder is that brutality does not occur more often. This may be why senior officers instinctively minimize incidents of brutality. Compared with the provocations, they seem excusable (Sparrow, Moore, and Kennedy, 1990).

Third, police officers are convinced that they have been put in a no-win position: responsible for keeping society safe, yet unfairly and unpredictably limited in their ability to do so. They know from bitter experience about turnstile justice, as well known drug dealers, robbers, car thieves, gang 'enforcers,' and wife-abusers go back onto the streets within hours of arrest or get light sentences though plea bargains that mock any pretence of justice. And it is not only the police who have this opinion. They hear it from their friends and families, from business leaders, from the media, from politicians, and even from presidential candidates.

All of this provides an excuse for the police to take matters into their own hands, to cut through the 'bullshit' of legal procedures in order to provide the safety that the public desperately wants (Sparrow et al.,

1990; Skolnick, 1966). The fact is that the public expects impossible things of its police: it wants the police to protect the good and punish the bad, not recognizing that the police may not be able to distinguish between the two accurately. As the police remark tellingly, a liberal is a conservative who has not been mugged.

In the face of these deeply ingrained attitudes, reinforced by inconsistent messages from the public, it is unreasonable to expect that police officers will not sometimes act without due consideration for the rights of others. In such an environment, the threat of disciplinary punishment is remote and uncertain. Officers soon learn that as long as the people abused are relatively powerless, or already at risk in the eyes of the law, and that force is not grossly excessive, they are unlikely to be caught, let alone punished. Nor are their peers, supervisors, or many in the public likely to complain.

To create more responsible policing, thereby minimizing the chances that abuses of power will occur, what is needed is to insist that police forces are held accountable for the behaviour of their members. This means that police organizations must be required to manage themselves in ways that effectively discourage and minimize abuses of power. They must accept responsibility for moulding the organization's occupational culture. When misconduct occurs, blame must not fall exclusively on the rank and file but must be shared by managers for failing to prevent misconduct from occurring.

The public is not aware that during the past twenty-five years, since 1967 and the publication of the report of the President's Commission on Law Enforcement and Criminal Justice, police have become accustomed to outside examination of operational policies (United States, President's Commission, 1967). It is now standard procedure for departments to cooperate with non-police experts in evaluating the effectiveness of basic programs, such as foot patrols, mobile deployment, criminal investigation procedures, targeting high-risk offenders, and training in the use of deadly force (Bayley, 1994; Weatheritt, 1986).

The police solicit and accept outside examination of operational policies despite the fact that findings have often been inconvenient, upsetting traditional canons of management and strategy. For example, research has consistently failed to support the argument of most police chiefs that adding more police will reduce crime and produce safer communities (Loftin and McDowall, 1982; Gurr, 1979; Lane, 1980; Walker, 1989). Research has cast doubt on the value of random motorized patrol, where radio-dispatched police cars slowly drive through designated beats on the expectation that their visible presence will deter crime (Kelling, Pate, Diekman, and Brown, 1974; Kelling, 1985; and Morris and Heal, 1981). Research has also called into question the value of reducing response times to emergency calls for service and the skills required in order to be a productive criminal investigator (Tien, Simon, and Larson, 1978; Spelman and Brown, 1981; Chaiken, Greenwood, and Petersilia, 1977).

As a result of this flood of civilian evaluation of standard police practices, police managers in many countries are now actively engaged in rethinking basic strategies. The most notable new programs are community- and problem-oriented policing (Goldstein, 1990; Skolnick and Bayley, 1988). These programs call for more, not less, participation by the public in the design and targeting of police operations. Rather than resenting and rejecting the appraisals of outsiders, police officials are beginning to recognize the value of associating the public, now often referred to as 'customers,' in assessing the appropriateness of local police operations. In other words, what police instinctively resist as 'civilian review' in the area of police misconduct is now accepted routinely with respect to operational matters. Not just accepted, but advocated as essential to effective crime prevention.

On the surface this seems paradoxical. Why should civilian oversight be rejected in one area and encouraged in another? The answer to the question contains fundamental lessons for how to design civilian oversight with respect to police misconduct. Civilian review has become well established with respect to operational matters for four reasons.

1 It is policy focused. The police establishment can accept civilian review as long as it focuses on policies rather than on people. Policies are debatable, changeable, and subject to reconsideration. People, however, are protected by constitutional guarantees of due process. What happens to the careers of individuals is very sensitive, and the status of people who make decisions about them, as well as the procedures they follow, raise instinctive concerns in all of us.
2 It is expert. It has been undertaken by trained social scientists with the active participation of police managers. It has not done by amateurs.
3 It is factual. Civilian review of policy has been based on careful, systematic, rigorous examination of facts. It has been guided by the discipline of science, not considerations of politics or representation.
4 It does not usurp police decision-making authority. Policy studies

have undoubtedly made the police uncomfortable, but they have not threatened their autonomy. Research findings are at best non-binding recommendations. Police have been left to deal with them as they see fit. Their formal authority has not been threatened or negotiated away as a condition of the research being conducted.

If this analysis is correct, it has major implications for the design of effective and acceptable processes of civilian review of police conduct.

Principles of Responsible Policing

The failure to change the way police organizations are run is the problem; making police leaders accountable for management is the solution. How can this be accomplished? Here are six straightforward principles:

FIRST: THERE MUST BE FULL-TIME, NON-POLITICAL, CIVILIAN OVERSIGHT OF THE POLICE

After my strictures about the limitations of civilian review, this principle may seem surprising and contradictory. Not so. Civilian review is not wrong in principle, it is wrong in practice. Given the record of the police, discipline cannot be left to the police. Whatever the true level of misconduct, people need to be reassured that someone is independently monitoring the conduct of the police. When police reflexively oppose civilian review, they contribute to undermining their own standing. They lack credibility; they look like the fox guarding the henhouse.

It also follows that oversight cannot be left to normal political processes, such as legislative hearings or executive investigations, for they too have obviously been inattentive and ineffective. A new mechanism of oversight is needed, one which is independent of the police and gives them its full-time attention.

SECOND: THE PRIMARY PURPOSE OF INDEPENDENT OVERSIGHT IS TO
EVALUATE THE PERFORMANCE OF THE LEADERS OF POLICE ORGANIZATIONS
WITH RESPECT TO THE PREVENTION OF MISCONDUCT

The problem with most proposals for civilian review is that they focus on erring front-line personnel. What civilian oversight must do instead is to determine whether the organization has pursued policies that minimize misconduct. Rather than holding the feet of operational police officers to the fire, it should roast the managers (Goldsmith, 1991c). The critical question for civilian review is not whether a particular officer struck Rodney King, but whether police managers created an organization that increased the likelihood that any officer would engage in beating Rodney King. The purpose of outside supervision is to blow the whistle on leadership when it fails to live up to its managerial responsibilities for creating a disciplined workforce.

It is easy to say that police forces need to be held accountable for their management so as to minimize misconduct. What does that involve? What kinds of management policies affect whether abuses of power take place? Here are seventeen questions and suggestions:

1 Is the chief repeatedly and unequivocally on the record against the violation of civil rights and due process, especially the excessive use of force?

2 Is the chief willing to admit departmental shortcomings and to apologize to individuals or groups for mistakes made?

3 Has the department publicly specified the values or moral standards by which all its activities should be judged? In effect, has it stated its moral as opposed to its legal or functional purpose?

4 Does the department hold supervisors responsible for the misconduct of subordinates, right up the entire chain of command in the case of very serious and persistent abuses?

5 Has the department in good faith made efforts to diversify recruitment?

6 Has the department begun training in multiculturalism so as to enhance the ability of officers to empathize with people different from themselves? A new and powerful recommendation for how this might be done has come from the Ontario, Canada, Race Relations and Policing Task Force (1989). It suggested requiring recruits, as a condition of employment, to serve a two- or three-month internship in a community organization in a minority neighbourhood. Alternatively, internships could be made a regular part of recruit training. These proposals offer a far more meaningful way of expanding the intellectual and emotional horizons of young recruits than the usual canned lectures on 'multiculturalism.' Police readily admit that there is no substitute for on-the-job training in learning about policing. Can this be less true of learning about the diverse people that police deal with?

7 Does officer training constantly stress the manner of police action, rather than just its official outcome? Are the ethical dilemmas of law enforcement in the real world explored?

8 Does the department take advantage of cases of misconduct to re-train and re-emphasize lessons in proper behaviour? This can be done through printed circulars, case studies, video instruction, in-service classes, group discussions, and lectures at roll-calls.

9 Does the department have an early-warning system for spotting officers who may be headed for serious trouble? The Christopher Commission (1991) found in Los Angeles that a small proportion of all officers were responsible for a majority of public complaints. Over a four-year period, forty-four officers, none of them women, had six or more allegations. In Kansas City, too, twenty-five officers out of twelve hundred were responsible for half the six hundred complaints filed during a recent year. Findings like these have led several police departments, notably Chicago, Houston, and Kansas City, to set up monitoring systems to keep track of officers who receive repeated complaints. Kansas City now requires commanding officers to be notified whenever an officer gets three or more complaints in a six-month period. These officers must attend a special eight-hour class.

10 Does the department encourage the public to lodge complaints by treating them sympathetically and making the complaint process simple and responsive? For example, does the department publicize the way a complaint can be made? Does it train officers who are responsible for receiving complaints to be sympathetic rather than defensive or dismissive? Does it inform complainants of the result of its investigations?

11 Does the department actively solicit comments from people, especial-ly in communities known to distrust the police, about the perform-ance of officers? In police parlance, is the department proactive in assessing the opinions of the communities it serves? For example, does it leave self-addressed forms with people who have solicited police service so that they may record their satisfaction with the police action? Does it have supervisors call back to citizens to deter-mine whether they were pleased or displeased with what the police did?

12 Are departmental disciplinary proceedings speedy and uncompli-cated, as well as fair and impartial?

13 Does the department have procedures that encourage non-coercive

conciliation of disputes? Many complaints are matters of misunderstanding rather than real misconduct. They can be cleared up through frank discussions between police and citizens. Often citizens only what to express their point of view, to vent their sense of grievance, while officers want to citizens to know why they really had no choice and had to do what they did. A great deal of anger and hostility can be dissipated when people say, 'Oh, I didn't know that,' or 'I guess I overreacted, I'm sorry.'

14 Does the department have an active, well-staffed internal investigations unit made up of the best personnel in the department? Is internal affairs a dead-end job or a choice posting for ambitious officers?
15 Does the department encourage officers to be responsible for the conduct of one another? Do officers feel that they can advise, caution, and restrain colleagues without being resented? Are there mechanisms for peer counselling?
16 Do procedures exist whereby officers can bring questionable behaviour of other officers to the attention of supervisors without being stigmatized? Do supervisors seek out peer-group appraisals of individual performance?
17 Finally, does the department analyse patterns of complaints in order to prevent future abuses? For example, do they know whether a disproportionate number of complaints come from particular sorts of people, places, or police activities?

If a police department can answer all these questions affirmatively, it is unlikely that it has a brutality problem. Misconduct is not an accident; it is the result of organizational inattention, uncommitted leadership, and lack of managerial expertise.

THIRD: DECISIONS ABOUT POLICE DISCIPLINE MUST REMAIN THE EXCLUSIVE PREROGATIVE OF THE CHIEF OF POLICE

Outsiders are ill situated and ill equipped to control behaviour as well as police managers can. The point of civilian review is to strengthen the resolve and capacity of police managers, not to supplant them. The power of civilian review comes from publicity, as in the case of operational policy research. It comes from providing independent testimony about disciplinary performance. By rendering the performance of the police visible to the public, civilian review forces police managers to face up to their responsibilities.

This principle does not preclude civilian review agencies from examining individual cases. Indeed, they must do so, because that is the only way they can evaluate what a police force is doing. They must have the power to review all cases, to make independent investigations where called for, and they must be allowed to make recommendations. From this it follows that review agencies must have staffs of trained investigators, that they must have unlimited access to all police records and personnel, and that they must have power to subpoena. The point to bear in mind, however, is that the purpose of review is not to see that justice is done in particular cases, but to determine whether the police department is acting fairly in many cases (Lewis, 1991).

FOURTH: POLICE CHIEFS AND THEIR SENIOR STAFFS SHOULD NOT HAVE TENURE

To be made accountable, chiefs must be dismissable from their managerial posts, although they should retain their civil service status as police officers.

FIFTH: CIVILIAN REVIEW AGENCIES SHOULD NOT HAVE THE POWER TO HIRE OR FIRE THE CHIEFS OR THEIR SENIOR STAFF

Appointment and dismissal should remain the prerogative of elected politicians. Just as civilian review should not undermine police responsibility for discipline, it should also not take over the responsibilities of elected officials. If a community's elected leaders choose to keep irresponsible police leaders, they may. In democratic political systems, police are ultimately accountable to the people. The value of civilian review is that it ensures that these essentially political decisions are guided by informed analysis.

SIXTH: CIVILIAN REVIEW MUST BE EXPERT

This means that members of such agencies should be appointed rather than elected. Furthermore, members must be supported by staff trained and experienced in both policy evaluation and criminal investigation. Review staffs, to discharge their new and more important function of overseeing management and policy, should not be monopolized by criminal investigators, as has tended to be the practice. The implication of this principle is that effective civilian review cannot be obtained on the cheap.

Although these principles for ensuring an accountable police force are easy to understand, their implementation in different countries will vary according to local circumstances. The United States, for example, will have a particularly difficult time because it has at least 13,058 police agencies that report crime data regularly to the FBI (United States, Department of Justice, 1990). Creation of a policy-focused police-conduct civilian review commission for each of these would be impractical and expensive. To ensure that everyone in the United States was protected by appropriate civilian review, state governments should consider legislation that would mandate creation of civilian review boards for all jurisdictions over a certain size, supplemented by regional boards covering groups of smaller police forces. Under such a scheme, Nevada might have one; New York State would need several, not including those in its major cities. Alternatively, review of departmental management with respect to discipline in small forces might be undertaken by civilian boards in nearby metropolitan areas.

Countries with fewer separate police jurisdictions, like Australia with eight, Japan with forty-seven, and Britain with forty-three, would have an easier time (Bayley, 1992). Canada may be in the best position because of its system of police service boards and police commissions (Stenning, 1981c). With appropriate training and expert staff, they could provide ongoing independent supervision of police management of discipline as well as service delivery.

Success Is Possible

To get serious about preventing police misconduct, communities must give up their single-minded attachment to deterrence. Punishing a few 'rotten apples' is simply not enough. The more powerful remedy, which is also likely to be more acceptable to the police, is to require public but expert evaluation of the performance of police managers in shaping organizational culture. This does not require a redistribution of either disciplinary or political power. Police must be sovereign in discipline; elected politicians must retain the right to hire and fire police chiefs.

The police organization is the key to obtaining high levels of conduct. Police autonomy is essential to obtaining the willing participation of police in this task. And civilian review is necessary for assuring the public that police leaders are measuring up to their managerial responsibilities. Following these precepts, police forces can be made reliably accountable at last.

Necessary but Not Sufficient: The Role of Public Complaints Procedures in Police Accountability

ANDREW GOLDSMITH

A public complaints procedure for dealing with civilian dissatisfaction concerning police conduct is only one means of formally addressing the issue of police accountability. Criminal prosecutions, disciplinary proceedings, and civil actions against police officers (Clayton and Tomlinson, 1987) provide other channels for concerns of this nature. In principle at least, there are also political channels for challenging police action and seeking redress (see Jefferson and Grimshaw, 1984; Lustgarten, 1986; Stenning, 1981a). In addition, the media can play a significant role in contributing to the sense of scandal and urgency that prompts other accountability mechanisms into life (Sherman, 1978; Skolnick and McCoy, 1984; Ericson, Baranek, and Chan, 1987) Nevertheless, debates concerning trends in, causes of, and solutions to complaints against police conduct in many respects have come to symbolize the entire question of police accountability (Goode, 1991). Institutionally, public complaints procedures have provided the obvious formal channel for the reception of grievances from ordinary members of the population.

In this respect, public complaints procedures represent the preeminent, if not for all practical purposes the exclusive, grassroots mechanism for citizen input on a wide variety of policing practices (Goldsmith, 1991a). Discipline is typically closed to external gaze, and criminal prosecutions are brought and directed by the state. Individual legal actions by citizens are commonly dogged by problems of delay and expense. Aside from these options, the constitutional landscape of public policing suggests a definite preference for an arms-length relationship between police, government, and members of the public (Jefferson and Grimshaw, 1984; Lustgarten, 1986; Stenning, 1981). In recent times, some emphasis has been given by senior police officers and government policy-makers to initiatives under the rubric of 'community policing' (such as Neighbourhood Watch and other public security programs). However, in view of the limited objectives of many such programs and the evidence that there is often considerable police and bureaucratic dominance of such schemes (T. Bennett, 1990), there is no obvious challenge in principle to the structured opportunity that public complaints procedures provide for ordinary citizens to make a direct input on matters of policing directly affecting their lives. The scope and performance of these procedures, then, are issues of vital importance.

The object of this essay is to provide an overview of the contribution that procedures for public complaints against police make to the larger question of police accountability. I propose to do this first by looking at the recent history of complaints procedures in a number of Western countries, relating changes and conflicts to the wider public concerns of the time. The objectives and expectations of complaints systems are then discussed, with particular focus on the problems that have emerged in attempts to implement these expectations. These problems are explored in terms of the persistent difficulties the police face in maintaining public confidence on the question of accountability. In examining the possibilities and prospects for significant reform in this area, the essay further pursues an argument (Goldsmith, 1991b) concerned with the importance of the *informational* as well as *sanctional* significance of complaints for the improvement of police policy and operations. It goes beyond a functional analysis to examine the changing nature of police discourse and the impact these changes have for discussions of complaints procedures and police accountability.

By way of explanation, this essay attempts to provide a comparative perspective on the questions addressed. It refers at different stages to developments in Australia, Canada, the United States, and the United Kingdom by way of illustration of general themes and issues. The case for drawing such comparisons has been made elsewhere (Goldsmith, 1991c), and will not be repeated here.

The Concept of Accountability

Before turning to an account of some significant themes in the debates about police accountability over the past three decades or so, it makes sense to consider accountability conceptually, so as to appreciate the basis upon which discussions on how best to deal with complaints against police have come to represent the larger question of accountability. In so doing, an understanding of the limitations of a wholesale reliance upon complaints procedures for the maintenance of accountability should begin to emerge.

The concept of accountability in the police setting is generally discussed in relation to the notion of police discretion (see Goldstein, 1977; Brown, 1981). The existence of discretion is said to necessitate the operation of effective accountability mechanisms to ensure compliance with defined standards of behaviour. Police accountability can therefore be said to refer to 'processes whereby the behaviour of police is brought into conformity with the requirements of the encapsulating society' (Bayley, 1985: 160). These processes can take a number of forms, and they vary as to the degree of external influence they bring to bear. While accountability can be 'passive,' taking the form of *ex post facto* explanations for particular actions or policies, it can also permit direct external input into the determination of policies. This latter, 'active' form of accountability is similarly directed to achieving compliance with behavioural standards, but it is obviously more intrusive in form and hence threatening to the degree of organizational autonomy of the target agency than the former 'passive' approach. As the subsequent discussion suggests, the debate around public complaints procedures reflects many of the tensions that permeate attempts to alter the balance along the 'passive–active' continuum of accountability.

As well as the concern about *conformity to particular standards* inherent in the notion of accountability, there is also the dimension of the *range of issues* that falls to be considered. Increasingly, it can be argued, an expanded meaning has been given to accountability in the police context, whereby a broader range of matters is envisaged to be subject to accountability than just the control of discretion by individual officers in operational matters. Normative considerations affecting this expanded range of issues arise from contexts other than the law or disciplinary codes. This enlarged sense of accountability has previously been described as follows: 'Accountability, in its broadest sense, includes much more than responsibility for determining policies in discretionary areas. It covers every aspect of administration of an agency, including, for example, its operating efficiency, its hiring and promotion practices, and its financial management. Accountability encompasses as well responsibility for the conduct of individual employees – for the use which they make of their authority and for their integrity' (Goldstein, 1977: 131). It is clear from this approach that accountability presupposes an interest in system-wide issues, as well as matters arising from specific acts by individual officers. While this distinction is largely artificial, it does illustrate the possibility of pursuing accountability at different levels of organizational generality or abstraction, as well as seeing police work as the result of a number of interrelated organizational processes. Thus, a legalistic preoccupation with the conformity or otherwise of individual officers to substantive or procedural standards is only a very partial and incomplete approach to the issue of accountability. The familiar demand within traditional mechanisms of accountability for strongly punitive treatment of offenders in individual complaints ignores a number of considerations, including the most fundamental of all: 'Both the police and the public become so preoccupied with identifying wrongdoing and taking disciplinary action against errant officers that they lose sight of the primary objective of control, which is to achieve maximum conformity with legal requirements, establishing policies, and prevailing standards of propriety' (Goldstein, 1977: 160). Thus, the multifaceted nature of the task of ensuring conformity to established standards of policing should not be lost sight of in any balanced and effective mechanism of accountability.

A Recent History of Complaints against Police

Two relevant observations arise from an examination of the history of the modern police institution in virtually any Western, English-speaking country since 1829. The first is the persistent and pervasive nature of police misconduct as an organizational and public problem. Histories of individual police forces are replete with accounts of instances of petty thievery, corruption, drunkenness, and brutality committed by rank-and-file police officers (Critchley, 1978; Fogelson, 1977; McQuilton, 1987). The discovery of such occurrences resulted often in dismissal or criminal prosecution of individual officers under the militaristic style of discipline practised in nineteenth-century police forces. Police histories in the twentieth century are similarly replete with examples of misconduct and corruption of various kinds, often receiving the attention of the media and becoming matters of official and public concern (Sherman, 1978; Fitzgerald, 1989). The reasons for the persistence of this behaviour are diverse and complex, reflecting among other things the uncertainty surrounding the police mandate and the difficulty of regulating operational police discretion (Smith and Gray, 1983; Goldsmith, 1990). As a consequence however, various forms of misconduct have come to constitute a perennial problem for police administrators from a disciplinary as well as public relations perspective.

A second observation is that for much of this institutional police history, public discussions of the 'problem' of police accountability have often focused upon the role and possible contribution of different complaints procedures in remedying deficiencies in accountability and community relations (Goode, 1991; Scarman, 1983). Public attention and the recommendations of official inquiries have been addressed to the need to alter the existing complaints systems, tending thereby to displace more fundamental questions concerning popular political control of the police (McMahan and Ericson, 1984). In reviewing now the post-Second World War experience with questions of police accountability and complaints, some possible explanations for this apparent preference for changes to complaints procedures will be considered.

THE APPARENT FALLIBILITY OF THE POLICE

It is widely accepted that between the late 1950s (in the case of the United States at least) and the early 1970s (in the instances of Australia and Canada), there was a discernible deterioration in relations between the police and at least certain segments of the population. A variety of social factors have been mentioned by way of explanation, including the impact of postwar immigration from countries with quite different cultural traditions, the development of civil rights consciousness in the United States in the early 1960s and slightly later in other places, the Vietnam War protest movement, and, more generally, the growing practice of mass civil demonstrations on a range of issues (Terrill, 1991). In addition to these pressures from socially deviant groups, among more traditional sectors there was growing concern about rising crime rates and the apparent increases in public disorder, fuelled very often by sensationalist media reports. There was also growing concern among civil liberties groups with the documented cases of police brutality, harassment, and racism (Chevigny, 1969), and the increased prevalence of motor vehicles meant that more ordinary citizens were coming into contact with police than in the past.

Whatever the respective contributions of these factors might have been, their combined effect was to make police conduct and accountability issues of public concern and debate on an unprecedented scale. The explanation for the degree to which enthusiasm for reform has dwelt upon the prospects offered by different forms of complaints mechanisms is not exactly clear, but there are features of the wider context of police developments which help to make sense of this phenomenon.

Although appearing under different rubrics, the official statements of many senior police officers over the past hundred years or so have stressed the arm's-length relationship that they believe is appropriate between the police and the community, including its agencies of government. The police, it is argued, should be 'above politics.' In the United Kingdom as well as Australia and Canada, the doctrine of constabulary independence has exercised considerable influence not just over the thinking and practices of senior police but also the courts and governments (Marshall, 1965; Jefferson and Grimshaw, 1984; Lustgarten, 1986; Stenning, 1981). This doctrine, while controversial and undoubtedly subject to some relaxation in more recent years (see Stenning, 1981), has been based upon the idea that the police constable's primary obligation is to 'the law.' In this way, police have sought to perpetuate the notion of the unseemliness of police involvement in political matters, whether in the form of involvement in specific controversies or government attempts at political direction.

While American police history reveals some rather long-standing and overt linkages between police forces and local politics (Walker, 1977), the various ongoing attempts to professionalize the police departments since the 1920s and 1930s suggest some parallels with the United Kingdom, Canada, and Australia (Goldstein, 1977; Manning, 1977). The thrust of the 'professionalization' phenomenon includes the suggestion that the police possess unique skills and expertise which differentiate them from others on questions of law and order and that self-regulation is the appropriate model of accountability (Brown, 1981). The influence of this phenomenon has not been confined to the United States, as an examination of police reform rhetoric in other countries reveals (Reiner, 1985).

The result of these two trends, it is suggested, has been to serve to insulate the police from outside influence. This has been particularly true at the level of police policy, whereas various scholars have commented upon the perhaps inevitable but nevertheless diffuse influence of community values and expectations upon operational styles of policing (Wilson, 1969; Brown, 1981). In this environment, public complaints procedures, especially those that rely exclusively or predominantly upon *internal* investigations, appear relatively unthreatening to the organization and administration of police forces. The distinction between internal and external complaints mechanisms will be discussed further in the next section. However, there are a number of characteristics of the complaints process that help to explain the relative prominence of complaints issues in accountability debates. Before proceeding, one factor which ought to be mentioned, although the evidence is impressionistic, is the high degree of interest shown by lawyers in the reform of the complaints system. Lawyers, particularly those of a civil libertarian orientation, are well aware of the drawbacks of various forms of litigation as means of providing accountability to individuals and see in changes to complaint procedures an alternative, individual case-based method for providing what ought to be relatively expeditious justice in civil rights issues around policing. This would seem to have been the case at least in Australia; see Goode, 1991; Australia Law Reform Commission, 1975.

Complaints traditionally have taken the form of individual complaints about the actions of particular officers. Aggrieved citizens have had to initiate complaints in their own name concerning particular actions of police officers, rather than raising matters of general policy or administration. Typically, the officers complained about have been rank-and-file officers or at least those directly engaged in dealings with members of the public. Thus, because the focus has been on operational incidents, the targets have almost always been identifiable. Complaints in this way have become 'personified.' From a senior police perspective, this approach has facilitated resort to disciplinary measures, and in some cases criminal prosecution, as a means of dealing publicly with problems raised by complaints. Disciplinary and criminal proceedings, however, tend to isolate offenders by concentrating upon notions of personal responsibility and culpability for particular actions, resulting in sanctions against individuals officers in cases of established wrongdoing. In this state of affairs, there is no admission of more pervasive organizational factors at work in explaining the action giving rise to the grievance, so that the domain of police administrators in relation to setting matters of policy emerges unscathed. Complaints viewed in this way become handmaidens of internal police discipline, rather than 'windows' into the organization.

Using terminology from the sociology of policing, the focus on individual complaints echoes the dominance in police and official circles for a long time (Fitzgerald, 1989) of the 'bad apple' theory of police deviance. This theory suggests that deviance by police officers must be analysed in individual, exceptional terms, so that the appropriate organizational response to individual misconduct is to deal with that individual separately, akin to removing a rotten apple from a barrel in order to avoid tainting the other apples. From the perspective of a military-style organization, this approach preserves the integrity of the administrative hierarchy and does not call into question the basic objectives or established policies of the organization. While this is done presumably to protect the legitimacy of the organization as well as the authority of senior police officers, its retrospective, individualistic, and often punitive orientation arguably does little to allay public concerns in the face of evidence of widespread, ongoing misconduct (Fitzgerald, 1989; Punch, 1985).

That public debates concerning police accountability should arise from specific complaints or allegations concerning police conduct should scarcely be surprising (Sherman, 1978). This pattern is observable in each of the countries considered, reflecting the way in which most matters arise for attention and debate (Goldsmith and Farson, 1987; Marguire, 1991). When one examines the history of complaints procedures in the United Kingdom, for example, the prominence of such matters in accountability debates in striking, and in particular, the relationship between complaints procedures and public confidence in the police. Complaints were a key issue in the 1908, 1929, and 1962 royal commissions, which looked into police practices following public criticism and concerns about relationships with the community. The third reference of the 1962 commission reflected this perceived link 'to consider, (3) the relationship of the police with the public and the means of ensuring that complaints by the public against the police are effectively dealt with' (United Kingdom, Royal Commission on the Police, 1962: iv). The majority of the 1962 commission members decided against recommending the establishment of an independent investigative system for complaints, preferring to tighten internal disciplinary procedures and those for dealing with complaints. A minority favoured an independent mechanism along the lines of the Scandinavian ombudsman (Critchley, 1978).

Revelations of police corruption in the 1970s and the racial nature of the urban riots of the early 1980s continued to raise in the United Kingdom the theme of a close connection between police relations with the public and the nature of the complaints system. It was in 1972 that the Metropolitan Police established for the first time a separate investigation unit (A10) for dealing with complaints, while 1977 saw the creation of the Police Complaints Board, the first non-police body specifically involved to some degree with public complaints. Ongoing public confidence problems, particularly with black youths, played a role in the subsequent creation of a Police Complaints Authority in 1985, following criticisms of the previous system by Lord Scarman (Scarman, 1982).

In North America, demands for movement away from the police investigating complaints against themselves began as early as the late 1950s, following the identification of problems between police and blacks in Philadelphia by the American Council of Civil Liberties (Terrill, 1991). The 1960s saw a series of largely unsuccessful civilian review boards attempt to shore up declining public confidence in the police as race relations problems were compounded by repeated revelations of pervasive, ongoing police brutality and misconduct (Chevigny, 1969). The 1970s and 1980s have witnessed the persistent nature of the civilian review issue in the face of ongoing public controversies concerning police excesses of one kind or another (Terrill, 1991).

In the case of Canada, the origin of demands for changes to the complaints systems can be found in Toronto in the early 1970s, when allegations of police misconduct with respect to certain minority groups resulted in the Maloney report of 1975, which was charged solely with examining police complaint procedures (Goldsmith and Farson, 1987; Lewis, 1991). One of the principal recommendations of that report was the establishment of an independent complaints commissioner. It took several more inquiries and ongoing concerns about police relations with visible minority groups before legislation establishing such an office became effective in December 1981.

The Australian experience with changes to complaints against the police has not been driven by the same degree of police–public relations problems evident elsewhere, owing more perhaps to revelations of police corruption and misconduct generally (Fitzgerald, 1989). It has also been a topic of keen interest to law reformers in Australia, whose interest to some degree seems to have been driven by a desire to rationalize criminal investigative procedure generally as well as an awareness of developments in other countries (ALRC, 1975; Goode, 1991). More recently, in the late 1980s and early 1990s, the discovery of massive police corruption in one state police force (Fitzgerald, 1989) and the findings of the Royal Commission into Aboriginal Deaths in Custody (Australia, 1991) have only underlined the need for public scepticism towards the idea of the police being entrusted with the task of investigating themselves. The Australian findings unearthed almost unfathomable depths of mistrust among Aboriginals towards internal investigations. The final report (vol. 4, p. 129) refers to the 'reluctance, if not paralysis, that seems to descend on many police officers when called on to investigate other police officers.' Such perceptions are scarcely confined to Aboriginal groups.

This review points to the clear coincidence across several countries between debate and reform in the area of police-community relations and changes to the system for dealing with complaints against police. Generally speaking, this focus on complaints has been at the expense of wider debates about the democratic control of policing, particularly at a local level. Such debates have been more evident in some countries (for the United Kingdom see Jefferson and Grimshaw, 1984; Spencer, 1985) than in others (such as Australia) where debates of this nature have been relatively absent. In contrast to the United States, Canada, and the United Kingdom, Australia has strongly centralized police forces, each state having its own force. Criminal law is mainly a matter of state law. For reasons which are not clear, there has been relatively little debate of the kind evident in other jurisdictions, about the need to 'democratize' and 'decentralize' policing (Jefferson and Grimshaw, 1984; Spencer, 1985). A recent trend towards decentralization in some forces seems more a reflection of management philosophy than any concession obtained at the expense of managerial control. This, of course, seems paradoxical in such a centralized police system. Perhaps, however, it helps to explain the degree of emphasis given to complaint procedures in Australian law reform.

Either with or without such debates about the democratic control of policing, complaints seem to have provided a focal point for concerns about accountability across a wide range of community groups. While as targets of complaints, police officers have scarcely revelled in public debate addressing the need to tighten such procedures, it seems likely that organizationally this option is viewed by the police as far less threatening than structural challenges to the relationships between the police, government, and the community, which have traditionally been strongly resisted (Jefferson and Grimshaw, 1984).

Objectives, Expectations, and Experiences

Confirmation for the view that complaints have come to represent in large measure the wider question of police accountability can be found in recent attempts to specify the main objectives of public complaints procedures. Maguire and Corbett (1991: 13) list four objectives, without any pretence that their list is definitive:

1 The maintenance (through punishment or general deterrence) of 'discipline in the ranks'
2 The satisfaction of complainants
3 The maintenance of public confidence in the police
4 The provision of 'feedback from consumers' to police managers

A number of remarks can be made in respect to this list. As a preliminary observation, however, it seems plausible to suggest that without any attempt to rank these objectives overall, the maintenance of public confidence must surely underlie the efforts made to realize the other objectives. The moral authority of the police cannot be reduced simply to questions of legal power or administrative efficiency, as Radelet recognizes: 'Efficient administration is not necessarily effective administration from the point of view of community relations. Efficiency may become an end in itself, which dehumanizes administration and creates serious internal or external problems. Police *effectiveness* in social control is closely linked with their moral authority; it is dependent in large degree on community support' (1980: 304). In this context, a 'key question is how to channel grievances constructively, inside and outside the department' (ibid.: 304).

In terms of the contribution complaints can make to police discipline, it is a commonplace of police scholarship that the idea of the police as developed by Sir Robert Peel and applied subsequently owes a considerable amount to the military model of organization and discipline (Critchley, 1978). One aspect of the police borrowing of this model has been the importance attached until the present by senior police officers to retaining sole control over the discipline. This has meant that irrespective of the source of the original complaint, the police hierarchy must assume responsibility for taking action to deal with the complaint. This approach has had two corollaries; first, that internal discipline has tended to take priority over the concerns of the complainant, while, second, the tendency has been to react punitively towards the officer concerned, without obvious regard to wider issue of administrative practice and public confidence.

These corollaries have pointed to the difficulties associated with grafting a complaints procedure onto a disciplinary system, particularly when signs appear of the public having different expectations of the complaints procedure from those of the senior police management. So long as the complaints procedures remained entirely internal, largely secretive affairs, leading in the case of substantiated complaints to discipline, the authority of police management was not threatened. It has only been since demands have been made for various forms of external investigation or review of complaints that the military model has fallen into question, provoking a lot of resistance among rank-and-file police officers as well as senior police managers to the idea of external involvement. It is only comparatively recently that persistent public demands for greater external involvement in complaints procedures have succeeded to any degree in moving the approach away from a military-style approach (Goldsmith, 1991c).

The degree of police resistance to this challenge of their prerogatives has meant that the reception of civilian complaints bodies of various kinds has not been generally smooth. These bodies have found themselves to be the victims of campaigns, often successful, to close them down or severely curtail their power (Terrill, 1991; Freckelton, 1991). It has also meant that very often these bodies have had to strike delicate balances between their public function with respect to complaints and police administrative and disciplinary requirements, a task fraught with extreme difficulty, given the degree of police opposition to their existence in principle as well as fact. Often the result has been an ineffective, and ultimately unsuccessful, compromise arrangement (Fitzgerald, 1989; Goldsmith, 1991b; Finnane, 1990).

This insistence by police on maintaining discipline can be seen to have mixed consequences for the satisfaction of complaints. While there is comparatively little survey information on this topic, some recent results and anecdotal accounts point to a variety of motives for complaining. While one might predict that a desire to see the responsible officer punished would dominate the reasons complainants gave, Maguire and Corbett's recent study of complaints (1951) in regional police forces in the United Kingdom found that only a minority of complainants felt especially vindictive towards the officers involved. Less than one-quarter of complainants wanted the officer formally disciplined. Other motivations included making a point (20 per cent), 'ticking off' the officer (18 per cent), and an apology (20 per cent) (ibid.: 57). Their survey of complainants in London showed a similar range of motives, with still a minority 'out for blood' even when the complaints concerned assaults by police officers. Seventy-eight per cent of complainants in that survey mentioned among their reasons for complaining the desire to stop it happening to somebody else (1991: 167). These kind of results would seem to indicate that satisfaction of complainants and the maintenance of discipline require a more diverse and sensitive system for dealing with complaints than just a reliance on police discipline. It therefore has not been surprising to see greater emphasis in recent times on conciliation and other forms of informal resolution (Corbett, 1991). However, it would be wrong to regard these alternatives as simply individualistic, less punitive options to a sanctions-based disciplinary system. The reasons given by complainants indicate the need for greater attention to systemic responses to problems of which individual complaints are only symptoms.

COMPLAINTS AS INFORMATION

The strategic importance of complaints, viewed as forms of feedback on the performance of the police organization, is one function that has tended to be ignored (Goldsmith, 1991b), although there have been some encouraging signs of a change of attitude, particularly in situations where there is a mission-oriented external body involved in dealing with complaints (Goldsmith, 1991b; Maguire and Corbett, 1991). Quite obviously, the value of the information derivable from complaints will depend on the success the body in question has in attracting complaints from members of the public with grievances against the police and on the ways in which this information is processed and analysed once complaints have been collected. While the second point refers to matters that go to police efficiency as well as public trust, the first consideration raises fundamentally the question of public confidence in the complaints process and, therefore, public trust in the police.

One of the profound ironies of policing is that while the stock-in-trade of police work is information, there is plenty of evidence that police have been reluctant to take seriously the information provided by would-be complainants and complainants (Goldsmith, 1991b). While it might be said that such information is not welcomed because it bears no relevance to the solving of crime or the maintenance of order, such a perspective ignores the link between public trust and the willing provision of information: 'There is an inconsistency between lamenting, on the one hand, the apathy of the public regarding problems that loom large for the police, and on the other hand resisting the right and obligation of citizens to complain about what they perceive as improper police conduct' (Radelet, 1980: 305). It also ignores the potential relevance of information from complaints that bears upon issues of the effectiveness of police operations. For example, complaints may point to certain sorts of telephone requests for assistance not receiving adequate follow-up. As well as posing a public relations issue, such information raises questions of resource allocation and provides a measure of public concerns in particular neighbourhoods. A sympathetic method for the collection and handling of complaints would seem to offer the prospect of more public cooperation in the forms of provision of information more directly related to operational matters. The two sorts of information, in other words, are not unrelated.

There are many reasons why citizens do not complain. Without going into the various reasons (see Goldsmith, 1991b), one factor evident in a range of different jurisdictions has been a fundamental lack of confidence in complaints procedures operated by the police. In this sense, an absence of complaints would seem a greater cause for concern than the phenomenon of a rise in reported complaints. As I noted in an earlier piece, 'it seems probable that citizens least often complain directly to the police when public confidence in the police is low: in other words, when there is most need for complaints to be gathered and analysed systematically' (ibid.: 21). While it is difficult to estimate the degree of underreporting, the past history of internal complaints systems (ibid.) has scarcely provided material encouragement for citizens to complain, and the survey evidence (which is admittedly limited) suggests that lack of confidence in the complaints system is the most common reason given by citizens for not complaining (London Police Strategy Unit, 1987). The indicators then point to a likely problem of underreporting, an impression consistent with the evidence of the establishment of informal police monitoring schemes (McMahon and Ericson, 1984; London, Police Strategy Unit, 1987) and the persistent nature of demands for more external, civilian-staffed complaints mechanisms (Goldsmith, 1991c).

THE 'CONSUMER' PERSPECTIVE

The 'consumer feedback' justification for complaints procedures poses the interesting issues of how many dissatisfied 'consumers' of the criminal justice system are not complaining, who they are, and whether their exclusion is warranted in any way. Certainly, there is a view among rank-and-file officers that the sort of persons who complain are essentially troublemakers, either simply 'anti-police' or cynical exploiters seeking leverage in respect of charges laid against them (Maguire and Corbett, 1991). This stance, of course, tells more about the nature and extent of police hostility towards complainants than anything about those who do *not* complain. The fact remains that to complain requires some sense of personal capability or power, a fact which disadvantages the less articulate and those intimidated by bureaucracies of any kind, but especially ones such as the police which command so much power and authority by comparison with ordinary individuals (Goldsmith, 1991b).

The exclusion of the powerless from the complaints system poses the question whether it is defensible for any accountability system to exclude any citizen or group of citizens. Phrased in terms of 'citizenship,' the answer to this question should be obvious. The view that public accountability of the police 'should mean all of the public, the powerless as well as the powerful' (Radelet, 1980: 303) is a persuasive one. The following comment by Hogg and Findlay concerning the relationship between accountability and the 'consumers' of police powers points, by implication, to the critical role offered by complaints procedures in securing at least some measure of accountability for these vulnerable groups: 'The real test of police accountability and responsiveness to the community must lie in their relationships with those with whom they have the most frequent contact, groups who currently tend to be the least favoured by police stereotypes and working images' (1988: 52). If accountability is an objective in criminal justice, then the exclusion from a complaints mechanism of those groups to whom Radlet, and Hogg and Findlay, refer seems entirely unacceptable in a democratic society.

To return to the question of accounting to those who *have* complained, the fact of complaining is scarcely the end of the story, as any examination of the substantiation figures or the degree of complainant satisfaction with complaints mechanisms will reveal. There seems to have been an almost institutionalized reluctance in some police forces to take complaints seriously enough to record them, let alone investigate them seriously (Goldsmith, 1991b). This same reluctance would appear to make sense of the legion of criticisms levelled against internal investigations of complaints against police (ibid.). In this regard, serious attention must be paid to the consequences of the 'police culture' (see Goldsmith, 1990), which not only seems to maintain an 'us against them' syndrome, but which also serves to frustrate the ability of investigators (whether they be internal or external) to obtain the cooperation of officers during investigations of complaints (Bayley, 1985). I will return to the occupational dimension later in this essay.

One of the most potent criticisms that can be made about a complaints mechanism is its inability to substantiate a significant number of complaints. If one accepts that virtually all complaints stem from a genuine sense of grievance (Maguire and Corbett, 1991) and that the majority of complainants are not liars, the low substantiation figures (Goldsmith, 1991b) are difficult to explain, especially to complainants whose sense of injustice is strong and whose trust in the police is limited or practically non-existent (Waddington and Braddock, 1991). A Cook's tour of the problems of legal proof associated with substantiating a complaint is unlikely to provide much satisfaction to those whose sense of justice has been offended. Although the reasons for low substantiation of complaints are complex and diverse, they are essentially *legal* reasons that do little to address the subjective situation of complainants or sceptical onlookers of the process.

It has been argued that a consequence of the legalistic nature of official complaints discourse is to downplay the scope and significance of these subjective positions (McMahon, 1988). This leaves the complaints system with credibility problems and does little to provide any sense of police accountability. This analysis of the human face of the complaints process accords with the disturbing degree of dissatisfaction voiced by more than two-thirds of the complainants in Maguire and Corbett's (1991) recent British study. Interestingly, Maguire and Corbett analyse this finding in terms of a pervasive communications problem; complainants frequently felt left out of the process and left in the dark in terms of knowing how their case was progressing. Another way of expressing this point might be that complainants experienced the complaints system in question as providing very little sense of empowerment (Merry, 1990). A perceived absence of empowerment would seem to undercut the very rationale factor such a procedure. Without some sense of 'making a difference,' a complainant is likely to view singleminded proceduralism in the context of low substantiation rates as tantamount to the pointlessness of the overall process.

The Quest for Sufficiency

Predicting the future of complaints mechanisms in terms of their contribution to police accountability is difficult. One of the few certainties about institutional reforms in the area of policing is that achieving consensus about what ought to be done is almost impossible and, in any event, unlikely to last long if it is even approximated. In such a dynamic environment, one is forced back to an examination of funda-mental issues concerning the nature of police work and the exercise of police discretion. Michael Brown notes:

> If there is a lesson to be learned from the experiences of the most recent gener-ation of reformers, it is that simply enveloping policemen in a maze of institu-tional controls without grappling with the grimy realities of police work does not necessarily promote accountability and may only exacerbate matters ... Yet no one should entertain any illusions about the outcome of any effort at reform. Police work inevitably entails the arbitrary use of power: brutality, corruption, the violation of individual rights, and the penchant to take the law into one's own hands, to use it as a tool to right wrongs and attain 'justice.' It is mislead-ing and naive to think these abuses of power can ever be entirely eliminated, for they are the products of an occupation based on coercion. And as long as the police continue to wield broad coercive powers, the relationship between the police and the communities they serve will be characterized by a dialectical process in which the demand for external control by the public is contradicted by an effort of the police to limit such control. (1981: 303–5)

Brown concludes this analysis of police reform: 'What is needed is a system of institutions which will permit continued reflection on the ends of police work and encourage responsiveness, while forcing the policeman to re-examine continually the contradiction between the ends he serves and the means he uses to attain them (ibid: 304). This analysis bears two points of significance for the role of complaints mechanisms. One is the insufficiency of any conceivable complaints procedure to adequately meet the problems identified by Brown. The other is the potential contribution that complaints mechanisms can make to the reflective processes advocated by Brown and as a means of ensuring responsiveness to external concerns.

The largely individualistic focus of complaints procedures has already been noted. Even with the indications of some complaints bodies exhib-iting a more systemic approach to the analysis of complaints, the struc-tural location of these bodies and the degree of political influence they can exercise, which are the product of their resources as well as their constitutional and legal status, constrain the degree to which they can highlight, let alone have an impact on, the wider considerations that frame the debates on police accountability (see Freckelton, 1991). There was never the intention that complaints mechanisms should challenge the fundamental responsibility of the police for the prevention of crime and enforcement of the law, by calling into question the traditional arrangements for accountability or by putting forward a more authoritative account of the reasons for the problems facing the police. The notion of checks and balances in respect of policing, of which complaints procedures constitute only a part, implies an essentially shared perspective by the community, allowing for some variation in emphasis and a recognition of the potential for excesses from time to time. This does not mean that changes in complaints mechanisms do not serve as barometers of wider factors concerning the role of police and their accountability, as I have discussed above, but it does suggest the importance of realism in terms of what we can plausibly expect of complaints procedures. While recognizing the necessity for complaints mechanisms of some kind, we should not lose sight of the need for additional methods of tackling these wider considerations.

The advantage presented by complaints mechanisms is their established and, in some shape or form, accepted presence. A case does not have to be made for their creation, only for the extent of their powers and whether they should be partly or wholly external in form. They are expressly designed to allow members of the public to voice concerns and dissatisfactions about matters arising from operational policing. Another way of conceptualising their role is as listening posts. The idea of 'listening posts' naturally would seem to suggest 'hearing' as a consequence. As various elements of this essay suggests, this is all too infrequently true of procedures for dealing with complaints against the police. The theme of the capacity of the police to 'hear' different groups is also relevant in terms of the section later in this essay addressing the declining authority of police discourse.

The need for grassroots mechanisms for providing feedback to the police has been identified by David Bayley (1989) as a response to demands for community policing. Whether community policing is interpreted as consultation or participation in the formulation of police policy, the importance of treating complaints seriously under any commitment to community policing should be obvious (Goldsmith, 1991a). The challenge remains to persuade those groups within the community affected by police activity that these procedures are in some sense empowering. Persuasion of this kind will not emerge from official statements about the formal powers of the system in place, but rather from perceptions that the system in practice does make some difference, which will depend on a number of conspicuous results from the lodging of complaints by members of groups sceptical towards the system in place. This is a point which, at least in some jurisdictions, senior police officers and some in government seem not to have recognized. (My familiarity with recent debates concerning the adequacy of existing arrangements for handling complaints against police in the Australian state of Victoria points to a deeply held institutional reluctance by both the police and the police ombudsman to construe the issue in other than legalistic ways.)

A natural enough question in recent times, in the face of ongoing problems of police legitimacy and the record surrounding internal police investigations of complaints, has been whether external involvement in the investigation and determination of complaints offers any prospect of an improvement in public confidence in complaints systems and the police generally. Several points can be made. It must be admitted that there is no evidence that external investigation will improve significantly the substantiation rates of complaints investigated, in that there is research to suggest that the 'blue curtain' of police solidarity will close in the face of internal as well as external investigations (Maguire and Corbett, 1991; Smith and Gray, 1983), thus frustrating any attempts to thoroughly pursue allegations against police officers. Where there has been previous evidence of absolute incompetence or lack of will in the conduct of internal investigations (Fitzgerald, 1989), substantiation of complaints could only be expected to improve through external involvement. Nevertheless the police culture remains a real obstacle.

One clear advantage of external participation is the substance it lends to the perception that investigation of complaints will be impartially carried out, a basis for public confidence which has continued to elude the most determined efforts of internal investigations departments to justify their continued dominance of complaints investigations. Two familiar justifications for the status quo have been the presumed superiority of internal investigations, arising from an attributed better access to the police organization through familiarity with its ways of operation, and flowing from the competence of specialist police investigators. These claims have received the support of some police scholars, such as Bayley (1985, and in this volume). However, the experience of the past decade or so with civilian investigators working in ombudsmen's offices and specialist police complaints authorities suggests that police no longer at least are the sole repository of investigative skills relevant to the investigation of complaints (Lewis, 1991). The issue of *police expertise* is a broader one, to which I return shortly.

The question of the optimal complaints system cannot be definitively answered. The needs in particular situations will vary, according to the degree and nature of the problems arising between the police and members of the community. In some situations, relations may be so bad as to warrant a fully independent system for the investigation and determination of complaints, including the imposition of discipline on officers, while others may be adequately met by the provision of an element of external supervision, along the lines of early ombudsman models (see Goldsmith, 1988, 1991b), leaving the essential responsibility for investigation and determination to the police themselves. What is critical in assessing these different forms for the investigation of complaints is their significance in terms of public perceptions and their contribution to public confidence in the police. While senior police and bureaucrats may be convinced by their own formalistic, self-referential defences of the current arrangements, ongoing problems in police–community relations continue to indict this reasoning and underline the deficiencies of the existing procedures. It is trite, but insufficiently appreciated, that public confidence cannot be legislated or mandated in some other way, but has to be earned. While the basis on which public trust in complaints mechanisms can be earned will vary, to ignore this factor altogether is a fundamental error. To return to Brown's comment (1981) concerning the need for mechanisms that ensure continuing attention to the objectives of policing and responsiveness to external concerns, a complaints mechanism that does not command the respect of most citizens and is therefore ignored by them will not possess the capacity to work towards these objectives.

The Declining Authority of Police Discourse

This essay has stressed so far the twin points that complaints operate in one sense as units of feedback on the effectiveness and efficiency of operational policing and also represent an opportunity to address the more fundamental but also elusive notion of police–community relations. It was suggested that the two are not unrelated, in that the former was unlikely to be provided in the absence of some degree of public trust and faith in police procedures. A willingness to listen to complainants, it was also suggested, might result in a greater readiness by members of the public to provide criminal intelligence to the police. It has been suggested that one consequence of the drying up of criminal intelligence can be a resort by police to more overt, militaristic styles of policing (Lea and Young, 1982, 1984). In this way, the connection between information from the public, complaints procedures, and public confidence in the police seems incontrovertible.

However, it is important to place the notion of information (in this case, arising from complaints) as feedback into perspective by contrasting a preoccupation with administrative efficiency in terms of organizational objectives with one that pays explicit attention to values and the diversity of interests and opinions evidenced with regard to police issues. While police administration was perhaps among one of the last areas in the public sector to emulate business practice in various ways, there can be little doubt that trends in the business sector now find their parallel in many instances in policing (Bradley, Walker, and Wilkie 1986). The penetration of such concepts as 'management by objectives' and 'decentralization,' and greater reliance on civilian managers to conduct the financial and other affairs of police forces point to the impact of ideas of this kind. Corresponding to this 'managerialism' is the recognition that there is a wealth of unanalysed information available to the police, which offers dividends in terms of realizing the objectives of the organization (Tremblay and Rochon, 1991). On this view, information provides a basis for 'fine-tuning' police effectiveness.

In general terms, it is not possible to fault this particular analytical approach to information, of whatever kind, available to police organizations. Where it may be criticized is when it becomes the *only* legitimate way of dealing with information, in other words, when concerns that are not internally generated but which raise fundamental questions about the ends and methods of policing are not recognized or, if recognized, not addressed. While there is a valid case to be made for the aggregation of complaints for the purpose of identifying patterns of behaviour, permitting the recommendation of changes to the way in which certain police practices are carried out (Goldsmith, 1991b), more needs to be known about the impact of such information and kind of analysis for rendering the police more accountable to community standards. Although much more of this systemic analysis could be done, the fact remains that it seems to be on the increase largely if not wholly driven by the movement to more managerialism within policing (Maguire and Corbett, 1991). The danger posed by this trend, I suggest, is that from a police perspective it encourages the belief that this kind of analysis is preferable to other methods of accountability because of the control exercisable over the variables considered relevant and because it is arguably more scientific (Tremblay and Rochon, 1991). In this account, questions raising issues of value and opinion are stripped of significance, leaving only questions of 'objective fact' and 'cause' for consideration.

In contrast to this scientific approach to policing stands the declining authority of police accounts concerning the problem of crime and the priorities for law and order. The social issues that contributed to the problematization of police accountability from the 1960s through to the 1980s have served to undermine police legitimacy not only on operational questions but also on the level of *discourse*. By challenges to police discourse, I refer to challenges to the authority (and hence persuasiveness) of the ways in which the police have customarily described and explained events in their world. The emergence of disparate groups articulating divergent accounts of the nature of police work in relation to public problems has called into question the view of police work as 'scientific,' the legitimate preserve of 'professional' police officers with particular 'expertise' in matters of law enforcement. While the rhetoric of police professionalism and, more recently, managerialism, has sought to emphasize the peculiar competence that is the police's alone, socioeconomic and political upheavals in the postwar period have challenged the explanatory omnipotence of the police world-view. The tendencies of Daniel Bell's 'post-industrial society' towards the scientification of public policy (Bell, 1973) have come under the microscope of new social and political movements, including feminism, the 'green' movement, and gay groups, whose experiences and perspective on policing stand in often stark contrast to the official police rhetoric (see McMahon and Ericson, 1984; London Police Strategy Unit, 1987; Waddington and Braddock, 1991). One way in which these two perspectives might be construed is in terms of the much-invoked but not always well-understood distinction between modernity and post-modernism. Stephen White (1991) refers to post-modernism's growing incredulity towards metanarratives, its concerns with the dangers of societal rationalization, and the appearance of new values and social movements, as three defining elements of this perspective. 'Metanarratives' refer to taken-for-granted assumptions about the world, upon which knowledge claims are customarily founded. Each of these factors could be explored in some length in relation to policing, but this is not possible here. For another excellent account of post-modernism as a critique and alternative strategy, see McGowan (1991).

The interesting question for present purposes is: where does this leave the issue of police accountability and specifically the question of complaints? One implication of this challenge to the authority of police knowledge or discourse is that accountability mechanisms of whatever kind must contemplate the existence of different discourses on issues of law and order, emerging from these new social movements and other groups interested in policing questions. The appearance of competing discourses suggests that different groups are increasingly articulate and willing to construe as political, rather than factual, issues that were previously the preserve of police knowledge and expertise. It might therefore be predicted that traditional approaches to complaints, and especially those largely dependent on internal investigations, will have even less success than previously in terms of shoring up public confidence. Indeed, it might be assumed that these changes will further highlight the overall inadequacy of complaints procedures as the principal vehicle for citizen participation or input, leading to renewed and more concerted calls for changes to the constitutional arrangements governing police accountability. At the very least, this threat to police discourse would seem to demand a very open, externally run system for the investigation and determination of complaints, and one with a clear mandate to explore and address broader issues of policing, going beyond the immediate circumstances of individual complaints. In this latter regard, a power to conduct investigations of this kind would have to be matched by the resources and political independence necessary to make such a formal power significant at the level of practice. While the costs of achieving police legitimacy in this way might be high (accepting that it is realizable at least to some greater degree than is the case at present), the social costs of not at last striving to achieve it may well be higher (Scarman, 1983; Lea and Young, 1982).

Conclusion

Two words readily encountered in debates surrounding police accountability and complaint procedures are 'community' and 'citizen.' These notions have traditionally evoked thoughts of social homogeneity and an essential social and political equality between individuals. In keeping with these ideas, an 'objectification' of knowledge was possible, under which a broad range of social issues, including law and order, could be delegated to those with the appropriate expertise to response to these issues. Any grievance emerging from the public body concerning the performance of these experts was either in response to relatively minor issues amenable to self-regulation, and accepted as legitimate criticism, or came from 'irrational' marginal elements whose understanding of the complexities of the issues was in doubt and whose motives were almost certainly suspect.

Whereas complaints procedures for handling public grievances against police officers originated in the period just described, in the form of internal investigations of an often secretive kind, they have sustained enormous ongoing pressure to change from various quarters. The formal changes sought, and in varying degrees implemented, have reflected a trend towards the 'externalization' of complaints procedures, in response to persistent doubts surrounding the effectiveness of the traditional approach. This persistent scepticism towards police self-regulation represents one face of a broader public scepticism towards police 'objectivity' and 'expertise.'

The growing evident diversity within public life has meant that the concepts of 'citizen' and 'community' beg the question far more than they once did. Mounting evidence of social and political inequality has exposed the abstract and highly arbitrary nature of citizenship, while a variety of tendencies has pointed to the existence of 'communities' rather than any single community. We should not therefore be surprised by the rising number of public complaints or the evidence of mass mistrust of these procedures. These are merely symptomatic of a more widespread problem of public confidence in the police. It needs to be appreciated in this climate that there are limits to what complaints procedures can achieve in terms of furthering police accountability.

Recent experience with internal investigation to the contrary, it is not possible to presume that external complaints mechanisms will *necessarily* be more effective in substantiating complaints. Police attempts at self-regulation may improve (see Goldsmith, 1991b). However, it is difficult to imagine many groups placing their trust in internal procedures for the foreseeable future on the basis of that recent experience. External mechanisms at least offer a fresh basis on which to establish public confidence in the mechanism, aside from feelings arising directly from contact with police. Even so, without explicitly recasting the scope of operation of these mechanisms, by way of wide-ranging powers of inquiry, the individualistic and reactive nature of complaints procedures, often without any power to direct the laying of disciplinary charges, indicates the real limits upon the capacity of such procedures to act as mechanisms of accountability. This capacity would appear to shrink even further in the face of the growing pluralistic nature of public debate on policing matters. Further attention will inevitably be required on the issue of mechanisms of police accountability generally. The idea of an arms-length relationship between police and public is conspicuously under assault. Such deliberations, however, will take place alongside the ongoing demand and need specifically for a complaints mechanism to deal with individual grievances. For these reasons, complaints mechanisms by themselves will remain necessary but not sufficient to the challenge of police accountability.

The News Media and Account Ability in Criminal Justice

RICHARD V. ERICSON

News media are central to the process by which people's sentiments and understandings about government institutions are elicited and organized. News is a discourse of government accountability, of official obligation to describe, assess, justify, excuse, and recommend courses of action. The majority of news sources are government officials (Sigal, 1973; Ericson, Baranek, and Chan, 1991). Usually the official imprint of a government agency is required before something is regarded as news at all, and government agencies predominate in setting the news agenda and sustaining particular versions of events (Molotch and Lester, 1975; Glasgow University Media Group, 1976, 1980; Gitlin, 1980; Fishman, 1980; Ericson, Baranek, and Chan, 1989). Moreover, the majority of government and other news sources address some aspect of law and the administration of justice, including criminal justice. In a survey of news content in Toronto, Ericson, Baranek, and Chan (1991) found that approximately one-half of newspaper and television news items, and two-thirds of radio news items, addressed aspects of crime, deviance, legal regulation, and justice. These considerations suggest that analysis of how the news media participate in processes of accountability is central to an understanding of accountability in criminal justice.

The essay is organized as follows. I initially discuss the concept of accountability. I then consider the various institutions that comprise criminal justice. I argue that the news media do not stand apart from the various arenas in which people seek criminal justice, but are integral to their everyday practices. Hence, the news media are best conceptualized as part of criminal justice rather than as external reporters on criminal justice. With this concept, I analyse criminal justice as a communication process involving strategic practices in secrecy and revelation that both exclude and include the news media. Whether a crime or criminal justice practice is publicized is shown to be related to the strategic interests of the parties involved and their 'account ability' or capacity to explain their activities in a credible manner. Account ability is related to the social, cultural, and spatial aspects of how news is produced and distributed and to the peculiar requirements of the format of news communications. Social, cultural, spatial, and communications format dimensions create different environments of account ability across the various organizational contexts of criminal justice, for example, among policing, prosecution, adjudication, punishment, and lawmaking.

Accountability and Account Ability

Accountability entails an obligation to give an account of activities within one's ambit of responsibility. There are myriad sources of obligation, for example, law, administrative procedure, custom, fiscal parameters, morality, structures of authority, and reciprocity based on friendship and trust. Accountable also means capable of being accounted for or subject to explanation. Such capability entails a narrative or record of events and an explanation of events – legitimate causes, justifications, excuses, blame, and remedies – that demonstrate one has acted in a credible manner.

These two definitions of accountability point to a fundamental feature of social order. Social life is made possible through sets of obligations and by criteria through which one can demonstrate that the obligations are being met. Obligations and criteria for meeting them are represented in customs, norms, rules, and laws. Accountability is articulated through discourses of rights and obligations, and the work of all government officials is directed at making claims to 'symmetry between rights and obligations, the one being the justification of the other' (Giddens, 1984: 30). However, 'no such symmetry necessarily exists in practice' (ibid.). In everyday interaction, human beings are reflexive, knowledgable agents who perpetually adjust their senses of rights and obligations to organizational contingencies such as knowledge resources, fiscal resources, political interests, authority structures, communications formats, and occupational cultures.

The asymmetry in practice, resulting from organizational contin-gencies, suggests that we also need to pay attention to *account ability*: the capacity to provide a record of activities that explains them in a credible manner so that they appear to satisfy the rights and obligations of *accountability*. Clearly, the formal obligation to give an account does not ensure uniformity in the ability to give an account. The ability varies, for example, by what has to be accounted for; who makes the demand (the basis of the demand, the authority of those making the demand); who is the intended audience (only those making the demand, or other publics); and the spatial, social, cultural, and communications format capacities to make an account.

Account ability is a matter of strategic intervention and 'negotiating control' (Ericson et al., 1989). Accountability is not an end in itself, but a means to other ends, part of a broader effort to achieve complex, interrelated institutional goals and interests. Account ability is not part of a unidirectional power game with zero-sum consequences. It varies with all of the dimensions enumerated above, and shifts with each occasion and each matter to be accounted for. Involving the production and communication of knowledge across myriad institutional settings, processes of account ability, and criteria of accountability are inevitably equivocal, uncertain, transitory, conflictual, and contradictory. As a matter of strategic interaction and negotiating control, account ability always invokes practices of secrecy and revelation operating in tandem. Every act of publicity for accountability is also an act of selection and distortion in which some things are left out and some alternative formu-lations are ignored; every act of secrecy for accountability is also an act of selection in which some things are given out and some alternative formulations are explored.

Bok (1982; 179) observes, 'if officials make public only what they want citizens to know, then publicity becomes a sham and accountability meaningless.' She poses the question asked by J.S. Mill in *Considerations on Representative Government*: without publicity, how can citizens check or encourage what they are not permitted to see? In some circum-stances, however, secrecy and deception are vital. Plato pointed to this in *Republic* and even suggested it is a privilege exclusive to public authorities: 'Then, it's appropriate for rulers, if for anyone at all, to lie for the benefit of the city in cases involving enemies or citizens, while all the rest must not put their hands to anything of the sort.' Publicity might advance the project of an enemy. It can be used to manipulate public opinion in favour of particular interests and against the public interest. It can be used as a tool of injustice, inflicting unduly harsh punishment on those judged as deviants and hurting innocent persons labelled as deviants. Organizations require shelter from publicity in order to arrive at reasoned choices and to carry them out. Transparency of decision-making can cripple the policy-making process, while secrecy can serve rationality and efficiency because many policies require deliberation and an element of surprise in order to be effective.

The law is not only an important source of obligations and criteria of accountability, but also an important part of account ability. That is, law is not only bounded rules and administrative machinery, but also 'a species of social imagination ... constitutive of social realities rather than merely reflective of them' (Geertz, 1983). Moreover, in its news and other mass media appearances, law provides a 'vocabulary with which we rationalize our actions to others and ourselves' (Macauley, 1987: 185). People learn about law from television and other media of popular culture as well as from direct experience in the legal system. As a practical tool of account ability and a social discourse of accountability, law may be recognized as valid more through the ways it is 'mediated' in popular culture than through its formal procedures or substantive content as constituted in legal culture (Mathiesen, 1987; Goodrich, 1986; Macauley, 1987).

Criminal Justice and News Media

Criminal justice is a complex institution comprised of diverse organizations, communications media, and people. The organizations include, for example, politicians and their staffs at the legislature involved in lawmaking; policy officials in government departments; police; courts; correctional agencies; and myriad public and private community organizations involved in policing, service delivery, policy, and interest group politics. The membership, roles, and functions of people in these organizations frequently overlap. Morover, the criminal justice institution not only has a complex life of its own, it is constituted by and helps to constitute other institutions in the social structure. While analysts must respect the integrity of the criminal justice institution, they also need to take into account its relatedness as a social institution.

Relatedness is evident in the relations between criminal justice and news media. Indeed, as I show in subsequent sections, there are many respects in which the news media can be conceived as *part of* criminal justice. At the level of practical organization and everyday activities it becomes clear that the news forms part of the accountability structure of criminal justice and must be understood as such. On criminal justice news beats – at police headquarters, the courts, the legislature – the news media become part of the culture or symbolic organization of thought. Journalists and their sources share cultural values and templates for thinking. The templates include a focus on moral conflicts and their resolution, the isolation of conflicts into particular events involving individual protagonists (individualization and personalization), and ensuring that the conflicts are resolved by constituted authorities in accordance with proper procedures. As such, criminal law and news function as cultural devices for the coordination of institutional activities or 'ordering,' and offer a particular discourse of accountability.

The news media are not only part of the symbolic organization of thought, but social organization as well. Journalists are part of the spatial arrangement on news beats; for example, they have offices in police and court buildings. They develop social networks with criminal justice officials that span roles and hierarchy. They operate with particular communications technologies, media, and formats that influence how criminal justice officials approach their activities and communications about them. Criminal justice officials learn to control their space, social relations, and communications formats, tailoring them to their own requirements to the point where news becomes a useful part of their work. Through ongoing involvement with journalists, criminal justice officials are able to refine their account ability in the terms of news discourse, which in turn helps them to achieve accountability to the publics that concern them.

While the details of how accountability is accomplished through the news are provided in subsequent sections, it is worthwhile at this juncture to provide some illustrations in the case of police–news media relations (see generally Chibnall, 1977; Fishman, 1980, 1981; Wheeler, 1986; Ericson, 1989, 1991; Ericson et al., 1989: ch. 3).

In a leading study of news making, Roscho (1975: 63) observes that 'the mass-media reporter is prototypically an observer, describing the issues others frame, the problems they raise, the solutions they offer, the actions they take, the conflicts in which they engage. Thus, the nature of news as a form of knowledge makes the reporter dependent upon news sources for most of the knowledge he will transpose into media content.' It is too simplistic to say that the reporter is the only an 'observer' of what goes on in the source organization. The members of any given organization are themselves 'observers' of virtually all their organizational activity, because they deal with already socially constructed knowledge rather than participate directly in the activity being constructed. In the police organization (Ericson, 1982, 1993; Miyazawa, 1992), the typical scenario involves the patrol officer talking to a complainant about an event that occurred previously. Often the victim did not participate in the event directly (for example, she was absent when her house was broken into), and the patrol officer, also not directly involved, is not able to make direct observations. The patrol officer makes an occurrence reported that is read and possibly amended by a staff sergeant, and it is then possibly sent on to a detective sergeant, who again reads it and possibly makes amendments. If detectives are assigned to work on it they may seek further accounts from the complainant, try to generate witnesses, and talk to a suspect who can come closest to giving a first-hand account. Any accounts generated are scrutinized further, and possibly amended, at the detective-sergeant and detective-inspector levels. At all levels the participants in this process serve as 'reporters' of socially constructed knowledge and 'editors' of the documentary realities they have been presented with. Like the journalist, they are rarely dealing with observed activity 'in nature,' but rather with symbolical versions of reality constructed by others.

The journalist is literally given an 'office' (Weber, 1964) by the source organization, and in that sense has a defined role to play as much as any other member of the police organization. In that role she is privy to knowledge relevant to the role, just as other members are privy to knowledge pertinent to their roles. For example, the police constable has some knowledge exclusive to his role. The chief of police is not aware of a lot of this knowledge, just as the constable is not aware of much knowledge available to the chief. Similarly, the police reporter develops knowledge exclusive to her role, as part of the division of labour within the police organization. While the reporter may be several steps removed from the symbolically constructed reality she reports on – and is frequently forced to rely upon the organizationally mediated texts of front-line police personnel and public-relations officers – senior administrators, including the chief of police, are in the same position of being at the nth level of knowledge production regarding work on individual occurrences or internal practices and politics.

Regular reporters on the police beat establish working relations and friendships with a much wider range of police officers – including those in the police hierarchy and elite members of the force – than the vast majority of police officers (Ericson et al., 1989). They write articles for police newspapers and magazines, sit on the committee to nominate the police officer of the month, organize parties for police and reporters, and arrange for police officers to appear on special broadcasts such as 'talk shows.' Reporters sometimes consult with police officers about the advisability of including or excluding knowledge from their stories. They give police officers tips on investigations in exchange for exclusive stories when the timing is right. They give police access to their films and video tapes as these might identify suspects or otherwise help with investigations. They engage in helpful editing, for example, blocking the telecast of an item involving a police officer who is working undercover and who does not want to be identified publicly as a police officer. Special efforts are made to write stories favourable to the police when there are serious allegations of police misconduct. Care is taken to cite investigating officers in news stories, playing on their egos in exchange for the play they give the reporter by revealing the latest update on their investigations. Coverage is given to police news conferences regarding crackdowns or particular problems.

In sum, police reporters willingly join with members of the force in accomplishing their policing tasks. The journalist, within the role she negotiates and establishes as part of the police organization, becomes a component in the process of knowledge production and distribution. Like those in other roles, she has considerable control over what she decides to attend to, how much attention it deserves, how it should be constructed, and so on. She is a *participant* in the account ability of the police, giving meaning to the texts of the police organization. In turn news texts enter back into the police organization to affect social relations and practices there. The reporter is *interdependent* with police officers regarding knowledge production and communication both inside and outside the police organizations. Reporters' social participation and cultural affinities with the police have several important policing functions. First, reporters provide direct assistance to the police. For example, they communicate warnings about emergencies. They help the police by asking the public for knowledge about suspects, missing persons, and events they may have witnessed, both on an individual case basis and in institutional formats such as 'America's Most Wanted,' and 'Crime Stoppers' (Carriere and Ericson, 1989). They join the police in law enforcement crackdowns, such as the annual Christmas crackdown on impaired driving in Canada, by publicizing news conferences announcing the programs, showing the police at work dealing with drivers, and providing daily tallies of the results of their efforts. Second, reporters promote favourable organizational and occupational images that provide a symbolic canopy of accountability for the police. In news, as in other mass media products, much of ordinary life is portrayed through extraordinary events of police work (Williams, 1989). While most police work is routine and even boring (Ericson, 1982), the news media dramatize it and give it ceremonial force. Cathected scenarios of the police at work have promotional value for the police because they often show them to be quiet *effective* crime fighters (Marsh, 1988), and because they foster a sympathetic, *affective* response in people towards what is seen as dangerous work requiring heroic effort (Gunter and Wober, 1988: 61).

Even routine reporting of crime events has a 'performative character' and promotional value (Fishman, 1980, 1981). As Wheeler's study (1986) of a police public relations unit discovered, the police-produced news occurrence report constructs 'the occurrence as criminal, thereby making the police action seem sensible, proper, and officially authorized.' In this way the account provides 'the procedures for not knowing certain events, namely those events that are not relevant to the bureaucratic organization.' The news thus depicts the world as rife with crime and the police as *the* authority for keeping the lid on it. It makes the role of the police self-evident, and their efforts at controlling crime appear objective, compassionate, and effective. As Wheeler (1986) observes, this news 'discourse is fundamental to the work of the police, and its adoption by the news media means that the news media are also part of police work ... crime discourse is a tremendous resource, since it makes the power differentials [in policing] unactionable. After all, who would believe that the work of the police is anything short of proper, when that is the message that is conveyed day after day with the production of news release after news release and their adoption by the news media?' (ibid.: 54). This discourse is even more powerful than the 'good news' arm of the police public affairs unit – the 'Police Week' events, crime prevention displays at shopping malls, and school essays on the role of the police – because that material is obviously self-laudatory, whereas the 'eternal recurrence' (Rock, 1973) of crime releases is not.

Third, the news media contribute to management by police of their organization internally as well as externally. They do so by policing the police as a mechanism of regulation and compliance, urging police accountability. The important point in this regard is that while policing the police creates organizational trouble for the police in the particular instance, it serves police accountability structures and management practices in the long term and the aggregate.

While the police are shown in some news contexts as engaged in dramatic feats of crime detection and penal suppression, they are also portrayed in other contexts as inefficient, beset by internal conflicts and management problems, and as having members who use illegal procedures and are corrupt (Punch, 1985; Reiner, 1985; Ericson, 1989). While the shock value of a major news media exposé refers more to their own cultural template of what the police should be doing rather than to what the police do in the normal course of events, the daily presence of news items on police deviance indicates a much more difficult and tenuous relationship between journalists and police than most researchers (for example, Fishman, 1980, 1981; Hall, Critcher, Jefferson, Clarke, and Roberts, 1978) have suggested. It is not only major corruption scandals that create problems for the police. Incessant attention by the news media to the inability of the police to solve a particular notorious crime can create organizational trouble. Regular features such as 'Crime Stoppers' deal with difficult-to-solve crimes, most of which remain unsolved after appearing in the program, thereby underscoring the limits of the capability of police to clear crimes by arrest (Carriere and Ericson, 1989). Even apparently innocuous news items, such as those dealing with the police union–management contract negotiations, can tarnish the image of the police or at least cast them in a different light. 'Police who negotiate with the city "through the media," for example, can no longer distinguish their front region image of dedication as selfless protectors of the people from their back region haggling for more sick days, vacation time, and higher salaries' (Meyrowitz, 1985: 149; see also, Ericson et al., 1989: 164–6).

Contemporary administered societies are obsessed with procedural propriety or accountability in all institutions, and showing conformity to formal mechanisms of accountability has become a primary requirement for sustaining legitimacy (Habermas, 1975; Giddens, 1984). Indeed bureaucracy itself is essentially the tireless reflexive elaboration of procedures designed to ensure that people are acting as they should (Weber, 1964: 196–244; Dandeker, 1990). This obsession with procedure is accentuated in relation to the police organization because of its centrality to the state's representations of rule-governed order. Journalists focus on procedural propriety because the police symbolize the state's moral authority, and because in the exercise of this role the police are legally authorized by the state to engage in certain manipulative, intru-

sive, coercive, and violent practices. Police use of such practices provides a barometer by which to gauge the state's performance in all
lesser exercises of authority.

While the news emphasis on policing the police creates organizational
trouble for the police, 'the existence of the media as apparently independent, impartial and ever-vigilant watchdogs on behalf of the public
interest is conducive to the legitimation of these apparatuses (but not
individuals working within them). The process of legitimation could
never be effective if the media were seen as mere propaganda factories'
(Reiner, 1985: 139). The police can turn the news frame of procedural
impropriety to advantage, incorporating it into their work. Such coverage is useful is discovering problems, leading to the refinement of rules
and procedures. Sustained negative coverage of the inability to solve a
particular type of crime, and/or of problems in an investigative unit
dealing with that type of crime, can often be transmuted through negotiation into additional personnel and technological resources. News
attention to individual officers accused of wrongdoing can justify the
dismissal of officers who may have been found wanting on other
grounds. The rituals of expunging rotten apples offset the possibility of
a structural critique of the organization as a rotting barrel, thereby
contributing to its legitimacy (Ericson, 1981; Punch, 1985).

Communications and Account Ability

Account ability in criminal justice, as in any other social institution, is
a matter of communications. Communications are the means by which
knowledge is made common. The means include institutions, people,
media, formats, language, and trust. Communications do not stand
apart from reality. There is not first reality and then second communication about it. Communications participate in the formation and change
of reality. Facts arise out of communications practices, the ways in
which institutions, people, media, formats, language, and trust organize
experience.

Communications involve knowledge that is concealed as well as
revealed, and the social meaning of knowledge is a product of the
factors that have limited the exchange. Knowledge becomes power
through the ability to control its distribution, through practices of
secrecy, confidence, censorship, and publicity.

Secrecy is a property of knowledge, the property that it is intentionally withheld from others (Scheppele, 1988). It is not a property of individuals and groups, and it is always located in social contexts. These contexts involve not only private spaces, which usually come to mind when we visualize secrecy, but also public spaces, for example, when the police go undercover to regulate crowd behaviour at sporting events (Marx, 1988) and public demonstrations (Fleming, 1983). Secrets create *social* spaces that are shared and others that are partitioned, alliances and divisions, friends and enemies. In partitioning, dividing, and creating outsiders, secrecy provides for privacy. Privacy is a condition in which individuals or organizations can free themselves from the demands and expectations of others, and secrecy is one of the methods an individual or organization may use to attain this condition. Privacy refers to 'those places, spaces and matters upon or into which others may not intrude without the consent of the person or organization to whom they are designated as belonging' (Reiss, 1987: 20). As Bok (1982: 10–11) notes, 'Privacy need not hide, and secrecy hides far more than what is private. A private garden need not be a secret garden; a private life need not be a secret life.' Both confidence and censorship involve communications to an exclusive group of others while maintaining secrecy to outsiders. A confidence involves communication to the unauthorized that which is normally communicated only to the authorized, with the expectation that it is not to be made known to still others. Trust is crucial here. Censorship is a restriction on publicizing more broadly that which is made public in one narrower context, for example, publicity bans on courtroom proceedings.

Publicity is the disclosure of knowledge. However, publicity is never 'pure' in the sense of being a perfect communication or what Habermas terms an 'ideal speech situation.' Publicity itself involves enclosure on knowledge, because it is restricted by communications formats, knowledgability of audiences, misinterpretations, errors, and so on. Publicity is always simultaneously a procedure to know and not to know. It is always partial and must always be understood in terms of the factors that limit it.

As indicated in the previous discussion of police–media relations, reporters do not limit themselves to the official, formal settings of criminal justice proceedings. Reporters become part of the private world of criminal justice organizations, and in some respects they are more knowledgeable about that world than employed members of these organizations. Hence, it is wrong to say 'reporters expose themselves *only* to settings in which formally organized transactions occur' (Fishman, 1980;

emphasis added). The *primary* exposure of most reporters may be in such front-region settings, but these are not the exclusive settings of their work (Ericson et al., 1987, 1989). Moreover, as seen in the above distinction between secrecy and privacy, it is not just a matter of what reporters expose themselves to. Access to private spaces does not necessarily yield reportable material because relevant knowledge is still enclosed (secrecy) or disclosed with the understanding it will not be published (confidence). Thus, in Rubinstein's view (1973: 7) the police reporter's back-region 'access to the police is assured by his pledge not to reveal what he knows of police work.' However, official, formal front-region access may also fail to yield reportable material because what is there is censored (legally or otherwise restricted), or it is highly formatted, enclosed, and partial. The nature and degree of access for the journalist is always at issue, varying in time and place within a criminal justice organization, by the type of organization and by the type of knowledge sought (Ericson, 1994). Too much secrecy and privacy can become 'the ultimate generalized privilege' (Williams, 1976), enabling avoidance of accountability and the accumulation of power. At the same time secrecy and privacy are essential to the secure existence of human beings and their organizations, for their capacity to act and to maintain competitive advantage: 'No organization seems possible – whether that of the personality, a family or friendship, or more formal organizations, including the state – without its private matters or secrets. For the capacity to act is predicated in part on preserving a unique form of organization that sets in apart from others. Morever, any competitive advantage one may have stems from being able to "keep others guessing." There appears to be an implied threat even in sharing that information with others; its disclosure makes one vulnerable' (Reiss, 1987: 27–8).

In many circumstances an organization achieves accountability by keeping secrets, delaying revelation, and censoring aspects of what is revealed. Organizations require time and spaces to foster and contemplate policy options, to avoid harm to others who may be affected by different options, to avoid giving unfair gains to others who may capitalize on knowledge disclosed in advance, and to maintain the strategic value of surprise that comes with controlling the time and place of revelation. Accountability is a matter of justified practices of secrecy, confidence, censorship, and publicity. Justification is focused on whether criminal justice officials think news in a particular case will be helpful or harmful: whether it will enhance their capacity to act and to maintain strategic advantage over others (Ericson et al., 1989).

Criminal justice officials treat news with scepticism, and yet they take it seriously. They complain bitterly about being misrepresented, but feel compelled to make another representation the next time they are asked. The explanation for this behaviour lies in the realization that as public officials they do not have the option to ignore the news media entirely and that they can turn the news to advantage to constitute their authority, and to promote and protect the image of their organization as accountable. Hence, they are more concerned about news that is influential and helpful than about news that is accurate and impartial. Objectivity is less important than objectives. Since total secrecy is neither desirable nor possible, the common approach is to patrol the facts through selection and deception. Selection is an offensive strategy, trying to bring to news attention particular events and particular formulations of those events. By keeping reporters preoccupied with things they are bound to be interested in, and by easing their workload in the process, criminal justice officials can offset the likelihood of serious incursions into their private spheres. Thus, criminal justice officials have begun taking a much more proactive approach to the news media. As one police officer observed, 'I think that the more we disclose, the more we control' (ibid.: 142). By this he meant there is a need to do journalists' work for them, to provide an avalanche of stories and to format them within news discourse, in order to establish control of the environment.

Officials have been observed going to great lengths to hold news conferences for the purpose of fitting the format requirements of television visuals and the factual update needs of all news outlets, without actually revealing anything of substance (ibid.: 144–8). Even when there was a clear intention to remain secret, the response was to give a reason for not revealing what journalists wished to know. This was often done through formulaic accounts, such as the statement that revelation would 'interfere with an investigation or evidence.' While such accounts reflected real concerns, they also served as very convenient justifications for secrecy. Thus, a police officer observed, with reference to the 'interference with an investigation or evidence' justification, that 'if the police don't want to bothered with you, I guess they can tell you that ... Legally, you have to more or less accept that. And what can you do? The police have said that's the situation and you're not in a position to take it beyond that, but, quite often it is a "snowjob." I know that. And I suppose the media know that. They're not fooling anybody but they have to accept it' (ibid.: 128).

While such account ability practices are part of everyday relations between criminal justice officials and journalists, they are occasionally revealed more dramatically in major scandals and retrospective accounts of how they were handled in public culture. Thus, Chibnall (1979: 147) observes with respect to corruption scandals at Scotland Yard:

In his celebrated Dimbleby Lecture on BBC television in 1973, Sir Robert Mark (1973) virtually denied the association between pornography and police corruption although he was well aware of its existence. He admitted sometime later that his aim had been the restoration of morale with the CID [Criminal Investigation Division], which was also a factor in his attack on unscrupulous elements within the legal profession.

'I was like a surgeon who had to cut out a major cancer without telling the patient, in other words I had got to do great execution against the CID while at the same time maintaining their morale and to some extent maintaining public belief in them. Well this isn't a simple operation, you know, you've got to ... mask your real intentions behind your words occasionally. I would have thought that this was a classic example of walking that very dangerous tight-rope but producing the results that we wanted to produce.' (BBC interview, 12 July 1977)

Sir Robert also provides an illustration of another purpose of selective publicity: giving the appearance of veracity. All efforts at communication require a degree of trust between senders and receivers. Ironically, sometimes it is necessary to deceive in order to sustain the belief that one is still trustworthy. The appearance of veracity becomes more important than veracity itself. Hence, Sir Robert says that on occasion 'police/public relations are not governed by the truth necessarily. They are governed by the appearance of truth' (*Listener*, 25 August 1966, quoted by Chibnall, 1977: 173).

The appearance of truth is important for legitimacy. Regardless of legal, constitutional, and administrative niceties, legitimacy is central to how criminal justice officials approach publicity. News is considered to be an agency for promoting and sustaining the legitimacy of law and legal institutions. Thus, a court official we interviewed expressed a view similar to that of Atiyah (1983), who argues that the more mystery surrounding the law, the greater its powers of social cohesion. This official asserted that it is the *duty* of reporters, as part of the court system, to promote public confidence in it. The place of reporters in the system is 'the job of keeping the administration of justice respectable in the minds of the public. And, instead of dealing with the story, some-how keep in mind that the public has to be kept confident in the legal system ... [G]enerally the system has to be promoted and the press have a real responsibility to promote it.'

Proactive publicity is not only directed at damage control. Publicity is also a means of forcing a party with whom one is in conflict to pro-vide their own account of the matter. The opponent is placed in a defensive posture, forced to set the record straight, and to polish the tarnished image. Secrecy breeds rumours (Shibutani, 1966), and it is sometimes better to quash them with publicity. Indeed, the very fact of non-cooperation can be more stigmatic than responding with something that is negative.

Criminal justice officials may wish to disclose knowledge to reporters, but be unable to do so because of particular circumstances or legal requirements. A particular official may favour publicity, but feel organizationally constrained to avoid it. This situation arises, for example, when the police have made controversial arrests and laid charges, but cannot speak about matters before the courts.

Officials often want to explain their activity in organizational and structural terms, but refrain from doing so because of the perceived need to sustain particular myths and values. For example, in face of criticism about efficiency in law enforcement, or wishing to bring credit to hard-working members, it would be illuminating to talk about orga-nizational pressures on police officers. However, there is a perceived need to sustain a view publicly that law enforcement is more or less complete and even-handed, not a matter of organizational structures and situational contingencies. Hence, the police officer should not talk about other realities of her work, for example, that it is selective and partial in accordance with fiscal, social, cultural, and political con-straints.

Officials also locate decisions to keep things to themselves in elements of the public culture external to their organization. In the face of domi-nant cultural frames regarding the status of particular groups, it is difficult to communicate facts that conflict with these dominant values. For example, it is deemed difficult to convey facts about the criminal activities of members of particular racial or ethnic minorities because of possible racist overtones. Similarly, a police official we interviewed said that during a panic about attacks on women, it was difficult to com-municate statistics indicating there was no increase in murders involv-ing female victims because it appeared as a slight on the dominant media frame of the plight of victimized women in the more general political context of the status of women. 'Our murders of women that year in this city were half of what they were the previous year. But, first of all, how do you play a statistical game with a young girl's life? It is just a dangerous thing to do.'

News Culture and Account Ability

The preceding illustration of how a police news source felt silenced by prevailing sentiments in political culture indicates that there can be strong cultural influences on account ability in criminal justice organizations. Criminal justice officials seeking accountability through the news media must engage the cultural templates of news. These templates are based on three elements: dominant culture, the occupational culture of reporters, and the media formats available. These three elements work in combination to establish what is newsworthy, and the terms within which various sources can speak. Unless the criminal justice official learns to speak with the cultural template of news discourse, he not only will fail to appear accountable, he may not appear in the news at all.

In trying to appear accountable through the news media, the criminal justice official must engage the 'bad news' format and its dual meaning. First, she must recognize that if she is to participate as a regular news source, she will be subjecting herself and her organization to recurrent imputations of deviance and efforts at control. That is, she must come to terms with the fact that the cultural template of news involves a focus on procedural propriety in her organization and attendant moral assessments of her as an authority. Second, she must learn to handle the fact that the news accounts themselves will be routinely experienced as 'bad': inaccurate, distorted, unfair, biased, and wrong. It is imperative to handle this fact because, as bad as the news might be in terms of quality of knowledge, it is a powerful force in society. It must be taken earnestly by all those who wish to be represented in public conversations and even more so by all those who are compelled to engage the news as an essential component of control over their organizational environment.

Journalists focus on what is out of place: the deviant, equivocal, and unpredictable. They attend to the more calamitous happenings in social institutions that have proved difficult to classify or that contradict standard expectations in the social structure about efficiency, rights, and the distribution of power. As such news does not provide instruction on *'how things are'* as much as *'where they fit'* into the order of things (Hartley, 1982; Hall, 1979: 325). Things that do not fit are focused on, and persons responsible for them are called to account. Journalists consider questions of accountability primarily in terms of specific and sporadic incidents of procedural deviance, not in terms of significant and systematic processes of government. The minor fraud is featured, and major decisions are overlooked. For example, in reporting on the deliberations of a public accounts committee at the legislature, reporters focused on a minor scandal involving eight thousand dollars, and ignored a long discussion of the accountability of Crown corporations worth eight hundred million dollars (Ericson et al., 1989: 209).

This procedural emphasis obviously involves moral assessment. News is a discourse of procedural *propriety*. A focus on inefficiency, denial of rights, or abuse of authority is always with an eye on whether the parties involved are morally corrupt and therefore lacking in legitimacy. While formatting news as a morality play involving leading public officials serves dramatic storytelling purposes and sustains the news as a kind of social narrative, it also functions as an important means of allocating responsibility for action and attributing accountability (Wagner-Pacifici, 1986).

The focus on procedural propriety addresses the hierarchy of authority and the legitimacy of authorities. Legitimacy depends on the ability of authorities to make convincing *claims*, arguments that they are acting in accordance with laws and social norms (Habermas, 1975). Questions of legitimacy revolve around procedural norms, procedural propriety, and the search for and sanctioning of procedural strays. Especially regarding the legitimacy of the state, this obsession with procedure is expressed in terms of the constitutionality and legality of decisions. Hence, the news focuses in particular on criminal justice and other legal authorities in their efforts at achieving procedural regularity in other social institutions as well as their own. The news offers a pervasive and persuasive means by which authorities attempt to obtain wider consent for their activities. Moral authority is always subject to *consent*, legitimacy or deference to authority is always something that is *granted*, and the news media are at the fulcrum of this legitimation process in criminal justice and society at large.

In this discourse of procedure, morality and authority, the news focuses on individual authorities who are institutionally defined as accountable. Like the law itself, news individualizes and personalizes the locus responsibility for action. It gravitates towards spokespersons who are officially designated as being in positions of authority within their respective organizations. These 'authorized knowers' (Tuchman, 1978) are therefore not selected solely or even largely in terms of journalistic criteria, but rather in terms of the administrative mechanisms for accountability within the source organization. For example, within a police force we studied (Ericson et al., 1989: ch. 3), only officers of senior rank, and officers working in public affairs, were allowed to serve as news sources without specific authorization. The force's administrative procedure on media relations designated as regular news sources only 'a Unit Commander, an Inspector or person of higher rank, a person acting as Unit Commander or Inspector, a person in charge of a unit in the absence of a Unit Commander, [and] a person authorized to issue news releases.' This administrative procedure conveys a definite view of the forces' hierarchy of credibility. Their 'authorized personnel' are legally inscribed in this document as authorized knowers for news purposes. Thus, the news tendency to cite authorized knowers elevated in the hierarchy of credibility – for example, the police chief more than the individual police constable – is not simply a matter of the persons to whom reporters 'naturally' gravitate for their own purposes, but is prescribed by the source organization itself. Criminal justice 'personalities' in the news are selected and rehearsed by their own organizations to be actors on the public stage. They recognize that their organization's accountability depends very much on their account ability as personalized celebrities in public political culture.

Another significant feature of news culture is its peculiar criterion of objectivity. Objectivity consists of a point–counterpoint format: one source makes an allegation of procedural impropriety, the source subject to the allegation makes a counterpoint, and truth is held to reside somewhere in between. Tuchman (1978) refers to this as the 'strategic ritual of objectivity' because journalists are usually only interested in point–counterpoint *representations* by their sources rather than gathering their own independent evidence. Indeed, journalists will not even pursue independent evidence that would sort out the claims of the parties in dispute because then they would have no story within their point–counterpoint format (Ericson et al., 1987). Ironically, the journalistic version of objectivity creates a form of self-enclosure, in which they fail to examine documentary sources routinely available to them and restrict content to performative utterances from two sides in a controversy. With respect to news sources, the strategic ritual of objectivity tends to 'encourage rhetoric or even demagoguery, at least to the degree that spokesmen in a controversy are aware that their arguments are not likely to be questioned' (Epstein, 1974: 265).

In this cultural context of news work, news becomes a dramatic production involving leading actors in ongoing public performances. Another major feature of news formats, encouraged especially by the advent and advance of television, is dramatization. Increasingly, the dramatization formats of fictional entertainment programming permeate television documentaries and news. This is seen, for example, in the increasing popularity of television news features and television serials such as 'Crime Stoppers,' 'America's Most Wanted,' 'Top Cop,' 'Cops,' and 'American Detectives' that re-enact 'real' crimes using the conventional techniques of fictional entertainment programming. It is also seen in a news conference we observed, at which 'Barney Miller' (Hal Linden) was sworn in by the chief of police as an honorary detective, as part of a publicity campaign connected with the 'Police Games' being held at a local sports stadium. Capitalizing on fictional representations of policing, a deputy chief spoke at length about Linden's role in improving the police image. The image of the police in television drama was used to sell the 'fact' that the local police were doing a good job (Ericson et al., 1989: 151).

We have reached a point where news that is relatively discursive and unadorned with sensational and dramatic constructions fails to hold audiences, and therefore fails to sell goods (Seaton, 1980: 96–7). Hence, news, like the advertising system that supports it, moves in the direction of non-discursive, entertaining formats of presentation. As a television news producer informed us in interview, drawing a parallel to his own packaging of the news, 'Kellogg's does not spend most of its money on cornflakes, but rather on the cornflakes' box' (Ericson et al., 1987: 86). Indeed the news focus on sensational crime, and on cathected scenarios of police responding to it, is in part explained by the entertainment value. A survey of newspapers in Ontario found that the greater the advertising space in the newspaper the greater the emphasis on crime news (Dussuyer, 1979: 100).

The dramatic formatting leads to more than mere entertainment. We live in a dramatized world in which, thanks to the mass media, we experience more depictions of crime, law enforcement, and punishment in a few days than our forbears would have experienced in a lifetime. Drama has become 'habitual experience' (Williams, 1989: 4), and it forms an important part of the comprehension of mass media (Robinson and Levy, 1986: 91). The 'dramatization of consciousness' (Williams, 1989) influences both our mentalities (cognition) and sensibilities (emotions).

Dramatization is an important part of the account ability of criminal justice officials seeking accountability (Sparks, 1992). Techniques for dramatizing *effectiveness* range from releasing statistics on arrest, conviction, or recidivism to allowing television crews to picture criminal justice operatives at work. At times this dramatization is very strategic and important, as when the police position television crews behind them at strike-bound industries and public demonstrations in order to sustain the desired angle, one that shows the full force of their strength and its apparent invincibility (Halloran, Elliott, and Murdock, 1970; Gitlin, 1980; Tumber, 1982). Criminal justice officials also work hard to dramatize affectiveness, making emotional appeals that will elicit both ideological and practical support. This is accomplished, for example, by police encouraging victims or relatives of victims of crime to cooperate with reporters to publicize their plight, generating empathy, and, it is hoped, also sources of information to solve their case (Ericson et al., 1989: 151). It is also accomplished in regular re-enactments of crimes, such as those in 'Crime Stopper' programs, which are aimed at generating informants as well as empathy for criminal justice operatives (Carriere and Ericson, 1989). The police funeral remains *the* dramatic display for emotional appeal, and it has become one of the great contemporary public spectacles of state authority and moral consensus (Manning, 1977; Taylor, 1986).

The dramatization of effectiveness and affectiveness blends in many instances. For example, law and order campaigns regarding violence play on the alternative registers of fear and the need for efficient repression (Chibnall, 1977; Hall et al., 1978; Pearson, 1983). The crackdown on impaired driving in many Western jurisdictions over the past decade can also be seen in these terms (Gusfield, 1981). Nightly tallies of the success of police spot checks are blended with advertising and individual news reports dramatizing the terror of the drunken driver. As an official of the Ontario attorney general's office described to us in an interview, the news media were instrumental in his agency's campaign to intensify the criminalization and greater punishment of this activity (Ericson et al., 1989: 195). As he commented regarding the extensive news space given to this topic year in and year out, 'We couldn't buy that space with all the money in the world,' and even if they could buy it in the form of advertising it would not be as effective as the news, because of the more neutral appearance of news.

Since, in order to appear accountable to the public, criminal justice officials cannot avoid the news media, they cannot avoid participating in the dramatization of their work. In a dramatized world, there is no less dramatized place or format to escape to in the public sphere. News media formats fundamentally shape the ways criminal justice officials think, speak, organize, act, and account for their actions.

The Organization of News and Account Ability

Social institutions, and the organizations that comprise them, vary substantially in their need to be involved with the news media to achieve accountability, and therefore in how they organize in relation to the news system. For example, large corporations and business enterprises are not subject to a regular news beat system and have considerable power to stay out of the news when it does not serve their advertising purposes (ibid.: ch. 5). In contrast, the criminal justice institution is subject to a regular news beat system and cannot avoid intensive daily involvement with the news media as part of its operations. However, even within a particular institution such as criminal justice, there is enormous variation in how different organizations relate to the news media. The primary source of reality for news is not what is displayed or what happens in the real world. The reality of news is embedded in the nature and type of influences – spatial, social, cultural, and those created by the communications format – that develop between journalists and sources on each specific news beat. Each beat has a distinct environment of account ability, as is evident in the following comparison of prison, court, police, and legislative beats.

Prisons are relatively closed institutions for news. It is rare to find a regular 'prison beat reporter,' the exceptions being communities where prisons are dominant (as with the *Whig-Standard* in Kingston, Ontario) or where there are special ties between the prison administration and a particular local news outlet (as occurred in Chicago over a twenty-five-year period – see Jacobs, 1977). Prisons are run in terms more of administrative discretion than of external review and public accountability. This veil of administrative decency, combined with the obvious spatial control of prison life, has effectively kept out the news media on a routine basis. This observation is borne out by content studies that indicate that stories emanating from prisons, or about prisons, are rare statistically compared with court coverage and especially police coverage (Graber, 1980; Garofalo, 1981; Ericson et al., 1991; Doyle, 1993; but see Lotz, 1991).

Courts are relatively less closed. Reporters are given an office, and they develop ongoing relations with reporters from other news organizations, and with sources, in a distinctive beat culture. However, they are restricted to particular public physical spaces (they have access to the courtroom, for example, but not the Crown attorney's office during plea-bargaining sessions) and to particular documents. These restrictions emanate from a combination of formal legal and administrative control, work expediency, and norms of propriety that evolve among journalists and their sources (Epstein, 1975; Fishman, 1980; Drechsel, 1983; Ericson et al., 1989).

Key actors in the court are reluctant to divulge knowledge because they feel legally restricted from doing so or have been socialized into being reticent about talking to the news media about their cases. For example, Crown attorneys typically limit their accounts to the basic details of what is already 'on the record' in the case. Judges refuse to 'second-guess' their decisions to a reporter, and they are reluctant to talk about issues on a regular basis for fear of tainting the image of their office as independent, although the reticence may be changing with the greater participation of judges in public policy following the advent of the Canadian Charter of Rights and Freedoms.

The reporter is left to convey what the court organization has pre-established as public information, knowable through its presentation in settings on public display, such as the courtroom. However, the courtroom itself is enclosed in various ways. There is an elaborate hierarchy of place, dress, speech, and turn-taking in talking (Carlen, 1976; Mc-Barnet, 1981; Ericson and Baranek, 1982: ch. 6). The law allows publicity bans in certain circumstances. Judges and court officials sometimes arrange informally to hold hearings at times and under conditions that exclude reporters (Ericson et al., 1989: ch. 2). The threat of being charged with contempt of court for uttering the inappropriate is pervasive (ibid.). Electronic recording devices that might allow an independent record are prohibited or highly restricted.

The restrictions placed on electronic media are signs that court administrators, judges, and the legal profession persist in their preference for the more literate and formal logic of print to accomplish accountability. Printed documents and texts mediate transactions and decisions in the court, and the same is expected of news texts. The court beat remains oriented to print. There the term 'press room' is not anachronistic. Hence, with the exception of one television journalist and one freelance, no regular reporters on a court beat we observed represented broadcast news organizations (ibid.). The hope of court sources is that print journalism can provide accountability in their terms: greater depth, a permanent record, and subtle influence on other media, legal agents, and public opinion.

Channelled into the spatial, social, cultural, and communications format grooves of court organization, reporters are typically silent about the workings of their sources' private culture, about how they actually manage to get their work done. *As a member* of that private culture, the regular court reporter is bound to join with court officials in reproducing the formal legal rationality, even if he knows that the system works in terms of other criteria. For the journalist, parsimony takes precedence over testimony. He limits himself to a particular focus: criminal trials; the big case; a few facts blended with quotable quotes from officials; outcomes rather than process; emphasizing not what is important in legal reasoning, but what is important for the display of formal legal rationality. The news media cannot penetrate legal form through coverage that is restricted to the courtroom, and therefore they cannot help but underpin the court's account ability in that form. The police are much more open to the news media than the courts. Since I have already provided detailed descriptions of police–media relations in previous sections, I will focus here on reasons why the police are more open than other criminal justice bureaucracies. These reasons include the value of news as knowledge to the police, the fact that the police bureaucracy is large and diverse and therefore porous, and the fact that the police have symbolic importance as a vehicle for the accountability of government in general.

Compared with other areas of government, the courts are not very reliant on news. The knowledge the courts need to make decisions is gathered and formatted by officials in the legal system 'more thoroughly and exhaustively than the press could' (Drechsel, 1983: 21–4), and therefore the substance of news is seen as poor or unreliable knowledge. Moreover, relatively contained in their tasks and discourse, the courts are not too reliant on the news media for legitimacy. In contrast, as we have seen already, the police have several instrumental needs for news. News has value in helping the police mobilize informants, handle emergencies, and effect law enforcement crackdowns. News is also important in sustaining the occupational and organizational ideologies of police work as these generate public empathy and support, boost the morale of members, and allow the police to function as major players in public political culture.

The police cannot in any case be as closed to the news media as the courts because of differences in their organization and activity. As we have seen, in spite of a beat office arrangement, systematized release of news, and extensive regulations on relations with the media, the large police bureaucracy is very porous for publicity. Some reporters have more vertical and horizontal mobility in the police force than do police members, with elaborate social networks that allow them to go through, past, or around established channels. In addition to the forms of reciprocity in these relations that provide leaks and scoops, reporters can obtain alternative knowledge from disgruntled individual officers, and also from a police association or union in conflict with management and the police commission. Moreover, other official agencies with responsibility for police activity, such as the police commission, public complaints system, and coroner's office, serve as sources of alternative knowledge. Likewise, individual citizens and citizens' interest groups in conflict with the police are sources of alternative knowledge, useful in forcing police accountability. In a bureaucratic police organization having myriad daily contacts with the public, control of knowledge is inevitably partial. While the police bureaucracy develops elaborate devices to indicate that it is in command, control remains elusive. The work of the organization does not get done simply in terms of where the parties are supposed to connect on the organizational chart. It is accomplished through a complex web of relations, affinities, trust, and reciprocity.

The police are also in a different position than the courts with respect to the entire system of government accountability. Their pervasive presence as government agents who guarantee security, and their coercive powers, ensure that the police stand at the forefront of public debates about government. Exhibiting the government's moral authority in their everyday decisions, and featured prominently in public debates about the relation between the individual and the state, the police are used by the news media to represent government accountability more generally. In the face of this, the police have little choice but to allow reasonable access to the news media. While this openness may also entail efforts to exert more control over the news media, it is also a sign that the police recognize the need to be relatively open and accountable.

The legislative beat, which is the locus of criminal law and law-making, is the most open arena of criminal justice. At the legislature the news media, and their formats of account ability, dominate. They are the primary reference not only because they cannot be avoided, but also because politicians and senior civil servants recognize the importance of the news media to the authority of their office and to their ability to stay in office. The news media must be engaged routinely, for example, in legislative sessions and at election time. Civil servants must always speak with one eye on ministry positions as they reflect the minister's image. While there are many mechanisms for secrecy and controlled disclosure – ranging from the Official Secrets Acts to highly formatted settings such as royal commissions, other official inquires, and question periods in the House – these are often ineffective and heavily influenced by the news media because news coverage is *the* priority for myriad interests seeking image, recognition, presence, and influence.

The emphasis on obtaining publicity leads politicians, political staffs, and senior officials to conform to news criteria and discourse as ends in themselves. Much more than the court officials, or even the police administrator, regular sources at the legislature are ready, willing, and able to speak to reporters on the reporters' terms. As a member of a provincial legislature said to us in an interview, 'I talk to everybody [in the news media] on their terms as much as possible. When they want to talk, not when I want to talk. Try to accommodate them' (Ericson et al., 1989: 234).

News is so crucial that the legislative environment takes on the character of news, often consisting more of fragmented conversations than reasoned debates. For example, question period in the House is in effect a daily news conference driven by the news agenda for accountability. Political staffs and ministry officials scrutinize the news to find out what the latest problem is and, thus, to determine what questions politicians should ask in the House. Asking the right question yields coverage, which is used in turn to develop further questions. Even if knowledge of the problem is lost in the process, the visibility of the political party and its personalities, and, it is hoped, their accountability, is implanted in the public mind.

All types of news media participate actively at the legislature. However, in contrast to the print orientation at the courts, the legislature is dominated by television. While quality newspapers are treated as a source of authority, politicians and officials use television to express their authority. Television has become accepted as the most pervasive, believable, and influential medium, and news sources at the legislature go to great lengths to prepare every detail of their television appearances (Ericson et al., 1989: ch. 4). At the legislature secrecy and publicity are related to the ideology of television formats, which reduce everything to a matter of style, form, and image.

It is hard to see a judge or police administrator in the same light of media stardom as a politician. The judge and police administrator patrol their respective symbolic boundaries in terms of a more distant institutional authority. The politician relies more directly on personal symbolic images, in the hope of scaling new heights, and perhaps eventually reaching the pinnacle of institutional authority. Squarely in the hands of journalists, the politician is acutely aware that her task is the most treacherous. The others are more protected by their institution's routinized ways for appearing accountable, and they have occasion to be grateful for that.

In these circumstances, politicians and other sources on the legislative beat are forced into taking a very intensive proactive stance with the news media. There is knowledge overload on the beat, making access very competitive. On the police beat, and especially the court beat, it is typically reporters who pester sources and sometimes have difficulty getting the story they want. On the legislative beat it is typically the opposite, as a plethora of sources pester reporters and often have difficulty getting the story they want.

Politicians and government ministers have substantial public-relations staffs. These staffs do extensive work for journalists, in effect serving as their researchers. There is also extensive use of paid advertising as a supplement to news work, directed simultaneously at public education, directing people to services, and promoting the good work of government (see Singer, 1986, who documents that the government of Canada is the leading advertiser in the country, while the government of Ontario ranks sixth).

In spite of myriad offensive strategies of news management, sources at the legislature remain vulnerable to publicity about their lack of accountability. They are especially vulnerable because here more than anywhere else news is a disclosure of accountability, perpetually casting its searchlight for procedural strays and focusing its spotlight on those strays it identifies. They are also vulnerable because there are myriad interest groups who use the legislature to put their own causes on the political stage, and who are only too willing to help the media identify strays and to leak knowledge to them. The legislature is a 'nudge-

nudge' world of innuendo, gossip, and leaks where networks of confidence and selective disclosure alternatively threaten and form accountability.

As with regular reporters on the police beat, the only way to manage this situation at the legislature is to join the world of back-region confidences and establish ongoing relations with reporters and news outlets. Cultural elements of trust, reciprocity, and ideological affinity are much more effective aspects of account ability than spatial or other organizational arrangements. At the legislature more than anywhere else, relations with journalists are something to be worked at rather than taken for granted, and sustained public-relations 'stroking' is essential.

Conclusions

Accountability, as an obligation on criminal justice officials to publicize and explain their activities, must be understood in the context of their account ability, or capacity to fulfil that obligation. Account ability varies by communications format, cultures, and ways of organizing available to journalists and their sources in criminal justice, and these elements in turn shape their obligations of accountability. The reality of accountability in criminal justice is embedded in the communications practices, and cultural and social relations, that develop between journalists and their sources on each specific news beat. These practices and relations must be understood in order to evaluate whether criminal justice officials are accountable to the public.

Security Services, Constitutional Structure, and Varieties of Accountability in Canada and Australia

LAURENCE LUSTGARTEN

Some Conceptual Issues

Accountability is a multifaceted concept that has been used in a range of ways by various writers (for example, Day and Klein, 1987; Marshall, 1984). This chapter does not attempt to contribute to theoretical debate about the concept, at any rate not at an abstract level. Instead, I shall treat accountability as synonymous with 'responsibility' in the sense well known to public lawyers and political scientists, that of responsible government. That is to say, accountability is part of the process by which the administrative state explains and justifies its actions and ultimately subordinates itself to the elected representatives of the people. In the British tradition of public law (which Canada and Australia have inherited), the archetype of this process is individual ministerial responsibility to Parliament for the actions of a department of government that the minister heads. Increasingly, however, government business is undertaken by a range of bodies that do not fit this simple model. In postwar Britain the first class of such agencies was the nationalized industries, now mostly sold off; much more important are what have been called 'quangos' but are better described as 'fringe organizations,' which carry out functions of the central government but are not housed in any ministry and, hence, not directly under the control of ministers who can answer for their operations to Parliament. The usual list of such bodies includes everything from the Arts Council to the Equal Opportunities Commission to (truly) the Banana Trade Advisory Committee (for a useful discussion, see Craig, 1989: 71–91).

What is not usually appreciated is that, constitutionally speaking, security and intelligence agencies, if not entirely unique, belong in this category as well. In earlier times, a case could have been made for uniqueness, on the grounds that their lack of statutory existence and the exclusion of Parliament from any role in debating their activities, let alone superintending them, took them out of the realm of responsible government entirely. However, internal security agencies are no longer creatures of the prerogative (royal or otherwise). In Canada and Australia – the major Westminster-style democracies that are the subject of this essay – they have been placed on a statutory footing, by the Canadian Security Intelligence Act [1984] (CSIS Act) and the Australian Security Intelligence Organization Act [1979] (ASIO Act), respectively. In Britain the Security Service Act [1989] has done the same.

Nonetheless, although in each state there are significant variations in the relations between the executive and the agencies, in Canada, Australia, and Britain the security service is unmistakably placed under the control of a director who, though subject to ministerial direction, is also and in varying ways insulated from direct subordination to any politician. Thus, quite apart from whatever secrecy may genuinely be required, there is no place for classical ministerial responsibility, and hence new mechanisms of political accountability have had to be created. Ideally these would simultaneously safeguard necessary independence while preventing it from degenerating into irresponsibility. In this essay I review and critically evaluate the contrasting legislation, institutions, and practices that have emerged since the late 1970s.

The emphasis on 'Westminster-style democracies' and 'the British public law tradition' is quite deliberate. Accountability does not exist in a constitutional vacuum; indeed, to put the point more positively, the forms of accountability that exist in any particular polity are critically dependent on constitutional structure. For present purposes, the most important feature of the Westminster model is that it is a parliamentary system. This means that the government of the day – the political executive – is formed from the personnel of those elected to the legislature, and the executive's continuance in office depends on its ability to command continued support from the majority of the legislature. Historically this gave primacy to the legislature, which was able to declare its lack of 'confidence' in the administration, which it would vote out of office if one of its key policies was seen to fail. No election followed, however: a new government would be formed, often containing many of the same individuals in ministerial posts, which would command the 'confidence,' namely majority support, of the elected House. In Britain this process had its heyday in the 1850s, when five administrations were formed in seven years, with only one election supervening; it happens with remarkable regularity in contemporary Italy, which has had fifty governments since the Second World War.

This legislative dominance should logically give parliaments effective control over the activities of government. Political reality has stood theory on its head, however. That reality is the organization of electoral politics on partisan lines. This seems to be a product historically, if not logically, of democratic suffrage; in any case, the crystallization of disciplined political parties in Britain occurred in the 1880s, the same decade that saw a major expansion (falling, however, well short of total inclusion) of the male electorate. The result has been that party affiliation determines who is elected to the legislature, and rigid party discipline is imposed on those who arrive there. Furthermore, far from being the dominant partner or even an effective watchdog over the executive, the main function of parliamentarians in the Westminster system is to maintain their party in office. As Turpin recently observed, 'It is indeed a paradoxical feature of the modern constitution that for control and accountability of government we rely mainly upon an elected House in which the majority see it as their principal function to maintain the government in power' (1990: 424). This is, of course, true of all parliamentary systems, but the Westminster-model states – again historically, rather than logically – have added a peculiar twist. With the exception of the Australian Senate, they are virtually alone in resisting proportional representation, or, more precisely, retaining a system of first-past-the-post election in single-member constituencies. The result is single-party government, which makes party discipline and maintenance of the administration in office far easier than where coalitions are the rule. Thus, a system of government that theoretically gives omnipotence to the legislature has, as that legislature came to be chosen by the full electorate, produced a body that is shackled to and by the executive. Our understanding of mechanisms of accountability with respect to any government activity must start with a recognition of this fact.

Another key feature to note is the elitism of British political culture, also part of the imperial legacy to Canada and Australia, which they only began to shed in the 1970s (Galnoor, 1977: 282, and ch. 16). Within this culture, the conduct of government is seen as something for knowledgable and well-intentioned (and often well-connected) initiates.

The masses are let in on the act only to the extent that is good for them or is politically unavoidable. This culture pervades the entire administration, and it is responsible among other things for the obsessive secrecy of the British government, which remains virtually alone among Western democracies in its steadfast refusal to enact access or freedom of information legislation. And the bewitching brew of unrestricted executive discretion mixed with secrecy is at its most potent in those areas where the 'mysteries of state' (Bok, 1982: 171–5) are most jealously guarded by all governments: foreign relations, military matters, and 'national security.' A nice illustration is that even now Australia, which unlike Canada maintains an external intelligence agency, has refused to place it on a statutory footing even though the Australian Security Intelligence Organization (ASIO), the internal security agency, was made a statutory body fifteen years ago. A legal charter would imply limitations, no matter how expansively the mandate was expressed, that the political and administrative elites have regarded as unacceptable.

Thus, an executive that has sought determinedly to keep all matters concerning the operation of security and intelligence agencies hidden from Parliament and the public has, by virtue of its control over Parliament, generally been able to do so. To the extent that matters have been prised open, the lever has been *scandal*: the political fallout from misconduct by the agencies, particularly where at least some of those victimized were opposition politicians who later achieved office (Whitaker, 1991, 1992). Thus, the idea of responsible government has been most attenuated in the area of security, and there were simply no precedents or models available when, in the late 1970s, Canada and Australia slowly began to grapple with the need to get some kind of grip on agencies and activities that seemed 'out of control,' 'a law unto themselves,' and to be engaging in activities that in some instances threatened the health of democracy itself.

It is necessary to judge kindly when evaluating the results, for the wheel had to be invented before it could turn. A remote parallel is with the police, who in modern times have claimed a form of 'independence' from direct political control (Lustgarten, 1986). However, the police are far more visible, immediate in their impact, are locally connected, and have always had a statutory organizational foundation. Hence, the experience with police governance has not been much of a resource. This is particularly true in Canada, because separation of the security service from the national police force was one of the major reforms of the CSIS

Act [RSC 1985]. The developments in the accountability of security services of the past fifteen years have been of major long-term constitutional significance, going well beyond the specific area of security.

The only nation in the English-speaking world that has had any experience with formal structures of legislative accountability for security and intelligence agencies is the United States, but this is precisely the one source that could not provide a useful model. The United States possesses not only the oldest written constitution in the world, but also one of the most unusual. Its rigid separation of powers between the executive and the legislature differs radically from the parliamentary system that is the norm throughout the democratic world. One might assume that because the president is granted full 'executive power' by Sections I and II of Article I of the Constitution, as well as being made commander-in-chief of the armed forces, his power in relation to war and national security would be plenary, with the Congress excluded entirely; and indeed some occupants of the office have come close to asserting such power. But this claim, which one critic rightly castigated as that of an 'imperial presidency' (Schlesinger, 1974), ignores both the constitutional text and the political realities.

At the simplest level, the commander-in-chief cannot declare war, which requires Congressional declaration, nor enter into binding treaties, which require approval of two-thirds of the senators present at the vote. (By contrast, in Britain and Canada, the Crown makes treaties without need for legislative approval, though they do not become part of domestic law.) More important is that the executive cannot spend money without legislative approval; the power of 'appropriation' is conferred upon the Congress and involves highly detailed considerations of proposals for expenditure by both Houses of Congress.

The political reality is that Congress, particularly during the past two decades, is often controlled politically by a party different from that of the president. Thus, there is every incentive for the legislature to query and challenge the actions of executive bodies such as security agencies, whose heads, like all important American public officials, are not civil servants but are rather appointed by the incoming president and retain office only so long as he wishes. And Congress can exert pressure when faced with non-cooperation or evasion by threatening the lifeblood of any organization: money. Much more than partisan wrangling is involved. Partly because an ethos of legislative independence has arisen from the co-equal branches of government created by the Constitution, and partly because of the regional nature and weak party structure of American politics, legislators are far more willing to strike out on their own, and far less susceptible to political control by the executive, than in the Westminster-style democracies. Canada may be moving to a point midway between the United States and Britain in this respect.

This does not produce unremitting conflict between the two branches, particularly as there often is a dominant consensus about foreign policy and security issues in the United States. Nonetheless, after Congress asserted itself in the 1970s, successive presidents have had to accept, however reluctantly, the existence of both ad hoc Congressional investigative committees and two permanent committees for oversight of the Central Intelligence Agency (CIA). This is reinforced by a 1980 statute that requires all intelligence agencies to keep the committees 'fully and currently informed of all intelligence activities ... including any significant anticipated intelligence activity.' This was an amendment to the CIA charter, the National Security Act [1947]. The FBI, which is responsible for counter-intelligence within the United States, was also subject to some Congressional scrutiny and a considerably executive overhaul of its directing principles in the 1970s (Elliff, 1979).

Quite apart from the other constitutional constraints already noted, Westminster-type Parliaments that lack American Congressional fiscal powers cannot hope to exert equivalent supervision over security agencies. The struggle for accountability, therefore, must take place on several planes simultaneously. In an extraordinarily impressive paper that covers a wide range of security-governance issues, Reg Whitaker has identified three dimensions of accountability: executive, legislative, and public (Whitaker, 1991: 650–3). This essay will concentrate on the first two. In particular, the accountability that may be achieved through statutory mechanisms of individual complaints and (particularly in relation to security clearances) appeals will not be discussed. Nor will there be any detailed discussion of the role of the press and other media in exposing abuses or otherwise stimulating public interest in keeping security agencies under careful scrutiny, although there is clearly an overlap between legislative and public accountability here. My research has concentrated on the structure and actual functioning of governmental mechanisms; a completely different project, involving monitoring media output and interviewing those involved, would be required before any conclusions on their role and impact could be reached. And any such analysis would require extended consideration of the laws suppressing access to and publication of information, such as the notorious Official Secrets Acts that have at various times been on the statute books of all three nations.

The one gap in Whitaker's analysis is consideration of the constitutional context, which the first section of the present essay has sought to provide. A primary conclusion to be drawn from the constitutional perspective is that there are severe limits to legislative accountability in the Westminster model. It follows that those who seek to keep a close eye on security and intelligence agencies will have to follow two strategies, alternatively or in parallel. One is to rely particulary heavily on institutions within the executive branch, though that may raise a host of other objections. The second is to invent new devices to overcome the legislature's limitations, and then link them either to the legislature itself or to the wider public.

The final question that must be addressed in this section is the most basic: why is accountability important? This can be briefly answered at two levels: that of the conduct of any aspect of government and that of security and intelligence agencies particularly. At the first, accountability is a requirement or prerequisite of a functioning democracy; those entrusted with state power must be made to submit to the scrutiny, criticism, and direction of the citizenry, who are represented by those they elect. This principle, which is not primarily concerned with efficiency but rather with legitimacy, applies to all areas of state activity, regardless of their wider impact on public life.

In relation to security and intelligence services, however, the need for a more or less continuous form of accountability – which may variously and interchangeably be described as supervision, oversight, or review – is at a practical level much more profound. Apart from the armed forces, which in Western democracies have been kept effectively subordinated, security services are potentially the greatest threat to the functioning of democracy. They present two distinct potential dangers. The first is that they become a tool of the government in power to be unleashed against its political opponents, under the guise of protecting the security of the state. The second is that they become an independent centre of power in their own right, choosing targets and harassing or destroying individuals or organizations whose policies or ideology they oppose. The mechanisms of governance must therefore ensure both due independence and a close rein – what Whitaker calls 'a delicate balance ... which is neither too "hands-on" nor too "arm's length"' (1991: 657). Failure in either direction may have dangerous consequences.

Executive Accountability

General Provisions

The particularly striking thing about the controls that have been established within the executive branch of government in Australia is the extent to which the legislation seeks to build in protection for the director general (DG). More particularly, it establishes procedures designed to make it very difficult for both the relevant minister (the attorney general) or the government generally to manipulate ASIO for political or personal self-interest.

The first provision, Section 7(2) of the ASIO Act [1979], requires the prime minister to consult the leader of the opposition before appointing a DG, which is presumably intended to ensure a broad consensus both on the general direction the organization will take and on the standing of the person who will lead it. The DG has substantially more secure tenure of office than his counterparts in Canada and the United Kingdom. He or she is appointed for a period specified at the outset, the others serve at pleasure (Section 9(1) of the ASIO Act [1979], Section 2(1) of the Security Service Act [RSC 1989] (SSA), and Section 4(2) of the CSIS Act [RSC 1985]).

Once in post, the DG, though subject both to specific ministerial directives and to more general guidelines relating to the functions and powers of the agency, Sections 8(2) and 8A of the ASIO Act, is equipped with certain weapons for bureaucratic and political in-fighting. First, Section 8(3) allows that the DG may require that *any* direction be put in writing. This is shrewdly calculated to prevent a minister from denying the existence of any direction that may be thought improper or otherwise be politically embarrassing; it is also a significant deterrent to any attempt at misuse of the organization in the first place. Presumably, any purported direction not put on paper upon request may be treated as a nullity. Responsibility is thus placed squarely on the shoulders of the minister, where it belongs.

Secondy, and more precisely, the DG's opinion on whether collection or communication of intelligence about a person is justified on security grounds, in accordance with Section 8(5), cannot be overridden except by a written direction from the minister setting out his or her reasons for so doing. As with all written directions, a copy must be sent directly to the inspector general (of who more later), but in this unique instance, following section 8(6), a copy must be sent to the prime minister as well. The narrow aim here is clearly to prevent a politician from harassing political or personal antagonists. The broader one is to ensure the primacy of the non-political (in the partisan sense) judgment of the agency about what constitutes a security matter: statutory interference by a minister immediately becomes a matter for the review authority and his own political superior. The minister must therefore think long and hard, and feel himself on very firm ground, before intervening in this sphere. In both instances, protection of the agency's independence is sought by raising the political costs of interference, and particularly by preventing its occurrence in secrecy. Finally, in Section 8(4), the minister is simply forbidden from overriding advice given to the Cabinet and other government ministers on security matters.

The Inspector General

While the Australian system seeks to protect ASIO from interference by politicians, it also attempts to give the executive the capability of checking abuses by ASIO. In 1986, as part of the package of reforms growing out of the second royal commission, the Labor government created the office of inspector general of security (IG). This official, whose appointment also requires consultation with the leader of the opposition (Inspector-General of Intelligence and Security Act, Section 6 [1986]) is given a very wide remit. He or she is concerned with compliance with law and 'property' or activities; with effectiveness and appropriateness of procedures in relation to legality and propriety; and with 'consistency with human rights' (Sections 4 and 8). The objects of the act are described as assisting *ministers* in oversight and review of these matters, and the primary audience for the IG's work, and the recipients of the reports that emerge from his inquiries, is the executive branch. Even where the report was triggered by an individual's complaint, all the complainant is entitled to receive is a written response which contains no material that either the IG or the minister believe would prejudice the nation's security, defence, or foreign relations (Section 24). Clearly the IG is no whistle blower. Nor does the office possess remedial powers. The agency head is expected to act upon the report, and if the IG thinks the response is inadequate or inappropriate, he may discuss the matter with the minister and prepare a further report to be sent to the prime minister (Section 24). Ministerial pressure rather than public outcry is envisaged as the main form of influence and correction.

The IG is not limited to responding to complaints; he is permitted to act on his 'own motion.' What is most unusual is that this proactive capability is not limited to ASIO: the IG's jurisdiction extends to the entire security and intelligence establishment, including the Defence Signals Directorate, the external intelligence service (ASIS), the Office of National Assessments, and the Joint Intelligence Organization within the Department of Defence (Section 8). Various provisions impose slightly different restrictions on the review of each particular agency. No other review agency anywhere, however, has been granted such extensive jurisdiction, a point to which I shall return at the conclusion of this essay.

With such a wide range of matters to consider, and so many agencies under his superintendence, one would expect the IG to be extremely active. Not so. The office's reported expenditure in 1987–8 was just over A$250,000; the IG has virtually no staff, and his initial public annual report was largely devoted to his problems in finding suitable office accommodation. His second report consisted of two and one-half pages, of which only one paragraph discussed public requests or complaints. Apart from one complaint involving procedures of security assessment in the public service, all were dismissed. The inspector general has not conducted any inquiries of his 'own motion' (Australia, Inspector-General, 1987, 1988).

Social scientists tend to denigrate the importance of the character and outlook of individuals in influencing the workings of institutions. Historians, more taken with the quirkiness and contingency of events, allow such idiosyncratic factors greater weight. I side with the historians. This point will emerge again later in this essay; at present I shall merely contend that the apparent inactivity of the Australian inspector general is in significant measure the result of the approach taken by the first appointee to the post.

Mr Neil McInnes[2] had an extensive background in intelligence and defence-related matters as a government official – not the sort of background to encourage deep scepticism about security agencies. He also seemed markedly conservative, taking the view that the civil disobedience campaign of obstruction of logging in the Tasmanian wilderness, which involved some destruction of tractors and large-scale lying in front of trucks, constituted 'politically motivated violence,' which is part of ASIO's statutory mandate. (It was reassuring to be told that ASIO itself resolutely refused to get involved.)

McInnes seemed very resistant to individual complaints about agency misconduct, and he gave the impression that the complainant would have to present a very substantial case before he would take it seriously. He seemed untroubled by the obvious evidentiary difficulties this would entail. He did, however, place great emphasis on what he called the 'monitoring procedures' he had established to satisfy himself that agencies were behaving properly. These are not mentioned at all in his annual report and seemed to consist of looking at a random sample of files to determine whether they formed a satisfactory basis for the agency's conduct. However, Mr McInnes claimed that his own background in intelligence permitted him to be confident that he knew what to look for and how to find it. He also stated that if he needed staff to assist him in an extended inquiry, he could obtain them from the equivalent of the Privy Council Office, or from another security agency, making use of the bureaucratic reality of interagency rivalry to ensure a thorough investigation.

Unless one takes Mr McInnes's assurances on trust, the Australian inspector general may be described as a powerful gun that has yet to be fired. The potential of the office is great, but it awaits an incumbent prepared to make use of it before its effectiveness may be judged. Mr McInnes was not reappointed. His successor, also appointed from within government circles, has been considerably more active, and his annual reports are very much more extensive (Lustgarten and Leigh, 1994).

CANADA

The Canadian approach to executive accountability has been markedly different from that of the United Kingdom. The solicitor general's department is given an explicit statutory role, not only in the sense that the minister may issue directions to the director of the Canadian Security Intelligence Service (CSIS), but also in that the deputy minister – the department's senior civil servant – must be consulted by the director on general policy matters and whenever the issuance of directions requires consultation; this is stated in Sections 6(2) and 7(1) of the Act [RSC 1985]. Hence, the solicitor general's office has a police and security branch, with several people who are engaged full-time in liaising with CSIS on matters ranging from operational policy to particular requests to tap telephones, reading 'correspondence flows,' and advising the minister.[3] Even more intensely involved, and the centre-piece of the new executive mechanisms, is the inspector general (IG), whose office was created by the CSIS Act [RSC 1985].

The IG does not exist to serve the public, which never sees his reports. Nor does he report to Parliament, and he was, in fact, extremely reticent in providing information to a parliamentary committee established in 1990 to review the operation of the CSIS Act. Rather, the IG serves as a sort of auditor for the minister, a function which is directly traceable to the scandals of the 1970s. 'The history of the security services in Canada is that they kept secrets from everyone, including Ministers.'[4] Hence, the IG's main task in a fundamental sense is to ensure that ministerial responsibility is real – that is, either that the minister is actually aware of what CSIS is doing and how it is doing it or, if something goes wrong and a public row ensures, that he or she can say, 'I know there is a problem and the IG is looking into it.'

There are two dimensions to the IG's work. One, which from a bare reading of the CSIS Act might seem predominant, but emerged in interview as less important, is the issuance of a certificate that itself covers two matters. The first is whether he is satisfied with the director's statutorily required annual report. The second is whether in his opinion CSIS has engaged in any operational activities that are either unauthorized by the act or ministerial directions, or have involved 'an unreasonable or unnecessary exercise by the Service of any of its powers' (CSIS Act [RSC 1985] Section 33). This mandate requires the IG to make value judgments, and he recognized that 'there is a great deal of grey, rather than black and white in "unreasonable and unnecessary."' This remit leads him to see himself as a sort of 'conscience of the minister,' urging the latter and the deputy minister to 'think hard' about any matter that might raise doubts.

The IG forms his judgments not simply by reacting to the director's report, but by a structured program of research into CSIS's operations. This second dimension, the heart of his work, consists of six or seven major projects of a thousand or more hours each which are undertaken annually. These are based on a three- to five-year work program, worked out in conjunction with the solicitor general's office and the Security Intelligence Review Committee (discussed below), a coordinated exercise designed to avoid repeating problems that initially arose of duplication or directed 'tasking' (Canada, House of Commons, Special Committee, 1990: 141–2). The IG will pick a particular topic, for example, use of human sources, and look at both policy and actual practice. This entails both reading files and interviewing officers. The IG is given a statutory right of access to all CSIS material relating to the scope of his jurisdiction, according to Section 31(1), although this does not include information relating to financial audit. The present incumbent expressed confidence that his office had the capacity to 'go into the bowels of CSIS,' and that it would be very difficult to conceal discreditable matters from him.

It should perhaps be emphasized that the IG is neither a whistle blower nor in any sense an avenue of public accountability. The office is designed for monitoring compliance with statutory and ministerial standards and for a policy evaluation of the service's work. If it functions effectively, it should avoid political embarrassment for the minister and possibly the government as a whole. It is impossible from the outside to judge how well the IG has carried out its task over the years, though it may be revealing that while officials in the solicitor general's office were quite critical of aspects of SIRC's work, they found little to fault with the IG. What does seem clear, however, is that the Canadian system places the minister in a far more central role than in either Australia or (especially) the United Kingdom, and it has also tried to give him or her the tools to do the job properly. In this sense, paradoxically, it has remained closest to the traditional Westminster concept of ministerial responsibility; but it has also tried to make that responsibility real.

Legislative Accountability

In *The Adventure of Silver Blaze*, Sherlock Holmes remarked on 'the curious incident of the dog in the night time.' But, said Watson, 'the dog did nothing in the night time.' 'That was the curious incident.' Likewise parliamentary accountability for security. This section is devoted to a record of debate, official rejection, and only the very beginnings of an experiment in direct parliamentary involvement. It also considers much the most interesting development – that of an agency which is separate from Parliament but reporting to it, yet at the same time possesses a high public profile. It is here that parliamentary and public accountability converge.

AUSTRALIA

Only in Australia has a body for legislative oversight been created. Its establishment was described independently by interviewees inside and outside government as 'a sop to the Labor Left.' In other words, the

Labor government as a whole was not committed to the idea, which indeed had been explicitly rejected by the royal commission whose recommendations strongly influenced the reforms introduced in 1986 (Australia, Royal Commission, 1985: ch. 17, esp. par. 17.34). However, there is a long history of distrust of ASIO within the Labor party, which came within one vote of adopting abolition of the organization as official policy in 1971. This distrust was fuelled by the publication of a secret annex to Mr Justice Hope's report which revealed that ASIO had been supplying intelligence material about Labor politicians and other Left figures to a right-wing pressure group (Marr, 1984: 15–16, 269). Perhaps uniquely in parliamentary democracies, the Australian Labor party is organized into identified factions, so that a particular MP will be described as of 'the New South Wales Right' or the 'Victorian Left.' The Left faction secured the creation of a parliamentary committee, but one hedged about with major restrictions on its jurisdiction and powers. Though rare, joint committees (whose members are drawn from the House of Representatives and Senate) have a considerable pedigree in Australia: the Joint Committee on Foreign Affairs and Defence was established in 1952, and one on the National Crime Authority in 1984 (Sibraa, 1987). The inclusion of senators allows representation of the Australian Democrats, who have failed to elect any MPs; it also removes some of the discipline of the whips, which operates much more tightly on MPs than on senators.

The committee operates under two major kinds of restrictions. The first is that it cannot initiate inquires on its own. It can act only upon a reference from the attorney general (the minister responsible for ASIO) or, according to Section 92C(2) of the ASIO Act [1979] upon a motion by either House. Despite the possibility of an opposition majority in the Senate, the latter is highly unlikely to be passed over government opposition, so essentially the committee will require government approval before it can do anything.

Second, it is forbidden to inquire into certain crucial matters, notably anything that, following Section 92C(4)C, is 'operationally sensitive,' which specially includes anything 'that relates to intelligence collection methods or sources of information.' Hence, infiltration, telephone tapping, or other forms of intrusion on privacy, and virtually anything concerning current projects, will be beyond its scope. Section 92C(4)(a) also excludes it from examining anything relating to the obtaining or communicating of foreign intelligence by ASIO, which would exclude significant aspects of relations with foreign intelligence organizations.

A cynical view is that these restrictions were included by the government to nobble the joint committee at the outset. It may be said, however, that the Liberal opposition fought its establishment strongly, and that such concessions may possibly ensure its survival in the long term (Sibraa, 1987). In any case, a combination of difficulties in obtaining physically secure premises, getting its security clearance for its secretariat, and the disruption of membership caused by retirements and two federal elections meant that the committee was not launched until May 1990. Opposition parties are now participating in the committee. It had to manage without a full-time secretariat until July 1991. Its first inquiry concerned the appropriate treatment of information held by ASIO in relation to the Archives Act [1983]. It has received periodic briefings from the organization in private, and it has discussed matters of public concern, such as the exchanges of information with the discredited and now disbanded Queensland Special Branch, with the acting director-general.[5] It would be premature to offer an evaluation of the efficacy of this approach to oversight based on such limited historical experience. However, since the five-year review committee established by the Canadian legislation recommended establishment of a permanent parliamentary subcommittee on security and intelligence (Canada, House of Commons, Special Committee, 1990: ch. 14) – a recommendation the government has firmly thrust aside (Canada, Solicitor General, 1991: 79) – it is worth considering the arguments surrounding the direct participation of parliamentarians in this area.

The primary criterion in support is that, however well served by a body acting on Parliament's behalf, only MPs themselves can ensure that the questions they want answered are asked and the matters they want investigated are attended to. (The underlying justification of principle is that those chosen by the citizenry should determine priorities and participate in the process of controlling administration.) It is a point that has some force, but there are several that must be set against it.

Many of the counter-arguments derive from the nature of parliamentarians as active politicians. As one member of Parliament said, 'there are no votes in security,' meaning that it is not an area from which party advantage or personal recognition can be gained. Hence, when compared with analogous matters like defence or foreign policy, it is relatively low in the pecking order and unlikely to engage the long-time attention of an able and/or ambitious MP. This exacerbates the normal problem of turnover which afflicts parliamentary committees generally, depriving them of the expertise members gain only after several years of immersion in the subject. There is also an unfortunate tendency – to which MPs will admit in private discussions but which seems to be an occupational affliction – to 'playing to the gallery' or 'grandstanding': saying or doing things with an eye to media publicity rather than in an effort to make a genuine contribution. A closely related problem is that of partisan point-scoring and rigidity, both of which derive from the need to maintain the government's, opposition's, or individual MP's hold on or chance for office by discrediting those on the other side. Members of the Canadian special committee of all three parties emphasized that their effort, which produced a large number of recommendations that were almost all unanimous, was unusual in avoiding these problems. Lack of political pressure, absence of members with highly polarized or high-profile views, and a deliberate effort to achieve consensus in order to maximize the impact of the report were offered as explanations.[6] These factors are unlikely to be ever-present when a body with a shifting membership exists on a permanent basis.

Finally, it should be emphasized that the 'expertise' of parliamentarians can be too readily exaggerated, because their job allows them only a limited time to devote to any particular subject, even if they are given that brief for an extended period. The only practical answer is to ensure the provision of adequate support staff, which has been a matter of great contention between Parliament and the executive in all Westminster-style democracies in the 1980s and 1990s. A committee on security matters raises particular difficulties, because the agencies will be chary of cooperating unless their fears about leaks can be allayed. In Australia and the United States, vetting elected representatives is regarded as unacceptable in principle, but there is a corresponding insistence on careful scrutiny of committee staffers. Where there already exists, as in Canada, a group of security-cleared people working full-time for a body issuing public reports on which Parliament may act (Rankin, 1990; Gill, 1989b), assembling a separate group seems somewhat redundant.

Even more telling is the view that membership on such a committee would compromise the work of an MP. Participation entails respect for the secrecy of the information received, and the MP who is dissatisfied with the picture that emerges is placed in an impossible position. He or she cannot offer public criticism supported by reasoned argument without violating that condition; and silence can then be readily misinterpreted, or deliberately misrepresented, as approval. And if criticisms or dissatisfaction aired in camera are ignored by the security agency, the MP lacks the normal means of generating pressure by means of public campaigning and media publicity. These restrictions may be acceptable for a priest hearing confession, but they negate the function of a public representative. They can become co-optation with a vengeance.

Thus, the case for review by parliamentarians seems rather weak, particularly if most of the purported benefits could be achieved as effectively by other means. And its creation would be positively retrograde if done as an *alternative* to a more effective, if innovatory, body. The Australian inspector general is one which has yet to prove itself. The Canadian Security Intelligence Review Committee (SIRC) is a very different matter.

CANADA

Unlike the IG, SIRC has not only received substantial media coverage but also scholarly analysis. These evaluations have been positive. It has had a demonstrable influence on important issues of security policy, for example, in curtailing CSIS's 'counter-subversion' activities (Gill, 1989a); it took, in its early years, a high public profile as a gadfly to CSIS; and it deliberately courted, and to some extent fostered, a civil liberties constituency which has taken an interest in security matters unparalleled elsewhere, for example, by supporting conferences on security matters (see Franks, 1989b; Hanks and McCamus, 1989). The five-year review committee thought highly enough of its work to recommend substantial enlargements of its functions and budget (Canada, House of Commons, Special Committee, 1990: ch. 11). The only discordant notes were expressed by certain officials who (unattributably) criticized some of its work as 'shallow' and 'headline grabbing.' However, these critics also emphasized that they supported the existence of SIRC as an institution, while being unhappy with aspects of its performance.

SIRC, then, is generally accounted a success. It is important to specify what this means. Success for an institution of accountability is not easily measurable, indeed, it is not susceptible to precise measurement. It entails having a significant impact on an organization whose operations are perforce hidden from public view and altering the climate of public opinion and interest within which the organization functions. Perhaps its most important elements are:

1 Ensuring compliance with legal restrictions and norms of respect for

democracy and human rights. Public censure and reversal of decisions will have some effect in this direction, but greater long-term impact will be achieved if the organization is helped to respond positively and begin to internalize those norms, rather than responding defensively by either rejecting the criticism or looking for ways around the standards.

2 To achieve sufficient public authority and credibility so that when it concludes that the organization is behaving creditably, that conclusion is believed and rational people abandon their fears and suspicions about what is being done (to themselves or to others). This function of reassurance is also valuable politically to the organization, since it should increase support, or at least minimize opposition, when it seeks greater resources.

In order to achieve this credibility, it is probably necessary for the review body to 'take on' the organization publicly and be seen to defend civil liberties aggressively. This point was fully appreciated by SIRC and particularly its first chairman, Ronald Atkey; and the notably unworshipful tone of its early annual reports, coupled with Atkey's critical comments made during appearances on television, helped it achieve credibility with unusual speed.

3 To stimulate greater public interest in the problems surrounding the activities of the agency it covers – in this case, of bringing security and intelligence issues more visibly onto the public agenda. It should also raise new issues and alert the interested public to where developments are likely to occur. In parallel, it should encourage and bring into the often closed systems of bureaucracy fresh thinking from other sources. An important spin-off of this last contribution is to stimulate the agency's leadership to rethink and review its main activities and their rationales.

4 Finally, to accomplish the foregoing with the minimum practicable adverse impact on the ability of the organization to do its work effectively.

Accepting that SIRC has been generally successful on these criteria, what aspects of its structure, powers, and relations with the wider political environment have contributed in an important way? SIRC is a constitutional innovation that stands in unusual relation to both executive and legislative branches of government. It is independent of the executive, though providing it with secret reports. It is also, as the parliamentary review committee described it (Canada, House of Commons, Special Committee, 1990: 156–60) a 'surrogate' for, rather than responsible to, Parliament. This may in some ways be unsatisfactory, but at least it is unconstrained both by the unfortunate side-effects of partisan politics and by the public nature of parliamentary process.

SIRC can conduct its reviews and investigations under conditions of necessary secrecy, and it has been non-partisan in approach and, by convention, multipartisan in its composition. Section 34 of the CSIS Act [RSC 1985] requires that the prime minister consult with the leaders of all parties with more than twelve seats before making any appointment to SIRC. At the outset, however, it was accepted that there be one member from each of the two opposition parties, and that consultation occur in relation to all appointments, regardless of party. There was some controversy about whether proper consultation had occurred when the present chairman was appointed, but this seems to have been the result of a misunderstanding, not a flouting of the convention. Though committee members must be privy councillors, in some cases they have attained that status only as a result of appointment; the government is not limited in its choice to a small group of establishment-minded people.

Though they serve only part-time, SIRC members are assisted by a substantial full-time staff that, after initial learning difficulties, has developed substantial expertise in the workings of the agency they review. In accordance with Section 39 of the CSIS Act SIRC enjoys a statutory right to full access to CSIS files and related material. Although Cabinet documents are excluded from this access (which has provoked some criticism), in practice the solicitor general has given assurances that Cabinet decisions will be passed on to SIRC as ministerial directions (Canada, SIRC, 1989: Appendix A, 62).

SIRC can initiate investigations in response to public complaints and either conduct a review of specific activities of the service or direct the IG to do so, without the necessity of a prior complaint. This proactive capacity is particularly critical in the security field, where private individuals so often lack the hard knowledge necessary to establish any sort of prima facie case of wrongdoing.

Finally, SIRC can make full use of the mechanism of publicity to propagate its view that some thing or things are unsatisfactory and require change. Its annual reports, though delivered to the solicitor general, are required to be laid before Parliament within fifteen days (Section 53 of the CSIS Act); and these, particularly in the early years, were often combatative in tone to the extent that one critic thought that

SIRC took unfair advantage of its position, because 'CSIS couldn't answer back.' SIRC may also present special reports to the minister that are not intended to be published, and indeed the parliamentary review committee was refused copies on the grounds that the CSIS Act (Section 54) forbade their release (Canada, House of Commons, Special Committee, 1990: 158–60). Nevertheless, summaries of SIRC's view of the issues raised in these reports may appear in its public pronouncements and will be reflected in the general stance it takes towards the service. Two of SIRC's reports have been compiled on the understanding that they would be publicly released, but this is exceptional.

Conclusions

One can, then, identify eight features that seem necessary for an effective accountability mechanism in the security and intelligence field. These are:

1 Independence from the executive
2 Proactive capacity
3 Membership representative of the spectrum of political parties, but acting in a non-partisan manner
4 Access to information about all aspects of the agency's activities
5 The ability to maintain secrecy where necessary
6 Institutional expertise, which is intimately tied to
7 Adequate support staff, working full-time
8 The capacity to campaign, that is, to use the media to build up support for its position

The SIRC structure and relationships could certainly stand improvement. In particular, the complaints of the parliamentary review committee (Canada, House of Commons, Special Committee 1990) seem well founded. Although SIRC should remain the prime mover in relation to review, it should be open to Parliament to 'task' it when some matter arises that causes concern. Parliament should also be able to evaluate SIRC's own product, which means having access to some material now denied to it. Whether this requires establishment of a permanent committee of some kind is another matter.

The eight features here identified may be necessary conditions for the success of a review body, but are they sufficient? One of the points emphasized repeatedly by people I interviewed – whether officials, academics, or those associated with SIRC itself[7] – was the importance of individual personalities and political attitudes. SIRC began its operations quite coincidentally with the arrival of the first Progressive Conservative government in over two decades. The PCs, as a party, therefore did not have the kind of establishment mentality, including a close psychological identification with the security apparatus, that one would find among their British counterparts. The first chairman and moving figure was a 'Red Tory' and a member of the board of the Canadian Civil Liberties Association. His successor, whose political image is very different, also described himself to me as a 'Red Tory.' Thus, the government made no attempt to pack the committee with people predisposed to acquiescence in CSIS's outlook. Moreover, Ronald Atkey placed great emphasis on proceeding consensually and avoiding partisan division. Partly under his influence, and partly as a matter of self-education, some other members altered their views.[8] Good collegial relations have prevailed. There is no way that this chemistry could have been predicted, and it certainly cannot be created by statute. A body split by rancorous relationships and ideological differences would have had little practical impact or public respect. To an immeasurable but important extent, Canada has been lucky. And it is certainly possible, particularly in Britain, to envisage that a government compelled by public pressure to establish a review body, would pack it with people content with the status quo and insensitive to human-rights considerations. There is no magic in institutions, although badly designed institutions can predictably fail.

Rather than engaging in a superficially attractive but specious league table ranking of the accountability systems of the two nations, it is more valuable to conclude by identifying one serious defect common to all the institutions of accountability discussed in this essay, with the exception of the Australian inspector general. Review or oversight is *institutional*, rather than *functional*. That is to say, a particular agency – CSIS or ASIO – is the subject of the attention of a particular body. However, other agencies may be engaging in activities very like those of the subject agency, but because they occur within a different institutional framework, no one has jurisdiction to review them. Awareness of this problem underlay the recommendation of the Canadian parliamentary review committee that the Communications Security Establishment (CSE), the signals intercept body that has the technical capacity to monitor vast amounts of telephone traffic, be put under SIRC's review jurisdiction. At the moment, said the committee, 'to all intents and purposes [it] is unaccountable' (Canada, House of Commons, Special Committee, 1990: 153). This is bad enough, but even worse is the possibility that an unreviewed agency will be deliberately given tasks that a review body might object to. Hence, review must be structured around functions or activities, regardless of who performs them. That this raises considerable bureaucratic difficulties cannot be ignored, especially in Canada where at least with respect to CSIS there is also an active watchdog within the ministry. Functional review would cut across government departments – solicitor general, external affairs, and possibly the Privy Council Office, and defence. It might also undermine the separation, so painfully achieved in 1984, between CSIS and the RCMP, since the latter is clearly involved in gathering and storing intelligence about security threats in the context of terrorism. In any case, the distinction between criminal and security intelligence is so fine that its validity is doubtful (Farson, 1991a).

Nonetheless, while the difficulties may be acknowledged, they do not invalidate the main point. Establishing a structure of functional review, comprehensively covering all the activities of all actors on the security and intelligence stage, is the major challenge to accountability in this decade.

Note: The research for this chapter was conducted in 1990, and the first draft of the manuscript completed in 1991. While there have been a number of subsequent developments of importance in all jurisdictions considered in the essay since then (as to which, see Lustgarten and Leigh, 1994), the general structures for accountability of the security services in each of the jurisdictions remain as described in the chapter.

Notes

1 For a comparison that includes recent developments in the United Kingdom, see Lustgarten and Leigh, 1994 (esp. ch. 13–16).
2 The succeeding paragraphs are based on an interview held on 30 March 1989 in Canberra with the inspector general, whose frankness was much appreciated.
3 I wish to thank Mr Victor Gooch, director of security policy, and Mr James

Kitching, senior adviser on security policy in the solicitor general's office, for taking the time to answer a wide range of questions in an extended interview.

4 Ss. 30–33. I am grateful to Mr Richard Thompson, inspector general, and Mr Michael de Rosenroll, deputy inspector general, for the information provided in an interview of nearly three hours. All quotations in the following paragraphs are from this interview.

5 I should like to thank Ms Ann Hazelton, secretary to the parliamentary joint committee, for the information reported in this paragraph and for sending me copies of media releases issued by the committee.

6 These comments, and other remarks attributed to MPs, emerged in interviews with Blaine Thacker, chairman of the review committee and a Progressive Conservative; Derek Lee, Liberal; and John Brewin, NDP.

7 Interviews with SIRC personnel included John Bassett and Ronald Atkey, the present and former chairmen; Jean Jacques Blais, member since 1984; Maurice Archdeacon, executive secretary; Maurice Klein and John Smith, senior research officers. I am deeply grateful for the amount of time all these people took to discuss the issues with me, and for their engaging candour.

8 M. Blais was particularly frank about his own change of outlook and emphasized the role of Mr Atkey, in this respect.

The Noble Lie Revisited: Parliament's Five-Year Review of the CSIS Act

Instrument of Change or Weak Link in the Chain of Accountability?

STUART FARSON

When Walter Bagehot wrote his famous treatise on the English Constitution more than a century and a quarter ago as Canadians were joining confederation, he made a particular effort to distinguish between the realities and the appearances of British politics. In particular, he observed that the idea of a separation of powers protecting British freedoms was a fiction. The 'efficient secret' of the English Constitution, he opined, lay in the fact that executive and legislative powers were almost completely fused and embodied in the Cabinet (Bagehot, 1968: 65–6). No mention was made of measures to ensure that this body was answerable for its conduct to either the legislature or to the electorate. Nor was there a need to dwell on the fortunes of political parties.

Later, well after Bagehot's death, power began to shift away from the Commons floor, where ministers were accountable *in* and *to* Parliament, to the bureaucracies in Whitehall, and to the growing party machines. It was exactly at that point, as R.H.S. Crossland so perceptively observed, that 'the sceptic whose chief pleasure was the deflating of myths and the exposure of democratic pretensions, was himself admitted to the literary establishment; and the book in which he achieved such an exact separation of political myth from political reality became a part of the dignified facade behind which a new "efficient secret" could operate' (ibid.: 37). Ironically, it was radical theorists and left-wing reformers who propagated the new mythology. Instead of seeing *The English Constitution* as a model for prying behind the facade to observe the technique of power, they viewed it as a classical account of how British democracy worked, and ought to work. They continued to see the Cabinet through Bagehot's eyes and missed its secret links to party and bureaucracy alike (ibid.: 38–9). Nor did they notice that the independent-minded MP had left the political stage.

The new mythology of power was given further embodiment through the publication of A.V. Dicey's *Introduction to the Study of the Law of the Constitution*. Its conception of parliamentary sovereignty and discussion of that convenient conventional catch-all – the rule of law – provided the dominant paradigm for liberal democratic government without hinder for the best part of a century. In recent years, several critics have severely challenged this paradigm. Their criticism has varied not only in terms of source and intensity, but also in the way proposals for reform have been levied. In the United States, for example, the 'critical legal studies movement' has censured the rule of law on grounds of incoherence, inconsistency, and self-contradiction (Altman, 1990: 57). In Britain, where the notion of accountability is more intrinsic to the concept, particulary regarding the relationship between law and politics, critical scholars have exposed Dicey's notions of parliamentary sovereignty and the rule of law as a 'noble lie' (Harden and Lewis: 1986). Nevertheless, though they perceive the executive to be essentially unaccountable and incapable of being checked in practice, Harden and Lewis have argued that the idea of the rule of law retains merit. They posit that it can be made to work with certain fundamental modifications because it encompasses ideals and sentiments that transcend the historical moment. Essential to such a reinterpretation is the notion that the governed must have the capacity to evaluate both the would-be policies of the executive as well as past practices, if representation is to have meaning and to legitimize governance. For Harden and Lewis the *sine qua non* of such a position is access to information, not through notions of ministerial responsibility to Parliament, which they see as incapable of working adequately, but as of right through law that is reviewable in court by the judiciary, and in the legislature through statutory obligations imposed by such measures as sunset clauses.

In Canada there has yet been no all-encompassing critique of the constitution or of executive–legislative behaviour. This has been, in part, because both the constitution and parliamentary practice have been in a state of flux for more than a decade. Would-be critics, therefore, have faced the dilemma of how to deal with a moving target. Despite these difficulties there have been major criticisms of the rule of law and of executive and parliamentary practice. These criticisms have led, in turn, to innovative models of administrative law. These have encompassed new mechanisms of public and parliamentary accountability and, more recently, a frequently more strident pursuit of the public interest by parliamentarians. One such critique was provided by the Commission of Inquiry Concerning Certain Activities of the Royal Canadian Mounted Police (Canada, Commission of Inquiry, 1981 a, b – hereafter the McDonald commission). This inquiry firmly established that internal and external mechanisms of accountability governing Canada's security service did not work and that individual rights and freedoms were seriously at risk. To redress the balance, the McDonald commission proposed a new administrative model for their accomplishment, an important ingredient of which was the introduction of a new intermediary, an independent investigatory body with access to the secret world and its documentation. Significantly, the commission believed that this body should be directly accountable to both Parliament and the responsible minister. However, when the Canadian Security Intelligence Service Act [RSC 1985] and Security Offences Act [RSC 1985] were enacted in 1984, the Security Intelligence Review Committee (SIRC) was required to report only to the solicitor general of Canada, and through that office to Parliament.

The new legislation contained seldom-used provisions that obliged Parliament to review the law governing security intelligence practices and the enforcement of security offences after the law had been in force for five years. This essay focuses on those quasi-sunset provisions with a view to evaluating their capacity to analyse the policies and practices of the executive. In so doing, it does not consider all the dimensions of the five-year review process. Rather, it concentrates on whether the mechanisms provide Parliament with an enhanced level of sovereignty and allow it to obtain better information than through the convention of ministerial responsibility. In this regard, it looks closely at the new administrative model of accountability that was introduced through the auspices of SIRC and evaluates whether it provides the necessary flow of information to Parliament.

The Canadian Oversight System[1]

The political oversight system governing Canada's security and intelligence community has recently been restructured on the executive side. For several decades the Cabinet Committee on Security and Intelligence (CCSI), comprised of senior ministers and chaired by the prime minister, supposedly managed the intelligence process. Though it seldom met regularly, the CCSI ostensibly set objectives and provided policy direction for both the foreign intelligence and security sectors. In practice, most of this work was performed by bureaucrats within the Interdepartmental Committee of Security and Intelligence (ICSI) and the various middle-management committees and subcommittees that supported it. In 1993 the Campbell government revamped the Cabinet committee system and eliminated the CCSI. When the new Liberal administration took office later that year, it did not reincarnate the CCSI but allotted its responsibilities to the full Cabinet.

Individual ministers have direct responsibility for the agencies under their respective ministerial portfolios. Control of such agencies is effected by internal systems of direction and accountability and by internal audit mechanisms, largely under the control of the Treasury Board. On the foreign intelligence side, none of the organizations responsible for collecting or assessing intelligence is established by statute. Consequently, ministerial responsibility is drawn from the legislation governing the operation of the Department of Foreign Affairs (DFA) and the Department of National Defence (DND). The Communications Security Establishment (CSE), which is responsible for collecting signals intelligence and for ensuring the security of government communications, represents an exception to this rule. While its operational budget is included in DND's annual estimates, its operational directions stem from the deputy clerk (security and intelligence, and counsel) in the Privy Council Office. On the security side, the solicitor general derives responsibility for the Royal Canadian Mounted Police (RCMP) and Canadian Security Intelligence Services (CSIS) through the act providing for the ministerial office and the legislation establishing CSIS and the RCMP. Security measures conducted by the Department of Immigration, Transport Canada, and other departments originate in their respective statutes.

Special mechanisms have been put in place regarding CSIS. To assure the solicitor general that the service does not overstep its mandate, the CSIS Act [RSC 1985] established the office of the inspector general of CSIS. Its incumbent is a member of the Department of the Solicitor General and reports to its deputy minister. While the primary job of the inspector general is to measure the service's compliance with its operational policies, the office also has a capacity to monitor the efficacy of the organization. There is an important benefit in having the inspector general conduct reviews and provide certification instead of other persons in the solicitor general's secretariat. The legislation, rather than ministerial direction, specifically authorizes the incumbent to see documents belonging to the service and to receive explanations from its director and employees. Nevertheless, the size of the inspector general's staff, coupled with the breadth of the service's functions, make it impossible for the incumbent to certify compliance with all aspects of CSIS's mandate.

Legislative oversight is *theoretically* effected in three ways. By convention the Cabinet is collectively responsible and accountable to Parliament for the decisions it takes collectively on security and intelligence matters. Likewise, ministers are individually responsible and accountable for the actions of people in the departments and agencies they direct. Finally, a variety of parliamentary committees has the technical authority to review aspects of Canada's security and intelligence community. On the foreign intelligence side, the standing committees of the Senate and the House of Commons that concern themselves with foreign affairs and national defence are most relevant. On the security side, those concerning justice are most important, while those covering immigration and transport occasionally discuss security issues. Though seldom used as a legislative mechanism for overseeing the intelligence community, the Public Accounts Committee of the House of Commons has considered security and intelligence matters during its reviews of the auditor general's annual reports (Canada, House of Commons, Public Accounts Committee, 1991: 12–16).

The office of auditor general was established in 1976 by the Auditor General Act to provide an external and independent audit of government departments and agencies. To date these audits, which are provided directly to Parliament, not to the executive, have taken two forms. One consists of independent assessments of annual statements of government departments and agencies. The purpose of such statements is to assess the accuracy of the accounts produced by internal auditors. The other concerns an assessment of how well departments spend their money. These 'value-for-money' audits are conducted according to a schedule established by the auditor general. While the RCMP has undergone such an audit, the one scheduled for CSIS in 1993 was not conducted. The executive branch has been extremely reluctant to allow an independent audit by a body over which it has little reporting control. It suggested, however, that the audit could be conducted under the auspices of SIRC. Apparently, the auditor general rejected this approach because it might limit the office's independence.[2]

The Canadian Parliament has historically paid more attention to domestic security than to foreign intelligence. This is not surprising given the RCMP security service's history of infringing on individual rights and freedoms and the fact that matters of domestic security have been more broadly discussed by the Canadian public. In addition, there is now specific legislation to concentrate Parliament's mind on the subject. In fact, the adoption of the CSIS Act [RSC 1985] and the Security Offences Act [RSC 1985] placed specific obligations on Parliament regarding oversight. On the one hand, it required the solicitor general to table SIRC's annual reports with Parliament. Given the current Standing Orders of Parliament, this obliges the committee of appropriate jurisdiction, the Standing Committee on Justice and the Solicitor General (hereafter the 'Standing committee'), to review them. On the other hand, the CSIS Act [RSC 1985] specifically mandated Parliament to establish a special committee to conduct a comprehensive review after the legislation had been in force for five years.

The Security Intelligence Review Committee (SIRC) was also established by the 1984 legislation. While its members must be privy councillors, none can have a current association with the executive branch or be a parliamentarian. When nominating someone to SIRC, the prime minister must by law consult with opposition party leaders – not merely advise them who has been chosen – before making any appointment. Though this was done initially, there is evidence of non-compliance regarding some subsequent Tory appointments and of the positions becoming places for patronage (Cadieux, 1990).[3] The principal functions of SIRC are similar to those of the inspector general. The legislation authorizes SIRC to review the activities of CSIS and to provide the solicitor general with such reports as the minister directs. To complete its review, SIRC – like the inspector general – has the right to see all documents in the hands of the service, excepting Cabinet confidences. In practice, the reviews have attempted to cover issues of legality and propriety as well as those of effectiveness and efficiency. SIRC also acts as an independent tribunal for hearing complaints against the CSIS, over denials of security clearances and citizenship, and regarding matters relating to the deportation of landed immigrants and refugees on security grounds.

Past Assessments of Parliamentary Oversight

As part of his contribution to the McDonald commission, C.E.S. Franks (1979) assessed Parliament's capacity to provide legislative oversight of security matters. He concluded that there was cause for both optimism and concern. On the positive side, he noted that oversight had been reasonably effective, and that Parliament had shown a consistent concern for the rights and liberties of Canadians. Also, Parliament had played an important role in establishing commissions of inquiry. However, on the negative side, Franks thought there was considerable cause for alarm. Significantly, he concluded that Parliament had failed to control security activity:

The record shows that parliamentary discussion is spotty and partial, with some issues being flogged to death, while others have been ignored. Debate, questions and committee consideration have usually concentrated on a few, and often unimportant aspects of the problem. On changes in security organizations, and the implications of General Dare's letter, for example, the opposition chased after straw men and failed to uncover the real and disturbing issues. There has never been a full debate on security matters, and the government has never publicly informed Parliament of the policies, programmes and activities of the security branch. (1979: 65)

Franks believed existing problems were caused by Parliament and the public not having adequate information and knowledge to develop informed discussion. 'Secrecy,' he concluded, 'remains an obstacle to effective Parliamentary control' (ibid.).

When the McDonald commission made proposals about how Canada's domestic security system should be administered and overseen, it recommended dividing the functions between a new civilian security intelligence service and the RCMP. Furthermore, both institutions were to be placed under the purview of a parliamentary committee specially established for that purpose. The commission observed that 'the Parliamentary Committee should be as much concerned with the effectiveness of security intelligence organization as with the legality or propriety of its operations. Gaps in the security or intelligence system should be of as much concern to this Committee as alleged excesses of security surveillance' (Canada, Commission of Inquiry, 1981a: 899). When the Trudeau government devised legislation, it did not take this advice. Instead, it proposed SIRC, which successive governments have conveniently but incorrectly viewed as Parliament's surrogate (Canada, Solicitor General, 1991: 68, 77).

When Bill C-157 went to the Senate for review, the special committee chaired by Michael Pitfield, the former chief clerk of the Privy Council, did not attempt to change the system for monitoring and reviewing CSIS as proposed by the draft legislation. Instead of recommending direct accountability to Parliament, the Senate committee contributed to the notion of SIRC being a surrogate for first-hand review by the House of Commons. Clearly, the Senate committee did not trust those in the lower house with direct access to the secret world. Regarding the use of a special committee, it noted that one could be beneficial but posited that

There are many practical difficulties involved. A Parliamentary Committee would likely duplicate much of the efforts of the SIRC. Further, parliamentary committees are notoriously subject to the vagaries of time, changes in membership and overwork. There is also the problem of maintaining the security of information. This has reference in part to the possibility of partisan motivations in some members; but it also refers to the general question of whether that type of committee can maintain the requisite confidentiality by reason of the nature of its proceedings. (Canada, Senate, 1983: 32)

On these grounds the Pitfield committee argued against the establishment of even a parliamentary committee to work in tandem with SIRC. Nevertheless, it did observe that SIRC's annual reports would be tabled with Parliament and that the existing Standing Orders of the House of Commons required such reports to be referred automatically to the relevant standing committee. In this regard, the Senate committee optimistically asserted: 'Although such a committee would be relying on a report, and would not have original access to agency records, we expect that the quality and comprehensiveness of information which Parliament will receive about the operations of the security intelligence system will be greatly improved, thereby achieving some of the objectives of a special committee. This would also likely stimulate a useful public debate on these issues' (ibid.). The Pitfield committee's final conclusion proposed that Parliament conduct a thorough review of the legislation after it had been in operation for five years. Such a review, it observed naively, 'would go a considerable way toward ensuring that the legislation is working as Parliament intends it to operate' (ibid.: 35). This recommendation found expression in Bill C-9, the legislation that was eventually adopted by Parliament. Thus, while the Senate had contributed to the notion of SIRC as a parliamentary surrogate, it was also the agent that incorporated the concept of a quasi-sunset provision in the statute.

The Five-Year Review

The Special Committee of the House of Commons on the Review of the Canadian Security Intelligence Service Act and the Security Offences Act (hereafter the 'Special committee') completed its obligation to provide a 'comprehensive review of the provision and operation' of the two acts in September 1990, when it tabled its report in Parliament (Canada, House of Commons, Special Committee, 1990). During its review, it employed several strategies to inform itself. Besides receiving more than sixty submissions and hearing testimony from more than fifty witnesses, it requested several in camera briefings from government departments on specific subjects. To augment the limited information it received from government witnesses, it initiated the practice of following up every meeting with detailed written questions requiring departmental responses. In addition, the special committee benefited from many informal discussions with representatives of foreign governments. It met with a senior Australian parliamentarian visiting Ottawa who was involved in parliamentary oversight in his country. It visited the Australian embassy in Washington and talked with members and staff there and with a former head of that country's Office of National Assessments. Also in Washington, it talked with current and former senior American intelligence officials, representatives of the Department of Justice, staff of the Library of Congress, and leading academics. In addition, the special committee visited the secure facilities of the Intelligence Oversight Committee of the House of Representatives where it talked at length about the American experience with members and staff. In Ottawa, it had discussions with Swedish officials about new legislation in that country.

The special committee also visited Canadian institutions. It met with intelligence officials and staff at the Canadian embassy in Washington. It had meetings at the headquarters and regional offices (Vancouver only) of both CSIS and the National Security Investigation Directorate (NSID) of the RCMP. In addition, the committee's staff conducted confidential research interviews, developed comprehensive briefing materials, met with staff of the Federal Court and undertook several research projects that included the mailing of a questionnaire to complaints to SIRC. Outside legal analysis was also commissioned.

The special committee's report may suggest that the special committee did more than fulfil Parliament's mandate. Its more than two hundred pages covered most of the provisions of the legislation in one way, shape, or form. Most of the 117 recommendations addressed changes that the special committee thought desirable in the operation of the two acts. The remainder dealt with broader security and intelligence issues of direct relevance to the legislation studied. Nevertheless, important questions remain: Was Parliament, in fact, able to evaluate the quintessential aspects of the review satisfactorily? And was the review truly comprehensive in nature? The following sections address these issues directly.

Final Link in the Chain

In the CSIS Act [RSC 1985] and the Security Offences Act [RSC 1985], Parliament reserved for itself the quintessential function of checking that the whole mechanism of accountability worked. In this regard, SIRC's role as an independent 'watchdog' was central. Since the legislation came into force in 1984, much has been written about both the general scheme by which controls and modes of accountability were to be effected under the CSIS Act [RSC 1985] (Atkey, 1989; Bellemare, 1985; Blais, 1989, 1989; Chung, 1985; Farson, 1991b; Franks, 1989a; Rankin, 1986; Weller, 1988; Whitaker, 1991). In addition, some authors have concentrated on the individual review components of the system (Gill, 1989b; Ryan, 1989) and the Security Offences Act [RSC 1985] (Brodeur, 1991a; Farson, 1991b). This literature is consistent on two points. It reveals that the system of accountability as a whole is complex and countervailing in design and is comprised of many interlocking actors (such as the solicitor general, minister of national defence, secretary of state for foreign affairs, director of CSIS, deputy solicitor general, commissioner of the RCMP, inspector general of CSIS, SIRC, and justices of the Federal Court). However, it largely overlooks Parliament's ongoing and eventual role.

Parliament's role deserves more careful examination from two perspectives. On the one hand, did Parliament's adoption of the CSIS Act [RSC 1985] limit its original responsibilities for oversight of security and intelligence matters? On the other hand, did the establishment of SIRC under the CSIS Act [RSC 1985] create a surrogate for parliamentary oversight?

A close examination of the various sections of the CSIS Act [RSC 1985] and the Security Offences Act [RSC 1985] reveals that while practical impediments may affect Parliament's capacity, there are no legal restrictions limiting its oversight of security and intelligence activities. To the contrary, the CSIS Act [RSC 1985] clarified, extended, and confirmed Parliament's role of oversight in this regard. In addition to requiring that SIRC's annual report be tabled in Parliament, Section 56(1) of the CSIS Act [RSC 1985] and Section 7(1) of the Security Offences Act [RSC 1985] placed an obligation on Parliament to conduct a comprehensive review of the provisions and operation of the respective acts and delegated this responsibility to a committee. Sections 56(2) and 7(2) respectively completed the accountability chain by requiring the committee to table its report in Parliament.

While there is an implicit expectation in the CSIS Act [RSC 1985] that SIRC will keep 'a public eye' on CSIS on a day-to-day basis (a point explicitly made by SIRC, as will be shown later), the argument that the CSIS Act [RSC 1985] established SIRC as a surrogate for parliamentary oversight cannot be sustained over either the short or the long term. While the CSIS Act [RSC 1985] obliged SIRC to conduct certain reviews and required it to table an annual report in Parliament, the minister's explanatory notes accompanying the initial bill (C-157) made it clear that Parliament would play a continuing annual role. These observed that 'under current Parliamentary rules, the annual report of the Security Intelligence Review Committee submitted to Parliament will be referred to the appropriate Parliamentary Standing Committee. Parliament will, therefore, have both the opportunity and the responsibility to review the report and assess the activities of CSIS' (Canada, Solicitor General, 1983: 16). In fact, shortly after the passage of the CSIS Act [RSC 1985], the House of Commons completed a review of its procedure and extended the capacity of standing committees by expanding their powers in conducting inquiries and reviews of matters under their jurisdiction. Hitherto, committees could only examine matters at appropriate moments, such as when SIRC's annual reports were referred to the standing committee. Thereafter, the rules gave standing committees the discretion to decide when to make inquiries (Canada, House of Commons, 1989: no. 108, p. 68). Importantly, they also extended the accountability process by requiring the government to respond to committee reports within a fixed period when specifically requested to do so (ibid.: no. 109).

It seems evident from the CSIS Act [RSC 1985] that Parliament intended that it should play a different role over the longer term from the one it had adopted during the early years. The CSIS Act [RSC 1985] initially allowed Parliament to stand back from its normal responsibilities for oversight and to fulfil a largely supervisory function. During the years 1984 to 1989 this was to monitor the 'watchdogs.' Parliament's obligation to establish a committee after the acts had been in operation for five years removed the luxury of continuing such a role. The requirement to provide a comprehensive review of the two acts meant that Parliament had to return to the front line of the oversight business. To effect this return Parliament provided the special committee with all the powers that it normally affords standing committees.

The Special Committee's Key Decisions

After its appointment, the special committee considered several matters that were of critical and interlocking importance. An immediate question concerned the political style or tone that it would adopt. Should it be confrontational or not? Equally pressing was the issue of how the special committee should interpret its mandate. In particular, what did the phrase 'a comprehensive review of the provisions and operation of the Act' mean? These matters posed immediate questions about the list of materials and briefings the special committee would need to have. Of particular importance in this regard were questions about how it would get access to such information that the special committee considered necessary to complete a comprehensive review and what powers it had available to force such access should the executive be unwilling to be forthcoming. Finally, the special committee had to decide how to organize itself given the time restraints placed upon it by Parliament's Order of Reference.

THE QUESTION OF POLITICAL STYLE

While generalizations on such matters are particularly difficult to draw, two factors affect the style adopted by parliamentary committees. One encompasses the experience, attitudes, and standing that the chair has in his or her respective party. The other incorporates the length of time individual members have been in Parliament and the attitudes they hold. In the special committee's case, several forces combined to produce the style adopted. In the first instance, the chair of the special committee, Blaine Thacker, had previously chaired the first five-year review conducted by Parliament that covered the Access to Information Act [RSC 1985] and the Privacy Act [RSC 1985]. This committee had adopted a confrontational style. It had produced a very comprehensive review, but its recommendations had largely been ignored by the government (Canada, House of Commons, Standing Committee, 1987; Canada, Department of Justice, 1987a). By the time of his appointment Thacker had already decided that he would not be seeking re-election. He was, therefore, under less political constraint than he might otherwise have been. Such matters led him to think very carefully about how Parliament's best interests could be served. His view was that a confrontational approach would not obtain greater access to information. It would simply cause the doors to be bolted tighter and allow the government to run the clock out on the special committee. In addition, his previous five-year review experience led him to have certain concerns about the power of bureaucrats. Thacker believed that they caused too many good ideas to be lost. As a result, he considered that a special committee needed to operate as a 'poor-man's royal commission' by providing as much public information as possible to counterbalance the power and opinion of senior bureaucrats. Furthermore, Thacker did not look at the special committee's activity as the final phase of the process, but as one step in Parliament's continuing role of oversight. Parliament could always take a more confrontational approach at a later stage. Given what he perceived to be a change in the mood of Parliament and the executive in the mid-1980s to allow parliamentarians to study aspects of policy and legislation in more depth, Thacker believed that the special committee had an obligation to test the willingness of the government both to be more forthcoming and to allow backbenchers to contribute more. He therefore concluded that the special committee should try to work in cooperation with, and build the trust of, the executive, and should adopt a collective, non-partisan approach internally.

Members of the special committee came to embrace the chair's view. Luck played some part in this. In their selection of members for the special committee, both opposition party whips gave precedence to MPs who currently acted as their respective critics on the solicitor general or who already participated on the standing committee. Two opposition members whose style was normally more confrontational and partisan than collegial either were not on the special committee or left it shortly after the hearing process commenced. In the first instance, John Brewin replaced Svend Robinson as the New Democratic Party's (NDP) critic in January 1989. Shortly after the start, John Nunziata left the special committee to pursue the leadership of the Liberal party. This meant that once Bob Horner had retired because of illness, all the remaining members of the special committee were relative newcomers to the House (though not necessarily to politics).

Observation of, and conversations with, the members of the special committee suggest that newer members of the House of Commons now believe that committees operating in a collegial and non-partisan fashion are better able to serve Parliament and the public interest. While it can be posited that such a view may show a certain political naivety, and attitudes may change as experience in federal politics becomes greater, the success of the non-partisan approach necessarily depends on how governments respond to the work of committees. Whatever the case, members of the special committee stuck firm throughout their deliberations. Though the special committee often took time to find a consensus, it never resorted to a vote.

THE QUESTION OF THE MANDATE

It may be assumed that when Parliament included the phrase 'a comprehensive review' in Section 56 of the CSIS Act [RSC 1985] and Section 7 of the Security Offences Act [RSC 1985], it had something particular in mind. The phrase added little to the powers then available to standing committees. Its inclusion, therefore, must have been intended to reinforce those existing powers and to provide the greatest flexibility of interpretation.

It must be remembered that when Parliament established the special committee in 1989, it gave to the committee all the powers of a standing committee. Besides the authority to call for people, papers, and records, and the recently introduced capacity to initiate inquiries at its own discretion and to demand a formal response from the government, these now also included specific and extensive powers of review. Section 108(2) of the *Standing Orders* allows standing committees to review and report on:

(a) the statute law relating to the department assigned to them;
(b) the program and policy objectives of the department and its effectiveness in the implementation of same;
(c) the immediate, medium and long-term expenditure plans and the effectiveness of implementation of same by the department;
(d) an analysis of the relative success of the department, as measured by the results obtained as compared with its stated objectives; and

(e) other matters, relating to the mandate, management, organization or operation of the department, *as the committee deems fit*. (Canada, House of Commons, 1989: 66) (emphasis added)

Exactly how far flexibility of interpretation extended was an important question for the special committee. Was the review confined, as the solicitor general posited in his testimony, to 'the operation of an act and an organization called the Canadian Security Intelligence Service' (Canada, House of Commons, Special Committee, 1989–90: no. 2; p. 18)? The special committee believed it had a wider mandate and concluded that it should not be bound by the government's parameters on two grounds. First, the special committee held that it should follow the precedent established by Parliament during the five-year review of the Access to Information Act [RSC 1985] and the Privacy Act [RSC 1985]. That committee had interpreted 'provisions' to mean 'sections of the Act' and the term 'operation of the Act' to include both 'functions and consequences of the Act.' Second, it believed that it was necessary to adopt a wider, functional perspective. The committee's staff had posed the available options for determining a broad or narrow mandate in the following way:

This is not as simple a choice as it first appears, because the choice affects more than merely the breadth of the study. It implies the adoption of a specific approach or perspective. At issue is whether the Committee will decide to give primary emphasis to a functional or structural analysis. The latter would allow for a limited examination of how the Acts are operating and how the sections of the Acts are affecting the efficacy or propriety of CSIS and the RCMP activities. While such analyses are important, your research staff believes very strongly that the Committee's work should be more broadly based. Two arguments serve to make the point. First, even if CSIS and the RCMP do all that can be asked of them as effectively and efficiently as possible, the system of security may still fail if the intelligence gathered is not assessed, disseminated and acted upon in an adequate and timely fashion. Second, even if the system of accountability and control over CSIS and the RCMP were themselves watertight, the civil liberties of Canadians might still be in serious jeopardy because some other agency of government or some private organization had been subcontracted by government to do work that oversight agencies and Parliament would frown upon (Farson and Rosen, 1989: 1).

The special committee interpreted its mandate in the widest possible way. It saw its job as looking not only at the workings of CSIS, but at the activities of all the other organizations and bodies that were included or implied in the two acts. In this regard, the role of the minister, his department, the inspector general of CSIS, SIRC, the Federal Court, the RCMP, and its oversight bodies were to be handled with equal scrutiny and impartiality. The special committee also recognized that it needed to look beyond the workings of the two acts themselves. It had also to examine their implications and consequences. For this reason it attempted, with little success, to obtain information on how the CSE worked with CSIS and the RCMP and about the relationship between provincial police intelligence units and the RCMP.

THE QUESTION OF WHAT TO SEE

The special committee also took steps to identify what materials it should review. Several points underpinned its thinking on this matter. The special committee had to assume that it could not rely on anyone's word about how well or poorly the acts were working. To provide an impartial assessment, it had to treat members of the review mechanisms in the same way it handled members of the security and intelligence community. Also, the special committee decided that it should examine, *at the very minimum*, a representative random sample of all documents that constituted accounting mechanisms and which were identified in the two acts (such as a selection of director's reports, certificates and reports of the two holders of the office of inspector general, and the various types of SIRC reports). Finally, it wanted to see all directions provided by the minister to CSIS.

THE QUESTION OF ACCESS

Perhaps not surprisingly, it quickly became clear to the special committee that there would continue to be a difference of opinion between the executive and Parliament over access to sensitive information. Though the solicitor general went on record as suggesting that his officials would cooperate fully with the special committee and its staff and that he wanted to continue the process initiated by his predecessor of 'demystifying' CSIS, he also qualified his statement by saying that such cooperation would be 'consistent with national security concerns' and that 'confidentiality must be maintained in the interest of protecting private lives of Canadian citizens' (Canada, House of Commons, Special

Committee, 1989–90: no. 2; pp. 14–16). When asked directly by John Nunziata, then still the Liberal party's critic, whether he would give the special committee the same access as SIRC received, the solicitor general merely observed that 'as the Committee proceeds with its work over the next few weeks, it will be able to specify the documents or the information it needs to do its work. At that point, we can sit down together and make an objective decision in the light of the two restrictions that were maintained earlier' (ibid.: 17).

The committee quickly established the limitations that would be placed on the solicitor general's cooperation when committee staff, with the chairman's authority, asked to meet informally with an identified group of government employees. The solicitor general's department refused to allow these meetings, which included ones with the former director of CSIS and others who had held senior intelligence- and security-related positions. Instead, it offered discussions with two senior officials, one in the ministry and one in the RCMP. The committee declined this invitation. Subsequently, the solicitor general's department required all staff contacts to be channelled through its CSIS Act Review Division (CARD). While the bureaucrats explained this in terms of administrative efficiency, it had the effect of controlling not only what information flowed to the special committee but the timing of the release of that information. It also allowed CARD to screen the responses of the various government agencies under scrutiny and to weed out any discrepancies or inconsistencies in their submissions to the special committee. Significantly, it also provided an avenue by which the government could run the clock out on the special committee while appearing to comply with its requests.[4]

The special committee and its staff were initially of the view that SIRC and the inspector general did similar things but for different masters. If the inspector general was the solicitor general's 'eyes and ears' on the service, then, so the argument went, SIRC was 'Parliament's man.' This perception of SIRC probably stemmed from four things. First, SIRC was generally thought, with some justification, to be the independent watchdog on the service. Second, SIRC's annual reports were tabled in Parliament. These supposedly provided Parliament with sufficient information for its standing committee to assess the activities of CSIS and thus to maintain the delicate balance between the requirements of security and those of democracy (Canada, Solicitor General, 1983: 15–16). Third, despite contrary comments made to the special committee in private, SIRC continued to lead Parliament to the conclusion that it worked on its behalf. Finally, SIRC was quick off the mark both to forward its recommendations for amending the CSIS Act [RSC 1985] to the special committee and to commence a dialogue with it, an action that was to have both positive and negative implications (Canada, SIRC, 1989).

It was hardly surprising, therefore, that the special committee went looking to SIRC for help in resolving its access to information problems. At an early informal meeting, the special committee asked SIRC whether it would provide the special committee with access to its materials. SIRC expressed the view that while it wanted to be helpful, it believed it was not authorized by the act to supply the special committee with information that was not already in its annual reports or in versions of reports released under the Access to Information Act [RSC 1985]. In particular, it was SIRC's view that copies of reports sent to the solicitor general, as all SIRC's reports must be, were the property of the minister, and would have to be released by him.[5]

While SIRC helped the special committee in many ways, it fell far short of being an open book to Parliament, despite its stated wishes to the contrary. Clear confirmation of this point can be seen from the records of the standing committee when SIRC appeared on its 1990–91 estimates (Canada, House of Commons, Standing Committee, 1990). In his opening remarks to the standing committee, SIRC's chair confirmed the prevalent view of the review committee when he said: 'I would like to assure you and the members of your committee my colleagues and I continue to believe that in much of what we do, particularly our work reviewing CSIS operational activities, we act on your behalf. We will continue to examine CSIS activities thoroughly and to try both to ask CSIS the questions you would want us to ask and to answer the questions you put to us as completely and openly as possible' (ibid.: 5). However, Saul Cherniack later clarified the difficulty that SIRC had not only in getting its message out at the most propitious time but in speaking unequivocally to Parliament:

I think our responsibility is to Parliament, period – through Parliament to the public. We can ensure that what we have to say will come to Parliament and the public through our annual report, which is once a year. There may be occasions, and I think there have been occasions, when we have felt that something was urgent enough to make a report on a specific item during the year. The only opportunity we have had to do it under the act was to send a section 54 report to the Solicitor General, who did not have to publish it. *So we do not have a guarantee that it will get to Parliament and therefore to the public.* (Ibid.: 22) (emphasis added)

These statements were of crucial interest to the special committee for they posed what were arguably the most important questions of the entire review: Did SIRC, in fact, ask the questions that Parliament would want to have asked on its behalf? And would and could it provide full and open answers to the questions posed to it by Parliament?

Grave concerns on these counts were raised by members of the standing committee who were also members of the special committee when they examined SIRC's report on CSIS's 'report on the Innu Interview and the Native Extremism Investigation.' Brewin, for the NDP, considered SIRC's failure to show that it had 'taken a hard look at whether CSIS had any justification whatever for getting into the kind of broad investigation of native groups in Canada it did' constituted a 'glaring omission' (ibid.: 13–14). On this score, Cherniack responded that while SIRC had established that CSIS had complied with the requirements of Section 12 to have 'reasonable grounds to suspect,' it had not justified the extent of the service's activity (ibid.: 14). Jean-Jacques Blais acknowledged that SIRC had not done that inquiry (ibid.). It had only responded to the issue about the Innu, which Svend Robinson had originally raised in the standing committee and with SIRC later by letter.[6] Paule Gauthier simply admitted that the report was not their best work (ibid.: 14).

Brewin went on to ask whether there was any way that members of Parliament could get the complete report. On this score Cherniack replied:

I regret the fact that the act limits us to only one time a year when we can address Parliament in our annual report. That is the only place in the act; the only occasion when we are able to speak directly to Parliament is through that annual report. Otherwise we have no right and no access, no passageway to get to Parliament. I think the act really ought to provide that on occasion we may do that, but it does not say that.

So we must rely on our report going under section 54 to the Solicitor General, and then it is up to him to decide whether or not to inform you, or the extent to which he will. Then the censorship you found in that Innu report was that of the department, not of us. (ibid.: 15)

Blais added that the current process on Section 54 reports was to maximize through negotiation the amount that could be made publicly available. He acknowledged that in the Innu report 'we did not pursue that process as aggressively as possible' (ibid.: 16).

Ken Atkinson, for the government benches, asked for more details on how the Innu investigation got started and about the complaints process specifically. His answer revealed that a request from a member of Parliament got treated quite differently from one by the official representative of the Assembly of First Nations. An MP's request instigated a Section 54 report, while George Erasmus's letter requesting a response from SIRC was treated abruptly as a complaint requiring a further letter to the director of CSIS before any action could be taken by SIRC. Atkinson also asked about how the Innu investigation was conducted by SIRC and was informed that staff had conducted some interviews with the parties involved (ibid.: 16–17). The special committee was later able to confirm that the interviewing process had been one-sided. The recipients of the CSIS interview had *not* been contacted by SIRC staff![7]

Another government member, Wilton Littlechild, himself a Native Canadian also asked for more details on the Innu investigation. In particular, he wanted to know why SIRC members did not think it was one of their best reports. In response, Gauthier qualified her original statement by saying that she believed the looseness was not in the report itself, but in terms of its presentation. She went on to observe that 'we still have our next annual report, and we will do our best to have it made as clear as possible to show the public what we have done and what was the real investigation we made' (ibid.: 24).

Finally, on the second round of questions, Brewin came to the nub of the matter. His concern was not that the solicitor general had tried to cover up an inadequate performance by CSIS, but rather that SIRC had remained silent on the solicitor general's later comments on the matter. A news release by the solicitor general's staff had stated that SIRC had concluded that there was 'no evidence of any misconduct by service employees.' This, he believed, had left the intentionally unambiguous impression that SIRC had cleared CSIS. Brewin claimed SIRC's failure to challenge publicly the solicitor general's incorrect impression raised serious questions of confidence in SIRC. He asked whether SIRC had privately communicated its displeasure to the solicitor general. The dialogue that followed between the chairman of SIRC and MP John Brewin is worth citing in full as it removes any doubt about the real relationship between SIRC and Parliament:

Mr Bassett: We are not going to answer that. We do not reveal what in confidence we may or may not –
Mr Brewin: In answer to a perfectly reasonable question from a Member of Parliament when you are before –.
Mr Bassett: No. It is a perfectly reasonable question but I am not going to give you an answer. I am not going to reveal in public –
Mr Brewin: I only asked you whether you had communicated. I did not ask what you had said.
Mr Bassett: That is none of your business.
Mr Brewin: He says it's none of my business. Is that what are you saying?
Mr Bassett: I say that when we have a private communication with the Solicitor General I am not going to release in public what discussion may have taken place.
Mr Brewin: Or even whether it took place.
Mr Bassett: No I am not.
Mr Brewin: We have a problem, Mr. Bassett. My strong view is that if you are a servant of Parliament you have an obligation to tell us at least whether a conversation took place. (Ibid.: 30)

It is best not to leave the matter there. Does SIRC's annual report for 1989–90 both clarify the position and move to solve the problems? Obviously, it does in part. The report does explicitly contest the impression provided by the solicitor general (Canada, SIRC, 1990: 27–31). In addition, it states that there will be new arrangements regarding the release of Section 54 reports to the solicitor general. These are to encompass the preparation of two reports, one a top-secret version for bureaucratic consumption, the other a version that the solicitor general could release immediately to the public should he wish to do so (ibid.: 33). However, despite these commitments, no public versions have yet been released.

Two important questions remain unanswered. First, what caused SIRC to dwell on this matter further? Was it of its own volition that SIRC took action or was it because of the concern shown by the two parliamentary committees? Only SIRC knows the full answer to this. However, the really important question only pertains to SIRC tangentially. Earlier mention was made that the solicitor general's department was responsible for providing a news release. That news release not only stated that the solicitor general was making available SIRC's report to the public, but also that he had written to the chairs of both the standing committee and the special committee. In those letters, he said that he was 'pleased to note that the SIRC report confirm[ed] that the Canadian Security Intelligence Service [had] acted reasonably and in accordance with its mandate.'[8] SIRC's annual report stated that 'A statement in the Solicitor General's news release, namely that we found no evidence of any misconduct by Service employees, does not reflect our conclusions. In our report, this statement refers to only one of the activities we examined. Indeed, we did conclude there had been a breach of regulations' (Canada, SIRC, 1990: 28). The matter of whether the solicitor general deliberately misled the House of Commons and, if so, whether this might be considered as a question of privilege, must therefore be addressed. At issue is not so much whether he did mislead, and consequently if this constituted contempt, but whether the House of Commons could have taken action if he had. It is to be recalled that by the time SIRC's report had been tabled in Parliament the author of the letters, Pierre Blais, had been replaced by Pierre Cadieux as solicitor general. In these circumstances, three points raised by Franks in his earlier study (1979: 21) take on renewed relevance. First, in 1977 the speaker of the House of Commons had ruled that previous incumbents could not be held responsible for answering on issues after they had left office. Second, the same ruling also exempted current office holders from answering for previous incumbents. Finally, an issue of privilege had been raised in 1978 over a letter written some years earlier by a former solicitor general about assurances that the RCMP did not make a practice of opening mail. In this instance the speaker ruled that the member had been misled and that there was a question of privilege involved. However, on this occasion the House of Commons voted down a motion to have the matter studied by a committee.

THE QUESTION OF POWERS

After the solicitor general's initial appearance on 31 October 1989, the special committee sought legal counsel regarding its entitlement to have information provided by officials of the government of Canada. The response of counsel was sufficient to suggest that Parliament might hold certain legal trumps that could be employed to tip the balance in favour of greater accountability, should it wish to use them. These included the following points. First, the 'privileges, immunities and powers' of the House of Commons as established by Section 18 of the Constitution Act [1867] and Section 4 of the Parliament of Canada Act [RSC 1985] include *the right to start inquiries.* Second, the only limitation on a committee's right to call anyone before it concerns whether the inquiry falls within Parliament's legislative competence and the committee's mandate. Third, the power to send for papers and records appears to be unlimited. Fourth, in the case of the special committee, Section 19 of the CSIS Act [RSC 1985] appears to reinforce the general powers of committees. While it proscribes unauthorized disclosure of security-related information by CSIS, it also permits the release of such information by the service where the disclosure is 'for the purposes of the performance of its duties and functions under this Act or the *administration* of enforcement of this Act (emphasis added). It was counsel's opinion that the parliamentary review fell squarely within the administration of the act and constituted an authorized disclosure. Fifth, there is nothing in the CSIS Act [RSC 1985] that impedes the inspector general, SIRC, or their respective staffs from releasing sensitive material to the special committee. Sixth, it would not be a breach of the Official Secrets Act [RSC 1985] for anyone to release sensitive materials to the special committee as long as it related to the committee's mandate. Finally, in camera proceedings are protected by parliamentary privilege. 'Leaks' could be dealt with in a manner to be determined by the House.[9]

The Question of Time

When Parliament enacted the legislation in 1984, it imposed a statutory restriction on the length of time Parliament could take to conduct its review. This probably had much to do with the fact that many within government had been overly concerned by the length of time that the McDonald commission had taken to complete its work and the costs it incurred. The statutory time restraint was open to some interpretive flexibility. However, the special committee was informed that governmental approval to extend the deadline was unlikely to be forthcoming because of other political pressures.

By the time the special committee had agreed on what it wanted to see, and it was clear that it was unlikely to be given ready access to these documents, half of the time available to the committee had elapsed.[10] The special committee now found itself (some might say, manoeuvred) in an impossible position. Whatever the case, the belief that a broad approach was necessary, coupled with the slow progress of the first five months, meant that there was an incredible amount of work to do in the remaining period. It meant that a legal battle with the executive would be out of the question. With careful handling, any legal action could be extended beyond the reporting deadline of the special committee. It was assessed that even if the special committee received access to all the materials it wanted, it could not process them with the staff available. The special committee, therefore, determined that it would have to establish a *modus vivendi* with the executive over the access to documents and briefings and to do the best job that was possible under the circumstances. It was in this context that detailed written questions were sent to government witnesses – elected and non-elected alike – requiring written responses.

Conclusions

Important steps were taken by the special committee to rectify the deficiencies observed by Franks (1979). There is now a body of parliamentarians – albeit one severely diminished by the last federal election – and staff who are much better informed about the policies and programs of the secret world. They have had a full debate – albeit in private – of the important issues, and the product of that debate, though carefully nuanced and abbreviated, has now been made public (Canada, House of Commons, Special Committee, 1990). Significantly, these individuals are now well versed in the questions that Parliament must keep asking, the problems of government secrecy, and the tactics that bureaucrats use to frustrate them. They are also much wiser about the powers of Parliament and how Parliament can devise strategies for getting access to information.

On a more pessimistic note, Parliament is still a weak link in the accountability chain. It never managed to see any of the mechanisms prescribed in the CSIS Act [RSC 1985] for rendering accounts (that is, the director's annual reports, the inspector general's certificates and other reports, SIRC's reports) in their uncensored form, which it perceived to be essential to the review. In this regard, members of the special committee were not much better placed than any citizen using the Access to Information Act [RSC 1985]. Nor did Parliament see whether the service was being given clear, concise, and proper directions.[11] Consequently, it was never able to state categorically that the system of accountability and responsibility worked properly. As a result, it was unable to provide a truly comprehensive review of all the major actors in the process. This was particularly worrisome regarding the duplication of roles between SIRC and the inspector general of CSIS. If SIRC was not able to talk directly to Parliament, why was there a need for the inspector general? Did this not mean a duplication of costly resources and hence a failure to monitor CSIS adequately on an annual basis? The failure to provide a special committee's 'seal of approval' in this instance is most unfortunate and will detract over the long term from the confidence that Canadians place in these institutions. Also on a pessimistic note is that the government has chosen to ignore every single recommendation for statutory change made by the special committee (Canada, Solicitor General, 1991). This speaks volumes about the previous executive's view of parliamentary practice and accountability in Canada.

While many of the special committee's recommendations were of a technical nature for improving particular aspects of the system, a few were critical to ensuring proper parliamentary oversight in the future. Of central importance was the recommendation to treat security and intelligence matters as a special case (as the American Congress has done for years and the British Parliament appears now to be doing) by establishing a permanent subcommittee of the standing committee (Canada, House of Commons, Special Committee, 1990: recommendation 107). This would ensure that a small group of MPs would provide continuing parliamentary oversight of security and intelligence organizations and their review bodies, and would extend – albeit largely in private – their knowledge of the secret world. This is a prudent step for the government. Its majority on the standing committee can control the reporting output of the subcommittee. In this way, political partisanship would be kept in check but not the flow of crucial information to the House of Commons. Such information could provide the necessary balance to ever more powerful bureaucratic opinion. It is also prudent for the security and intelligence community. The American experience has shown that despite a bumpy start, both Congress and the intelligence community now believe oversight has worked to their respective advantages.[12] It is the essential first step for rectifying current deficiencies. Though resisted by the government, Parliament has shown its independence on this score by establishing a new Sub-Committee on National Security under the standing committee.

The special committee's recommendation that the subcommittee should have a small *permanent* (though not necessarily full-time) expert staff is not an unnecessary expense. It is essential to the process. Security and intelligence is a complex world requiring constant familiarity. Such staff would not duplicate SIRC's work. They could look behind SIRC's annual reports and the other documents in SIRC's possession (such as the annual reports of the director, the certificates and reports of the inspector general, and ministerial directions) with a view to keeping busy parliamentarians properly briefed. They would ensure that parliamentarians were routinely alerted to the questions that need to be asked and to matters requiring further probing.

The government, in fairness, was not entirely negative. It agreed to some of the special committee's recommendations and incorporated certain measures through executive order that will enhance both accountability to Parliament and public knowledge of security and intelligence matters. Nevertheless, many commitments remain unfulfilled. With regard to the CSE, the government acknowledged that it was considering some 'additional capacity for review' and that it would make a public announcement once a decision had been made (Canada, Solicitor General, 1991: 55). By the end of its mandate in 1993, no such proposals had been forthcoming. The government also agreed to provide Parliament with an annual statement concerning the national security issues facing the country at the time of the Main Estimates (ibid.: 78). This process was begun in 1992 and has allowed for some debate on the floor of the House of Commons and for questioning of the solicitor general by both the standing committee and its new subcommittee. Nevertheless, the quality of the annual statements is not satisfactory. As they stand, the statements look more like public relations outputs than useful sources of information about threats facing the nation. In addition, there supposedly will be a further comprehensive review of the legislation beginning in 1998 (ibid.: 79) On this score there is cause for concern. The new administration is under no obligation to follow through on the previous government's commitments and has not yet revealed what its intentions are.

It should be noted that the special committee did not advocate SIRC's replacement by the subcommittee. Rather, it recommended that SIRC should continue doing all its current functions under the CSIS Act [RSC 1985] and more so (see especially, recommendations 87, 88, 90, 105). The additional functions would allow SIRC to ask many more of the questions that Parliament believes should be asked. It should also be stressed that the special committee did not merely recommend that SIRC's powers of review be increased without qualification as SIRC seemed to imply (Canada, SIRC, 1990: 1). Recommendations 92 and 93 would make SIRC properly and fully accountable to Parliament in the way that the McDonald commission had originally intended. They would allow SIRC to talk freely and directly with Parliament at a moment of SIRC's or Parliament's choosing, not the solicitor general's. Given the government's reluctance to increase SIRC's powers of review, the new subcommittee will be left alone to call other members of the security and intelligence community to account.

Parliament now has sufficient legal trumps to force access to the information that it considers essential for the proper and full account-ability of actors designated in the CSIS Act [RSC 1985] and the Security Offences Act [RSC 1985]. In fact, former members of the special commit-tee have subsequently exhibited a greater willingness to use their exist-ing parliamentary powers. Witness the response of the standing com-mittee to both the special committee's recommendation regarding the establishment of a permanent subcommittee in the face of opposition by the government (Canada, Solicitor General, 1991: 79) and the response of the standing committee to the refusal of the solicitor general to release an uncensored version of a document relating to homicides committed by two escaped inmates from separate Canadian peniten-tiaries (Canada, House of Commons, Standing Committee, 1991; Rideout, 1993: 106). Consequently, a frontal assault on the walls of secrecy built by Canada's security and intelligence community may not be necessary for Parliament's needs. Parliament may simply decide to go through its supposed entry into the secret world, SIRC. All that is necessary in this regard is the combined political will to do so. It needs no additional legal help.

Notes

1 The term 'oversight' is frequently used in American government; less so where Westminster-style systems operate. The terms 'ministerial respon-sibility,' 'accountability,' and 'control are often used ambiguously. 'Oversight' is used here to imply a combination of mechanisms producing accountability and control.

2 Confidential interview; 2 March 1994.

3 Members of the special committee that reviewed the CSIS Act were not concerned by this breach. The chair, for instance, interpreted the relevant section to imply that each party could nominate members.

4 Some very important information came to the committee's attention only

after its report had been drafted. This indicated that it had been misled by a minister over the existence of a working group and the work it had already produced.

5 Information provided at an informal meeting of the special committee with SIRC, 12 Oct. 1989.

6 It had not taken into consideration the complaint made directly to it by George Erasmus on behalf of Native Canadians. Correspondence between SIRC and Mr Erasmus indicates that SIRC was not prepared to conduct an inquiry on that score until Mr Erasmus had first complained to the director of CSIS.

7 This was established through telephone interviews by the author.

8 Letter from the solicitor general, 5 February 1990.

9 Correspondence from the law clerk and parliamentary counsel to the chairman of the special committee, 4 Dec. 1989.

10 In addition, the committee was not fully staffed until it was at least five months into its mandate.

11 The special committee was briefed on ministerial directives, but it was not shown the actual documents.

12 This was confirmed by all the various people that the special committee met in Washington.

Accountability for Corporate Crime

FRANK PEARCE

Within the global economy as a whole, and within the advanced national economies particularly, very large corporations are now the major economic actors (Knox and Agnew, 1989: 192). Thus, for example, in the United States, virtually all businesses are limited liability corporations. The top one hundred of these receive a significantly greater share of manufacturing profits than all of the rest put together (Coleman, 1989: 14) and the top five hundred are responsible for over 75 per cent of all sales, receive in excess of 50 per cent of profits, and own nearly 90 per cent of all assets (Cherry, D'Onofrio, Kurddas, Michi, Mosely, and Naples, 1987: 311).

If corporations play such a key economic role, we are confronted with a number of questions related to accountability. First, what exactly are corporations? Second, to which individuals or institutions are they formally accountable for their activities? Third, to what extent, to whom, and by what mechanisms can they actually be made accountable? Finally, what role, if any, is played by the criminal law in securing this accountability?

In the first part of this essay the meaning of accountability is addressed. This is followed by a discussion of neoclassical economic and legal representations of the nature of the corporation and of market-oriented solutions to the problem of regulation, particularly of occupational safety and health. These are criticized at some length and we then move to a model based more upon political economy and sociology. This argues that any kind of effective regulation requires a redistribution of powers within the enterprises and between different social classes and social groups and that the state may need to intervene actively. In the case of occupational safety and health in the United States, effective regulation requires strong trade unions and entrenched workers' rights, the use of administrative sanctions, and of the civil and the criminal courts, and that the state itself may need to take over certain production processes.

Corporations and Accountability

A business corporation is a body corporate, incorporated under a relevant statute, that can function as a trading enterprise oriented to making profits for its shareholders. Legally it consists of the corporation itself, which for legal purposes (but sometimes substantively) is construed as a separate entity with its own 'legal' personality; its shareholders, who have bought (and can sell) a stake in the company and are entitled to a dividend, but who have limited liability; its directors, who are legally responsible for setting its policy goals, determining its organization and the kind of business it does; and its managers, who range from its chief executive to those responsible for the day-to-day activities of its specific plants, factories, or supermarket stores. Directors always, and many managers often, constitute the 'directing mind' of the organization. Lower level employees are not usually considered as part of the corporation, although as its 'hands' their actions may involve it in certain kinds of vicarious liability.

'Providing an account' can signify a number of different activities. It may involve a mandatory detailed, documented representation of what an individual or group has done and why they have done so in some area of activity when they knew, in advance, that they would be subject to this requirement and where their interlocutor has the capacity to independently check their representations. Audits of all kinds tend to be of this nature. If the individual or group, however, rather than its audience 'is primarily or exclusively determining what kind of information will be disseminated, how, when and to whom' (Stenning, this volume) then an account may be little more than a public relations gloss, obscuring as much as it reveals.

In the case of the corporation, problems of accountability may relate to the relation between owners and managers, to the different positions of employer and employee, or to the relationship between the corporation and the local community or the state. While the 'accounts' rendered to all groups by corporate executives may have a flavour of public relations, because of the existence of accountability mechanisms in the first sense, they are least likely to be only this in the case of shareholders. If those affected by decisions do not have a right to require accounts that deal with their questions, as is so often true in the case of other 'stakeholders' (Goyder, 1987), such an employees and local communities, then we are likely to be more firmly in the realm of 'public relations.' In fact, without a dialogical relationship between those providing and those requesting accounts, which entails some kind of equality, ideological discourses will be generated (Habermas, 1970). Discourses are, in this sense, ideological when they are, albeit often subconsciously, structured around a relatively powerful agent's presumption that its self-defined interest are legitimate and primary. The interests of others will be attended to in ways that take account of their 'voice' only when they have the power to have their concerns taken seriously. Significantly less powerful interests will either be discounted or defined by categories from within the ideological discourse and not from any statements produced by their own 'voice.'

If agents who share similar interests are talking about others, then they may collusively, but perhaps unselfconsciously, construct accounts of their own and these others' actions which are self-justificatory and may occlude certain arguably important factors and levels of analysis. An account, after all, is often a verbal justification and explanation of an outcome in which someone has been implicated, which involves little more than the construction of a *post factum* narrative in which different individuals, including the person providing the account, are ascribed various subject positions and certain actions and events are correlated with each other in a way that assumes them to be causally related. Such an account may be sincere, but sincerity is no guarantee of adequacy (Mills, 1940: Lyman and Scott, 1968), above all when it is part of a ('motivated') ideological discourse. If, for example, we examine the explanation by Union Carbide Corporation (UCC) of the Bhopal disaster, in which thousands of Indian people were killed and injured, we find UCC's discourse premised upon a concept of Indian backwardness. This allegedly was responsible for poor maintenance and management, poor planning procedures, inadequate control over population movements, and a purported act of sabotage by an irrational, disgruntled employee. What is thereby elided is UCC's own role in siting, designing, and monitoring an inherently unsafe production process and then letting it run down. The company's own production workers had identified the hazardous nature of this plant, but they were ignored. These 'stakeholders' were not viewed as legitimate 'voices,' as sources of 'serious statements' (Pearce and Tombs, 1989, 1992).

How then can corporations be made accountable for their conduct? What role can and should markets and/or the state play in regulating it? First, we will turn to some of the answers provided by neoclassical economists and their allies in the 'law and economics' school.

The Corporation's Economy

For neoclassical economists, the pursuit of self-interest in free market situations leads to the efficient production and allocation of scarce economic goods and services, enhances individual self-satisfaction, and promotes liberty and freedom of choice. Economic agents make contracts which involve the exchange of goods and services and in turn produce goods and services. In functioning adequately, these generate differences in the amount of resources that people have at their disposal. This is perfectly acceptable, however, since these in turn can be deployed to maximize the utilities produced within the system as a whole.

Law is used to facilitate these 'natural' activities of economically rational agents and helps provide, through the courts, an objective price constraint that tells these actors what it will cost them to obtain a certain good. Thus, the functioning of the different markets involving such legal persons as shareholders, employees, customers, and the corporate entity, in combination with the right of such persons to challenge violations of their rights in the civil courts, will constitute an adequate and socially efficient mechanism for producing self-interested but socially responsible behaviour. In this view, then, in so far as law is concerned, the *modus operandi* of civil law is, or should be, paradigmatic even if, on occasion, the criminal law may be used (Posner, 1980: 416–17; Kelman 1987: 120). The criminal law (and imprisonment), however, may be the appropriate mechanism to stop some (impecunious) 'predators' (and/or irrational 'ideologically motivated' extremists?) from destroying the possibility of community and of 'constructive' economic activity.[1] An economic and social system based on markets and the civil law and protected by the police power of the state will be rational, efficient, and just (Kelman, 1987: 121–2).

Not all economic relations are best organized via ad hoc and temporary contractual relationships. There are always transaction costs – 'search and information costs, bargaining and decision costs, policing and enforcement costs' (Dahlman, 1979: 148) – incurred in creating and monitoring contracts. Therefore, it may be more rational for an entrepreneur, or for groups of investigators, to develop permanent, centralized, authoritative organizations rather than to continuously renegotiate and monitor contracts made with independent agents. While both entrepreneurs and investors are concerned with the activities of lower level employees, investors are also concerned with those who actively control corporations. After all, the advantages provided to investors by limited liability – the ability to reduce risk by buying and selling shares in diverse kinds of economic activity and with potential losses limited, in each case, by the sums tied up in those particular shares – have as a matched concomitant the disadvantages ensuing from the wide spread of their interests. Investors, however, can be protected from managerial (in)discretion by the established mechanisms of corporate governance and by the managers' need to maintain the value of company shares in the stock market and the enterprise's general creditworthiness.

In this thinking, firms, including corporations, arise, survive, and grow when they are the most efficient way for private citizens to organize profit-making enterprises. Current trends to concentration in parts of industry in the United States indicate emerging economies of scale, the result of engineering and production developments, new distribution techniques, or new control and management techniques (Bork, 1978: 205–6; Williamson, 1975: 101, 102, 104; Posner, 1976: 96). Conglomerate companies, for example, are 'capitalism's creative response' to the limit of the capital market in relation to the firm. This provides an internal rather than an external control mechanism, with the constitutional authority and expertise to make detailed evaluations of the performance of each of its operating parts; it can make fine-tuning as well as discrete adjustments; the costs of intervention by the conglomerate's central office are relatively low (Williamson, 1975: 159; and Williamson, 1985: 284).

Furthermore, contrary to the position taken, for example, by Stigler in the 1950s (1952), neoclassicists now claim that market forces are at work whatever the degree of concentration of industry. A perfectly contestable market characterized by optimal behaviour can exist within a full range of industry structures, including even oligopoly (Bork, 1978: 221–2). In part because of the growth of international competition, *potential* entry into the market disciplines behaviour almost as effectively as would actual competition *within* the market (Baumol, 1982; Bailey, 1981). This analysis vastly extends the domain of the invisible hand.

It is important to recognize that this discourse tells us little about the actual organizational structure of corporations (Pearce, 1993), neither do we learn much about how or why the economy as a whole is organized in a particular way – of the relations between different enterprises, or between enterprises and employees and the community as a whole, or the role that the state plays in organizing these. It is to these issues that we now turn.

Regulation: Corporate Governance, the Market, or Regulatory Agencies?

Neoclassicists believe that when a free market is working efficiently general social welfare is maximized, and, thus, no one can be made better off without making someone else worse off, and that 'under perfect competition private and social costs will be equal' (Stigler, 1972, cited in Coase, 1988). Then, if transaction costs are assumed to be zero and the rights of the various parties are well defined, disputes between any two independent economic agents about the mutual effects of their activities can always be resolved in ways which maximize social production. In doing so 'it does not matter what the law is since people can always negotiate without cost to acquire, subdivide, and combine rights whenever this would increase the value of production' (Coase, 1988: 14). Moreover, while in any specific interactive harm situation some individual may have a first-line entitlement and hence receive a greater benefit, there is no reason to believe that they will be favoured recurrently and non-randomly (Kelman, 1987: 67–8; Tushnet, 1993).

Such arrangements may be facilitated by state agencies collating and distributing useful information, but unfortunately these agencies rarely restrict themselves to these activities. They often engage in detailed regulation of economic activity, thereby posing tremendous dangers to the working of market rationality and hence efficiency. Although state intervention is usually justified as being necessary to correct allocative problems resulting from *market failure,* in fact it does little to correct these (see Stigler, 1971; Peltzman, 1976). Rather, through their relation to regulatory agencies, small groups of highly motivated and well-organized economic and political actors can extract rents, and this, along with the bureaucratic costs of (essentially irrelevant) regulation, leads to increased prices (Weidenbaum and de Fina, 1978; Weaver, 1978; Wilson, 1980; for critiques, see Noble, 1986: 115–16; Pearce and Tombs, 1992). Regulation, therefore, is best achieved by a combination of market forces and litigation, rather than by the action of governmental agencies. To illustrate these arguments let us turn to the neoclassical analysis of occupational safety and health.

In this view, the Occupational Safety and Health Act has had little impact on job risk levels. This is because the activities of the Occupational Safety and Health Administration (OSHA) are unlikely to change the behaviour of those who own and/or control businesses, both because of its ineffectiveness in imposing sanctions (Smith, 1976: 63–4) and because, given its legalistic command-and-control approach to regulation, it tends to impose uniform high standards and to rely on engineering controls rather than personal protection devices. This differs significantly from the more economically rational practice routinely adopted by employers (and preferred by employees) of developing situation-specific flexible standards and the use of less expensive and less restrictive personal protection devices.

Occupational safety and health is best viewed as a good, bought and sold as part of the wage bargain (Viscusi, 1983: 35). Then, in the absence of market rigidities produced by governmental or trade union activities, the forces of supply and demand can determine the level and kinds of risk faced by individual workers, the level of investment in occupational health and safety, and the approaches taken to control hazards (Dickens, 1984). Employers offer safe and healthy work when they offer jobs, but jobs combine different levels of risk and wages. Some are very safe with relatively low wages, others involve high risks and high wages. In possession of sufficient information to make a rational choice and with sufficient freedom to choose other less risky jobs, some workers who 'do not value additional safety very highly relative to additional income – whether because they are poor, have high pain thresholds, or just do not care' (Smith, 1982: 213), knowingly select hazardous jobs because they receive substantially better compensation than they would in safer ones (Viscusi, 1979, 1983). This arrangement is efficient and democratic because it optimizes individual liberty and simultaneously leads to a socially optimal level of risk and protection. In an equilibrium situation, a worker's total compensation (wages plus the marginal cost of safety per worker) will be equal to the value of the worker's marginal product. Although the supply of safety will then approximate workers' demands for protection and the resource costs of reducing risk, some other market imperfections need to be remedied. For example, workers need accurate information about health hazards and this could be achieved by labelling laws and information programs and/or by changing liability laws so that workers can sue employers to recover the costs of work-related disease if employers cannot demonstrate due diligence (Smith, 1982: 330–4). The incentives of firms to invest in safety are diminished by the practice of the workers' compensation system of allowing them to pool their risks and benefits, but this could be eliminated either by experience rating of all firms or by requiring small deductibles from employers (ibid.: 326–9; Chelius, 1977: 63–9). The most socially efficient health and safety standards will be realized when employers find the level of expenditure on safety that is equal to the expenditure incurred by accidents. The latter is calculated by adding together the costs of damage to property, of training new workers, of increased insurance premiums, of workers' compensation, of anticipated costs of litigation, and of paying workers increased wages because they know that they are engaging in relatively dangerous work (Oi, 1977).

The most that regulatory agencies can realistically do is to set performance hazard standards or develop injury taxes (ibid.). Not surprisingly, then, some advocates of market-based incentives argue that the existence of this market mechanism allows for the dismantling of OSHA and the restoration of the private system that dominated health and safety before 1970, albeit with a somewhat reformed workers' compensation program (Chelius, 1977).

Neoclassical Theories of Regulation: A Critique

There are many objections to these analyses and the attendant suggestions for changes in modes of regulation. For example, how, *in practice*, are individual corporations regulated? After all, even if the legal form of the corporation helps it to make sufficient profits to satisfy its shareholders by surviving and growing, how do its different groups of shareholders, its directors and chief executives relate to each other? Of equal importance is the question: how do they and the corporation relate to other 'stakeholders' such as its employees, customers, and suppliers?

Corporate law focuses on problem created by 'the ability of corporate actors to abuse their discretion to take advantage of one another'

(Simon, 1990: 338–89), particularly with the potentially predatory relationship of executive officers to creditors and shareholders (Glasbeek, 1995). But even here, the principal internal mechanisms 'to protect shareholders from managerial discretion ... fiduciary rights and voting rights' at best function with only limited effectiveness (Simon, 1990: 392–4; Condon, 1992) and the external market mechanisms are imperfect instruments, because company reports and audits can to some extent be manipulated and future earnings can only be estimated somewhat crudely. Furthermore, the take-over threat is difficult to regulate – if it is too easy it may exploit some shareholders, and if it is too difficult management may be able to (expensively) insulate itself from the threat. Moreover, the outcome of many takeover bids is determined by the decisions of the major economic players, even if they formally control only a minority of stocks and shares (Latham, 1960: 226; Zeitlin, 1989: 30–6, 66). Thus, even for investors, accountability is at best imperfect. From the perspective of the economy as a whole (one absent from the concerns of individual actors), corporate take-overs and reorganizations are expensive and involve an extremely high opportunity cost in terms of a poor use of money which could be used for productive investment (Adams and Brock, 1991: 108–9).

As we have seen, much of the American economy is characterized by a very high degree of concentration. Even if aspects of the neoclassical explanations for this fact have some plausibility, they do not exhaust the reasons why firms grow or develop particular organizational forms. In oligopolistic situations firms have little incentive to worry about market pressure – to compete via price or technical innovation. They can engage in 'predation' and increase the entry size of firms necessary for market entry. They can make suppliers, competitors, customers, communities, and indeed countries follow their dictates (Adams and Brock, 1986, 1987, 1989, and 1991). Their power has been magnified by their integration through the military–industrial complex, facilitating the exercise of monopsonic power and an exercise of political power which influences the structure of the state and markets (Powell, 1990; Abolafia and Biggart, 1992)[2]. Such power makes it possible to demand concessions from communities, states, and even desperate countries, such as union-free workplaces, environmental deregulation, and financial incentives. If this is true of countries, communities, and firms, it is, of course, even truer of individual workers negotiating their wages and conditions of work with employers.

Individuals may try to obtain adequate wages and safe conditions of work by acting individualistically, by moving to areas where their skills are in short supply. A more collective response to unsafe conditions may be to demand 'higher wages' and compensation for occupationally induced ill health. Although these activities might lead management to offer alternative working arrangements, these would still be limited by management's expertise and subordinated to the goal of maximizing profits and growth. Furthermore, these strategies would only be effective if there were realistic access to alternative employment and if there were a labour shortage in the firm's area. But much of the time, and particularly in many hazardous jobs, there is a chronic oversupply of labour, and this is apt to shape a worker's 'preferences about the tradeoff between safety and wages, ability to choose among jobs, and ability to mount and sustain legal action' (Noble, 1986: 213). Indeed, even Viscusi acknowledges that 'workers may have limited job mobility, which will impede their attempt to leave a hazardous job' (Viscusi, 1983: 182–3, n. 4).

In many circumstances an efficient firm is a safe firm, and conversely an inefficient, poorly run enterprise is likely to be characterized by carelessness and disorder in matters of safety. Therefore, as a way of encouraging safer and more ecologically sound business practices, it may take a great deal of tactical sense to appeal to the employer's self-interest by proclaiming that 'safety pays.' A well-organized enterprise may wish to avoid the inconvenience through accidents of 'lost production time, loss of a trained employee, and increased compensation or increased insurance costs' (Frank, 1985: 42), and it may find that recovering and recycling chemicals is cheaper than allowing them to contaminate the workplace or the local environment (Elkins, 1989: 3). Unfortunately, however, such safe practices may be expensive, both in terms of the additional employee time required to work safely and of the capital investment required to engineer safe environments. Cheapness, not efficiency, for example, is the reason employers try to individualize solutions to many problems by making employees wear (often uncomfortable) personal protection devices. And if employees fail to wear these – whatever the productivity pressures – accidents or illnesses can be blamed on them (Tombs, 1989.) Moreover, such practices and investments will only be economically rational for a particular company if its competitors also follow these practices, but this is unlikely unless such standards are forced on them (Pearce, 1990). It is not surprising, then, that when OSHA became less active in enforcing standards, occupational accidents in the United States were recorded as rising (*Globe and Mail* 21 November B5; 1991: Reiman, 1990: 57–64).

How could one guarantee that workers and regulatory agencies would have access to accurate information about company affairs? Firms from the smallest to the largest routinely fabricate evidence about accident rates and falsify samples used to assess the condition of work places.[3] Presumably, then, it would require an independent monitoring or firms' activities and the ready accessibility of this information. For insurance and workmen's compensation to have any effect, compensation levels must be high, something always opposed by employers (Barth and Hunt, 1982). For an injury tax to work, the tariff must be significant. For litigation to be effective, courts would have to be sympathetic to those who are injured. Resources would need to be made available to equalize workers and employers in the competition for legal help. The rules regulating responsibility would have to be changed. For example, strict liability might replace negligence as the legal standard for damage suits, thereby liberalizing the conditions under which workers could sue employers. Employers could be held responsible for system failures (such as design flaws or random and uncontrollable breakdowns), as well as for gross negligence. This could result in a large number of successful class-action suits over occupational diseases such as silicosis and hazards such as hearing loss. In the long run substantial damages from these suits could provide incentives for employers to prevent hazards. But these might damage, or be perceived to damage, the viability of many industries and lead to a new legal regime that then restricted workers' rights, as in cases involving silicosis and asbestosis (Noble, 1986: 214–15). Thus, such solutions are themselves likely to generate conflict and, as Harold Barnett (1992) has shown, inevitably raise the issue of what determines state conduct and what are appropriate political strategies. In fact, the success of any or all of these measures would require a combination of significant legal rights to those who are now relatively powerless, substantial legal aid, the coercive power of worker-oriented regulatory agencies (Pearce and Tombs, 1990, 1992), and strong trade unions (Dawson, Wilman, Bamford, and Clinton, 1988). All of these are changes that such theorists wish to avoid.

It is fundamental to the system that whichever job a worker goes to, the employer, and not the worker, dictates the conditions of work there. Because workers do not own and operate their own means of production, they have no choice but to work for one or other employer. The differences of power between an employer and an employee, the very different mobilities of labour and capital, and the right that capital retains to determine how and where profits are invested – particularly in an era of globalization of investment decisions – suggests that employers and employees have little unity of interest. Indeed, the claim that there is such a unity of interest between then may create situations which result in 'death by consensus' (Glasbeek and Tucker, 1992).

The market situations of employers and workers are fundamentally different; the former are merely choosing to risk (thanks to limited liability, only some of) their own or somebody else's capital, whereas workers have to routinely risk life, limb, and their general health. It is for this reason that it is the general standard of workplace safety that is the central issue for workers – that is, whether or not employers as a class are forced to provide safe workplaces – and not merely the safety of workplaces relative to each other. The question needs to be reframed. It should not be: 'How do workers choose risk at work and how could they make this choice more efficiently?' It should be 'How can working conditions and institutional arrangements be changed so that workers do not have to make such a choice?' (Draper, 1991: 129).

This leads us also to question the working assumption within the neoclassical school of economics that in order to calculate costs and benefits, to produce a social *accounting* of activities, it is enough to restrict oneself (firms as) producers, employees as 'formally free' owners (Marx, 1965: 169) of their capacity to labour, and (citizens as) paying consumers (Pearce, 1990). Profitability, for example, is calculated as the difference between the revenue accruing *to* an enterprise and the costs which *it* incurs, but economics 'is concerned with the efficient use of resources, and many economic activities which may be non-commercial (i.e. non-profitable for the enterprises concerned) may prove still to be *economic* – in the sense that for the economy as a whole the total gains exceed the total costs incurred' (Donaldson and Farquar, 1988: 141; Waring, 1988; 292–3). The full costs of plant closings and de-industrialization (Bluestone and Harrison, 1982), for example, are not accounted for, or accounted in, narrow commercial forms of accounting.

Such accounting is a particularly poor basis for evaluating the impact of occupational accidents and disease. It is morally repugnant and economically problematic to assume that a monetary sign is an adequate signifier of a set of possibly incommensurate values – of whether an individual, his or her spouse and/or children will have jobs at all; of what will be their standard of living and for how long; of what are the possible effects on their health and on the environment of engaging in particular kinds of production, or not. True, risk analysis can legitimately be used to compare a particular risk with other similar kinds or risks for the same group of individuals. Thus, it may be reasonable to calculate and compare the effects of different ways of organizing a particular mining operation on mine accidents. For example, safer working conditions may reduce risk, but risk may be increased by a concomitant increase in hours worked underground (Braithwaite, 1985: 169–79). Here, like is being compared with like, and the same individuals enjoy the costs and benefits in each case. It is often much more difficult to provide exact comparisons, and more usually those who enjoy the most benefits are not those that suffer the greater risk. Deciding on the costs and benefits of particular courses of action is, therefore, inherently political and should only be decided politically (Irwin, Smith, and Griffith, 1982; Griffiths, 1981). Such decisions may also entail the examination of alternative economic forms. For example, a nationalized mining system with safety inspection in the hands of workers themselves is a way of organizing mining that is both relatively safe and economically efficient (in the broad and even narrow sense of economic efficiency) (Labour Research Department, 1989; Beynon, Hudson, and Sadler, 1991). That current criteria for decision-making are rarely seen as forms of political choice among potentially viable options is an example of the 'unpolitics' of so much economic analysis and practice (Crenson, 1962).

Countervailing Powers: Occupational Safety and Health in the United States – A Brief Contextual History

This reminds us again of the difficulties in making corporations accountable to those on whom they impinge and, relatedly, in controlling the way that such corporations actually function. The regulatory strategies that flow from neoclassical theory are unlikely to lead to safe workplaces or many other socially desirable outcomes. Because employers are motivated by the desire and need to maximize profits, and since they are more powerful than workers, they will not spontaneously provide safe workplaces. In these situations they will have to be forced to do so, but the pressure to make them do this can be exerted in a number of different ways.

To explore these issues, rather than using the law and economics view of regulation or the (in some ways similar) left instrumentalist view of the state (Barnett, 1992), I will draw upon structuralist Marxism.

In this view the state, state agencies, and the law are best viewed as condensations of class relations and as sites of struggle (Jessop, 1982, 1990; Pearce, 1985, 1993). State agencies are more amenable to the goals and strategies of the more powerful groups, yet they are not totally closed to the aspirations of the less favoured groups. Law, for example, may indeed currently favour capital more than labour, but it does so in specific ways that are the anything but inevitable outcome of previous struggles themselves conducted on a historically conditioned terrain. Both the form and content of American labour law are the outcome of a number of different social conflicts and of different attempts by lawyers to systematize the law, to create consistency and closure within it, and to do so in ways that did not obviously compromise its claim to autonomy (Woodiwiss, 1991). Similarly, regulatory agencies only function effectively if they too are *represented* as essentially autonomous, and if, in practice, they *exhibit* a certain relative autonomy, that is if they are 'hegemonic apparatuses' (Mahon, 1977, 1979).

A group and its ideology are hegemonic insofar as it and others are 'persuaded' of the value of its leadership, its conception of the problems that need to be solved, and its sense of the range of feasible solutions to these problems (Gramsci, 1971). Thus, we find that those associated with the deregulation movement did not see themselves as representative of special interests but rather as objective commentators, speaking for the common interest from a place allegedly outside of ideology.[4] These rationalizations are more easily sustained when alternative viewpoints and modes of organization are actively (and coercively) marginalized.

In the United States, as in most other Western countries, the rate of serious and fatal work-related injuries and illnesses peaked in earlier days of industrialization (Trachtenberg, 1982: 91; Beaumont and Leopold, 1982: 102–3).[5] Then, trade union struggles, pressure from socialists, and the move from a disorganized to a more organized capitalism led to some significant changes. 'Progressive' reformers attempted to improve sanitation and the quality of food and to regulate the age of workers and the hours worked. Far-sighted employers designed some safer machinery and 'educated' workers in safe practices, while individualizing the causes of accidents. Trade unionists reluctantly compromised with corporate capital to develop a workers' compensation system on the latter's terms. During the 1930s, the Department of Labor, with strong ties to organized labour during this, the most nearly tripartite phase of corporate liberalism (Woodiwiss, 1991), developed some relatively ineffective state 'legislation designed to prevent conditions endangering the health of workers' (Rosner and Markowitz, 1989: 95).

Occupational health and safety was then generally neglected until the passing of the Occupational Health and Safety Act in 1970 (Berman, 1978). Although legislation had been initially proposed by radical discontented rank-and-file workers and by activist trade union leaders (Donnelly, 1982: 18–19; Szasz, 1984: 105; Aglietta, 1979), it was Richard Nixon who eventually opportunistically supported and passed a much weakened Occupational Safety and Health Act. The new Occupational Safety and Health Administration was underresourced, uncritically adopted pre-existing business-generated standards (Stellman and Daum, 1973: 9–11), and its inspections and enforcement activities, initially at least, were directed mainly against small businesses (Szasz, 1984: 108). Nevertheless, the act created a general duty for employers 'to furnish to each of his employees employment and a place of employment which are free from recognized hazards that are causing or are likely to cause death or serious physical harm to his employees' (Section 5a). Initially, OSHA inspections were both proactive and reactive to either injuries or disasters or to complaints from individual workers, trade unions, or even anonymous callers. Inspectors gave no notice that they were going to inspect premises and had statutory right of access to it and to its safety records. OSHA was provided with a range of types of offence (non-serious, serious, failure-to-abate, repeated, and wilful), and a relatively flexible range of fines which could be imposed and increased in severity automatically. The OSH Act also created employee rights 'to participate in standard setting, workplace inspections, and the monitoring of hazards; to have access to information about hazards and agency findings; to appeal certain agency rulings to a newly created Occupational Safety and Health Review Commission (OSHRC) and to the courts and to oppose certain kinds of employer appeals; and to be protected from employer discrimination for exercising these rights' (Noble, 1986: 95).

While OSHA legitimated occupational health and safety concerns and provided a mobilizing basis for trade unions, it usually failed to impose maximum penalties and many early citations were for easily observable but relatively trivial violations. Furthermore, every observed violation had to be recorded and, less happily, there was an obligation to make a formal finding of guilt. This latter provision removed from the inspector the kind of discretion, and negotiating power that, contrary to Kagan (1984), is routine in most police work. However, such practices helped to provide reasons (and justifications or excuses) for the climate of opposition to OSHA which developed into the vocal deregulatory movement (Wilson, 1985).

Although the arguments of the deregulationists' did not, at first, affect what happened within the production process and did not have much influence on OSHA, they were much more significant at the general political level. During the Carter administration, President Carter himself, Congress, and the Supreme Court all acted to constrain the activities of OSHA, and organized labour lost political and economic power. Reasonable questions about the relative effectiveness of different regulatory strategies were subtly redefined as issues resolved through the application of very narrowly construed cost–benefit analyses.

When Reagan came to power, a crucial and antagonistic hegemonic apparatus (Mahon, 1976, 1979), the Office of Management and Budget, gained effective control over many regulatory agencies. Occupational safety and health were subject to a process of deregulation. A new unambiguously pro-business secretary of labor and a pro-business OSHA director were appointed, and Viscusi became a consultant to OSHA. The budget, number of inspectors, inspections, and follow-up inspections were all cut, and workers' rights and inputs curtailed (Calavita, 1983: 441–3; Navarro, 1983: 523). Deregulation as a whole was a victory for the interests of corporate capital and its owners, and it certainly helped redistribute income in their favour (Noble, 1986; Edsall, 1984). The Bush administration continued to pursue similar policies (Phillips, 1991).

Beyond OSHA?

In the United States there is still a high rate of occupationally induced injuries, illnesses, and deaths, all too many of which are avoidable:

10,000 people still die on the job each year. Every day another 11,000 workers are injured seriously enough that they lose work time or have to restrict their work activity. The lost work-day rate is actually climbing, up 65 per cent between 1972 and 1989.

Americans remain unprotected from most toxic chemicals common in today's workplaces. Between 1,000 and 3,000 new substances appear every year. Many are toxic, some are lethal, and the vast majority are unregulated by OSHA. As a result, in addition to accidental deaths, occupational diseases kill a substantial number of workers. According to the Office of Technology Assessment (OTA) the most common estimate is 100,000 such deaths yearly, but because information is crude and monitoring primitive, no one knows how prevalent occupational diseases really are. (Noble, 1992: 44)

This carnage is caused, I would argue, by management practices which are often irresponsible – the safety records of similar companies in the United States can vary by a factor of six (Wilson, 1985: 4) – and also often illegal.[6]

While it is notoriously difficult to assess the impact of regulatory regimes, Mendeloff, by no means an unqualified supporter of OSHA's *modus operandi*, writing in 1979, argued (contrary to Smith, 1979: 63–4), that in its early days, OSHA had a considerable, and generally positive, effect on occupational safety. First, as OSHA came to concentrate on large establishments and on the most accident-prone industries, it began to inspect annually the workplaces of a third of all of those covered by the act. Virtually all of those working in high-risk industries, where violations were frequently dangerous and subject to relatively large fines, were thus inspected annually. Second, there was an increased awareness of hazards by workers and unions and consequent demands for time-consuming and potentially punitive OSHA inspections. The possibility that this might occur often led management to pre-emptively take greater care. Finally, safety-conscious managers were able to use OSHA regulations and the possibility of inspections to argue for greater attention to safety. Mendeloff 'guestimated' that private-sector expenditures that would not have occurred in the absence of OSHA have amounted to between $500 million and $1 billion annually' (1979: 88). Furthermore, there is evidence that there were some improvements even into the early 1980s (Szasz, 1986).

Overall, then, there are somewhat contradictory findings on the effectiveness of OSHA. But, at best, there have only been a few periods when it has been allowed to be effective. This is partly because of weaknesses in the original legislation. Workers were never 'guaranteed compensation for participating in inspections. The law did not protect their right to refuse hazardous work. Workers were not given a role to play in the selection of company health and safety professionals. Instead, all these things remained subject to collective bargaining' (Noble, 1986: 98). Therefore, since companies will rarely spontaneously create safe workplaces, it is essential that effective pressure is brought to bear on them by an adequate enforcement policy. This can be done in one or both of two ways. First, the state can use fines to discourage employers from violating standards. If this approach is chosen, penalties must be stiff, inspections comprehensive, and policy consistent. The rational employer who is out of compliance and contemplating investing in health and safety should consider (1) the odds of being inspected each year; (2) the probability that once he or she is inspected, the violation will be detected; and (3) the size of the penalty that will be assessed if the employer's violation is cited. If the odds on inspection are low, the penalties minimal, and/or policy too erratic to be predictable, the economically rational employer would be advised to violate standards with high compliance costs.

'Alternatively, the state can create and subsidize a variety of implant mechanisms through which workers can participate in a decentralized enforcement effort, such as mandatory health and safety committees, safety representatives, and employee-run occupational health clinics. Field inspections can then be linked to worker participation in in-plant institutions to take advantage of worker knowledge, maintain motivation, and facilitate involvement in decision making over the work environment. (Noble, 1986: 197)

Noble's third alternative, taking elements of both strategies, was put in place in Sweden in the 1970s and the 1980s. At that time, Sweden had a high-wage, relatively skilled, highly productive Fordist/Postfordist economy with low unemployment, few low-wage jobs, and a strong welfare state (Clegg, 1990: 225–30). Given their high average pay, their social wage (including such items as free health care, social welfare payments, unemployment payments, child care provisions, and maternity and paternity leave), their good working conditions, and their short working week, Swedish workers were among the best rewarded workers in the world. Unions won the right to representation on the boards of most companies and to bargain over the organization of many aspects of the work situation. Shop stewards and safety representatives were given significant powers and protection. Under the Work Environment Act [1977], safety representatives and safety committees could play an active role in the planning of new premises, work processes, and working methods and, famously, the former had the right to unilaterally stop any dangerous process until an inspector arrived (Navarro, 1983; Tucker, 1992). (Such a 'right to act' is actually already *formally* acknowledged to some extent by the United States Supreme Court (Noble, 1992: 50).) There was a massive increase in safety representatives and safety committees and the right to stop work has been exercised, but the threat of doing so is more significant than its actual exercise. Similarly, the

threat that the inspectorate might close a factory has been more significant than the actual exercise of this power (Navarro, 1983: 555). Capital
was to some extent 'compliant.' This, incidentally, shows that there are
crucial differences between what are allegedly equivalent 'compliance'
systems (Pearce and Tombs, 1990, 1992).

Occupational health services improved dramatically and were under
the control of safety committees. The evidence on accident rates is less
clear. Although these have not worsened in the past decade, they do not
seem to have improved dramatically. In fact, reforms do not seem to
have been translated into new workplace practices. Capital and the
labour inspectorate have focused on designing safety into new processes, but they have not sought a significant input from workers and
their unions. Safety committees have been more involved with immediate workshop issues than in the planning of the production process, and
even there they have lacked effective power – only a minority of their
complaints and recommendations are acted upon (Tucker, 1992: 110–11).
Indeed, without a more direct challenge to the power of capital – crucially its right to manage – such an outcome was perhaps to be expected. Nevertheless, here we have a different form of economic organization that is also efficient and, in this case, much improved employment
and working conditions for workers. It becomes clear why a devolution
of power and control to unionized workplaces is a crucial *aspect* of any
effective strategy to improve occupational safety and health in any
country. Legal forms may facilitate this, but its success requires effective
social organization.

Civil and Criminal Law

Whichever strategy is used, there would be a need for an enforcement
agency that was well staffed and provided with adequate powers of
enforcement (Pearce and Tombs, 1989, 1990, 1992). If OSHA had the
power and authority to frequently, both reactively and proactively,
inspect all workplaces, record all violations, and routinely engage in
follow-up inspections, and if all workplaces required a licence from
OSHA (or from a body licensed in turn by OSHA), which could be
withdrawn if there were evidence of occupational safety or health
violations, then OSHA could be much more effective.

Currently, most offences against OSHA are prosecuted as civil offences according to a standard of strict liability. For example, failure to

correct a violation for which a citation had been issued could result in a civil penalty of up to $1,000 a day. Although this makes these offences relatively easy to prosecute, the fact that they are civil offences makes it more likely that they will be construed as merely regulatory offences, as *mala prohibita*, the unavoidable side-effect of doing business, and not 'true crimes.' However, both the content of laws and the nature of such legal distinctions as those between acts which are *mala in se* and *mala prohibita*, between crimes, torts, and administrative sanctions, are conventional, time-bound social products without an intrinsic substantive meaning that transcends their social or historical contexts (Sutherland, 1945; Blum-West and Carter, 1983; Bergman, 1991; Pearce, 1992).

For there to be a public recognition of both the avoidability and the seriousness of the harm resulting from business misconduct, it is important that killing and injuring at work can and should be *frequently* (but not exclusively) subject to criminal sanctions. As Glasbeek and Rowlands have argued (1979), violations of occupational health and safety regulations that may lead to occupational accidents or ill health are as much real crimes as assault and homicide. Defining them as crimes demonstrates that a society actually values workers' lives and that it is unwilling to tolerate either managerial carelessness or underinvestment within the production process.

Although criminal penalties do exist under OSHA, they are rarely imposed, and they are limited to *wilful* violations of safety regulations, which *demonstrably* lead to the *death* of an employee, when 'fines of up to $10,000 and up to six months' imprisonment' (Noble, 1986: 95) could be imposed.[7] But a more general criminalization strategy is not without precedent in the United States; for a period in Wisconsin and New York around the turn of the century, the criminalization of these violations was normal (Frank, 1985).

In Britain, criminal prosecution is routinely used in such cases. On occasion, a standard of *criminal* strict liability is also used. This was not adopted because of an indifference to the guilt or innocence of particular employers, but rather because a higher standard of proof would allow many culpable people to escape prosecution and, hence, undermine the deterrent effect of sanctioning conduct that might lead to serious injury or death. What applies in the case of a shopkeeper selling decayed foods, applies equally to many offences involving occupational health:

With respect to at least some strict liability offences, it can be said that there exists a great danger to *each* of a considerable number of individuals. Offences of selling decayed foods are an example. Also, the penalty imposed on the shopkeeper is certainly such as to cause him less distress than would be caused to each of a number of individuals if they were poisoned ...

It is not essential that ... the penalty in question must be a relatively small one ... [if judges] *know* that a considerable number of offences will be committed unless there is a deterring example ... [and] nothing else would work (Honderich, 1976: 77)

American scholars sometimes challenge strict liability because, it is claimed, its use violates the requirement that crimes should involve an element of *mens rea* as well as *actus reus* (Hall, 1947). Yet, ironically, in 1989 over 50 per cent of the inmates of federal prisons in the United States and 20 per cent of those in local jails were there for drug offences (United States Department of Justice, 1990), in which issues of *mens rea* rarely arise (Skolnick, 1966; Manning, 1980). Furthermore, drug trafficking convictions are often secured because the accused is allegedly found to be in possession of a relatively large amount of a drug and/or because illegal entrapment strategies have been used (Marx, 1981). Admittedly, this does not provide a perfect parallel with offences against occupational safety and health; a better example is the treatment of traffic offences (Pearce and Tombs, 1990).[8]

It may well be the case that the dominant legal disclosure is so resistant to such a strategy that for many offences administrative and/or civil penalties are the best that can be achieved, and hence the most practical, if criminal intent cannot be demonstrated (Walker, 1995). This does not mean that there may not be many situations where issues of intent should, or can, be neglected. Prosecutions can, have, and should take account of whether or not violations are part of a pattern, whether employers have failed to rectify problems, indicating a willful or reckless disregard of regulations and/or the seriousness of the consequences of the violations. Furthermore, the ease with some kind of *mens rea* can be ascribed depends on both the legal framework of duties and the structure of business enterprises. This leads us directly back to the issue of corporate criminal liability, because most businesses are limited liability corporations.

In American law, corporations, theoretically at least, can be held liable for most criminal offences (Leigh, 1969). American courts have attributed criminal liability to corporations for crimes requiring negligence or intent, and the United States Supreme Court has held that the corporation could be held liable for the acts of its agents when in their occupational role they illegally act on behalf of, or for the benefit of, the corporation. That is to say that the civil law principles of *respondeat superior* (let the master reply) was transplanted into criminal law. Thus, the term 'corporate crime' has a substantive meaning in American law, a meaning clarified by Kramer:

By the concept of 'corporate crime,' then, we wish to focus attention on criminal acts (of omission or commission) which are the result of deliberate decision making (or culpable negligence) of those who occupy structural positions within the organization as corporate executives or managers. These decisions are organizationally based – made in accordance with the normative goals (primarily corporate profit), standard operating procedures, and cultural norms of the organization – and are intended to benefit the corporation itself. (Kramer, 1984: 18)

In the early 1980s the Ford Motor Company was charged (unsuccessfully) with reckless homicide for the defective design of the gas tank of the Ford Pinto (Dowie, 1979; Cullen, Maakestad, and Cavender, 1987). Then, in June 1985 in Illinois, the Film Recovery System Corporation and its parent company, Metallic Marketing Inc., were convicted of involuntary manslaughter and fourteen counts of reckless conduct, and fined $14,000 each, after a worker died at its factory from cyanide fumes. Three of its executives were also convicted of murder and fourteen counts of reckless conduct and received twenty-six-year sentences. The judge ruled that the president and the managers of Film Recovery Systems knew that their acts would cause a strong probability of death or great bodily harm – conditions of murder in the Illinois statute. Ironically, six months before the worker's death, the company had been exempted (under Reaganite regulations) from inspection by the Occupational Safety and Health Administration because, according to the company's logs, it had a better-than-average safety record. On appeal, the verdicts were set aside and a new trial ordered. This was based on the kind of technicality that shows legal formalism and anthropomorphism at its worst. The state court of appeals argued that since the evidence and facts used in both convictions were the same, then they should not have produced different criminal convictions – murder for the managers and involuntary manslaughter for the corporation. The usual reluctance to charge a corporation with murder because of its ostensible inability to serve a sentence or to be executed came back to haunt the prosecutors in this case.[9]

Although, as I have argued, it is essential that on some occasions criminal prosecutions should be used against the corporate entity alone, an effective deterrence strategy also requires that the corporate veil be pierced and that executive and directors be prosecuted (Geis and Di Mento, 1993). What renders this more possible is that company law has become increasingly specific about the duties and responsibilities of those who control corporations. For example, corporate fund managers are personally responsible for certain non-prudent actions in relation to their management of funds under the Employee Retirement Income Security Act [1974] (Meyer, 1986). The law could also become more rigorous about the duties of those responsible for the management of safety, making it easier to determine individual and corporate responsibility for disasters and accidents. As argued elsewhere (Pearce, 1993; Pearce and Tombs, 1990), companies could be forced to tighten up and improve their organizational structure and their management of health and safety by clarifying where responsibilities lie and by extending the range of crimes or offences for which executives would be liable. Indeed, such a system would accord with much American federal jurisprudence, in which corporate 'liability will be imposed whenever an officer or agent, in doing the acts complained of, was engaged in exercising corporate powers and acting within the course and scope of his employment, provided that he thereby intended to benefit the corporation' (Leigh, 1969: 116; see also Barrile, 1992). This has the advantage that it makes it much more difficult for management to claim that it did not know what was happening or for it to practice 'willful blindness' (Wilson, 1979). However, in line with earlier observations, employees also need the protection of their unions and/or whistleblowing legislation if they are able to protect themselves from the impersonal subtle pressure of the bottom line and the not-so-subtle, off-the-record pressure to disobey official company policy for greater profits.

These suggestions involve a move away from the idea that the corporation is simply a private entity. Its activities depend on and, in turn, affect a whole series of stakeholders – shareholders, employees, suppliers, customers, local communities, and the national state. Indeed, its rights, its duties, and its privileges are dependent on the power of the state. This returns us to the question of how to make corporations accountable to these stakeholders. External mechanisms include federal chartering and much stricter licensing conditions. They also include a restructuring of the laws and institutions associated with investment and with the distribution of corporate revenue and profits (Block, 1992).

Active participation by stakeholders in the formulation of regulatory policy is important. Participation by state-owned enterprises in the economy, or indeed state control of the economy, may also be important mechanisms to control conduct and generate information (Pearce, 1987; Pearce and Snider, 1995). As suggested earlier, internally, accountability would involve a corporation documenting, explaining, and justifying its specific activities to its various stakeholders. This would only be credible insofar as this involved some kind of genuine dialogue, and this, in turn, would require the empowering of these stakeholders. One way to achieve this is through a restructuring of corporate governance, for example, by requiring that employees and equity holders should both elect 35 per cent of corporate boards and other groups should elect 30 per cent (Block, 1992: 289). Another might include the (defeated) Swedish suggestion to use worker funds to socialize the ownership of the enterprises themselves (Meidner, 1978; Ambrahamson and Brostom, 1980).

Conclusion

In this chapter I have tried to achieve a number of related goals. First, I have sought to determine what accountability might mean in the case of corporate organizations. Second, I have examined different methods by which such accountability might be achieved. I have engaged in a detailed discussion and critique of how a currently dominant perspective in law, that associated with the 'law and economics' movement, has dealt with the issue of corporate accountability. This required an exploration of its understanding of the nature of the corporation and the economy. Then, in part by drawing on this critique and in part by drawing on other work, including my own, I have developed an alternative set of suggestions as to how some elementary forms of accountability might be achieved. To make these arguments more concrete, I have focused particulary on issues concerning occupational safety and health in the United States.

In my view, accountability to different stakeholders will only be realizeable if there are significant changes in the *modus operandi* of the state and its regulatory agencies, including a commitment to actively use the criminal law in the case of violations of the laws governing occupational safety and health; a redistribution of powers within corporations and within the economy as a whole, and within society more generally; and significant changes in the legal framework through which corporations are chartered, governed, and organized. These suggestions are quite feasible. Indeed, there are excellent precedents for many of them in the organization and registration of economic life in other Western societies. The problem lies in inequalities of political and economic power and in a lack of political will. It remains a scandal that so much carnage is still associated with people's need to earn their livelihood. Nevertheless, this essay can be ended on a cautiously optimistic note. Some positive moves are currently being made by the Clinton administration. It has proposed a Comprehensive Occupational Safety and Health Reform Act (Noble, 1992). According to recent reports, this bill

would require employers to establish joint safety and health committees that would include employees. The bill would extend OSHA coverage to state and local public employees who are now excluded from coverage, except in the 23 states that have their own OSHA program.

In addition, the bill would: give workers the right to refuse unsafe work; mandate that OSHA issue final standards on key hazards, and update permissible exposure limits on toxic substances; give workers the right to challenge weak citations and weak settlements; improve construction safety; and strengthen federal oversight of state plans. (*Corporate Crime Reporter*, 1994: 7)

Notes

1 For Posner criminal (or civil penalty) liability is appropriate for crimes committed by individuals acting as agents of corporations or other associations but not if they were acting on their own behalf (1980: 417). He takes it as self-evident that corporations cannot be imprisoned but equivalent punishments can be, and have been, developed (Box 1983; Braithwaite, 1984).

2 This degree of concentration is also, in part, the effect of four merger movements. The first, from 1898–1902, peaked about a thousand mergers per year, the second (1925–9) at fifteen hundred, the third (1955–69) at twenty-five hundred, the latest (1980–8) peaked at just under forty-five hundred. Between 1980 and 1988 there were 26,671 mergers and acquisitions involving assets worth $1,083.4 billion (Jones 1982: 9; Adams and Brock 1989: 12, 13).

3 For example, five hundred companies were fined five million dollars for

tampering with the coal dust samples used to gauge miners' risk of black lung disease, including $500,000 for Peabody Coal, the largest producer in the United States (*Globe and Mail*, 8 April 1991). For other routine falsification of test results see Clarke (1990: 148–9), Braithwaite (1984), and Di Mento (1986).

4 Weidenbaum, for example, made the extraordinary claim that the 'Task Force on Regulatory Relief' (set up by, that most ideological and business-oriented and business-dependent of presidents, Ronald Reagan), 'did not have any interest group constituency to protect and defend. Its only constituency is the president and the president's program for rationalizing regulation' (cited in Noble, 1992: 160).

5 The United States had a particularly high fatality rate – in construction, agriculture, and mining more than twice that of England, Germany, and France; see Rosner and Markowitz (1989: xi).

6 American estimates of injuries caused by violations of safety codes vary between 10 and 45 per cent (Mendeloff, 1979: 115; Coleman, 1989: 7). These are probably underestimates, since in-depth investigations by the Health and Safety Executive found that more than 60 per cent of occupationally related deaths in different occupations in the United Kingdom were mainly the result of management's failure to fulfill its (far from onerous) statutory duties (Pearce and Tombs, 1990).

7 Although in recent years, maximum penalties (both civil and criminal) have been increased, these are still rarely imposed, and even if they are, they are then usually reduced on appeal (by as much as 96 per cent). Furthermore, fines are often not even collected (Brill, 1992: 66–9).

8 For a discussion of other and more fundamental problems with the very categories of, and distinction between, *mens rea* and *actus reus* and with the concept of strict liability see Lacey, Wells, and Meure (1990) and Kelman (1987).

9 *Illinois v Stephen O'Neil, Film Recovery Systems, Inc., Metallic Marketing Systems, Ind., Charles Kirshbaum, and Daniel Rodriguez* [1990]. Reversals on appeal are common in corporate criminal cases including regulatory cases (for example, asbestos manufactures) and work-related deaths and negligence (*People v Warner-Lambert Co.* [1980 & 1981].

Alternative Accountabilities: Examples from Securities Regulation

MARY CONDON

This essay attempts to show, by examining accountability in the social and historical location of Ontario securities markets, that the concept of accountability, as it is employed in the criminal justice literature, has been too narrowly defined. It argues for a shift of emphasis to a broader understanding of the phenomenon, with implications for recasting the framework in which issues of who is to be made accountable, for what, and how, are considered. The essay attempts to refocus the agenda of scholars concerned about accountability.

Accounting for the Use of a Concept

In the Introduction to this volume, Stenning provides a generic definition of accountability as comprising a 'requirement to give an account.' Although a power relationship between provider and receiver of the account is implicit in this formulation, Stenning is careful to distinguish the phenomenon of accountability from that of control, because the requirement to provide an account of itself implies nothing about the response from its receiver. Similarly, of course, there are ways to control that do not rely on the production of accounts. The generic definition, not surprisingly, is also silent about the particulars of who or what is to give the account, to whom or what it is to be given and of what it is to consist. There is a substantial literature on accountability in the criminal justice field which applies this generic definition to a variety of substantive areas (Stenning, 1983, 1986; Edwards, 1964, 1984; Goldsmith, 1991c). However, one of the central arguments of this essay is that these applications have been driven and shaped by an acceptance of the distinction drawn in liberal political theory between the public and private realms. The influence of this fundamental distinction has been to narrow unduly the scope of activities subject to accountability research and to ignore the realities of the way power is distributed in modern society. Accordingly, a reassessment of the fundamental premises of accountability research in the criminal justice field is timely. Let us first briefly explain the link between liberal theory and accountability scholarship.

The Public/Private Distinction: A Consequential Divide

The public/private distinction has been at the core of liberal theory since its inception. As Gardbaum (1992: 759) points out: 'Liberal political theory predated modern society. It should not be forgotten that the original problem to which liberalism was offered as the solution, and thus the *raison d'être* of the liberal state, was the protection of individuals from *each other*. The solution was to confront actors of roughly equal power with the deterring concentration of power that is the state.

In fact, the aspect of this protection that received the most attention in the age of pre-classical liberalism was the 'sanctity of private property' (Mensch, 1982: 20). Yet, if individuals and their property required protection from the encroachments of others in a 'realm of pure private autonomy' (Mensch, 1982: 22), they also had to be ensured freedom from intrusion by the state. In this way there emerged what Gardbaum (1992: 759) describes as 'the schizophrenic liberal view of politics as both the sole guarantor and the major enemy of freedom.' However, the state *was* entrusted with the problem of 'maintaining public order and serving clearly delineated public functions' (Mensch, 1982: 23). This legitimate and 'carefully delimited' (Kelman, 1987: 259) public realm and that of the private were 'vacuum-bounded' and completely separate. As Kelman expresses it, 'The mainstream position is that there is a fairly distinct line between the domain of intentional choice and freedom (private life, contract) and the domain of coerced choicelessness (public law, mandatory law, subjection to political sovereignty)' (ibid.: 102).

Not surprisingly, the task of policing the definition and maintenance of the boundary between the realms of private rights and public power fell to the courts. Mensch points out that 'to the classics, freedom *meant* the legal guarantee that rights and powers would be protected as absolute within their own sphere, but that no rightholder/powerholder would be allowed to invade the sphere of another' (1982: 23–4). The power of the rule of law to resolve 'the conflict between freedom as private, civil right and freedom as public participation in a democracy' depended on the 'objective' discovery of the boundary between public and private by means of specific common-law doctrine. The exercise of public power was legitimate insofar as it rested on legal authority. It was this 'supposed objectivity that gave the appearance of coherence and reality to the legal (and social/political) model of bounded rights and powers' (ibid.: 26). The liberal theory of law, therefore, was conceived as a 'normative enterprise ... distinct from politics and morality both in method and content.' It followed that there were 'meaningful criteria for ascertaining the truth of a proposition of law' (Gardbaum, 1992: 736).

The twentieth-century phenomenon of increased and explicit government regulation by law of economic and social activity has not occasioned any fundamental rethinking by mainstream political and legal theorists of the validity of the public/private distinction. Thus, Tollefson (1991: 716) draws a distinction between 'classical' and 'pluralist' liberalism, but argues that both are characterized by a 'private/public dichotomization of the relationship between the state and civil society.' State regulation in areas like occupational health and safety and the environment may have had some redistributive effects, but these could be encompassed within what Kelman (1987: 259) describes as 'the collective desire to frame distributive outcomes that is always part of liberal consciousness.' With respect to legal theory, Mensch (1982: 32) argues that American legal thought 'continues to be premised on the distinction between private law and public law. Private law is still assumed to be *about* private actors with private rights, making private choices, even though sophisticated judges tend quite frankly to refer to public policy when justifying private-law decision making.'

Within the liberal world-view, the growth of economic regulation and, in particular, the discretionary, 'public interest' powers for regulatory agencies associated with it, did mean a greatly enhanced role for public law, concerned as it was with the 'pragmatic control of public power' (Hancher and Moran, 1989: 280). In this context, the task of the courts has become that of distinguishing between legitimate and illegitimate exercises of discretion on the part of regulatory agencies. This enterprise maintains continuity with classical liberalism's formulation of the superiority of the rule of law, administered by courts, over the decision-making of public agencies with statutory powers.

The Public/Private Distinction and Accountability

The plausibility of the public/private distinction has, in fact, been questioned by a body of legal critique beginning with the legal realist movement in the early twentieth century (Mensch, 1982: 26–9) and taken up more recently by critical legal scholars (Kelman, 1987: 103–10). This critique revolves around the twin arguments that the public state actually facilitates and enables the pursuit of private rights and that the exercise of so-called private rights may have public, and often coercive, consequences. However, this critique has not penetrated the literature on accountability, so that the public/private distinction continues to undergird studies of accountability and accountability mechanisms in much criminal justice research and policy-making. Acceptance of the distinction has meant that those who study accountability have assumed the phenomenon to possess the following features:

First, research endeavours focus on ensuring that agents of the *state*, such as the police, prosecutors, and regulatory agencies, are sufficiently accountable for actions that encroach on private powers or rights. As Gardbaum puts it, 'It is still only the state, the one concentration [of power] with the duty and mandate to protect our freedom from others, that is officially deemed a threat to it'(1992: 759). For Hutchinson (1990: 381–2), it is this 'philosophy of distrust,' which characterizes liberal theories of the state, that underlies the expectation that public officials act as 'communal angels in the service of heavenly ambition.'

Second, agents of the state are to be rendered accountable for actions taken pursuant to explicit grants of discretionary power. These discretionary powers are accorded to agents of the state in recognition of the need for flexibility and the capacity to adjust the application of rules in regulating an increasingly complex and dynamic social world (Galligan, 1986: 84). Thus, mechanisms of accountability are put in place for the primary purpose of curtailing the power of agents of the state, by requiring them to answer for how they exercise their discretion. As suggested above, the rule of law, considered the antithesis of discretionary power, is the pre-eminent device for curtailing this power and policing illegitimate exercises of discretion, which violate the 'extra-state realm of individual autonomy' (Hutchinson, 1990: 402; McBarnet, 1981: 162–5).

Third, institutionally, the channels of accountability are assumed to flow to other, more powerful and well-established organs of the state. The traditional distinctions drawn among forms of accountability are those of (a) legal (judicial review by courts); (b) political (to legislatures), and (c) administrative (to higher or external levels of state bureaucracy) accountability (Stenning, 1986: 286). To reiterate, the 'deterring concentration of power' that characterizes the state, through its various institutions, is considered to be the best guarantor of adequate accountability. That the state has taken over the field here is evidenced by the preoccupation in the regulatory literature with the problem of avoiding the 'capture' of regulatory agencies (Ayres and Braithwaite, 1991; Stigler, 1988; Kolko, 1963; Moran, 1986). One interpretation of analysts' concern with this issue is that it stems from an understanding of 'capture' as a situation where the state agent has become accountable to a non-state entity, often one of its regulatory constituents. As Hancher and Moran point out (1989: 274), the idea of capture only makes sense in the context of accepting a distinction between the public and private realms. The assumption that there should exist 'an inviolable sphere' of public authority implies that the only legitimate form of accountability is to another institution of the state.

Fourth, in part because of the focus on exercises of discretion specifically provided for by law, and in part because the institutions of the state to which accountability is rendered are often external to the agency providing the accounts, the accountability mechanisms studied, evaluated, and recommended by justice researchers tend to be *problem* driven and mobilized in reaction to specific complaints. In other words, mechanisms of accountability become activated *after* the order sought to be achieved by criminal justice and regulatory officials has broken down. The best example of this phenomenon is the variety of police complaints commissions that have been established, at local and national levels in many countries, to respond to calls that the police be accountable for their discretionary activities (Goldsmith, 1991c). Another example is the practice of rendering senior prosecutors accountable by means of questions raised in legislatures about their decisions (Edwards, 1984). Let us turn then to examine the application of these distinguishing features to the context of the regulation of securities markets in Ontario.

Accountability in Ontario Securities Markets

The initial sale to investors of the securities of public companies, and their subsequent trading by market intermediaries on behalf of those investors, is the subject of regulation embodied in the Ontario Securities Act [1990]. It should be clear by now how the topic of accountability would traditionally be addressed in the social context of Ontario securities markets. In all likelihood, the focus would be on the exercise of the range of discretionary powers granted by this securities statute to the government agency accorded regulatory responsibility since the 1940s, the Ontario Securities Commission (OSC). Research would be undertaken into the extent, practice, and deficiencies of its accountability to the courts or to the legislature (Janisch, 1989). However, such a view of the appropriate scope of accountability research in this field would, even as an empirical matter, be misguided.

In the first place, and most obviously, the *content* of the securities statute is predominantly concerned with the accountability, not of the state agency, but of corporations and market intermediaries, in the sense that they are required by law to provide financial and other information about their activities while selling securities to investors. Despite the fact that the phenomenon of securities regulation can easily be understood as a kind of institutionalized accountability for corporations and market intermediaries, a discourse of accountability has been almost completely absent from political, regulatory, and academic consideration of the obligations for disclosure contained in the Ontario securities statute and the accompanying regulations. In other words, the extent to which corporations are thereby being made accountable for their activities by the imposition of requirements for disclosure is not made an issue in political or regulatory debate about the scope or application of these requirements. Now, the point that the public/private distinction has operated to assist corporations to escape scrutiny is one that has been made by a number of commentators. For example, Hutchinson (1990: 396) asserts that 'corporations are doubly insulated from public scrutiny and control; they can resist attempts at administrative regulation by calling the courts in aid [to challenge the administrative acts of government], and they can largely rely on the courts not to interfere with their own activities. The public/private distinction frustrates rather than facilitates any democratic aspiration or practice in corporate affairs.'

Such commentators argue that analytical attention should be reoriented to corporate practices because of the 'social reality of power' (ibid.: 396; Kelman, 1987: 109). While I endorse the view that there is serious 'potential for abuse' (Hutchinson, 1990: 396) of the increasingly public power and status available to legally private corporate organizations, my point here is rather that the narrowing effects of the public/private distinction on accountability scholarship has prevented an adequate description and evaluation of potential and *actual* mechanisms of accountability imposed on corporations by means of, for example, the dictates of securities regulation. The difficulty is accentuated by the fact that, in this sphere, neither regulators nor regulated describe what is happening as accountability. In that disclosure regulations are a mechanism for 'doing accounting' they clearly are systems of accountability. We need to begin, therefore, to specify the ways in which corporations are being, or can be, made accountable for their activities.

This argument is heightened by the point that in the context of the regulation of corporations by securities legislation, the distinction drawn by Stenning between control and accountability is of considerable relevance (Stenning, 1986: 285–6). Securities legislation provides to the OSC a variety of enforcement and sanctioning powers, which clearly allow for the opportunity to exercise control over corporations and/or their significant actors. But it has become a truism of criminological wisdom that examining the law and practice of applying formal and punitive sanctions, such as orders to cease trading or prosecutions for insider trading, will not provide a complete picture of a regulatory process or regulatory power (Reiss, 1984b). Thus, we shall see that there are a variety of statutory strategies for rendering corporations accountable, which would not be apparent by examining only powers of enforcement. In fact, the first Ontario Securities Act [1990] properly so-called, in 1945 (c. 22), eschewed powers of enforcement of any substance in favour of the imposition of requirements for disclosure.

A second reason that a focus on the relationship of the state agency to courts and legislatures would provide an inadequate description of strategies for accountability in Ontario securities markets is the presence of several self-regulatory organizations (SROs) in the field (Stenning, Shearing, Addario, and Condon, 1990). The number and nature of these organizations has fluctuated in the period since the OSC was established. The Toronto Stock Exchange (TSE) and the Investment Dealers Association (IDA) already existed by that time, and the Broker Dealers Association (now largely defunct) was created by statute in 1947 to regulate the activities of those market intermediaries who were prominent in the promotion and trading of mining and natural resource securities.

Incorporated by statute, the Toronto Stock Exchange is recognized by the OSC for the purpose of running a stock exchange. It has the power both to 'specify the terms on which shares are admitted to trading on the exchange' (Dey and Makuch, 1979: 1407–8) and to regulate the activities of its members, 'including admission to membership, business carried on by members, capital requirements for continued membership, directors and shareholders of members, affiliated companies, trading procedures ... and relations with customers.' According to Dey and Makuch (1979: 1408), 'Members of the IDA are generally the larger well-recognized firms that perform most of the underwriting and trading of non-speculative securities.' Like the TSE, the IDA also regulates the capital requirements and trading practices of its members. As associations whose members are brokerage and investment houses, these non-state regulators can be seen *both* as possessors of consequential social and economic power *and* as alternative guarantors of accountability (Shearing, 1992a). Their existence and activities bear out Hancher and Moran's point (1989: 297) that 'the study of regulatory power cannot be furthered by an artificial division between "public" and "private" spheres. An organizational perspective on regulation allows us to go beyond "capture" theory, to examine the process by which powerful organizations, both state and non-state, gain, maintain, and sometimes lose their dominant positions within regulatory space.'

While there is room for debate about the appropriateness of a reliance on self-regulation (Dey and Makuch, 1979; Abolafia, 1985; Stenning et al., 1990; Moran, 1986), the point to be made here is that, as an empirical fact, SROs share with the government agency a responsibility for ensuring corporate and market-intermediary accountability. We shall return to this issue in subsequent sections.

Thus, to begin to address the implications of corporate disclosure legislation and practice for our present understanding of the phenomenon of accountability, it is proposed to examine examples of disclosure regulation in Ontario securities markets following the introduction of the 1966 Securities Act [1966]. This statute was important in that it marked the first acceptance of disclosure of information as a comprehensive regulatory strategy for the market (Condon, 1991: 109–206; Williamson, 1966). The choice of disclosure as the prevailing regulatory strategy is of obvious significance for the study of accountability, although it is not usually considered in this light. A significant portion of this essay will consist of a case study of conflict over reforming important aspects of this disclosure orientation during the 1970s. Among other things, this study demonstrates the difficulties of using legal concepts to achieve definitive accountability. It should be noted that these issues are not only of historical interest, because disclosure of information remains the cornerstone of regulatory policy for securities markets in Canada and elsewhere. Examination of this historical period will provide a framework to understand more recent developments in market accountability[1] and, more significantly, the possibilities for broadening and deepening contemporary debate about the characteristics of corporate accountability.

Disclosure as Routine Practice

In the 1966 statute the paradigmatic example of imposing requirements for disclosure on corporations was on the occasion of a primary (initial) distribution of shares to the public. By Section 35 of the act, no such 'trading in the course of a primary distribution' could take place until both a preliminary prospectus and a prospectus had been filed with the OSC and a receipt (approval) obtained from the commission. The prospectus was required to contain 'full, true and plain disclosure' of all 'material' facts at the disposal of the corporation (Section 41) and Section 43 identified the financial statements that must accompany the prospectus. Section 46 required a prospectus to contain a report on the accompanying financial statements by an accountant who was 'acceptable to the Director' of the OSC, which should state whether in the opinion of such accountant the relevant financial statements 'present fairly the financial position of the company in accordance with generally accepted accounting principles applied on a consistent basis.' Leaving aside considerations of the content and adequacy of this disclosure, about which there is ongoing debate (Nixon, 1963: 348–9), it is important to appreciate the difference between this approach to accountability and the traditional features of accountability already noted. By requiring disclosure of information as a prerequisite for access to the marketplace, the accountability thereby imposed on corporations is of a proactive kind. It emphasizes the prevention of subsequent problems attributable to insufficient information, rather than a reaction to the emergence of these problems. That this is a different approach from the traditional one of rendering actors accountable *after* a problem has occurred is evidenced by Makens's comment (1984: 448) concerning state regulatory activity in the United States: 'It has been said that the best allocation of scarce state securities regulatory resources is fighting fraud through enforcement, not fighting reams of prospectuses used in offerings in which little if any fraud may be involved.'

Makens was writing in the context of a debate about the appropriateness of imposing state 'merit' regulation (that is, a requirement that issuers demonstrate the 'fairness' of an investment opportunity) *on top of* federal disclosure regulation (administered by the Securities and Exchange Commission) in the United States. However, since the argument against state regulation is that the 'federal disclosure system provides adequate protection in public offerings' (ibid.), this buttresses the point that the form of accountability that characterizes the operation of the securities market in Canada generally and in the United States is qualitatively different from the conventional approach of criminal justice.

Moreover, there is agreement among commentators (Johnston, 1977; Bray, 1967: 415) that a significant effect of the 1966 act in Ontario was increased regulation of secondary trading in securities; that is, continued trading of securities on the market after the unique event of their initial issuance. Once again, the nature of this regulation was the obligation to provide current information on corporate activities to shareholders and investors. Part XII of the act instituted the system of continuous disclosure of financial information. By Section 120, a corporation was to file with the commission comparative financial statements 'relating separately to the latest completed financial year and the financial year preceding it.' Section 129 described the requirements for interim (semiannual) corporate financial statements.

Significant details of the requirements for continuous disclosure evidence an implicit legislative concern for issues of accountability. For example, as with the prospectus, these financial statements were to be accompanied by a report of the company auditor. This provision for validation by an independent auditor can be seen to be inspired by concern for accountability in at least two ways. First, the independent auditor functions as a guarantor of the accuracy of corporate financial statements. Second, the existence of the auditor allows for the identification of an individual to be rendered accountable for deficiencies in those statements. Even more significantly, compliance with the requirements for continuous disclosure was possible by filing with the OSC financial statements and auditors' reports sent by corporations to their shareholders. In other words, these accountability requirements of the Securities Act could be fulfilled by recourse to existing routine activities of the corporation, disclosing information for other purposes to its owners, in fulfilment of other legal requirements. Thus, Bray (1975: 240) argued that 'it is apparent that the draftsmen attempted to tailor the requirements to the kind of regular disclosure then being made by prudent management to its shareholders.' It may indeed be possible to criticize the adequacy of these requirements for continuous disclosure, from the point of view of the timing of their production or the adequacy of their substance, but the point to note is that the proactive, routine, and multipurpose nature of the provisions displays a different approach to accountability from that typically found in the criminal justice model.

Apart from the requirements for initial and continuing corporate disclosure set out in the statute, the securities commission established a further avenue of accountability to deal with occasions when there were 'material changes or developments'[2] in the affairs of the corporation, which information should, according to the OSC, be made available to investors. This was the so-called timely disclosure policy, introduced in September 1968. The introduction of this policy laid the foundations for the subsequent struggle over the meaning of a 'material' change, which was a key aspect of attempts to reform the Securities Act in the 1970s. We shall look at this struggle in more detail shortly; for now it is sufficient to note that the policy, by requiring 'immediate disclosure of all material and significant information through the news media,' allowed for a further proactive mechanism of accountability to become embedded in corporate practice. As Emerson, a practitioner and commentator on securities regulation, put it (1973: 463), 'compliance with timely disclosure policies is, in most instances, good corporate practice in any event. Not only does timely disclosure avoid securities violations for trading by insiders, it also satisfies the trading market's demands for corporate news, promotes corporate goals by creating publicity and avoids sanctions against the corporation, including suspension of trading, by either securities commissions or exchanges.'

While these sentiments ultimately provide no guarantee of corporate compliance with disclosure requirements, it is significant that the same disclosure obligations are presented as fulfilling multiple functions within the corporate context. One of these functions, though not explicitly described as such by Emerson, is clearly that of a framework for ensuring corporate accountability. Finally, it is worth briefly noting that the preferred way to regulate corporate take-overs in Ontario has been, ever since this period, by requiring the offeror to provide specified information to the offeree shareholders about the proposed transaction, to assist them in deciding whether to tender their shares (Securities Act, 1966, Part IX, and Ontario Reg. 101/67, No. 56).

In view of the argument so far, it would not be surprising to find that market participants other than corporate issuers were rendered accountable by means of routine requirements for disclosure. The statute under discussion gave the OSC the responsibility 'to register and regulate underwriters; that is, those persons or companies who promote the distribution of securities to the public' (*Ontario Securities Commission Bulletin* (*OSCB*), January 1967: 13). Underwriters are typically members of a self-regulatory organization such as the IDA. The two main regulatory strategies employed by the OSC in developing its policy 'on the standards that must be maintained by these registrants' were the establishment of a requirement for underwriters to have a minimum amount of capital at their disposal, along with various disclosure requirements. Thus, the policy provided that:

5(b) All applicants for registration as underwriters must name the officer or officers who will be in active charge of the company's affairs. The experience of such officer or officers in underwriting in the last three years must be shown in detail. The method of operation of the company by its officers and directors and the extent of supervision over its affairs to be exercised by each of them and other relevant details shall be disclosed.

5(c) Applications for registration or renewal as an underwriter must be accompanied by an audited annual financial statement and a profit and loss statement as of the same date. (*OSCB*, July 1968: 150)

Once again we notice how disclosure of routine corporate information becomes the preferred technique of regulation. Although not described as such, requiring disclosure of this information as a prerequisite to registration is clearly an attempt to enforce the accountability of underwriters for their activities.

The most contentious issue in debate prior to the enactment of the 1966 statute was the proposal that the OSC be granted the power to oversee the activities of the TSE. The Windfall report (Ontario, Royal Commission, 1965: 100–18; Condon, 1991: 127–44) had criticized the absence of control over exercises of discretion by the TSE. Ultimately, the power of the OSC under Section 139 to 'make any direction, order, determination or ruling ... with respect to any bylaw, ruling, instruction or regulation of any such stock exchange' was a compromise resulting specifically from considerable opposition in the securities industry to elimination of the practice of primary distribution of mining stocks on the TSE, with the exchange as sole reviewer of prospectuses (Condon,

1991: 40–1, 113–34). In the event, in the years after 1966 examples of regulation of the TSE by the commission were rare. One of them, however, was the February 1969 policy on registration of market intermediaries. This provided that

> the three self-regulating bodies shall notify the Commission immediately upon becoming satisfied that a material infraction has occurred of the capital or financial or other record-keeping requirements of their body, or the Commission, or suspected violations of the Securities Act, the Criminal Code or conduct otherwise affecting their fitness for continued registration. The self-regulating bodies shall also report to the Commission quarterly all instances which the self-regulating bodies viewed as immaterial together with the steps taken to remedy or deal with them.

Here we see requirements for disclosure imposed both on SRO *members*, as a means of evaluating their continued fitness for registration, as well as on the SROs themselves. With respect to the latter issue, while this policy provided the SROs themselves with scope to regulate their members, the quid pro quo for this responsibility was the imposition of routine reporting requirements on these organizations. The mechanism for their accountability to the OSC became built into and a part of *their own* ongoing regulatory activities.

Thus, repeated examples of the regulation of corporate issuers and market intermediaries by means of the 1966 Securities Act demonstrate that the mechanisms of accountability relied on were neither driven by after-the-fact discoveries of problems in the marketplace, nor wholly separable from other routine activities performed by these market actors. The successful intertwining of these mechanisms for achieving accountability with, for example, corporate efforts to achieve access to the market to raise capital, or the provision of information to owners of the corporation, may be one reason for the invisibility of a discourse of accountability in the practice and analysis of securities regulation. Accountability 'work' is continually being done, however, in ways that highlight the deficiency of conventional understandings of the components of accountability.

Accountability to Whom and Why

We have shown that such accountability as exists in Ontario securities markets takes place by and large through practices of routine disclosure imposed on corporations and market intermediaries. This belies the prevailing view in scholarship on accountability that the appropriate subject for scrutiny is the accountability of state agencies by means of isolated, after-the-fact mechanisms. Another assumption of the prevailing approach, which flows from the distrust accorded to the exercise by the state of its discretionary power, is that the purpose of strategies of accountability is primarily to act as a restraint on that power. Furthermore, only other institutions of the state are appropriate to enforce that accountability. Let us now address more explicitly the extent to which these assumptions are translatable to the accountability of corporations and market intermediaries by means of the tenets and practice of securities law.

Political debate around the introduction and strengthening of the requirements for disclosure in the 1966 statute suggests clearly that the significance of these requirements lay, to a great extent, in their capacity to encourage participation by investors in the stock markets. For example, while discussing the securities commission's practices with respect to reviewing the information in prospectuses, before the Royal Commission on Banking and Finance in 1962, the OSC Registrar pointed out that 'the Commission do never accept [sic] the bare "general corporate purposes" [as an answer to the requirement to disclose the nature of the business to be transacted] ... We ask them to expand, to enlarge ... not just so that the Commission knows the answer, but so that the member of the public, the investor, who has this prospectus placed in his hands can understand from this plain and full disclosure what the corporate venture is to be' (Canada, Royal Commission, 1962: 1557–9).

Recall also the establishment of the OSC's policy on timely disclosure in 1968. This policy began with the assertion that the topic of timely disclosure was 'one of great concern to all parties interested in securities, whether as investors, as executives, or regulatory bodies.' It continued, 'It is essential that all investors be placed on an equal footing insofar as knowledge of the material facts regarding the company which has securities in the hands of the public.' The value of disclosure to the investment and trading plans of investors is likewise evidenced by Bray's comment (1967: 420) that the rationale for the system of continuing disclosure was that 'every purchaser immediately becomes a potential seller entitled to information.' A similar preoccupation is asserted by Emerson (1973: 402–3, 463) to the effect that 'unless disclosure is effectively communicated to the investor, the fundamental purpose of the continuing disclosure system is not achieved.'

In its final report, the Royal Commission on Banking and Finance made explicit the link between disclosure, investor participation, and public confidence. The main preoccupation of the royal commission with respect to securities markets was with the encouragement of more widespread ownership of listed stock. The key to this goal of increased ownership was increased to be the enhancement of public confidence in securities markets. Thus, for instance, 'certain features of stock exchange operations in Canada are problematic when, to the extent that they engender investor distrust of common stocks, these factors inhibit the growth of Canadian share ownership' (Canada, Royal Commission, 1964: 341). One of the primary conditions for encouraging this wider ownership was identified as 'public knowledge and information' (Condon, 1991: 116–23).

For other formulations of the objectives of the disclosure system, we turn to Williamson (1966: 5) who argued that 'confidence in individual companies and in securities markets generally rests on adequate information. And the efficient investment of institutional and individual funds is not possible without a constant flow of information to facilitate continuous evaluation of portfolios.' Similarly, Baillie (1973: 370), later to become chair of the commission, states that 'the essential point is that disclosure is not an end in itself, but a means of contributing to the efficiency of the securities markets, both primary and secondary.'

All these examples serve to reinforce the point that the principal express rationale for statutory and policy-based requirements for disclosure in securities markets is the economic and political objective of the maintenance and encouragement of participation by investors in the market, rather than that of exercising control over corporations and market intermediaries *per se*. In other words, the achievement of corporate accountability for its own sake has not been the primary *raison d'être* of statutory requirements for disclosure. This suggests that struggle over what and how to disclose is likely to take place on the terrain of achieving investor participation rather than that of restraining the power of corporations.

The foregoing sheds some further light on the role of the commission, the state regulator. The OSC's position may best be understood as that of a broker and disseminator of information, whose ultimate destination is investors and the marketplace. The role of the state in securities regulation is not necessarily to be the repository of accounts, as the conventional model would suggest, but rather to *enable* the accountability of corporations and intermediaries to the market and investors generally.[3] Thus, with respect to corporations, the state can be considered as in part a facilitator of access to investment funds, for which accountability is a prerequisite, rather than an institution or set of institutions to whom accountability is owed, as a guarantee against untrammelled corporate power (Sunstein, 1990; Shearing, 1992b). Recognizing that, in securities markets, investors and the market might be more consequential repositories of accountability than the state regulator broadens our view of the possible entities to whom accounts can be rendered and who could be guarantors of accountability.

We have already pointed out that if institutions of government are not the only occupiers of the field of enforcing accountability, a possible alternative candidate is a self-regulatory organization. The existence of these organizations in the Ontario scheme of securities regulation removes the OSC's monopoly here, and it also opens up the possibility for contests among guarantors of accountability over who is to act as the funnel for information (Hancher and Moran, 1989: 275–6). A simple example was raised explicitly by the OSC's 1968 policy on timely disclosure. In the course of establishing its own policy, the commission pointed out that the TSE had a 'timely disclosure' policy 'substantially to the same effect.' Therefore, 'compliance with the requirements of the Exchange by companies whose securities are listed thereon will normally be viewed as compliance with the Commission's policy.' The implication of these other possibilities is that, if the focus is only on accountability to the state, we may miss the existence of, and possibilities for, significant exercises of accountability by other entities.

To sum up, such accountability as exists for the activities of corporations in this sphere is most likely not an end in itself, but imposed and complied with for reasons to do with the economic health of the organization and the market. In this sense, the phenomenon of accountability is facilitative rather than restraining. Because of this, the most effective guarantor of that accountability may not necessarily be an institution of the state, conventionally understood, but a variety of non-state organizations and individuals. Now, in the same way that there may be a contest over guarantors of accountability, there has also been in this field an ongoing struggle over the substance of that accountability. This issue is the subject of the next section.

Accountability as Contested Space

It has been mentioned already that one of the most controversial features of the reform of the 1966 act during the 1970s, culminating in the passage of the 1978 Securities Act (c. 47), was the manner of regulating 'timely disclosure' by corporations of relevant information not included in their most recent periodic reports. The significance of this issue revolved around the growing importance attached to up-to-date information in making investment decisions. The matter had, as we have seen, first been dealt with by the OSC in its 1968 policy concerning timely disclosure. It is proposed to examine in some detail this reform debate, involving a succession of bills, concerning how to ensure timely disclosure of material information. As a case study of regulatory reform, not only does it provide illumination of the role of the interests subject to regulation in the reform process (Condon, 1992), but more particularly, the debate was clearly very consequential for the extent of corporate accountability. Interestingly, this language is conspicuous by its absence in the arguments of participants. The debate is also significant in its demonstration of the variation possible in the use of disclosure of information as a strategy of accountability and the ambiguity that characterizes attempts to render corporations accountable by means of legal requirements in statutes or policies. These ambiguities revolved around the timing, content, manner, and guarantors of disclosure of information. Finally, the prominent role of interest groups in the debate, characterized as it was by the production of several versions of the statute, illustrates the potential for regulated entities to proactively shape the accountability to which they are subject (McBarnet and Whelan, 1991; Hancher and Moran, 1989).

BEGINNINGS

The OSC's merger report (Ontario Securities Commission, 1970), completed three years after enactment of the 1966 statute, is usually credited as the public beginning of the process of reform that led to the 1978 Securities Act. Focusing as it did on the problems of private placements[4] and take-overs, the merger report had little to say on the subject of timely disclosure, save a recommendation that the OSC's policy of timely disclosure be replaced by a system of 'timely amendments' to a document to be called a cornerstone prospectus. The major difference from the then-existing policy was that timely amendments would be required 'essentially at or immediately following' (OSC, 1970: par. 2.29) the relevant event or change, rather than before the fact.

The importance of the OSC's role in legislative change is indicated by the fact that it was responsible for drafting several versions of the statute, of which there were six in the course of the decade. Bill 154, presented to the legislature in 1972, took the recommendation in the merger study a step further by defining the circumstances in which an amendment to a cornerstone prospectus would be required. It was established by Section 66 of the bill that this would be necessary 'where a material change occurs in the affairs of a reporting issuer, that makes untrue or misleading any statement of a material fact in a cornerstone prospectus.' The attempt in Bill 154 to give content to the concept of a 'material change,' around which debate over the meaning of timely disclosure now revolved, was attacked by prominent interests who responded to its appearance.

The TSE disagreed that the subjective requirement that a material change make 'untrue or misleading' the material facts in a cornerstone prospectus would result in disclosure of all appropriate information. This was because there 'could be new developments in a company's affairs which would be of the greatest significance to investors but which might not have any direct relation to facts stated in the company's cornerstone statement.' Instead the TSE brief, in response to the circulation of Bill 154, recommended that a material change be considered to be any 'transaction or occurrence in the affairs of the company which may reasonably be expected to have a material effect on the market price of any class of securities of the company' (Toronto Stock Exchange, 1973: 10–12).

We shall see in a moment to what extent the TSE was successful in arguing that only developments *internal* to a company, which might reasonably affect the market *price* for its shares, should be considered material changes. Overall, however, the TSE's contribution lay in its successful argument for the substitution of more apparently 'objective' tests for determining what changes were material, and to be accounted for, for the more nebulous 'untrue or misleading' standard. All definitions of a possible content for the concept of material change, however, included the discretionary criterion of 'reasonableness.' It is also noteworthy, in view of the argument in the previous section, that the exchange argued on the terrain of what information was significant for investors (Baillie, 1973: 360). Linked to this was the TSE's reliance on market processes for guaranteeing disclosure rather than the preparation of unwieldy documents, reviewed by the OSC. Thus, the TSE argued that the cornerstone statement would be of 'limited benefit' as a source of current information for investors, and that the information provided by a combination of timely disclosure and the market would be considerably more effective (TSE, 1973: 10–11). Of course, reliance on non-state, market processes to provide for the accountability of corporations for material developments in their activities might well have had the effect of bolstering the TSE's position as an alternative guarantor of order, because it was more closely involved in the operation of the market. The same result might accrue, indirectly, from acceptance of its alternative definition of a material change.

The main thrust of the Canadian Manufacturers Association's (CMA) response to Bill 154 was a strong stance against the merger report's proposal for a continuously updated cornerstone statement. Consistent with this position, it proposed that continuous reporting should not be required concerning any matters 'going beyond what is presently required by the TSE policy on timely disclosure,' which as we have seen, involved a 'market impact' test of materiality (Emerson, 1973: 460–1).

WHAT IS MATERIAL?

When Bill 75 was published in 1974, the 'untrue or misleading' criterion for the disclosure of a material change had vanished in favour of a definition, as stated in Section 1(1)20, consisting of 'a fact or change that might reasonably be expected to have a significant effect on the market *value* of a security.' In subsisting 'market value' for 'market price' as the relevant test, the formulation in Bill 75 was not at one with the TSE's recommendation (Alboini, 1980: 534). Even more significantly, both the TSE proposal *and* the original OSC policy had limited material changes to those 'in the affairs of a company' which could affect price (or value, in the case of the OSC). The absence in the formulation in Bill 75 of the requirement that the relevant changes be *internal* to the company broadened considerably the scope of events or facts that companies would be required to disclose.

Not surprisingly, the TSE responded negatively to these formulations in Bill 75 concerning 'market value' and external effects. In its written brief, the exchange repeated its argument that these interpretations of the content of 'material change' were unduly broad, with price being a 'more objective and determinable test' of whether an event has a 'significant effect' than that of value (TSE, 1974). The IDA, while agreeing that timely disclosure and dissemination of material facts were 'important factors in the maintenance of efficient financial markets,' interpreted the requirement in Section 73 for 'plain and accurate disclosure' of material changes as invoking a 'continuing burden of prospectus disclosure' amounting to the maintenance of an ongoing prospectus. The IDA alleged that the 'cost of this to a large multinational company, or relative to its resources, even to a junior company, will be a serious impediment to such companies becoming reporting issuers' (Investment Dealers Association, 1974).

As well as the question of the content of material changes, the TSE and IDA identified a problem concerning the *timing* of disclosures. This problem centred around the risk that premature disclosure 'could negate a business opportunity.' The TSE's position was that 'corporate management must be entitled to withhold information if disclosure would be unduly detrimental to the interests of the issuer,' even if the absence of information was not in the short-term (as opposed to long-term) interests of shareholders. In fact Section 73(3) of the bill made provision for this scenario, requiring that in such a situation a 'confidential report' giving the information and reasons for non-disclosure be delivered to the OSC. Both the TSE and IDA were against this, because there was no obligation on the agency to keep the matter confidential and internal agency procedures might pose a risk for issuers of improper disclosure. Furthermore, the TSE argued, 'administrative bodies should not be put in a position of having to re-evaluate this managerial function some time after events have occurred.' The TSE's argument was, therefore, that the extent of accountability should be governed by the business interests of the corporation, which were to be within the competence of the corporation itself to identify. Similarly, its argument for a limited role for the state in situations of confidential information was an attempt to curtail levels of business accountability to government.

The response of Bill 98, in 1975, to these submissions on issues such as the definition of material changes and the timing of disclosure, was mixed. The external feature of the definition (that is, that it was not limited to changes *in* the affairs of the company) was maintained. However, the relevant 'significant effect' was now, in accordance with the TSE submission, declared to be on the 'market price' rather than the 'market value' of the securities. With respect to *when* an issuer would be free from the obligation to make disclosures of material change, the TSE's argument that withholding information should be possible in certain circumstances appeared to carry some weight. Section 73(3) of Bill 75 had read: 'Where in the opinion of the reporting issuer the disclosure required by subsections 1 and 2 would be unduly detrimental to the interests of the reporting issuer without significant benefit to its present or prospective security holders, it shall forthwith deliver to the Commission the report required under subsection 2 marked "confidential" together with written reasons for non-disclosure.'

In Bill 98, the phrase 'without significant benefit to its present or prospective shareholders' was omitted, thus expanding the possibilities for companies to withhold on the grounds of detriment to the issuer, to include those occasions where the information *would* be of 'significant benefit' to the shareholders. However, the bill did retain the obligation, which had not met with the favour of the IDA and TSE, that where information was being withheld, a confidential report accompanied by reasons had to be submitted to the OSC. Bray (1975: 267), vice-chair of the OSC, explained this as follows:

The draftsman's position is that every material fact ought to be disclosed on a timely basis to the public or in the long term unless some extraordinary circumstances exist. Trading in the securities of that issuer ought to be halted until such time as the issuer finds it possible to make disclosure. There is no question but that these provisions are designed to afford the Commission the opportunity of considering the facts and making the decision as to whether trading ought to be halted. The subsequent 10 day reports are aimed at urging the issuer to make disclosure. The discretion as to whether there should be disclosure is in the issuer but the discretion to determine whether trading should continue is in the Commission ... In Bill 98, the responsibility of the reporting issuer is to investors as well as to shareholders. Its obligations is [sic] to furnish this information to the Commission for the benefit of prospective purchasers of its securities in the secondary markets as well as holders of the securities.

Thus, the agency's aim continued to be to take into account the interests of 'prospective security holders' despite the removal of this phrase from Section 73(3). These remarks by Bray lend support to two issues already raised. The first is a reiteration of the argument made in the previous section that the role of the state agency here is to facilitate corporate accountability to investors and the market. Second, this passage shows us the analytical distinction between control and accountability at work. While accountability encompasses the decision, whether made by the corporation or the OSC, concerning whether material must be disclosed, the resource available to the OSC to halt trading in the shares if dissatisfied with the level of accountability is clearly an opportunity to exercise control over the issuer corporation.

FINAL DEFINITIONAL BATTLES: THE STANDING COMMITTEE ON THE
ADMINISTRATION OF JUSTICE

A gap of some two years occurred between the death of Bill 98 and the
introduction of the first version of Bill 7 into the Ontario legislature in
February 1978. This bill was characterized by the innovation of separate
definitions for a material fact and a material change. The latter encompassed a 'change in the business or operations of the issuer' that did or
could reasonably be expected to affect market price. This was the formulation supported by the TSE in its briefs on Bills 154 and 75 and was
a narrowing of the terms of Bill 98. By the time Bill 7 was presented for
second reading in April 1978, a series of further amendments had been
made, which were said to have resulted from 'many meetings' held, at
the request of the minister, by the chair and vice-chair of the OSC with
'interested parties' to discuss their comments on the draft. One significant amendment was a further revised definition of a material change
that was now formulated, apparently in the interests of 'clarity and
precision', as follows: ' "Material change" where used in relation to the
affairs of an issuer means a change in the business, operations or capital
of the issuer that would reasonably be expected to have a significant
effect on the market price or value of any of the securities of the issuer
and includes a decision to implement such a change made by the board
of directors of the issuer, or by senior management of the issuer who
believe that confirmation of the decision by the board of directors is
probable.'

In providing explicitly that changes in corporate capitalization would
fulfil the characteristics of a material change, this formulation was a
more inclusive version than previous ones. Dispute over whether the
relevant effect should more appropriately be on the market value or the
market price of the issuer's securities was solved by including both
alternatives in the amended definition. Similarly, the future-oriented
component of the formulation was presumably intended to broaden the
scope of the disclosure requirement in the interests of enhanced knowledge by investors. However, as we shall see, the definition did not
appease those to be affected by the requirements.

After the second reading, Bill 7 went before the Legislature's Standing
Committee on the Adminstration of Justice, giving interest groups a last
chance to influence the terms of the bill. The question of the interpretation of a material change generated considerable dispute at this committee stage. The most negative response came from a brief submitted

jointly by a group of seven major Canadian corporations (Algoma Steel, Inco, MacMillan Bloedel, Molson, Noranda, SteelCo, and TransCanada Pipelines). The concept of material change in the bill was alleged by this group to be very vague, and its brief (hereinafter referred to as the joint brief) proposed that a concept of 'material event,' that is, 'discrete events specific to an issuer' be substituted for the former. Furthermore, the test of materiality should be those events that a 'businessman assesses as likely to have a significant effect on the *business* or *assets* of his company,' rather than on the price or value of company securities, since the latter was information he was less likely to know (Algoma et al., 1978). In making a distinction between business and financial knowledge, the brief was both proposing that power should reside in businesspeople to make the appropriate judgments about what to disclose, and assuming that 'business knowledge' would be a more restrictive formulation than the one in the legislation. In terms of accountability, this is an argument that businesspeople should only be accountable for information relating to the internal business of the company, and that it should be within their own judgment to decide on an ongoing basis the limits of this accountability.

Apart from adverting to its own role as 'perhaps the leader in Canada in the development of timely disclosure requirements,' the TSE's statement before the Standing Committee on the Administration of Justice focused on the 'difficulties raised in determining when a material change has occurred.' In contrast to its position on Bill 75, which criticized the discretionary aspects of disclosure of material change, with particular reference to the OSC's reaction to the decision to keep certain information confidential, it now 'welcomed ... discussions with officials of and counsel to public companies to assist in ensuring that disclosure is made fairly and properly.' In addition, the exchange professed itself 'certain that the Commission will use its powers wisely and judiciously to ensure that these problems do not become so burdensome that the commercial world is unable to function.' These remarks serve both to call attention to the OSC's facilitative, as opposed to restraining, role in producing corporate accountability *and* to promote the TSE's own role as an alternative guarantor of that accountability.

The joint brief's advocacy of the business judgment test was disputed by the OSC, in its appearance before the committee. As Bray, the vice-chair, put it, 'I know the argument on the other side is that businessmen are better able to make business judgments but the whole thrust of the Act is a market-oriented Act and market price is the thing that really affects the judgment of investors as opposed to the business judgments which must, of course, sway the judgment of the management of the company' (Law Society of Upper Canada, 1978: 206). This comment is interesting for its reiteration that accountability to *investors* by the provision of information affecting the market price was the ultimate objective of the requirements for disclosure of material changes. Baillie, the chair of the OSC, also argued for the effect on market price as the criterion, on the basis of the purposes of other provisions within the securities statute. Thus, with respect to the requirement that a corporation not disclose confidential information before there is general disclosure to the marketplace, 'it seems to me appropriate for government to lay down the rule that information which ... is going to affect the market price of securities should be kept strictly confidential' and 'that kind of constraint should not be imposed except as to information that will affect the market.'

From the point of view of accountability, one of the interesting features of the reaction to the joint brief's proposal of a 'business judgment' approach to giving content to material change was the lack of certainty about whether this test would be more or less onerous for corporate issuers. Clearly, Algoma *et al.* suggested it in the belief that it was a more restricted obligation to provide accounts. Sometime after these corporations had presented their views, the New Democratic Party (NDP) spokesperson on the standing committee, James Renwick, moved an amendment to the definition of material change in the bill. His proposed definition was 'material change, where used in relation to the affairs of an issuer means (a) a change in the business operations or capital of the issuer that would reasonably be expected to have a significant effect thereon, or (b) a decision to implement such a change made by the board of directors of the issuer or by senior management of the issuer who believe that confirmation of the decision by the board of directors is probable.' Thus, the relevant significant effect was to be on 'the business operations or capital of the issuer' rather than on the market price or value. The similarity of this wording to that of the proposals in the joint brief did not go unnoticed by the rest of the participants in the debate. Although there is some irony in the possibility of an alliance between seven major Canadian industrial corporations and the NDP on this issue, what is significant is that the *meaning* attributed to the substantially similar proposal by the two sets of participants was very different.

Renwick understood a definition of material change that focused its significant effect on market price to be a restrictive one and argued that 'there are many changes ... which have a significant effect on the business operations or capital of the issuer but do not necessarily have an effect on market price or value ... but are of interest to a person who is an investor in or intending to invest in that company.' He went on, 'there are many areas in which, for the purpose of the principle of disclosure and timely disclosure, that the more an investor knows the better off he is with respect to these matters.' Thus, Renwick's concern, once again, was to identify an appropriate level of accountability to investors by means of the material change requirements.

Renwick's amendment provoked opposition from the Board of Trade, the Canadian Bankers' Association, and various members of the standing committee, including the minister himself. Arguments here centred on the opposition erected between effects on business operations and effects on market price. The conclusion was drawn that, because the purpose of securities legislation was to deal with the market place and its effect on the investor, the material changes that were relevant were those that affected the market. Thus, the minister pointed out that the issue was not which possibility provided a higher or lower threshold of disclosure, but the 'key thing is that the ones [material changes] that should be caught in all cases are ones that affect the market.' Renwick responded by arguing that 'continuous disclosure and timely disclosure and the evergreen prospectus is very, very important and is the guts of all progressive securities legislation.' He argued that his amendment (requiring disclosure if there was a significant effect on the business or operations of the issuer) was necessary 'if we want ... to make a significant step toward further protection of the investing public.'

As for the ultimate resolution of this controversy, comments by Baillie, chair of the OSC, to the Law Society Panel on Securities Legislation (Law Society of Upper Canada, 1978: 19) are revealing:

The reason we bogged down for five or six weeks on the definition of material change is because there was a motion ... jointly sponsored by the two minority parties, for a change in the definition, ... that would in our judgment have significantly expanded the scope of the items caught by that definition. And sooner than have that more onerous approach put into the Bill we hung in for five or six weeks and finally that approach was defeated yesterday in a vote. So I think you can take it that we are aware of the difficulties that are involved for business, or could be involved, in compliance with unduly onerous requirements in this Act.

However, before the Standing Committee on the Administration of Justice itself, Baillie argued that it was 'inappropriate to analyse the issue on the basis of whether more or less would be heard about the internal affairs of a corporation.' This was because the OSC would supplement the statutory obligation with 'continuous encouragement on a policy basis for corporations to make wider information available.' Renwick's amendment was ultimately unsuccessful, so the version of the definition of material change enacted into law was that inserted before the second reading of Bill 7.

Undoubtedly, the reform debate we have described in some detail raises a number of issues that would be of interest from the point of view of conventional scholarship on accountability. Is there evidence here of the OSC, the government agency, having been 'captured' by its dominant constituents? Is it inappropriate from the point of view of accountability for the OSC to expand statutory provisions by means of policy statements, as Baillie suggests? However, this debate can be seen to tell us something more fundamental about the phenomenon of accountability. To say that accountability is to be found in routine corporate practices is not by any means to say that there is no dispute over the scope of that accountability.

There seems no doubt that corporate organizations, whether characterized as public or private, mobilized around this debate because of its repercussions for the situation of corporate accountability. Those who were to be subject to requirements for accountability were proactive in shaping its contours. While we will not here attempt an evaluation of which organizations were 'winners' or 'losers' with respect to the ultimate outcome, the point is that the nature and scope of corporate accountability here was available for prolonged negotiation and renegotiation. The shifting terrain of the debate, from concern with market price or market value as the relevant 'triggers' for accountability, to the distinction between financial and business knowledge, was the product of a number of uncertainties and competing interpretations. These included uncertainty about the information that would be useful for investors, uncertainty about the abilities of management to provide useful information, and uncertainty about the consequences of particular definitions of material change for the content and level of accountability produced. One matter about which there was little uncertainty was that the ultimate destination of the information accounted for was investors and the market, rather than the government agency itself. However, an important feature of the debate concerned who or what would ultimately facilitate the provision of that information; the market, a state agency, or a hybrid self-regulatory organization.

The other area of dispute, that of what kind of knowledge or information was to be accounted for, is of great significance for conclusions about the role of law and legal rules in accountability. The conventional view is that legal rules operate as a check on, and an antidote to, discretionary powers. However, this case study reveals that the attempt to formulate legal rules, such as 'what is a material change?' is riven with ambiguity and the possibility of multiple interpretations. Different formulations of the definition would produce different results for the substance of accountability and the *same* formulation could be interpreted in diverse ways to equally produce different results. Legal rules, far from producing a definitive substance of accountability, may rather operate to provide room to manoeuvre for those subject to the requirements and make possible a continuously ambiguous and contested accountability.

Conclusion

Corporate accountability in securities markets is typically not problem-driven, but embedded in routine practice. The information provided by corporations about their activities serves a number of functions, and the usual motivation for imposing accountability – that of the restraint of power – is not accorded a very high profile. As a result of the various purposes served by providing information, corporate disclosure is not predominantly aimed at the government agency, the OSC, but beyond it, to investors and the market. Accountability in securities markets is given content through the dynamic interaction between regulators and regulated organizations and, because of the open-textured nature of legal concepts, is subject to significant shifts in the meaning of the requirements imposed. Disputes over the appropriate content of corporate accountability in securities markets take place on the terrain of the nature and purpose of securities law generally, as opposed to, for example, the opportunities for restraint of corporate power. One lesson to be learned from this is the importance of *context* in finding and evaluating mechanisms of accountability, since the scope, attributes, and form of accountability may vary in different social and legal locations. In other words, in both searching out and making recommendations about the nature of accountability in various social and economic locations, we should not be bound to existing forms of accountability that are, after all, institutionally and historically specific. We have recounted how the characteristics traditionally associated with accountability in criminal justice developed historically, and how these characteristics are deficient in terms of framing the 'real world' of accountability in Ontario securities markets, because they work largely to render that accountability invisible. The accountability we have discovered is more partial, elusive, and ambiguous than can be encompassed in the traditional model, with its focus on clear lines of hierarchical authority, explicit grants of discretion, and incident-driven triggers for accountability.

For those who see merit in the arguments of this essay, there are a range of possible responses. One is to engage in a more fine-grained analysis of the provisions for disclosure imposed on corporations by securities regulation, to make a determination of the adequacy of corporate accountability in this sphere. There is a lot of scope for such an analysis, whose first step is of course to recognize the requirements for disclosure *as* an opportunity for accountability. A variety of normative judgments could be made, for example, about the extent to which securities regulation should be about the restraint of corporate power for its own sake. On the issue of who or what is the appropriate guarantor of accountability, the respective roles of the state, SROs, and the market need to be assessed, bearing in mind that the issue of who is to guarantee or enforce accountability cannot be separated from the *purpose* of that accountability. A scheme of accountability that is to be responsive to the needs of investors may need to distinguish among different kinds of investors, in terms of their differential access to resources and expertise. Allied to this set of issues is the possibility of taking up the criticism of some commentators that shareholders and investors are not the only corporate constituency to whom information should be provided.

A more general response is to incorporate the assertions made here about different ways of seeing accountability in securities markets into such research in criminal justice generally. This is a more difficult task, in large part because of the point made earlier about the need to be sensitive to *context* in describing and evaluating that accountability. At the least, this essay is a plea for a more creative and fine-grained approach to the problem of accountability. This may involve seeing it in the context of other purposes served by information, which may require the involvement of a mix of public and private institutions in enforcing it, but which should not discount the need for sensitivity to the possibility of less hierarchical, more democratic, accountability exercised over powerful organizations, whether public or private, in all spheres of social and economic life.

Acknowledgement. I would like to thank the Centre for Socio-Legal Studies, University of Oxford, for its hospitality while this essay was written. Thanks are also due to the Laidlaw Foundation and the Solicitor-General of Canada, through its sustaining grant to the Centre of Criminology, University of Toronto, for their funding during the research stage.

Notes

1 Examples of controversial OSC policy here include its recently established Policy 9:1 dealing with related party transactions, and its requirement that issuers provide a management discussion and analysis document along with other periodic reporting documents (OSC Policy S.10). More generally, the advent of institutional investors as key players in securities markets creates new dimensions to issues of corporate accountability (Coffee, 1991), as does the recent debate about corporate responsibility to its non-shareholding, stakeholding constituencies.

2 These included actual or proposed changes in control of the company, actual or proposed acquisitions or dispositions of material assets, proposed take-overs, mergers, consolidations, amalgamations or reorganizations, material discoveries, changes or developments in the company's resources, technology, products or contracts that could materially affect the earnings of the company upwards or downwards, indicated changes in earnings upwards or downwards of more than recent average size, and changes in dividends. See *OSCB*, September 1968: 192–3.

3 This should not be taken as meaning that the 'market' and 'investors generally' are necessarily interchangeable concepts. The idea of the market is that all participants get the same information at the same time, and the market is often understood as a surrogate for investors generally, but the reality may be that those with most resources to expend will get the information more quickly. The importance of this point is reinforced by the growing presence of institutional investors in the market-place (Coffee, 1991).

4 Under securities legislation, it is possible to avoid the disclosure requirements occasioned by the public sale of securities by offering the securities to particular investors (such as financial institutions) or offering them by means of transactions of more than a particular price.

Canadian Public Inquiries and Accountability

KENT ROACH

> I am the Royal Commission of Kissing,
> Appointed by Gladstone in '74;
> The rest of my colleagues are buried or missing;
> Our Minutes were lost in the last Great War.
> But still I'm a Royal Commission,
> My task I intend to see through,
> Though I know, as an old politician,
> Not much will be done if I do.
> A.P. Herbert 'Pageant of Parliament' in *Mild and Bitter* (1936)

The idea that public inquiries can be effective instruments of accountability may seem implausible. The appointment of a public inquiry is often a means of deferring a political problem while the inquiry takes a number of years to hold public hearings and research and write its report. Although the release of a report may focus public attention on a problem, there is no guarantee that the inquiry's proposals will be implemented. Inquiries have no formal powers to issue sanctions and no continuing role in investigating the subjects they examine. In responding to past events, prosecutions to impose penal, regulatory, or civil sanctions seem more effective in bringing home tangible consequences to those who should be made accountable for their actions. In terms of regulating future events, bureaucratic and legislative structures seem better able to influence the consciousness and behaviour of officials who should be held accountable for their actions.

This essay will explore what is distinctive and valuable about the accountability that is promoted by public inquiries. The focus will be on the relationship between the institutional characteristics of public inquiries and the type of accountability they promote. Public inquiries are a hybrid of judicial, executive, and legislative institutions, and it will be argued that their unique institutional features allow them to hold individuals and especially organizations and society accountable in ways that courts, administrators, and legislatures cannot.

First, I will outline three different processes of accountability and suggest how the institutional features of public inquiries may allow them to hold individuals, organizations, and society accountable for the events being investigated. Second, I will test the existence of these forms of accountability by examining three recent Canadian public inquiries appointed in response to concerns about the behaviour of actors in the criminal process: an inquiry appointed to investigate suspected illegalities by the Royal Canadian Mounted Police (RCMP; Canada, Commission of Inquiry Concerning Certain Activities of the RCMP, hereafter McDonald Commission, 1981a, b), an inquiry to examine the wrongful conviction of Donald Marshall Jr (Nova Scotia, Royal Commission on the Donald Marshall, Jr Prosecution, hereafter Marshall Commission, 1989), and an inquiry to examine the relationship between the administration of justice and Aboriginal people (Manitoba, Public inquiry into the Administration of Justice and Aboriginal people, hereafter Aboriginal Justice Inquiry or AJI, 1991a, b).[1] Finally, I will offer some thoughts about the future of public inquiries in Canada.

At present, the ability of public inquiries to investigate suspected wrongdoing is being challenged as unfair to the individuals investigated (Ontario, Law Reform Commission, 1992; Alberta, Law Reform Institute, 1992). At the same time, however, criticisms are heard that inquiries do not punish wrongdoers sufficiently and are an ineffective policy response to wrongdoing. I will suggest that understanding the distinctive ability of inquiries to hold organizations and society accountable helps to resolve these two lines of criticism. Moreover, it indicates where public inquiries have the potential to make important and unique contributions to the supervision of actors in the criminal process.

Three Processes of Accountability

Because accountability is an elusive phenomenon, it is helpful to attempt to define different types of accountability. Literal accountability refers to a process in which individuals are forced to account for their actions. Organizational accountability refers to a process where organizations are called to account for events and policy failures. Finally, social accountability refers to a complex process that depends on social recognition of the problem being investigated and subsequent demands by the interested public that individuals, organizations and society account for their response to the problem.

LITERAL ACCOUNTABILITY

The most obvious form of accountability occurs when a body with legal powers compels individuals to provide an account of their actions. Stenning has stressed literal accountability by arguing that 'the key element of accountability is a requirement to give an account' (this volume). Public inquiries have long had legal powers to compel individuals to testify and produce relevant evidence, but these powers have become more controversial with the growing concern that people suspected of wrongdoing should not be forced to incriminate themselves.

In 1176 the first public inquiry into the administration of government was held with the Inquest of Sheriffs. Henry II commissioned barons to take evidence under oath concerning suspected misconduct in collecting taxes and tributes. The inquest's royal commission stated that the sheriffs must attend and 'shall take an oath ... that they will speak the truth' and that the suspects should cooperate so that 'inquisition be made' about the sheriffs' conduct (Clokie and Robinson, 1969: 220). The sheriffs were thus forced to account for their actions when collecting taxes.

With the rise of Parliament and the common law courts, the powers of inquiries to compel testimony began to be criticized as 'inquisitorial,' 'continental,' and dangerous to the liberties of individuals (Dicey, 1885; Moore, 1913). Legal commentators from Coke to Dicey stressed that inquiries departed from the protections that individuals enjoyed under the common law, most importantly the right of a person accused of a crime to refuse to testify. A legal consensus developed in the mid-nineteenth century that subjects could not be compelled to testify by virtue of an inquiry's royal commission (Clokie and Robinson, 1969: 85–6). Soon after, however, legislation was introduced in Canada giving public inquiries statutory powers to compel testimony and the production of documents and other evidence (Alberta, Law Reform Commission, 1991: 3–4). Public inquiries continue to have powers to compel people suspected of wrongdoing to testify and account for their activities. Although partial abolition of these powers has been recommended (Canada, Law Reform Commission, or LRC, 1977; Ontario, LRC, 1992), recalcitrant witnesses can still be punished or even indefinitely detained until they answer an inquiry's questions or produce relevant evidence.

The legal powers that public inquiries have to require people to account under oath for their actions should not be underestimated. Anyone with evidence relevant to the mandate of an inquiry can be compelled to testify and produce evidence. They need not be presented with a formal charge or accusation. Even if coercive legal powers are not exercised, their existence may encourage individuals to cooperate with an inquiry when they might not otherwise answer questions (Ontario, LRC, 1992: 190).

Despite the importance of the legal power to call individuals to give accounts, a central argument of this essay will be that this literal, legalistic, and individualistic form of accountability does not exhaust the accountability processes of public inquiries. Public inquiries can promote at least two other forms of accountability that are not as dependent on legal powers to force individuals to give accounts for their actions.

ORGANIZATIONAL ACCOUNTABILITY

Organizational accountability refers to a process whereby organizations are called to account for events and risk being held responsible for either their actions or inactions. Although organizations may be made accountable in part by compelling officials within them to explain their actions, the focus is not on holding the officials accountable as individuals for their actions. As Salter has noted, 'Government officials, departmental spokespeople, members of parliament and others who are not themselves 'on trial' can be brought before an inquiry and asked to account for their actions. Moreover, the structure of decision-making within which they function can also be introduced as pertinent evidence' (1990: 174–5). She concludes that 'in most public inquiries about 'wrongdoing,' the factors that encourage 'wrongdoing' are as important as the conduct of the individuals involved' (ibid.: 186).

The literal act of calling officials to give accounts may not be necessary to hold organizations accountable for their policy failures. Research into organizational structures and direct observation of organizational behaviour can play an important role in assessing how organizations carry out their mandate. If this research is carried out by competent and independent people, it may be more effective than the 'account ability' (Ericson, 1981a) of officials to explain and justify their actions. Because inquiries are not bound by restrictive rules governing the admissibility of evidence, they are in a position to generate evidence by commissioning research into organizational structures. Most major Canadian inquiries have researchers prepare studies that are written in part to influence the conclusions of the commissioners (Cairns, 1990) and can incorporate radical aspects of academic and social debate (Salter, 1990).

Public inquiries also have the ability to research organizational and social problems because they are not subject to the initiation and control of parties to a dispute.[2] The state, by exercising its discretion to appoint a public inquiry, mandates a problem to be examined and the official investigation cannot be short-circuited by a settlement or plea bargain between the affected interests. Some individuals may be granted rights to respond to allegations by calling evidence and cross-examining witnesses as if they were in court. Nevertheless, public inquiries remain inquisitorial institutions, set in motion by the state to investigate a specified matter. They are more concerned with the development of state policy than with resolving disputes between parties (Damaska, 1986: 123).

Although public inquiries are often called on to make findings of fact and evaluative conclusions about past events, they do not need to adjudicate in the sense of applying pre-existing standards or expressing their conclusions in the binary form of verdicts of liability (Macdonald, 1980). In fact, inquiries in Canada are often instructed not to express any conclusion of civil or criminal liability and federal jurisdiction over criminal law and procedure precludes them from making such findings (*Re Nelles and Grange* [1984]). Although most legal theorists accept that courts make law when faced with difficult cases, a public inquiry has a greater capacity to engage in quasi-legislative activity by openly articulating new standards of proper conduct and applying them to past events. Such departures from adjudicative standards may not seem fair to individuals who are criticized, but they may help stimulate organizational reform.

Public inquiries differ from both legislatures and courts in the sense that they only make recommendations and do not have the power or the responsibility to implement their decisions. For example, a finding of misconduct by an inquiry does not necessarily lead to the imposition of formal sanctions. Likewise, reform proposals do not necessarily have to be expressed in a legislative format or be acceptable to the government. They can be designed to stimulate public debate (Le Dain, 1973).

Some courts, mainly in the United States and India, have attempted institutional reform litigation, which places custodial institutions and the police on trial for their organizational failures (Chayes, 1976; Roach, 1994a: ch. 13). This form of litigation encounters arguments that the judiciary is not competent because it is bound by adversarial and adjudicative standards, which limit its ability to investigate organizational problems (Horowitz, 1977). In any event, most courts continue to put individuals, not organizations, on trial. They stress individual responsibility for wrongs and not the structural shortcomings of institutions, even if only organizational reform can prevent similar wrongs in the future (Roach, 1991). Robardet has commented that courts see events as 'the outcome of a linear process' that enables them 'to identify who is the responsible actor of an act.' This 'who-done-it' form of analysis, however, 'detracts ... from the attention that must be paid to interrelations between actions and actors within complex organization ... [it] means assuming that an act always has an identifiable author, rather than being primarily the product of the activity of an organization or the product of a complex process' (Robardet, 1990: 125).

When courts rely on adversarial presentation of evidence and apply pre-existing standards of legal liability to discrete events, they often engage in an individualistic form of analysis. In contrast, public inquiries may be more inclined to accept organizational and sociological explanations of events because they are able to conduct their own investigation and form their own standards of proper conduct. There is, of course, no iron law of institutional determinism. It is possible for inquiries to be drawn to individualistic and legalistic analysis (Wells, 1991) and for courts to engage in organizational and sociological analysis (Chayes, 1976). Nevertheless, such behaviour departs from the norm and is not encouraged by the structure of each institution.

SOCIAL ACCOUNTABILITY

This process of accountability does not rely on legal powers to call individuals to account or an official assessment of organizational behaviour. Stenning (in this volume) identifies 'moral accountability' as perceptions by officials that they are 'obligated by pressures from interest groups, the media or the public generally, to give accounts.' He is sceptical whether these perceptions, which are not based on formal legal obligations, 'can be regarded as accountability in the usually accepted sense of the word.' They may simply be an opportunity for officials to engage in public relations and control their own agenda. Although moral or social accountability is the most intangible of the accountability processes, I will suggest that public inquiries can contribute to a process of attitudinal change in which the interested public begins to demand answers about officially recognized problems. Individuals and organizations that may not be legally compelled to account for themselves may nevertheless feel obligated by pressures generated by the inquiry to be prepared to give an account of their actions or inactions in responding to an identified problem. This form of accountability is especially important because it can affect perceptions and behaviour long after the inquiry has ended.

Le Dain has identified this social accountability process as the 'social function' of a public inquiry. He argues that 'there is much more than law and governmental action involved in the social response to a problem' and that inquiries can have 'an effect on perceptions, attitudes and behaviour' (1973: 85). The term 'social accountability' emphasizes that it is the interested public and not an official body with legal powers that is perceived as demanding an account. The immediate sanction is not a legal one but rather the anxiety and embarrassment caused by public criticism. Social accountability is related to non-carceral forms of social control that rely on perceptions of being under surveillance rather than the imposition of coercive legal sanctions (Foucault, 1979; Reiss, 1984a).

Although the social function of an inquiry does not rely on coercive state powers, it should not be underestimated as either a force for reform or oppression. Social accountability is not necessarily directed only at officials; it can make others in society believe they are vulnerable to give an account of their actions or attitudes. The McCarthy investigations into 'un-American activities' stand as an example of social accountability gone bad. These investigations departed from adjudicative standards and held people accountable for the 'crime' of having unpopular political views.[3] The effects of McCarthyism were not limited to those who were subpoenaed to testify before the official inquiry and who attempted to explain their political beliefs to the committee. McCarthyism was so oppressive precisely because it spread beyond the official work of the inquiry and encouraged people in government, universities, labour unions, and the entertainment industry to hold themselves and others accountable for their political beliefs (Pells, 1985: 262).

Some institutional features of public inquiries lend themselves to the promotion of social accountability. A public inquiry's 'personnel, powers, procedures, mandate and goals may be tailored *ad hoc* to deal with almost any situation' (Macdonald, 1980: 370). Commissioners can be appointed because of their particular expertise or because they represent a group affected by the problem the inquiry investigates. Once appointed, they are not expected to be as impartial as judges in their deliberations. Influenced by informal consultation and research studies, they can play an advocacy role and attempt to legitimate perceptions that a structural problem exists and that there is a social obligation to respond. Because inquiries are temporary and act in an independent fashion, they are more unpredictable than the bureaucracy (Trebilcock et al., 1982: 37–50). In Canada public inquiries have at times adopted radical critiques of existing institutions and society (Salter, 1990). They have also promoted innovative and broad forms of public participation by conducting town hall meetings in remote communities and prisons.

SUMMARY

Public inquiries are unique institutions. They have inquisitorial powers to engage in state-mandated investigations like the executive, but they are not subject to the bureaucracy's hierarchical control and organizational interest. Like courts, they are independent bodies who examine past events, but they are not bound by the judiciary's obligation to adjudicate by applying pre-existing standards or to act in a passive manner within an adversarial system. The institutional features of inquiries give them the potential to make distinctive, but perhaps underappreciated, contributions to accountability.

I have made distinctions between literal, organizational, and social accountability, and it will be important in the discussion that follows to identify which process of accountability is being discussed. For example, the discretionary appointment of public inquiries by the cabinet would seem to be a major handicap to their ability to hold individuals accountable. A government that wished to avoid creating a body which, once appointed, could call officials into account could simply refuse to let the genie out of the bottle.[4]

Sustained public and political pressure to appoint an inquiry, however, may help lay the foundation for organizational and social accountability. Governments will not always appoint public inquiries, but when they do, they will officially confirm perceptions of structural problems. The act of appointing an inquiry may then begin a process of self-reflection and self-criticism that can exert influence long after the legal powers of the inquiry to compel accounts have been exhausted.

Three Inquiries and Their Processes of Accountability

Public inquiries have institutional features that can, in theory, promote literal, organizational, and social accountability for the problems they investigate. These observations will now be tested in light of the experience of three recent public inquiries held in Canada to investigate problems in the criminal process. I will examine the factors that led to the appointment of each inquiry, the procedures they adopted, and the response of other institutions such as courts. My purpose will be to link the institutional features of the inquiries to the types of accountability they promoted.

THE INQUIRY ON THE ACTIVITIES OF THE ROYAL CANADIAN MOUNTED POLICE

The existence of illegal activities by members of the RCMP first came to public attention through criminal proceedings. A former member of the force's security service testified in his 1976 trial that he had 'done worse things for the RCMP than plant bombs,' including a break-in to steal documents (Sawatsky, 1980: 279). This led to further investigations by the media and the police. Charges were subsequently laid against three police officers respecting a break-in to a union's office, and in 1977 the officers pleaded guilty and received an absolute discharge. The effect of the 1976 trial in promoting accountability was unusual. The accused could not have been compelled to testify, and the matters he mentioned were not legally relevant to the charge he faced. The entry of guilty pleas in 1977 was more typical of the limitations of the criminal trial as an instrument of accountability. Party control of the proceedings meant that there was no public examination of either the event or its context. The lenient sanction reflects a belief that the illegality was mitigated by its organizational context even though that context was not subject to public scrutiny.

These two criminal cases led to the appointment of a public inquiry by the Quebec government and parliamentary questions about ministerial knowledge about illegal activity. Some within the RCMP welcomed the appointment of a federal public inquiry. They believed it would benefit the force if the illegalities were not examined as isolated incidents in the criminal courts, but 'in the calmer atmosphere of a Commission of Inquiry' (Canada, McDonald Commission, 1981a: vol. 1; 10). They accurately predicted that at an inquiry, the force would have 'the time and the opportunity to present a broad detailed explanation of our operating procedures, properly set in historical context and illustrating an inadequate working mandate' (ibid.) They might not have expected, however, that the inquiry would take an organizational approach to wrongdoing and successfully propose that security intelligence activities be transferred from the force to a new civilian intelligence agency.

The federal public inquiry was appointed in July of 1977 to be chaired by David McDonald, a judge of the Alberta Court of Queen's Bench. From the start, the McDonald commission faced legal and political challenges that it was not independent from the government of the day. Matters were not helped when a court challenge based on allegations that the commissioners were biased because of ties to the governing party was rejected on the basis that a public inquiry need not be free from bias because it was only an advisory body that did not exercise quasi-judicial powers (*Re Copeland* [1978]). The commission made efforts to redeem its reputation for independence by insisting on public disclosure of most of its hearings and demanding access to Cabinet information (*Re Commission of Inquiry* [1979]). The independence of an inquiry from executive interference is essential to its credibility as a mechanism of accountability.

The commission's mandate had two sections: one charged with the investigation of wrongdoing and the other with broader policy issues. Much of the commission's activities and report reflected this two-track strategy. Most of the evidence about wrongdoing was heard in judicial-style hearings where witnesses were represented by counsel. The evidence collected in these hearings formed the basis for the commission's third report, which they described as 'essentially a catalogue of incidents,' some of which were not released because of a concern about fair trials in the future (Canada, McDonald Commission, 1981b: 2).

Although public attention was focused on the commission's formal hearings to determine the extent of wrongdoing, the bulk of its work was devoted to assessing the adequacy of the RCMP's policies and procedures and the legal and organizational framework of its security intelligence activities. The heart of the commission's report was its two-volume second report, which focused on general operating procedures, not specific incidents of wrongdoing. Its early chapters were devoted to what was referred to as 'institutionalized wrongdoing,' and the rest presented a detailed policy plan to govern security intelligence activities in the future. Although it made some reference to evidence revealed in the judicial-style hearings, much of the information about the RCMP as an institution came from the commission's research program. The commissioners reported that their visits to security operations gave them 'a sense of the organization that we would not otherwise have had' (ibid.: 1981a: 26) and that they had received 'important insights' from 'hearing the testimony of a large number of Force personnel, studying the Force's management and personnel systems, seeing at first hand the recruit training programme in Regina and studying the curriculum' (ibid.: 688–9). This approach to gathering information may help explain why the commission took an organizational view of the police misconduct it discovered. As Goldsmith has commented,

From the perspective of organizational analysis, the extent to which the commission delved into the traditions, structures and personnel practices of the RCMP, in its attempt to explain institutionalized disrespect for the Rule of Law and responsible government is interesting. The 'bad apple' theory of police deviance was largely jettisoned in favour of a consideration of the organizational and occupational characteristics of the RCMP and its members. For example, the Commission noted the RCMP's 'definite quality of insularity' and its evident difficulty in accepting and working with 'outsiders.' Indeed, the RCMP displayed a number of characteristics 'normally associated with a religious order,' the commission concluded. (Goldsmith, 1985: 42)

This organizational approach was reflected in the commission's central recommendation that a civilian intelligence agency replace the RCMP's security service.

Even though the commission's third report dealt with specific acts of wrongdoing, it also took an organizational approach to wrongdoing. The report started with exploring the knowledge ministers and senior officials had of illegal activities, rather than concentrating on the activities of field operatives. When an activity was examined, the commission addressed whether it was an independent act or one that was part of an accepted systemic practice. The commission was not bound by legal standards of liability and drew a distinction between unacceptable or improper activities and those 'not authorized by the law.' They noted,

'No body of jurisprudence exists to guide us in weighing the conduct of members when we are assessing 'acceptability' or 'propriety' apart from the commission of offenses. The fact of rebuke by a Commission of Inquiry may itself serve as a warning to the members and to other members in the future not to engage in such conduct' (Canada, Mc-Donald Commission, 1981b: 5–6). The report, both in its criticisms of specific members and its general comments about the RCMP, was intended to establish new standards of organizational accountability in the future.

There can be a tension between organizational accountability and attempts to control and punish the behaviour of individuals. The commission's investigation into the organizational failure of the security service hindered attempts to punish individual officers for wrongdoing. The four years the commission took to complete its work delayed the institution of criminal proceedings. Two days after the report was released, the government released two legal opinions, one from a retired judge of the Supreme Court of Canada, that disagreed with the commission's conclusion that some criminal offences had been committed. These opinions stressed that activities should only be prosecuted if they were specifically prohibited by law and criticized the commission's conclusions that the activities were illegal because they were not authorized by law.[5] When asked about his awareness of illegal activities, Prime Minister Trudeau argued that the differences between the legal opinions and the McDonald commission indicated that the RCMP was acting in a 'grey area of the law' and that whether there were illegalities could only be known 'the day [an officer] will be sentenced and he will have lost all his appeals' (*Globe and Mail*, 29 August 1981). Regardless of the merits of this debate (Mewett, 1981), it illustrates how a commission's conclusions that there have been illegal activities are vulnerable to charges that it did not apply legal standards in a criminal trial context. At the same time, the ability of a commission to declare improper what is not necessarily illegal may be effective in holding organizations accountable for wrongdoing.

The McDonald commission was more successful in assessing the organizational deficiencies of the RCMP than in holding individuals accountable for wrongs. Its organizational focus was criticized for excusing wrongful conduct by focusing on the larger context and making it more difficult to punish individual officers.[6] Nevertheless, the commission was successful in creating organizational responsibility for wrongdoing and advocating organizational change.

THE INQUIRY INTO THE PROSECUTION OF DONALD MARSHALL, JR

The appointment of a public inquiry to examine the wrongful conviction of Donald Marshall, Jr, can be related to the shortcomings of criminal and civil courts as instruments of accountability.

Concerns about the accuracy of Marshall's 1971 murder conviction arose in the early 1980s and in 1982 the minister of justice ordered the Nova Scotia Court of Appeal to consider the original conviction as if Marshall was taking a fresh appeal. In 1983 the court reversed Marshall's conviction after hearing evidence that Roy Ebsary, not Marshall, killed Sandy Seale. The Court of Appeal did not consider any of the factors that contributed to Marshall's wrongful conviction except to attempt in a controversial aside to blame Marshall for his own wrongful conviction (*R v Marshall* [1983]). The Marshall commission subsequently concluded that the 1983 reference should not have been heard as an appeal because such a procedure confined the court to the issue of 'guilt or innocence, and not to the factors leading to the wrongful conviction' (Nova Scotia, Marshall Commission, 1989: 115). The ability and inclination of any court to consider the broad range of individual, institutional, and systemic factors that contributed to Marshall's wrongful conviction is quite limited.[7] Courts will not investigate matters in the same manner as public inquiries, nor are they likely to make detailed reform proposals.

After his conviction was overturned, Marshall sued the Sydney police force that investigated his case. He abandoned this civil action because of the costs of litigation[8] and to facilitate negotiations with the government over compensation. The civil courts again failed as an instrument of accountability when the investigating officer in the Marshall case abandoned a defamation action against journalists who claimed he had intimidated witnesses (*Toronto Star*, 8 June 1986). It had been hoped that both civil suits would provide a vehicle for a public examination of the investigation which led to Marshall's wrongful conviction. A public inquiry was appointed in 1984, but was short-circuited when Marshall and the government agreed to settle for $270,000 in compensation. This inquiry functioned more as a civil proceeding controlled by the parties than as a public investigation. It was later discovered that a senior justice official wrote to the judge heading the 1984 inquiry in an attempt to convince him not to examine the police investigation (Nova Scotia, Marshall Commission, 1989: 135). Public inquiries must be free from executive interference, limited mandates, and party control if they are to be effective instruments of accountability.

In October of 1986, three judges from outside of Nova Scotia were appointed as a royal commission charged with examining the police investigation, prosecution, conviction, and sentencing of Marshall 'and such other related matters which the Commissioners consider relevant to the Inquiry.' In its organization and report, the Marshall commission took a two-track strategy remarkably similar to the one the McDonald commission had taken almost a decade earlier. Formal hearings were held to determine what went wrong in Marshall's case. The commission, under the heading of 'Factual Findings,' criticized the conduct of various named officials who had been involved in Marshall's case. They stressed individual responsibility and proceeded on the basis that the miscarriage of justice was an isolated event that would have been avoided if the actors in the criminal process had only acted competently and fairly. For example, the trial judge's legal error in restricting cross-examination of a witness who falsely claimed he saw Marshall stab Seale prevented the 'full and complete cross-examination' that the commission confidently concluded would have led to the witness recanting his false accusation and the jury acquitting Marshall (ibid.: 79). In short, the formal hearings were used to identify discrete acts that led to Marshall's wrongful conviction and the individuals responsible for them.

The second part of the commission's report dealt with the institutional and social context of Marshall's wrongful conviction. Much of the information contained in this part was obtained from the commission's research studies on policing, prosecutions, and the treatment of minorities in the Nova Scotia criminal justice system, and from a consultative conference. It stressed organizational and social responsibility for Marshall's wrongful treatment and made recommendations for the institutional reform of policing and prosecutions and the establishment of a Native criminal court.

The different orientation of the first and second parts of the report is reflected in the treatment of the role of racism in Marshall's wrongful conviction. The formal hearings were not an effective means to hold individuals and groups accountable for racist prejudices towards Marshall. As one of Marshall's lawyers admitted, 'Lawyers deal with facts. We rarely try to get at intangibles such as racism and the formal proceeding is not well suited to it' (*Globe and Mail*, 26 October 1987). Attempts to question Ebsary and a witness who testified against

Marshall at his 1971 trial about their views and assumptions about Aboriginal people were terminated by the commissioners as irrelevant (Wildsmith, 1991: 98–9). The commission also rejected attempts to make the town of Sydney accountable for its attitudes towards its Aboriginal and black minorities (Nova Scotia, Marshall Commission, 1989: 162). The commission did draw the conclusion that the behaviour of the investigating detective and Marshall's own lawyers had been adversely affected by Marshall's race. Bruce Wildsmith, who acted as counsel at the inquiry for the Union of Nova Scotia Indians, has stated that the reasons for the commission's conclusion about these individuals 'are sketchy,' and 'the record contained no evidence of outright, direct, deliberate racial bias or discrimination against Marshall' (Wildsmith, 1991: 108–9).

The commission's approach to racism differs in the second part of this report, which relies on the research studies and the consultative conference more than the testimony at the formal hearings. The focus is not so much on a search for whether individuals had racist attitudes, but on broader institutional and social factors that disadvantage racial minorities in the criminal process. Wildsmith has noted that in its factual findings the commission focused on 'individual racism' through inferences about human behaviour, while in the second part it 'addressed institutional and structural racism' through attention to 'statistics, the comments of others and the complaints and feelings of minorities' (Wildsmith, 1991: 106, 111, 113). He also reports that the commissioners were influenced by their informal visit to the Membertou Reserve where Marshall and his family lived.

The Marshall commission arguably was able to combine the tasks of holding individuals accountable as well as organizations and society. Through its hearings and in its factual findings, the commission criticized the behaviour of almost every person in the criminal process who handled the case. The police, the prosecutor, the defence counsel, the trial judge, and the Court of Appeal were all harshly criticized. To the extent that an inquiry can administer informal sanctions through public criticism, the Marshall commission exercised its powers to the fullest. Still, there were concerns about the lack of formal sanctions and calls for the investigating detective to be charged with the criminal offence of obstruction of justice (Kaiser, 1990). As happened with many cases the McDonald commission investigated, it was eventually decided that there was not enough evidence to commence such a criminal prosecution (*Globe and Mail*, 27 October 1990).

Unlike the McDonald commission, which was able to examine all relevant officials including the prime minister, the Marshall commission faced some legal obstacles in demanding that individuals give an account of their actions. Because of a Criminal Code provision (section 649) that makes it an offence for a juror to disclose any information about a jury's deliberation except in an investigation or trial for obstruction of justice, the jury of twelve white men who wrongfully convicted Marshall could not be called to explain their actions even though one juror had been reported as giving an overtly racist explanation for Marshall's conviction.[9] The jury was not even criticized in the commission's report. The commission did note that Marshall's discomfort and hesitancy in being questioned in English at his trial may have led the jury to regard his 'demeanour as a negative factor and that may have influenced the ultimate disposition' (Nova Scotia, Marshall Commission, 1989: 171). This finding, however, was only mentioned in the second, more policy-oriented part of the report.

The commission ordered the judges who sat on the 1983 reference to testify, but the judges refused and obtained a judgment from the Supreme Court of Canada that compelling them to testify would violate the constitutional principle of judicial independence (*MacKeigan v Hickman* [1989]). The court reasoned that judges must not fear that they will be required by the executive or legislative branches of government to explain and defend their judgments. This decision reflects a concern that accountability will lead to control and influence and a belief that judicial independence is more important than judicial accountability. Even though the judges could not be legally compelled to testify, the commission strongly criticized them for defending the system at Marshall's expense and ignoring evidence that suggested that the police, prosecutor, and trial judge were at fault. The chief justice was also criticized for allowing a judge who had been attorney general when Marshall was wrongfully convicted to sit on the 1983 reference (Nova Scotia, Marshall Commission, 1989: 124–7). The Canadian Judicial Council, a self-disciplinary body of judges, subsequently held a hearing and determined that there were not sufficient grounds to remove from office those of the judges who remained on the bench.[10] As was the case in the aftermath of the McDonald commission, institutions that had to implement sanctions had a much more difficult time condemning the behaviour of officials than did the public inquiries.

Moving away from the accountability of individuals, how did the Marshall commission encourage the collective accountability of organizations? The prosecution system was examined through two research studies and a comparison between the way the Marshall case was handled and two other cases involving prominent politicians. The commission concluded that the Nova Scotia attorney general's department had 'a deep-rooted and unwritten code that status is important, and that one is not blind to influence in enforcing the law' (ibid.: 220–1). Like the McDonald commission before it, the Marshall commission used its own research to make conclusions that individual acts of wrongdoing were rooted in organizational flaws and offered a detailed blueprint for organizational reform by recommending that prosecutions be supervised by a director of public prosecutions with significant functional independence from the elected attorney general. This reform proposal has been implemented, as was the McDonald commission's recommendation for the introduction of a civilian security intelligence agency.[11]

By researching and discussing racism, the Marshall commission sought to promote an increased sense of accountability in all levels of society for the treatment of racial minorities. It recommended that all participants in the criminal process be educated in race relations. Such education would invite people to question themselves about their attitudes and assumptions. It also encouraged institutions to re-evaluate their treatment of minority groups. In documenting the institution of an affirmative action program for indigenous black and Micmac students at Dalhousie Law School, Devlin and Mackay have commented: 'Although Dalhousie Law School was never identified as a player in the Donald Marshall Affair, it might perhaps be suggested that there was a sense of guilt by institutional association given that many of those that had been involved had been graduates of the school and somewhere along the way Dalhousie as an institution had failed to sensitize its students to some of the basics of professional responsibility' (1991: 301). This sense of 'guilt by institutional association' reflects social accountability. People who were not called to account at the inquiry nevertheless began to develop a sense of responsibility for the officially recognized problem of racism.

The Marshall commission, by following a similar two-track structure to that of the McDonald commission, was able to hold individuals and organizations responsible for the wrongful conviction of Marshall. Its formal hearings culminating in factual findings demonstrate, much more than those of the McDonald commission, the legal tradition of focusing on individual responsibility for events that could also be explained by organizational or sociological analysis. Research studies and informal consultations laid the foundation for the organizational and sociological analysis in the second half of the commission's report. This type of analysis was crucial in allowing the commission to produce recommendations for organizational change and to have the social function of raising awareness about the treatment of racial minorities in the criminal justice system.

THE MANITOBA ABORIGINAL JUSTICE INQUIRY

Two events led to the appointment of Manitoba's Aboriginal Justice Inquiry (AJI) in April of 1988. The first was controversy over the investigation of the 1971 death of an Aboriginal youth, Helen Betty Osborne, and subsequent prosecutions in which only one of four men implicated in her abduction and killing was convicted of murder. The second event was the shooting of an Aboriginal man, J.J. Harper, in an encounter with a member of the Winnipeg police force. An internal police board exonerated the officer within twenty-four hours of the shooting, holding that the gun had discharged accidentally as Harper was assaulting the officer. Soon after the inquiry was appointed, a judge presiding at an inquest also determined that the shooting was accidental.

As in the Marshall case, dissatisfaction with the ability of courts to hold individuals and organizations accountable for their behaviour produced a demand for the appointment of a public inquiry. At the same time, the inquiry was also appointed in response to perceptions of mistreatment of the province's Aboriginal people in all aspects of the criminal justice system. More than in Nova Scotia, the specific events were seen as symptoms of larger social and political problems. The inquiry was chaired by two judges, one of whom is one of the few Aboriginal people on the bench in Canada. It was given a broad mandate to investigate 'the relationship between the administration of justice and aboriginal peoples of Manitoba,' including the possibility of 'systemic discrimination against aboriginal people in the justice system' and 'whether there are alternative methods of dealing with aboriginal persons involved with the law' (Manitoba, 1991a: 763).

As was the case with both the McDonald and Marshall commissions, the Manitoba inquiry responded to its mandate with a two-track organization and report. The Osborne and Harper killings were examined in formal hearings where witnesses were compelled to testify under oath and were often represented by counsel. Although Osborne's mother, her tribal band, the RCMP, and the Indigenous Women's Collective were granted standing, the man convicted of her murder was not. This demonstrates how the inquiry differed from the criminal trial in not being subject to party control or a focus on individual responsibility. The man convicted of Osborne's murder later refused to testify before the inquiry on pain of being held in contempt (*Toronto Star*, 11 August 1989). As was the case with the judges who refused to testify at the Marshall inquiry, a failure to achieve literal accountability did not exhaust the accountability processes of the Manitoba inquiry.

The other part of the commission's report was directed at the broader issue of the relationship of Aboriginal people to all aspects of the administration of justice. Community hearings were held in thirty-six Aboriginal communities including twenty remote communities, seven other Manitoba communities, and five provincial correctional institutions, with over a thousand people making informal presentations (Manitoba, AJI, 1991a: 5). The commissioners explained that they took an informal approach to encourage 'frank and open expressions of opinion,' especially from Aboriginal people who were 'alienated from, and intimi-dated by, the formal court system.' They also explained that in these hearings they 'did not attempt to make determinations of 'fact' about individual incidents and injustices that were related to us. Our primary concern was to learn how the legal system was working, what people felt about the system and if people were being well served by it' (ibid.: 5). To this end, the general findings of the commission made liberal use of direct quotes from the participants at the community hearings. In addition to the hearings, research projects were undertaken, including surveys of judges, prosecutors, defence lawyers, and inmates, and an empirical study comparing the treatment of Aboriginal and non-Aboriginal accused in the courts. A symposium was held on tribal courts, as was a conference of Aboriginal elders.

The Manitoba inquiry was arguably able to hold individuals, organizations, and society accountable for their roles with respect to the Osborne and Harper deaths. Not only were the men who abducted Osborne and participated in her killing held accountable, but so were the investigating police force, the Department of Indian and Northern Affairs, and the people in the northern Manitoba community of The Pas who knew about the killing but kept quiet. Likewise, the officer involved in the Harper shooting was held accountable, but so too was the Winnipeg police force. Both events were portrayed as symptoms of systemic racism towards Aboriginal people, and to this extent Canadian society was held accountable for the way its attitudes and actions contributed to the deaths.

An important feature of the commission's conclusions about individual and organizational responsibility in the Osborne and Harper cases was that they departed from pre-existing legal standards in judging conduct. Although the hearings were conducted in a judicial fashion, the commission exercised a quasi-legislative function in order to hold, for example, that all four men involved in her abduction 'are morally, if not legally, responsible for Betty Osborne's murder' (Manitoba, AJI, 1991b: 22) and that a person who knew of the killing but did not tell the police had 'a warped sense of social responsibility' (ibid.: 50).

Unlike the Marshall commission, which stressed individual responsibility in its account of what happened, the Manitoba commission was more concerned with the organizational and social context of wrongdoing. For example, in its formal hearings the commission heard evidence about the treatment of Aboriginal people in The Pas, the town where Osborne was killed, and in its report it criticized the segregation and racism that was a 'well-ingrained and accepted part of life in The Pas' (ibid.: 91). The Marshall commission had resisted similar attempts to hold the town of Sydney accountable.

The report on Harper's death proceeded in a similar fashion. The commission called individual police officers involved in the incident and the subsequent investigation to account for their actions,[12] including allegations about racist jokes circulating among police. Officers were criticized for unnecessarily drawing their guns and for not using proper methods in investigating Harper's death. Again, the commission appealed both to legal standards and to those of their own making. They determined that Constable Cross did not have 'reasonable and probable grounds to stop Harper' (ibid.: 32) and that Harper was legally justified in resisting an illegal arrest (ibid.: 35). As to the actual encounter between Cross and Harper, however, they declared that Cross exhibited 'poor judgment' by 'his unnecessary approach and inappropriate attempt to detain Harper ... which set in motion the chain of events which resulted in Harper's death' (ibid.: 32 and 38). Moving from individual accountability, the Winnipeg police were held accountable for exonerating Cross before they knew all the evidence, for using race as a means to identify suspects, for deficient cross-cultural training, and for insufficient efforts in recruiting Aboriginal officers.

The larger part of the Manitoba report, dealing with the relation between Aboriginal people and the justice system, stressed the historical treatment of Aboriginal people in Canadian society and their over-representation among those apprehended and punished in the criminal justice system. Institutions such as the police, the courts, the Department of Indian Affairs, and the correctional services were all criticized for their failure to provide culturally sensitive services.

The report, especially in its chapters detailing the history of Aboriginal peoples, Aboriginal rights, Aboriginal over-representation in the criminal justice system, and the need for separate and comprehensive Aboriginal justice systems, went beyond holding organizations accountable and stressed a sense of social responsibility for the treatment of Aboriginal people. The commission conceived of its role as one of advocacy of Aboriginal self-government (Manitoba, AJI, 1991a: 3). Although many of the commission's recommendations were directed at 'provincial and federal governments,' they were in another sense directed at everyone in Canada in an attempt to make known the injustices of the past and create support for Aboriginal self-government in the future. Geoffrey York commented that the hearing process had 'opened the eyes of thousands of Manitobans who had blindly supported the police and the justice system. As a forum for public education, the inquiry has been unprecedented in its scope and influence ... The inquiry has forced Manitobans to confront their assumptions about fairness and neutrality among those who enforce and adjudicate the law (*Globe and Mail*, 4 November 1989). It is difficult to verify this observation, or whether attitudinal change will have any effect on hehaviour. Nevertheless, it does suggest that the 'social function' (Le Dain, 1973: 73) of the Manitoba inquiry was crucial. Increased awareness may produce the conditions for social accountability if people begin to question their own attitudes and behaviour and those of others. Even though the federal and provincial governments have initially rejected the commission's recommendations for a separate Aboriginal justice system, its work may have helped create increased social concern and vigilance about the treatment of Aboriginal people.

SUMMARY

All three inquiries adopted a two-part structure, with one part focusing on the assessment of past events through formal hearings and the other charged with investigating the broader organizational and social context. The Marshall commission focused on individual responsibility in its formal hearings even though it was unable to require the judges and jury to account in a literal sense for their mistreatment of Marshall. The Manitoba Aboriginal Justice Inquiry was more concerned with promoting social accountability for the treatment of Aboriginal people and viewed even individual misconduct as a symptom of larger social and political problems. The McDonald commission was mainly concerned with organizational accountability and to this end focused on a detailed examination of the organizational structure of the RCMP and proposals for a new civilian security intelligence agency.

The Future of Canadian Public Inquiries

The commissions examined above demonstrate how inquiries can act as instruments of accountability in situations where courts and the executive may not be as effective. In all three cases, inquiries held formal hearings that forced individuals to account for their actions. Moreover, the inquiries examined the organizational and social context of wrongdoing by engaging in investigation and research and holding informal hearings. In contrast, the courts did not fully explore either the events or their contexts, and the executive would probably not have been trusted to examine matters in which it was implicated.

Many of the institutional features that allow public inquiries to hold individuals accountable can also threaten their civil rights. Inquiries can compel people suspected of wrongdoing to testify against themselves and can accept evidence that would not be admissible in court. Concerns about the fairness of inquiries have led to recent judicial decisions in Canada holding that an inquiry into suspicious deaths at a hospital could not 'name names' and that a provincial inquiry appointed to determine if there were illegal dealings between named individuals and government officials was an improper substitute for criminal proceedings (*Re Nelles and Grange* [1984]; *Starr v Houlden* [1990]). A justice of the Supreme Court of Canada has argued extrajudicially that inquiries aimed at the alleged wrongdoing of specific individuals are unfair and invalid because they operate without the protections of the criminal process (Sopinka, 1990: 3). The modern trend in Canada is to place more restrictions on the activities of public inquiries (Roach, 1994b), and there is evidence of this trend in the inquiries examined above. The Marshall inquiry was not allowed to examine judges about their activities, and a police officer went to court and obtained a ruling that he could refuse to answer questions at the Manitoba inquiry if the answers would result in self-incrimination (Manitoba, AJI, 1991b: 4).

Will civil libertarian restrictions inhibit the ability of public inquiries to act as instruments of accountability? In answering this question, it is important to distinguish between different types of accountability. It will likely become more difficult in the future to compel individuals suspected of wrongdoing to testify before an inquiry (Ontario, Law Reform Commission, 1992: 191–200). This will, of course, mean that accountability in a literal sense will be diminished. As was shown in both the Marshall and Manitoba inquiries, however, those immune from being called to account may not be immune from criticism. In any event, restrictions on the ability to hold individuals accountable in a literal sense may encourage inquiries to focus on the responsibility of organizations and society for wrongdoing. Public inquiries are well suited for this task. They do not have to rely on formal hearings with adversarial procedures, but can gather evidence from a wide range of sources and create their own evidence by commissioning research.

Although concerns about the fairness of public inquiries have prominence at present, somewhat conflicting concerns that inquiries are too soft on individuals can also be heard. The McDonald commission was criticized for not facilitating subsequent criminal prosecutions, and there were calls for criminal prosecutions of police officers during and after the Marshall and Manitoba inquiries. Some believe that successful criminal prosecutions are necessary for true accountability, but this mistakes accountability for the ability to sanction individuals for wrongdoing or to control their behaviour in the future (Stenning, in this volume). Those who criticize inquiries as being too soft on individuals also ignore that inquiries are uniquely suited to holding organizations and society accountable in ways that courts cannot. In part, this is because inquiries are not bound by adjudicative standards and can openly establish their own standards of proper conduct. They are also not restricted in the type of evidence they consider or the need for it to be presented in an adversarial fashion. Perhaps most importantly, inquiries do not have to implement their judgments.

The risk of unfairness can be mitigated if inquiries focus their critical gaze on organizations and society, not individuals. Inquiries can hold organizations accountable for their failures, and this can encourage organizational change. In fact, the greatest legacy of the inquiries examined here may be the organizational change they encouraged. Inquiries can also play a role in social accountability by influencing attitudes among interested members of the public that encourage them to hold governments and others accountable for what have become officially recognized problems. Such accountability can last long after the inquiry is terminated and does not rely on formal legal powers to compel an account.

The future of public inquiries may depend on whether the processes of organizational and social accountability identified in this essay are appreciated as valuable and distinctive. Civil libertarian restrictions may prevent public inquiries from calling individuals suspected of wrongdoing to account for their actions in a literal sense, and this will increase reliance on organizational and sociological analysis. If organizational and social accountability are dismissed as too soft and intangible, so too may public inquiries be dismissed.

Acknowledgment. I thank Jamie Benidickson, the late John Edwards, Peter Russell, and Philip Stenning who provided helpful and challenging comments on an earlier draft of this essay.

Notes

1 Public inquiries have played an important role in other jurisdictions. For example, the deaths of Aboriginal prisoners in Australia resulted in a royal commission. In Great Britain, discovery of the wrongful convictions of the 'Guildford Four' and the 'Birmingham Six' in part led to the creation of the Royal Commission on Criminal Justice. That commission, unlike the Australian commission and the Canadian ones examined here, did not have the mandate to investigate the causes of the past events.
2 In a leading case, the Ontario Court of Appeal criticized a trial judge for taking an active role in exploring possible design defects in a car. Evans, JA stated, 'A trial is not intended to be a scientific exploration with the presiding Judge assuming the role of a research director; it is a forum established for the purpose of providing justice for the litigants' (*Phillips v Ford Motor Co.* [1971] (at 657)).

The Supreme Court of Canada has implicitly recognized differences between the courts' passive role and the more active role of public inquiries when in a recent reference case they stated, 'We have not been presented with any probative evidence that the police acted improperly ... Nor has evidence been presented that there was inadequate disclosure '(*Reference re Milgaard (Can)* [1992]). An inquiry, of course, would not have to rely on the evidence that was presented to it, but could collect its own evidence. In the wake of the court's decision that Milgaard's conviction could not be sustained, there were numerous calls for the appointment of a public inquiry to investigate the police investigation, the prosecution, and the appeal process.

3 The congressional inquiries into 'un-American activities' attempted 'to do by exposure what may not be done by legislation – punish men for associations and beliefs' (Barth, 1955: 22). McCarthy and his associates inevitably framed their questions not with regard to pre-existing legal standards, but rather those of their own making. This is illustrated when they attempted to obtain a perjury conviction of a witness who denied he had been 'a sympathizer or any kind of promoter of communism or communist interests.' The indictment was quickly thrown out by the courts for being too vague (ibid.: 109).

4 This situation can be contrasted with those jurisdictions where coroners' inquests are mandated by legislation in certain circumstances such as the deaths of inmates (Manson, 1988).

5 A federal/provincial committee of senior criminal justice officials echoed these criticisms in declining prosecutions. They stated that 'the Commission's original terms of reference caused them to enter into their deliberations on the basis of a false premise – a belief that it was appropriate to search for activity that was 'not authorized or provided for by law' rather than searching for activity that was 'prohibited by law' (Federal/ Provincial Committee, 1983: 1).

6 Only the attorney general of Quebec launched criminal prosecutions. The RCMP did not follow the commission's recommendations that twelve officers be disciplined, in part because eight of them had retired (Canada, Department of Justice, 1983: 16).

7 The Court of Appeal apparently balked at being given a broader mandate to state whether additional evidence warranted any action being taken in respect of Marshall's conviction (Nova Scotia, Marshall Commission, 1989: 114). Even this question did not explicitly require the court to consider the factors that contributed to the wrongful conviction, and it would have been extraordinary for the court to have ordered compensation for Marshall or reforms to prevent similar miscarriages of justice.

The criminal courts that dealt with Ebsary also did not investigate why Marshall had been wrongfully convicted. Bound by standards that gave the accused the benefit of a reasonable doubt, they did not even unequivocally exonerate Marshall or Seale. Ebsary was charged with manslaughter, not murder, and it took three trials before his claims of self-defence were rejected and a conviction entered.

8 It was reported that Marshall would be required to post $50,000 in security for costs before the courts would consider his civil suit (*Toronto Star*, 29 December 1983). Under Anglo-Canadian rules of civil procedure, liti-

gants may be forced before trial to post security for the costs that they will have to pay the opposing side if they are unsuccessful at trial.

9 One juror, after denying that prejudice had anything to do with Marshall's conviction, stated, 'With one redskin and one negro involved — it was like two dogs in a field — you know one of them was going to kill the other. I would expect more from a white person. We are more civilized' (*Toronto Star*, 9 June 1986).

10 The judge who had been attorney general at the time of Marshall's conviction and the chief justice who had assigned him to sit on the 1983 case had retired by this time and the Canadian Judicial Council determined it had no jurisdiction to consider the conduct of retired judges. Retirements also prevented individuals criticized by the McDonald commission from facing disciplinary proceedings. The retirement phenomenon underlines the importance of organizational accountability as opposed to attempts to sanction individuals.

The disciplinary panel's decision not to recommend that the remaining judges be removed from office has been strongly criticized (University of New Brunswick, 1991). Nevertheless, all the parties to the proceedings, including Marshall's lawyer, agreed that the extreme sanction of removing the judges from office was not appropriate.

11 Following the recommendations of the Marshall commission, Nova Scotia introduced the office of a director of public prosecutions [S.N.S. 1990 c.21]. Likewise, the federal government acted on the recommendations of the McDonald commission that a civilian security intelligence agency be created (SC, 1984, c. 21).

12 The police officer in charge of the investigation of Harper's death committed suicide the day before his testimony was scheduled to begin, and his suicide note was introduced as evidence in the hearing (*Globe and Mail*, 4 November 1989). During the McDonald commission, an inspector in charge of the security service in Winnipeg also committed suicide shortly after testifying before the inquiry (*Globe and Mail*, 7 May 1980). These tragic events demonstrate the effects that having to account for actions in a public inquiry have on some people.

The Office of Attorney General – New Levels of Public Expectations and Accountability[1]

JOHN LL.J. EDWARDS

In recent years, several major developments have occurred which challenge the traditional functions and powers associated with the office of attorney general in the countries of the Commonwealth. Some of these have merely added fresh examples of issues explored in an essay which I wrote on this topic fifteen years ago (Edwards, 1977). Others, however, have surfaced for the first time in the intervening years. In some respects, such as the entrenchment of the Charter of Rights and Freedoms in the Canadian Constitution Act [1982], and parallel initiatives in many parts of the Commonwealth towards constitutionalizing basic human rights, the role of the attorney general as 'guardian of the public interest' has scarcely evoked any serious attention.

During the same period there has been increasing evidence of disagreement between the courts and the law officers in the area of judicial reviewability of prosecutorial decisions made by the attorney general or his agents, the Crown or state prosecutors. In 1977 the House of Lords, in its landmark decision in *Gouriet v Union of Post Office Workers* [1978], disavowed any jurisdiction in the courts to review the exercise by the law officers of their prerogative discretionary powers. Over the intervening years, however, this decision has been assailed from many perspectives, not the least of which has seen the adoption, across the entire Commonwealth spectrum, of the doctrine of abuse of process that was first enunciated by the same court in *Connelly v DPP* [1964]. The task of reconciling these patently divergent theories has yet to be undertaken by the court that originally spawned them. In the meantime, attention must be paid to the constant chipping away at the fundamental principle established in the *Gouriet* [1978] case, as well as the long-term ramifications of the abuse of process doctrine as justification for asserting the judicial reviewability of prosecutorial decisions. More on this subject later.

Not all member countries of the Commonwealth have, as a central feature of their criminal justice systems, an office of director of public (or criminal) prosecutions, but those jurisdictions that do not have such an office must now be in a clear minority. In the vast majority of Commonwealth countries the basic characteristics of the office, and in particular the relationship between the director of public prosecutions (DPP) and the attorney general or minister of justice, and between the DPP and the government, are spelled out in the respective constitutions, thus underlining the critical importance of the position in the legal machinery of government. The wide disparity of constitutional arrangements on this subject in different parts of the Commonwealth was reviewed in my earlier work (Edwards, 1977). Later on I shall try to update this mosaic which, quite frankly, bewildered me when I first encountered it.

What is of considerable interest is the surge of activity in this field by those older member states, such as Australia and Canada, which for so many years had seemingly never felt the necessity to examine, let alone alter, their existing systems of criminal prosecutions. Experience with the royal commission on the Donald Marshall, Jr, prosecution in Nova Scotia (Nova Scotia, Royal Commission, 1989), from whose recommendations emerged the first statutorily independent office of director of public prosecutions anywhere in Canada, suggests that it is only a matter of time and political enlightenment before this significant reform is adopted in all the other provinces, and federally, across the country. In Australia, the process of change had begun several years earlier with the state of Victoria and the Commonwealth government leading the way. Notable differences, however, are evident in their respective approaches to the basic elements of independence and accountability. As to these, whether we are speaking of the office of attorney general or that of the director of public prosecutions, it is very apparent that important questions arise from the new directions reflected in the Australian and Canadian initiatives. These basic elements need to be addressed by every jurisdiction, no matter which model was originally adopted or is in place as of this moment.

I include in this exercise England and Wales, which gave birth, as far back as 1879, to the original office of director of public prosecutions. As is probably well known by now, after a mere 150 years or so of intermittent debate, the Westminster Parliament in 1985 inaugurated a dramatic turn-around by establishing for the first time in its history a system of full-time state prosecutors acting under the overall direction of the director of public prosecutions who, in turn, remains subject to the supervision and control of the attorney general. Scotland, whose indigenous system of criminal justice, dating back to the seventeenth century, long precedes that of nearly every other country in the Commonwealth, must have experienced more than a fleeting spasm of national pride in seeing its neighbour embrace the principle of a single national prosecution service for England and Wales controlled and directed by the director of public prosecutions.

Far from signifying a total merger of institutions involving the police and prosecutors, certain features continue to distinguish the prevailing systems within England and Scotland, respectively. And these differences mark an apparent divergence of approach to some of the ever-present central questions that every jurisdiction in the Commonwealth must resolve to meet its particular circumstances. Whether the differences are more apparent than real remains an open question. I propose to revert to some of these differences more fully below, but for now let me identify the issues that continue to plague many countries. Thus, should departmental control over the conduct of police in criminal cases and that of supervising prosecutors be unified or be completely separate? Irrespective of ministerial responsibility for the police and prosecutors as distinct entities, should the investigating police have an acknowledged right to determine whether or not to set the criminal process in motion by laying a formal complaint before a justice of the peace (or magistrate), and this notwithstanding the attorney general's undoubted right to decide whether the ensuing criminal prosecution should be continued or terminated by entering a stay of proceedings?

These very familiar questions were thoroughly canvassed and resolved, or so it was thought, so far as English criminal justice is concerned, by the Royal Commission on Criminal Procedure (1981). Its principal recommendations are to be found reflected in the statutory landmark, the Prosecution of Offences Act [1985]. Before the ink on the statute book had scarcely dried, the same old questions resurfaced in the wake of an unprecedented erosion of public confidence that resulted from the handling of what came to be known as the 'Birmingham Six,' the 'Guildford Four,' and the 'Maguire' cases, and the wrongful incarceration over many years of alleged members of the Irish Republican Army. These flagrant miscarriages of justice spread across the entire system, from the original police investigation and the seriously flawed scientific evidence to the appellate process. No professional group was immune from the outburst of public criticism that fed upon the spate of revelations. So, once again, an embarrassed government resorted to the traditional method of neutralizing, for a while at least, hostile public opinion, namely, the creation of yet another royal commission. Judging by the dramatic and unexpected nature of the reforms advocated by the legal professional bodies in their submissions to the Royal Commission on Criminal Justice (1993), major changes were envisaged in some of the areas with which this essay is concerned. The commission's recommendations have been released, but the final report contains no structural proposals that could be described as fundamental.

On another very specific subject, I confess to being disappointed at the slowness with which attorneys general have taken the bold initiative of making publicly available the policy guidelines that shape individual decisions in matters of prosecution. In my book, *The Attorney General, Politics, and the Public Interest* (1984), I traced the origin of this major contribution towards full public accountability for prosecution decisions. In doing so, I recognized the leadership shown by the attorney general of the Commonwealth of Australia (in 1982) and by the attorney general of England and Wales (in 1983). My own country, Canada, with the occasional exception, had lagged sadly behind in this kind of endeavour but the release by the attorney general of Canada, in 1993, of the federal justice department's 'Guidelines for the Making of Decisions in the Prosecution Process' is to be applauded. Equally impressive, though not publicly disclosed, was the unprecedented scale of the consultation process that preceded the manual's public availability.

Before leaving this introductory note on the subject of public dissemination of prosecution guidelines, I want to emphasize the central place that the principle of full pre-trial disclosure must be accorded in any such prosecution policy statements. Much as it may offend the more reactionary exponents of prosecutorial responsibilities, the time has come to recognize the damaging effects, in terms of public confidence, of any perception that the state is prepared to seek convictions even at the expense of placing the accused at an acute disadvantage by withholding evidence that could benefit his defence. For too long, in many jurisdictions, the prevailing principle has been that the provision of pre-trial disclosure to counsel representing the accused was a matter of grace and favour. In Canada, the turning point in this outmoded thinking came with the decision of the Supreme Court of Canada in the

Stinchcombe case [1991]. Noting that, despite recommendations by the Law Reform Commission of Canada for legislative action on this subject (Canada, Law Reform Commission, 1984) Parliament has been content to leave the development of the law of disclosure to the courts, the Supreme Court of Canada has now chosen to do just that. In a unanimous judgment, the justices based the new principles for disclosure squarely within the accused's ability to make 'full answer and defence,' which right, the Supreme Court pointed out, 'has acquired new vigour by virtue of its inclusion in section 7 of the Canadian Charter of Rights and Freedoms [1982] as one of the principles of fundamental justice.' As the chief prosecutor in every jurisdiction, the attorney general bears the primary responsibility to see to it that this philosophy is fully reflected in the operating guidelines that govern the individual prosecutor's discretionary authority. Most recently, the final report of the broadly based Advisory Committee to the Attorney General of Ontario, chaired by the former doyen of criminal law judges in Canada, Honourable G. Arthur Martin (Ontario, Advisory Committee, 1993), was publicly released. Its far-reaching recommendations, with respect to charge screening, disclosure, and resolution discussions, will reverberate across and beyond Canada.

Associated with many of the issues I have introduced in the previous paragraphs is a relatively new development that concerns the extent to which an attorney general and his agents, be they the director of public prosecutions, Crown Counsel, or state prosecutors, are amenable to the disciplinary processes of the professional body that is responsible for maintaining minimum standards of professional conduct. The universality of these standards in any particular jurisdiction is not in issue. What cannot be ignored, however, are the serious constitutional issues that emerge from the shadows if the breadth of the professional body's disciplinary powers are expanded in a way that crosses the boundary line between (a) the prosecutor as an ordinary member of the legal profession who, like his colleagues in the defence bar, specializes in the practice of criminal law, and (b) the state or Crown prosecutor in his capacity as the public embodiment of the attorney general's constitutional powers and prerogatives in the area of criminal law. To clarify the true character of this demarcation line was the challenge presented a few years ago before the British Columbia Court of Appeal in *Re Hoem and the Law Society of BC* [1985]. No one questioned the statement made by that court that 'the researches of counsel have turned up no case in which a governing body of the legal profession has asserted the power to discipline an attorney general, or counsel instructed by him, in respect of the exercise of prosecutorial discretion.' Such a lack of authority no longer prevails in Canada, but the decisions by the courts in one province have in no way deterred the governing bodies in some other parts of the country from pressing forward with their claims to exercise another level of supervisory accountability over the attorney general and his agents, to which I now turn.

A New Level of Accountability

How far does the disciplinary arm of the legal profession's governing body extend to the actions of the attorney general or his agents, particularly in the area of prosecutorial discretion?

The emergence of this question as an additional level of accountability, over and above that of parliamentary accountability and judicial review-ability, should not be dismissed as an abstract academic problem. Up to now, this potentially new field of conflict involving the attorney general and the pertinent governing body of the legal profession has manifested itself only in Canada and Australia. And even in these countries the subject has scarcely been recognized as a pressing issue among the rank and file of the legal profession, let alone amidst the wider public. That it will nevertheless do so, in the fullness of time, would seem to be inevitable, so this is an opportune moment to take stock of what is involved.

To begin with, it may be useful to recall the solitary instance in which an English attorney general was held to be amenable to answer charges of unprofessional conduct before the benchers of his inn of court. In what at the time, thirty years ago, was considered to be a situation without precedent, Sir John Hobson, attorney general in the Harold Macmillan administration, did not challenge the jurisdiction of his fellow benchers in the Inner Temple to adjudicate charges against him of unprofessional conduct in the handling of the *Enaharo* case (*R. v Brixton (Governor) and Another, Ex parte Enaharo* [1963]). The original complaint arose out of the heated controversy engendered by the Gov-ermment's refusal to grant political asylum to Chief Enaharo of Nigeria. The specific allegations directed against the attorney general were that, in the course of habeas corpus proceedings that preceded the deporta-tion of Enaharo to stand trial for treason in Nigeria, Hobson had presented an affidavit sworn by the home secretary which he, the attorney general, knew to be inaccurate and misleading. The affidavit had failed to disclose that the Nigerian government had informed the home secretary that senior English counsel, whom Enaharo had wished to represent him before the Nigerian courts, was to be excluded from the country. Among the alternative dispositions available to the Inner Temple benchers were a reprimand, suspension or disbarment. The attorney general was represented by counsel and gave evidence refuting the allegations made against him. At the conclusion of the hearing the assembled masters of the Inn of Court found that the charges were unfounded and that there were no grounds for criticizing the attorney general's conduct.

Shortly thereafter, in 1965, and perhaps prompted by the events just described involving the attorney general of England and Wales, the flamboyant Minister of Justice and Attorney General of Quebec Claude Wagner found himself having to meet charges of unprofessional conduct arising out of a speech, made at a public meeting, in which Wagner had sought to awaken the conscience of the bar to the widespread erosion of public respect for the bench and bar. The complaint in this case was lodged by the judge whose conduct had been attacked in the course of the minister's speech. An essential part of the attorney general's unsuccessful defence before the Montreal Bar Council was that his actions were outside the disciplinary jurisdiction of the professional body. There followed a series of convoluted appeal proceedings culminating in a very brief judgment by the Quebec Court of Appeal, in *Barreau de Montreal v Wagner* [1968], declaring that the disciplinary powers of the bar did not extend to the minister of justice when exercising the executive powers of the Crown.

My own reading of the two cases suggests that the circumstances of the *Enaharo* case are clearly distinguishable from those just described in relation to Claude Wagner in Quebec in 1965. Both of the complaints in the case involving the English attorney general referred directly to judicial proceedings and the professional conduct of the senior law officer in his handling of those processes. The political implications of the *Enaharo* case were properly the subject of debate and accountability in the House of Commons. The professional conduct of the attorney general, however, was concerned with his observance of the appropriate standards by which every lawyer is subject to the assessment of his peers. Hobson enjoyed no preferential status in this regard, simply because he was the incumbent attorney general. An additional complication, regrettably not addressed by the Quebec Court of Appeal in the *Wagner* case, arises if the attorney general also happens to occupy the portfolio of minister of justice or its equivalent. In this essay I intend to focus my attention on the amenability of the attorney general *qua* attorney general, and that of his agents, to the professional judgment of their peers with respect to decisions made under the umbrella of prosecutorial discretion.

Much confusion exists on this subject. The phrase 'prosecutorial discretion' is often used as if there existed a universal understanding of what it encompasses. Unfortunately, this is far from being an accepted fact. To avoid any misconceptions as to my basic premise, I understand the concept of prosecutorial discretion to include, but not to be restricted to, decisions by the attorney general or any agent of the attorney general as to (a) preliminary questions of law that derive from the definitional, substantive, procedural, or jurisdictional aspects of the offence(s) in question; (b) the sufficiency of the evidence collected by the police and which is legally admissible to support the proposed charge(s); and (c) whether the prosecution or its termination is called for in the public interest. The challenges at present being mounted by various of the provincial law societies in Canada are directed towards one or more of the above instances of prosecutorial discretion. Other aspects, such as the decision to grant statutory consent to the commencement of criminal proceedings, to exercise the right of appeal against conviction or sentence, or to proceed summarily or by indictment, have not figured prominently in the debate.

Without going into the details, I interpret the Canadian trend, whenever it has surfaced, as an attempt to legitimize the exercise of disciplinary jurisdiction with respect to the professional competence of the crown prosecutor in particular cases. Thus, in the case previously referred to (*Re Hoem et al.* [1985]) involving criminal proceedings against municipal politicians, the Law Society of British Columbia took the position that Crown counsel should have appreciated that there was no evidence to prove material allegations, and therefore the charges should not have been proceeded with. Even this assertion on the facts was highly questionable (see *Gillen v Law Society of BC* [1985]), but the appeal court chose to reject the Law Society's position on more fundamental grounds, saying:

The concession that the Law Society has no concern with policy considerations is significant ... The limit suggested by the Law Society in that passage is that it is within its powers to determine whether there was a legal foundation for a prosecution. If that were so it would mean in practice that the Law Society rather than the Attorney General would be the final arbiter as to what is an adequate legal foundation – the determination whether there is legal foundation for a charge will always be open to doubts, disputes and differences of opinion, and that is essentially a question of policy whether any given set of facts justifies a prosecution. It is not in the public interest that that determination should be made by the Law Society rather than the duly appointed Law Officers of the Crown ... The distinction sought to be made between the exercise of the discretion, and the question whether the lawyer was competent in performing the work leading up to its exercise is an unworkable one – the separation cannot feasibly be made. (Ibid.: 253–5)

In this passage, the appellate court was emphasizing the importance of keeping in mind the distinction between two essentially separate issues. Blurring of the boundary line separating the two issues should prompt a strong reaction on the part of any attorney general conscious of the importance of defending his independent status in matters of prosecution. Thus, there should be no serious question raised if what is at issue is the professional conduct of the prosecutor in the handling of a case as it proceeds through the criminal courts. If the alleged breach of ethical standards consists of, for example, misleading the court, pressuring Crown witnesses as to their forthcoming testimony, or failing to observe the essential requirements of pre-trial disclosure to the defence, no exemption based on the office should protect the prosecutor from his or her accountability to the disciplinary processes that extend to all members of the profession.

By virtue of the very office that is under scrutiny, there is an inherent expectation that every Crown or state prosecutor will demonstrate his compliance with the fundamental principles of fairness and justice in relation to the accused before, during, and after the trial and the appeal process. The boundary line is crossed if the body seeking to exercise the disciplinary review powers of the law society focuses its attention on the *decisions* made by the prosecutor in charge of the case. Such decisions are invariably an amalgam of many considerations including, but never confined to, an assessment of the available evidence and the pertinent law. Whatever may be the theoretical chronology of an individual prosecutor's exercise of the discretionary powers associated with his office, there will always be a consideration of the 'public interest' or 'public policy' dimensions of the individual case.

Increasingly, the dimensions of these prominent factors are spelled out in some detail in the policy guidelines issued by the attorney general or the director of public prosecutions. For any law society to claim for itself the right to judge what, in any particular set of circumstances, is or is not in the public interest demonstrates the dangers of sacrificing to another body the constitutional independence and its concurrent responsibilities historically associated with the office of the attorney general. For the same reasons given by the court of appeal in the *Hoem* [1985] case, any attempt to separate the interrelated stages in the prosecutor's decision-making process is both impractical and devoid of any sustainable principle. Each stage, in practical terms, is so interwoven with the others that any attempt by a disciplinary committee to isolate parts of the process from the others would quickly demonstrate the futility of such a review procedure.

I can find no justification for subjecting the attorney general and his prosecutorial agents to yet another layer of accountability. Difficult as it may be in the ordinary run-of-the-mill cases to maintain the demarcation line that I described earlier, especially in the face of claims that what is at issue is nothing more than a simple matter of professional conduct, the larger constitutional ramifications should not be ignored. At the same time, I disapprove strongly of any legislative immunity that is designed to insulate the holder of the office of attorney general from *all* forms of professional accountability. In the case involving Sir John Hobson in 1963 no such claim to total immunity from the disciplinary processes of the Inner Temple was made. All the more reason, therefore, to react adversely to the provision, still extant, in Section 13(3) of the Law Society of Upper Canada Act [RSO 1990] which states, 'No person who is or has been the Minister of Justice and Attorney General for Ontario is subject to any disciplinary proceedings of the Society or to any penalty imposed in Convocation or in a committee of benchers for anything done by him while exercising the functions of such office.' There may be other examples of this kind of extraordinary protection conferred on attorneys general in other parts of the Commonwealth, but I am unable to cite any other historical precedents for this kind of immunity. To say the least, it seems incongruous to confer upon every attorney general in Ontario the ex officio rank of a bencher of the governing body and simultaneously clothe the same person with total immunity from the disciplinary powers of the law society. In my opinion, the Ontario provision cited above, or any parallel enactments, should be totally removed from the statute book.

This underlying philosophy is in stark contrast to the landmark decision of the Supreme Court of Canada in *Nelles v R in right of Ontario et al.* [1989]. After examining the common law precedents and traditional arguments supporting the principle that the attorney general and Crown prosecutors enjoy absolute immunity from civil liability for malicious prosecution, the Supreme Court (by a majority) ruled that such immunity could no longer be justified in the interests of public policy. As the majority judgment concluded, 'The inherent difficulty in proving a case of malicious prosecution, combined with the mechanisms available ... to weed out meritless claims, is sufficient to ensure that the Attorney General and Crown Attorneys will not be hindered in the proper execution of their important duties' (ibid.: 199). The adverse reactions of prosecutors across Canada to the ruling in *Nelles* was to be expected, but this attitude could not be supported rationally. Having previously argued in favour of the reform, I welcome this additional form of public accountability encompassing the office of attorney general and its prosecutorial agents. In handing down its decision the Supreme Court of Canada believed it was breaking new ground so far as Commonwealth countries are concerned.

New Dimensions to the Principles of Independence and Accountability as They Relate to the Attorney General and Director of Public Prosecutions

There are few areas of greater importance in maintaining public confidence in government than the ordinary citizen's respect for the administration of justice. That respect, when accorded, springs from the depth of the ordinary person's basic values and hopes. Violate those values and you quickly begin to see the erosion of society's confidence in those to whom the enormous powers of government have been entrusted. Nowhere is this more evident than in the institution and conduct of criminal prosecutions. Among the central criteria by which a country's justice system is publicly judged are fairness and evenhandedness in criminal proceedings, the absence of any perception of bias or political interference on the part of those exercising police and prosecutorial authority, as well as professional competence and integrity throughout the system. As often as not the public focus will be directed towards the highest echelons in the system and, particularly, those holding the critical offices of attorney general and director of public prosecutions.

This is where the ultimate authority for prosecuting crimes is vested and from which source is delegated the broad range of discretionary powers exercised daily by the state's prosecutors.

In earlier writings on this subject (Edwards, 1977), I warned against any attempt to fully understand the bewildering series of alternative arrangements for the offices of attorney general and director of public prosecutions, as reflected in the respective constitutions of Commonwealth countries, without reference to the prevailing political context of each individual country. The sheer magnitude of the exercise explains why I intend to follow the same sound advice today. Buried beneath these constitutional arrangements, but ready to erupt once the surface is scratched, are the broad principles of independence and accountability. What has engaged my attention more recently (Edwards, 1989), is the flurry of major reforms instituted in Australia, Canada, and Britain, countries which for so many years had adhered, rather complacently, to the status quo with regard to their respective machinery of criminal prosecutions.

The prelude to major institutional changes can usually be traced to public dissatisfaction with, or worse, the collapse of public confidence in, the existing structures of government. So it was in Australia in the 1970s. Commencing with indications of possible involvement by the federal Crown solicitor's office in Western Australia in a highly organized system of tax evasion, to the series of scandals involving political figures and members of the judiciary in the activities of organized crime, Australia was subjected to the embarrassing findings of one royal commission after another. Public confidence in the normal machinery of justice was shaken to the point that special prosecutors were appointed, with total independence from the attorney general, under new legislation providing for such extraordinary appointments. Significantly, the transition from ad hoc special prosecutors to the establishment of a permanent statutory office of director of public prosecutions was foreseen and strongly advocated by each of the special prosecutors appointed by the Australian government. With this kind of momentum building up for radical reform, the pressures for change were inescapable. The state of Victoria was first off the mark with the smooth passage of its Director of Public Prosecutions Act [1982]. The following year saw the Commonwealth of Australia introduce legislation on the same subject, and this enactment too [1983] proceeded quickly through both houses of the legislature without amendment or indeed much debate. The particular provisions of both measures demand careful attention if the nuances of the legislation are to be fully appreciated. This comparative exercise will quickly demonstrate the striking disparities between the federal and state philosophies on the questions of independence and accountability.

Subsequent initiatives by the other states in Australia reflect a strong preference for the model originally embodied in the state of Victoria enactment in 1982. It envisages a totally independent director of public prosecutions of the kind familiar to many of the countries of the Commonwealth. Time, however, will tell whether the assumed independence claimed for the director of public prosecutions in the state of Victoria is reconcilable with the terms of Section 9(2) of the parent statute declaring the director to be 'responsible to the Attorney General for the due performance of his functions under this Act or any other Act.'

Turning to the philosophy reflected in the Commonwealth of Australia statute of 1983, the most notable provision is Section 8(1), which states unequivocally that 'in the performance of the Director's functions and in the exercise of the Director's powers, the Director is subject to such directions or guidelines as the Attorney General, after consultation with the Director, gives or furnishes to the Director in writing.' Opportunity is provided for the director to express his reactions to any proposed directive before the attorney general's views are finalized and committed to written form. When the exchange of ideas has run its course the instructions of the attorney general must always prevail. Even more fundamentally, the two jurisdictions in Australia diverge markedly on the issue of involvement in the handling of a particular case. Experience has taught us that public scrutiny is likely to be magnified proportionately if the accused is a political or other public figure and questions of non-prosecution or non-enforcement of the criminal law become the subject of public comment in the media or in the legislature.

It is in these kinds of exceptional circumstances that confidence in the doctrine of ministerial accountability is put to its most severe test. The state of Victoria, and those other jurisdictions (for example, Queensland [1984]; New South Wales [1986]) that have followed its example in their sensitiveness to the perceptions of political interference, have legislatively deprived the 'independent' director of public prosecutions of any right to issue guidelines or directives in relation to individual cases. He must be content with the formulation of general policy directives. In sharp contrast to this statutory policy of enveloping the attorney general and director of public prosecutions in a shroud of total insulation from decision-making with respect to individual cases, the Commonwealth of Australia expressly authorizes its attorney general to give the federal director of public prosecutions directions in individual cases. Such directions, however, it is important to note, must always be made in writing. Sceptics will not readily be assuaged by this requirement. The real sting is contained in the supplemental requirement that the attorney general's written instructions to the director of public prosecutions be published expeditiously in the *Official Gazette* and, in addition, be communicated directly to the House of Representatives. Some delay is permitted if this is necessary to safeguard the interests of the accused or potential witnesses. Such postponement has to be justified before the House of Representatives when the case has finally been disposed of. There has been, as yet, little enough experience in Australia to determine the practical effects of these innovative reforms. Nevertheless, I want to revert shortly to the inherent nexus between these mandatory obligations placed upon the attorney general and the effectiveness of the doctrine of ministerial accountability.

Understandably, the Australian debates on the measures just described are replete with references to the difference between their indigenous solutions to the problems associated with public prosecutions and that which defines the original office of director of public prosecutions established for England and Wales in 1879. If for no better reason than its antiquity and the experience it represents, the English office is often used as a talisman by which all later versions of that office are assessed. In considering the significance of the major reforms instituted by the Prosecution of Offences Act [1985] and any new directions which the English criminal justice system may be destined to take in the wake of the report of the Royal Commission on Criminal Justice (1993), it is important to remember that it is the language of the original statute of 1879 that, to this day, authoritatively defines the status of the director of public prosecutions for England and Wales and that office holder's constitutional relationship to the attorney general.

Despite frequent changes over the intervening years to the subordinate regulations in the field of prosecutions, the essential character of this relationship is expressed in Section 2 of the 1879 enactment, which speaks of the director acting 'under the superintendence of the attorney general' and 'as may be directed in a special case by the Attorney General.' In what has come to be regarded as an authoritative exposition of the respective responsibilities of the two offices, speaking in the

House of Commons in 1979, then Attorney General Sir Michael Havers, declared:

My responsibility for superintendence of the duties of the Director does not require me to exercise a day-to-day control and specific approval of every decision he takes. The Director makes many decisions in the course of his duties which he does not refer to me but nevertheless I am still responsible for his actions in the sense that I am answerable in the House for what he does. Superintendence means that I must have regard to the overall prosecution policy which he pursues. My relationship is such that I require to be told in advance of the major, difficult, and from the public interest point of view, the more important matters so that should the need arise I am in the position to exercise my ultimate power of direction. (*House of Commons Debates*, vol. 176, Written Answers, cols. 87–8).

Whenever there is envisaged a system of collaboration between the attorney general and the director of public prosecutions in the decision-making process, as exhibited in the Australian legislation referred to earlier, it is impractical to define with much greater particularity than in the above-quoted passage the circumstances wherein consultation is mandated. Obviously, any such consultation must precede the making of final decisions, otherwise the attorney general will be placed in the invidious position of having to defend the exercise of discretionary authority without having had the benefit beforehand of ascertaining the facts and law involved, assessing the dimensions of the public interest, and rendering his own decision whether to approve or reject the director's advice and recommendations.

In this regard, the former English attorney general was at pains to emphasize that his ultimate power to give directions had to be viewed in conjunction with his ultimate responsibility to defend his actions before the pertinent legislative body. Regrettably, it must be acknowledged that few champions are to be found nowadays who are ready to extol the demonstrated value of parliamentary accountability as a key element in controlling the exercise of prosecutorial discretion. Such lack of support for this principle is readily explained by the relative infrequency of such public challenges, and the customary inadequacy of the questioner's preparation and determination to elicit the full picture of what took place prior to making the decision to prosecute or to stay the proceedings. Something more concrete is called for if we are to inject real backbone into the principle of ministerial accountability for prosecutorial decisions.

Because I retain a fundamental commitment to this constitutional principle as a central element of parliamentary democracy, I find myself favourably drawn to the aspects of openness of the Commonwealth of Australia's approach to the accountability of the attorney general. Thus, according to the federal statute (No. 113 of 1983, Section 8), whenever the attorney general chooses to intervene in a particular case and to give instructions to his subordinate, the director of public prosecutions, such instructions must be committed to writing and, subject to reasonable delay if it is shown that the interests of the accused or a witness may be seriously prejudiced, the written instructions must be made available for public information. This process necessarily mandates (a) the publication of the attorney general's written directive, with any accompanying reasons, in the government's *Official Gazette* (or its equivalent) and (b) tabling the same information promptly in the legislature. The contrast between, on the one hand, this kind of specific obligation to publicly disclose the thinking behind questionable decisions and, on the other, the veil of secrecy that prevents any realistic assessment of the values and variables operating at the time of decision-making makes it imperative that every jurisdiction take a good hard look at the Australian initiatives and then ask themselves, can we justify not accepting a similar degree of total prosecutorial accountability?

Not for one moment am I suggesting that this process represents a panacea for all the weaknesses in the doctrine of parliamentary responsibility as it relates to the office of attorney general. That doctrine should not be relied upon as the single foundation stone on which the attorney general's accountability can be guaranteed. As this essay recognizes, there are several lines of accountability that must be taken into account by any attorney general wishing to fulfil his or her constitutional obligations as the responsible member of the executive. Requiring any interventionist directions in an individual case to be committed to writing and published will not, in one stroke, secure the twin goals of openness and accountability. Nevertheless, this reform has the potential for making a major contribution towards both these central objectives.

In my previous writings, I have warned against any tendency to place exaggerated, even exclusive, faith in the independent characteristics of the office as provided for by statute or in a country's constitution. Of no less significance, and in my opinion even greater importance, are the personal qualities of the office holder and that person's commitment to meeting the highest expectations of ordinary people in terms of personal integrity, impartiality, and steadfastness in the face of pressures from whatever quarter.

Even if we assume the possibility of exercising the independent powers of the director of public prosecutions' office with such elevated personal qualities, the principle of total independence without the accompanying sanction of parliamentary accountability is, to my mind, too high a price for any society to pay in achieving the goal of keeping partisan political pressures away from the exercise of prosecutorial discretion. To observe, however, what often amounts to no more than paying lip-service to the principle of ministerial accountability does little to reinforce public confidence in the integrity of prosecutorial decisions. When questions are directed towards the responsible minister, usually the attorney general, one major flaw that emerges repeatedly is the absence of hard evidence associating the attorney general directly with the controversial decision, whatever form it may take. It is this absence of any real basis for invoking effective sanctions against the attorney general or other responsible minister that prompts many critics to pour scorn on the principle of ministerial accountability as it relates to the office of attorney general. Instances of an attorney general publicly acknowledging his or her direct involvement in a case, with commensurate personal responsibility, are few and far between.

If, therefore, the principle of accountability is viewed as an essential component in preserving the independence of prosecutorial decision-making, a solution must be found that will overcome the major flaw to which I have referred above. The answer to this problem lies in the imposition of a statutory duty upon the attorney general to commit to writing his decision to intervene in a particular case and to do so as an essential part of communicating his decision to the otherwise independent director of public prosecutions. Obviously, the greater the statutory insulation of the director from any interference by the attorney general so, in turn, does the doctrine of ministerial accountability assume a more theoretical quality and become of less practical importance. These conclusions were the essence of my principal recommendations to the Nova Scotia Royal Commission on the Donald Marshall, Jr, Prosecution in 1988 (Edwards, 1989). In due course they became incorporated in the legislation enacted by that province in 1990 establishing, for the first time anywhere in Canada, a statutorily independent office of public prosecutions [1990].

The legislation adheres closely to that enacted by the Commonwealth of Australia in 1983 and rejects the totally independent model exemplified in many Commonwealth countries and which has been adopted by the states of Victoria, New South Wales, Queensland, and South Australia. As I indicated at the beginning of this essay, it is disappointing to have to record the absence of any similar initiative in other parts of Canada. While providing in its 'purposes of the Act' clause for 'the independence of the Director of Public Prosecutions and the public prosecution service,' the Nova Scotia statute authorizes the attorney general, after consultation with the Director of public prosecutions, to issue instructions in a particular prosecution. These must be in writing and must be published as soon as practicable in the *Royal Gazette* except where, in the opinion of the director of public prosecutions, publication would not be in the best interests of the administration of justice, in which case the director, instead, shall publish as much information concerning the instructions as he considers appropriate in his next annual report to the Legislative Assembly. Looking at the various Australian statutes and their remarkably divergent approaches to this question, what is lacking, especially in those instances where the annual report of the director of public prosecutions is designated as the time and place in which to disclose the issuance of particular directives, is the special effectiveness that I associate with the contemporaneous public disclosure of what is going on in the offices of the attorney general and of the director of public prosecutions. The passage of time somehow diminishes the bite that can be exhibited when the conduct of a minister or public official is examined close to the time of its actual occurrence.

Nothing said in the preceding paragraphs should preclude either of the senior state officials, personally or through counsel, making a public statement in court by way of explanation as to the decision that has been taken. The same observation applies to a situation where the attorney general is of a mind to make a formal statement on the floor of the legislature. There is no conflict of principle between the discretionary initiative that has always been at the disposal of an attorney general 'to go public' and the mandatory obligation that, in my opinion, should be imposed by statute to ensure that the written records of the attorney's or the director's directives are made available for public scrutiny.

In the same vein, there is an ever-growing necessity for making publicly accessible the relevant considerations and criteria that enter into prosecutorial decision-making. Ever so slowly the movement towards this laudable goal is gaining new adherents with the attorneys general of the United States, England and Wales, Australia, and, more recently, Canada leading the way. The potential significance of specific guidelines is discussed further below in the context of the question of judicial review of prosecutorial decisions.

Before leaving this aspect of the topic, it is worth noting how fragile the Canadian initiative in establishing its first statutorily independent director of public prosecutions might turn out to be. Barely three years after the office was created, the newly elected government of Nova Scotia, representing a different political party, launched an independent review of both the legislation establishing the office and the first director's handling of several high-profile cases. During that short period of time the director of public prosecution's office has received more than its fair share of misconceived criticism. The principal criterion dictating the public response in Nova Scotia to the new office has been the failure rate of prosecutions in which the director himself has been closely associated. To anyone acquainted with the history of the earliest years of the same office in England and Wales from 1879 onwards (see Edwards, 1964: ch. 17), it all sounds like a familiar refrain. The annual reports to Parliament by the English director of public prosecutions between 1884 and 1894 should be required reading for every modern holder of the office, as well as any person who is called upon by government to examine its operation and to make recommendations. What cannot be doubted is that future reform in this area across Canada will be significantly influenced by the outcome of the current Nova Scotia review (see Ghiz and Archibald, 1994).

Judicial Review of the Attorney General's Actions

Surveying the most notable legal developments within the Commonwealth in the past twenty-five years, a prime candidate for inclusion in any such list must surely be the growth in judicial readiness to review the exercise of discretionary power by the executive arm of government. What was once a fairly restricted and straightforward jurisdiction has been expanded in more recent times to what has aptly been described as a 'terminological lottery' (Williams, 1986: 105). Judicial review is now predicated on a combination of basic elements as to which many formulae have been advanced by way of explaining the circumstances in which the courts are prepared to intervene. Among the more prominent of these triggering conditions are indications of illegality, irrationality, or procedural impropriety on the part of the executive's decision-maker. Other broad-ranging concepts invoked by the courts to justify their intervention include the unreasonableness of the executive's position or the manifestation of unfairness in the process of decision-making. Also lurking in the shadows is the determination whether the subject-matter of the exercise is itself justiciable and amenable to judicial review by the courts. My concern in this essay is to examine the application of this growing trend towards an interventionist approach on the part of the judiciary with special reference to the broad range of discretionary powers exercisable by the attorney general and his agents.

Given the fluid state in which the law of judicial review can at present be described, and the inevitability of its continuing evolution, there are certain central questions that must be addressed as they relate to the office of attorney general. First, in terms of 'justiciability' and 'judicial reviewability,' what significance should be attached to the historical fact that many of the attorney general's prosecutorial powers derive from the prerogative, as opposed to the legislative, source of governmental authority? Second, in light of the courts' widespread adoption of the doctrine of abuse of process as an expression of its inherent jurisdiction to control its own processes, how far is this development reconcilable with the attorney general's historic right to determine all questions relating to the institution or discontinuance of criminal prosecutions? Although, as we shall see, there is a certain amount of overlapping in the judicial precedents that touch on these questions, it will be advisable, in the first instance, to treat them separately.

JUDICIAL REVIEW AND THE PREROGATIVE

The long-standing unwillingness of the courts to review executive decisions based on the royal prerogative has recently undergone radical reappraisal in many Commonwealth jurisdictions. In Canada this reconsideration was encouraged by the broad language of Section 32 of that country's Charter of Rights and Freedoms [1982]. In *Operation Dismantle Inc. v R* [1985], the Supreme Court of Canada interpreted this constitutional provision as signifying that all activities of the executive branch of government, regardless of the source of the legal authority on which they are based, are subject to the scrutiny of the courts if it is established that any of the Charter's enumerated rights or freedoms have been infringed, denied, or imperilled.

In the absence of such a constitutional mandate in England, the House of Lords in the GCHQ case (*Council of Civil Service Unions v Minister for the Civil Service* [1985]), held that 'if the subject matter in respect of which prerogative power is exercised is justiciable ... the controlling factor in determining whether the exercise of prerogative power is subject to judicial review is not its source but its subject matter' (at 407). Subsequent cases in England and elsewhere have revealed the difficulties in applying this principle, not only in terms of identifying which prerogative powers are 'by their very nature' not susceptible to judicial review, but also in terms of what the purview of any such review should be: see, for example, *R v Home Secretary ex p. Bentley* [1993]; *Burt v Governor General* [1992]; and *Githunguri v Republic of Kenya* [1986].

Even allowing for this uncertainty (see Williams, 1986 for an insightful review), what does seem to be uniformly accepted by the highest courts is that adherence to the principle of fairness does not mean that it is open to the courts to determine whether a particular policy or a particular decision is fair. Rather, the ambit of judicial review is to be confined to determining whether the *process* of exercising the discretionary power and the *manner* in which prerogative decisions are made and carried into effect reflect the duty to act fairly. There are no absolutes, and it is generally recognized that the extent of such a duty will vary greatly from case to case.

It is interesting to note that among the catalogue of excluded categories, referred to in the leading English and Canadian cases, no reference is made to the prerogative powers historically associated with the law officers of the Crown. Of most relevance to the administration of criminal justice are the power to initiate and to stay criminal proceedings and (under Canadian law at least) to prefer a direct indictment; the exclusive authority to grant immunity to witnesses who agree to appear on behalf of the Crown; and the right to appear ex officio as 'guardian of the public interest' to protect or enforce public rights. I do not propose to explore the current state of each of these discretionary powers here. Instead, I shall endeavour to identify the more general strands of development in the area of judicial reviewability as these relate to the office of attorney general, wherever these have emerged in recent years.

In 1977 a major constitutional crisis, involving the attorney general and the judiciary, was gathering steam in the United Kingdom. Its echoes rapidly reverberated throughout the Commonwealth and are still to be heard from time to time. The instigation for this confrontation was the view trenchantly expressed by Lord Denning, MR in *Gouriet v Union of Post Office Workers* [1977]. Presiding over the Court of Appeal on that occasion, Lord Denning claimed that, in matters pertaining to the institution of civil proceedings for injunctive relief against threatened breaches of the law, courts have the right to review the attorney general's decision and, if necessary, to substitute their own views for that of the senior law officer of the Crown. As is now well known, each of the law lords, in the subsequent appeal to the House of Lords [1978], categorically rejected any jurisdiction on the part of the courts to review and control the attorney general's decisions in matters affecting public rights and the public interest generally. Delivering the lead judgment, Lord Wilberforce declared it to be 'a fundamental principle of English law that private rights can be asserted by individuals, but that public rights can only be asserted by the Attorney General as representing the public. In terms of constitutional law, the rights of the public are vested in the Crown, and the Attorney General enforces them as an officer of the Crown ... That it is the exclusive right of the Attorney General to represent the public interest – even where individuals might be interested in a larger view of the matter – is not technical, not procedural, not fictional. It is constitutional ... it is also wise' ([1978] at 477, 481).

The theme running throughout all the *Gouriet* judgments in the House of Lords is the rejection of the invitation to stake out a jurisdictional claim whereby the decisions of the attorney general, in the exercise of his prerogative authority, could become the subject of disputation in the courts. In the words of Lord Fraser, 'If the Attorney-General were to commit a serious error of judgment by withholding consent to relator proceedings in a case where he ought to have given it, the remedy must in my opinion lie in the political field by enforcing his responsibility to Parliament and not in the legal field through the courts. That is appropriate because his error would not be an error of law but would be one of political judgment, using the expression, of course, not in a party sense but in the sense of weighing the relative importance of different aspects of the public interest. Such matters are not appropriate for decision in the courts' (ibid.: 524).

In emphasizing the remedy of parliamentary accountability, in contradistinction to judicial accountability, as the proper avenue to follow where a challenge is mounted against the attorney general's decision to withhold his fiat in relator proceedings, the views expressed by the law lords in *Gouriet* [1978] seem to be out of step with the position taken by the same court in the later *GCHQ* case (*Council of Civil Service Unions v*

Minister for the Civil Service [1985], opening the door as it did to a general reviewability of prerogative decisions made by any sector of the executive branch of government.

This new judicial philosophy stands in marked contrast to the same court's refusal in the *Gouriet* case to undertake precisely such an exercise with respect to prerogative decisions of the attorney general in matters affecting public rights and the public interest. The apparent divergence in judicial doctrine, represented by the two cases, was not addressed in the *GCHQ* case (*Council of Civil Service Unions v Minister for the Civil Service* [1985]) and it will be recalled that the prerogative powers associated with the office of attorney general do not appear among the list of excluded categories which the House of Lords has suggested might not be amenable to judicial assessment and review. This singular omission may or may not have been deliberate, but there already exist a number of instances, drawn from different countries in the Commonwealth, that indicate a judicial disposition to tread carefully when encroaching upon those clearly defined prerogative powers that historically are associated with the office of the attorney general in England and Wales. The principal body of evidence that supports this conclusion derives from the mounting volume of judicial precedents applying what has come to be known as the abuse of process doctrine. In analyzing those precedents, a special watch should be focused on parallels with the principles of judicial review as formulated in the broader context just concluded.

ABUSE OF PROCESS AND JUDICIAL REVIEW

The advent of the modern doctrine that there exists an inherent power in the courts to prevent abuses of their process, even to the extent of staying the trial of an indictment that has been properly filed, is generally attributed to Lord Devlin's judgment in the House of Lords case of *Connelly v Director of Public Prosecutions* [1964]. Reinforcement of the doctrine by the House of Lords in *D.D.P. v Humphreys* [1977] and by the Judicial Committee of the Privy Council in *Bell v D.P.P. of Jamaica* [1985], coupled with similar pronouncements of the highest appellate courts in Canada, Australia, and New Zealand, leave little room for doubt that the abuse of process doctrine is now an integral part of the common law.

Of all these jurisdictions the Canadian courts appear to have contributed the most guidance in determining the exact scope of the doctrine and what limits prescribe its availability in the circumstances of a particular case. And even there the story of the doctrine's evolution has not been straight sailing. After the general principle was first tentatively invoked by a provincial court of appeal in 1969, it was not until its decision in *Rourke v The Queen* [1977] that the Supreme Court of Canada gave the abuse of process doctrine what many observers felt was a confusing and, at best, ambivalent endorsement. Speaking for the majority of the court, in a five-to-four decision, Pigeon, J concluded that:

I cannot admit of any general discretionary power to stay proceedings regularly instituted because the prosecution is considered oppressive. In fact, I think the correct view is that which was expressed as follows by Viscount Dilhorne in *DPP v Humphreys* [1976] 2 All ER 497:

A judge must keep out of the arena. He should not have or appear to have any responsibility for the institution of a prosecution. The functions of prosecutors and of judges must not be blurred ... If there is the power which my noble and learned friends think there is to stop a prosecution *in limine* it is my view a power that should only be exercised in the most exceptional circumstances. (Ibid.: 510–11)

Two schools of thought emerged in the Supreme Court of Canada as the justices wrestled with this new frontier of judicial involvement in the administration of criminal justice. Set against the principle reflected in the passage quoted above was the interpretation of abuse of process as a wide-ranging technique for control by the criminal courts of criminal procedure, a technique illustrated but not limited by the special pleas of *autrefois acquit* and *convict, res judicata,* and issue estoppel. Although not couched in this precise language, one senses the same underlying tug of war going on in courts across the Commonwealth, as they come to decide upon the application of abuse of process in particular cases. The latest pronouncement on the present state of Canadian law on the subject is contained in the judgment of former Chief Justice Dickson, speaking for a unanimous Supreme Court in *R v Jewitt* [1985]. Acknowledging the uncertainty that surrounded the common law position as to the availability of a stay of proceedings to remedy abuse of process, Dickson, CJ adopted the conclusion of the Ontario Court of Appeal in *R v Young* [1984]: 'There is a residual discretion in a trial court judge to stay proceedings where compelling an accused to stand trial would violate those fundamental principles of justice which underlie the community's sense of fair play and decency and to prevent the abuse of a court's process through oppressive or vexatious proceedings' (ibid.: 31). Dickson, CJ added that this is a power *which can be exercised only in the clearest of cases*' (my emphasis) (*Jewitt* [1985]: 14).

The development of the doctrine of abuse of process has been invoked in the Canadian courts to an extent not paralleled in other common law jurisdictions. There is an additional element that explains this prominence, namely the Charter of Rights and Freedoms [1982], and especially the extremely broad interpretation accorded to Section 7 of the Charter since it was first invoked before the Supreme Court. That provision declares, 'Everyone has the right to life, liberty and security of the person and the right not to be deprived thereof except in accordance with the principles of fundamental justice.' Despite the widespread opinion, expressed by provincial appellate courts, that the common law doctrine of abuse of process has now been subsumed in the above section of the Charter, with all the remedies available under its Section 24, there are outstanding questions as to the onus of proof that are yet to be ruled on by the Supreme Court of Canada. No less importantly, we have yet to discover how far the Supreme Court justices, as opposed to the lower courts, are disposed to press their claims to oversee the exercise of prosecutorial discretion under the jurisdictional umbrella of the Charter of Rights and especially the potent Section 7.

On the present available evidence the Canadian Supreme Court appears to be working in tandem with its counterpart, the High Court of Australia. Beginning with *Barton v The Queen* [1980/81], the justices of Australia's highest court squarely addressed the conflict of principles inherent in the constitutional question as to who, ultimately, determines where the line is to be drawn between the executive and judicial functions in supervising matters of prosecution. On the particular issue before it in *Barton*, the High Court justices upheld the New South Wales attorney general's right to file an ex officio indictment, with a majority inclined towards the view that 'a trial held without antecedent committal proceedings, unless justified on strong and powerful grounds, must necessarily be considered unfair' (ibid.: 100). Perceptions change, and I venture to suggest that little, if any, support exists today for such an extreme position. Relying on the House of Lords speeches in *Connelly* [1964] and *D.P.P. v Humphreys* [1977], the Australian High Court showed no equivocation in declaring the existence, as an integral part of Australian common law, of the power in the superior courts to prevent an abuse of process in criminal cases and to ensure the right of the accused to a fair trial. At the same time, the Australian justices expressly disavowed any intention on their part to examine the attorney general's original decision, under his prerogative powers, to launch the criminal prosecution, stating, 'The courts exercise no control over the Attorney General's decision to commence criminal proceedings, but once he does so, the courts will control those proceedings so as to ensure that the accused receives a fair trial' [1980] 147 CLR 75, 96.

Similar judicial statements, reconciling the principles that underlie the constitutional separation of functions as they involve the attorney general and the courts, are to be found in the law reports of many Commonwealth jurisdictions. Repetition, however, does not conceal the simplistic character of the dividing line expressed by the High Court of Australia in the passage quoted above from *Barton v The Queen* [1980/81]. Just exactly what is comprehended in the phrase 'the Attorney General's *decision* to commence criminal proceedings' is far from clear. Earlier in this essay, when discussing the problems surrounding the scope for the law society's disciplinary jurisdiction as it relates to the attorney general and public prosecutors, I tried to stress the importance of preventing the governing body from intruding upon a range of subsidiary issues that are part and parcel of the discretionary power entrusted to the attorney general to institute or to stay a criminal prosecution. Legal, evidentiary, and policy questions are incapable of being assigned to wholly separate compartments within the decision to commence or halt criminal proceedings. Therein lies the same danger that I perceive exists in not keeping a vigilant eye on the extent of judicial interpretation of abuse of process. If the resolution by any court of that question involves a substantial constraint on the attorney general's discretionary powers, whether to institute or to stay the proceedings, and whether at large or in a particular case, there should be no reluctance on the part of any attorney general to confront the underlying constitutional question of the separation of functions in the administration of justice.

It is important to assess how far the courts are now prepared to go in pressing their claims to supervise the prosecuting arm of the state with the goal of ensuring a fair trial. It is now generally accepted that, as Lord Diplock observed in *R v Sang* [1980] at 437, 'the fairness of a trial is not all one-sided; it requires that those who are undoubtedly guilty should be convicted as well as that those about whose guilt there is any reasonable doubt should be acquitted.' Consequently, whereas at first there was a distinct impression that the courts viewed delay on the part of the prosecution solely from the perspective of whether it was justifiable or not, this approach has now been replaced with a more stringent test as to whether the delay on the part of the prosecution has resulted in the defendant being substantially prejudiced in the preparation or conduct of his or her defence. Different jurisdictions appear to agree that the reneging by a prosecutor on an agreement to extend immunity from prosecution to an accused in return for cooperation that is in fact given constitutes improper conduct and an abuse of process. More recently, the English Divisional Court, following an all-too-rare review of a wide range of Commonwealth cases on the issue before the court, ruled that the prosecution of a person who has received a promise, undertaking, or representation *by the police* that he will not be prosecuted is capable of being an abuse of process, and his committal to the Crown court to stand trial in breach of such a promise may be questioned in judicial review proceedings (*R v Croydon Justices, ex p. Dean*) [1993].

Considerably more reluctance is evident, at least in Canada, on the part of the courts to question the route chosen by the attorney general or his agents in launching a prosecution, whether by way of a preliminary hearing or by direct indictment. Although the question has yet to be determined in the Supreme Court of Canada, both the Ontario and Manitoba Courts of Appeal have ruled that the principles of fundamental justice, now entrenched in Section 7 of the Charter of Rights [1982], are not per se violated by the attorney general exercising his long-established right to prefer an indictment directly, thus depriving the accused of the opportunity to cross-examine key Crown witnesses by way of a preliminary hearing. Two important caveats, however, suggest a recognition on the part of the provincial appellate courts that there are no absolutes on this question. In declining on the grounds of the separation of constitutional functions, to recognize any power in the courts to review the prosecutorial functions of the attorney general, the chief justice of Manitoba in *Balderstone v R* [1984] qualified this immunity by reference to the caveat 'barring flagrant impropriety' (at 534). This is an emotive phrase that judges in several jurisdictions have invoked to describe the principle of last resort when assessing the fairness of the adjudicative process.

More specific dimensions are contained in the important ruling of the Ontario Court of Appeal in *Re Regina and Arviv* [1985]. After acknowledging what has been said, in countless authorities, to be the unfettered jurisdiction of the attorney general to exercise his discretion in resorting to a direct indictment, Martin, JA (speaking for the court) declared: 'The preferring of a direct indictment under s. 507(3) of the [Criminal] Code *in combination with* the failure of the Crown to make adequate disclosure might, however, result in an accused being unable to make full answer and defence at his trial, thereby contravening s. 7 of the Charter and enabling the trial judge to fashion a remedy under s. 24(1)' (underlining of the Court; at 404). The same court, in the later case of *R v Ertel* [1988], put the whole issue in an even broader context, stating that 'the power of the Attorney-General to prefer an indictment is in accord with the principles of fundamental justice and forms part of the large arsenal of discretionary powers that the chief law enforcement officers must possess in order to effectively discharge their high constitutional duties. In the exercise of these discretionary powers the Attorney-General is accountable to Parliament or the legislature and the exercise of the power may be reviewed by a court of competent jurisdiction if it results in a denial or infringement of a constitutionally protected right' (ibid.: 415).

The accountability of the attorney general to Parliament or the legislature has not figured in this essay as prominently as the subject deserves. The introduction of the Charter of Rights [1982] as part of the Canadian Constitution, however, may have resulted in diminishing the parliamentary role in holding the attorney general to account for his or her actions, especially in the discharge of prosecutorial functions, and there is reason to believe that the passage quoted from *R. v Ertel* [1988] would receive the universal support of the Canadian judiciary, including the members of the present Supreme Court of Canada.

Bearing in mind the major changes in the modern approach to judicial reviewability subscribed to by the leading appellate courts in the Commonwealth, the question remains as to whether the incorporation into legislation of the attorney general's former prerogative powers automatically precludes any consideration of the original source of the same powers? It is my feeling that the historical roots of the attorney general's prerogative authority to commence or to stay criminal proceedings continue to exert a major constraint upon the judiciary, no matter which Commonwealth country is involved. Relying upon the original source of the attorney general's discretionary powers as justification for treating the subject as one of the 'excluded categories' beyond the reach of judicial review, it might also be thought, would be substantially diminished if these discretionary elements were now to be found embedded in statute law. How valid are these impressions?

Looking at the cases decided in the English courts since the enactment of the Prosecution of Offences Act [1985] with its detailed provisions governing the duties, powers, and responsibilities of the 'new' director of public prosecutions and the members of the Crown Prosecution Service, there is nothing that suggests a declaration of 'open season' on the part of the judiciary to review the exercise of prosecutorial powers. On the contrary, the approach has been uniformly circumspect and heavily weighted towards concentrating on the process of decision-making, as opposed to evaluating the particular decision. For example, in the recent case of *R v DPP ex parte B (a minor)* [1993], the Divisional Court was invited to review the decision of a Crown prosecutor who had refused to discontinue the prosecution of a minor. The police had earlier decided against administering a caution in the particular circumstances. The approach, reflected in the court's decision, is consistent with that expressed in several other recent cases which have explored the limits of judicial review in prosecution matters. According to Watkins, LJ:

I find it very difficult to envisage, with regard to that policy [of cautioning], a circumstance, fraud or dishonesty apart possibly, which would allow a challenge to a decision to prosecute or to continue proceedings unless it could be demonstrated in the case of a juvenile, that there had been either a total disregard of the policy or, contrary to it, a lack of inquiry into the circumstances and background of the person, previous offences, general character and so on, by the prosecutor and later by the Crown Prosecution Service ...'

   Therefore, although the C.P.S. decision may in principle be reviewed, in practice it is rarely likely to be successfully reviewed ... my view as to the position of adults, on the other hand, in this respect is that judicial review of a decision not to discontinue a prosecution is unlikely to be available. The danger of opening too wide the door of review of the discretion to continue a prosecution is manifest and such review, if it exists, must, therefore, be confined to very narrow limits. (Ibid., 770–1)

To summarize what has been happening on the judicial review front as it relates to actions taken by, or in the name of, the attorney general, I would describe the underlying constitutional questions as relatively dormant at this time. There have been the occasional skirmishes on the edges of the battleground. The *Gouriet* [1978] principle of the attorney general's total insulation from judicial review in exercising his prerogative authority is no longer sustainable in its entirety. Where the encroachment springs from adherence to the abuse of process doctrine there is no intrinsic reason to bemoan the new order. There are obvious pitfalls of excessive judicial ardour in wanting to oversee every aspect of the administration of justice. The most effective response to such potential excesses is to determine, in advance, the ground upon which the constitutional duties and prerogatives of the attorney general should be defended as a matter of principle. This essay, in part, has been concerned to provide some guidance in anticipation of these future conflicts.

Chief Legal Adviser to Government and Guardian of the Public Interest

The attorney general's additional responsibilities as the government's chief legal adviser and as guardian of the public interest are undoubtedly the least discussed and least well understood of the office's functions. Difficult questions have arisen in many jurisdictions around the organization (centralized or dispersed among government departments) and superintendence of these functions by the attorney general. Recent tendencies in some countries (for example, Australia) towards commercialization of some of the legal services for which the attorney general is responsible threaten to fragment still further the unified role traditionally vested in the attorney general as the chief legal adviser to the Crown, its executive council, its individual minister, and all the branches of government.

Equally importantly, there appears to be a lack of appreciation among politicians, treasury mandarins, and members of the government legal service alike in many jurisdictions as to the full scope of these responsibilities in the overall machinery of government and the importance of assuring the political independence with which the senior law officer discharges these advisory functions. The all-too-common tendency to view the attorney general and his department as no more than the law firm that is always on call to serve the interests of the political party that is in power at the time provides a fertile environment for subtle and not-so-subtle political pressures to be brought to bear on the attorney general and his staff with respect to the exercise of these functions. The practice, in many Commonwealth countries, whereby the deputy minister in the attorney general's department is appointed by the prime minister, can easily encourage such attitudes and practices.

It requires a very strong attorney general, fully cognizant of the history of the office, and confident of his or her constitutional position, to withstand such pressures. There should never be any doubt, however, as to the single line of accountability that flows upwards to the desk of the attorney general, as the accountable minister of the Crown. Regrettably, there is evidence that many new incumbents come into the office of the attorney general without the requisite appreciation of these issues, and a greater commitment to the appropriate principles, and to educating all concerned about them, seems to be called for in many, if not most, jurisdictions.

With the advent of human rights as a subject of increased public debate in every part of the Commonwealth, another major dimension has been added to the attorney general's variegated functions. The question arises as to what are the proper principles that should guide an attorney general in fulfilling his role as 'guardian of the public interest' with respect to maintaining fundamental rights and freedoms. The idea of exploring ways and means to expand the judicial enforcement of human rights, by incorporating well-established international norms into the domestic laws of each country, has captured the imagination of senior members of the judiciary in several continents. Testimony to this fact is provided by the many conferences specifically devoted to this enterprise, which have typically concluded with the public release of formal statements committing participant countries towards bringing the principles of fundamental human rights into the daily consciousness of domestic courts and public officials alike.

This commitment to the implementation of basic human rights has, of course, been reflected not only in many of the independence constitutions of countries of the Commonwealth, but also in the adoption or consideration of constitutional rights documents by some of the older members of the Commonwealth. By its adoption, in 1960, of a statutory Bill of Rights [RSC 1985], and its subsequent incorporation of an entrenched Charter of Rights and Freedoms [1982] into its patriated constitution in 1982, Canada can be regarded as a leader among this latter group. While New Zealand has chosen to reject the entrenched option in favour of a declaratory but unenforceable New Zealand Bill of Rights [1990], discussions are still going on in Australia about what is the appropriate approach to the recognition and implementation of human rights in that country.

The simmering debate that has been going on in the United Kingdom for many years on the question of whether to adopt a judicially enforceable Bill of Rights, must be viewed in light of that country's decision to become a signatory to the European Convention on Human Rights in 1950 and its consistent acceptance, since 1966, of the jurisdiction of the European Court of Human Rights. Implementation of human rights through a regional rather than a domestic tribunal, however, has not been without its problems or critics. In particular, the tedious and cumbersome nature of the present procedures to enforce the European Convention, and what the English lord chief justice has referred to as the 'humiliation' of having decisions in this area imposed on the British courts by a court in Strasbourg (Taylor, 1933: 329), has led senior members of the judiciary in that country to urge incorporation of the convention into domestic law, so that its implementation can be in the hands of British judges (see for example, Bingham, 1992). The current political climate in the United Kingdom suggests that such a fundamental reform may not be far off.

Promulgation of constitutional or statutory human rights provisions is, of course, an important indication of good intentions. Nevertheless, the gulf between theory and practice in the matter of ensuring adherence to human rights precepts is illustrated daily across the Commonwealth, to the point that ordinary citizens may be forgiven if they entertain reservations as to the practical value of texts that enunciate rights and freedoms but provide no effective sanctions where violations are shown to have occurred. In this respect, however, there are encouraging signs, in many jurisdictions, of an increased judicial creativity and reformist zeal in this area. The momentous entrenchment of the Charter of Rights and Freedoms [1982] in the Canadian constitution, for instance, has produced a notable transformation in judicial thinking, both in terms of direction and in the methods of legal reasoning. In fact, in demonstrating their readiness to venture down unfamiliar paths in which the interplay between legal, political, and social considerations becomes very apparent, there have been occasions when the predilections of individual justices have demonstrated, sometimes to an acute degree, the dangers of exaggerating the judicial power to override the will of Parliament. More recently, however, members of the Canadian Supreme Court have exhibited a more restrained approach to the judicial task of interpreting the Charter of Rights [1982] and balancing conflicting values in the process.

The prospect of an increased commitment by the judiciary throughout the Commonwealth to securing adherence to internationally recognized human rights norms is a trend that must be warmly welcomed. But it is equally important to consider the attorney general's expansive role, with historic roots in the common law, as one of the state's principal 'guardians of the public interest.' In my earlier work (Edwards, 1964, 1984), I have described the wide range of circumstances in which the attorney general is clothed with authority to represent the public interest and to appear ex officio in court to protect or enforce public rights. Notwithstanding the more generous approach evinced by the courts and law reform bodies in various parts of the Commonwealth on the subject of *locus standi*, there remains a constitutional responsibility on the part of the attorney general to intervene directly, in the courts or otherwise, if he deems public rights to be in jeopardy.

Basic human rights provisions confer public rights and not private rights in the procedural sense of conferring standing before the courts, and every individual citizen is entitled, without additional qualifications, to invoke human rights provisions in his or her own cause. The absence or failure of a citizen to set human rights laws in motion, however, in no way precludes the attorney general from exercising his prerogative powers to ensure conformity with what are quintessentially public rights. Indeed, if the title 'guardian of the public interest' is to gain credence as something more than a high-sounding but empty formula, it calls for recognition by every attorney general that his or her constitutional duties demand a constant regard for the impact of human rights proclamations on every branch of the country's internal laws. In a state where these provisions are constitutionally entrenched they form part of the 'supreme law' of the land and, to borrow the words of a former chief justice of Canada, this means that 'these values are higher, more sacred than other public interests' (Dickson, 1983: 185). The message for attorneys general should be basically the same where something short of constitutional entrenchment exists but there are other forms of national commitment to the principles of universal human rights.

To be more specific, in discharging his role as chief legal adviser to the government, if the issues that give rise to consultation with the attorney general are strictly matters of law few serious problems can be anticipated in acknowledging the paramountcy of the first law officer's opinion. Where, however, legal and policy issues are intertwined and the policy aspects involve adherence or non-adherence to the legal standards incorporated in human rights provisions, the situation may well arise in which the ministry responsible for the policies at stake, and its legal advisers, take a diametrically different position to that subscribed to by the attorney general. How should this impasse be dealt with? If I may be permitted to draw on my previously expressed views on this question, in the context of the Canadian Charter of Rights and Freedoms [1982]:

'the first Law Officer may choose to defer to the policy position taken by the other branch of the Executive. If so, this will be by choice and not through any constitutional obligation to confine himself to expressing a legal opinion in the narrowest sense of that expression. The Attorney General is entitled to oppose the policy of his ministerial colleagues at every stage of its formulation and implementation including discussions with the appropriate cabinet committee or in the cabinet itself. If the full weight of the Attorney General's office is to be sustained it must be seen that the so-called policy imperatives derive from the legal implications of the proposed policy. Nowhere is this likely to be more apparent than if the proposed legislative or executive action is calculated to invite a major Charter challenge. For the government to reject the Attorney General's advice would be quite exceptional and, in my view, should lead the Attorney General to question seriously his commitment to serve the Government as its chief legal adviser. This threat should not be lightly undertaken but if the claim to the title of 'guardian of the public interest' is to be reinforced it must be shown that the Attorney General is totally committed to upholding the 'supreme law' as the embodiment of society's deepest convictions.' (Edwards, 1987: 52–3)

Should the application of the human rights provisions and related jurisprudence be less than clear and the prospect is entertained of referring the dispute to the courts for resolution, what further responsibility derives from the special constitutional position occupied by the attorney general? Viewed from the narrow perspective of his role as the minister responsible for regulating all litigation involving the government, or any ministry or agency of the government, it will suffice if the attorney general ensures that the government is represented by counsel in the ensuing litigation. Beyond this minimal stance, in my view, lies the larger constitutional duty to ensure that the wider public interest is adequately represented, particularly in determining the ambit of a hotly contested human rights provision. Furthermore, as I have previously suggested:

It not enough to assume that a public spirited citizen or interest group will step forward to assert a Charter challenge. Merely ensuring that the necessary funding is forthcoming to maintain such a suit, including the costs of providing legal counsel to represent the citizens' claims, is not sufficient. These alternatives may be sufficient to meet most of the claims deserving support and recognition. The door, however, must be left open, in my judgment, for the extraordinary demonstration of the Attorney General's independent status and independent responsibilities by way of active representation in the courts, in his own person if that is necessary, to argue the case on behalf of the public interest.

Steps to ensure that the government's more restricted interests are adequately represented can readily be accomplished through senior departmental counsel. It could be argued that the objective described above could just as readily be discharged by engaging the services of independent counsel, drawn from the ranks of the private Bar. This suggestion is deserving of implementation in appropriate circumstances. My concern, however, is not merely to observe the minimum dictates of adequate representation on behalf of the maligned citizen, or a specially disadvantaged or threatened group in society, but to underline the significance that attaches to the unique constitutional place occupied by the office of the Attorney General in Canada and in so doing to strengthen in the public mind an awareness of the Attorney General's determination to uphold the essential qualities of this historic office.' (ibid.: 53–4)

Those remarks have equal application to every member state in the Commonwealth. They define what I consider to be the constitutional mandate of the attorney general to assume a leadership role in sustaining public rights in general and fundamental human rights in particular. Experience to date suggests that, where there is strong evidence of the violation of human rights, the role of public advocate in pursuing judicial remedies has been left to non-governmental organizations or private groups to spearhead. The existence of such bodies, in the various regions of the Commonwealth, has been largely instrumental in generating a heightened public awareness of the whole question of human rights.

There has never been a time in which the judiciary has been more vocal in examining different ways whereby the common law courts themselves can, in the words of one English judge, 'insist upon and secure a high degree of priority for those central rights which broadly find their place in the principal substantive provisions of the European Convention on Human Rights and Fundamental Freedoms' (Laws, 1993: 60). Each approach has been focused on the judicial initiatives that are now being increasingly recognized. Without in any way seeking to diminish the significance of those noteworthy developments, my purpose is to underline the challenge facing every attorney general throughout the Commonwealth to assert, by personal example, the traditional leading role of the office of the attorney general as 'guardian of the public interest' in upholding the fundamental rights of every citizen and, if necessary, actively representing this noble cause before the courts.

Note

1 This is an abridged version of a discussion paper prepared for the meeting of Commonwealth Law Ministers in Grand Baie, Mauritius, in November 1993. The editor thanks the Commonwealth Legal Secretariat for permission to include it in this volume.

Prosecutorial Accountability in Canada

DON STUART

The focus of this essay is on the accountability of trial prosecutors in Canada, with particular reference to the practical realities of prosecuting in Toronto in the province of Ontario. Toronto is a congested metropolitan area of some three and a half million people. The concept of 'accountability' does not necessarily imply 'control' (Stenning, 1986: 285–6). If 'accountability' were merely used to refer to an ability to give an account, there would be little meaning in a conclusion that a prosecutor is accountable. Accountability will here rather be used in the sense of a liability or obligation to give an account, which certainly points to external control. The source of obligation could be legal, but also political or administrative, in the sense of internal job-related consequences for non-compliance (ibid.: 286).

Prosecutorial Arrangements and Powers in Canada

The historical origins and establishment of the Canadian system of Crown prosecutors has been well described elsewhere (Grosman, 1969: ch. 2; Stenning, 1986: Part 1).

Although Canada, since 1892, has had a Criminal Code that applies across the country, there is a complex division of prosecutorial authority between federal and provincial jurisdictions. Although Canada still has in principle a system of private prosecution in which any individual can prosecute, in practice the vast majority of criminal prosecutions are conducted by salaried Crown attorneys under the authority of provincial attorneys general. The attorneys general are elected politicians who also serve in Cabinet.

The authority for prosecution of criminal offences is but one of the responsibilities of the attorney general (see for example, Section 5 of the Minister of the Ontario Attorney General Act) [RSO 1990]. On a day-to-day basis, the vast bulk of criminal prosecutions are conducted by individual Crown prosecutors who act as agents for the attorney general. Unlike district attorneys in the United States, Crown prosecutors in Canada are appointed, not elected. Unlike district attorneys, they have no separate investigatory arm and are thus forced to rely exclusively on investigation by police forces.

The Canadian tradition is that prosecutors play a quasijudicial role in a special relation to the court. The role of prosecuting counsel is that of 'ministers of justice' rather than partisan advocates. The most frequently quoted description is that of Mr Justice Rand for the Supreme Court of Canada in *Boucher v. The Queen*:

It cannot be over-emphasized that the purpose of a criminal prosecution is not to obtain a conviction. It is to lay before a jury what the Crown considers to be credible evidence relevant to what is alleged to be a crime. Counsel have a duty to see that all available legal proof of the facts is presented; it should be done firmly and pressed to its limit but also done fairly. The role of the prosecutor excludes any notion of winning or losing; his function is a matter of public duty than which in civil life there can be none charged with greater personal responsibility. It is to be efficiently performed with a sense of the dignity, the seriousness and the justness of our judicial proceedings. [1955] SCR 16, at 23–4

Similarly the Canadian Bar Association describes the duties of a prosecutor as follows:

When engaged as a prosecutor, the lawyer's prime duty is not to seek a conviction, but to present before the trial court all available credible evidence relevant to the alleged crime in order that justice may be done through a fair trial upon the merits. The prosecutor exercises a public function involving much discretion and power and must act fairly and dispassionately. The prosecutor should not do anything that might prevent the accused from being represented by counsel or communicating with counsel and, to the extent required by law and accepted practice, should make timely disclosure to the accused or defence counsel (or the court if the accused is not represented) of all relevant facts and known witnesses, whether tending to show guilt or innocence, or that would affect the punishment of the accused. (Canadian Bar Association, 1988: 37)

Most Canadian prosecutors would reject the view of one United States prosecutor that 'your true purpose is to convict the guilty man who sits at the defence table, and to go for the jugular as viciously and as rapidly as possible ... You must never forget that your goal is total annihilation' (Luban, 1988: 59, 17).

Canadian legislatures and Parliament have repeatedly attempted over the years to declare criteria on which police discretion is to be exercised in a wide variety of contexts such as powers to search, arrest, and release prior to trial. In stunning contrast, Crown attorneys have virtually unfettered discretion as to when to charge, what to charge, and when the charge should be reduced or dropped (see generally Morgan, 1986; Stenning, 1986: 199–329). Common law powers such as the right to withdraw a charge, give discovery to defence counsel, and accept a plea bargain have been largely unlimited by the courts. So too, statutory powers such as the right to take over a private prosecution, to enter a stay of proceedings, or to decide in the case of dual offences to proceed by way of indictment or by way of summary conviction (which has important implications for the accused, such as the right to choose a jury trial and as to the maximum penalty) are simply given to the attorney general or the agents without any statutory guidelines. The Law Reform Commission of Canada (Canada, LRC, 1990) has recently recommended that guidelines be published, although their recommendation is that they not be imposed by legislatures.

All Crown attorneys have this panoply of powers. The few special prosecutorial powers which can only be exercised at the discretion of the attorney general are also unlimited. Such powers include the power to directly indict to avoid a preliminary inquiry or where there has been a discharge at a preliminary inquiry, consent to prosecute in the case of some offences such as wilful promotion of hatred, and nudity in a public place, and also permission to make an application to have an accused declared a dangerous offender, leading to indeterminate detention.

Attorney General's Accountability to the Executive and to Parliament

In England, the attorney general is not a member of Cabinet, and there is now an entrenched constitutional convention that the attorney general's exercise of prosecutorial authority is to be independent and free of political consideration. It has long been clear that the English attorney general may seek the advice of Cabinet but is not required to do so and not bound to follow that advice. The authoritative statement of the relationship between the attorney general and cabinet is that of Lord Shawcross, a former attorney general of England, writing in 1951:

I think the true doctrine is that it is the duty of an Attorney-General, in deciding whether or not to authorise the prosecution, to acquaint himself with all the relevant facts, including, for instance, the effect which the prosecution, successful or unsuccessful as the case may be, would have upon public morale and order, and with any other consideration affecting public policy. In order so to inform himself, he may, although I do not think he is obliged to, consult with any of his colleagues in the government, and indeed, as Lord Simon once said, he would in some cases be a fool if he did not. On the other hand, the assistance of his colleagues is confined to informing him of particular considerations which might affect his own decision, and does not consist, and must not consist, in telling him what that decision ought to be. The responsibility for the eventual decision rests with the Attorney-General, and he is not to be put, and is not put, under pressure by his colleagues in the matter. Nor, of course, can the Attorney-General shift his responsibility for making the decision on to the shoulders of his colleagues. If political considerations which in the broad sense that I have indicated affect government in the abstract arise it is the Attorney-General, applying his judicial mind, who has to be the sole judge of those considerations' (quoted in Edwards, 1964: 223)

In Canada, the extent to which attorneys general are independent is less clear, because they are members of Cabinet and also have traditionally been given responsibility for matters far wider than that of prosecutorial authority. Nevertheless, in recent years a constitutional convention of independence has emerged. In 1968, Chief Justice McRuer, author of *Report Number One* of the Royal Commission Inquiry into Civil Rights in the province of Ontario (henceforth McRuer Report) wrote:

The Attorney General must be answerable to the Legislature and it is better that he be answerable as a Minister of the Crown. Notwithstanding that this is so, he must of necessity occupy a different position politically from all other Ministers of the Crown. As the Queen's Attorney he occupies an office with judicial attributes and in that office he is responsible to the Queen and not responsible to the Government. He must decide when to prosecute and when to discontinue a prosecution. In making such decisions he is not under the jurisdiction of the Cabinet nor should such decisions be influenced by political considerations. They are decisions made as the Queen's Attorney, not as a member of the government of the day. (Ontario, McRuer Report, 1968: vol. 2, 933–4)

More recently, several Canadian attorneys general have re-asserted the convention that the exercise of prosecutorial authority by an attorney general is an independent one free of political considerations. For example, the former minister of justice of Canada, Mr Ron Basford, stated this in the House of Commons: 'The first principle, in my view, is that there must be excluded any consideration based upon narrow, partisan views, or based upon the political consequences to me or to others. In arriving at a decision on such a sensitive issue as this, the Attorney General is entitled to seek information and advice from others but in no way is he directed by his colleagues in the government or by parliament itself' (Canada, House of Commons Debates, vol. 121, p. 3882, 17 March, 1978).

So too, former attorney general of Ontario, Ian Scott, wrote the following in 1987:

Issues of whether to institute or discontinue a prosecution are not matters of government policy. The Premier and Cabinet have no power to direct whether a particular prosecution should be pursued or whether a particular appeal should be undertaken. These decisions rest solely with the Attorney General, who must be regarded for these purposes as an independent officer, exercising a function that in many ways resembles the functions of a judge.

Questions of prosecution policy are legal issues and, while considerations of the public interest are vital in determining these questions, prosecutorial decisions must be made according to legal criteria. The Attorney General's assessment of the public interest must absolutely exclude any consideration of the political implications of a particular decision. Public respect for the rule of law demands that prosecutorial decisions be made objectively, without regard to possible political consequences. (Scott, 1987: 190)

Since the convention is that the attorney general has no obligation to discuss prosecutorial decisions with Cabinet, the attorney general could not be said to be truly accountable to Cabinet (see too Stenning, 1986: 295). Given a well-entrenched convention respecting the secrecy of Cabinet deliberations, the extent of political accountability by an attorney general to Cabinet will never be known. Few attorneys general may be prepared to sacrifice their own political careers by assertions of independence in the face of Cabinet objections. In 1988, the attorney general of British Columbia did, however, give as a reason for his resignation the attempted interference from the Cabinet in his independent prosecutorial responsibility for determining whether particular charges should be laid (Canada, LRC, 1990: 2). Stenning (1986: 300) suspects that the attorney general can be considered accountable to Cabinet, especially when cases are thought by the Cabinet to have important political implications and also in the sense that an attorney general who insists upon exercising prosecutorial authority in ways which do not command the confidence of the Cabinet or the prime minister may be liable to be dismissed from office.

The attorney general is politically accountable to the legislature through ministerial responsibility to answer questions in question period and to face possible censure by the House. However, there is room for considerable scepticism as to the effectiveness of this accountability (ibid.: 301–6; Cohen, 1977: 188). The parliamentary question period does not provide a mechanism to ensure that the minister will in fact give direct answers or answers which provide sufficient background for an assessment as to whether the answer is satisfactory. Questions in the legislature will often be after the fact (Edwards, 1964: 224–5) and will often be ducked by reliance on the *sub judice* rule, which ensures that, in the interests of a fair trial, there should be no comment on a matter still before the court. From the point of view of an accused, this form of accountability is highly unlikely to be an effective remedy for abuse. Stenning explains this very well:

In the pressure of business with which Legislatures are involved, they inevitably can and do become far removed from the stream of run-of-the-mill criminal prosecutions which are processed through the inferior courts every day. The volume and low visibility of these cases (which form the vast bulk of all criminal cases heard by the courts) make it fairly easy for abuses to go undetected by the politicians, and ensure that parliamentary control over such abuses is unlikely to be very consistently effective. In these circumstances, a judge or magistrate is undoubtedly in a far better position to check such abuses than a busy politician. (Stenning, 1971: 179–80)

Edwards (1980: 69–70) has suggested that the convention that the attorney general be free from political influences should be understood in the sense of free from partisan political considerations, which he defines as 'designed to protect or advance the retention of constitutional power by the incumbent government and its political supporters.' Edwards suggests that the attorney general may have regard to 'non-partisan' political considerations such as the 'maintenance of harmonious international relations between states, the reduction of strife between ethnic groups, the maintenance of industrial peace and generally interests of the public at large.' Stenning (1983: 438–9) seems well justified in retorting that this distinction between partisan and non-partisan decisions is one of degree rather than kind.

Concerns about the independence of the attorney general from partisan political influences and the need to reduce potential conflicts of interest has recently led the Law Reform Commission of Canada (1990: 53–5) to recommend the creation of a new office of director of public prosecutions, who would be an appointed professional with tenure and not a member of Cabinet. Such an office has recently been established in Nova Scotia as a result of the Marshall inquiry (Nova Scotia, Royal Commission on the Donald Marshall, Jr, Prosecution, 1989), which raised questions concerning the attorney general's decision not to lay charges against a member of the provincial Cabinet.

Accountability of the Crown Attorney to the Attorney General

All Crown attorneys, whether full- or part-time, are employed by the attorney general and are clearly administratively responsible to him or her, given that the attorney general has the power to terminate their employment.

A claim has been made (Armstrong and Chasse, 1975: 162–4) that Ontario Crown attorneys enjoy constitutional status independent of the attorney general largely by virtue of a special history of appointment under Section 2 of the Upper Canada County Attorneys Act, 1857. This claim has been persuasively refuted on historical and other grounds (Stenning, 1986: 289–90, 308–10). However, there is clearly a modern convention under which attorneys general rarely involve themselves in individual prosecutions. This was explained by a former attorney general of Ontario, Mr John Clement as follows:

It has never been suggested, however, that the Attorney General assume responsibility for the day-to-day administration of justice. Under our system, the

Attorney General is ultimately responsible to the people while local Crown Attorneys are granted a broad and generous area of unfettered discretion in criminal prosecutions. Subject only to very wide and general guidelines as to policy, the Crown Attorney is free to decide whether or not to launch a prosecution, the manner in which it will be prosecuted and how he will handle the matter at trial. In all these matters and in the general administration of justice within his jurisdiction, the Crown attorney knows that he has more than enough authority to respond adequately to the situations in which he is involved. (Cited in Chasse, 1982: 83)

Of course in practice this deference does not remove the right of the attorney general to intervene in any particular case.

Most attorneys general content themselves with issuing policy guidelines on specific matters. Just how general and non-binding they are can be gauged by considering two Ontario examples.

As of 1 January, 1988, the Ministry of the Attorney General issued ten principles applicable to plea discussions. One of these principles related to expediency: 'Expediency in reducing workload is not acceptable as a reason for accepting a plea to a lesser offence or to a lesser number of offences. Expediency in this sense does not include weaknesses in the Crown's case on the major charge or charges, which may be a valid reason for accepting a plea to a lesser offence or to a lesser number of offences' (Ontario, Ministry of the Attorney General, 1988: Policy No. P-1, par. 2). However, the guideline ended with the following paragraph designed not to fetter discretion: 'These principles are not rules to be applied rigidly or to be considered binding in every situation. However, although a Crown Attorney must have a free and unfettered discretion as to how to apply these principles, the Crown Attorney also has a continuing responsibility to conduct all plea discussions in accordance with their spirit' (ibid.).

A 20 March 1984 direction as to the prosecution of cases of domestic violence encourages Crown attorneys to proceed with a prosecution against the wishes of the complainant: 'The Crown Attorney should accede to a request by the complainant not to proceed only after giving the request careful and serious consideration. This is clearly in line with the view that domestic violence is in the realm of other criminal offences and must be treated as equally serious, and not regarded as solely a private family matter' (Ontario, Ministry of the Attorney General, 1984: 2). However, the director of crown attorneys was quick to add that a Crown attorney continues to have the jurisdiction to withdraw the charge 'when circumstances warrant.' The directive added a number of factors to be considered although they were said not to be exhaustive (ibid.: 2–3):

1 The strength of the Crown's case
2 The history, if any, of prior violent behaviour of the accused
3 The extent of injuries suffered by the battered wife
4 The reasons why the battered wife wishes not to proceed with the prosecution
5 The evidence of any harassment by the husband or others on his behalf after the charge was laid
6 The results of an interview between Crown counsel and the battered spouse during which Crown counsel discusses the public wrong aspect of domestic violence and tries to answer any concerns the battered spouse may have.

These guidelines from the attorney general were not binding on the particular Crown attorney or the court. They have since been revised (see now Ontario, Ministry of the Attorney General, 1994: Policies No. R-1 and No. SP-1). If a Crown attorney were to ignore them it seems self-evident that there might well be job-related consequences. In this sense, the guidelines set up administrative accountability to the attorney general.

A researcher who conducted a series of interviews with Crown attorneys in Ontario (Grosman, 1969: 3) suggests that their discretion is much more likely to be influenced by administrative demands and informal social relations, particularly those with the police.

A full-time prosecutor in Toronto, typically receiving twelve case briefs from the police the day before the scheduled trials, has little option but to trust the police and little time to consider the nuances of policy directives from the attorney general. The individual prosecutor is often entirely on his or her own. In such a pressure-cooker environment, it would be disingenuous to deny the lure of expediency in accepting guilty pleas. Given special training and emphasis on the difficult and important job of prosecuting domestic assault cases, prosecutors feel under tremendous pressure not to withdraw such a charge. There are certainly cases, however, for example, where there is no admission from an accused and the victim is not in court and has evaded service of a subpoena, when to proceed would be utterly futile. Most experienced prosecutors indicate that the best chance of proceeding successfully with a domestic assault prosecution where the victim is available but reluctant to proceed is not by the use of aggressive cross-examination tactics through 'adverse witness' evidence rules, but rather through a proper and sensitive interview with the victim, prior to the trial, to persuade the victim to proceed. Yet the unfortunate reality in busy metropolitan courts is that sometimes such interviews are simply not possible.

There is some legal authority for the proposition that an attorney general cannot legally pre-empt prosecutorial discretion. In *R v Catagas* [1977] the issue before the Manitoba Court of Appeal was whether the prosecution of an Aboriginal person for breach of the Migratory Birds Convention Act [RSC 1985] of Canada constituted an abuse of process because it was contrary to an internally promulgated policy of non-prosecution of Aboriginal persons in the province of Manitoba. The court refused to stay the prosecution, on the basis that the purported dispensing power by executive action in favour of a particular group was void and of no effect. The court speaks eloquently of the need to preserve a notion of prosecutorial discretion:

The other point is that nothing here stated is intended to curtail or affect the matter of prosecutorial discretion. Not every infraction of the law, as everybody knows, results in the institution of criminal proceedings ... An Attorney General, faced with circumstances indicating only technical guilt of a serious offence but actual guilt of a less serious offence, may decide to prosecute on the latter and not on the former ... But in all these instances the prosecutorial discretion is exercised in relation to a specific case. It is the particular facts of a given case that call that discretion into play. But that is a far different thing from the granting of a blanket dispensation in favour of a particular group or race ... The Crown may not by Executive action dispense with laws. The matter is as simple as that, and nearly three centuries of legal and constitutional history stand as the foundation for that principle. [1978] 38 CCC (2d) 296, at 301

Prosecutor's Liability against Civil Suits

Can an accused aggrieved by the conduct of the attorney general or the Crown prosecutor recover monetary damages in a civil suit?

Until the recent landmark ruling of the Supreme Court of Canada in *Nelles v Ontario* [1989], the weight of judicial authority, particularly in Ontario, was that prosecutors had an absolute immunity against such actions. In 1981, the plaintiff, Susan Nelles, a nurse, was charged with four counts of first degree murder in connection with the mysterious deaths of a number of infants at the hospital at which she worked. After a lengthy preliminary inquiry she was discharged on all four counts on the basis that the evidence adduced was insufficient to commit her to trial. She later brought a civil action against the Crown in right of Ontario, the attorney general of Ontario, and several police officers. The claim was framed in negligence, malicious prosecution, and false imprisonment, and also alleged a violation of Charter rights. A pre-trial motion succeeded in having the action dismissed. In confirming this ruling, the Ontario Court of Appeal held that the attorney general and his Crown attorneys had an absolute immunity from suits for damages in respect of their conduct of prosecutorial functions. The majority of the Supreme Court confirmed that under Section 5(6) of the Ontario Proceedings Against the Crown Act [RSO 1990], the Crown was exempt from any proceedings relating to liability for prosecutorial decisions. However, the court ruled that the attorney general in a personal capacity and Crown attorneys were not absolutely immune from civil suits in that they were liable for malicious prosecution. However the court appears to confirm absolute immunity against suits based on errors in judgment or professional negligence.

Writing for the majority, Mr Justice Lamer held that an absolute immunity was not justified in the interests of public policy. It would have the effect of negating a private right of action and, in some cases, might bar a remedy under the Canadian Charter of Rights and Freedoms [1982]. It would threaten the individual rights of citizens who have been wrongly and maliciously prosecuted. The court indicated that there were three policy reasons advanced to justify an absolute immunity for prosecutors: the rule encouraged public trust in the fairness and impartiality of those involved in the prosecutorial function, the threat of personal liability for tortious conduct would have a chilling effect on the prosecutor's exercise of discretion, and to permit civil suits against prosecutors would invite a flood of frivolous litigation. The court recognized some merit to these considerations but determined that they had to give way to the right of a private citizen to seek a remedy when the prosecutor acts maliciously and causes damage to the victim. Lamer, J pointed out that the tort of malicious prosecution requires proof of an absence of reasonable and probable cause for commencing the proceedings and also proof of an improper purpose or motive. Such a motive involved an abuse of the system of criminal justice for ends it was not designed to serve and an abuse of the office of the attorney general and his agents, the Crown attorneys. The inherent difficulty in proving a case of malicious prosecution, combined with the mechanisms available within the system of civil procedure to weed out meritless claims, was sufficient, according to the court, to ensure that the attorney general and Crown attorneys would not be hindered in the proper execution of their important public duties. Attempts to qualify prosecutorial immunity in the United States by, for example, drawing lines at various prosecutorial functions, had proven unsuccessful and unprincipled. Most commentators have similarly rejected the case for absolute immunity of Crown prosecutors (for example, Price, 1985; Hogg, 1989: 153). It has never been clear why Crown law officers should have absolute immunity while police officers do not, particularly when the police may in some prosecutions be acting on the instructions of Crown attorneys.

Since *Nelles* [1989], an accused can therefore hold the attorney general and/or the prosecutors personally legally accountable by a civil suit if there is proof on a balance of probabilities of a malicious prosecution. Apart from the considerable hurdles to such actions mentioned by the Supreme Court, other considerations suggest that the remedy will likely be largely ineffective (Stenning, 1986: 347; Hogg, 1989: 511). Actions for malicious prosecution cannot be brought where there was a conviction. They require a plaintiff prepared to undertake the notoriously high costs of such litigation. Furthermore, experience throughout the common law world indicates that actions for malicious prosecution rarely succeed. They are no remedy against the incompetent or negligent Crown attorney. There is thus still a contrast with the civil liability of police officers who, in addition to liability for malicious prosecution, face potential liability for breaches of duties of care or statutory duty.

It is still too early to verify the claims of some Crown prosecutors in Ontario that *Nelles* [1989] has indeed resulted in a number of vexatious law suits, especially from those defence counsel who conduct their practice as street fighters and are now prepared to add the threat of a civil suit to their arsenal of intimidation tactics in their fight against the Crown attorneys. One suspects, however, for the reasons already given, that such concerns will turn out to be largely groundless. The Supreme Court itself noted that the province of Quebec has allowed suits against the attorney general and Crown prosecutors since 1986, and there has been no evidence of a flood of claims.

Judicial Review

In the case of the vast bulk of prosecutorial conduct in trial courts, the above picture is one of most limited accountability in any of the senses of legal, political, or administrative accountability. It seems clear that the most important form of accountability of Crown attorneys lies in the discretion and power of trial judges to control the criminal process over which they preside.

Trial judges have always been prepared to exercise an overriding discretion to control the trial process itself in various rulings on matters of fair procedure and the application of the rules of evidence. However, prior to the enactment of the Charter of Rights and Freedoms [1982], courts showed extreme reluctance to review the exercise of the unlimited powers of discretion given to Crown attorneys. The reluctance has been based on a notion of separation of powers. There are also concerns that the administration of criminal justice would be jeopardized by endless applications for review and would transfer too much discretion to judges.

In *Smythe* [1971] the accused, charged with income tax evasion, relied on the protection of equality before the law in the Canadian Bill of Rights to challenge a provision under the Income Tax Amendment Act [1970, 1971, 1972] under which the Crown had an absolute discretion to proceed by way of indictment rather than by summary conviction proceedings. The Crown option in this case to proceed by way of indictment was particularly significant, in that such proceedings carried a minimum penalty of two months' imprisonment. For the Supreme Court of Canada, Chief Justice Fauteux rejected the challenge. The manner in which the attorney general exercised discretion could only be questioned in the legislature. Enforcement of the criminal law would be 'impossible' unless someone in authority was vested with discretionary power. Both before and after the Bill of Rights [RSC 1985], the attorney general's discretion to elect the mode of procedure was held to be part of the British and Canadian conception of equality before the law.

In *Rourke* [1977], Mr Justice Pigeon for the majority of the Supreme Court of Canada flatly held that there was no general discretionary power in the courts of criminal jurisdiction to stay proceedings that had been regularly instituted on the grounds that the prosecution was considered 'oppressive.' His Lordship pointed to the dangers in the exercise of an uncertain discretion by all courts and a threat to the independence of the judiciary.

Now, under the entrenched Charter, which is the supreme law, review of the exercise of discretion of prosecutors or an attorney general can no longer be resisted on the basis of a doctrine of separation of powers. In *Operation Dismantle* [1985], the Supreme Court confirmed that decisions of the executive branch of government, including Cabinet decisions, are subject to review by the courts under the Charter. Courts have, however, continued to resist frontal attacks, based on the Charter, on discretionary powers of prosecutors (and police), although they have accepted that the exercise of power in particular, exceptional case may require judicial intervention.

Beare [1988] is the leading authority. The Saskatchewan Court of Appeal had struck down the power of police under the Criminal Code [RSC 1985] to fingerprint in cases where the police have reasonable and probable grounds to believe that a person has committed an indictable offence. The Saskatchewan court held that this gave too much discretion to police officers, and the provision should require an officer to show reasonable and probable grounds for believing fingerprinting was necessary. On appeal, the Supreme Court of Canada, through Mr Justice LaForest, disagreed and reversed:

The existence of the discretion conferred by the statutory provisions does not, in my view, offend principles of fundamental justice. Discretion is an essential feature of the criminal justice system. A system that attempted to eliminate discretion would be unworkably complex and rigid. Police necessarily exercise discretion in deciding when to lay charges, to arrest and to conduct incidental searches, as prosecutors do in deciding whether or not to withdraw a charge, enter a stay, consent to an adjournment, proceed by way of indictment or summary conviction, launch an appeal and so on.

The Criminal Code provides no guidelines for the exercise of discretion in any of these areas. The day-to-day operation of law enforcement and the criminal justice system nonetheless depends upon the exercise of that discretion. *Beare v R* [1988] at 116

The court added, however, that there would be a remedy under Section 24 of the Charter where it was established in a particular case that police or prosecutorial discretion had been exercised 'for improper or arbitrary motives.'

Lower courts have consistently held that the significant power given to the attorney general to directly indict, even where an accused has been discharged at a preliminary inquiry, is not *per se* contrary to the Charter, but that a court may intervene in a particular case to avoid a violation of the Charter or an 'abuse of process' (Stuart, 1991: 99). Similarly, it has been held that the court should not interfere with the exercise of a stay of prosecution by an attorney general, in the absence of evidence of 'flagrant impropriety' (ibid.).

The power to intervene in the case of particular conduct by a prosecutor (or police officer) is now generally litigated under an application to 'stay as an abuse of process' or, less often, as a denial of equality before the law under Section 15 of the Charter of Rights [1982]. In both cases, such challenges face an uphill battle.

At face value, the majority decision in *Rourke* [1977] had sounded the death knell to any doctrine that there was a residual power of trial judges to stay proceedings as an abuse of process. However, some courts, particularly at the trial level, persisted in distinguishing *Rourke* [1977]. Finally, in *Jewitt* [1985], Chief Justice Dickson, speaking for a panel of seven judges of the Supreme Court of Canada, went out of his way to resolve the long-festering issue and held that there is a residual power of trial judges to control their own processes by entering a stay as an abuse of process. The courts could not transfer to the executive the responsibility for seeing that the process of law was not abused. The court determined that a stay should be granted where 'compelling an accused to stand trial would violate those fundamental principles of justice which underlie the community's sense of fair play and decency' or where the proceedings are 'oppressive or vexatious.' The Supreme Court also asserted the caveat that it was a power which should be exercised only in the 'clearest of cases.'

The doctrine of stay as an abuse of process was broadened by the ruling of Madame Justice Wilson for a unanimous Supreme Court in *Keyowski* [1988] that prosecutorial conduct and proper motivation are 'but two of many factors to be taken into account.' Many rulings rejecting applications for a stay have turned on the lack of evidence of bad faith, and, therefore, earlier decisions should be considered with caution.

The notion that proceedings can be stayed as an abuse of process only 'in the clearest of cases' may be a case of the remedial tail wagging the dog. Being too wedded to the dramatic remedy of stay may have made the courts too cautious in assessing claims of abuse. Interestingly, in *Hamilton* [1992] a trial judge refused the remedy of a stay in a case where a Crown attorney had given an abusive opening address to the jury, which had extended far beyond a summary of the evidence to be heard. Instead of a stay, the trial judge declared a mistrial. The end result was the same, as the Crown subsequently decided to offer no further evidence.

Judging solely by reported case law, trial judges have been far more prepared than courts of appeal to stay a criminal prosecution as an abuse of process. The record of the Ontario Court of Appeal is particularly conservative (Stuart, 1991: 104–5). For example, that court refused to enter a stay against a direct indictment for first degree murder, where the Supreme Court of Canada had ordered committal for trial on a charge of second degree murder and overturned a stay by a trial judge of an incest charge laid two days after an acquittal on a charge of sexual assault against a daughter.

Unfortunately, the most recent ruling from the Supreme Court of Canada also points to non-intervention. In *Scott* [1991] a Crown attorney entered a stay in a drugs case to avoid an unfavourable evidentiary ruling that would have revealed an informer's identity and immediately recommenced the same proceedings in another court. The Supreme Court ruled six to three that the conduct should not result in a stay as an abuse of process. On the evidence, the minority view is compelling. This was surely the type of undue manipulation of the judicial process that the power to stay is designed to control. The Crown had the option of calling no evidence and appealing the resulting acquittal.

The practical effect of *Scott* [1990] may be that applications to stay as an abuse of process will now hardly ever succeed. This would be disappointing, as the stay as an abuse is the major vehicle for holding trial prosecutors to account. It also seems clear that the principles upon which the doctrine rests are highly contentious and confused (*Stuart*, 1991: 100–3).

Discriminatory Law Enforcement Contrary to Section 15 of the Charter

Under Section 15(1) of the Charter, 'Every individual is equal before and under the law and has the right to the equal protection and equal benefit of the law without discrimination and, in particular, without discrimination based on race, national or ethnic origin, colour, religion, sex, age or mental or physical disability.'

In *Andrews v Law Society of British Columbia* [1989], the Supreme Court decided that the words 'without discrimination' were a form of qualifier built into Section 15 with the result that a challenge under that section must demonstrate not just inequality but also discrimination. Discrimination is defined as a 'distinction, whether intentional or not, but based on grounds relating to personal characteristics of the individual or group, which has the effect of imposing burdens, obligations, or disadvantages on such individual or group not imposed upon others, or which withholds or limits access to opportunities, benefits, and advantages available to other member of society' (Andrews [1989] at 174).

In *Turpin* [1989], Wilson, J for the Supreme Court expressly rejected the proposition that there was a fundamental principle under Section 15 that the criminal law apply equally throughout the country. Mere geographical inequality would not establish a violation of Section 15. There would also have to be proof that the distinction was discriminatory in purpose or effect.

Thus far, courts have resisted attempts to use the equality guarantee in Section 15 to protect against discriminatory law enforcement by the police or prosecutors in a particular case. An argument that enforcement was discretionary will not do. There will have to be clear evidence of discrimination. The lack of success of such claims thus far suggests that criminal courts will continue to be an inadequate forum for consideration of such serious, but difficult-to-substantiate charges as racism. The charter is not a panacea and will be no substitute for such special inquiries as the Manitoba Aboriginal justice inquiry (1991a, b), which substantiated systemic racism in the Manitoba justice system. That inquiry took three years and cost three million dollars.

The Right to Be Tried within a Reasonable Time under Section 11(b) of the Charter

Prior to the enactment of Section 11(b), there were few statutory limitation periods in criminal prosecutions in Canada. Since Section 11(b), anyone charged with an offence has the right 'to be tried within a reasonable time.' There have been literally thousands of cases regarding this right since 1982. The Section 11(b) challenge may also be the most politically charged, because the court's constitutional duty to assess delay necessarily involves the judiciary in direct assessment of administrative and political decisions as to the deployment of scarce public resources. In this determination, the conduct of the prosecutor is front and centre.

In the Supreme Court's leading decision in *Askov* [1990], the court determined that there were four groups of factors to be considered: the length of the delay, explanation for the delay, waiver, and prejudice to the accused (for a detailed consideration, see Stuart, 1991: 230–46). Under the group of factors entitled 'explanation for the delay,' the court directs consideration of delays attributable to the Crown, which will weigh in favour of an accused, and also systemic or institutional delays – delay caused by lack of resources such as courtrooms, judges, and Crown counsel – which will also weigh against the Crown. In the case of institutional delay, the court fashioned a test of comparing jurisdictions across Canada under which it is necessary to have in mind a rough comparison with the best districts of comparable geography, population, and resources. In *Askov* [1990] itself, the court stayed charges of conspiracy to extort and weapons charges on the basis of a delay of almost two years between the preliminary hearing and the trial caused by a lack of facilities in the Brampton court district, which, from the point of view of delay, said the court, was the worst district not only in Canada but, so far as studies indicated, 'anywhere north of the Rio Grande.' The court indicated that the period of delay in such a case should have been in the range of some six to eight months.

After *Askov* [1990], some 100,000 criminal charges were permanently stayed in Ontario alone, including thousands of impaired driving charges, and a substantial number of assaults, fraud, sexual assault, and drug-related charges. In *Bennett* [1991] the Ontario Court of Appeal called for restraint in the exercise of the Section 11(b) discretion by trial judges, holding that the six- to eight-month period mentioned in *Askov* [1990] had been wrongly interpreted as a mechanical limitation. Trial judges were expected to exercise judgment in the remedy of stay and to do their best to apply each of the factors mentioned in *Askov* [1990].

In July 1991 one of the Supreme Court judges in the Askov case, Mr Justice Cory, told a legal conference in Cambridge, England, that the court had known that *Askov* [1990] would have an impact but had not anticipated the huge implications. It was not long before the Supreme Court changed direction. In *Morin* [1992], in holding that a delay of fourteen and a half months for an impaired driving trial did not violate Section 11(b), the Supreme Court refocused its approach by emphasizing the interest of society in having serious offences brought to trial, that administrative guidelines are not limitation periods, and the importance of evidence of prejudice. Since *Morin* [1992] the deluge of cases being stayed for unreasonable delay has become a trickle. The court may have got cold feet too quickly. Despite the change in direction, *Askov* [1990] is still important for its major effect on the chronic problem of court delay, especially in Ontario. When the judges began throwing out thousands of valid charges because of delay, politicians were forced to react. New resources were quickly directed at courts and new management strategies employed. The Charter had been used to force a major reassessment of a long-festering problem.

Right to Discover: Section 7 of the Charter

Where a decision-maker has the ability to keep the factual basis for the decision secret, there can be no true accountability.

Until very recently in Canada the accused has had little right to discovery of all aspects of the Crown case (Stenning, 1986: 22–225, 251–4; Stuart, 1991: 107–13). There are few statutory rights to discovery. Although defence counsel see a preliminary inquiry as an important instrument of discovery that allows cross-examination of Crown witnesses on oath, such inquiries occur only in a very small minority of criminal cases and are sometimes waived. At common law the position is that pre-trial discovery is in the absolute discretion of the Crown, while discovery at trial is in the discretion of the court.

The recognition of the power of trial judges to order a discovery apart from a specific statutory power to do so is relatively recent. The Law Reform Commission of Canada (Canada, LRC, 1984) long advocated a formal legislature procedure for pre-trial disclosure, but the legislature has thus far left it to the courts. There have long been signs that attitudes are changing. Most attorneys general have issued generous disclosure guidelines. The problem with a system of voluntary disclosure is that it tends to differ from region to region and from prosecutor to prosecutor.

Since the 1982 entrenchment of the charter, there has been an emerging yet uncertain trend towards the recognition of a constitutional right to discovery. This movement has now culminated in the far-reaching decision of the Supreme Court of Canada in *Stinchcombe* [1991] to impose a broad legal duty on the Crown to disclose all relevant information subject only to a limited and reviewable discretion to withhold.

Mr Justice Sopinka, on behalf of a unanimous court, pointed to the role of the prosecutor outlined by Mr Justice Rand in *Boucher v. The Queen* [1955], under which prosecution is a matter of public duty which excludes any notion of winning or losing. It followed that the fruits of the investigation which are in the possession of counsel for the Crown are not its property for use in securing a conviction but the property of the public to be used to ensure that justice is done. In contrast, the defence had no obligation to assist the prosecution and was entitled to assume a purely adversarial role. The absence of its duty to disclose could be justified as being consistent with that role. The court saw no valid practical reason not to impose a broad duty of disclosure. Indeed, discovery experiments across the country had shown that there was a significant increase in the number of cases settled and pleas of guilty entered or charges withdrawn. There was in any event an overriding concern that failure to disclose could impede the ability of the accused to make full answer and defence. This common law right had acquired 'new vigour' by virtue of its inclusion in Section 7 of the Charter as one of the principles of fundamental justice. The court referred to the recent Marshall commission report (Nova Scotia, Royal Commission on the Donald Marshall, Jr, Prosecution, 1989), in which the commissioners had found that lack of disclosure of prior inconsistent statements to the defence counsel had been an important contributing factor in the miscarriage of justice that had occurred in the wrongful murder conviction of an Aboriginal accused. The court made it quite clear that the Crown is under a general legal duty to disclose all relevant information whether inculpatory or exculpatory and whether the Crown intends to introduce it as evidence or not.

The obligation to disclose imposed by the Supreme Court is not absolute, and it is subject of some discretion of Crown counsel relating both to the timing of disclosure and the withholding of certain information. Rules of privilege must be respected and the Crown has a duty to protect the identities of informers. The Crown need not produce what is clearly irrelevant, but should err on the side of inclusion. In rare cases, disclosure can be delayed if it will impede an ongoing investigation. The Crown's exercise of discretion is reviewable by the trial judge at the initiation of defence counsel.

It is still too early to tell what scope of remedies will be employed. In *Stinchcombe* [1991] itself, a new trial was ordered where key statements of a witness had not been provided to the defence counsel, and the trial judge had refused to order that they be provided. Other remedies could include, in an ongoing trial, orders for full discovery, a mistrial, or even a stay of proceedings.

Stinchcombe [1991] is a decision of immense importance to the accountability of Crown prosecutors. The decision as to whether to provide discovery has tended to be an individual one, with little visibility in the review process by more senior prosecutors or by the courts. Very clearly now, failure to disclose will have important legal consequences to the outcome of trials, and in this sense Crown attorneys have been held accountable. Once again the power of the Charter has forced a long-overdue reform in the criminal justice system.

There are some legitimate concerns about the decision. Ferguson (1992), while generally applauding the decision, points to the difficulty of an accused being able to discover what things the Crown has decided are not relevant, the reality that often the lack of disclosure is by the police, the apparent ruling in *Stinchcombe* [1991] that the obligations for disclosure by the Crown will only be triggered by a request by or on behalf of the accused, and the present limitation of the scheme to indictable offences. However, Gover (1992), a senior Crown prosecutor, points to concern about the lack of guidance as to the meaning of relevant information, practical and legal difficulties in the requirement that disclosure occur before the accused is called up to plead, to the possibility that summary conviction proceedings will be unjustifiably distinguished when the penalties are often the same, and to the lack of guidance as to the nature of defence requests for disclosure. The constitutional right to full disclosure has proved particularly controversial where defence counsel attempt to gain access to medical records of complainants of assault. It may well be that a new form of qualified privilege for such records will emerge.

Code of Professional Conduct for Crown Prosecutors

One feature common to each of the forms of political, legal, and administrative accountability is that they are after the event and by their nature in response to improper conduct. It may well be that the best hope for true accountability of Crown attorneys lies in better recruitment, training, and professional formation.

In this respect, there have been some encouraging signs. In 1991, the office of the director of criminal prosecutions under the Ministry of the Attorney General of Ontario (1991) circulated a 'Proposed Code of Professional Standards and Enforcement Procedures.' The objective of the draft code was a statement of the principles underlying the duties of an agent of the attorney general, for the purposes of education and guidance, and as a bliss for fair and proper enforcement of the professional standard it would declare. It also aimed to maintain public confidence in the administration of justice in Ontario and to facilitate accountability to the public. The draft document envisaged a mission statement of the role of Crown prosecutors as ministers of justice rather than partisan advocates, and also included standards to regulate relations with other Crown attorneys, defence counsel, the court, the accused, victims, and the police. The proposed statement of minimum standards expected of Crown attorneys extended to conduct outside the course of duty, dealing with such matters as the ability of a Crown attorney to participate in partisan political acts and post-employment conduct. Topics included relations with the media, the public and public interest groups, responsibilities to participate in continuing legal education, and issues of confidentiality and conflict of interest. The 'Proposed Code' has never been officially adopted, however.

Such initiatives seem most worthwhile and to be encouraged. However, that new and difficult issues will be faced is clear when one considers whether a recent out-of-court statement by a Crown prosecutor should be the subject of professional regulation and/or discipline. In December 1991 Mr Norman Douglas, a senior prosecutor, prosecuted a controversial campus rape trial in Kingston, Ontario, involving four counts of sexual assault (two on the same victim). The accused and the three alleged victims were all students of the same university. In the case of two of the victims there was evidence of consensual sexual intercourse both before and after the events that were the subject of the charge. Following a trial before a judge alone, the accused was acquitted on all counts (*Van Oostrom* [1991]). In a lengthy oral judgment, the trial judge indicated he had a reasonable doubt on the issue of consent in each of the four counts and that an expert called by the Crown respecting the rape trauma syndrome had little probative worth in the circumstances of the case.

Immediately after the verdict, Mr Douglas gave a brief television interview expressing satisfaction that the trial and the judge had been fair. However, a week later he gave an interview to the local newspaper (*Whig-Standard*, 21 December, 1991) reportedly indicating that, with the consent of the complainants, he was ready to 'start from scratch.' He furthermore released a six-page statement to the press, recounting how the trial judge had chuckled at the Crown's argument that there is a myth that false reports of rape occur because women are fickle and vengeful. The statement indicated that Mr Douglas had decided to express his views on the crime of campus rape because it was all too prevalent, all too ignored, and it worried him because he had three daughters about to go to university. In his view, campus rape was in a unique class all on its own: 'My bottom line is that universities are a world in themselves that breed and foster rapes by "normal" red-blooded college males on vulnerable co-eds. Campuses are hunting grounds. There are no restrictions and you don't have to worry about going over your limit. It's open season' (ibid.). He spoke about the prevalence of campus rape and the realities which make it an underreported offence, and pointed out that, according to his expert witness, 42 per cent of women date-raped on campus have a consensual sexual experience with the assailant after the date rape. He said he found her to be one of the most impressive expert witnesses he had ever seen in twenty years and decried the fact that the trial judge, who was 'enamored with the defence counsel's approach throughout the trial,' made short shrift of the expert's opinion. The prosecutor then explained how challenging campus rape cases are for prosecutors and made a strong plea that the justice system needs more sensitivity and more enlightment on these issues surrounding the epidemic of violence against women in our society. He ended his statement with a plea that we all think and 'dialogue' about these issues.

Reaction to this statement was swift. A local group of defence counsel wrote to the attorney general asking that the Crown prosecutor be reprimanded or dismissed, indicating that his remarks about the judge were 'scandalous,' had 'no legitimate motive,' and were 'in fact deliberately misleading to the public about the legal situation' (*Toronto Star*, 4 January 1992).

Support was also expressed, however, for the statement of the Crown attorney. A group of female law students applauded the decision to appeal (*Whig-Standard*, 25 January 1992). Although the prosecutor may have breached traditional professional protocol, those same protocols had been used to 'silence the disenfranchised and further entrench the powers of the already powerful.' They applauded the Crown attorney for his great courage and unusual insight and extolled the virtues of making public the internal workings of the law in courtrooms.

Following a six-month investigation, the office of the attorney general announced that Mr Douglas had done nothing improper. He had not breached law society rules or any rule of law concerning public criticism of court judgments and 'did not transgress the role of Crown counsel' (*Whig-Standard*, 24 June 1992).

There may be little cause for complaint in the fact that the Crown attorney criticized the trial judge. The Ontario Court of Appeal has established that there is no offence of contempt in the form of scandalizing the court (*Kopyto* [1988]. That court held that such an offence was an unconstitutional violation of the Charter right to freedom of expression and that the courts could withstand robust criticism. There may, however, be more cause for concern about whether the Crown attorney's statement and action was in the best traditions of the Crown attorney as a minister of justice. His comment must be seen in the context of the reality that this was indeed a most controversial trial in which there had been vandalism of the accused's home, daubing of slogans on the courtroom steps, and an attempt by a group of protestors that, at the very least, amounted to harassment of the accused as he was driven away. The development of minimum professional standards might ensure that such difficult cases will not arise in the future. There are, of course, no guarantees. Mr Douglas does not appear to have heeded his own advice. A year previous to his newspaper statement he instructed his fellow Crown attorneys to take care when speaking to the media: 'Our remedy when we disagree with the decision is to appeal. There is nothing inappropriate in telling the media that we disagree with the judge's decision and we will be giving consideration to an appeal. Nor is there anything wrong in commenting generally on issues relating to the administration of justice. It is entirely inappropriate and improper to publicly criticize a specific decision or a specific judge' (*Law Times*, 3 February, 1992).

Conclusion

This essay has found that there is little effective legal, political, or administrative accountability for prosecutors. At the apex of the Canadian system, the attorney general is politically accountable in the legislature, but this is largely ineffective. The office is not free from considerations of political expediency hidden from public scrutiny.

Front-line prosecutors have wide powers and, especially given administrative realities and the tradition of a prosecutor as an independent 'Minister of justice,' largely unfettered discretion as to how and whom to charge. Canadian prosecutors now risk civil suits for malicious prosecution, but it has proved to be a small risk. The most important form of legal accountability lies indirectly in the power of judges to stay a prosecution as an abuse of process. Unfortunately, the judicial record has been one of conservative deference. The entrenchment of the Canadian Charter of Rights and Freedoms [1982] has brought important new forms of accountability. Prosecutors frequently now find their conduct in issue, particularly when trial judges interpret the new constitutional rights of accused to be tried within a reasonable time and to full disclosure in advance of the trial. This is not to say that the Charter is a panacea. Clearly it has not proved a successful vehicle to deal with such serious allegations as racism.

The picture of little prosecutorial accountability described in this essay cries out for reform. These changes should not just be to laws and legal institutions. Clearly the law is only one answer and one that is often unsatisfactory. Perhaps the best hope for true accountability of prosecutors lies in improved recruitment, training, and professional formation. There also needs to be wide public debate.

Judicial Accountability in Canada

IAN GREENE

Typically, when a judge is asked who he or she is accountable to, the answer will be 'to God,' 'to my conscience' or 'to the public.'[1]

Judges do think of themselves as accountable, but not according to the usual standards of line accountability. One of the best descriptions of the lack of line accountability regarding judges has been drafted by R. MacGregor Dawson and Norman Ward:

The unique functions which the judiciary perform in the government make it imperative that judges should be given a different position from that of the great majority of government officials ... Judicial independence ... involves the removal of most of the punitive influences which surround ordinary officials, particularly for the enforcement of political responsibility, which usually imply the power of a superior to remonstrate, reprimand, and even remove from office ... To this political irresponsibility is added a civil and criminal irresponsibility as well. Under the common law a judge is not liable to civil or criminal action for acts committed within his jurisdiction while performing his judicial duties. (Dawson and Ward, 1970: 395–6)

Dawson and Ward explain how this absence of line accountability is for the greater public good of ensuring that judges can make decisions independently and impartially, without fear of a superior looking over their shoulder and without fear of the possibility of an angry litigant, upon losing a case, harassing them. This theme of the importance of making judges 'politically irresponsible' for the greater good for the polity is more extensively developed in Dawson's doctoral dissertation, *The Principle of Official Independence* (1922: 28 ff). Here, Dawson explains how removing the fetters of political responsibility not only encourages independence of thought, but stimulates the highest standards of performance among professionals who are used to self-discipline and who resent imposed discipline.

Some of the less-positive sides of the independence theme are explored by Don K. Price in *The Scientific Estate* (1965). Price analyses the independence given by governments over the centuries first to the clergy in government employ, then to lawyers and judges, and most recently to scientists. This independence, according to Price, is required as much because it is demanded by these experts as it is given for the good of society. Experts insist on a fair degree of autonomy as a condition of working for government. Therefore, Price claims, experts in government employ often have a fair amount of scope to set their own agendas, and their agendas are not necessarily in the best interests of society as a whole.

In this essay it will be argued that judges are accountable in a number of ways that are often overlooked, but that the whole issue of judicial accountability needs far more careful consideration by the judges themselves. The essay begins with a reconsideration of the concept of accountability, then moves to an analysis of judicial independence before the various actual mechanisms of accountability are appraised.

An Approach to Accountability

Accountability in the public sector is too often thought of purely in terms of line accountability. Line accountability means having to answer for one's actions to a supervisor who is in turn answerable to a senior supervisor and so on right up to the minister who is answerable to Parliament, which is answerable to the people at election time. At each point along this bureaucratic structure of command supervisors may enforce their authority by taking disciplinary action against disobedient or ineffective subordinates. Subordinates, however, may not be held to account for anything not contained in their job descriptions or required of them by law; the superior–inferior relationship is a legal one.

A related form of accountability, according to conventional wisdom, is budget accountability. Every administrative office in government has a budget, and the office supervisor is accountable to superiors both for recommending a workable draft budget, and for ensuring that the budget, once approved by the legislature, is not overspent.

Line and budget accountability are sometimes resented by officials with independence because they imply control (Stenning, this volume). However, the concept of control itself is often misunderstood. As Peter Drucker has written, 'Control is above all a principle of economy. It means allocation of efforts where they can produce the most results with the minimum of energy' (1968: 220). Some studies about accountability have suggested that organizations in the public sector are not accountable merely by having strict standards of line or budget accountability. Line and budget accountability are merely two possible mechanisms that can be used, where appropriate, to encourage the ultimate aim of quality performance (Rieselbach, 1970; Greene, 1982, 1988a).

Expectations regarding the nature of quality performance will vary according to the purpose of a public sector organization, but, in general, quality performance can be measured according to the following criteria, but with different combinations of emphases in different organizations:

- Fairness – the extent to which a public organization accommodates the practice of established principles of justice pertinent to the institution in question
- Efficiency – the degree to which a public organization has the capacity to produce practical, effective, and cost-efficient policies to resolve the problems it faces (and organizations that encourage and reward their personnel for generating problem-solving ideas are more likely to be efficient according to Zussman and Jabes, 1989)
- Responsiveness – the degree to which a public organization can quickly meet the legitimate needs of those it was established to serve
- Answerability – the degree to which a public organization can demonstrate that the organization is performing at an optimal level.

These indicators of performance vary in relative importance depending on the purpose of the organization. In a court, for example, fairness is the most important indicator of quality performance, whereas in a hospital efficiency and responsiveness are relatively more important.

From this perspective, a public service is not accountable simply by having a rigid command structure which can prove that employees are fulfilling their job descriptions and are spending the taxpayers' funds within a pre-approved budget. To be accountable for quality performance, a public service needs to respect the relevant principles of fairness in its operations, to have the capacity to devise solutions to the problems it encounters that work and are cost-effective, to respond quickly, flexibly, and creatively to changing public needs, and to publicly demonstrate its competence. Accountability means being able to show optimum performance according to each of the four criteria.

According to this approach, then, that judges are not responsible to politicians does not mean that they cannot be accountable; it means that indicators of accountability other than line accountability must be relied on. In fact, as Bruce Smith has noted, the independence of some government organizations may actually enhance accountability by encouraging these organizations to be stronger and therefore more efficient and effective (Smith, 1971: 17 ff). At this point, it is worthwhile taking a closer look at the prime reason why line accountability is not an appropriate indicator of performance for the judiciary – judicial independence.

Judicial Independence

During the latter part of the thirteenth century, King Edward I of England appointed a royal commission to investigate charges that many of the royal judges, most of whom were clerics, were corrupt. The commission found that a number of the judges were guilty of corruption – for example, because of accepting bribes – and as a result they were fired. Some of the replacement judges were members of the nascent legal profession, and they developed a reputation for ably fulfilling their judicial responsibilities. By midway through the fourteenth century, it had become a time-honoured tradition that the royal judges should be appointed from among the ranks of lawyers (Dawson, 1968).

From that time until judicial independence was recognized by English legislation in 1700, the royal judges struggled for greater independence, meaning non-interference from anyone – especially from the Crown – in their decision-making. They succeeded in winning independence sooner than in continental Europe partly because of the ascendance of the rule-of-law aspect of the political philosophy of liberalism. John Locke, for example, embraced judicial independence so that the law would not 'be varied in particular cases, but [there should be] one rule for rich and poor, for the favourite at court and the countryman at plough' (1690: 81). As well, like all professionals, the judges took pride in their work and resented any interference from blundering kings and queens that made their decisions look less than proficient. Moreover, the judges were used to a great deal of autonomy from their previous careers in private practice (Dawson, 1968; Price, 1965; Shetreet, 1976).

In 1985 the Supreme Court of Canada had occasion to define the meaning of judicial independence in the *Valente* [1985] decision. The issue was whether provincially appointed judges are 'independent and impartial' as required by the Canadian Charter of Rights and Freedoms [1982], even though they do not have the same constitutional and statutory guarantees of their independence as judges in higher courts. Mr Justice Gerald Le Dain, who wrote the decision for the unanimous six-member panel of the Supreme Court of Canada, identified three 'essential conditions' for judicial independence: security of tenure, financial security, and institutional independence. He derived these conditions from his review of the history and development of the idea of judicial independence in the United Kingdom and in Canada.

Security of tenure must be protected, he reasoned, by judicial appointment that is 'secure against interference by the executive or other appointing authority in a discretionary or arbitrary fashion' ([1985] (at 698)). Thus, judges must have appointments tenable 'during good behaviour,' which means that they may be removed only for cause after the recommendation of an independent review process that provides judges accused of impropriety with a fair hearing. Financial security must be guaranteed through legislation that provides judges with a right to a salary and, where appropriate, to a pension. As well, the executive or legislature may not manipulate judicial salaries to attempt control over the judges. Institutional independence means that judges have a right to control matters directly affecting adjudication, such as 'assignment of judges, sittings of the court, and court lists – as well as the related matters of allocation of court rooms and direction of the administrative staff engaged in carrying out these functions' (ibid.: 709).

One of the administrative issues with which Canadian judges have been struggling over the past several decades is the extent to which judges ought to control the administration of courts. In 1981 a report produced for the Canadian Judicial Council and the Canadian Judges Conference by then Chief Justice Jules Deschênes of the Quebec Superior Court recommended that the courts should eventually become independent agencies under the control of judges (Deschênes, 1981). Deschênes was of the opinion that judicial control of all aspects of court administration could be justified by the principle of judicial independence. However, a survey of judges at all levels in Ontario and Alberta, conducted in the early 1980s, showed that only about a third of the judiciary would agree with Deschênes that judicial independence has such far-reaching implications for administration (Greene, 1988a: 156). This question was settled, from a legal perspective, in the *Valente* [1985] decision. Le Dain noted Deschênes's recommendations and concluded that although complete judicial control of the courts 'may well be highly desirable,' such control is not essential to the requirement for judicial independence in Section 11(d) of the Charter ([1985] (at 708–12)).

In 1986 the Supreme Court made another decision regarding judicial independence that provided the court with a platform from which to broaden judicial control over court administration in the future, should the court choose to take such a path (*The Queen v Beauregard* [1986]). The majority decision in the *Beauregard* [1986] case was written by then Chief Justice Brian Dickson, and it was accepted unanimously by the court in relation to the issue of judicial independence. The case was initiated by Mr Justice Marc Beauregard, who was appointed a justice of the Quebec Superior Court in 1975 at a time when a contributory pension plan was being put into effect for the federally appointed judges of the provincial superior courts. Beauregard and the judges appointed after him would have to contribute 7 per cent of their income to the judges' pension plan, but judges sitting prior to Beauregard's appointment were 'grandfathered' regarding the pension contributions, and would have to contribute only 1.5 per cent of their salaries to the pension fund. At the same time, the judges received a 39 per cent salary increase. Beauregard was unhappy that he had missed the cut-off date for being 'grandfathered,' and sued for violation of judicial independence. His argument was that being required by Parliament to contribute 7 per cent of his salary to a pension fund constituted legislative and executive tampering with his salary contrary to the principle of judicial independence.

Dickson, CJ, found that neither the legislature nor the executive was attempting to influence Beauregard's decisions through establishing the contributory pension scheme; there had to be an arbitrary cut-off date, and it was simply unfortunate for Beauregard that he fell on the wrong side of it. More importantly, Dickson wrote that in Canada judicial independence has two purposes – to provide judges with the liberty to decide the cases that come before them impartially, and to enable judges to fulfil their institutional role of protecting Canada's constitution against legislative and executive encroachment. Thus, the judiciary must be 'completely separate in authority and function from *all* other participants in the justice system' (ibid.: 73). It is this dictum that might be used by future supreme courts to expand judicial authority in the administration of courts, should they choose to do so (Greene, 1988b).

The *Valente* [1985] decision illustrates why line accountability would be inappropriate as a mechanism of accountability for judges. Line accountability is enforced through the power of supervisors to discipline those who report to them through promotions, demotions, or firings, and to reward compliance with salary increases. Judges' salaries are set by law and apply to all judges at the same level in a particular jurisdiction. For example, in April 1994 all puisne (regular) judges of the provincial superior courts earned $155,800 per year, while the chief and associate chief judges of these courts all earned an extra $14,800 per year. Judicial independence, as defined in *Valente* [1985], would be violated if certain judges were awarded salary increments for demonstrated ability, or were demoted for having too many decisions overturned on appeal, or were promoted or demoted as a result of their administrative record. A judge can only be removed from office after a judicial inquiry finds that the judge engaged in behaviour not appropriate for a judge. According to the Constitution Act [1867], federally appointed judges in the provincial courts may be removed only through a joint address of the House of Commons and Senate; the *Valente* [1985] decision stipulates that in addition, such procedures could be instituted only after a judicial inquiry.

Budget accountability is currently not an issue facing Canadian judges. One reason provincial attorneys general and federal ministers of justice, as well as many judges, have been sceptical about the recommendations of former Chief Justice Deschênes is that if judges were to control the administration of courts, some form of budget accountability for the courts would have to be devised that did not interfere with judicial independence. According to the Deschênes plan, the minister would act as a 'conduit' for the courts regarding budget accountability (Deschênes, 1981: 5), but Deschênes was silent about how independently administered courts would be accountable for the quality of their administration.

In the United States the federal courts won administrative autonomy early in this century. The federal judges are collectively responsible for the administration of courts and for drafting and administering the budget for their courts. Administrative autonomy, however, has been purchased at the price of having to account for the budget. The judges must lobby, like other government services, for a fair share of the federal budget; this is a role that they do not relish and are not particularly good at. And some judges must invest time in learning the skills of administration (Fish, 1973: 206 ff). In some state courts in the United States the judiciary has been delegated responsibility for the administration of courts, but the judges are expected to account for their administrative decisions in judicial confirmation elections. These elections, however, are often fought on issues that have little to do with the administrative responsibilities of judges, leaving problems of judicial administrative accountability unresolved (Thompson, 1986).

That the Deschênes recommendations generated more questions than answers about accountability may be one reason that there has been no legislative attempt to institute them.

Mechanisms of Accountability for Judges

There are a number of other mechanisms of accountability – actual and potential – that may be more appropriate for Canadian judges than line accountability or budget accountability; each of them may be more or less effective depending on the circumstances. They are analysed below according to whether they are formal, self-imposed, or potential.

FORMAL MECHANISMS OF ACCOUNTABILITY

Formal mechanisms of accountability for Canadian judges consist of procedures for appointment and promotion, the office of the chief justice, and judicial councils. As well, there have been experiments with management advisory committees for the courts, and new developments in continuing education and the production of annual reports are welcome innovations.

Appointment and Promotion

Judicial appointment procedures can be thought of as a front-end mechanism of accountability. In our system, once judges are appointed there is nothing that can be done to remove them as long as they attend court, hear and decide the cases on their lists, are polite to litigants, and do not get convicted of a serious offence, get involved in politics, or behave in such a way that their moral principles are called into question (Russell, 1987: 176). An appointment procedure that results in the selection of the best possible candidates for judgeships in the first place is therefore necessary to promote optimum judicial performance.

Until recently judicial appointments were determined primarily by political patronage. Fortunately, there were enough good lawyers who were owed favours by the parties controlling the federal and provincial governments in Canada that a number of good judicial appointments were made, along with some very inappropriate ones (ibid: 113 ff). The main problem was that the pool of available talent was often limited to supporters of the party in power.

Canada's constitution gives the federal Cabinet the power to appoint the 750 or so provincial superior trial court judges, the 126 provincial and territorial court of appeal judges, the 34 judges of the Federal Court, the 25 judges of the Tax Court, and the 9 judges of the Supreme Court of Canada. The provincial cabinets have the power to appoint judges in the provincial court systems below the level of the superior and district courts, and there are currently about one thousand of these provincially appointed judges. Beginning in the 1970s the provinces began to establish non-partisan appointment procedures. There are three basic approaches: judicial nominating committees that search out the best candidates to recommend to the attorney general for appointment (Ontario and Quebec), provincial judicial councils that screen applications which come to them and make recommendations to the attorney general (Alberta and British Columbia), and judicial councils that comment on the qualifications of candidates proposed by the attorney general (Saskatchewan and Newfoundland). In spite of these improvements, in 1895 the Canadian Bar Association reported that patronage still remained an important factor in provincial judicial appointments in Nova Scotia, New Brunswick, Prince Edward Island, Manitoba, and Saskatchewan (McCormick and Greene, in 1990: 37–9).

Patronage also remains a factor in many federal judicial appointments, although some improvements have been made over the past three decades. Changes to the old patronage system began in the 1970s when the federal minister of justice established a system of nation-wide contacts with prominent lawyers and judges to recruit outstanding candidates. As well, the names of potential appointees were given to a committee of the Canadian Bar Association for comment. In 1988 the justice minister established a system of provincial and territorial assessment committees; the committees were set up to advise the minister whether potential federal appointees are qualified for the job. These five-member committees represent the judiciary, the legal profession, the provincial or territorial attorney general, and the federal minister of justice. Their major weakness is that they are limited to commenting on names put forward by the minister of justice, who tends to put forward the names of the party faithful. A recent study has shown that the Conservative government of the 1980s tended to appoint judges who were known supporters of the Progressive Conservative party to all courts with federal judges except the Supreme Court of Canada (Russell and Ziegel, 1989). Unlike the procedures in Ontario and Quebec, the federal assessment committees cannot advertise for applications.

The new selection procedure in Ontario, which was established by the Liberal attorney general in 1989, and continued under the New Democratic party administration, is arguably the best in the country in terms of recruiting the most able candidates for the bench. The judicial appointments advisory committee is composed of fourteen persons from across Ontario; although it includes representatives of the legal profession and the judiciary, half of its members are non-lawyers and half are women. The chair is a university professor who has been a leading advocate of court reform in Canada. When vacancies in the provincial bench occur, the committee advertises extensively for applicants and has found no shortage of would-be judges among lawyers of ten years' standing or more. Applicants must fill out detailed application forms, and those who are short-listed are interviewed. The committee looks not only for candidates who have high academic and professional qualifications, but also for candidates who demonstrate compassion and who have a demonstrated record of community service.

The committee has endeavoured to recommend to the Ontario Judicial Council and the attorney general candidates who would create a more representative judiciary – a bench that more closely resembles the ethnic and gender diversification of Ontario society (McCormick and Greene, 1990: 253–4). Until now, the federal and provincial judiciaries have tended to over-represent those of English and French ethnicities and those from the middle and upper socioeconomic brackets, and 93 per cent of Canadian judges in 1990 were men (ibid.: 59 ff). A judiciary is more likely to be accountable in the sense of demonstrating optimum performance if the selection procedure is designed both to select the most qualified candidates for judicial office, and candidates who more broadly represent the entire community. A degree of representativeness is important because when the law is unclear, judges fill in the gaps and, in effect, make policy. They are more likely to make policy that is acceptable to the political community the more they are representative of that community (Strayer, 2983: 297 ff).

The Role of the Chief Judge or Chief Justice

Chief judges are selected by the provincial attorneys general to head courts staffed by provincially appointed judges, while chief justices are selected by the prime minister to head courts staffed by federally appointed judges. The larger courts also have associate chief judges and associate chief justices. The duties of these offices are administrative rather than supervisory. In multijudge courts they organize the system for assigning cases to judges, and in travelling courts they set the judges' travelling schedules. In appeal courts they decide the make-up of the appeal panels and the assignment of cases to panels, and they determine the system for selecting which judge will write the majority decision for the panel.

Chief judges and justices are typically described by the puisne (regular) judges and justices as 'first among equals.' Because of judicial independence, it is not proper for the chief to try to influence puisne judges regarding their decisions about particular cases (except if the chief is a member of an appeal panel, in which case each member of the panel may try to persuade other panel members). Regarding case-flow duties other than assigning cases and setting schedules, the regular judges think of the chief judge or justice as someone who can make suggestions but who cannot give orders. In a 1980 survey of Ontario judges at all levels, nearly two-thirds of the judges thought that the chief judges and justices should *not* play a major supervisory role regarding the case-flow management duties of the regular judges and justices (Greene, 1988a).

In spite of these limitations on the authority of the chief judges and justices, they can often serve to promote accountability simply by having informal chats with puisne judges about whom some criticism has been received. If a chief receives a complaint about a judge's behaviour, having a word with the judge in question might resolve the problem. The chief has no formal authority to discipline or suspend, but can have a great deal of influence through moral suasion, depending on the personality of the chief and the openness of the puisne judge to the chief's counsel. This approach to accountability may be an example of what

Marshall (1978) refers to as an 'explanatory and cooperative' style of accountability.

Judicial councils:
[It] was recently recognized by [British] Lord Chancellor Hailsham [that judges] occasionally become subject to what he called 'judges' disease, that is to say a condition of which the symptoms may be pomposity, irritability, talkativeness, proneness to obiter dicta [that is, statements not necessary for the decision in the case], a tendency to take short-cuts'... When judicial self-restraint and self-restraint and self-control fail, or when litigants believe them to have failed, there is a need for an independent forum in which complaints about judicial performance can be considered. (Pannick, 1987: 75–6)

The Canadian Judicial Council, consisting of all federally appointed chief justices and judges and associate chief judges and justices, was established by Parliament in 1971, both to promote judicial education and to deal with complaints about federally appointed judges. In 1994 this body consisted of thirty-five judges. It is chaired by the Chief Justice of the Supreme Court of Canada. If the council receives a complaint for which there is enough evidence to warrant an inquiry, it has the power to conduct the inquiry and if necessary, to recommend removal of a judge. Prior to the creation of the council, complaints about federally appointed judges were dealt with by the minister of justice, who would establish a judicial inquiry into the conduct of a judge if the evidence warranted such a procedure. Since 1867 no Canadian superior court judge has ever been removed, although the joint-address procedure was initiated for the removal of Mr Justice Leo Landreville in 1966; Landreville, however, resigned before he was removed. A royal commission inquiry had found that Landreville's behaviour prior to becoming a judge, as mayor of Sudbury, had not been to the standard required of a judge (Russell, 1987: 176 ff). In England only one superior court judge has been removed since the official recognition of judicial independence in 1700.

During the 1992–3 fiscal year, the council received 127 complaints, but only one produced enough evidence to warrant an inquiry. The matter concerned a complaint from a chief justice that a judge in his court had become unable to carry out his duties because of 'age or infirmity' (Canadian Judicial Council, 1993: 16). At the time of writing, the inquiry had not taken place. It should be noted, however, that with regard to at least eight other complaints, either the Judicial Conduct Committee of the council or its chair were critical of individual judges for matters such as sexist remarks or undue delays in rendering decisions, but were satisfied that the judges in question regretted their behaviour and took steps to change (Canadian Judicial Council, 1993: 11–16).

Prior to 1993 only two inquiries had been conducted by the council. The first, in 1982, was a result of remarks made by Mr Justice Thomas Berger of the British Columbia Supreme Court at a university convocation in late 1981. Berger criticized the 5 November, 1981 constitutional accord, and his remarks also appeared in the *Globe and Mail*. The council reprimanded Berger for his foray into politics, but concluded that his behaviour had not constituted an offence serious enough to warrant removal. Berger eventually resigned in any case (McCormick and Greene, 1990: 51).

The second inquiry, in 1990, was in the aftermath of the Donald Marshall, Jr, affair. In 1983 the Nova Scotia Court of Appeal acquitted Marshall of murder after he had been wrongly convicted and had spent eleven years in jail, but in 1988 a royal commission found that the court had wrongly blamed Marshall for being partly responsible for the miscarriage of justice (Nova Scotia, Royal Commission on the Donald Marshall, Jr, Prosecution, 1989: vol. 1, p. 125). As a result, the attorney general of Nova Scotia requested an inquiry by the Canadian Judicial Council. The council concluded that there had been no judicial misconduct on the part of three continuing members of the Nova Scotia Court of Appeal. However, the inquiry committee which the council had established concluded that the judges had been guilty both of legal error and inappropriate comments. 'But neither legal error nor inappropriate language are grounds for removal of a judge from office' (Canadian Judicial Council, 1991: 14).

The provinces have all established provincial judicial councils since the early 1970s. Typically, they are composed of all the federally and provincially appointed chief justices and chief judges, as well as the associate chiefs, in each province, sometimes with the addition of representation from the bar as well as from non-lawyers. These councils have the power to investigate complaints about provincially appointed judges, and they serve much the same function as the Canadian Judicial Council serves regarding federally appointed judges. Of the complaints received by these councils during the past few years, only a handful have produced evidence serious enough to warrant an inquiry (McCormick and Greene, 1990: 48–9). The most notorious was the inquiry conducted by Madame Justice Jean MacFarland in November 1993 about a complaint of sexual harassment against Ontario Provincial Court Judge Walter Hryciuk that was filed by Toronto's director of Crown attorneys; the inquiry took place on the recommendation of the Ontario Judicial Council. MacFarland recommended Hryciuk's removal because of rude remarks and behaviour towards several women. She concluded that such behaviour was not only unprofessional and inappropriate, but made it impossible for Hryciuk to appear impartial. Hryciuk applied for a judicial review of the findings, claiming that MacFarland exceeded her jurisdiction; no decision has been made at the time of writing.

The judicial councils have provided a formal avenue for dealing with complaints about judges, and, thus, they promote judicial accountability by discouraging unacceptable judicial performance. However, the existence of the councils is not well known to most Canadians, and probably many of those who have heard of one of the councils do not understand the division of responsibilities among the councils. A well-publicized office that acted as a central clearing house for complaints about judges might help to promote a higher degree of accountability in this respect.

Courts Advisory Committees

When someone is frustrated about an experience in court – and nearly 90 per cent of Canadians think that the justice system needs to be 'more sensitive and compassionate' (Canada Department of Justice, 1987b: 2–7) – it may be hard for that person to discover where to launch a complaint. If the criticism is about a particular judge, of course, then one of the judicial councils is appropriate. But if there is concern with lengthy delays, it is more difficult to find out where to complain. The attorney general, who is responsible for the administration of the entire provincial court system (including courts staffed by federally appointed judges) may fend off a complaint about delay by stating that pursuant to judicial independence, it is the judges who are responsible for administrative issues directly related to adjudication. If the complaint goes to the chief justice, he or she may respond that the judges have no control over the budgets for the courts, and therefore cannot intervene in obtaining the necessary resources to reduce delay. If pressed, both the chief justice and the attorney general might seek to blame the bar for unnecessary delays in any case (Greene, 1982). Most problems related to the administration of courts in the provincial court systems cannot be resolved without joint action involving the judiciary (federal and provincial), the attorney general, administrative officials in the courts, the bar, and the Crown attorneys.

To tackle problems of coordination and to provide a vehicle for public input into the improvement of the provincial courts system, the report of Mr Justice Thomas Zuber in 1987 recommended the establishment of courts management advisory committees at the provincial and regional levels in Ontario (Zuber, 1987). Such committees were actually established in 1991, and they have representation from the groups mentioned above as well as from the lay public. If these committees are given a clear and practical mandate, and if the potentially explosive problems relating to interpersonal relations on these committees are approached with tact, they could have a tremendous potential not only to promote better coordination among the various personnel involved in court activities, but to promote accountability. Similar committees in each of the six judicial circuits in England and Wales have had a positive impact from the perspective of all four performance indicators.[2] The Ontario experiment is worth watching.

Continuing Education

During the past two decades, several associations have been involved in organizing conferences and educational seminars for judges. The Canadian Judicial Council has organized educational seminars for federally appointed judges, and there are national and provincial associations for provincially appointed judges that have established impressive educational programs. As well, the Canadian Institute for the Administration of Justice has run a one-week seminar each year for new judges. These developments, while positive, have nevertheless left judicial education as a 'patchwork quilt,' in the words of former Ontario Chief Justice William Howland (Canadian Judicial Council, 1988). In an attempt to provide a more systematic structure for judicial education, in 1987 the Canadian Judicial Centre was established. The centre, known since 1991 as the National Centre for the Judiciary, has taken over some of the educational functions of other organizations and has established new judicial education initiatives such as early orientation seminars for new judges.

These educational seminars and conferences not only help to improve the quality of judgments by orienting new judges and helping established judges to keep abreast with developments in the law, they also provide forums in which judges can compare notes about improvements in court administration.

Annual Reports

It has become a tradition over the past decade or so for the chief justice of Ontario to present a report at the annual ceremonial opening of the courts in January of each year. The statement constitutes an annual report of the achievements of Ontario's judiciary, and it has become an important vehicle for demonstrating the accountability of the Ontario judiciary to the people of Ontario. The adoption of a similar tradition in other jurisdictions may help to promote judicial accountability.

Under Chief Justice Dickson, the Canadian Judicial Council produced its first annual report in 1988. Among other things, the council's reports present data summarizing the complaints received by the council, and without violating confidences, they review how the complaints were dealt with. Other activities of the council, most of which are directed to improving the quality of Canada's judicial system, are explained. These annual reports help to promote judicial accountability not only by publicly accounting for judicial performance and discipline, but by providing the judiciary with a vehicle for advertising its achievements.

Self-accountability

Most judges consider that self-accountability is a more important factor in encouraging quality judicial performance than the formal mechanisms of accountability discussed above (Paterson, 1983: 195 ff). Judges generally value the making of fair judgments and the writing of quality opinions not because of the possibility of remprimand from the chief justice or a judicial council, but because their self-esteem depends on their own assessments of themselves regarding how they measure up as judges.

EFFECT OF YEARS IN PRIVATE PRACTICE

On average, provincially appointed judges come to the bench with fifteen years' experience in the practice of law, while federally appointed judges average about twenty years' experience. Most often this experience is in private practice, although a few judges have worked only as Crown counsel or in the litigation department of a large corporation. For example, in Alberta about a quarter of the judges have had experience as a sole practitioner. Of the three-quarters of the judges who had worked in multilawyer firms, most had become partners before accepting a judgeship (McCormick and Greene, 1990: 59 ff).

What this background experience indicates is that most judges are used to self-discipline rather than discipline imposed from above. While in law practice, they became used to working long hours and to coping with a demanding schedule. It appears that for nearly half of Canada's judges, the desire to become a judge was in part motivated by the hope of not having to work so many evenings and weekends and to spend more time with their families (ibid.: 84 ff). After appointment, many of these judges, however, found themselves working the same lengthy hours as before, not because they were forced to, but because they were used to it and derived satisfaction from completing their work to standards that satisfied them.

PUBLIC OPINION AND MEDIA REPORTS

Judges tend to be sensitive to criticism of their judgments in newspapers and other media, and they value a public reputation as being fair, even if somewhat conservative (Griffith, 1977: 202–16). If a judge's decision or behaviour is criticized in the media, it is not considered appropriate for the judge to respond; a response could be considered as entering into the political fray in violation of judicial independence. However, media criticism of judges is rare, partly because until 1986, those criticizing the judiciary in the media might have been charged with contempt of court. The principle behind the contempt offence was that criticism of the judiciary (even if accurate) might cause the public to lose respect for the courts, and this loss of respect could have serious consequences for social order.

In 1986 a radical Toronto lawyer was charged by the Crown with 'scandalizing the court,' a form of statutory contempt. He had complained that the courts and the police stick together like 'Krazy Glue,' and his remarks were picked up by a reporter. He was acquitted in the Ontario Court of Appeal, which found that the Charter rights to freedom of expression took precedence over the law of contempt (*R v Kopyto* [1988]). With the relaxation of the law of contempt, the media may now act somewhat more freely in terms of publishing criticism of judicial decisions or behaviour. Such critiques may help to promote judicial accountability by providing consequences, in terms of a negative public image, for lapses in judicial performance.

THE ACADEMIC PRESS

Judges, and especially appeal court judges, generally try to keep abreast of the articles in the major law journals and to read books that comment on the judiciary. They are naturally pleased with articles that praise their decisions and are concerned about criticism of their reasoning. Even if an article in a law journal does not persuade a judge, it may encourage the judge to explain her or his reasoning more clearly and to spell out the thought process involved in decisions in more detail.

OPINIONS OF OTHER JUDGES

It is important for most judges to be respected by their colleagues on the bench. In a survey of the attitudes of Alberta judges at all levels, the judges were asked what the qualities are that cause a judge to gain the respect of his or her fellow judges. It was found that the judges valued 'the qualities of diligence and industry, of humaneness, of patience and courtesy, of a knowledge of the law and intelligence, of a sense of fair play and decisiveness [in that order]. At a somewhat lower level, they attach importance to clear writing, common sense, grasping the central elements of a cause, and a sense of humour' (McCormick and Greene, 1990: 115). It was also found that two-thirds of Alberta judges were 'collegial judges,' that is, they interact a fair amount with their colleagues and consult with them about how they carry out their responsibilities (ibid.: 144 ff). We can assume that peer pressure is not unimportant in encouraging higher standards of performance among judges.

Other Potential Mechanisms of Accountability

EVALUATIONS OF INDIVIDUAL JUDICIAL PERFORMANCE

It has been suggested by Peter Russell that an informal but rigorous system of evaluations of judges by the lawyers who appear in their courts, similar to student evaluations of professors, might assist judges to become aware of areas in which their effectiveness could be improved (1987: 189).

To be effective, such evaluations would have to be carried out professionally and with discretion. Evaluation forms would have to be produced such that the information they would record would be useful to judges, and not merely a popularity contest. Lawyers would need to feel confident that they could fill out the forms anonymously, and they would need to complete the forms honestly and consistently. The forms would have to be kept confidential and be given only to the judge they refer to. The judges would need to be provided with a system for analysing the results of the evaluations that would provide them with an accurate overview of the evaluations without consuming an unreasonable amount of their time.

PROGRAM EVALUATIONS

Program evaluation is a set of techniques used in public administration to investigate whether the programs of public organizations are actually fulfilling their goals. Program evaluations are now required by law at least every five years for all federal government programs, and program evaluations of provincial and municipal programs are becoming increasingly common. Although program evaluations are not a panacea for improving the performance of public organizations, under the right circumstances they can have a very positive impact (Rossi and Freeman, 1985). Program evaluation, if employed selectively, is a potentially important mechanism for promoting the increased accountability of the judiciary.

SURVEYS

Much could be learned from surveys of the views of Canadians who have had experience with the judicial system. A 1987 Department of Justice survey, for example, produced mixed results. On the one hand, three-quarters of the respondents thought that the average Canadian usually gets a fair deal under Canadian law, and two-thirds said that most people are treated with respect by the legal–judicial system. On the other hand, three-quarters said that the law favours the rich, 86 per cent said that the justice system needs to be more sensitive and compassionate, and 90 per cent said that the justice system is too complex for the average person to understand (Canada, Department of Justice, 1987b). Regular samplings of the opinions of litigants, witnesses, and the general public about the justice system might boost judicial accountability.

Can Judges Be Accountable?

If accountability is considered to be the demonstration of optimum performance with regard to fairness, efficiency, responsiveness, and answerability, judges can be accountable – but not through the usual mechanisms of line accountability and budget accountability. Judicial independence precludes the imposition of line accountability on judges. Budget accountability is not relevant where judges have no part in the budget process, and to involve judges in budgeting may create more problems than it would resolve.

To what extent do the present mechanisms of accountability result in real judicial accountability? Probably the most important accountability mechanism for the promotion of fairness is the self-discipline that judges have learned from their years in the practice of law prior to becoming judges. The habits learned through self-discipline are supported and encouraged by peer pressure, the need to be respected by fellow judges. Accountability for fairness is also promoted through commentaries on the quality of judicial decisions in the academic press. Media critiques of judicial decisions can be expected to become a more important factor of accountability, thanks to the loosening of the constraints of the doctrine of contempt. Opportunities for continuing judicial education have improved enormously during the past two decades, and they will continue to improve with the National Centre for the Judiciary coming into full operation. An astute chief judge or justice can often deal with legitimate complaints about judges in a diplomatic and effective manner. Where the intervention of the chief judge or justice is inappropriate or too late, judicial councils can play an important disciplinary function, fut their existence needs to be better publicized. Credible individual evaluations of judges by the lawyers who appear before them could provide judges with a valuable accountability tool.

Front-end accountability for fairness can be promoted through nonpartisan procedures of appointment designed to select the most capable candidates for judgeships and to encourage a judiciary that is representative of Canadian society. Although developments during the past two decades have been encouraging, Ontario's judicial appointment system stands out as exemplary to other jurisdictions, especially when compared with the system of appointments for federal judges.

Accountability for efficiency could be demonstrated through professional program evaluations of court services. Some thought might be given to a legislative requirement that all courts must undergo periodic independent evaluations. As Stenning (this volume) points out, it is often not enough to rely simply on the goodwill of independent agencies to institute adequate mechanisms of accountability.

Accountability for responsiveness could be encouraged through court management advisory committees, such as those currently being developed in Ontario. As well, much could be learned from regular and properly conducted surveys of litigants and witnesses.

Answerability could be encouraged through the production of annual reports by Canada's chief judges and chief justices, and by the heads of the various judicial organizations across Canada. The reports produced by the chief justice of Ontario at the opening of the courts each year, and the annual reports of the Canadian Judicial Council, provide useful models.

The judiciary can be more accountable than it currently is in spite of the inappropriateness of line accountability. Like all professionals, judges value their autonomy not only because autonomy is associated with judicial independence, but also because they enjoy autonomy and have become used to it through their prior career experiences. What is sometimes overlooked by judges, however, is that the institution of appropriate accountability mechanisms can actually enhance autonomy by discouraging outside 'tampering' with judicial administration. Courts that can demonstrate quality performance do not attract intervention from outside.

Notes

1 Source: more than 80 formal interviews with Canadian judges at all levels, 1980–94.
2 Interview with Mr Anthony Howard, courts administrator for the Lord Chancellor's Department in Manchester, 6 April 1992.

Achieving Accountability in Sentencing

ANTHONY N. DOOB AND JEAN-PAUL BRODEUR

Individual sentences handed down in criminal cases are criticized frequently and publicly in many countries. In Canada, sentences are most often criticized in terms of level of severity of the sentence. A majority of Canadians have been shown to have a generalized belief that sentences are too lenient (see, for example, Doob and Roberts, 1988). A careful analysis, however, suggests that in Canada, as in some other countries, this generalized belief does not translate reliably to a view about sentences handed down in individual cases. The generalized belief is based in part on misinformation and misunderstanding. A more sensitive view of the Canadian public would suggest that they, like many within the criminal justice system, find Canada's sentencing structure more confusing than lenient.

The phenomenon of the public apparently wanting harsher sentences is not solely a Canadian one. In the United States, a country that executes offenders, places many non-violent offenders in prison for decades, and incarcerates others for life without eligibility for parole, the public also wants harsher sentences (see Roberts, 1992, for a review). However, even in the United States, careful analyses of public attitudes suggest that, as in Canada, the public does not want harsher sentences than those *actually being handed down* (Diamond, 1989, 1990; Diamond and Stalans, 1989; Stalans, 1993).

Judges are increasingly criticized for handing down sentences that are apparently inconsistent with other sentences. In other words, concern is expressed about disparity. In this essay, we will largely be concerned with the problem of disparity in sentencing first of all, because it has often been claimed that the possibility of 'unequal treatment' in law is incompatible with the notion of justice. Although we believe that this claim is justified, we suggest that the more general concern is that punishments are being handed down in an unprincipled way.

We will specify what we generally mean by this. Building upon the ambiguity of the word 'unprincipled,' which may refer to a lack of both theoretical and ethical principles, we begin with an extreme example of unprincipled sentencing. Needless to say, this example illustrates sentencing disparity, because the probability that an offender convicted of similar offences would get a comparable sentence is almost zero. However, we deliberately chose it to provide an illustration of a complete failure of control over the sentencing process.

In Canada, a life sentence may have very different meanings depending on the offence for which it is imposed. A life sentence for first-degree murder involves spending twenty-five years in jail before being eligible to apply for parole. For second-degree murder, a life sentence means a period of incarceration of ten to twenty-five years before eligibility for parole, the length of this period being determined by the sentencing judge when he or she hands down the sentence. Finally, when a person is given a life sentence for manslaughter, he or she may apply for parole after a relatively short period of incarceration (usually seven years).

In 1986 a professional assassin agreed to be a witness for the prosecution against former accomplices who were members of a motorcycle gang. In return he was offered the following deal, the details of which were spelled out in a contract, of which researchers at the University of Montreal managed to obtain a copy (Gravel and Bordelais, 1993: Appendix): This hitman pleaded guilty to thirty-five counts of manslaughter committed between 1970 and 1985 which, taken together, involved forty-three victims. There is no doubt that all these offences were in reality first-degree murder, since they were perpetrated in cold blood and with premeditation (if his target was accompanied by a wife or a parent, he also killed them). Nevertheless, he was permitted to plead guilty to offences of manslaughter for which he was to receive a sentence of life imprisonment. However, in accordance with the agreement approved by the prosecutor and confirmed by the sentencing judge, his life sentence meant that he was to spend four years in full custody (with weekly money for expenses), two years of partial custody (with day passes to go to work outside of the prison), and, finally two years in a halfway house. After serving those eight years, only half of which involved full custody, he was to be released on parole in 1994.

The only way of attempting to justify such an affront to justice is to argue that this man's testimony was required to convict other killers. In other words, it is to reassert, within the framework of criminal justice, that the end justifies the means, in complete disregard of the fact that one of the basic purposes of the criminal law – indeed of any law – is precisely to deny that the end justifies the means. However, this prosecutorial strategy proved in fact to be counterproductive; few convictions were obtained by his testimony, since he completely lacked credibility as a witness. More importantly, he himself was more dangerous than any of the persons that he might have helped to convict. In sum, this is a particularly crude example of the disposition of a criminal case occurring without reference to anything that could be said to be remotely connected with principles of sentencing or of fundamental justice. A working group appointed by the government of Quebec to study the use of informers as Crown witnesses has recommended that all agreements between such informers and the Ministry of Justice take the official form of contracts like the one that was used with the professional assassin previously referred to (Quebec, 1992).

There is a natural tendency to explain away the problems of sentencing by asserting that, to a considerable extent, they are the result of a lack of knowledge. Hence, it is sometimes argued that the problems of disparity could be lessened, if not entirely solved, by providing additional information to judges about court practice and the 'tariffs' that are applied by their colleagues. In a similar fashion, it is argued that public criticism could be defused by better informing the general public about the role and responsibilities of courts and by disseminating accurate data on the level of severity of the sentences imposed by judges.

Such an analysis, we suggest, is fundamentally wrong. The problems with sentencing – disparity in particular – can be seen to relate to problems of accountability. The case that we just described really shows how deep are the problems of sentencing, which cannot be reduced to a lack of sentencing information that could be resolved by technology (for example, all judges having a lap-top computer displaying the sentencing practices of their colleagues). We argue that in many jurisdictions the state, by way of its sentencing judges, simply is not accountable for sentencing decisions. This is a rather strong statement to make, in particular when referring to a process that is often described as the most serious intrusion of the state into the lives of its citizens. We say it, however, not merely as a challenge to those responsible for sentencing policy, but because we believe that unless true accountability is built into the sentencing process, sentences will, over time, no longer be seen as legitimate.

Here a distinction must be drawn between legitimacy of sentencing for the public and its legitimacy for convicted offenders. When sentencing loses its legitimacy with regard to convicted offenders, this perception may also neutralize any efforts towards their treatment and rehabilitation or towards 'communicating' some censuring message to them (Duff, 1986; von Hirsch, 1993). Why should offenders feel inadequate when a professional killer is going to be released because he benefited from a good deal from the Crown? Their only inadequacy is that they failed to get a better lawyer. The impact upon offenders of cases such as the one we have described cannot be underestimated. We understand that rumours about the sentencing 'fix' spread like wildfire among inmates. Events like these must undermine any confidence inmates may have entertained in the criminal law, having reduced 'just sentencing' to a power play within an unprincipled and uncontrolled setting. With regard to the public legitimacy of the sentencing process, its erosion is well under way. A sizable majority of the public indicates that they believe that sentences generally are inappropriate (Roberts, 1992; Doob and Roberts, 1988). It may be that, in general, the public's view of the sentencing process is more in line with actual practice than it would appear (Doob and Roberts, 1988; Diamond and Stalans, 1989), but instances like the one described are probably salient when ordinary people are thinking about sentencing decisions.

A Definition of Accountability

Concerns about 'accountability' can be found in most countries with respect to most areas of the criminal justice system. Interestingly enough, however, for the most part non-elected judges' decisions are typically not discussed in these terms. The concept of accountability usually implies the possibility that people who cannot answer satisfactorily for their actions may be removed from their positions or submitted to disciplinary action (see the notion of 'line accountability' in Greene's essay in this book). It is often argued that line accountability is incompatible with judicial independence, which is believed to be an essential guarantee of judicial impartiality.

What is interesting in this debate is that the judiciary believes itself to be unique with respect to its independence. However, that is not the case, as is shown by this quotation from Lustgarten's classic book on governance of the police:

The contemporary controversy about the relationship between the police and democratic institutions of government takes place in a particular doctrinal and political context. It is dominated by a theory enshrined in the Police Act [1964], and the Court of Appeal decision in the first Blackburn case, and imbibed like mother's milk by all police officers in their training. This is the doctrine of police independence – the view that the police, uniquely among public officials, should not be under the ultimate control of democratically elected representatives of the public. (Lustgarten, 1986: 32)

With regard to our present discussion, it is particularly significant to note that the police, like the judiciary, claim to be unique among public officials. It would seem that many officials within the criminal justice system see their position as being uniquely incompatible with line accountability. Yet, this notion of line accountability has made remarkable progress in the field of policing and is generally seen as a necessary feature of law enforcement within the context of democracy. What among other things made this progress possible was the enactment of codes of police ethics, which specified both for the police and the public the principles and rules forming the base of police accountability.

All groups of professionals initially resist being made accountable. This reluctance is proportional to features of their professional culture that tend to conflict with accountability. There are two such features in the professional culture of judges. First, judges staunchly maintain that their judgments are the final expression of what they have to say on a particular case. Consequently they never comment on their judgments. We do not dispute that there may be very good reasons for their reluctance to add anything to their rulings. However, this trait of their professional culture does not foster accountability. Second, judges also claim not to be accountable for the consequences of their rulings. For instance, a judge refusing to put a wife beater on remand or giving him a sentence of probation would decline all responsibility for reprisals that this offender might use against his wife, after being released. Actually, a Quebec judge explicitly said in open court that he would not 'lose any sleep' over the fact that a wife beater that he had refused to put in preventive custody might kill his wife (*Montreal Gazette*, 7 January 1994).

Our guess is that if judges were asked to discuss their accountability they would do so in four ways. They might suggest that they are accountable 'to the law.' They might discuss the manner in which their decisions might be reviewed by higher courts (unless they were members of the highest court). They might discuss how they were 'accountable' for their own behaviour and how some other body – a judicial council, for example – could make them account for any behaviour that might be seen as inappropriate for a judge. And, finally, judges might refer to the notion that they, as members of society, were, in some indirect way, accountable to the public. In this context, it might be suggested that 'accountability' is achieved by way of the openness of our courts and the provision of explanations of decisions.

Before presenting our main criticism of this view of accountability, we will briefly comment on some of its alleged mechanisms. There are two problems with seeing appellate review as a mechanism promoting accountability. First, appellate review divorces a judge's performance from his or her person. It is exclusively a judge's ruling that is under review. Whatever may be the result of this review, it will generally have no consequence for the judge himself or herself, with the possible exception of a slight hurt to his or her pride. More importantly, the appellate process has to be triggered from within the adversarial court system. Even if a sentencing outcome profoundly offends justice, as was the case with the sentence imposed in the case we have described, it cannot be subject to appellate review when it is the result of an agreement between the prosecution and the defence. Only these two participants in the sentencing process can actually trigger the review.

Judicial councils are a paradigm case for a line of criticism that has been directed against police internal review: this kind of mechanism almost never produces sanctions against misconduct by an official and acts mostly as a shield against external criticism rather than as a defender of the public interest. Furthermore, we suspect that very few members of the public are even aware of the existence of judicial councils and that even fewer would dare to make a complaint against a member of the judiciary.

Lastly, judges have acknowledged being accountable 'to the law' or 'to the public.' Both notions are so vague that they may be devoid of any meaning. Yet, this very situation – the lack of meaning of accountability – is a risky one, because it allows public opinion and its media surrogates to fill in the vacuum with cries for accountability that are fueled more by blind indignation than careful deliberation of the nature of sentencing. A recent case that happened in Quebec bears witness to the risks of leaving judicial accountability undefined. In January 1994, a judge of the Quebec provincial court imposed a sentence of twenty-three months of incarceration on a man who had sexually abused his nine- or ten-year-old stepdaughter for a period of two and half years. The judge justified her comparatively light sentence by saying that the accused had preserved the virginity of his victim by resorting exclusively to sodomy and that she did not believe that having been sexually abused would leave the child with permanent psychological scars. The family involved in this case was Islamic and the judge argued that in her opinion the followers of this religion specially valued virginity in a woman and that this circumstance gave an additional extenuating weight to the fact that the aggressor refrained from having vaginal intercourse with his victim. As expected, the prosecution immediately appealed the judge's sentence. Nevertheless, this judge was subsequently promoted to be the administrative head of one level of court in the province.

This, however, was far from being the end of the matter. Selections from the court record of her judgment were publicly aired by radio stations and created an instant furor in Quebec. This furor was further exploited by 'hot line' radio broadcasters. Shortly thereafter the judge took a voluntary leave from the court. She had been about to rule in three other cases involving sexual abuse but, as a result of her leave, the cases had to be retried. In an exceptional move, the Quebec bar decided to complain to the Quebec judicial council and called for an inquiry into the judge's capacity to fulfil 'adequately and diligently her judicial duties' (*Montreal Gazette*, 17 February 1994). Although this judge's ruling appears difficult to defend, we believe that there should be an alternative to such 'street justice' as a means of fostering judicial accountability.

This leads us to what we consider to be the heart of the matter of judicial accountability. As we have already seen, accountability is often thought of as relating primarily to openness and legitimacy. If a person makes a decision that can be justified in some way, and the decision and the basis of it are open for public examination, and if deviations from legitimacy or openness can be corrected, then the decision-maker is seen by many as being accountable. Borrowing from Day and Klein (1987), we suggest that such an analysis ignores two fundamental aspects of accountability. Day and Klein suggest that

accountability is all about the construction of an agreed language or currency of discourse about conduct and performance, and the criteria that should be used in assessing them. (ibid.: 2)

Accountability implies both a shared set of expectations and a common currency of justifications. There has to be agreement about the context, the reason why one actor owes explanation to another since it is precisely this sense of obligation which translates the giving of accounts into accountability. Equally there has to be agreement about the language of justification, what constitutes good reason for explaining conduct ... In short, accountability, even at its simplest in the relationship between individuals, presupposes agreement both about what constitutes an acceptable performance and about the language of justification to be used by actors in defending their conduct. Furthermore, it implies a definition of the relationship between actors. To talk about accountability is to define who can call for an account, and who owes a duty of explanation. (ibid.: 5)

This view of accountability is innovative in that it goes beyond the traditional notion of responsibility and stresses that giving an account of one's behaviour implies using a medium that can be shared and understood by the party for which it is intended. The conditions for mutual understanding are said to be a shared set of expectations and a common currency of justifications.

Such a shared set of expectations and a common currency of justification is precisely what is completely lacking in the examples that we have discussed. The perspective that led to the extremely light sentence imposed on the professional assassin reflects a utilitarian approach to justice pushed to its absurd consequences, where the end of securing a few convictions justifies the means of granting quasi-immunity to a professional killer, at the expense of any value related to justice. The judge in the sexual assault cases was utterly confused over the issue of mitigation, particularly when it was raised in a context involving a perceived difference of culture.

Although in the remainder of this essay we shall focus on the problem of disparity as it currently arises in court and refer to sentencing principles and guidelines, it is very important to keep in mind that the lack of a common currency extends beyond differences of approach between judges and is responsible for an ever increasing credibility gap between the public and the courts. What we at present are witnessing in this regard is a process of alienation that feeds on itself. The more that sentencing disparity is reported to the public, the less the public understands the function of criminal justice. As the public is more confused about criminal justice, it is ever more likely to make contradictory demands on the system, to which the courts can only respond by increasing the inconsistency of their decisions. The issue of disparity is not a technical problem in search of ad hoc solutions. It challenges the ability of the courts to produce something that is and can be perceived as justice. We shall elaborate on these ideas later.

Disparity and Accountability for Sentencing Decisions

In its strictest sense, the term 'disparity' means simply variation. Variation in sentencing *per se* clearly is not seen as bad. We have variation in sentences handed down for different offences and variation in sentences handed down for different instances of the same offence. The issue, however, that needs to be addressed is how one evaluates this variation. When we hear about sentencing variation (across cases, across districts, or across types of offenders) and say that 'it makes sense' we are, in effect, saying that the variation that exists fits a set of principles (or a single principle) that we agree with. However, when we find systematic variation in sentencing that we cannot explain by any acceptable set of principles (such as variation in sentencing because of the race of the offender or victim), we might refer to that variation as unwarranted disparity in sentencing. A theory of sentencing, then, implies not only what should determine sentences, but what should not.

What then, in the area of sentencing, might be 'a shared set of expectations' or a 'common currency of justifications'? Simply put, it would be a 'theory' or a set of guiding principles on sentencing and an explanation of how the sentence followed from the guiding principles. But, one might ask, do we not have a theory of sentencing in most countries? Do we not say that sentences should denounce the crime, rehabilitate, deter (individually and generally), and, if appropriate, incapacitate the offender? Many courts have laid down such a basket of principles. The problem, of course, is that this does not constitute '*an* agreed upon language or currency.' It constitutes many. More directly, such an unordered and unweighted set of principles does *not* provide criteria for assessing the 'conduct and performance' – the sentence, in this case – of the judge.

A few years ago, one of us was asked in an informal conversation with one of Canada's more senior judges what the empirical evidence was for unwarranted disparity in sentencing in Canada. The judge patiently listened as the evidence was described. There was evidence of variation from one location to another that could only be described in terms of differences in local custom unrelated to any underlying differences in crime or socioeconomic conditions; there was evidence from 'simulation' exercises where large numbers of judges had been asked to indicate what sentence they would hand down in a particular case; and there was evidence that, depending on which purposes of sentencing they saw as paramount, different judges would emphasize different evidence, weigh various concerns differently, and come to different decisions about the appropriate sentence for a case.

The judge was told that the evidence suggested not so much that there was 'random' variation, but rather that two different judges, sentencing identical cases, could start with different principles and could arrive at dramatically different, but equally 'justifiable' sentences because their 'theories of sentencing' were different. We suggested that evidence such as this would suggest that the sentencing system was in need of some attention.

The judge's response was simple: 'Maybe both judges were right.' Our judge, of course, was correct. Both sentences were 'right' as long as the meaning of 'right' is that both sentences could be 'justified.' The sentences could be justified, but the judges were not accountable for their sentences.

Defining disparity as a sentence that cannot be justified is equivalent to defining disparity out of existence. What we actually have is a set of principles that sometimes flatly contradict one another and which, depending on the priority given to any subset of them, and depending on the exact manner of application, could be used to justify virtually any sentence within the legally permissible range for that offence. The point is made more forcefully by Nils Jareborg (1989) in a comment on many European sentencing laws:

Any jurisdiction which relies interchangeably upon two or more of these [standard purposes of sentencing] has an incoherent policy. In fact, it is normal that any of the mentioned types of policy is seen as sufficient for justifying a sentence. Like cases are then certainly treated differently but they are also treated alike — in relation to the disjunction of relevant policies. Disparity occurs only [under such incoherent policies] when the sentence depends on factors clearly irrelevant according to all the accepted sentencing policies. (ibid.: 11)

No one can with certainly answer the question as to whether disparity exists unless he knows what sentencing pattern is the right one and whether a certain sentence deviates from that pattern. (ibid.: 12)

Other than being within legislatively prescribed limits, sentencing fails on almost every criterion outlined by Day and Klein (1987) above.

It is almost completely devoid of expectations that can be seen as 'shared' among a set of sentencing judges, let alone between members of the public and the judge, or any other pairing of individuals or groups interested in the criminal process. Furthermore, it would be hard to argue that we have an agreed 'language of justification' for justifying sentences. Finally, we cannot even specify who can (or should) be called on for an explanation for a given sentencing decision. Sentencing is, in many countries, in trouble. And disparity is a symptom of that trouble.

What Forms Does Disparity Take?

The most common association to the term 'disparity in sentencing' is the situation where there is unwarranted variation in the sentences being handed down in two 'equivalent' cases. Data often demonstrate that different sentencing judges in the same jurisdiction hand down very different sentences in identical written hypothetical cases. This constitutes evidence of disparity that is relatively uncontroversial, since it is difficult to argue against the view that identical cases should be treated alike.

Not treating similar cases similarly is actually only one side of the coin. The reverse situation – treating cases that are significantly different from one another in a similar way – is also a form of disparity. For example, if it is agreed that a particular factor should affect sentences and if it can be shown that this factor is not being taken into account, then clearly we have a different, albeit less conspicuous, form of the same problem of disparity.

These two types of disparity in relation to a single category of offences (similar or different cases of robbery, for example) also apply across types of offences. Although it is not often thought of in the context of disparity, variation in sentencing patterns *across* types of offences raises problems of disparity that may be just as serious as intraoffence disparity. Disparity then becomes a *systematic* part of the sentencing process. For instance, if there are sound reasons to believe that two kinds of offences should have similar patterns of sentences and they do not, we have a type of cross-offence disparity that is analogous to intraoffence disparity. Similarly, if there are two offences that do have similar patterns of sentences, but there is an accepted view that they should not, we again have a form of disparity analogous to intraoffence disparity.

Individualized Sentencing

In most countries, 'individualization' of sentences is valued. That sentences should be determined by sentencing principles and by a concern for the specific facts of a case is a legitimate, indeed a necessary, requisite of sentencing. However, the individualization of sentences is more often used as a rhetorical device to disguise anarchy in sentencing as order and to market chaos as deliberation. The stronger justification for the individualization of sentencing is that the sentence should fit the individual offender.

Not only is it never asked whether sentencing can actually be tailored to fit individual offenders, but the history of sentencing theory shows that initially the individualization of sentences was introduced to allow sentencers to make a difference between two very broad categories of offenders and not between individual offenders.

One of the earliest treatises on the individualization of sentences was published in France at the end on the nineteenth century and translated into English in 1911 (Saleilles, 1911). Although it is much referred to, this treatise is seldom read. Its main subject is the difference between politically motivated crime, such as anarchist terrorism, and common criminality. Saleilles argued that the two phenomena should not be confused, and pushed this argument into the field of sentencing politically and profit-motivated offenders. Hence, what is meant by the individualization of sentencing is not that the intelligent fitting of different sanctions to fit the offenders – at the time of Saleilles's writing, there were few sanctions other than incarceration – but the opportunity to distinguish between two very broad categories of offenders. It deserves to be stressed that even in this very broad sense, Saleilles's advice was not heeded by most Western countries, which continue to treat politically motivated offenders as common criminals.

At its best, the individualizing of sentences would imply a process in which the purpose and principles of sentencing were clearly laid out. For example, sentencing in one jurisdiction might be governed by the principle that a sentence was to be proportionate to the harm actually done. Some form of standard for sentences would be set for different levels of harm for a particular offence. The judge, in individualizing the sentence, would then evaluate the harm done by the offender and then assess the appropriate penalty according to the agreed-upon standard.

Alternatively, if the primary purpose of the sentence was to rehabilitate the offender, judges would be obligated to assess the underlying factors that led the offender to commit the offence. Judges would then have to assess the evidence concerning the effectiveness of various treatments in dealing with the underlying cause of the offence and would then order the treatment most likely to 'rehabilitate' the offender. Neither of the sentencing tasks – under a proportionality model or a rehabilitation model – would be easy. And neither task could be carried out *completely* reliably. There would always be some variation.

But this is not what is typically meant by 'individualized' sentencing. The supporters of individualized sentencing often begin with the truism that 'no two cases are alike.' Though technically true, this statement implies that there is no consensus on which factors *should* be considered by the sentencing judge and which should not. The broadest definition of 'individualization' of sentences implies complete anarchy in sentencing: anything goes as long as an intelligent person can come up with a *post hoc* justification. A bit less anarchistic than this is the view that the judge first decides what the major goal of the sentence should be and then applies principles to achieve this goal.

Very few people, however, take an extreme view of the individualization of sentences. Most people would accept the view that there are some principles of sentencing, even though they might be reluctant to state these in such a way that there could be a shared understanding of what would justify a sentence.

Conditions for Accountability in Sentencing – the Need for a Theory of Sentencing

To have true accountability in sentencing, there must be a meaningful theory of sentences. Theory need not be understood as 'grand theorizing' in the context of sentencing. It might be characterized in three ways. First, in the simplest sense of the word, a theory is a set of assertions that describe a phenomenon accurately. Hence, a theory of sentencing would first attempt to present in a truthful way the reality of the sentencing process and the constraints that characterize the process. For example, in the overwhelming majority of cases, a sentencing hearing cannot last more than fifteen minutes because of the crushing volume of cases that the lower courts have to process. Judges must determine their sentence in a matter of minutes. Within such a context, the individualization of sentences can only be a noxious illusion, because the most basic conditions to achieve this goal are lacking. Typically, for example, there is no time for careful deliberation and weighing of the principles and facts. In other words, having an accurate depiction of the practice of sentencing is the starting point in trying to achieve the much vaunted ideal of 'truth in sentencing.'

Second, within the context of sentencing tradition, a theory of sentencing may refer to a set of principles on which to base sentencing decisions. A theory of sentencing must tell the decision-maker what principles are most important, and, by implication, what should not be given weight in the sentencing decision. In addition to 'truth,' which applies mostly to factual theories, there is the requirement that a theory must have consistency. This requisite applies equally to a set of norms, whether or not they are conceived of as sentencing principles, sentencing purposes, or sentencing guidelines (of whatever form). Hence, a theory of sentencing in this sense means simply a consistent set of sentencing norms.

Finally, the result of having a theory of sentencing can be described by using the words of Day and Klein that we quoted earlier. If we have a true perspective on the reality of sentencing, we also have a 'shared set of expectations' about what it can achieve and how it can do so. Also, a consistent set of sentencing principles will afford us the 'common currency of justifications' that is now completely lacking in the sentencing structures of many jurisdictions. We will now apply these concepts to the problems of sentencing.

Imagine a situation where there are two co-offenders who had identical roles in an offence, and one of the offenders had no previous convictions and the other had numerous recent convictions for similar offences. Let us first consider the case where they get quite different sentences – the one with the long criminal record getting a harsher sentence. We might be inclined, in many countries, to say that the existence of the difference in the sentences was not evidence of unwarranted disparity, since the one with the record was treated more harshly. However, implicit in such an evaluation is the principle that severity of sentence and criminal record should be correlated. Similarly, if they were to get identical sentences, whether one felt the outcome was appropriate would depend on one's 'theory' of sentencing.

Because, in reality, no two cases are *completely* identical, the lack of a theory of sentencing would, in theory, allow any sentence to be justified because, after all, it is the responsibility of the judge to 'individualize' sentences.

Another anecdote illustrates the problem of complex, unstated, 'incoherent' theories of individualized sentencing. In discussing the evidence for disparity with a group of judges one day, one of us noted that in one Canadian province, for some offences, there is a good deal of variation from judicial district to judicial district on the use of conditional discharges. A judge suggested that there might be important variation in these locations, such as the prevalence of the offence, the tolerance for it in the community, or other factors that would 'explain' the variation. Of course, the judge might well be right. But two observations can be made: 'justifying' such variation in this way implies that such factors *should* be part of sentencing policy. Furthermore, the discussion appeared to begin from the premise that the variation is acceptable ('because it is there') and to proceed to search for a post hoc explanation for it.

There is one final point which should be borne in mind with respect to the nature of a sentencing theory. In our earlier example, we have assumed that there normally is a correlation between the severity of a sentence and an offender's previous criminal record. This need not necessarily be so. One can imagine a situation where an offender with a shorter criminal record might be given a more severe sentence than an offender with a longer record committing a similar crime. In the case of a minor offence against property, some judges indicate that they like to give younger first-time offenders a 'short sharp shock' on the (empirically unsupported) belief that such 'treatment' will be an effective individual deterrent. The same judge might be more lenient towards a more experienced shoplifter believing that overpunishing minor offenders is a practice to be avoided. Our hypothetical judge might, in other cases (such as, violent offences against persons) treat the prior criminal record as an aggravating factor.

If applied consistently, this set of rules concerning the use of previous criminal convictions could still constitute part of a 'theory' of sentencing. The point that we want to stress is that a sentencing theory is not necessarily a simple-minded book of ready-to-use recipes. It is a rather detailed statement that attempts to spell out what is the desirable course of action in a variety of cases. This statement may be very complex, just as cases themselves are complex. Whether simple or complex, however, a theory of sentencing must be explicit.

Can Disparity Be Eliminated without the Difficulty of Agreeing on a Theory?

The simple answer to this question is probably yes. Certainly, if all sentences were mandatory ones specified in legislation, then it would be easy to see that all those found guilty of a given offence would get the same sentence. Discretion would probably have been shifted to the prosecution, so that the disparity would be created by decisions about charges. But, on the surface, there would be no disparity. The legislature might or might not have had a theory when it mandated certain sentences. There would not, however, be unwarranted variation in sentences for those found guilty of a given offence.

There have been other attempts to reduce or eliminate disparity in sentencing without specifying a theory. Perhaps the most notorious of these attempts is to be found in the United States federal criminal jurisdiction. Prior to implementing some fundamental changes in sentencing in the late 1980s, sentencing in the United States federal jurisdiction was seen as being somewhat chaotic. In the words of the first chairman of the United States Sentencing Commission:

The process of punishing persons convicted of federal criminal offences was so manifestly discretionary and so given to unwarranted sentencing disparity that when Congress finally passed legislation in 1984 to change that process, it called the prevailing system 'shameful' ... The root of the problem was that sentencing was the one function given to federal judges that was essentially ungoverned by law. (Wilkins, 1990: 214)

The problem, as many critics have pointed out, is that the United States Sentencing Commission took federal sentencing in the United States from a situation where it was 'ungoverned by law' to one where it was ungoverned by principles. The United States Sentencing Commission, in what is now probably its most frequently quoted statement of non-policy, said that it could not choose between a sentencing model based primarily on severity of the offence and one based on utilitarian goals, noting that 'adherents of these [two] points of view have urged the Commission to choose between them, to accord one primacy over the other. Such a choice would be profoundly difficult ... As a practical matter, in most sentencing decisions both philosophies may prove consistent with the same result' (United States Sentencing Commission, 1988: 1.3–1.4).'

A set of guidelines is then described. But where, especially in the absence of any overriding theory of sentencing, is the shared set of expectations governing the sentencing process and, more importantly, how could one possibly find a 'common currency of justifications' for a particular recommended sentence where there was no initial agreement on how sentences should be determined?

More to the point, even if judges attempted to follow such guidelines religiously and even if the guidelines were so unambiguous that judges could reliably determine what the guideline was for individual cases – and there is every reason to believe that neither of these conditions holds – the previously discussed problem of inter-offence disparity remains.

These problems have haunted the United States Sentencing Commission since its guidelines first were announced. The commission has the responsibility of amending its guidelines as the need arises. But, as F.W. Bennett noted, 'Decisions seem to be made on some amendments without any substantive reasons other than conclusionary statements that certain offence levels "need to be raised"' (1990: 149).

The amendment process made quite clear how difficult it was to work in a complex system without an overriding set of principles. Michael K. Block, as one of the original commissioners, had apparently been content to sign the original report endorsing an unprincipled approach to creating sentencing guidelines. Later, however, he indicated serious problems with such an approach. After citing example after example of 'arbitrary change[s] in sentencing policy' (1989: 221), Block suggested, after resigning from the commission, in testimony before the House of Representatives Subcommittee on Criminal Justice, that

The personal preferences of Sentencing Commissioners as to what is 'good' or 'right' or 'just' should not be the basis for the Commission's policy decisions. The basis of those decisions must be information and information in particular on the costs and benefits of various policy options. (Ibid.: 222)

What concerns me about these unsupported amendments is not only that the substantive changes may not be warranted, but also that the Commission's process for generating guideline amendments is developing in such a way as to hinder rational policy making ... The pure increases in offence levels in this amendment were not: 1) required, either explicitly or implicitly, by Congressional action, 2) responsive in any obvious manner to a problem that the Commission or its staff had identified in the operation of the initial guideline, or 3) intended to further the rationalizing of fraud sentencing begun in the initial guideline. (Ibid.: 451)

The commission's view that sentencing law can be made explicit (through the use of guidelines) without articulating principles for the original guidelines (or the changes in them) makes the role of the sentencing judge even more difficult. If the judge's role involves, in part, the giving of reasons for the sentences, there should be, as Ashworth (1984: 528) has suggested, 'a reconsideration of what should count as a reason.'

In any case, as matters stand now, many of the arguments about the guidelines, amendments to them, and justifications for departure can be seen as problems inevitable in a complex system without explicit, broadly accepted guiding principles.

As Nils Jareborg (1989: 10) noted a few years ago, 'In many countries, we find a penal system with a incoherent penal policy.' The goal of sentencing policy should be to achieve a level of coherence such that sentences and the policies that govern them make sense to all involved.

The problem of having a sentencing structure that does not make sense to all involved is well illustrated by a rather sad statement made by a New York judge in April 1993:

On one day last week I had to sentence a peasant woman from West Africa to 46 months in a drug case. The result for her young children will undoubtedly be, as she suggested, devastating. On the same day, I sentenced a man to 30 years as a second drug offender ... These two cases confirm my sense of depression about much of the cruelty I have been party to in connection with the 'war on drugs' ... I need a rest from the oppressive sense of futility that these drug cases leave ... I have therefore taken my name out of the wheel for drug cases ... This resolution leaves me uncomfortable since it shifts the 'dirty work' to other judges. At the moment, however, I simply cannot sentence another impoverished person whose destruction has no discernible effect on the drug trade ... I am just a tired old judge who has temporarily filled his quota of remorselessness. (Weinstein, 1993: 298)

Our criticism of the United States Sentencing Commission's work, then, should be put in the context of the present state of sentencing in many countries. In Canada, for example, although the Report of the Canadian Sentencing Commission was released in early 1987, there have been no major changes in the sentencing structure in the eight years following the report's release.

In many common law countries, then, the legislative arm of government has left the problem of disparity – and sentencing policy – to the courts. The courts have dealt primarily with one form of disparity: ranges for a given offence that are too wide. Thus, very severe (and in some countries very mild) sentences have been appealed and quite often 'pulled in' towards the centre of the distribution. Explanations are usually given for changes in individual sentences. When a sentence is made less severe, courts will often say something like 'insufficient weight was given to the goal of rehabilitating the offender.' If the sentence is too mild, the court will substitute 'deterrence' or 'the serious nature of the offence' for the words 'rehabilitating the offender.' In this way, courts, like legislatures, can avoid making policy but at the same time narrow the distribution of sentences somewhat.

From time to time, however, some courts in some jurisdictions have ventured timidly into the policy area. The result is what are sometimes called 'guideline' judgments, where the court of appeal has indicated some form of 'starting point' in sentencing offenders convicted of a particular kind of offence. As an approach to dealing with the problem of high levels of variation in sentences, this might seem to be an adequate solution to the problem of sentencing. Interestingly enough, however, it is clear that sometimes even the court that created a 'guideline' can have difficulty in following it in subsequent cases (Young, 1988). The reason for this is simple: without a theory, the court has no guidance in how to apply the rules to the next case it is faced with.

But such guideline judgments typically do not address a form of disparity we have already discussed: unexplained variation *across* types of offences. Without a theory – or an explicit set of principles – to guide sentencing, the public, offender, victim, and court have no way of deciding the relative severity of sentences across types of offences.

One of the terms of reference of the Canadian Sentencing Commission, on which we each served, was to recommend a new set of maximum sentences for all Criminal Code offences in Canada. Although some initial work was done on it in the early stages of the life of that commission, some of the more difficult decisions were made after the commission had agreed on a set of principles to guide sentencing decisions. The commission recommended that the seriousness of the offence be the primary determinant of the sentence. Thus, when the commissioners got to the point of deciding the maximum sentences for each offence the commission had a framework to apply to each offence.

The theory of sentencing that the commission had agreed upon gave 'a common currency' on which to evaluate each offence. Without agreement about what should be considered, any disagreement could never have been resolved adequately. It is possible that two reasonable people might not agree on the relative seriousness of the most serious instances of an offence. They might, for example, have to make a further policy decision: whether 'seriousness' connotes the amount of harm an offence has, or could have caused, or if it reflects some more abstract set of moral values. However, they would know that the ultimate decision should be guided by the definition they arrived at and then some assessment of the 'seriousness' of the two acts. The handing down of a sentence for an individual case reflects the same problems. Without a true theory of sentencing, accountability is not possible.

Problems of Implementation

We have insisted throughout on the need for a sentencing theory. Our insistence upon this need may, however, generate an imbalance that must be redressed. For the ancient philosophers, the human mind had two components – the intellect and the will. In stressing the importance of a sentencing theory for the creation of a framework for accountability with regard to sentencing, we might appear to favour the intellect over the will. This appearance is completely misleading, for we believe that accountability cannot be promoted only by developing a set of sentencing principles, however thoughtful they may be. Doing justice and thinking about it are not the same thing. A theory of criminal justice does not implement itself by virtue of its profundity. Its application is dependent on a political will to reform the sentencing process.

Few votes are to be gained by undertaking to reform criminal justice and fewer still will be obtained by lowering punishments for certain offences or for creating a coherent theory of sentencing. There are, in Canada, few signs that contradict the conclusion that the criminal justice system is generally the object of a benign neglect by the government. To be fair to our government, we are encouraged, from time to time, to see some small steps towards the creation of a process that might eventually lead to sentencing reform. It is not an easy process and not one that is likely to be done well if done quickly or in response to an apparent crisis. We look forward to seeing our own government (and others) make the difficult decisions that are necessary to move towards achieving accountability in sentencing.

Summary

We have suggested that the concepts of disparity and accountability are intimately related. Organizations and individuals are 'accountable' when there is a 'shared set of expectations' and 'common currency of justifications' for policy, decisions, or actions.

Although not often discussed in these terms, we have suggested that the major cause of disparity and general discontent in sentencing is that we do not have a set of principles to guide the development of sentencing policy and sentencing practice.

Efforts to deal with disparity without first addressing the issue of policy will not be doomed to *complete* failure, but will be severely limited in their effectiveness and ultimately will never be able to provide an adequate foundation for defining, understanding, and eliminating unwarranted disparity in sentencing.

Accountability and Justice in the English Prison System

ROD MORGAN AND MIKE MAGUIRE

Prisons pose problems of accountability that go beyond those raised by most other state agencies (Day and Klein, 1987). The essence of imprisonment is punishment through loss of liberty. The consequent duty upon the prison authorities to maintain security and prevent escapes necessarily requires that some restrictions be imposed on aspects of prisoners' lives and over the flow of information between the world of the prison and the wider community. Prisons are therefore relatively closed and total institutions (Goffman, 1961) within which it is all too easy for accountability to be denied, ostensibly in fulfilment of the prison mandate.

Moreover, prisoners are a discredited group whose rights as citizens are generally curtailed by statute and subtly undermined by the unwritten doctrine of 'less eligibility' – that is, because inmates are undergoing punishment, the conditions within prison should not be better than those they would experience outside (Webb and Webb, 1922: 88; McConville, 1981: 238–41; Garland, 1990). Because they stand condemned legally, they are judged deficient morally and of less account politically. In sum, legally responsible yet socially irresponsible, prisoners are peculiarly vulnerable to abuse. Theirs is not a world against which they can easily protest. They are not readily believed, and when their pleas regarding adverse conditions are shown to have substance it is often doubted that they deserve better.

It is because prisoners are peculiarly vulnerable that there is said to be a particular need to construct a legal framework for accountability in relation both to prisoners – in the form of positive rights (Richardson,

1985a) – and to prisons, in the form of legally enforceable standards (Casale, 1984; Gostin and Staunton, 1985; Casale and Plotnikoff, 1989). Furthermore, because prison security and order within prisons rest ultimately on coercion, prison policy is inevitably prey to accusations that the power of the state is being abused. Thus, debates about the adequacy of mechanisms for prison accountability, including complaints procedures and the redress of wrongs, are fierce and perennial. Nowhere has this been more true than in Britain in recent years.

Because one cannot be accountable *to* another without it being clear as to what one is accountable *for*, this essay will begin with a brief discussion of what it is that English prisons are supposed to deliver. We shall then review the various mechanisms through which accounts are made and draw some broad conclusions about their adequacy and prospects for the future.

Criminal Justice, Sentencing, and the Objectives of Imprisonment

In his 1952 review of the *English Prison System*, the then chairman of the Prison Commission referred with sympathy to English suspicion of 'systems' and illustrated the tradition by noting that little could be learned from English law about 'what place Parliament has assigned to the prison in its general order of battle for the attack on crime' (Fox, 1952: 3). Indeed, Fox considered it a merit that English prison administrators had been able over the previous sixty years to change so much within prisons with virtually no recourse to Parliament (*ibid.*: 3–4). This tradition has continued. However, it is doubtful whether the current director general of the Prison Service would glow with the same pride over his department's record in recent decades, even if much has changed in the absence of new legislation.

Though the service remains statutorily committed to the paramedical doctrine of 'treatment and training' (Prison Rules, 1964: Rule 1), in fact it has adopted a much more prosaic managerial statement of purpose (Prison Department, Circular Instruction 55/1984; see also Train, 1985) which owes little to the rehabilitative optimism of the 1950s and early 1960s. In Britain, as elsewhere, the growing belief that 'nothing works' (to paraphrase Lipton, Martinson, and Wilks, 1975), or that 'nothing works much better than anything else' (to paraphrase Brody, 1976) gave rise to a new doctrine of 'penal pessimism' (Cross, 1971); led to calls for the abandonment of 'treatment and training' in favour of 'humane containment' (King and Morgan, 1980); was buttressed by pleas for the parsimonious use of custody (Rutherford, 1984); and was underpinned by the ubiquitous call for offenders to get their 'just deserts' (von Hirsch, 1976; United Kingdom Home Office, 1990a, b).

These ideological struggles washed around the Prison Service throughout the 1970s but the statute remained unamended. Moreover, the organizational manifestations of treatment and training were preserved: namely, a dual system of 'local' prisons, which service the courts and in which sentenced prisoners are received and classified, and a variety of 'training' prisons, to which they are then allocated according to their 'treatment and training needs.' Even the opportunity presented by a major official inquiry (United Kingdom, Committee of Inquiry into the United Kingdom Prison Services, henceforth the May Report, 1979) passed without a radical alternative being adopted (King and Morgan, 1980; Bottoms, 1990).

The system remained inequitable, paternalistic, and unjust. Inequitable, because those prisoners deemed untrainable or untreatable – the untried and unsentenced, those sentenced to terms not considered long enough to make the effort worthwhile, and the recalcitrants who failed to settle in the training prisons and who were held to be beyond redemption – were excluded from the noble mission and consigned to the local prisons within which, as pressures on the system increased, less and less was provided. The local prisons, all of them Victorian, became squalid sinks, overcrowded and ill resourced. All the new buildings and most of the new prisoner programs went to the training prison sector, which for the most part, was shielded from overcrowding. They were called 'paternalistic', because within this system prisoners enjoyed 'privileges' not 'rights,' and the decisions made by staff about prisoners were made according to criteria that were seldom revealed, within procedures that lacked due process. They were viewed as 'unjust,' because the quality of life that prisoners enjoyed bore little or no relation to any legal theory informing the use of imprisonment. The untried, subject to the presumption of innocence, suffered the most oppressive conditions (King and Morgan, 1976; Casale and Plotnikoff, 1990; Morgan, 1994), while the medium and long-term sentenced population benefited from the modern prisons operating increasingly liberal regimes that had emerged during the 1960s and 1970s (King and Morgan, 1980). They were unjust also because as overcrowding got worse, so the executive released prisoners early (by increasing remission and introducing parole), thereby creating a more and more complicated disjunction between sentences passed and sentences served. In general, the shorter the sentence, the greater was the likelihood of parole, a phenomenon that increased the gap between short- and long-term prisoners in time actually served, a system described as 'double sentencing' (United Kingdom, Committee to Review the Parole System, henceforth the Carlisle Report, 1988; Maguire, 1992).

It is only during the 1990s that a meaningful connection has begun to be forged between the realism that in recent years has increasingly informed sentencing theory and the aims of the prison system. The catalyst was a series of major disturbances that took place in Strangeways Prison, Manchester, and other institutions in April 1990. The resulting inquiry (United Kingdom, Inquiry into Prison Disturbances, henceforth the Woolf Report, 1991) put forward as its central conclusion the proposition that, though prisons are the supreme creation of the criminal justice system, prisons in England and Wales are not well integrated into that system, nor are their policies wholly just or well calculated to fulfil the purposes of the courts in particular, and the criminal justice system in general.

This proposition is underpinned by the growing realism, already widespread in government circles, which can be summarized as the acceptance of four main arguments. First, it is now broadly agreed that imprisonment tends to debilitate rather than invigorate prisoners and, in particular, it undermines rather than enhances their personal responsibility (United Kingdom, Home Office, 1988 & 1990a, b). Second, if sentencers wish in some sense to improve offenders (better educate them, train them, or address some medical, psychological or social problem that they may have), then the last place one would ideally choose to undertake the task would be in prison. This is not to say that positive efforts should not be attempted within prisons; merely that the *use* of imprisonment is not justified by such purpose (United Kingdom, Home Office 1991a: par. 1.28).

Third, the potency of deterrence as a practical doctrine has been undermined by our understanding of the way in which the criminal justice system works. We know that by a process of attrition a remarkably small proportion of the offenders responsible for all the crime that is committed are actually caught, convicted, and punished (United Kingdom, Home Office, 1991c: 31). As a consequence, Beccaria's certainties are compromised (Beccaria, 1770). It is no longer plausible to imagine that some categories of offenders will be deterred by the unlikely prospect of their receiving a particular punishment (United Kingdom, Home Office, 1990a, b: par. 2.8). As for the experience of imprisonment acting as a deterrent, the reconviction statistics for released prisoners are depressingly familiar (United Kingdom, Home Office, 1990c: ch. 9).

Fourth, the adoption by the government of 'just deserts' as a sentencing model in Britain has meant that 'the first objective for all sentences is denunciation of and retribution for the crime' (United Kingdom, Home Office, 1990b: par. 2.9), with public protection added as a subsidiary aim particularly for offences of violence; Criminal Justice Act, [1991], section 1(2)(b). The implication of this delimited sentencing framework is that Paterson's dictum that offenders 'come to prison *as* a punishment, not *for* punishment' (Ruck, 1951: 23) has at long last started to be taken seriously. Lord Justice Woolf argues that we are entitled to assume that when prisoners are committed by the courts, the intention is that they should lose their liberty, but no more. Thus, if they 'are subjected to inhumane or degrading treatment,' then not only is an injustice being done (Woolf Report, 1991: par. 10.19) but, insofar as the result is that prisoners deteriorate, or leave prison 'in an embittered and disaffected state,' then the prison system is working against the overall purpose of the criminal justice system, which is the reduction of crime.

Woolf's message, then, was that prisoners remain citizens with rights and that justice – fairness and due process – should be an overriding characteristic of the prison system. He recommended a number of procedural and standard-setting measures that, in time, should lead to new statutory rules enforced by judicial review (ibid.: par. 12.117). This is a far cry from the mere privileges for prisoners associated with the 'treatment and training' philosophy.

Though the government claims to have accepted most of Woolf's principles and recommendations (United Kingdom, Home Office, 1991a) it remains to be seen to what extent it will implement them, particularly those involving structural changes such as the development of contracts between prisoners and prison managers, community prisons, and accredited prison standards. Nevertheless, at most points in the discussion that follows it is apparent that the drift from the rehabilitative framework of treatment and training, towards a more honestly punitive yet rights-oriented justice approach, has stimulated the demand for greater accountability at all levels of prisons policy.

Fiscal Crisis and Effectiveness and Efficiency in the Public Sector

Imprisonment is an expensive commodity. In 1989/90 the English prison system cost over £1.2 billion and the average cost of keeping a prisoner in custody was £321 per week (United Kingdom, Home Office, 1990d). Expenditure on prisons has risen by approximately 90 per cent in real terms since 1979, and the cost of keeping offenders in custody is about eighteen times as great as supervising them in the community (United Kingdom, Home Office, 1990b), a fact which – at least, until a recent volte-face by a punitive new home secretary – the Home Office has frequently tried to impress upon sentencers. Though the Conservative government that has been in office since 1979 always undertook to spend more on 'law and order' services while cutting public expenditure elsewhere (Conservative Party, 1979), it is nonetheless committed to the rigorous application of the three 'E's – effectiveness, efficiency, and economy – to all public sector services (United Kingdom, Prime Minister, 1984). This means formulating measurable objectives, costing all major functions and activities, monitoring the achievement of objectives at regular intervals, and looking for greater competition in the provision of services.

The Prison Department was undoubtedly in need of such attentions. In 1979, for example, a major official inquiry into the United Kingdom Prison Service found rudimentary financial accounting systems that were unable, for example, to cost the operation of individual establishments (May Report, 1979: par. 5.35). All that has changed dramatically. The annual report of the Prison Service now includes a welter of financial statistics, disaggregated by both function and establishment (United Kingdom, Home Office, 1990d: Appendix 6). However, as management information increased in quality and quantity, incisive eyes were focused on both the effectiveness and efficiency of what the service was achieving. All the evidence suggested that, despite the significant increase in expenditure and, in particular, the greatly reduced ratio of staff to prisoners, the delivery of measured services within prisons had either not improved or had deteriorated (Morgan, 1983; King and McDermott, 1989; McDermott and King, 1989). As a consequence, the previously unthinkable became thinkable: namely, that not just services within prison might be contracted out (that prospect had long been commended by advocates of 'normalization' – see King and Morgan, 1980: 121–33; Morgan and King, 1987), but the management of prisoners themselves might be undertaken by the private sector (United Kingdom, House of Commons, Home Affairs Committee, 1987b; United Kingdom, Home Office, 1988; Ryan and Ward, 1989)

Such an idea breaks a long and deeply entrenched tradition, still enshrined in the Prison Act [1952]. Since 1877, when they were brought under the control of the central government, prisons in England and Wales were the sole undivided financial and administrative responsibility of the Prison Department (subsequently called the Prison Service), a division within the Home Office. The Criminal Justice Act 1991 breached this monopoly. It provided for the development of a market in prison management and services. Although the financial terms of the first prisons to be contracted out to commercial management (the Wolds and Blakenhurst Prisons, run by Group 4 Security and United Kingdom Detention Services, respectively) have not been published, the tender documents setting out in some detail the regime to be provided have been made available (United Kingdom, Home Office, 1991b; United Kingdom, Home Office, 1992). The regime was planned to be far superior to any yet provided in a remand centre or local prison run by the Prison Service and, in spite of criticisms, has proved to be so (United Kingdom, HMCIP, 1993a). The comparison may not be fair, but it is nonetheless being made. The same issue is arising in relation to court escort services, the privatization of which is also provided for in the Criminal Justice Act [1991] (Section 80). Furthermore, the contracting out of services within state prisons – prison medical services, prisoners' food, prison education, and so on – is well advanced.

Contracting out all these services involves defining precisely what is required and what is to be provided for the purposes of preparing contracts. That process, as even commentators opposed in principle to privatization have conceded, may paradoxically lead standards to be defined and, thus, a level of accountability to be attained in both public and private prisons, far in advance of what has previously been achieved by the Prison Service (Ryan and Ward, 1989). Such gains, of course, have to be considered in light of other effects, such as a potential reduction in the legitimacy of the prison system as a whole (Sparks, 1994).

Prison Department Accountability to the Minister and to Parliament

The Prison Service operates within a wide-ranging legislative framework. The current statute, the Prison Act [1952], lays down the general duties of the prison authorities, provides for personnel, sets out the administration of prisons, allows for the confinement of prisoners, defines what a prison is, and empowers the minister to make rules for the management of prisons. The rules the minister makes are exercisable by statutory instrument and are therefore subject to annulment by resolution of Parliament. The current rules, which date from 1964 (SI no. 388, as amended), elaborate on issues covered by the Prison Act. In particular, they state the purposes of the system, describe some aspects of regimes (exercise, cells, privileges) and decision-making about prisoners (such as parole or early release), cover disciplinary procedures for staff and prisoners, and define the inspection duties of prison boards of visitors (see Loucks, 1993, for a detailed discussion of the rules).

The director general of the Prison Service is accountable to the minister (the home secretary) for the operation of his agency (the Prison Service became an agency outside the Home Office on 1 April 1993), and the minister is in turn accountable for prisons to Parliament. The service is required to produce an annual report for the minister, who in turn is required to lay it before Parliament (Prison Act [1952], Section 5). In fact, the act requires only a small proportion of the many facts and statistics that the service now incorporates in its annual report (the accommodation provided in each prison and the numbers of prisoners confined, prisoner employment and productivity, and punishments inflicted on prisoners for breaches of the disciplinary code). Current annual reports come in three parts, the first a prose account of policy and operations (United Kingdom, Home Office, 1990d), the second a statistical account of the prison population (United Kingdom, Home Office, 1990c), and the third a statistical account of offences committed against the prison disciplinary code and punishments inflicted (United Kingdom, Home Office, 1990e).

In comparison with the annual descriptive accounts produced by other jurisdictions (see van Zyl Smit and Dunkel, 1991, for a collection of accounts from twenty-four countries), the English annual reports are sophisticated and comprehensive. Nevertheless, they provide remarkably little information to enable the external observer to judge whether conditions in prisons have got worse or better. There are data on average hours per prisoner spent at work and on education or training, and the average number of prisoners sharing two or three to cells designed for one. However, there are few other data on the quality of regimes – for example, time out of cell, the frequency and duration of visiting arrangements, or the number of clothing exchanges that are achieved. Moreover, even when topics are covered, the data are frequently incomplete or superficial. The medical statistics, for example, contain no data on drug prescriptions, and the statistics on the prison disciplinary system lack data on pleas, requests for representation and how often it is granted, or the quantity as opposed to the type of penalty imposed (United Kingdom, Home Office, 1990e). Some of these deficiencies are made up in the form of written or oral answers given by the minister to ad hoc questions put down in Parliament and more and more material is becoming available from the Reports of the Prison Inspectorate (see below). Moreover, the Prison Service is embarking on the systematic collection of regime monitoring data (RMD), though these have yet to be used much in publications (see below), and the first act of the new agency has been to publish a *Business Plan* and a *Framework Document* including performance indicators (United Kingdom, Prison Service, 1993a, b).

Though the home secretary is constitutionally accountable for prisons to Parliament, he or she, like other ministers in charge of large and complex departments, is seldom expected to resign because of the mistakes or failings of subordinates. The minister is nevertheless still obliged to account to Parliament in an explanatory or amendatory sense (Turpin, 1989). In recent years such explanations or amendations have often been prompted as a result of the investigatory probings of Parliamentary committees, of which at least five have from time to time interested themselves in aspects of prisons policy. Examples of House of Commons reports include *The Reduction of Pressure on the Prison System* (Expenditure Committee, 1980); *Prison Education* (Education, Science, and Arts Committee, 1983); *Remands in Custody* (Home Affairs Committee, 1984); *Prison Medical Service* (Social Services Committee, 1986); and *The State and Use of Prisons* (Home Affairs Committee, 1987). These reports, and their accompanying volumes of evidence, often fill out and colour the generally bland sketches provided in the Prison Service annual reports.

The decision to make the Prison Service an agency outside Home Office restores the *status quo ante*. It also tackles an issue that in recent years has been controversial and is closely related to parliamentary accountability.

Prior to 1963, prisons were administered by what was in effect an agency, namely the Prison Commission. The case for integrating prisons administration within the Home Office was primarily on the grounds that this would better facilitate prisons planning within overall planning for criminal justice. There has always been controversy regarding the costs and benefits of this reorganization (May Report, 1979; Thomas, 1980), the detail of which does not concern us here. One cost of implementing it, however, has been the limitations upon the visible leadership that the director general has been able to provide to the Prison Service. This has not been a question merely of maintaining the corporate identity and morale of the service, important though that is. It appears also to have compromised the day-to-day public accountability of the service. During the siege lasting three and a half weeks at Strangeways Prison in April 1990, for example, information about what was happening was being given to the media by ministers, by Home Office press officers, and by officials of the prison officers' trade union both locally and nationally. The director general was silent and when eventually he gave a radio interview his account was halting and, as the subsequent investigation made clear, either seriously incomplete or inaccurate (Woolf Report, 1991: par. 3.223–4). This episode contrasts strikingly with the higher public profile that chief executives of prison services have in other jurisdictions (see, for example, Morgan, 1992b, on Sweden). Senior civil servants within the Prison Service have been discouraged by ministers, it appears, from adopting a high public profile.

Lord Justice Woolf's recommendation on this issue was that there should be a public 'compact' between the minister and the head of the Prison Service. The compact should be based on a published 'corporate plan ... which sets out clearly the tasks and objectives of the Service for the coming year ...' (Woolf Report, 1991: par. 12.47–8). The purpose of this device is to nail precisely what the Prison Service and the director general are accountable for. The 'contract' or 'compact' is to 'fix' the burden placed on the service. It is a perennial complaint of prison administrators that those who are responsible for running prisons are unable to control either the demands made on them or the resources with which they are able to meet those demands. At the same time, the sentencers who directly determine the size of the prison population have no responsibility for the consequences of their decisions. The reality, of course, is that politicians indirectly determine the size of the prison population. Thus, the burden that prison administrators have to bear is a political decision. Woolf's contract between the minister and the director general is designed to make that fact clear for all to see, and his recommendation has been implemented. What is not yet clear is whether agency status will more effectively insulate the service from day-to-day political interference and better stabilize the relationship between the demands placed on the service and resources provided to meet these demands. The early signs are not encouraging. The home secretary, Mr Michael Howard, announced during the summer of 1993 that prisons were to be made more 'austere.'

Her Majesty's Chief Inspector of Prisons

Until 1981 the prisons' inspectorate operated within the Prison Department. It was a tool of management and its reports were not published. However, in January 1981, in the interests of greater openness and public accountability (United Kingdom, House of Commons, Expenditure Committee, 1978; May Report, 1979), a new inspectorate was formed, independent of the Prison Department, albeit still within the Home Office. This arrangement was in some measure a reversion to the high-profile prisons' inspectorate of the nineteenth century, when the inspectors acted as agents of the central government enforcing compliance with prison legislation in the jails run by local authorities (for an account of the creation and early operation of the present inspectorate see Morgan, 1985).

Though the chief inspector of prisons is not fully independent – he is appointed by the minister responsible for prisons, his resources come from the same source and, hitherto, a high proportion of his staff have come on secondment from the Prison Service – successive chief inspectors have established a well-deserved reputation for conspicuous independence, forthrightly criticizing the conditions they have found and resolutely arguing for policies at variance with those being pursued by the service. Reports from the inspectorate are heavily drawn on in critical appraisals of the prison system produced by outsiders (see, for example, Stern, 1987; Casale and Plotnikoff, 1990; Council of Europe, 1991a: par. 203).

There have been three chief inspectors to date. The present incumbent is a judge with a flair for publicity, which he uses assiduously to make known the conclusions reached by his department and to promote the remedial policies he favours. His staff of approximately a dozen, plus a secretariat, includes specialist advisers (on such matters as provision of medical services, building, and farms and gardens). He is charged with reporting to the minister 'on the treatment of prisoners and conditions in prisons,' in accordance with Section 5A(3) of the Prison Act [1952], a duty elaborated in the inspectorate's 'charter' (United Kingdom, HMCIP, 1982: Appendix 1). The chief inspector has three main tasks: to conduct a regular inspection program, to undertake occasional 'thematic reviews' of aspects of policy, and to investigate major incidents.

The form and scale of the inspection program has evolved over the years. As the inspectorate's database has built up and its collective experience grown, the number of visits each year has increased. It now aims to visit every one of the approximately 130 institutions at least once every three years. In 1992/3, twenty-one full inspections (lasting four to five days each) and twenty short unannounced inspections (lasting two days each) were undertaken (United Kingdom, HMCIP, 1993c: Appendices 2 and 3). Short and long inspections result in reports, all of which are published, though generally some time after the inspections (currently about six months' later). When reports are published, the minister (the director general since agency status) issues a statement, sometimes indicating whether he agrees with the chief inspector's findings and accedes to the principal recommendations. He often does not accede, though he normally finds it necessary to say that he is addressing whatever problems the chief inspector has identified. When the chief inspector publishes a severely critical report (see United Kingdom, HMCIP, 1990a, b for particularly glaring examples) a good deal of media coverage is usually generated.

The idea of thematic reviews was recommended by the May committee (May Report, 1979: par. 5.62). This aspect of the inspectorate's work has been enormously important. The chief inspector has published reports on suicide in prisons (United Kingdom HMCIP, 1984a, 1990c), on the security classification of prisoners (United Kingdom, HMCIP, 1984b), on prisoners' complaints (United Kingdom, HMCIP, 1987b), on cell sanitation (United Kingdom, HMCIP, 1989) and on the quality of prisoner regimes (United Kingdom, HMCIP, 1993b). There is no doubt that continuous public pressure from the chief inspector has been highly influential in keeping some policy issues – notably the provision of cell sanitation and an end to 'slopping out' – in the forefront of the policy agenda. The chief inspector of prisons partnered Lord Justice Woolf for that part of his inquiry concerned with issues of background policy, and it is notable that on the day the inquiry report was published, the Home Secretary undertook to advance the date by which slopping out should end, from the recommended February 1996 (Woolf Report, 1991: par. 11.105; United Kingdom, HMCIP, 1989) to the end of 1994 (United Kingdom, HMCIP, 1991a: par. 6.7).

The third aspect of the inspectorate's work, the investigation of major incidents, suffers from considerable uncertainty about when it is appropriate for an incident to be investigated by the chief inspector and when it is right for the task to be undertaken from within the Prison Service. In the latter case, there is no publicly available account. The official province of the chief inspector is incidents 'which raise questions about the management of an establishment, or of the service as a whole' (United Kingdom, HMCIP, 1982: Appendix 1, par. 7), but it is difficult to see why, for example, he investigated widespread disturbances at several prisons in April and May of 1986 (United Kingdom, HMCIP, 1987a) but not the major disturbance at Risley Remand Centre in 1989 (United Kingdom, Home Office, 1990d).

Official Inquiries and Research Studies

From time to time events occur in prisons, as in other areas of public policy, of so serious a nature and with such profound implications for the direction of policy, that the government thinks it wise to appoint an independent inquiry. In England this may take the form of either a committee of inquiry or a judicial inquiry (a departmental inquiry headed by a judge, normally acting without judicial powers). In both cases, information is forced into the public domain. Official inquiries invariably shed light on some aspects of policy previously hidden, or they give a 'voice' (Hirschman, 1970) to actors previously not heard.

There have been three major independent inquiries in recent years: that headed by Sir John May into, *inter alia*, industrial disputes between the Prison Department and prison officers (May Report, 1979), that headed by Mr Peter Prior into the prison disciplinary system, following the overturning of much existing practice on judicial review (United Kingdom, Committee of Inquiry on the Prison Disciplinary System, henceforth the Prior Report, 1985), and the judicial inquiry undertaken by Lord Justice Woolf into the widespread disturbances at Strangeways Prison and elsewhere in April 1990 (Woolf Report, 1991).

Whenever an independent inquiry is appointed, the service and its policies are directly threatened. A major defence is erected in the form of an authoritative, well-documented, and voluminous written account of why existing policies, though not necessarily ideal, are nevertheless the best that could reasonably be pursued given existing circumstance and resources (for full discussion of the practical politics of the Woolf inquiry, see Morgan, 1991). This account is eventually published, and subsequently it provides an invaluable source of information for analysts (for example, United Kingdom, Home Office, 1979, 1984; United Kingdom, Prison Service, 1990). Thus, for example, the evidence to the May inquiry revealed that the department had in effect decided to abandon the provision of treatment and training facilities in local prisons (United Kingdom, Home Office, 1979: vol. 1).There was also a previously unpublished account of the condition of prisoner accommodation throughout the system, a vital source for anyone wishing to appraise the validity of the massive prison building program that took place during the 1980s. The evidence to the Prior committee included details on important aspects of adjudicatory decision-making not included in Prison Department annual reports (Prior Report, 1985: vol. 2) and the evidence to Woolf provides numerous references to data and internal Prison Service memoranda (for example, the circular instructions issued to prison governors informing them how some of their discretion is to be exercised) not normally available to persons outside the service.

Not all investigations or reviews of policy conducted within the service are kept hidden. For example, in 1984 a highly influential internal review on *Managing the Long-Term Prison System* (United Kingdom, Home Office, 1984) was published, which stimulated a series of studies, all of which have been published, on the operation of special units for difficult-to-manage long-term prisoners (United Kingdom, Home Office, 1987).

Small numbers of external researchers have been allowed lengthy access to prisons, resulting in in-depth studies on subjects such as the work of boards of visitors, the nominally independent 'watchdog' committees attached to each prison (Maguire and Vagg, 1984), race relations in prisons (Genders and Player, 1989), mentally disordered prisoners (Gunn, Maden, and Swinton, 1991), and the impact of legally qualified clerks upon prison adjudications (Jones and Morgan, 1990). Nevertheless, prisons remain a relatively difficult area for independent and critical researchers to work in. It is difficult to get access for research on topics that are not narrowly defined and which are not of immediate technical interest to prison administrators. There are a number of aspects of policy that would almost certainly be illuminated by critical independent evaluation – aspects of management, for example, including personnel policy and the deployment of uniformed staff (for a tantalizing overview see Woolf Report, 1991: Section 13), the use of 'control and restraint' techniques, the organization of prisoners' training and work, and resort to administrative segregation – about which current accounts are gravely deficient.

Prisoners' Rights: The Domestic and European Courts

A phrase often quoted in relation to prisoners' rights in the United Kingdom is Zellick's bald assertion (1978) that 'the law stops at the prison gates.' There was much truth in this at the time he was writing. A virtual 'hands off' policy had been adopted in judicial review, encapsulated in Lord Goddard's statement in *Arbon v Anderson* [1943] that 'it would be fatal to all discipline in prisons if governors and warders had to perform their duty always with the fear of an action before their eyes if they in any way deviated from the rules.' This view was confirmed thirty years later by Lord Denning in *Becker v Home Office* [1972] with the observation that 'if the courts were to entertain actions by disgruntled prisoners, the governor's life would be made intolerable.' It has long been established that even a clear breach of the Prison Rules gives no cause for action for breach of statutory duty, a ruling recently confirmed in *Hague v Deputy Governor of Parkhurst Prison* [1991].

The 1980s saw a considerable change in judicial responses to prisoners' actions. The landmark case of *R v Hull Prison Board of Visitors ex parte St Germain* [1979], in which it was found that the principles of natural justice had been breached in disciplinary hearings, heralded a series of successful challenges in both the domestic courts and the European Court of Human Rights to actions of the prison authorities (for reviews of these cases, see Richardson, 1985a, 1993; Owen and Livingstone, 1993). However, as Richardson, (1985a: 55) points out, these successes were limited principally to two specific areas, the prison disciplinary system and access to courts and lawyers. In the first of these, the British courts were able to draw on a body of decisions relating to procedures of tribunals in other fields (employment, tax, social services, and so on), while the second area was of direct interest to the legal profession. In other areas, such as prison conditions, the infliction of specific forms of treatment, transfer, release, and negligence by the authorities, the courts have continued to take a very cautious line in recognizing prisoners' rights, often allowing arguments of administrative necessity to outweigh the interests of individual prisoners.

Certainly the British courts have shown few signs of acceding to Richardson's argument (1985: 26) that, owing to the particular relationship of dependence between prisoners and the prison authorities that is created by the very fact of incarceration, prisoners should have special 'additional rights,' and the authorities special duties (for instance, adequately to house, feed, clothe, protect, or educate prisoners) recognized in law. Perhaps the clearest general statement by the courts on the subject of prisoners' rights is the widely quoted assertion by Lord Wilberforce in *Raymond v Honey* [1982] that a prisoner 'retains all civil rights which are not taken away expressly or by necessary implication.' But, of course, huge questions remain about the nature of citizens' rights in general in a country with no written constitution. And the phrase 'by necessary implication' is open to a broad range of interpretations.

In conclusion, despite the exceptions in the area of public law referred to above (particularly interventions in the disciplinary system), it is difficult to argue that the British courts have acted as an adequate protector of prisoners' rights. Richardson (1994) sums up the position succinctly, 'The ability of the private law to provide any real protection is greatly inhibited by the courts' attitude to the Prison Rules. There are no effective private law rights to sensible minimum standards ... With regard to inter-prisoner violence courts have been prepared to recognise special duties of protection on the part of the authorities, although they appear reluctant to find those duties breached. In the context of medical law, the fact of imprisonment has led the courts to accept a lower standard of care from the authorities' (ibid.: 90).

The situation in the European Court of Human Rights (ECHR) has been rather more encouraging from the prisoner's point of view. For example, the right to respect for correspondence, recognized in the key case of *Silver v UK* [1983], led to significant changes in the system of censorship, while recent cases concerning parole board decisions about prisoners serving discretionary (that is, non-murder) life sentences have led to the creation of a new independent and more open tribunal system for deciding such cases. Such concessions to European decisions have been made neither willingly nor swiftly, but in the end the government has had to bow to pressure. Moreover, the British courts have been gradually influenced by the positions adopted by the ECHR: subsequent decisions about prisoners' correspondence, for example, have certainly paid heed to the *Silver* [1983] decision. In sum, there is little doubt that the overall 'climate' has been affected by the existence of the ECHR and its interpretations of the written code of human rights to which Britain is a signatory.

Boards of Visitors and Prisoners' Complaints

Every prison in England and Wales is served by a board of visitors, a voluntary lay body appointed by the secretary of state, until recently with the triple role of satisfying itself as to the state of the prison, hearing prisoners' grievances (or 'applications'), and undertaking disciplinary hearings on the more serious charges. The last of these roles has now been removed from boards of visitors, following lengthy criticism both of boards' legal competence and of the incongruity of this punitive function with the other two 'watchdog' functions (Martin, 1975; MacKenna, 1983; Prior Report, 1985; Woolf Report, 1991; Morgan and Jones, 1991). Disciplinary hearings are now conducted solely by prison governors, though criminal offences committed in prison can be referred to the police with a view to prosecution in the courts.

Boards have few executive powers, but in theory they have the 'ear' of the home secretary and can make life uncomfortable for a prison governor who refuses to take note of their comments. However, their influence is principally at a local level, and while their comments quite frequently lead to minor improvements to regimes or to the solution of individual problems, they have a relatively weak collective voice (Maguire and Vagg, 1984; Maguire, 1985). Many of their criticisms refer to problems an individual governor is unable to solve (such as overcrowding, understaffing, the condition of buildings, or lack of recreational facilities) and which are more effectively targeted by the inspectorate. Moreover, their social composition – predominantly middle aged, white, and middle class – and their tendency to form close personal relationships with prison governors, tend to militate against their willingness to make sharp criticisms of local management (Thomas and Pooley, 1980; Maguire and Vagg, 1983, 1984). In the aftermath of riots or major incidents, this tendency has several times led to criticisms of boards for failure to act decisively or to protect prisoners from staff reprisals (for example, United Kingdom, Inquiry into the Cause and Circumstances, henceforth the Fowler Report, 1977; Thomas and Pooley, 1980; Martin, 1980; Woolf Report, 1991: par. 8.124–6). While attempts have been made over the past decade to sharpen the watchdog's teeth – such as by the formation of a more radical organization, the Association of Members of Boards of Visitors, by members concerned about the boards' ineffectiveness – their image among prisoners remains a poor one.

Arguably their most important function, at least until recently, has been the hearing of prisoners' complaints. While many institutions encourage prisoners to ventilate grievances first with members of staff, every prisoner has the right to approach the board directly. However, Maguire and Vagg (1984), who looked closely at the handling of complaints, found that many members did little more with complaints than record them in the 'applications book,' leaving staff to provide the response. More recently, it has become common practice for boards to send written replies, but again, investigations are carried out by staff and the board's role is primarily that of monitoring the system. And changes to internal systems of dealing with complaints are now marginalizing boards further in the process.

In 1990, following a thematic report by HM Chief Inspector of Prisons (1987b) and a report by a Home Office Working Group (1989), a new grievance system was introduced. This created an hierarchical method of dealing with complaints, whereby prisoners are expected to go first to a wing manager or duty governor with the option, if they are dissatisfied with the response, of appealing 'up the line' to governors and area managers. Stricter rules have been introduced on time limits for replies and the necessity for all replies to be in writing. While this has ironed out inefficiencies, it has put the emphasis firmly on internal methods of dealing with complaints. Recourse to a member of Parliament or the 'ombudsman' (Parliamentary Commissioner for Administration), as well as to judicial review, still exist as external alternatives, but these avenues are both time consuming and suitable only for certain kinds of complaint.

A more radical suggestion floated for many years has been the establishment of a specialist prisons ombudsman (Birkinshaw, 1985; United Kingdom, HMCIP, 1987b; United Kingdom, Home Office, 1989; Woolf Report, 1991). The government finally acceded to this recommendation and appointed the first incumbent in mid- 1994. The role envisaged goes well beyond that of a traditional ombudsman, whose remit is restricted to allegations of maladministration. The prison ombudsman will provide the apex of the system for dealing with all complaints, including those arising out of disciplinary hearings. The office is eventually to be placed on a statutory basis.

Prison Standards

One of the reasons why the courts have failed to recognize special rights in prisoners arising from the prison rules is that the rules are seldom specific (Zellick, 1981). For example, Rule 23 states that 'no room or cell shall be used as sleeping accommodation for a prisoner unless it has been certified,' but lays down no criteria for certification. Many rules also incorporate a wide discretion. For example, Rule 20 provides that 'an unconvicted prisoner may wear clothing of his own if and in so far as it is suitable, tidy and clean,' without defining what that means or placing any corollary obligation on the service to assist dependent unconvicted prisoners to keep their own clothes clean and tidy.

The consequence of this lack of specificity has been that, as the prison system has been subjected to population pressures ill matched by accommodation and other resources, there has been little to prevent the service from cramming a quart into a pint pot and depressing the quality of prisoners' lives accordingly. Some discretionary prison rules – for example, Rule 3(2) that 'unconvicted prisoners shall be kept out of contact with convicted prisoners as far as this can reasonably be done' – are honoured more in the breach, regularly, openly, and with impunity (Morgan and Barclay, 1989; Casale, 1994). It has been to put an effective check upon this back-sliding and to ensure the redirection of resources to those institutions and functions where they are most needed, that all the penal pressure groups and prison staff associations, as well as Parliamentary select committees, have advocated the adoption of specific minimum standards for prisons that can eventually be incorporated in a revised set of prison rules and made legally enforceable (Casale and Plotnikoff, 1989). Having first agreed to the suggestion that the Prison Service should prepare a draft code of standards (United Kingdom, Prison Service, 1990: par. 5.87), the government then recanted and argued vigorously against a code, on the grounds that 'it would be wholly unrealistic to expect any Government to endorse a legally enforceable code which it knew it could not comply with or which would require resources which it did not plan to provide' (ibid.: par. 5.91).

Lord Justice Woolf was not impressed by the service's arguments and recommended that a code be drafted, accompanied by a timetable for the achievement of particular standards. Moreover, when generally achieved, the code should become the 'subject of a Prison Rule and so enforceable by judicial review' (Woolf Report, 1991: par. 12). In response the government has undertaken to codify the various standards it claims already to have (United Kingdom, Home Office, 1991a: par. 6.14–15), but it is far from clear that what is proposed is that for which critics have long pressed or which Woolf recommended. For example, the government has not yet decided whether to have a single set of standards (ibid.: par. 6.20). Furthermore, it is not clear how whatever standards are adopted will relate to the undertaking 'to prepare a model regime for local prisons and remand centres' (ibid.: par. 7.17).

Nevertheless, there are signs of significant movement of policy on the 'standards' front. At the time of writing, a draft document setting out a 'Model Regime for Local Prisons and Remand Centres' was being circulated by the Prison Service. This lays down aspirational standards covering all aspects of prisoners' daily life (United Kingdom, Prison Service, 1991) and which, significantly, mirrors almost exactly the contractual obligations being met by Group 4 Security at the Wolds, the first privatized prison, which opened in April 1992 (United Kingdom, Home Office, 1991b). Moreover, a consultative document inviting views on a method to establish a general 'code of standards' has also been circulated (United Kingdom, Prison Service, 1992). Thus, though no timetable has been announced for the 'fundamental revision of the statutory framework for the Prison Service' that the government thinks 'desirable' (United Kingdom, Home Office, 1991a: par. 10.6), it appears that a policy momentum is developing for standards which it will be difficult to reverse (Casale, 1994).

Internal Accountability

Accountability *to* an external body depends not merely on a clear specification of what the Prison Service is to be accountable *for*, it also rests on an integrated chain of management accountability within the service (Day and Klein, 1987; Maguire, Vagg, and Morgan, 1985: Introduction). Two aspects of management accountability merit particular attention in this regard: contracts between governors and area managers, with the proposition that these might form the basis of a network of contracts extending down to individual prisoners, and regime monitoring. The two are closely related. Their effectiveness, too, rests ultimately on the adoption of a clear set of standards as discussed above.

THE DEVELOPMENT OF PRISONER AND STAFF 'CONTRACTS'

We have already made reference to Lord Justice Woolf's proposition, now implemented, that there be a 'compact' or 'contract' between the director general (in effect the Prison Service) and the minister. This is but one part of a network of contracts that Woolf proposed, building on those already agreed annually between prison governors and their area managers.

The purpose of governors' existing contracts is to 'set out clearly the functions of individual establishments, the level of service to be provided with respect to them, and how this is to be met within the resources available' (United Kingdom, Prison Service, 1990: par. 1.25). Contracts cover twenty-two specified functions, and some existing contracts are very precise, specifying what prisoners *will* get and, as Woolf argued, can *expect* to get (Woolf Report, 1991: par. 12.94–5). Woolf set great store by this arrangement, arguing that it should be developed as the vehicle for advancing the progress of 'accredited standards' (ibid.: par. 12.116) and providing the basis for a further set of contracts for prisoners and prison staff, mechanisms that 'would underline both the prisoner's and the establishment's responsibilities,' making 'clear what were his legitimate expectations ... in accord with the principles of justice' (ibid.: par. 12.129). The implication is that such 'legitimate expectations' might be the basis of judicial review.

The government has so far been reticent about this idea, though an experiment with prisoner 'compacts' (a legally less threatening term) is being conducted in 'selected establishments' (United Kingdom, Home Office, 1991a). The proposal has also been coolly received by external commentators. If the code of standards being formulated by the Prison Service is purely aspirational and if, as the minister has suggested, they are part of a program that may take twenty-five years to achieve, then an emphasis on individual prisoner compacts 'carries the danger of fragmenting prisoners' already fragile power as a group to complain or exert pressure to improve their conditions' (Casale, 1994).

REGIME MONITORING

For several years the Prison Service has been developing a regime monitoring database (RMD). This supports one of nine 'performance indicators' that the department currently employs (United Kingdom, Prison Service, 1990: par. 1.18), though none of the RMD have yet been reported in an annual report. Furthermore, the chief inspector of prisons does not yet regularly include RMD in the increasingly voluminous appendices that accompany his inspection reports. Indeed, there has been only one official published reference to RMD to date, namely the 'number of hours each week spent by prisoners in organized activities (work, education, chaplaincy, classes, PE, induction)' by 'type of establishment' for two successive years to 1991 (United Kingdom, Home Office, 1991a: Table 1).

This lack of use reflects the inadequacies of RMD as presently collected. They do not include certain activities (it is not possible, for example, to deduce how long prisoners spend out of their cells). They are subject to the familiar criticism of performance indicators, that only those routines easily quantified are included. And they are collected at an aggregate level (usually either whole prisons or living units within prisons), so that significant differences in regime which are often to be found between categories of prisoners are lost. There are also doubts about the accuracy of the data that every institution is now required to submit each week to the Prison Service headquarters. These deficiencies are to some extent evident from the passing references to RMD in the report of the Woolf inquiry (1991: see par. 4.25–6 and 7.22, for example).

That some RMD system is required is beyond question. It is a vital element in the accountability of the system. As critics have long since argued, the fact that neither the service nor the chief inspector of prisons systematically incorporate in their reports data on the quality of prisoners' daily routines means that those reports are of limited value: it is not possible to conclude whether conditions are improving or deteriorating and, therefore, whether value for money is being achieved (Morgan, 1985). However, it is not at all clear that the answer is to make the RMD system more complex than it already is. Were Lord Justice Woolf's recommendations regarding governors' contracts to be pursued, this should mean that a visible (for staff, prisoners, and outside commentators) statement of each prison's daily routine would be available and that each prisoner should know what he or she can legitimately expect in the way of time out of cell, choice of food, exchange of clothing, access to showers, workshop hours, and so on. Were this the case, the RMD could quite simply be inferred from the published contract, subject to a record kept of any *failure* to deliver the stated program.

The Council of Europe 'Torture' Committee

The European Committee for the Prevention of Torture and Inhuman or Degrading Treatment or Punishment (CPT) is the latest actor on the accountability stage for United Kingdom prisons. The committee was established in 1989 under a convention of the same name and was designed to assist the realization of the obligation, contained in Article 3 of the European Convention for the Protection of Fundamental Human Rights and Freedoms [1950] (ECHR), namely, that no one shall be subject to torture or inhuman or degrading treatment. The United

Kingdom has ratified the torture convention. This means that one of the members of the CPT is a British nominee and the United Kingdom is one of twenty-four Council of Europe states liable to be visited by the committee at short notice in order to inspect places of detention (for a full account of the constitution and procedures of the CPT see Evans and Morgan, 1992; for a broad assessment of its influence, see Morgan and Evans, 1994). The committee initially selected countries to be visited by lot and the United Kingdom was the third country to be visited, from 29 July to 10 August 1990.

The CPT has no formal powers other than rights of access to inspect custodial conditions or, in the event of a member state failing to cooperate or refusing to improve a situation in the light of the committee's recommendations, the adverse publicity that would result from a published statement. The purpose of the convention is to establish a positive dialogue with member states and encourage them to end unacceptable practices. In this spirit CPT reports are confidential to member states and, in normal circumstances, published only if the recipient government wishes it. However, most of the countries first visited have opted to publish, and that precedent may now prove difficult to resist.

The CPT report on the United Kingdom (Council of Europe, 1991a) has many complimentary things to say, not just about some of the institutions visited, but also some of the structural features of the prison system that have to do with accountability. For example, the system of prisoners complaints is said to be 'in principle very good,' and the disciplinary system is judged to be 'satisfactory.' Boards of visitors are described as a 'very important safeguard' and the reports of the chief inspector of prisons are said to be 'invariably of outstanding quality.' These are notable commendations. However, they have to be set alongside the most serious judgment yet to emerge in a published CPT report, namely that the cumulative consequence of the very bad conditions found for prisoners in three prisons – Brixton, Wandsworth, and Leeds – amounted to 'inhuman and degrading' treatment (ibid.: par. 57). The implication is that in the committee's view the combined conditions to which they draw attention – three prisoners crowded into cells designed for one, without integral sanitation (such that prisoners are forced to defecate and urinate in a pot without privacy), and scarcely any out-of-cell activities (confined to cells for up to twenty-three hours per day) – might constitute a breach of Article 3 of the ECHR.

The British government, though willing to acknowledge the undesirability of these conditions and though undertaking to do everything possible to eliminate them, does not accept the CPT judgment (Council of Europe, 1991b: par. 6). This is scarcely surprising. Were the British government to concede the appellation, it would almost certainly stimulate a flood of petitions under the ECHR machinery. Nevertheless, the CPT pronouncement will of itself almost certainly precipitate a trickle of such petitions. A further indication of the potency of the CPT as an accountability device can be found in the government's prompt announcement of plans to develop a 'Model Regime for Local Prisons and Remand Centres' (United Kingdom, Home Office, 1991a: par. 7.17). Significantly, the content of that 'model regime' is greatly superior to any regime currently delivered in the local prisons of which the CPT was so critical (United Kingdom, Prison Service, 1991).

Conclusion

Arguments about prison accountability in Britain typically conflate two issues that though separable in theory are less easy to distinguish in practice: first, the purposes of imprisonment, and, second, evaluation of the degree to which the purposes are being achieved. The Prison Service has for many years provided in its annual publications a full and clear account in relation to certain limited objectives. Data about escapes and absconds have provided an account in relation to security. Data on disciplinary offences and punishments have provided an account of order. Tables of statistics on reconvictions have provided a picture, albeit a dismal one, of the effectiveness of treatment and training. The paradigm shift that has taken place with regard to the philosophy of punishment, however, has meant that these limited accounts are no longer considered sufficient or even the most important. The just deserts approach to sentencing has meant that the quality of 'care' and 'justice' (particularly 'due process' in decision-making and grievance ventilation) have come to the fore, concepts that are multifaceted and inherently more difficult to measure. Added to this difficult enterprise has been the government's insistence that there be value for money in the provision of services.

The range and quality of the accounts provided by the Prison Service about the services it provides have markedly improved in recent years. These accounts have been supplemented by more incisive reports from inspectoral bodies. Furthermore, limited intervention by the domestic and European courts has bolstered the view that prisoners are entitled to certain provisions. However, a vigorous argument continues as to whether prisoners should have special rights and whether standards of care and justice in prisons should be more closely defined and, if breached, enforceable at law. The demand for yet more detailed accounts from the Prison Service is being made as part of an argument for an improved and justiciable standard of life for prisoners (Morgan, 1993).

Accountability and the National Parole Board

ALLAN MANSON

In 1976, while the Supreme Court of Canada was considering an appeal by a prisoner whose parole had been revoked without a hearing and without notice of the allegations against him, the chief justice was prompted to observe, 'The plain fact is that the Board claims a tyrannical authority that I believe is without precedent among administrative agencies empowered to deal with a person's liberty. It claims an unfettered power to deal with an inmate, almost as if he were a mere puppet on a string. What standards the statute indicates are, on the Board's contentions, for it to apply according to its appreciation and without accountability to the Courts' (*Mitchell v The Queen* [1976] at 577).[1] This statement was a scathing indictment of an agency operating within the context of a government that considered itself democratic and representative and a protector of individual liberties. Notwithstanding Chief Justice Laskin's graphic criticism of the National Parole Board's processes, the revocation was upheld by the majority of the court without examining the merits of the prisoner's claim.

Openness and accountability are common themes of discussions about officials and governmental agencies. Both concepts deal with the community's expectations of government and how the community scrutinizes government. The real content of openness and accountability in action usually undercuts their promise. Openness rarely means completely open. All governmental regimes recognize some degree of executive and national security privilege, and from that starting point, other manifestations of secrecy are often hidden within the layers of official bureaucracy. Accountability, however, seems ubiquitous. Assertions of so-called accountability cover the entire landscape of official activity. Occasionally, the rhetoric and reality of accountability intersect; sometimes by design, sometimes by coincidence, but often not at all. Accountability means different things to different people for different purposes.

Yet, the yardstick of accountability may be a useful way of examining and comparing governmental agencies. In this essay, I want to use the perspective of accountability to examine the operations of the National Parole Board ('the board'). The board is the Canadian agency responsible for making decisions about early release from imprisonment, including whether prisoners on conditional release should be returned to confinement. In most jurisdictions, vehicles for early release are established by statute. The mandate and structure of these agencies differ from jurisdiction to jurisdiction depending on the statutory authority that creates them and the array of functions allocated to the agency. There are significant similarities in the elements of decision-making[2] that make the Canadian experience a useful paradigm for considering how mechanisms of accountability may be developed in relation to parole.

Constructing a Functional Assessment of Accountability

Anyone can come forward to account and, therefore, may be viewed empirically as accountable. The question of accountability in relation to governmental activity is more complex. It raises questions of scrutiny and the ability to enforce conformity with stated objectives. The question of accountability usually arises in three ways. The first involves examining the source of accountability. If there is an obligation to account, is it a legal one that was created by statute or other legal authority and which can be enforced legally? Does it arise as a function of political necessity or moral imperative? These questions need to be asked but they do not advance the inquiry significantly.

The second common form of analysis of accountability is more informative because it measures accountability against three standards: (a) legal, (b) administrative, and (c) political. These are the various contexts within which someone may be called to account. While this way of mapping out the different techniques of accountability is useful for assessment or comparative purposes, it is only a descriptive structure, which categorizes, but adds nothing substantive to the consideration of accountability.

Another way of looking at accountability involves questioning the relationship between accountability and control. This inquiry assumes that an official or agency is accountable to those who can exercise control over it. The premise, although accurate, only addresses a part of what 'accountability' might mean. While control usually requires or includes accountability, the converse is not true. Short of control, there are a number of ways in which participation, influence, and scrutiny may be implemented, all of which may fit within an acceptable definition of 'accountability.' Moreover, some agencies, especially those with adjudicative mandates, require independence to properly pursue their statutory responsibilities. In these situations, control would be antithetical to the nature of the role and some other mechanism of accountability must necessarily be established.

The value in considering the relationship between control and accountability is that it directs our attention to the functional implications of accountability. If we start with the assumption that all techniques of accountability share one fundamental characteristic, the ability to call on an official or agency to disclose or explain, the relevant questions quickly rise to the surface:

1 Who can call on the agency to explain, and in what circumstances?
2 How complete an explanation can be compelled?
3 What remedies are available if the explanation is found to be deficient?

A functional assessment of accountability can be translated into other questions: accountable to whom? accountable to what extent? and with what possible results?

For the National Parole Board, the first step in a functional assessment will be delineating the set of people or institutions to whom the board may be accountable. For the purposes of this essay, we can determine them to be (a) the solicitor general and the Cabinet, (b) other governmental officials, (c) prisoners and parolees, (d) the public, and (e) victims of crimes. The extent of accountability must be assessed both in terms of the kinds of responses that the board can be compelled to make and the kinds of remedies that may be available. These questions are influenced, if not determined, by the context in which accountability is sought and the kind of mechanism of accountability employed. Yet, different people may resort to the same mechanism in an effort to demand accountability. For example, a member of the public, a victim of crime, or a government official may call for some form of public inquiry in response to a particular event. Ultimately, whether the responsible minister or other element of government responds, and how a response is crafted, will be a matter of political choice. Each participant may pull the same kind of lever, but some levers are 'more equal' than others. Another example is the role of the courts. The courts may be available to a number of protagonists representing diverse interests. But issues of standing, jurisdiction, justiciability, and remedial scope may determine the result for a particular litigant. Because a number of different people may call on the board to account, this discussion of accountability will be organized by mechanism and context.

The Constitutional Situation of the Board

In Canada the Constitution Act [1867] divides legislative and governmental powers between the federal and provincial authorities. With respect to corrections generally and parole in particular, specific responsibilities depend on the kind of institution in which a prisoner is confined. The Constitution Act [1867], Sections 91(27) and (28), empowers the federal Parliament to legislate in respect of the criminal law and gives it responsibility for the 'establishment, maintenance and management of penitentiaries'. The criminal law power has been interpreted broadly to include issues of release and remission. Provinces, however, in accordance with the Constitution Act [1867], Section 92(6) have authority over prisons, reformatories, and local jails. The Criminal Code determines the distinction between persons confined within the federal regime and those who remain within their respective provincial or territorial system. The division is based on length of sentence and, generally, persons sentenced to two years or more serve their sentences in federal penitentiaries.[3] An enabling provision in the federal statute permits provinces to establish provincial boards of parole to deal with the release of prisoners from provincial institutions but, to date, only British Columbia, Ontario, and Quebec have done so.[4] In any event, it is the federal structure that determines the essential elements of the release process for both federal and provincial prisoners.[5]

A Brief History of the National Parole Board[6]

Before 1899 a prisoner in Canada could achieve early release from imprisonment only as a result of accumulated remission or through the exercise of the royal prerogative of mercy in the form of an absolute or conditional pardon. Remission, credited by penitentiary administrators on the basis of 'good behaviour, diligence and industry,' was introduced in the Penitentiary Act [1868]. A prisoner could earn up to five days per month. Later, this was reduced to three days (Penitentiary Act [1883]. The royal prerogative, however, was a form of clemency with roots going back to the early Anglo-Saxon period.[7]

In 1899 the process of release was extended by the passage of the Ticket of Leave Act [1899], which empowered the governor general, on the advice of the minister of justice, to issue convicted persons licenses to be at liberty. The minister of justice was favoured over the originally proposed source of advice, the Cabinet, because it was felt that the 'high tradition' of the post would serve to insulate recommendations from political influence. In 1913 a separate Remission Service was established within the Ministry of Justice to deal with the granting and revoking of licences, the two major elements of the new process. Licences were subject to conditions. Breaches, or anticipated breaches, of the conditions resulted in recommitment. The original act, however, contained no criteria for decision-making concerning release. Ultimately, the perception of rising crime rates after the First World War produced formal, restrictive criteria of eligibility. By 1938 the Remission Service was the subject of severe criticism by the Archambault commission for the quality of its decisions concerning release, especially the information relied on and the apparent rejection of rehabilitation as an objective of release (Canada, Royal Commission to Investigate the Penal System of Canada, 1938: 236–41). The major factors that led to release were more-akin to clemency than release as a step towards re-integration: for example, health, mental and cognitive problems, questions about guilt and extraordinary provocation. Again, in 1956 another federally appointed inquiry commented on the inappropriate criteria employed by the Remission Service (Canada, Committee Appointed to Inquire into the Principles and Procedures Followed in the Remission Service of the Department of Justice, 1956: 35–6). As well as recommending a new system of granting remission to prisoners, the Fauteux committee recommended the establishment of a permanent parole board.

In 1959, following many of the Fauteux recommendations, an autonomous agency, the National Parole Board, was established with the responsibility for the discretionary early release of prisoners from confinement (Parole Act [1958]. The board consisted of five full-time members empowered in its 'absolute discretion' to grant parole if it considered that the prisoner had 'derived the maximum benefit from imprisonment and that the reform and rehabilitation of the inmate [would] be aided' (Parole Act [1958]: Section 5). The board was required at specified intervals to review the cases of all prisoners serving sentences of two or more years. Eligibility for parole was determined by stipulated periods with the general rule being one-third of sentence or four years, whichever was shorter. If parole was granted, the prisoner was permitted to be at large, subject to whatever conditions the board considered 'desirable,' until the sentence expired. While on parole, a breach of condition or new criminal conviction could result in suspension, revocation, or forfeiture, which would lead to recommitment to custody. The mechanisms of suspension and revocation were part of a discretionary process whereby a parolee could be apprehended as a result of a breach or apprehended breach of conditions and a decision made about whether the parole should be continued or revoked. With some modifications, these mechanisms have continued as part of the parole process until today.[8]

Between 1959 and 1970 the board was active. It granted 37,710 paroles and returned approximately 5,000 parolees to custody either as a result of revocation or forfeiture. During the period 1963 to 1970 the board claimed to have increased the rate of paroles from 29 per cent to 67 per cent of applications while experiencing a rise in the failure rate from 10 per cent to only 25 per cent (Street, 1971).

Since 1970 packages of amendments have expanded and changed the functions of the National Parole Board. The remission scheme, established at about the same time as the board came into existence, has been gradually turned inside out.[9] Until 1970 the prisoner was released free and clear of conditions when the accumulated remission credits plus the days served in custody equalled the total sentence. However, the Canadian Committee on Corrections in its 1969 report was impressed with the value of parole supervision. It recommended that the group of prisoners who did not receive early conditional release but were released by reason of remission should also be subject to conditions, supervision, and the potential sanction of recommitment (Canada, Canadian Committee on Corrections, 1969). On 1 August 1970, the regime of mandatory supervision was established. It required that all prisoners, except those serving life sentences, served their remission on the street subject to conditions.[10] The sanctions that applied to parole were made equally applicable to mandatory supervision.[11]

Amendments in 1977 effected a number of changes. Structurally, they altered the relationship of the National Parole Board to the National

Parole Service. Since 1959 officers of the service had been responsible for preparing cases that went to the board and for the subsequent supervision of parolees unless supervision was contracted to an outside agency. Within the parole process, it was the chairman of the National Parole Board who had supervisory control over the service. This relationship troubled the Senate committee (the Goldenberg committee) delegated in 1971 to examine parole (Canada, Senate, Standing Committee on Legal and Constitutional Affairs, henceforth Goldenberg Report, 1974: 70–1). The committee advocated a parole tribunal that would operate as an independent, autonomous agency. As part of this shift to independence, the committee recommended that the National Parole Service be removed from the direction of the board. This would, it was assumed, distance board decision-making from the preparation of cases. The 1977 amendments to the Parole Act and the Penitentiary Act placed the parole service within the administrative responsibility of the Corrections Service of Canada and answerable to the commissioner of corrections.

The most significant change to the board's function was the entrenchment in 1986 of the power to deny release on mandatory supervision, known colloquially as 'gating.' Originally, release on mandatory supervision was a matter of entitlement that related only to the amount of accumulated remission. The board could place conditions on the prisoner and could exercise the sanctions of suspension and revocation in response to breaches of those conditions, but it had no discretion in respect of the initial release. In the early 1980s the board was publicly criticized as a result of offences committed by a few prisoners on mandatory supervision. Perhaps in response to this improper attribution of fault, the board re-interpreted its powers of suspension and decided that it was empowered to suspend and revoke mandatory supervision 'to protect society' if the prisoner could be characterized as a threat to re-offend in a violent way. Because prisoners were entitled to be released, the board reasoned that it could not stop release but could execute suspension warrants immediately to return the prisoner to confinement pending a revocation decision. In late 1982 nine prisoners across Canada were selected and, upon their release, were suspended at the penitentiary gates. A number of these prisoners challenged their re-confinement.[12] Eventually, the Supreme Court of Canada ruled that the Parole Act [1958] did not include the power to suspend a prisoner released on mandatory supervision in the absence of some post-release conduct that justified it (*R. v Moore* [1983]). Even the phrase 'to protect the public' was not broad enough to encompass a denial of liberty simply on the basis of a prediction of future violence.

This was not the end of the 'gating' story. While the courts were still dealing with the issue, the government introduced a bill in the Senate, Bill S-32, which legislated the power in clear terms reminiscent of those applicable to the dangerous offender provisions in the Criminal Code [RSC 1985]. The bill passed the Senate but died on the order paper when Parliament prorogued in 1984 prior to a federal election. The legislation was re-introduced in 1985 and passed the House of Commons but was rejected by the Senate. In an extraordinary move, usually reserved for proclamations of war or the cessation of a public sector strike, the new government recalled Parliament in the summer of 1986 and passed the amendment to the Parole Act [1986] now known as the detention provisions. The board was empowered to deny release on mandatory supervision if it determined that it was likely that the prisoner would, according to Section 21.4(4) of the Parole Act, commit 'an offence causing the death of or serious harm to another person' before the expiration of the sentence. Experience with detention hearings has shown a large number of referrals and a high rate of detention. In 1990, 239 cases were referred to the board pursuant to these provisions, and 76.2 per cent of the prisoners were detained (Canada, Correctional Services Canada, 1991: 39).

The proclamation in force on 1 November 1992 of the new Corrections and Conditional Release Act [1992] provided a single statute governing both the penitentiary and parole regimes. As well as enacting a number of procedural changes, the new act also includes significant substantive changes. The federal system no longer permits prisoners to earn remission. The scheme of mandatory supervision is now called statutory release and, subject to detention, occurs after a prisoner has served two-thirds of his or her sentence (ibid.: section 127). Necessarily, revocation of parole or mandatory supervision (statutory release) no longer involves a loss of remission. Instead, the prisoner is recommitted to serve the balance of the sentence subject to another release on parole or statutory release after serving two-thirds of the portion remaining after revocation.[13]

The new act has also expanded considerably the detention net. The list of offences that may trigger the detention process is already extensive even to including the most basic form of assault so long as it was prosecuted by indictment. The new act adds 'serious drug offences' to the list. Detention may result if the prisoner is serving a sentence for a qualifying offence and there are 'reasonable grounds' to believe that 'the offender is likely to commit a serious drug offence before the expiration of the offender's sentence' (SC 1992, c. 20: Sections 129–32, and Schedule II). Certainly, it is questionable whether all drug offences can easily be grouped for sentencing purposes along with offences causing death or serious harm to another person. The specific offences listed within the category of 'serious drug offences' include all forms of trafficking, whether the substance is a narcotic or a controlled or restricted drug under the Food and Drugs Act (RSC 1985].[14] Both the offences included within the definition of 'serious drug' offender and the factors which the board must consider, in accordance with Section 132(2) (a), suggest that petty offenders, especially addicts, may fall easily within the grasp of the expanded provision, notwithstanding governmental rhetoric to the contrary.

Scrutiny through Inquiry

As with most agencies of government, some degree of scrutiny can be exercised by other organs of government. Often, this is effected by way of formal inquiry. Formal inquiries and internal reviews into early release have been conducted at the behest of ministers, parliamentarians, and the Senate. Curiously, the issues and mechanisms of early release must be one of the most examined areas of Canadian criminal justice. While the mechanism of the formal inquiry may be viewed as part of the board's accountability to its political masters, it also represents an attempt to respond to the need for public accountability.

Beginning with the Fauteux Report in 1956, there have been three inquiries devoted entirely to early release, appointed by the minister of justice (Fauteux Report, 1956), the solicitor general (Canada, Task Force on the Release of Inmates, henceforth Hugessen Report, 1972), and the Senate (Goldenberg Report, 1974). The general issues of sentencing and corrections have been addressed by the Ouimet committee (Canada, Canadian Committee on Corrections, henceforth Ouimet Report, 1969) and the Canadian Sentencing Commission (1987) both appointed by the government of the day. The Law Reform Commission of Canada has published working papers (Canada, LRC, 1974, 1975) and reports (Canada, LRC, 1976a, b, c) on sentencing and release. In recent years a number of internally based reviews have generated inquiries and reports which, to various degrees, examine aspects of parole. In this category, the principal effort has been the Corrections Law Review project of the solicitor general's office (see also D'Ombrain, 1985; and Canada, Task Force on Program Review, 1986). A significant portion of the 1988 Parliamentary committee report, commonly known as the Daubney report, was devoted to parole, mandatory supervision, and detention (Canada, House of Commons, Standing Committee on Justice and the Solicitor General, 1988).

Shelves can be filled with the materials these groups have produced. Some have clearly been the impetus of statutory change as the historical account above indicates with respect to the Fauteux and Ouimet committees. Other reports have been rejected. The decision to adopt or reject may, too often, be susceptible to political whim or misperception.

A formal inquiry is usually initiated as a result of a political perception that the public is concerned about its protection. Unfortunately, research has indicated that the Canadian public has an exaggerated picture of the amount of violent crime and the lenient manner in which the justice system responds to offenders (Canada, Canadian Sentencing Commission, 1987: 87–101). Particularly with respect to early release, public misperceptions can play a significant role. The newspaper headline announcing a killing committed by a person on parole naturally evokes concern about the parole system. However, the data suggest that the incidence of homicide by persons on parole is extremely rare. The follow-up study of 52,484 prisoners released on either full parole or mandatory supervision between 1975 and 1986 revealed that only 90 people, or 0.17 per cent, were recommitted for murder and 40 people, or 0.08 per cent, were recommitted for manslaughter (Canada, National Parole Board, 1987: vol. 2, Appendix E). Furthermore, of those recommitted as a result of homicide, only 15 per cent had originally been sent to penitentiary for a crime of violence against the person.[15] Once the distinction is made between those released through board discretion and those released by operation of law, the number of homicides over the eleven-year period drops to 42. It is true that if certain people had not been released, tragic results would not have ensued. However, on the data, it is a facile and unsupported conclusion to argue that tighter release procedures would have prevented any given homicide.

The inquiry may reveal important information and data that may encourage an informed debate. However, ultimate responses are still left in the hands of politicians who respond to public opinion. This may result in a distortion of the original study especially when data are open to different interpretations. A good example arises from the report of the Canadian Sentencing Commission (1987). The Sentencing Commission advocated the abolition of parole in favour of a system of presumptive sentencing guidelines accompanied by a form of remission-based release. This proposal was the subject of considerable debate and criticism (Cole and Manson, 1990: 442–51). The Sentencing Commission used statistics that showed a relatively equal success rate between prisoners released on parole and those released on mandatory supervision by reason of accumulated remission, to support the recommendation for the abolition of parole. A special committee of the Canadian Bar Association used the same data to argue that the board had been too reluctant in carrying out its release mandate and that success on mandatory supervision showed that many of those denied parole should have received it (Canadian Bar Association, 1988b). Thus, the same statistics were used to support the converse result, the retention of parole, including presumptive release of a segment of the penitentiary population after serving one-third of the sentence.

The Daubney report concluded that parole should be retained although the system was not 'functioning as well as it should' (1988: 187). The Corrections and Conditional Release Act [1992] appears to have ended the move towards abolition. At the same time, the act has rejected presumptive early release, although it provides for statutory release after two-thirds of the sentence. Both the Sentencing Commission report and the debate that it generated have fallen prey to a political judgment based on a perception of the public mood. The new legislation expands the detention function and provides mechanisms for increasing ineligibility periods.[16] Its provisions are intended to justify the press coverage that the government is 'getting tougher on parole.'[17] The act represents another example of incremental tightening that is consistent with the reactive history of parole evolution since 1959 but not justified by the evidence.[18]

Other forms of inquiry exist which, from time to time, provide windows into the operation of the parole system. At the internal level, investigations into specific incidents provide some degree of accountability to the relevant officials and the solicitor general, but these inquiries are usually not made public. For example, after a prisoner on an unescorted temporary absence pass killed a young woman, a board of investigation was appointed by the commissioner of corrections, 'in consultation with the Chairman of the National Parole Board' pursuant to Section 14 (formerly Section 12) of the Penitentiary Act [RSC 1985] (Canada, Board of Investigation, henceforth Pepino Report, 1988). The mandate of the investigation was to 'inquire into the complete circumstances surrounding the events preceding, during and following the declaration that an inmate on an unescorted temporary absence pass was unlawfully at large from Montgomery Centre.' Part of the inquiry examined the process by which the prisoner had been granted the pass, including the review conducted by the National Parole Board.

Inquests also provide an opportunity for a public forum of inquiry. Coroners or medical examiners have, in most provinces and territories, the discretion to call and conduct an inquiry into a death when it appears in the public interest to do so. Recommendations emanating from the inquest process are not enforceable, but they can add weight to arguments for change. The inquest itself can provide a useful vehicle for public scrutiny, except that there is no guarantee that all sides of an issue will be represented. Standing may be restricted to persons with a 'direct and substantial' interest in the inquest (Manson, 1988). This criterion will always be interpreted to include the board and the Correctional Service, but that does not ensure a full airing of all dimensions of the release issues.

With respect to deaths in which a person on conditional release was involved, a number of inquests have been conducted that directed attention to various aspects of the release process. In Ontario the inquests into the deaths of Tema Conter and Celia Ruygrok have produced recommendations about how information should be used and communicated within the release process (Daubney Report, 1988: 171, 199–200). The caseload of parole officers was the subject of comment at the inquest in Burnaby, British Columbia, into the deaths caused by the prisoner Foster (ibid., 1988: 197). The inquest, which lasted four and a half months, into the death of Christopher Stephenson, a young boy molested and killed by a man on mandatory supervision with a long record of violent pedophilic acts, produced numerous recommendations dealing with how the justice system responds to sex offenders. After evidence disclosed a number of administrative errors and failures to pass on relevant information, many of the recommendations were directed to the processes of release and detention.[19]

Scrutiny by the Courts

JUDICIAL REVIEW

The function of judicial review is, for the most part, limited to supervisory control that is distinct from appellate review. Historically, the extent to which a governmental body is amenable to judicial review has depended on the nature of the particular body. In the early years of the Board's existence it continued to be characterized in terms more appropriate to an executive or ministerial agency and, hence, external scrutiny of the board's conduct was conspicuously limited. The Fauteux committee recommended that the board be regarded as a 'quasi-judicial body' as compared with a 'Minister of the Crown acting in an exclusively administrative capacity.' The Parole Act [RSC, 1985], however, contained no provisions for hearings and expressly stated that the board was not required to hear personally from either the prisoner or someone speaking on his or her behalf before deciding to grant or revoke parole. The Supreme Court of Canada was content to describe a parole decision as 'altogether ... within the discretion of the Parole Board as an administrative matter' (*Ex Parte McCaud* [1965]).

By the mid-1970s questions began to arise about the fairness of a parole process that permitted issues of liberty to be determined in private and without any obligation to explain (*Howarth v National Parole Board* [1975]; *Mitchell v The Queen* [1976]). Mandatory statutory requirements could be enforced by way of habeas corpus if the error went to the legality of revocation (Cromwell, 1977), but otherwise prisoners could not claim resort to the common law protections of natural justice or the Canadian Bill of Rights [RSC 1985]. The new Federal Court Act [RSC 1985], intended to establish a modern era of administrative law review in the federal sphere, appeared to offer nothing to prisoners. While courts accepted that parole decisions had to be made fairly, this was no more than the rhetoric of legality, since no remedy was recognized that would enable a prisoner to enforce the obligation (*Ex Parte Beauchamp* [1971]).

It was not until 1979 and the acceptance by the Supreme Court of Canada of the duty of fairness that an opportunity for judicial scrutiny arose (*Nicholson v Haldimand–Norfolk Regional Board of Police Commissioners* [1979]; *Martineau v Matsqui Institution Disciplinary Board* [1980]. Dickson, J articulated what has become known as the 'spectrum analysis,' which places decision-making processes along a curve from the executive to the judicial depending on the statutory structure of the decision-maker, the function being exercised, and the interests at stake. As one moves closer to the judicial end of the spectrum, persons affected by decisions are increasingly entitled to procedural protections. As a result, there can no longer be any doubt that all prisoners are entitled to fairness in their treatment by the board, which includes, at a minimum, notice of adverse allegations and an opportunity to respond. By 1980 it was clear that alleged breaches of the duty to act fairly could be enforced by *certiorari* in the Federal Court of Canada.

The constitutional entrenchment of the Canadian Charter of Rights and Freedoms [1982] also provided a vehicle for scrutiny that has, to some extent, influenced the operation of the board. Certainly, the dominant feature of the post-Charter era is the prescription that governmental action must measure up to constitutional standards. Decisions revoking parole or mandatory supervision have been recognized in terms of the liberty interest they affect. They must conform with the principles of fundamental justice entrenched by Section 7 of the Charter [1982]. While there may be some question as to whether granting parole implicates the prisoner's liberty interest (Cole and Manson, 1990: 116–125), expanded conceptions of liberty and 'security of the person' (*R v Morgentaler* [1988] ch. 465) suggest that these decisions must be subject to the constraints of the 'principles of fundamental justice.'

The guarantee in Section 7 has been applied, in the context of parole, with respect to the procedural attributes of the process. The Federal Court of Appeal has suggested that, compared with the duty of fairness, fundamental justice provides 'enhanced' procedural protections (*Howard v Presiding Officer of Inmate Disciplinary Court of Stony Mountain Institution* [1985]). The meaning of an 'enhanced' protection is the subject of debate (Cole and Manson, 1990: 128–31). Although the Supreme Court of Canada has recognized that Section 7 of the Charter includes a substantive yardstick for review (*Reference Re: Section 94(2) of the Motor Vehicle Act* [1985]), that proposition was offered with respect to the constitutionality of legislation, and there has been no indication that decisions by tribunals will, or should, be subjected to substantive review.

In terms of assessing accountability, a number of good tests can be found examining how the courts have responded to provisions of the statutory framework and the way the board interprets them. The degree of deference shown to either the decision maker or the legislation can be considered as a diminution of the accountability function played by the courts. The current examples tend to cut in both directions. While mandatory time requirements used to be interpreted restrictively (*Ex Parte Collins* [1976]; *Re Grabina and the Queen* [1977]), the more recent approach is one of generosity towards the board. The detention provisions contain strict time frames within which referrals for the purpose of possible detention beyond the presumptive release date must be made. Throughout Sections 129 and 130 of the Corrections and Conditional Release Act [1992], all time requirements, whether they relate to the commissioner of corrections or the board, are cast in the apparently mandatory language of 'shall.' Curiously, the courts did not require strict conformity with the predecessors of these time requirements, but interpreted them indulgently unless the prisoner could show prejudice (*Cleary v Correctional Service of Canada* [1990]).

An example that shows a significant degree of accountability to the courts involved the issue of confidential information. A prisoner on parole from a life sentence was suspended on the basis of allegations that he had committed two sexual assaults (*Gough v National Parole Board* [1990]). At his post-suspension hearing, the board indicated that confidential information in its possession supported the allegations, but that in order to protect the informants the information could not be disclosed. As a result the prisoner was not told the names of the alleged victims or even the dates or places of the alleged assaults. Relying on a regulation that purported to authorize non-disclosure, the board revoked the prisoner's parole notwithstanding his denial of any wrongdoing.

After protracted litigation, Reed, J of the federal Court held that a revocation without providing greater details denied the prisoner his liberty without conformity to the principles of fundamental justice as guaranteed by Section 7 of the Charter [1982]. She concluded that the prisoner was 'entitled to sufficient detail respecting the allegations being made against him to enable him to respond intelligently thereto unless the respondent could demonstrate otherwise' (ibid.: 335). Moreover, the non-disclosure was not justified under Section 1 of the Charter [1982]. Reed, J concluded that the regulation which purportedly authorized the non-disclosure was over-broad and that no effort was made to satisfy the court that the assertions about the need for non-disclosure were true. As well, she questioned whether the board's dual role of decision-maker on the merits and arbiter of how much information should be disclosed could ever satisfy the requirements of Section 1 of the Charter [1982]. The revocation was quashed and the decision was upheld by the Federal Court of Appeal (*National Parole Board v Gough* [1991]).

An analysis of judicial review reveals another mechanism of accountability that has potential influence on two avenues of scrutiny. Section 22(1) of the former Parole Regulations permitted prisoners who have received certain negative decisions to seek a re-examination of that decision by other members of the board. The board attempted to argue that a court could not entertain judicial review of a decision until the prisoner had exhausted internal remedies by seeking a re-examination. The existence of an alternative remedy may be a factor that a court should consider in determining whether to intervene by way of judicial review. However, authority suggests that the alternative must be a parallel one, in the sense that it should provide the same scope for review and a similar remedial power (Evans, 1980: 426; see also Lewis, 1992: 147–9). Furthermore, there must be an entitlement to the alternative review. The Federal Court of Appeal, in *Pulice v National Parole Board* [1990], rejected the obstacle of the re-examination process in the case of a prisoner seeking judicial review of a denial of day parole. Since section 22(1) of the regulations did not specifically include this category of decision, the court reasoned that any prospect of internal review could not be characterized as an adequate alternative remedy.

The opportunity for internal review has given rise to a new division of the board that is formally constituted by section 147 of the new act. This division is empowered to review any decision of the board on procedural, jurisdictional, or legal grounds, and challenges can be based on the claim that a decision was the result of 'erroneous or incomplete' information. The board may argue that this appeal scheme is an alternative remedy that must be pursued before a prisoner can resort to judicial review, but the courts ought not to be too quick to accept this position. First, the board must demonstrate that there is a sufficient degree of independence in the appeal division to characterize its function as comparable to the external nature of judicial review. Second, the new scheme contains limits on the remedial powers of the appeal division that deny the prisoner the fuller scope of remedy available in the Trial Division of the Federal Court. In particular, Section 148(5) makes a decision of immediate release subject to the 'applicable policies of the board.' In other words, deference to policy is paramount to rectifying decision-making errors including errors of law, breach of statutory obligation, or even a failure to observe the principles of fundamental justice. For this reason alone, resort to the appeal division cannot be considered an alternative remedy. As well, the delay involved in pursuing an internal review will negate the efficacy of any subsequent judicial review.

SUING THE BOARD

There are no reported Canadian cases in which a member of the public has obtained a judgment for damages against the board in compensa-

tion for injury or loss suffered as a consequence of the parole process.[20]
This is not to say, however, that such an action could never be maintained. The issue of liability of a parole agency and the consequential
questions that arise from attempts to create immunity have become
topics of interest in American legal literature (Lowder, 1987/88; Aglon,
1990; Thompson, 1988/89). Canadian courts have been moving away
from traditional approaches that tended to insulate many elements of
the administration of justice from liability. Crown attorneys no longer
enjoy absolute immunity from claims of malicious prosecution (*Nelles
v Ontario* [1989]), and a police force is currently facing a claim based on
breach of a duty to warn potential victims of a serial rapist (*Jane Doe v
Metropolitan Toronto Board of Police Commissioners* [1990]). Conceivably,
the board could issue a decision so badly and defectively formulated
that it satisfied the criteria of a negligent breach of a statutory duty.

With respect to public agencies, like the board, Canadian law has
evolved from the position adopted by the House of Lords (*Home Office
v Dorset Yacht Co. Ltd.* [1970]). That court distinguished between policy
decisions, which would be immune from liability, and operational
functions, which, if negligently performed, could give rise to liability.
A plaintiff was required to show that it was reasonably foreseeable that
he or she would suffer injury as a result of the defendant's default. This
test suggested the need for some special or identifiable relationship
between the governmental defendant and the injured party. With respect to prisoners, Canadian courts have applied this approach. When
a prisoner released on a temporary absence pass caused injury to a
passenger in a motor vehicle accident, the action against the warden
who authorized the pass was dismissed on the ground that its issuance
was a matter of policy and that the warden could not have reasonably
foreseen the injuries that ensued (*Toews v MacKenzie* [1980).

In cases not involving prisoners, the inherent difficulty involved in
marking out the policy/operations boundary has produced a judicial
attitude more inclined to entertain claims against public authorities and
agencies. With respect to municipalities, one can observe a trend over
the past ten years that has expanded the potential scope of liability even
though the claim arises from a discretionary decision (*Barratt v District
of North Vancouver* [1980]; *City of Kamloops v Nielsen* [1984]). More recently, the Supreme Court of Canada in *Just v British Columbia* [1989], approved a two-step approach to claims of governmental negligence[21] that
requires, first, the identification of a relationship of proximity between
the defendant and the injured party such that 'in the contemplation of
the former, carelessness on his part may be likely to cause damage to

the latter' (at 1235). Second, the court must consider whether there are any factors that would negate or reduce the 'scope of the duty.' It is within the second consideration that the distinction between policy and operations would arise. In *Just* [1989], the court did not accept that a decision about road maintenance fit within the policy category even though it included budgetary considerations.

By finding the province liable in *Just* [1989], the court has severely restricted the exculpatory ambit of the policy/operations distinction. This move flows from a new attitude towards government and the many roles it plays in modern society. According to Cory, J, 'The need for distinguishing between a governmental policy decision and its operational implementation is thus clear. True policy decisions should be exempt from tortious claims so that governments are not restricted in making decisions based upon social, political or economic factors. However, the implementation of those decisions may well be subject to tortious claims' (*Just v British Columbia* [1989] at 1240–1). In determining where a particular decision falls, Cory, J offered some guidelines. Matters of policy usually emanate from 'persons of a high level of authority.' As well, budgetary allocations for departments or agencies are generally considered to be policy issues. However, neither of these characteristics are necessarily determinative. Moreover, a 'policy decision is open to challenge on the basis that it is not made in bona fide exercise of discretion' (ibid.: 1245).

With respect to decision-making about parole, questions of civil liability will relate primarily to the process by which decisions are made or communicated. Given the adjudicative nature of the mandate, there is little likelihood of a successful action against the board if all reasonably available material bearing on the relevant issues of risk is placed before it, and the board proceeds in a reasonable manner to consider it. Some assessments of future risk will prove to be wrong, but the test is one of negligence not perfection. Accordingly, if relevant material does not find its way into the file or is not considered by the board, a claim may be generated if a person suffers injury as a result of the decision. An argument may even be made that some information is so transparently incomplete that a decision cannot properly be formulated without additional data. Of course, it will always remain to be determined whether the person injured falls within the set of people whose injury should be reasonably foreseeable as a consequence of negligent decision-making.

Another potential source of a claim against the board may arise through the recognition of a duty to warn specific people of a clear risk to which they may be subjected as a result of a release decision. For example, if threats have been made which seem credible, there may be a duty to warn the person threatened (see, for example, *Jane Doe v Board of Commissioners of Police for the Municipality of Metropolitan Toronto* [1990, 1991]. It is more likely that this situation will arise in the case of someone who has not been granted early release but who must wait until his or her sentence expires before returning to the community. Hence, any duty to warn probably rests on the Correctional Service.

It is also worth considering whether a prisoner could sue the board. Again, the answer may be that a defective process that is sufficient to constitute negligence and that results in a denial of liberty is actionable. For example, assume an excellent candidate for parole who is denied early release because a negative report relating to another prisoner is mistakenly considered by the board. Unless all parole decisions are insulated from liability, damages should equally be available to this prisoner as to a member of the public who suffers injury as a result of someone's negligent release. Once the availability of damages for a negligent denial of release is accepted, other less extreme examples will likely satisfy the appropriate threshold. As well, claims for damages may be brought for violations of the Charter's guarantee of fundamental justice when liberty is at stake (Pilkington, 1987; Cooper-Stephenson, 1990). These claims, which may become known as constitutional torts, are distinct from a claim based on negligence.

Obviously, as a result of the modern attitude towards governmental liability, it is not surprising that the new Corrections and Constitutional Release Act [1992] addresses this issue. Section 154 provides: 'No criminal or civil proceedings lie against a member of the Board for anything done or said in good faith in the exercise or purported exercise of the functions of a member of the Board under this or any other Act of Parliament.' While this leaves open issues of malice, bad faith, or deliberate neglect, the prospect of suits against individual board members will be significantly reduced. Section 154, however, does not protect the board as a whole; internal processes and policies may still prove to be the subject matter of civil claims.

Accountability through the Appointment Process

While the board appears to be an autonomous agency with an independent statutory mandate, it is linked in a variety of ways with the solicitor general and the Cabinet. Many of these linkages can be viewed as forms of accountability. Regularly, the solicitor general and the chair of the National Parole Board appear before the House of Commons Standing Committee on Justice and the Solicitor General to respond to questions about new legislation, internal policy, or budget estimates. The degree of accountability is a function of how well the committee members are informed and prepared to perform their role.

At a more direct level, the appointment process provides a degree of accountability. The appointment of all members of the board and designation of the chair, vice-chair, and executive committee are effected by the governor in council (the Cabinet) upon the recommendation of the solicitor general. These appointments, pursuant to order-in-council, may extend for up to ten years but are usually for five years. During their currency, they are revocable only for cause. They are also renewable. However, the process of appointment and renewal may raise questions of political allegiance rather than accountability.

The security of the order-in-council appointment is important if a decision-maker is to exercise the degree of independence needed to make fair and impartial decisions. Many appointees to the National Parole Board have been known more for their partisan political efforts than their relevant experience (Daubney Report, 1988: 168–9). When this factor is combined with the prospect of renewal, the existence of adequate independence may be questionable. Certainly, with respect to judges, the discretion to extend appointments beyond usual retirement age can be sufficient to place judicial independence in jeopardy when pension entitlements have not yet been satisfied (*R v Valente* [1985]. A similar question can be asked about the process for appointing and renewing parole board members. The potential for deference to one's master may not be consistent with the role of an independent adjudicator exercising an important statutory mandate.[22]

Section 105(1) of the new act provides the only statutory appointment criteria: 'Members appointed to the Board shall be significantly diverse in their backgrounds to be able to collectively represent community values and views in the work of the Board and to inform the community with respect to unescorted temporary absence, parole and statutory release.' In 1991 the solicitor general of the day suggested that appointment by politicians creates full accountability at the next election. With specific reference to the Parole Board, he said: 'They're all accountable. We're accountable because we make the appointments.'[23] It is unlikely that the collapse of his party in the 1993 election proves his point. Until the board can free itself from both the reality and the appearance of patronage appointments, it will fail to engender the confidence that its mandate requires.

Accountability through Participation

Board hearings have been conducted in private. As a result, participation was restricted to the board members, the prisoner and counsel, and the case management team. Victims could not be present, although they could submit material in writing. The new act expands the board's role in making information available to victims and will permit, in appropriate cases, attendance at hearings by observers. Section 142 permits the board to provide a victim[24] with information including eligibility dates, dates for reviews, conditions of any release, and the prisoner's destination on release. Section 140(4) of the legislation empowers the board to permit individuals to attend hearings as observers 'after taking into account the offender's views' and after considering whether the person's presence will have an adverse or disruptive affect on the hearing. The ability to attend as an observer appears to include victims. Still, permission requires a conclusion by the board that the person's presence will not 'adversely affect an appropriate balance between that person's or the public's interest in knowing and the public's interest in the effective re-integration of the offender into society.' This provision recognizes that, in some situations, the uncontrolled dissemination of information about a release decision may significantly impair the likelihood of success. It should be noted that, unlike courts, the board has no power of contempt that could be used to enforce a non-publication order.

An important example of inappropriate participation beyond that which the statute permits is the case of *Bains*, in which the prisoner was granted day parole from a sentence for attempted murder (*Bains v National Parole Board* [1989]). After the decision, but before its implementation, representations were made to the chair of the board by the original trial judge, the prosecuting Crown, the attorney general of Ontario, and the deputy attorney general, denouncing the release decision and urging a re-consideration. As a result, the chair ordered that the prisoner not be released until the board reviewed its decision. On the evidence, it appeared that the observations offered by the various officials who intervened were not new but were issues with which the board was familiar. Muldoon, J held: 'The considerations shown herein to have been invoked by the board's chairman are extraneous to the board's lawfully-formulated conclusions about the applicant's character, conduct and progress toward apparent rehabilitation' (*Bains v National Parole Board* [1989] at 348). Accordingly, he concluded that the original release decision should be implemented without considering whether, in other circumstances, there might be power to nullify a previously formulated decision. While the attempts to influence the process after a release decision was made did not succeed in *Bains*, the decision does not foreclose a similar effort based on what might be considered to be new information. However, the argument remains that a decision, properly formulated with regard to the relevant factors, cannot be disturbed (see, however, *Beaumier v National Parole Board* [1981]; *Re McDonald and the Queen* [1981]). Certainly, when an attempt to reverse a board decision would result in a denial of liberty, courts should ensure that the parole process is not subverted by inappropriate forms of external influence masked as new information.

A more difficult issue arose in *Veysey v Millhaven Institution* [1993] where the board purported to suspend the parolee after receiving an opinion from treatment staff involved in the parolee's post-release treatment program. The parolee had participated conscientiously in the program that was a condition of his parole. Perhaps not surprisingly, given the previous record of offences, a psychiatrist considered that the parolee represented a high risk to re-offend. Based on this opinion, and without any evidence of negative post-release conduct, the board suspended Veysey's parole pending a post-suspension hearing. Before that hearing, he was released on habeas corpus by Hurley, J, who concluded that there was no statutory authority to suspend or revoke simply because the board receives an opinion contrary to its own earlier assessment of risk. The parolee may be compelled to participate in programs as conditions of release, but the board cannot compel success or even 'significant improvement' (ibid.: 278). The assessment of risk is the board's function.

Conclusion

The discussion above indicates some of the available windows of scrutiny into the operations of the National Parole Board. The extension of judicial review to the parole process has removed some of the arbitrariness that disturbed Chief Justice Laskin back in 1976. Yet, it must be remembered that the scope of judicial review is limited, for the most part, to issues of jurisdiction and procedure. The advent of the Charter [1982] has added another dimension to judicial review, but these constitutionally entrenched norms operate mostly in the procedural realm.[25] Much of what takes place day-to-day can remain insulated from judicial scrutiny by careful attention to the statutory framework and internal decision-making policy. When coupled with the recognition that the majority of board members do not come to their responsibilities with relevant criminal justice experience (Daubney Report, 1988: 168–9),[26] the restricted scope of judicial scrutiny is cause for concern. This insulation is compounded by the limited degree of legal representation available to prisoners in many provinces.

At the political level, the board is regularly exposed to examination and inquiry. These forms of scrutiny are easily manipulated to fit public opinion. Hence, legislation and internal policy continue to tighten the parole process, sometimes without regard to the evidence. From the public perspective, accurate information about parole, parolees, and the parole process is necessary to ensure that public opinion is not distorted by media accounts of blood and mayhem. Various inquiries, commissions, and committees have attempted to put hard data in front of the community, but, again, the accessibility of this material can be controlled by the media, who may not find it interesting. With respect to victims, the new act will provide some opportunity for participation. However, as has been noted recently by the British Columbia Court of Appeal, the criminal process was not designed, nor is it suitable for healing the wounds of past injury (*R v Sweeney et al.* [1992], per Wood, JA).

The Corrections and Conditional Release Act [1992] includes, for the first time, a statutory statement of purpose, which reads: 'The purpose of conditional release is to contribute to the maintenance of a just, peaceful and safe society by means of decisions on the timing and conditions of release that will best facilitate the rehabilitation of offenders and their reintegration into the community as law-abiding citizens.' In other words, the National Parole Board is in the release business. However, since 1959, the board and its functions have grown in ways that are not consistent with being in the release business. This is especially true of the ever-expanding detention process that has fundamentally redefined the role of the board. Frankness is an important element of any process. If accountability means exposing an agency to scrutiny, effective accountability requires some guarantee of a frank and serious response to what is found, not simply new slogans to fuel an already distorted public perception.

Notes

1 The critical issue in *Mitchell* [1976] was the ability of the courts to examine revocation decisions of the National Parole Board. The majority of judges insulated the board from scrutiny by relying either on narrow conceptions of the scope of habeas corpus review or by using strained arguments to preclude the use of *certiorari* in aid. In dissent, Laskin, CJC (with Spence and Dickson, JJ concurring) argued for a more flexible remedial response that would permit greater scrutiny of board processes. A decade later the Laskin view was adopted unanimously by a differently constituted Supreme Court in *R v Miller* [1985]. For a discussion of these two cases, see Cole and Manson, 1990: 93–9.

2 For an interesting capsulized account of release systems in various European, North American, and Australian jurisdictions, see United Kingdom, Report of the Review Committee, 1988: 16–28.

3 See Criminal Code, Section 731. In 1841, the Provincial Statutes of Canada (4 and 5 Vict, c. 24), provided that persons serving sentences 'not exceeding two years' would serve them in 'Common Gaol or House of Correction,' while at that time, the penitentiary was reserved for sentences at least seven years in length.

4 Part II of the federal Parole Act Regulations, SOR/78–628, as amended, provided the relevant eligibility, review, and revocation details applicable to provincial parole boards. Since 1 November 1992, see *Regulations Respecting Corrections and the Conditional Release and Detention of Offenders*, Canada Gazette, Part I, 5 Sept. 1992.

5 Until recently, the relevant statute was the Parole Act [RSC 1985]. This has now been superseded by Part II of the Corrections and Conditional Release Act [1992] discussed below. For federal prisoners, this enactment merged all statutory provisions dealing with both the penitentiary and parole regimes.

6 For a detailed history, see Cole and Manson, 1990: 159–88.

7 For a history and discussion of the royal prerogative and the pardoning power, see ibid.: 399–415.

8 Forfeiture, the automatic recommitment upon conviction while at large for an offence punishable by imprisonment for two years or more,

was abolished in 1977, Criminal Law Amendment Act, 1976–7: Section 32.

9 It started with a statutory credit equal to one-quarter of the sentence supplemented by the potential to earn three more days each month. In 1977 this was changed to an earned remission scheme whereby a prisoner could earn up to 15 days per month based on conduct and participation.

10 Shortly after the introduction of mandatory supervision, the chairman of the National Parole Board estimated that the new function of supervising this group of prisoners would double the annual number of released prisoners under the jurisdiction of the board. He estimated that while about 3,000 prisoners would be released annually on parole, another 3,000 would be released on mandatory supervision (Street, 1971). This prediction has not come to pass. Of the 52,484 prisoners released under the supervision of the National Parole Board between 1975 and 1986, 18,746 (28 per cent) were released on full parole and 33,738 (72 per cent) were released on mandatory supervision.

11 At the same time, the consequences of recommitment were expanded to include loss of all statutory remission that stood to the prisoner's credit on the date of release. (Parole Act [1970]: Sections 20 and 21).

12 *R v Moore* [1983]; *Oag v R* [1983]; *Truscott v Director of Mountain Institution* [1983]; *Noonan v National Parole Board* [1983].

13 Section 138(1) provides that the prisoner be recommitted to 'serve the portion of the term of imprisonment that remained unexpired on the day on which the parole or statutory release was terminated or revoked.' Section 138(2) provides that the revoked prisoner 'is not eligible for statutory release until after serving two-thirds of the unexpired portion of the sentence.'

14 The act, first presented to Parliament in 1991 as Bill C-36, also included in Schedule II the curious offence of failing to disclose a previous prescription. This offence, found in Section 38.1 of the Food and Drugs Act [RSC 1985] (as amended by Section 194 of the Criminal Law Amendment Act [1985]) is known on the street as 'double doctoring.' It was deleted from Bill C-36 after committee hearings.

15 The board's breakdown of data categorized robbery separately from crimes of violence against the person. Fifty-nine people, or 45.4 per cent of the group, had been paroled from a sentence imposed for robbery (Canada, National Parole Board, 1987: vol. 2, Appendix E, Figure 3).

16 Section 741.2 of the Criminal Code [RSC 1985] empowers a sentencing judge faced with an offender who has been convicted of one of the scheduled offences to increase the period of ineligibility for parole to one-half

of the sentence or ten years, whichever is less. The trigger for the increase is the judge's determination that 'having regard to the circumstances of the commission of the offences and the character and circumstances of the offender, that the expression of society's denunciation of the offences or the objective of specific or general deterrence' requires that a greater portion of the sentence be served before release; Sections 125 and 126 of the new act provide for accelerated reviews at first eligibility of non-violent and non-drug offenders serving their first penitentiary term.

17 Evidence of Fred Gibson, chair of the National Parole Board, before the House of Commons Standing Committee on Justice and the Solicitor General, 28 Nov. 1991, 18: 29. Also see *Globe and Mail*, 9 Oct. 1991, p. 1.

18 Of the 122 people detained up to 30 Sept. 1989 and subsequently released either at warrant expiry or on mandatory supervision, with or without a residence requirement pursuant to Section 21.4(4) (b), 29 per cent were re-admitted to penitentiary but only 10 per cent had been convicted of a new indictable offence. See Evidence of Fred Gibson, chair of the National Parole Board, before Standing Committee on Justice and the Solicitor General, 30 Oct. 1990, 49: 8–9.

19 See Jury Recommendations, Inquest into the Death of Christopher Stephenson, Brampton, Ontario, 22 Jan. 1993. The principal recommendation was that Canada adopt a 'sexual predator' statute, like the state of Washington, which would permit indefinite detention after a sentence had been completed. For a discussion of such legislation, see Greenlees (1991) and *University of Puget Sound Law Review* (1991/92).

20 The author cannot say whether any settlements have been made either *ex gratia* or as a result of the commencement of litigation.

21 Borrowed from the decision of Lord Wilberforce in *Anns v Merton London Borough Council* [1978]. This decision has been approved by the Supreme Court on a number of occasions: *City of Kamloops v Nielsen* [1984]; *Laurentide Motels Ltd. v Beauport (City)* [1989]; *Rothfield v Manolakos* [1989]. However, the House of Lords departed from it recently in *Murphy v Brentwood District Council* [1991].

22 The Canadian Bar Association task force report, *The Independence of Federal Administration Tribunals and Agencies in Canada* (1990), recommended that appointments to a specified list of Schedule A adjudicative tribunals, including the National Parole Board, should be 'during good behaviour until retirement age.' More significantly, the report recommended the establishment of an Office of the Commissioner for Federal Tribunal and Agencies, which would be responsible for the screening of candidates for appointment to Schedule A tribunals and that the ultimate nomination be

by the minister of justice not the minister responsible for the tribunal or agency.

23 Evidence of Doug Lewis, solicitor general of Canada, before the House of Commons Standing Committee on Justice and the Solicitor General, 26 Nov. 1991, 16: 32.

24 'Victim' is defined as 'a person to whom harm was done or who suffered physical or emotional damage as a result of the commission of the offence.'

25 This is not to say that a statutory provision cannot be substantively unconstitutional in terms of Section 7 or that a decision cannot result in arbitrary detention contrary to Section 9 or perhaps even cruel and unusual treatment or punishment as prohibited by Section 12.

26 The Daubney report (1988) indicates that in 1987, only 46.7 per cent of permanent and temporary board members 'had held criminal justice-related occupations prior to their appointments.'

Prospects for Accountability in Canadian Aboriginal Justice Systems

ROGER F. McDONNELL

Many Aboriginal communities and regional organizations are currently engaged in investigations that are intended to assist in an assessment of their problems with existing legislation, court procedures, and policing practices. These investigations promise to provide guidance in the design of alternate justice systems that will address Aboriginal needs in a realistic and culturally meaningful manner. Some have begun to shed valuable light on the complex issues involved, and it is our purpose here to examine aspects of these investigations to better understand what might be meant by 'accountability' in an alternate Aboriginal justice system.[1]

The challenges that face us are several, since accountability can assume radically different forms according to the frame of reference employed. For present purposes we invoke two such frameworks to make clear just how divergent these forms are in their entailments and also to show how intertwined they are. As it turns out, diverse modalities of accountability do not, in the contemporary Aboriginal context, provide grounds for clear choice.

The frames of reference, which reflect different forms of accountability, centre on the individual and on the collectivity. The ethical norms that might allow us to account rationally for the value of accomplished deeds and also guide us when we are faced with the necessity of choosing and acting, have a distinctive character in either case. However, whether emphasis on the individual or the collective must be considered as mutually exclusive options or whether they can be articulated in some manner remains an intensely debated issue among moral philosophers, political theorists, and others.[2] Some see coexistence as a possibility, others most decidedly do not. From the vantage of anthropology, anomalies and contradictions are the focus of many of the most creative moves in the symbolic expression of any culture. Consequently, at this historical stage, there is something to be said for loosening the grip of theory and allowing those we theorize *about* to assume control of the conversation. Theory, after all, may never show us how to go on or how best to conclude anything about fitting square pegs into round holes. The symbolic–interpretive creations of culture, however, do this all the time, and we should thus reflect more on what this might mean for our endeavour than we have in the past.

The essay is presented in four main parts. Each part is intended to serve as a way of framing and introducing the next, with the hope that we can progressively appreciate the kind of problem that accountability is for us today. Our overall purpose is both to broaden our understanding of what is involved and to indicate why, with regard to notions like accountability, it is no longer possible to reason out – in Enlightenment fashion – solutions to these problems from afar. The next section provides one way of appreciating the rise of collective rights by tracing the recent evolution of the notion of planned development and the social initiatives and interventions occurring at the level of the state.[3] Many of the issues raised find expression in the case study of the James Bay Cree, which follows. The next section widens the framework by exploring accountability and self-determination in the context of the heterogeneity and diversity that exist within and between all contemporary Aboriginal communities, and the essay concludes with a general discussion of tradition, the state, and the problem of accountability in Aboriginal Canada.

Modernization and the Rise of Collective Rights

In the 1950s it was confidently supposed that all societies of the world were converging on some modernized, fully developed stage. As then imagined, the so-called theory of modernization had two distinct features. On the one hand, all progress and development were thought to require a functionally integrated set of values, institutions, and attitudes. Central to this set was the idea that collective well-being was best ensured when individuals were free to creatively pursue their interests, however these might be construed. This embellishment of the long-standing emphasis on the individual received particularly wide circulation in 1948, when it was included as a central consideration in the United Nations Covenant of Human Rights [1948]. On the other hand, the theory of modernization was reiteratively hostile to the idea of continuity, in the sense that all traditions and conventions not thought conducive to modernization were considered as obstacles to be eradicated or neutralized.

The deficiencies of this perspective on development were soon challenged on several grounds, not the least of which was that the planned-for changes were not taking place. In addition, the so-called obstacles of tradition were proving to be far more resilient and central to the course of change than had been originally supposed. Among other things, the concept of a social formation composed of individuals who were somehow interchangeable and equal simply did not exist in most societies whose social imagination was not a product of a Western heritage or modern state formation. Indeed, most societies, including many partial societies in modern states, set off much of their social file against a moral framework of complementary duties and obligations that draw people into structured relationships on the basis of conventions of recognized differences between them. Objectionable and scandalous conduct is often recognized to occur in such a context when people begin to behave as if they *were* interchangeably the same.

Thus, social and cultural traditions – or rather their transformation and elaboration – came to be appreciated as one of the keys to meaningful, constructive development. Western intellectuals, along with a growing number of disenchanted Western-educated leaders of emerging states, argued strongly for a pluralist approach to modernization. Instead of one converging plane, there were to be many parallel streams, each moving forward according to the distinct values, priorities, and institutions already in place in the traditions of the people whose future development it would be.

The idea of development thus became less a matter of replacing old traditions with new techniques, ideas, values, and institutions, and rather more a matter of elaborating and transforming whatever happened to be in place. Partly because of this shift in thinking there were several amendments introduced to the Covenant of Human Rights throughout the 1960s. Most of these were intended to preserve and maintain the features of culture, tradition, and social formation that were judged important in any people's attempts at collective development. The 'right to self-determination', also introduced at this time, features exactly this collective connotation and association with the social *and* the cultural.

Some Impacts of the Cree-Naskapi Act: A Case Study

The transformation in thought about development and certain kinds of state intervention described above is apparent in the events following the proposed hydroelectric development of northern Quebec in the early 1970s. Initially, there was an attempt on the part of the Quebec government to ignore not only collective rights but also any claim to the land on the part of its Aboriginal inhabitants. This, however, proved to be seriously misguided; Quebec had failed to recognize the legal strength of the Native position in the Canadian context or the force of the emerging Native leadership. Consequently, they were obliged to come to terms.

In 1975 this resulted in the nine (eight were recognized at the time) Cree communities coming to an arrangement with both the provincial government of Quebec and the federal government of Canada. What became known as the James Bay and Northern Quebec Agreement (JBNQA) coincided with the emergence of political and administrative organizations known, respectively, as the Grand Council of the Crees (GCC) and the Cree Regional Authority (CRA). These two bodies were to be held responsible for the collective interests and concerns of all the communities.

Prior to this period, Cree leadership and administration in the region was focused on the band. Indeed, it was only in the 1960s that it had begun to perform even a few of the broad range of services required of it today. Thus, it was virtually overnight that an aggregation of Cree bands were forged into a regional organization in 1975. It is important to realize that this organization arose in a context of resisting various non-Cree governmental and industrial initiatives, and it continues to be most cohesively focused when responding to such external initiatives. As this examination of accountability progresses, it will become clear why it is so much more difficult for Cree and other Aboriginal groups in Canada to achieve anything like such sharpness of focus when trying to develop and deal with internal initiatives.

The JBNQA placed the Cree in a position to influence subsequent developments in a variety of areas including land use, health care, education, municipal government, and social services. It also provided room for them to assume the initiative regarding subsequent legislative developments as well as the future shape of the administration of justice in the region.

The scope of Cree legislative powers were subsequently elaborated in the Cree-Naskapi (of Quebec) Act [1984]. Since that time, Cree have been regularly monitoring their own difficulties in implementing the act and have encouraged investigations to assist them in assessing their problems with present legislation, court processes, and policing procedures, as well as providing guidance in redesigning a system for themselves that would address their needs in a realistic and culturally meaningful manner.

The investigation that explored the relationship between Cree society and the present justice system was highly instructive (La Prairie, 1991). One of the most striking findings involved the extremely limited reliance that Cree typically placed on the justice system in resolving problems among themselves. Typically, people did not respond directly to aggression or deviant conduct and when they did respond, they seldom involved the courts. Cree police (in the employ of the Sureté du Québec) were called upon by Cree mainly to prevent material and physical damage. Cree were seldom concerned to have the police follow through with a full investigation. The general expectation was that the dynamic of conflict would eventually run its course and that one would only prolong it – and perhaps provoke an amplification – by invoking the full process of the justice system.

This disinclination to fully use existing justice facilities is partly understandable by reference to the fact that victims and offenders were usually intimately related. The lack of social distance between protagonists appears to have directly influenced their reluctance to hand a dispute over to the impartiality of the courts. To bear witness or simply to charge someone because their actions transgress a formal law is to deny not only the protagonists' history of interaction but also the *future* interaction they imagine with each other. From this vantage, the courts are often viewed less as a means of resolving an issue than as an avoidable complication of it.

One result of this is that people generally want police to intervene in a partial and circumscribed manner. They want offending behaviour to cease without engaging the whole process of making a statement, encouraging a formal charge, and making a court appearance as a witness. In other words, people are inclined to report offensive behaviour and call in the assistance of the police without any intention of engaging the whole apparatus of the system. In many respects Cree police accommodate this – especially when the offence is more disorderly and disruptive than criminal in nature. Overall, only one-third of the reports of a potentially criminal nature are officially recorded as occurrences in the police files. Of the total number of incidents reported to police, between 40 per cent and 60 per cent involve interpersonal disturbances, although only 12 per cent of these are eventually processed as occurrences.[4] Incidents of mischief, theft, and breaking and entering are reported far less frequently, although proportionally they assume a far higher percentage in the occurrence reports. In one community, mischief, theft, and breaking and entering combined consisted of only 15 per cent of the total reports to the police; however, they involved 66 per cent of the official occurrences reported in the police files.

This disparity reflects several things simultaneously: a disinclination on the part of the community to pursue certain kinds of offences through the court system, an accommodation of this disinclination on the part of the police, and an overwhelming bias of police training towards property-related offences.[5] It also raises some important questions regarding the development of an alternate Cree justice system, since the very idea of justice can hardly be dissociated from its impartial application. It resists even the suggestion of favouritism or prejudice entering into the imbricated process of arraignment, prosecution, and judgment. The entire sequence rests on the understood capacity to recognize events that are contrary to existing law, the collection of facts for the purpose of determining responsibility for the occurrence of these events, and a judgment of those facts in relation to particular persons regardless of their social position or relation to others in society. The entire process, in other words, is understood to hinge on a fact–law relationship, and with respect to this relationship all members of society are to be considered equal.

Equality, however, is not the only condition. The relationship between functionaries of the system and those who are drawn into it is meant to be that of strangers. Indeed, as Bauman (1990) observes, the general design of the state, including its justice apparatus, is largely devoted to an articulation of relations between "strangers" or at least people whose relationship to each other – whether this be by way of rank, occupation, kinship, friendship, or enmity – is largely viewed in terms of individual rights and equality before the law. In most urban settings, of course, being a stranger to one's neighbours describes the social condition of most, whether they like it or not. Between the public and its officials, however, a cultivated distance and unrelatedness is the preferred social relationship. In the justice system, for instance, should it transpire that functionaries and protagonists are related (socially, politically, or economically), the former may well be disqualified from further involvement in the proceedings.

Cree police, however, could not be farther from such a situation in the practice of their duties. Not only do they know the community members intimately, they are typically related as kinsmen to a large number of them. And nothing whatever in their training prepares them to deal with such abiding ambivalence. They are unavoidably partial towards the community, without having had any training to deal with such a profoundly indecisive and uncertain situation in executing their mandate.

The overall consequence is that the existing justice system is underused. Very largely this is because people do not want police to proceed as police in a great many interpersonal disturbances. At the same time, interpersonal disturbances are a very prominent concern and all communities would like to stop the seemingly endless cycle of abuse, violence, and argument that affects the lives of so many. The result is that the police are criticized for not being more effective even though, because of their relationship to the communities they serve and the nature of those communities, a solution through the existing system is resisted, and the problems remain distinctly social in character.

Among Cree there remains a widely held and deeply felt conviction that something must be done regarding interpersonal disturbances. But many feel they are not being appropriately served in this regard and believe, rather vaguely, that this is a deficiency on the part of the justice system as it now exists. The question is what should be done and what guides should be used in developing alternatives? Without modification in either their formulation or application, certain premises and expectations of the present justice system seem clearly inappropriate in the context of contemporary Cree communities. They are also of very questionable suitability for other Aboriginal communities.

Consider, for instance, the following examples from different sectors of Aboriginal Canada. They are meant to briefly illustrate the experienced inadequacy of present justice processes, the desire to explore alternative processes that realistically address and meaningfully reflect contemporary needs, and the importance of trying to incorporate traditional considerations into future developments. They are also an attempt to expand the concept of justice to include a range of social issues that, although not necessarily implicated by the law, are recognized by Aboriginal groups to have a direct bearing on any solution of enduring value to the communities in question.

This broader approach to issues of justice is, in part, reflected in the current attempts to improve the delivery of justice services to Aboriginal communities. It is also clearly accommodated by the guidelines and objectives of the "diversion program" as reported by La Prairie (1992: Appendix 3). Among other things, these guidelines encourage disclosure of certain kinds of offences, such as spousal assault and sexual abuse, in order to steer resolution more directly towards the possibility of reconciliation, rehabilitation of offenders, and general community well-being. They also encourage the incorporation of traditional values and customs to aid in this process.

In numerous places across the country – from Yukon to the Maritimes – various initiatives have been developed along the above lines by different Aboriginal communities. For the most part, and with varying degrees of success, however, these have resulted in attempts to graft local institutional creations to existing justice procedures. The Teslin Tlingit Justice Council, for example, serves the court in such a capacity. It is composed of clan leaders who, within limits set by the judge, decide on sentencing and are responsible for supervising the outcome which, to date, may include house arrest, restitution, and participation in treatment (ibid.: 83–5). Rather similar approaches have been developed in British Columbia, Ontario, and the Maritimes. A recent evaluation of a Mi'kmaq community in Nova Scotia also reveals very strong parallels (Clairmont, 1993).

In our view, the similarity of the Aboriginal response suggests that the prevailing context of justice administration tends to annul the promise of the guidelines and efface the enormous diversity of both history and tradition traversing this vast area. This also seems to be partly reflected in a progress report on the administration of justice recently distributed by Pauktuutit, the national Inuit women's organization (Pauktuutit, 1993). Like most other Aboriginal groups, they stressed that their concern was to develop policy statements and programs within the justice system that would faithfully exhibit the values and needs of their own society. However, although Inuit experience with domestic violence, sexual abuse, and substance abuse was very similar to that of more southern Aboriginal communities, and although it was felt that the present justice system's treatment of these difficulties was inadequate or counter-productive, Pauktuutit was of the view that southern Aboriginal models of justice did not point in a meaningful direction for them. Indeed, they acknowledged important regional variations and differences of cultural emphasis among themselves and recognized that any solutions and alternatives that might be devised would necessarily reflect these internal differences if their objectives were to be realized. They are still engaged in the process on how best to explore and create the meaningful alternatives they feel are required.

Over the past ten years, an Ojibwa community on the shores of Lake Winnipeg has self-consciously attempted to develop an alternative to the justice system which, it felt, was misdirected in emphasis and too narrow in scope to deal with the complexities of their social problems. It began, like so many others, in thinking that the community could work within the existing system. The thinking of this group followed from the idea that a good deal of family violence, substance abuse, and other forms of dysfunctional conduct were symptomatic of a deeper malaise rooted in a persuasive pattern of intergenerational sexual abuse in which 75 per cent of the community were involved as victims. As recently reported by Ross (1993), a fundamental aspect of their strategy in breaking this pattern is to make victimizers acknowledge the harm their conduct has generated and to affirm in their minds their responsibility to their victims, to the families subsequently affected by the victim's conduct, and to the community at large. This is a very tall order for, in a sense, what they are trying to do is create (or rekindle) a positive sense of community for those who have become actively inconsiderate of the well-being of those with whom they live.

If the Cree or any of the others mentioned here are to develop appropriate alternatives for themselves, it will be necessary to have a clear and realistic sense of both the nature of the communities they occupy and the kinds of traditions and conventions that might be useful guides for developing justice institutions that would better serve their needs. If they do not embrace the importance of impartiality, perhaps they have another ethic that would serve as well in reconciling differences and attempting to ensure peaceful social relations among themselves. If so, what standards and criteria do they employ in assessing whether individuals are conducting themselves appropriately and what mechanisms do they possess for taking people to account for misconduct in such a context? Such a self-determining initiative, however, introduces a whole series of fundamental challenges.

Self-Determination, Accountability, and the
Problem of Heterogeneity

We must hasten to put things in context here by saying we are not concerned with abstract 'self-determination' and the interminable quasiphilosophical, quasireligious discussions about emancipation, justice, and natural rights that seem to attend it. For our purposes, self-determination requires recognition by the state, since even in instances where separation is envisioned, some form of statehood is the imagined goal and, thus, the issue of internal variability of culture and ethnicity is simply postponed. The trick, as Taylor indicates below, is to imagine how any community (or partial society) can retain its distinctiveness and move forward according to its own lights yet still be linked to the state in some meaningful manner. What the modern state and its occupants very clearly need 'is to recover a sense of significant differentiation, so that its partial communities ... can become ... important centres of concern and activity for their members in a way that connects them to the whole' (Taylor, 1979: 118).

Putting it this way, the state – whatever else it may be – must be an arrangement that nurtures internal diversity and is responsive to the dynamics both between and within the societies that compose it. It is an arrangement that must be, in other words, much more sensitive to its own internal dynamics. If it is to have a viable and relatively stable future, this would seem to be achievable only by increasing the state's sensitivity to its own history, thereby opening it to periodic reassessments of how it might best nurture the evolving diversity within. Even should this occur in some form, however, some problems will be endemic, and we would like to discuss two of them that bear directly on the present concern.

HETEROGENEITY AND DIVERSITY

The first problem involves the heterogeneity of every community and indeed every tradition. Sociolinguists, for instance, have even gone so far as to suggest that some form of grammatical, verbal distinction of genre or difference in speaking pattern corresponding to men and women in the same speech community may well be universal (see Sherzer, 1987). This allows for the possibility that even within the most intimate and integrated communities there are significant differences. Men and women may not only speak differently about the same things, they may have different meanings for the same words used and, in some well-documented instances, employ entirely different vocabularies when speaking on just about anything at all. The same can be said for assessed priorities and matters of value, and here one can easily ramify internal divergence according to age, status, occupation, and so forth. The point is hardly incidental. What it brings into focus is that every society is composed of collateral, subjascent, and superordinate perspectives rather than a single social perspective. This implies that virtually *no culture remains uncontested from within*, regardless of what rhetoric of seamless wholeness it might employ when representing itself to others.

The importance of registering internal heterogeneity is not to weaken the concept of community nor to cunningly reintroduce the idea that the populace really is an aggregation of individuals after all. At any historical juncture, one perspective tends to prevail and to determine initiatives that other, subjascent perspectives respond to, without losing their contrary and distinctive character in the process. Rather, the importance of acknowledging a community's internal diversity is that the community as a whole is asymmetrically situated with respect to changing circumstances. In other words, as the community is drawn in by history, it may be easier (or, conversely, more difficult) to respond positively and to advantage from some sectors or positions in society than from others. This has serious implications for the whole question of accountability.

We have already seen that the Inuit are well aware of their own internal variability and believe it to be a crucial consideration when addressing contemporary issues. Such variability could, however, be found in virtually every language and culture grouping. Certainly the Cree are no exception to the kind of internal variability of tradition alluded to above. From coastal to inland groups and from north to south there existed important and acknowledged differences of dialect, sensibility, use of resources, size of groups, mobility, extent of involvement in wage employment, opportunities and inclinations for cooperative endeavours, and so forth. Since this diverse heritage roughly corresponds to the diversity of contemporary Cree communities, it is undeniably of potential significance in understanding the response of these communities to what has been happening to them; obviously it constitutes a resource to draw on in any regional- or community-specific project of development they may devise for themselves.

For purposes of this discussion, however, we wish to set aside this order of variability so that we might better concentrate on certain general features of the traditional means of achieving social order and harmonious interaction. One of the principle things to bear in mind here is that a Cree sense of order hinged largely on an understanding of morality rather than polity or legality. For a person to fall within the moral order, there were certain associated premises and expectations. What we have to say here focuses specifically on Cree material. However, the overall emphasis and contrasts apply to Aboriginal Canada generally. This should be kept in mind.

Most crucial of these premises appears to have been that the people of a tent or a camp had a reciprocal claim on each other's food resources. Typically, the act of sharing implied an already established base of cooperative conduct between those involved; but cooperative conduct, especially in the hunt, could also lead to sharing and the formation of a new and broadened moral sphere of orderly conduct. This link between sharing and an expectation of orderly conduct is critical and, in an important sense, sharing meant that two parties were prepared to be accountable to each other in terms of the moral order. Conversely, to refuse to share was a major breach of existing or pending solidarity; it signified that orderly, cooperative conduct could not be expected between the parties concerned.

To be accountable within the framework of the Cree moral order meant that a person assumed a position within a structured set of positions. Everyone within the moral sphere was distinguished according to age and social gender as indicated by way of kin terms. These terms were associated with complementary sets of duties, obligations, and regulations that systematically emphasized differences of conduct appropriate between paired sets of kin such as father and daughter, say, or grandmother and grandson. What specific categories of people could eat, where they slept in a camp, what they were expected to do, with whom they were expected to do it and where, were all different, one to the other. Thus, instead of an impartial application of common law and a notion like equality being the principle moral and political measure of propriety, it was this set of differences and their associated duties and obligations that constituted and guided moral conduct. There was, in brief, *no common law or set of regulations and constraints that bound everyone equally.*

The general effect of this differentiating emphasis was integrative; it drew people together who by cultural convention were defined in terms of complementary differences. This is crucial to stress; the differences were based on convention not ability. The practices of men and women, the old and the young, were set off from each other in such a way that much could not be produced or brought to completion without others. By defining people as different according to their practices and proclivities – men bend snowshoe frames, women fill them; older people eat this part of a bear, younger eat that part – the members of the group were construed as *interdependent*. Among the Cree, for example, this view was encouraged in the very earliest rituals that introduced a child into the nature of Cree social life. The evaluative stress was not on the individual or on an autonomous 'self,' rather it was on a sort of inter-self in which people viewed themselves in relation to others and as a contributing part to something larger than themselves. Here again, the general effect was integrative.

Where people got upset and found conduct offensive was, in the main, when the premise of solidarity underlying the recognition of these differences was placed in question (that is, when they were either ignored or not maintained). As indicated, such behaviour denied all grounds for cooperative conduct and was the opposite of intimate, trusting cooperation which, in Cree terms, is one of the meanings attributed to the English word 'respect.' However, 'disrespect' could also occur when people failed to conduct themselves appropriately in relation to a particular category of 'other.' Such conduct did not so much challenge the moral order in its entirety as jeopardize a particular relationship. People who were treated inappropriately considered it disrespectful. The result could be anger which, in Cree terms, was an act governed by sentiment, dangerously unpredictable, and beyond the moral order.

BANDS AND TRIBES

The second problem involves prominent differences between communities regarding their internal political relations and their respective consciousness of themselves as a distinct entity capable of acting together for common benefit. We need only mention two broad types to indicate the organizational variability and diverse sensibilities that are involved when addressing the traditional Aboriginal situation: the so-called band and tribal societies. In Canada, the first of these predominates throughout the subarctic, the second is generally found south of the subarctic and along the southern coastal regions.

Band societies are notoriously labile in the traditional setting. For our purposes they could be characterized as quasiwholes, since they possessed weakly developed internal lines of authority at the band level and a correspondingly high degree of autonomy at the level of the domestic kin groups that composed them. Bands, as such, had only broadly defined interests in common (usually seasonal concerns over cooperative trading or hunting ventures). Typically leadership over the groups composing the band was task-specific and did not endure. Pervasive social influence simply did not extend beyond a small cluster of domestic groups. Consequently, for any number of reasons, domestic groups (and sometimes individuals) moved from one band to another with relative ease. For most of the subarctic region, there is evidence of considerable geographical movement across both social and dialect boundaries.

Tribal societies, by contrast, had a far more developed sense of membership and identity. They were also more hierarchical in composition and structure. Typically they had an ideology of nested units in which lineages (or something of the kind) composed the clans, and clans were the principle units of organization of the tribe. At each level there were representative positions that served to voice the interests of the lineage within the affairs of the clan or the clan within the tribe. The incumbents of the representative positions at each level were recognized authorities on many matters of collective concern. Not only were they authorized to speak on behalf of others on a whole range of issues, their decisions often had binding force. In contrast to band societies, furthermore, the units of tribal organization were neither so easily detached nor so easily incorporated should they come from elsewhere. This is not to say tribal organization was closed because tribes could – and frequently did – forge relations with other tribes, and there are several well-documented examples of this sort of alliance or confederacy. But members of a tribe had a much more developed sense of the coherence and integrity of the tribe *qua* tribe and, in contrast to band societies, could be decidedly less casual about such detachments or incorporations.

Perhaps the most significant contrast to be stressed here involves perspectives on authority. Band societies typically do not recognize any enduring authority at the level of the band. Rather they recognize centres of influence by which each member chooses to be swayed or not, as circumstances and leaders arise. Indeed, band leaders are well known for their inability to command or coerce a following. They, quite literally, are a product of followership, and if people cannot be persuaded to follow some initiative or enterprise then leadership simply dissipates. Relative to tribal society, therefore, the structure and political consciousness of a band is acephalous. It simply lacks any sense of permanent and pervasive representation at the level of the band and, in accord with this, it may also lack any clear sense of its own bounded-ness and durability as a social entity.

The importance of all this for the present discussion is that whatever opportunities exist to articulate special collective interests within a state organization, there are some traditional polities that are far less able to voice their interests in a manner that even roughly corresponds to their traditional institutions and political imagination. The reason is simple enough. Regardless of how solicitous and accommodating the state may be, it is necessarily disposed to deal with representatives of discrete populations and this, to a very large extent, is just what band societies do not possess. Thus, the self-determination of bands cannot be achieved without introducing considerations that are radically at odds with band organization. Indeed, if we are to judge from the current tendencies of consultants, bureaucrats, and media hacks – not to men-tion the various Aboriginal political leaders caught up in their discourse – it would appear that the self-determination of bands cannot even be thought without first thinking of them as quasitribes. All general talk of 'Native traditions' that gives sweeping reference to authoritative councils of 'elders,' codified rules and regulations, or tribal court sys-tems (with the presumption that someone within the community might be in a position to pass judgment on another), would thus seem to be rather more than just narrowly simplistic. It could also seem to indicate we are approaching a real conceptual limit on our ability to positively imagine a future for the self-determination of certain band-associated traditions within the state.

The above contrast between band and tribe is a formal one, and it should therefore be expected that distinctions are not nearly so sharply evident in actual situations. Still, a band form of organization is over-whelmingly apparent in the traditions of many Aboriginal groups, and we would like to draw out some specific implications of this in terms of what amounts to a band theory of social influence. Current Cree aspirations to develop along certain lines will serve as our thematic reference.

An ambition of every Cree in the traditional setting was to be able to anticipate and accommodate the world in an orderly manner. Order, however, was not simply there in the material or social world as some-thing to be learned about and applied. Rather, it was understood as a continuous achievement over the uncertainties of life. A hunter could never be complacent about his knowledge of animals and there were certainly times when interaction directed by sentiment was unavoidable.

The ability to deal with uncertainty was recognized to be a measure of a person's 'power' which, in turn, was understood as a product of a special relationship between that person and a spirit being. For most, such ability was simply evident in a capacity to cope adequately from season to season and year to year. However, a few were able to distinguish themselves by foretelling the future, influencing the weather, avoiding disasters that afflict others, or diverting the ill intentions of people from afar. They could be spoken of as people who were autonomous, who did not need others.

The status and prestige granted to persons with exceptional ability usually did not exceed the hunting group of which they were members. At most, they would carry their status and influence in a relatively narrow social sphere involving those groups with which they were in regular cooperative contact. This narrowness of social influence followed from the Cree belief that exceptional ability was derived from a source beyond society. It was not, therefore, understood to be a product of those relations that defined the moral order and for this reason, despite all the benefits that might follow from exceptional ability, it possessed an unpredictable and dangerous potential. This potential left open the possibility that, instead of conducting themselves according to the moral responsibilities of an 'older brother,' an 'uncle,' or a 'father,' people might act according to their own narrow desires, regardless – or even at the expense – of the well-being of other group members.

There were only a few ways in which this ambiguity could be offset. One was to avoid giving any impression of forcing or coercing others to do one's bidding. This general disinclination to give or receive an authoritative directive is evident in the very earliest documentary record for the general region. The strategy was to persuade. Any attempt to coerce would provoke large questions, because an act of coercion carried with it the open possibility that somebody was pursuing his or her interests regardless of the interests and concerns of others. Another way to offset ambiguity was to exercise exceptional ability for the tangible benefit of the group as a whole; this might manifest itself in resisting outside threats or in being able to anticipate and avoid potentially detrimental situations. Yet another way was to ensure that the quality and quantity of a person's contribution to collective well-being was never translated into a one-sided benefit, especially a one-sided material benefit. Thus, every member, according to need rather than capability or actual contribution and regardless of age or gender, had claim to a share of the produce of the group.

This manner of ensuring to group members that exceptional ability was, in a sense, an ability *for* them had several political implications. Central among these was that high status was narrowly circumscribed. People did not achieve high status unless it was demonstrably clear that their abilities were being directed to the collective well-being of the group. And such status was not maintained unless this was *continuously* demonstrated to be the case. This meant that those in infrequent contact did not assume that their respective abilities would necessarily be employed on behalf of each other. Indeed, since their abilities were already being exercised on behalf of specific groups, a Cree 'sociologic' would permit the inference that they might also be employed at the expense of all other groups.

In short, exceptional ability was morally suspect. There had to be a continuous demonstration of its beneficial application for the group for it to be received as trustworthy and the appropriate status granted. In these broad terms social influence was restricted and, for the most part, specific to a group. There was no enduring overarching position of influence that drew in even so much as an entire trapping community. To be sure, there were certain projects involving most or all of a community, and there would be one or a few who would direct the activities of the others in such situations. However, these were seasonal occurrences at most, and social influence did not extend beyond the project.

All of the above constitutes the substrate of the contemporary situation, with the difference that the traditional associative link between status, influence, decision-making, and collective well-being now exists less in experience than in the contemporary social imagination. Communities today are run as 'Bands,' an administrative creation of government that bears little or no relationship to the more traditional bands discussed earlier. The position of Chief now serves largely as a liaison to regional, provincial, and federal authorities, and as a conduit to various funding agencies. The social qualifications that previously were so closely linked to high status have, over the past few decades, become almost completely displaced by educational requirements. In addition, an increasingly wage-oriented, sedentary, and youthful population is now acutely aware that finite budgets and limited employment opportunities are distributed neither equally nor according to need. Inevitably, many feel their interests and concerns being left out of account, and progressively the administrator-leader is becoming, if we might put it so, a position of influence without status. Consequently, contemporary leadership often measures poorly when set against the moral probity surrounding the image that many Aboriginal people have of traditional leadership.

Partly in an effort to redress this lack, several Cree communities have even formed committees of elderly people for the purpose of providing direction and balanced judgment along traditional lines – for providing, in other words, the terms in which future decisions will be made in the hopes that the results will appear more satisfactorily directed towards the collective well-being than at present. These advisory committees, of course, do not represent a traditional institution at all. Rather they are a response to the evident absence in the contemporary setting of the kind of guidance, stability, and moral order that Cree strongly believe characterized life in the recent past. However, as most elderly people are quick to remark, there is little in their experience that has prepared them to assess the kind of domestic mayhem that is now so prevalent in their communities.

This last point is brought out most cogently by La Prairie (1992) in her report on justice issues in the Yukon. She remarks that not only is it the case that elders may harbour values not necessarily shared by other sectors of the community population, but 'the group over whom elders would exercise control in justice matters are the group likely to hold them in the lowest esteem. Those who most often identify elders as the appropriate group to assume control over justice by forming elders panels and elders councils are the middle-age people who hold elders in positions of respect and authority. The groups most often involved as offenders in the criminal justice system, youth and young people, do not necessarily share these perceptions' (ibid.: 112).

Tradition, the State, and the Problem of Accountability

A consideration that follows directly from the preceding discussion centres on the fact that all Native societies, regardless of their respective traditional heritage, have long since been drawn into a complex history of involvement with the state. This history, furthermore, has been asymmetrically experienced so that within each Native Canadian community there are radical divergencies in education, occupation, religious affiliation, political involvement, and so forth. This means that there are also quite different views on (and knowledge of), what passes for 'our traditions.' These traditions, we now know, are at the heart of considerations of 'self-determination.'

The importance of this is twofold. First, the rhetoric of self-determination makes no mention of the fact that at the community level there are a diverse plurality of potential 'selves' that might do the determining. Yet, it is now a commonplace in international development studies that the promise inherent in the shift to a 'self-determining' rationale has carried forward much of the original difficulty (see Griffin, 1981). The reason for this is that those who would administer and lead at the local or regional level have, in their education and through their experience, acquired a set of priorities and concerns that are far from representative. The result is that the general populace often feels very strongly that those who would establish priorities and implement policies on their behalf are strangers to their needs and desires, no less alien in their way than the state agencies that preceded them.

Second, the best that anyone can hope from the state is that it provide the mechanisms that permit communities to build on their own traditions and values in their attempts to respond and adapt to an ever-changing world. By definition the state cannot provide the substance of a community's response. However, it can hardly help but provide the general framework within which substantively distinct terms are expressed. And it is here, in the process of providing the framework for expressing distinctiveness and difference – we should even say for best expressing it – that every Aboriginal community is obliged to make its selection and develop its strategies of advantage and influence with regard *to* the state.

As we have indicated in the Cree example, there has been progressive development of a Cree administrative and political hierarchy in the past several decades. The decline of the fur market in the 1950s resulted in the convergence of various trapping communities; this was followed by the rise of administered bands in the 1960s and in 1975, the transformation of an aggregation of Cree bands emerged under the auspices of a regional authority after the JBNQA.

At each stage of the evolution of this hierarchy, new requirements and skills were expected of the incumbents who filled the available positions. The emphasis, however, was not directed inward on domestic and local issues; rather it was directed almost entirely outward. The focus was on learning the procedures and developing the strategies to effectively procure funding and garner advantage from provincial and federal agencies. For the most part, this external emphasis has also permitted a semblance of solidarity to be maintained between regional and community leadership, on the one hand, and between leadership generally and the Cree populace, on the other. An outward perspective, simply put, has provided the opportunity for the leadership to sustain the impression that the community is being externally thwarted in both voicing and realizing collective well-being.

There are, however, limits to maintaining this view of things. Some communities now wish to take over certain regional programs, just as many band members are not at all satisfied with the local provision of services. Part of the reason for this is that, in thinking about themselves and their needs, Cree leadership is inclined to do so in terms that are first and foremost influential in their dealings with non-Cree. It is here, for instance, where matters regarding 'tradition' are unavoidably drawn into a political discourse and, as already mentioned, it is certainly not uncommon to hear administrators and political leaders speaking of themselves and those they represent in terms that they know have wide currency among non-Cree but which, for all that, have little to do with their own social and cultural heritage.

The notion of a 'tribal court' is an obvious case in point. The model for this comes largely from the American situation and especially from the experience of certain Native American 'tribes' as understood in the sense already discussed at some length. But it is also a model that has been taken up by certain Cree largely because the lawyers, bureaucrats, and politicians with whom they are continuously negotiating possess a very generalized understanding of everything to do with Aboriginal peoples. It must also be stressed that many Cree politicians and administrators are composed of the educated young who have spent their time being trained by non-Cree and addressing problems that originate (at least in their formulation) beyond Cree society. For this reason, it cannot always be supposed that they are themselves outside of the traditionalist rhetoric they employ; nor are they particularly aware of just how inappropriate it might be in dealing with their own situation. In short, much is the product of a discourse between Cree and non-Cree and is geared largely to the limits of the latter. This is not at all the same as providing an agreeable, comprehensible or effective foundation for developing a community-based, socially realistic, and culturally meaningful alternative to what now exists, either in matters pertaining to justice or anything else. Indeed, it does little more than provide a model that non-Cree can understand. In the process it risks taking something that has been useful to Cree in handling their relations with non-Cree as if it were a model for Cree handling their relations with each other, a subtle but profound deflection of the hopes and ambitions of self-determination.

STATUS, RIGHTS, AND THE CIVIC TRADITION

We have now arrived at a stage where we can begin to appreciate the complexity and difficulty of addressing the notion of accountability. As we shall see, accountability has taken on its present form and character largely in opposition to virtually all traditions that preceded the emergence of the modern state. It has, in other words, developed in opposition to many of the traditions of those partial societies now embraced by state organizations. It is thus potentially at odds with prevailing thought on development and much political rhetoric regarding the idea that constructive and meaningful change can only be achieved by building on, elaborating, and preserving the traditions of those whose development it will be. But as we shall also see, this opposition is not the crucial problem surrounding accountability today.

Accountability is embraced by what has been rather loosely labelled the 'civic tradition,' something that has been associated with state development since early modern times (see Pocock, 1975; Robertson, 1983). From this vantage, the notion of accountability achieves meaning in relation to those attitudes, ideas, values, and perspectives that are often acknowledged as virtues in public service (that is, the recognition of individual rights, equality before the law, or an ethic of impartiality), which even today continue to receive attentive elaboration in the form of conflict-of-interest guidelines, say, or gender and employment issues in areas of justice, ethics, and public administration.

As several scholars (for example, Shennan, 1974; Skinner, 1989) have argued, the modern state came into being with a progressive shift in allegiance away from a single ruler towards a sort of abstract, collective singular that eventually came to be embodied in terms such as état, state or *Staat*. To make reference to the 'status' of a country was to remark on its overall well-being or *bon état*. Duties and obligations of individual subjects, as well as the idea of public influence were gradually and often contentiously realigned so that, as one author put it in 1516, 'the whole people must be above the King' (quoted in Skinner 1978: vol. 2, 120). Part of this realignment involved the secularization, as it were, of the notions of individual equality and universal humanity; old ideas, to be sure, but ones that retained an other-worldly association and application (namely equality in the kingdom of Heaven) until they obtruded into the stratified, hierarchical, and status-differentiated society of the late feudal (or early modern) era at the time that the modern state was emerging (Lewis, 1974: vol. 1, 195–7).[6]

Along with the rise of secular equality and the displaced importance of differences of status, role, and occupation, the modern notion of individual 'right' also emerged. As Daggers points out, this too involved a shift or displacement, 'for the concept of rights to appear and gain purchase, the status concepts had to lose their grip; and in order for this to happen, the idea that human beings are fundamentally alike had to displace the belief that differences in nationality, culture, or rank were rooted in natural differences between people' (Daggers 1989: 118).

What had been thought of as 'right or proper conduct' by reference to a differentiated moral or legal standard that was, so to speak, 'out there' in society progressively became conceived of as an attribute or property of each individual subject of the state. But whereas duties and obligations largely served to integrate people differentiated according to status and role, rights tend to atomize by setting the individual off against the encroaching activities of both other individuals and the state.

Thus, whatever else may be involved, accountability in its most prominent modern form requires a commitment to the notions of individuality, equality, and impartiality. This also means that an accountable person must be someone who is willing to situate himself or herself at the level of the social whole. In view of what we have learned about band society and custom, we know that high status and influence are inextricably linked with the capacity and inclination to contribute to the collective well-being (of the social whole). Consequently, in this respect the requisite level would seem to be met. Conversely, high status in a hunting setting is granted only on the condition that recipients voluntarily subordinate themselves to the *differentiated* framework defined by the duties and obligations of the moral order. This necessarily meant that a high status person did *not* interact with other members in their group from the vantage of the collectivity. Apart from the ethic of sharing produce according to need (which in any case applied to everyone in the group), a person capable of contributing to collective well-being registered his or her continued acceptability to the group by treating everyone in it differently (by reference to age, gender, and a vocabulary of kin terms).

This meant too that, regardless of the ability or status of any particular person, the traditional social whole was restricted in scope and, relative to the band or regional levels of organization traversing most aboriginal populations today, it was also very fragmented. The reason for this, as we have pointed out, is that high status and the influence associated with it required continued demonstration of both ability and voluntary subordination to the moral order. In the dispersed population of even three decades ago this meant relatively small groupings of people.

We have seen in the Cree example that in contemporary communities the leadership and those in influential and strategic positions are always having to contend with the charge that their actions are partisan, that because of their decisions and actions some grouping or other benefits more than the rest. Typically this charge points to the sort of restricted kin network that delineated high cooperation and mutual trust in the context of trapping communities in the past. However, such is the layered depth and awkwardness of interaction among most people in today's communities that almost anything in a person's history can be pointed at as the rationale for a decision to have gone one way rather than another. Why someone did or did not get a house, in other words, can be variously rationalized to promote the view that people in the service of the community are acquitting themselves in a very partial manner.

In reflecting on the options here it is instructive to examine some of the attempts to resolve this sort of thing as the so-called civic tradition began to emerge. One of the earliest illustrations is to be found in eleventh-century Europe where, in the context of emerging city-states, moves were being made beyond feudal society. These moves involved elected officials progressively displacing the influence of the occupants of noble houses, thus setting in motion a need to re-adjust the relations between ruler and ruled and, in the process, shifting both the character of social influence and the nature of accountability (Skinner, 1978: vol. 1, 3–4).

One of the central problems that this posed to the electorate was that nobody was logically situated at the required level or, rather, everyone was variously immersed in his own interests, priorities, and loyalties. The challenge was to find someone to expend public funds and administer common law for the benefit of all. But the process and, in a sense, the logic of finding such a person had to be created and the problem of doing so appears to have centred on how to find representatives of the whole who were not perpetually in danger of being perceived as *if* they were favouring certain parochial interests or were otherwise conducting themselves in a manner that did not appear equitable to all.

Several formal options existed. One not taken up, at least initially, was the schooling of a would-be incumbent in a 'civic tradition' that promoted the virtue and importance of administrative impartiality. Rather, the city-states in question developed a convention that entailed electing to public office a person who had no history of involvement with others in the city. The impartiality required for the position thus derived not from some supposed embrace of inner values but from the brute external fact of being a stranger. The disinterest that would ensure for the electorate a measure of impartiality in the administration of justice and in handling those disputes that inevitably arose from the convergence of different interests and loyalties in the life of the city was achieved by electing an incumbent from the citizenry of another city. Impartiality was thus achieved by selecting a person who had no history of partiality, and the social instability latent in representing the whole by one of its parts was overcome by selecting the part from another whole altogether.[7]

Interviews with contemporary Cree indicate similar leanings. When asked to suggest alternatives to the existing justice system, many recognized a formidable obstacle in finding people within the community who could both provide such crucial services as judging the conduct of others and do so in a manner that would not divide the community. The problem was not that there were no good and trustworthy people, rather it was one of achieving community acceptance. As several people observed, if local judges were *not* partisan, they would inevitably run up against those who thought they had a claim to some special consideration because of kinship or friendship. Conversely, if judges *were* partisan, they would run up against everyone else. It was their frequent conclusion that under such circumstances a person would probably have to move away from the community in order to do the job at all. It is also worth noting here that in many areas across the country the political agenda of certain Aboriginal leaders seeking to take over the justice system is cause for real alarm at the community level. Ross (1993) cites certain frightening abuses of band officials regarding intergenerational sexual activity. He also observes that some feel the devolution of authority for justice retains such possibilities for local abuse that it may actually produce an increase in social violence (ibid.: 14).

INTERSECTING TRADITIONS AND CONTENDING MODALITIES OF
ACCOUNTABILITY

In many modern states today there is, of course, a similar expectation regarding the impartial practices of public officials and elected representatives. A scandal is in the making if they do not continuously effect a distance from those individuals and interest groups with whom they may have some personal involvement. When such involvement arises, they are expected to dissociate. Procedures of a physical or symbolic character are often put in place to effect such removal. Police, for instance, are frequently stationed away from the community in which they were raised in order to offset the temptation to show preference to their former associates when enforcing the law. In the same vein, public officials are often obliged to take an oath of office binding their commitment to communal well-being or to follow conflict-of-interest guidelines and in various other ways ritually distance themselves from their own history of parochial involvements.

The ethical injunctions and attitudes of this so-called civic tradition pertain, we repeat, to the embracing level of the state. The history of the emergence of this tradition has clearly attempted to elevate the value of a perspective that is partial to no particular interest, that is committed to no value, that would elevate the concerns of no one group over any other in determining the interests of the state. This, of course, does not speak at all to the endless rumours and often turbulent attempts by special-interest groups to subordinate the "civic tradition" to their own concerns and ambitions. However, it is only recently that the values of other traditions are being granted the kind of elevated recognition that one finds today under the auspices of the right to self-determination.[8] Such a recognition rather awkwardly concedes that the collective well-being of individual members of the state requires the mediation of the social and cultural traditions of those partial societies that embrace individuals within the state. This is awkward, of course, because those traditions may not themselves recognize or embrace a "civic tradition." Indeed, there may be much in the idea of the ageless, genderless, statusless, occupationless abstraction of the individual that is found objectionable. There may also be much in the idea of impartiality that is meaningless, since articulate social life may hinge on conceding, permitting, or promoting certain things to, say, women and not men, the elderly but not the youthful, this lineage but not that one. The idea of accountability within this other tradition may thus take on an entirely different

474 Prospects in Canadian Aboriginal Justice Systems

character, one that may exercise a nuanced or even contradictory variance to that found in the "civic tradition."

Awkwardness, however, does not necessarily imply impossibility, and it is quite conceivable that the civic and the multiplicity of other-than-civic traditions could somehow coexist under certain conditions. The state, for instance, might simply not intrude beyond the boundaries of all those developing, self-determining societies that compose it. Impartiality and equality might be exercised only in the relations between substate societies or in relations between individuals from different societies. Otherwise, these societies might look after themselves, according to their own traditions.

The flaw in this is that we do not anywhere have merely societies subjacent to the state. Rather we have partial societies, which is to say societies that have a history – and typically a very protracted and involved one – *within* the state. Because of this, these societies do not represent some clear, monadic alternative even to themselves. They are intersected through and through with considerations that emanate from and reach out towards traditions beyond their own. Furthermore, this intersection has been so pervasive in certain areas that it is no longer possible to tell where one tradition leaves off and another begins. This is crucially true when it comes to what we have been calling the "civic tradition," for there are probably few members of any substate tradition that do not place very considerable value on an ethic of impartiality, equality before the law, and, in some measure, individual rights. It is precisely this that configures the problem of accountability. It is not a question of being faced with clear alternatives where one can say, "Here is where this takes place and there that takes place; here is where people think, believe, and evaluate matters in one way and there where they conduct themselves otherwise." Were this so we might, as indicated, begin to conceive of some way in which these clearly distinct traditions might articulate.

As it is, the very idea of contextual clarity is misleading. Indeed, with regard to accountability, it is grossly distorting to represent differences of tradition in terms of the clear and simple contrasts evident in the words of the Metis and Non-Status Indian Constitutional Review Committee, "The value system of the dominant socio-cultural system in Canada is liberalism which places emphasis on the individual, individual rights and private property. This is in contrast to the value system of Native peoples which places a far higher value on the collectivity or upon the community" (Ponting and Gibbins, 1986: 21).

We need only remind ourselves of the efforts of the Native Women's Association of Canada to insist that women receive a voice equal to that of men in recent constitutional/self-government deliberations to realize just how inept the above characterization actually is. Moreover, it dangerously oversimplifies and thereby conceals the complex sorts of mayhem that now pervade virtually all Aboriginal communities. This is not to deny a certain truth to the contrast relative to, say, the aggregation or perfect strangers that typically compose an urban Canadian setting. However, it hardly tells us anything much about how seriously in disarray this aspect of the so-called Native value system is in its present application. Canadian cities are full of urban refugees from the neglect, domestic violence, and sexual abuse of community life in many Aboriginal settlements.

This should not in any way dilute or weaken the thrust of conclusions arrived at three decades ago. For change to be of constructive advantage it must have meaning for those who will experience it, and an unquestionable condition of meaning is tradition. Still, as indicated, the traditions of any society are neither static, homogeneous, nor necessarily coherent. Certainly, Aboriginal societies in Canada would appear to be largely composed of people who simultaneously place value on both a 'civic tradition' and on traditions that in many respects are contradictory to this 'civic tradition.'

In consequence, there are contending modalities of accountability circulating in virtually everyone's mind, and the question for Aboriginal people is how to sort them out. From the outside it would seem that no non-Aboriginal could possibly be in a position to rationalize an adequate process with any condidence. There are simply too many imponderables and we already know the dangers of allowing a dialogue between Aboriginals and non-Aboriginals too much prominence. But, as we have also tried to make clear and as many Aboriginal people are now acutely aware, things are not greatly advanced by listening too intently to any single voice from the inside either, because contemporary Aboriginals themselves value and assess tradition quite differently depending on their place in the community. To put it otherwise, there is for Aboriginal communities in general no one now who can claim, with confidence and realistic advantage, to speak for the interests of the whole society when examining the best way to address relations *within*.

What has begun to emerge in many Aboriginal communities is the beginning of an internal dialogue involving people from many diverse sectors of contemporary populations (such as hunters, administrators, youth, women, Pentecostals, or Native spiritualists). This is to be applauded wherever it occurs since it seems the only hope for discovering in contemporary communities what substrate of cultural commonality such diversity might still possess. It also seems one of the few avenues for discovering a meaningful guide for developing institutions and arrangements that, although derived from the past, are intended to serve the needs of the present and the future. The results, however, cannot be anticipated in advance, and nothing will substitute for the evaluative weightings, priorities, and solutions that emerge from such community conversations. Developments so far seem very promising, and certainly some of the real challenges of what lies ahead are becoming clearer. However, as many Aboriginal communities are discovering, there are no shortcuts and no easy answers in developing their own cultural possibilities within present organizational arrangements.

Acknowledgment. I must record my gratitude to my colleague, Dr Sheila Van Wyck, for her very constructive criticism and advice during the writing of this piece.

Notes

1 The main source here will be the findings of phase 1 of the 'Justice for the Cree' Project among Cree of East James Bay in northern Quebec. This comprehensive contemporary study is presented in separate reports on the sociology of the present justice system (La Prairie, 1991), policing and alternate justice processes (Brodeur, 1991b), and the relevance of customary beliefs and practices (McDonnell, 1992). Reports and examples from other areas of the country will, however, also be introduced.
2 See, for example, Walzer (1983), White (1991), and Taylor (1989), to name only a few.
3 The mountainous literature surrounding the notion of "development" has received useful review at the hands of Kitching (1982), Robertson (1983), and Worsley (1984). Our remarks apply mainly to the failed application of the so-called Western theory of modernization. From the vantage point of the recipients, however, both the Western and Soviet versions were recognized as variants of an inappropriate European cultural thematic.
4 These figures vary, depending on the community.
5 See Brodeur (1991b) on police training in this context.

6 As Dumont (1985: 93–122) observes, these ideas go back to the Stoics and early Christians and are at the root of virtually all Western legal, political, and ethical thinking on the individual today. Nonetheless, the reasons for the secularization of the concepts of a universalized and equal humanity are still not convincingly settled (see Dumont 1970: 31–41; Burridge 1979: 144–90).

7 Very little was taken for granted in these early cases. Not only was the term of office short but elected officials were, at the end of their tenure, obliged to provide for the electorate an account of their financial dealings and legal judgments before they were permitted to leave the city and return home. In other words, incumbents were obliged to give a satisfactory account of themselves to complete their term of office.

8 We speak here from the vantage of current affairs and the juxtaposition we are trying to sketch from the admittedly narrow aperture of recent shifts in thought about development. An intricate and circuitous conversation involving both communitarian and individualist themes has been under way for a very long time. In a valiant attempt to provide resuscitation to an ailing liberal tradition, Kymlicka (1989) provides an interesting and useful review of many of the issues and protagonists.

Cases

Anns v. Merton London Borough Council [1978] A.C. 728
Arbon v. Anderson [1943] 1 K.B. 252
Andrews v. Law Society of British Columbia [1989] 1 S.C.R. 143

Bains v. National Parole Board [1989] 3 F.C. 450
Balderstone v. R. (1984) 8 C.C.C. (3rd) 532
Barratt v. District of North Vancouver [1980] 2 S.C.R. 418
Barreau de Montreal v. Wagner [1968] B.R. 235
Barton v. The Queen (1980/81) 147 C.L.R. 75
Beauchamp, Ex Parte (1971) 1 C.C.C. (2d) 101
Beaumier v. National Parole Board [1981] 1 F.C. 454
Becker v. Home Office [1972] 2 Q.B. 407
Bell v. D.P.P. of Jamaica [1985] A.C. 937
Boucher v. The Queen [1955] S.C.R. 16
Burt v. Governor General [1992] 3 N.Z.L.R. 672

City of Kamloops v. Neilsen [1984] 2 S.C.R. 2
Cleary v. Correctional Service of Canada (1990) 44 Admin.L.R. 142
Collins, Ex Parte (1977) 30 C.C.C. (2d) 460
Commission of Inquiry, Re (1979) 94 D.L.R. (3d) 365
Connelly v. D.P.P. [1964] A.C. 1254
Copeland, Re (1978) 88 D.L.R. (3d) 724
Council of Civil Service Unions v. Minister for the Civil Service
    ('G.C.H.Q. Case') [1985] A.C. 374

Director of Public Prosecutions *v.* Humphreys [1977] A.C. 1

Fisher *v.* Oldham [1930] 2 K.B. 364

Gaw and Yeomans, Re (1985) 14 C.C.C. (3d) 134
Gillen *v.* Law Society of British Columbia (1985) 63 B.C.L.R. 1
Githunguri *v.* Republic of Kenya [1986] L.R.C. (Const.) 618
Gough *v.* National Parole Board (1991) 3 C.R. (4th) 325
Gouriet *v.* Union of Post Office Workers [1977] Q.B. 729; [1978] A.C. 435
Grabina and The Queen, Re (1977) 34 C.C.C. (2d) 52

Hague *v.* Deputy Governor of Parkhurst Prison [1991] 3 All E.R. 733
Hoem and the Law Society of British Columbia, Re (1985) 20 C.C.C (3d)
    239
Home Office *v.* Dorset Yacht Co. Ltd. [1970] A.C. 1004
Howard *v.* Presiding Officer of Inmate Disciplinary Court of Stony
    Mountain Institution (1985) 45 C.R. (3d) 242
Howarth *v.* National Parole Board (1975) 18 C.C.C. (2d) 385

Illinois *v.* Stephen O'Neil, Film Recovery Systems, Inc. etc. [1990] 550
    N.E. 2d. 1090; 194 Ill. App 3d. 79

Jane Doe *v.* Metropolitan Toronto Board of Police Commissioners (1990)
    74 O.R. (2d) 225; (1991) 1 O.R. (3d) 416
Just *v.* British Columbia [1989] 2 S.C.R. 1228

Laurentide Motels Ltd. *v.* Beauport (City) [1989] 1 S.C.R. 705

MacKeigan *v.* Hickman (1989) 61 D.L.R. (4th) 688
Martineau *v.* Matsqui Institution Disciplinary Board [1980] 1 S.C.R. 602
McCaud, Ex Parte [1965] 1 C.C.C. 168
McDonald and The Queen, Re (1981) 56 C.C.C. (2d) 1
Mitchell *v.* The Queen [1976] 2 S.C.R. 570
Murphy *v.* Brentwood District Council [1991] 1 A.C. 414

National Parole Board *v.* Gough (1991) 3 C.R. (4th) 346
Nelles and Grange, Re (1984) 9 D.L.R. (4th) 79
Nelles *v.* R. in right of Ontario et al. [1989] 2 S.C.R. 170
Nicholson *v.* Haldimand-Norfolk Regional Board of Police Commission-
    ers, [1979] 1 S.C.R. 311

Noonan *v.* National Parole Board [1983] 2 F.C. 772

Oag *v.* R. (1983) 33 C.R. (3d) 111
Operation Dismantle Inc. *v.* R. [1985] 1 S.C.R. 441

People *v.* Warner-Lambert Co. (1980) 51 N.Y. 2d. 295; 414 N.E. 2d 660; 434
    N.Y.S. 2d 159
Phillips *v.* Ford Motor Co. [1971] 2 O.R. 637
Police *v.* National Parole Board (1990) 44 Admin. L.R. 236

The Queen *v.* Beauregard [1986] 2 S.C.R. 56

Raymond *v.* Honey [1982] 1 All E.R. 756
Reference re Section 94(2) of the Motor Vehicle Act (1985) 23 C.C.C. (3d)
    289
Reference re Milgaard (Can.) (1992) 90 D.L.R. (4th) 1
Rothfield *v.* Manolakos [1989] 2 S.C.R. 1259
Rourke *v.* The Queen (1977) 35 C.C.C (2d) 129
R. *v.* Askov [1990] 2 S.C.R. 1199
R. *v.* Beare [1988] 2 S.C.R. 387
R. *v.* Bennett (1991) 6 C.R. (4th) 22
R. *v.* Boucher [1955] S.C.R. 16
R. *v.* Brixton Prison (Governor) and Another, Ex parte Enahoro [1963] 2
    All E.R. 477
R. *v.* Catagas (1977) 38 C.C.C. (2d) 296
R. *v.* Commissioner of Police of the Metropolis, Ex parte Blackburn
    [1968] 2 Q.B. 118
R. *v.* Croydon Justices, Ex parte Dean [1993] 3 W.L.R. 198
R. *v.* Director of Public Prosecutions, Ex parte B (a minor) [1993] 1 All
    E.R. 756
R. *v.* Ertel (1988) 35 C.C.C. (3d) 398
R. *v.* Hamilton (1992) 10 C.R. (4th) 385
R. *v.* Home Secretary, Ex parte Bentley (1993) 143 *New Law Journal* L.R.
    1025–6
R. *v.* Hull Prison Board of Visitors, Ex parte St. Germain [1979] 3 All E.R.
    545
R. *v.* Jewitt (1985) 21 C.C.C. (3d) 7
R. *v.* Keyowski (1988) 40 C.C.C. (3d) 481
R. *v.* Kopyto (1988) 39 C.C.C. (3d) 1
R. *v.* Marshall (1983) 57 N.S.R. (2d) 286

Statutes

Australia

Commonwealth
Archives Act, 1983, No. 79
Australian Security Intelligence Organization Act, 1979, No. 113
Director of Public Prosecutions Act, 1983, No. 113
Inspector-General of Intelligence and Security Act, 1986, No. 101

New South Wales
Director of Public Prosecutions Act, 1986, No. 207

Queensland
Director of Public Prosecutions Act, 1984, No. 95

Victoria
Director of Public Prosecutions Act, 1982, No. 9848

Canada

Province of Canada (1840–1867)
    1841 (4 & 5 Vict.), c. 24
County Attorneys Act, 1857 (20 Vict.), c. 59

Canada (Federal) (1867 onwards)
Access to Information Act, RSC 1985, c. A-1
Auditor General Act, RSC 1985, c. A-17
Canadian Bill of Rights, RSC 1985, Appx. III
Canadian Charter of Rights and Freedoms, RSC 1985, Appx. II, No. 44,
    Schedule B, Part I

Constitution Act, 1867, RSC 1985, Appx. II, No. 5
Constitution Act, 1982, RSC 1985, Appx. II, No. 44, Schedule B
Corrections and Conditional Release Act, 1992, c. 20
Cree-Naskapi (of Quebec) Act, 1977, c. 18
Criminal Code, RSC 1985, c. C-46
Criminal Law Amendment Act, 1976–7, c. 51
Criminal Law Amendment Act, RSC 1985, c. 27 (1st Supp.)
Canadian Security Intelligence Service Act, RSC 1985, c. C-23
Department of the Solicitor General Act, RSC 1985, c. S-13
Federal Court Act, RSC 1985, c. F-7
Food and Drugs Act, RSC 1985, c. F-27
Government Organization Act, 1966–7, c. 25
Income Tax Amendment Act, 1970–1–2, c. 63
Migratory Birds Convention Act, RSC 1985, c. M-7
Official Secrets Act, RSC 1985, c. O-5
Parliament of Canada Act, RSC 1985, c. P-1
Parole Act, 1958, c. 38
Parole Act, RSC 1970, c. 31 (1st Supp.)
Parole Act, RSC 1985, c. P-2
Parole Amendment Act, 1986, c. 42
Penitentiary Act, 1867
Penitentiary Act, 1883
Penitentiary Act, RSC 1985, c. P-5
Privacy Act, RSC 1985, c. P-21
Royal Canadian Mounted Police Act, RCS 1985, c. R-10
Security Offences Act, RSC 1985, c. S-7
Ticket of Leave Act, 1899

Nova Scotia
Public Prosecutions Act, 1990, c. 21

Ontario
Law Society of Upper Canada Act , RSO 1990, c. L.8
Ministry of the Attorney General Act , RSO 1990, c. M.17
Proceedings Against the Crown Act, RSO 1990, c. P.27
Securities Act, RSO 1990, c. S.5

Europe

European Convention for the Protection of Human Rights and
Fundamental Freedoms, 1951

New Zealand

New Zealand Bill of Rights, 1990, No. 109
Sweden

Work Environment Act, 1977

United Nations

Covenant on Human Rights, 1948

United Kingdom

Criminal Justice Act, 1991, c. 53
Local Government Act, 1985, c. 51
Police Act, 1964, c. 48
Police and Criminal Evidence Act, 1984, c. 60
Police and Magistrates' Court Bill, 1994
Prison Act, 1952, c. 52
Prosecution of Offences Act, 1985, c. 23
Security Service Act, 1989, c. 5

United States of America

Employee Retirement and Income Security Act, 1974, U.S. Code 1988,
    Title 29, 1001 et seq.
National Security Act, 1947, c. 343, 61 Stat. 495
Occupational Safety and Health Act, 1970, U.S. Code 1988, Title 29,
    651 et seq.

References

Abel, R., ed. 1982. *The Politics of Informal Justice*. New York: Academic

Abolafia, M. 1985 'Self-Regulation as Market Maintenance: An Organisation Perspective,' in R.G. Noll, ed., *Regulatory Policy and the Social Sciences*, pp. 312–47. Berkeley: University of California Press

– and N. Biggart. 1992. 'Competitive Systems: A Sociological View,' in P. Ekins and M. Max-Neef, eds., *Real-Life Economics: Understanding Wealth Creation*, pp. 315–22. London: Routledge

Abrahamsson, B., and A. Brostrom. 1980. *The Rights of Labor*. Beverly Hills: Sage

Adams, W., and J. Brock. 1986. *The Bigness Complex: Industry, Labor, and Government in the American Economy*. New York: Pantheon

– 1987. 'Bigness and Social Efficiency: A Case Study of the U.S. Auto Industry,' in W.J. Samuels and A.S. Miller, eds., *Corporations and Society: Power and Responsibility*, pp. 219–37. New York: Greenwood

– 1989. *Dangerous Pursuits: Mergers and Acquisitions in the Age of Wall Street*. New York: Pantheon

– 1991. *Antitrust Economics on Trial: A Dialogue on the New Laissez-Faire*. Princeton: Princeton University Press

Adelberg, S., and C.D. Batson. 1978. 'Accountability and Helping: When Needs Exceed Resources.' *Journal of Personality and Social Psychology* 36: 343–50

Aglietta, M. 1979. *A Theory of Capitalist Regulation: The U.S. Experience*. London: New Left Books

Aglon, M. 1990. 'Washington's Discretionary Immunity Doctrine and Negligent Early Release Decisions: Parole and Work Release.' *Washington Law Review* 65: 619–37

Alberta Law Reform Institute. 1991. *Public Inquiries* (Issues Paper No. 3). Edmonton: Alberta Law Reform Institute
– 1992. *Proposals for the Reform of the Public Inquiries Act* (Report No. 62). Edmonton: Alberta Law Reform Institute
Alboini, V.P. 1980. *Ontario Securities Law.* Toronto. DeBoo
Algoma et al. (Joint Brief). 1978. *Brief to the Standing Committee on the Administration of Justice.* Toronto: Legislation of Ontario
Allport, G.W. 1937. *Personality: A Psychological Interpretation.* New York: Holt
Altman, A. 1990. *Critical Legal Studies: A Liberal Critique.* Princeton, N.J.: Princeton University Press
Anderson, P.A. 1981. 'Justifications and Precedents as Constraints in Foreign Policy Decision-Making.' *American Journal of Political Science* 25: 738–61
Andrews, A. 1992. *Review of Race Relations Practices of the Metropolitan Toronto Police Force.* Toronto: Metropolitan Toronto Audit Department
Armstrong, F., and K. Chasse. 1975. 'The Right to an Independent Prosecutor.' *Criminal Reports* (new series) 28: 160–210
Ashworth, A. 1984. 'Techniques of Guidance on Sentencing.' [1984] *Criminal Law Review* 519–30
Atiyah, P. 1983. *Law and Modern Society.* New York: Oxford University Press
Atkey, R. 1989. 'Accountability for Security Intelligence Activity in Canada: The New Structure,' in P. Hanks and J. D. McCamus, eds., *National Security: Surveillance and Accountability in a Democratic Society,* pp. 37–42. Cowansville: Les Editions Yvon Blais
Australia, Inspector-General of Intelligence and Security. 1987. *Annual Report, 1986–87.* Canberra. Government Publishing Service
– 1988. *Annual Report, 1987–88.* Canberra: Australian Government Publishing Service
Australia, Law Reform Commission. 1975. *Complaints Against the Police* (Report No. 1). Canberra: Australian Government Publishing Service
– Royal Commission of Inquiry into Aboriginal Deaths in Custody. 1991. *Report.* Canberra: Australian Government Publishing Service
– Royal Commission on Australia's Security and Intelligence Agencies. 1985. *Report on the Australian Security Intelligence Organization* (Hope Report). Canberra: Australian Government Publishing Service
Ayres, I., and J. Braithwaite. 1991. 'Tripartism: Regulatory Capture and Empowerment.' *Law and Social Inquiry* 16: 435–96
Bagehot, W. 1968. *The English Constitution.* London: Collins
Bailey, E. 1981. 'Contestability and the Design of Regulatory and Antitrust Policy.' *American Economic Review* 71: 178–83
Baillie, J.C. 1973. 'Securities Regulation in the Seventies,' in J.S. Ziegel, ed.,

Studies in Canadian Company Law, vol. 2, pp. 343–99. Toronto: Butterworths

– and V. Alboini. 1977–8. 'The National Sea Decision – Exploring the Parameters of Administrative Discretion,' *Canadian Business Law Journal* 2: 454–70

Bandura, A. 1977. 'Self-efficacy: Toward a Unifying Theory of Behavioral Change.' *Psychological Review* 84: 191–215

Barnett, H. 1992. 'Hazardous Waste, Distributional Conflict, and a Trilogy of Failures.' *Journal of Human Justice* 3: 93–110

Barrile, L. 1992. 'Has the Corporate Veil Really Been Pierced?' *Critical Criminologist* 4: 3–4

Barth, A. 1955. *Government by Investigation.* New York: Viking

Barth, P. (with H. Allan Hunt). 1982. *Workers' Compensation and Work Related Illnesses and Diseases.* Cambridge: MIT Press

Baskett, G.D. 1973. 'Interview Decisions as Determined by Competency and Attitude Similarity.' *Journal of Applied Psychology* 57: 343–5

Bauman, Z. 1990 'Modernity and Ambivalence,' in M. Featherstone, ed., *Global Culture: Nationalism, Globalization, and Modernity,* pp. 143–9. London: Sage

Baumeister, R.F. 1982. 'A Self-presentational View of Social Phenomena.' *Psychological Bulletin* 91: 3–26

Baumol, W. 1982. 'Contestable Markets: An Uprising in the Theory of Industry Structure.' *American Economic Review* 72: 1–15

Bayley, D.H. 1983. 'Accountability and Control of Police: Lessons for Britain,' in T. Bennett, ed., *The Future of Policing,* pp. 146–62. Cambridge: Cropwood Conferences Series No. 15

– 1985a. *Patterns of Policing: A Comparative International Perspective,* New Brunswick: Rutgers University Press

– 1985b. 'The Tactical Choices of Patrol Officers.' *Journal of Criminal Justice* 14: 329–48

– 1989. 'Community Policing in Australia: An Appraisal,' in D.T. Chappell and P. Wilson, eds., *Australian Policing: Contemporary Issues,* pp. 63–82. Sydney: Butterworths

– 1991. *Forces of Order.* Berkeley: University of California Press

– 1992. 'Comparative Organization of the Police in English-Speaking Countries,' in M. Tonry and N. Morris, eds., *Modern Policing,* Chicago: University of Chicago Press

– 1994. 'Police Brutality Abroad,' in H. Toch and W. Geller, eds., *Police Use of Excessive Force and Its Control: Key Issues Facing the Nation.* Washington, DC: National Institute of Justice

– and E. Bittner. 1984. 'Learning the Skills of Policing.' *Law and Contemporary Problems* 47: 35–59

– and J. Garofalo. 1989. 'The Management of Violence of Police Patrol Officers.' *Criminology* 27: 1–25

Beaumont, P.B., and J.W. Leopold. 1982. 'The State of Workplace Health and Safety in Britain,' in C. Jones and J. Stevenson, eds., *The Year Book of Social Policy in Britain*, pp. 102–3. London: Routledge and Kegan Paul

Beccaria, C. 1770. *An Essay on Crimes and Punishments*. London: Newberry

Bell, D. 1973. *The Coming of Post-Industrial Society*. New York: Basic Books

Bellemare, D. 1985. 'Le nouveau mandat d'enquête créé par la Loi sur le Service canadien du renseignement de sécurité.' *Revue générale de droit* 16: 335–61

Ben-Yoav, O., and D.G. Pruitt. 1984. 'Accountability to Constituents: A Two-edged Sword.' *Organizational Behavior and Human Performance* 34: 283–95

Bennett, F.W. 1990. 'A Direct Participant's Perspective on the Guideline Amendment Process.' *Federal Sentencing Reporter* 3: 148–51

Bennett, T. 1990. *Evaluating Neighbourhood Watch*. Aldershot: Gower

Bergman, D. 1991. *Deaths at Work: Accidents or Corporate Crime?* London: Workers Education Association

Berman, D.M. 1978. *Death on the Job*. New York: Monthly Review Press

Beynon, H., R. Hudson, and D. Sadler. 1991. *A Tale of Two Industries: The Contraction of Coal and Steel in the North East of England*. Milton Keynes: Open University Press

Birkinshaw, P. 1985. 'An Ombudsman for Prisoners,' in M. Maguire, J. Vagg, and R. Morgan, eds., *Accountability and Prisons: Opening Up a Closed World*, pp. 165–74. London: Travistock

Blais, J.J. 1989. 'The Political Accountability of Intelligence Agencies – Canada.' *Intelligence and National Security* 4: 108–18

Blake, W. 1793/1965. 'Proverbs of Hell,' in W. Erdman and H. Bloom, eds., *The Poetry and Prose of William Blake*, pp. 35–9. New York: Doubleday

Blau, P. 1964. *Exchange and Power in Social Life*. New York: Wiley

Block, F. 1992. 'Capitalism without Class Power.' *Politics and Society* 20: 277–303

Block, M.K. 1989. 'Emerging Problems in the Sentencing Commission's Approach to Guideline Amendments.' *Federal Sentencing Reporter* 1: 451–5

Bluestone, B., and B. Harrison. 1982. *The Deindustrialization of America*. New York: Basic Books

Blum-West, S., and T.J. Carter. 1983. 'Bringing White-Collar Crime Back in: An Examination of Crime and Torts.' *Social Problems* 30: 545–54

Bok, S. 1982. *Secrets: On the Ethics of Concealment and Revelation*. New York: Pantheon

Bork, R. 1978. *The Antitrust Paradox*. New York: Basic Books

Bottoms, A.E. 1990. 'The Aims of Imprisonment,' in *Justice, Guilt, and Forgiveness in the Penal System*. Edinburgh: Edinburgh University Centre for Theology and Public Issues, Paper No. 18

Bouza, A.V. 1990. *The Police Mystique*. New York: Plenum

Box, S. 1983. *Power, Crime, and Mystification*. London: Tavistock

Bradley, D., N. Walker, and R. Wilkie. 1986. *Managing the Police: Law, Organization, and Democracy.* Brighton: Wheatsheaf Books

Braithwaite, J. 1984. *Corporate Crime in the Pharmaceutical Industry.* London: Routledge and Kegan Paul

– 1985. *To Punish or Persuade: Enforcement of Coal Mine Safety.* Albany: State University of New York Press

– 1989. *Crime, Shame, and Reintegration*. Cambridge: Cambridge University Press

Bray, H.S. 1967. 'Recent Developments in Securities Administration in Ontario: The Securities Act, 1966,' in J.S. Ziegel, ed., *Studies in Canadian Company Law,* vol. 1, pp. 415–51. Toronto: Butterworths

– 1975. 'Ontario's Proposed Securities Act: An Overview. Its Purposes and Policy Premises.' *Ontario Securities Commission Bulletin,* October: 235–70

Brill, H. 1992. 'Government Breaks the Law: The Sabotaging of the Occupational Safety and Health Act.' *Social Justice* 19: 63–81

Brockner, J., and J.Z. Rubin. 1985. *Entrapment in Escalating Conflicts: A Social Psychological Analysis*. New York: Springer-Verlag

Brodeur, J.P. 1991a. 'Countering Terrorism in Canada,' in S. Farson, D. Stafford, and W.K. Wark, eds., *Security and Intelligence in a Changing World: New Perspectives for the 1990s,* pp. 182–200. London: Frank Cass

– 1991b. *Justice for the Cree: Policing and Alternative Dispute Resolution*. Quebec: Grand Council of the Crees (Quebec) and Cree Regional Authority

Brody, S. 1976. *The Effectiveness of Sentencing*: *A Review of Literature* (Home Office Research Study No. 35). London: HMSO

Brogden, M. 1977. 'A Police Authority: The Denial of Conflict.' *Sociological Review* 25: 325–49

Brown, M. 1981. *Working the Street: Police Discretion and the Dilemmas of Reform*. New York: Russell Sage Foundation

Burridge, K.O. L.B. 1979. *Someone, No One: An Essay on Individuality.* Princeton: Princeton University Press

Byrne, D., D. Nelson, and K. Reeves. 1966. 'Effects of Consensual Validation and Invalidation on Attraction as a Function of Verifiability.' *Journal of Experimental Social Psychology* 2: 98–107

Cadieux, F. 1990. *The Requirement to Consult in the CSIS Act*. Ottawa: Staff Report, CSIS Act Review, 25 April

Cairns, A. 1990. 'Reflections on Commission Research,' in P. Pross, I. Christie, and J. Yogis, eds., *Commissions of Inquiry,* pp. 87–108. Agincourt: Carswell

Calavita, K. 1983. 'The Demise of the Occupational Safety and Health Administration: A Case Study in Symbolic Action.' *Social Problems* 30: 437–48

California, Independent Commission on the Los Angeles Police Department.
1991. *Report*. Los Angeles: Independent Commission

Canada, Auditor General. 1990. *Report of the Auditor General of Canada to the
House of Commons*. Ottawa: Minister of Supply and Services

– Board of Investigation. 1988. (Chairwoman, J. Pepino) *Unlawfully at Large
Inmate on Unescorted Temporary Absence, Montgomery Centre*. Ottawa: Ministry
of the Solicitor General

– Canadian Committee on Corrections. 1969. (Chairman, R. Ouimet) *Toward
Unity: Criminal Justice and Corrections*. Ottawa: Queen's Printer

– Canadian Sentencing Commission. 1987. (Chairman J.R.O. Archambault) *Sentencing Reform: A Canadian Approach*. Ottawa: Minister of Supply and Services

– Commission of Inquiry Concerning Certain Activities of the Royal Canadian
Mounted Police. 1981a. (Chairman, D. McDonald) Second Report, *Freedom and
Security under the Law*, 2 vols. Ottawa: Minister of Supply and Services

– 1981b. (Chairman, D. McDonald) Third Report, *Certain RCMP Activities and the
Question of Governmental Knowledge*. Ottawa: Minister of Supply and Services

Canada, Committee to Inquire into the Principles and Procedures Followed in
the Remission Service of the Department of Justice. 1956. (Chairman, G. Fauteux) *Report*. Ottawa: Queen's Printer

– Correctional Services Canada. 1991. *Basic Facts about Corrections in Canada*.
Ottawa: Correctional Services Canada

– Department of Justice. 1983. *The Position of the Attorney General of Canada on
Certain Recommendations of the McDonald Commission*. Ottawa: Department of
Justice

– 1987a. *Access and Privacy: The Steps Ahead*. Ottawa: Minister of Supply and Services

– 1987b. *Survey of Public Attitudes Toward Justice Issues in Canada*. (Prepared by
Environics Research Group Ltd.) Ottawa: Department of Justice

Canada, House of Commons. 1989. *Standing Orders*. Ottawa: Canadian Government Publishing Centre

– Public Accounts Committee. 1991. *Minutes of Proceedings and Evidence*
(No. 7, October 10). Ottawa: House of Commons

– Special Committee on the Review of the Canadian Security Intelligence Service Act and the Security Offences Act. 1989–90. Minutes of Proceedings and
Evidence (Nos. 1–36). Ottawa: House of Commons

– 1990. *In Flux but Not in Crisis*. Ottawa: Queen's Printer

Canada, House of Commons, Standing Committee on Justice and the Solicitor
General. 1987. *Open and Shut: Enhancing the Right to Know and the Right to Pri-*

vacy: Report of the Standing Committee on Justice and Solicitor General on the Review of the Access to Information Act and the Privacy Act. Ottawa: Queen's Printer

– 1988. (Chairman, D. Daubney) *Taking Responsibility: Report on Its Review of Sentencing, Conditional Release, and Related Aspects of Corrections.* Ottawa: House of Commons

– 1990. *Minutes of Proceedings and Evidence* (Issue No. 29, April 10). Ottawa: House of Commons

– 1991. *Second Report* (October 9). Ottawa: House of Commons

Canada, Law Reform Commission. 1974. *Principles of Sentencing and Dispositions* (Working Paper No. 3). Ottawa: Information Canada

– 1975. *Imprisonment and Release* (Working Paper No. 11). Ottawa: Information Canada

– 1976a. *A Report on Dispositions and Sentences in the Criminal Process: Guidelines.* Ottawa: Information Canada

– 1976b. *The Parole Process: A Study of the National Parole Board* (by P. Carriere and S. Silverstone). Ottawa: Law Reform Commission of Canada

– 1976c. *Permission to be Slightly Free: A Study of the Granting, Refusing, and Withdrawing of Parole in Canadian Penitentiaries* (by P. Macnaughton-Smith). Ottawa: Supply and Services Canada

– 1977. *Commissions of Inquiry* (Working Paper No. 17). Ottawa: Minister of Supply and Services

– 1984. *Disclosure by the Prosecution* (Report No. 22). Ottawa: Minister of Supply and Services

– 1990. *Controlling Criminal Prosecutions: The Attorney General and the Crown Prosecutor* (Working Paper No. 62). Ottawa: Law Reform Commission of Canada

Canada, National Parole Board. 1987. *Briefing Book for Members of the Standing Committee on Justice and Solicitor General,* vol. 2. Ottawa: National Parole Board

– 1989a. *Decision Policies,* rev. ed. Ottawa: National Parole Board

– 1989b. *Report to the House of Commons Standing Committee on Justice and Solicitor General* (June 20). Ottawa: National Parole Board

– Royal Commission on Banking and Finance. 1962. *Evidence,* vol. 14. Ottawa, Queen's Printer

– 1964. *Report.* Ottawa: Queen's Printer

Canada, Royal Commission to Investigate the Penal System of Canada. 1938. (Chairman, W. Archambault) *Report.* Ottawa: Queen's Printer

– Security Intelligence Review Committee. 1989a. *Amending the CSIS Act: Proposals for the Special Committee of the House of Commons.* Ottawa: Minister of Supply and Services

– 1989b. *Annual Report, 1988–89.* Ottawa: SIRC

- 1990. *Annual Report, 1989–90*. Ottawa: Ministry of Supply and Services
Canada, Senate, Special Committee on the Canadian Security Intelligence
  Service. 1983. (Chairman, M. Pitfield) *Delicate Balance: A Security Intelligence
  Service in a Democratic Society.* Ottawa: Ministry of Supply and Services
- Standing Committee on Legal and Constitutional Affairs. 1974. (Chairman,
  Senator Goldenberg) *Parole in Canada*. Ottawa: Information Canada
Canada, Solicitor General. n.d. *Secretariat Mission*. Ottawa: Ministry of the Solici-
  tor General
- 1983. *Canadian Security Intelligence Service: Explanatory Notes*. Ottawa: Solicitor
  General of Canada
- 1990. *Corrections and Conditional Release – Directions for Reform*. Ottawa: Solici-
  tor General of Canada
- 1991. *On Course: National Security for the 1990s*. Ottawa: Minister of Supply and
  Services
- Independent Advisory Team on the Canadian Security Intelligence Service
  (Chairman, G.F. Osbaldeston). 1987. *People and Process in Transition*. Ottawa:
  Solicitor General of Canada
Canada, Task Force on Program Review. 1986. *Report*. Ottawa: Task Force on Pro-
  gram Review
Canada, Task Force on the Release of Inmates. 1972. (Chairman, J. Hugessen)
  Report. Ottawa: Task Force on Release of Inmates
- Treasury Board. 1989. *Enterprising Management: A Progress Report on IMAA*.
  Ottawa: Minister of Supply and Services
Canadian Bar Association. 1988a. *Code of Professional Conduct*. Ottawa: Canadian
  Bar Association
- Special Committee on Release and Imprisonment. 1988b. *Parole and Early
  Release*. Ottawa: Canadian Bar Association
- Task Force. 1990. *The Independence of Federal Administration Tribunals and Agen-
  cies in Canada*. Ottawa: Canadian Bar Association
Canadian Judicial Council. 1988. *Annual Report, 1987–88*. Ottawa: Canadian Judi-
  cial Council
- 1993. *Annual Report, 1992–93*. Ottawa: Canadian Judicial Council
Carlen, P. 1976. *Magistrates' Justice*. London: Martin Robertson
'Carlisle Report' – see United Kingdom, Committee to Review the Parole System
  in England and Wales, 1988
Carnevale, P.J. 1985. 'Accountability and the Dynamics of Group Presentation,'
  in E.J. Lawler, ed., *Advances in Group Process* 2: 227–48
Carriere, K., and R. Ericson. 1989. *Crime Stoppers: A Study in the Organization
  of Community Policing*. Toronto: Centre of Criminology, University of Toronto

Carter, D.L., A.D. Sapp, and D.W. Stephens. 1989. *The State of Police Education: Policy Direction for the 21st Century.* Washington: Police Executive Research Forum

Casale, S. 1984. *Minimum Standards for Prison Establishments.* London: NACRO

– 1994. 'Conditions and Standards,' in E. Player and M. Jenkins, eds., *Prisons after Woolf: Reform through Riot,* pp. 203–25. London: Routledge

– and J. Plotnikoff. 1989. *Minimum Standards in Prisons: A Programme for Change.* London: NACRO

– 1990. *Regimes for Remand Prisoners.* London: Prison Reform Trust

Chasse, K. 1982. 'The Role of the Prosecutor,' in S. Oxner, ed., *Criminal Justice,* pp. 79–99. Toronto: Carswell

Chayes, A. 1976. 'The Role of the Judge in Public Law Litigation.' *Harvard Law Review* 89: 1281–1316

Chelius, J.R. 1977. *Workplace Safety and Health.* Washington: American Enterprise Institute for Public Policy Research

Cherry, R., C. D'Onofrio, C. Kurddas, T.R. Michl, F. Moseley, and M.I. Naples, 1987. *The Imperilled Economy, Book 1: Macroeconomics from a Left Perspective.* New York: Union for Radical Political Economics

Chevigny, P. 1969. *Police Power: Police Abuses in New York City.* New York: Vintage

Chibnall, S. 1977. *Law-and-Order News.* London: Tavistock

– 1979. 'The Metropolitan Police and the News Media,' in S. Holdaway, ed., *The British Police,* pp. 135–49. London: Edward Arnold

Christopher Commission. 1991. *Report of the Independent Commission on the Los Angeles Police Department.* Los Angeles: Christopher Commission

Chung, D. 1985. 'Internal Security: Establishment of a Canadian Security Intelligence Service.' *Harvard International Law Journal* 26: 234–49

Cialdini, R.B., A. Levy, C.P. Herman, L.T. Kozlowski, and R.E. Petty. 1976. 'Elastic Shifts of Opinion: Determinants of Direction and Durability.' *Journal of Personality and Social Psychology* 34: 663–72

– R.E. Petty, and J.T. Cacioppo. 1981. 'Attitude and Attitude Change.' *Annual Review of Psychology* 32: 357–404

Clairmont, D. 1993. 'Diversion and the Shubencadie Band: Analysis and Interim Evaluation.' Unpublished ms.

Clark, I. 1991. 'Public Service Accountability: The Basic Bargain.' *Manager's Magazine* 2: 17–19, 60

Clarke, M. 1990. *Business Crime: Its Nature and Control.* Cambridge: Polity Press

Clayton, R. and H. Tomlinson. 1987. *Civil Actions against the Police.* London: Sweet and Maxwell

Clegg, S. 1990. *Modern Organizations: Organization Studies in the Postmodern World*. London: Sage

Clokie, H., and J. Robinson. 1969. *Royal Commissions of Inquiry*. New York: Octagon

Coase, R.H. 1988. *The Firm, the Market, and the Law*. Chicago: University of Chicago Press

Coffee, J.C. 1991. 'Liquidity versus Control: The Institutional Investor as Corporate Monitor.' *Columbia Law Review* 91: 1277–1368

Cohen, S.A. 1977. *Due Process of Law*. Toronto: Carswell

Cole, D., and A. Manson. 1990. *Release from Imprisonment: The Law of Sentencing, Parole, and Judicial Review*. Toronto: Carswell

Coleman, J. 1989. *The Criminal Elite*. New York: St Martin's Press

Condon, M.G. 1991. 'Ideas and Regulatory Practice: The Ontario Securities Commission: 1945–1978.' Doctor of Juridical Science Thesis, Faculty of Law, University of Toronto

– 1992. 'Following Up on Interests: The Private Agreement Exemption in Ontario Securities Law.' *Journal of Human Justice* 3: 36–55

Cooper-Stephenson, K. 1990. *Charter Damages Claims*. Toronto: Carswell

Corbett, C. 1991. 'Complaints against the Police: The New Procedure of Informal Resolution.' *Policing and Society* 2: 47–60

Council of Europe. 1991a. *Report to the United Kingdom Government on the Visit to the United Kingdom Carried Out by the European Committee for the Prevention of Torture and Inhuman or Degrading Treatment or Punishment from 29 July 1990 to 10 August 1990*. Strasbourg: Council of Europe

– 1991b. *Response of the United Kingdom Government to the Report of the European Committee for the Prevention of Torture and Inhuman or Degrading Treatment or Punishment (CPT) on its Visit to the United Kingdom from 29 July 1990 to 10 August 1990*. Strasbourg: Council of Europe

Craig, P. 1989. *Administrative Law*, 2nd ed. London: Sweet and Maxwell

Crenson, M.A. 1962. *The Unpolitics of Air Pollution: A Study of Non-Decision Making in the Cities*. Baltimore: Johns Hopkins University Press

Critchley, T.A. 1978. *A History of Police in England and Wales*, rev. ed. London: Constable

Cromwell, T. 1977. 'Habeas Corpus and Correctional Law.' *Queen's Law Journal* 3: 295–331

Cross, R. 1971. *Punishment, Prison, and the Public*. London: Stevens

Cullen, F.T., W.J. Maakestad, and G. Cavender. 1987. *Corporate Crime under Attack*. Cincinnati: Anderson

Currie, E. 1985. *Confronting Crime: An American Challenge*. New York: Pantheon

Daggers, R. 1989. 'Rights,' in T. Ball, J. Farr, and R.L. Handon, eds., *Political Inno-*

vation and Conceptual Change, pp. 292–308. Cambridge: Cambridge University Press

Dahlman, C.J. 1979. 'The Problem of Externality.' *Journal of Law and Economics* 22: 148

Damaska, M. 1986. *The Faces of Justice and State Authority.* New Haven: Yale University Press

Dandeker, C. 1990. *Surveillance, Power, and Modernity: Bureaucracy and Discipline from 1700 to the Present Day.* New York: St Martin's Press

'Daubney Report' – see Canada, House of Commons, Standing Committee on Justice and Solicitor General, 1988

Dawson, J.P. 1968. *Oracles of the Law.* Ann Arbor, Mich.: University of Michigan Law School

Dawson, R.M. 1922. *The Principle of Official Independence.* Toronto: Gundy

– and N. Ward. 1970. *The Government of Canada*, 5th ed. Toronto: University of Toronto Press

Dawson, S., P. Wilman, M. Bamford, and A. Clinton. 1988. *Safety at Work: The Limits of Self-Regulation.* Cambridge: Cambridge University Press

Day, P., and R. Klein. 1987. *Accountabilities: Five Public Services.* London and New York: Tavistock

Deschênes, Jules (with Carl Baar). 1981. *Masters in Their Own House: A Study on the Independent Judicial Administration of the Courts.* Ottawa: Canadian Judicial Council

Devlin, R., and W. Mackay. 1991. 'An Essay on Institutional Responsibility: The Indigenous Black and Micmac Programme at Dalhousie Law School.' *Dalhousie Law Journal* 14: 297–339

Dey, P.J., and S. Makuch. 1979. 'Government Supervision of Self-Regulatory Organisations in the Canadian Securities Industries,' in Philip Anisman et al., eds., *Proposals for a Securities Market Law for Canada*, vol. 3, pp. 1399–1484. Background Papers. Ottawa: Consumer and Corporate Affairs Canada

Di Mento, J. 1986. *Environmental Law and American Business: Dilemmas of Compliance.* New York: Plenum

Diamond, S.S. 1989. 'Using Psychology to Control Law: From Deceptive Advertising to Criminal Sentencing.' *Law and Human Behaviour* 13: 239–52

– 1990. 'Sentencing Decisions by Laypersons and Professional Judges.' *Law and Social Inquiry* 15: 191–221

– and L.J. Stalans. 1989. 'The Myth of Judicial Leniency in Sentencing.' *Behavioral Sciences and the Law* 7: 73–89

Dicey, A. 1961. *An Introduction to the Study of the Law of the Constitution*, 10th ed. London: Macmillan

– 1982. *Introduction to the Law of the Constitution.* Indianapolis: Liberty Classics

Dickson, The Hon. B. 1983. 'The Public Responsibilities of Lawyers.' *Manitoba Law Journal* 13: 175–88

D'Ombrain, N. 1985. 'The Justice System.' (Study Team Report to the Task Force on Program Review.) Ottawa: Task Force on Program Review

Doob, A.N., ed. 1993. *Thinking about Police Resources*. Toronto: Centre of Criminology, University of Toronto

– and J.V. Roberts. 1988. 'Public Punitiveness and Public Knowledge of the Facts: Some Canadian Surveys,' in N. Walker and M. Hough, eds., *Public Attitudes to Sentencing: Surveys from Five Countries*, pp. 111–33. Aldershot: Gower

Donaldson, P., and J. Farquar. 1988. *Understanding the Economy*. Harmondsworth: Penguin

Donnelly, P. 1982. 'The Origins of the Occupational Safety and Health Act of 1970.' *Social Problems* 30: 13–25

Dorn, N., K. Murji, and N. South. 1991. 'Mirroring the Market,' in R. Reiner and M. Cross, eds., *Beyond Law and Order: Criminal Justice Policy and Politics into the 1990s*, pp. 91–106. London: Macmillan

Dowie, M. 1979. 'Pinto Madness,' in J. Skolnick and E. Currie, eds., *Crisis in American Institutions*, 4th ed. Boston: Little Brown

Doyle, A. 1993. 'Breaking into Prison: News Sources and Correctional Institutions,' M.A. Dissertation, Centre of Criminology, University of Toronto

Draper, E. 1991. *Risky Business: Genetic Testing and Exclusionary Practices in the Hazardous Workplace*. Cambridge: Cambridge University Press

Drechsel, R. 1983. *News Making in the Trial Courts*. New York: Longman

Drucker, P.F. 1968. 'Control, Control, and Management,' in A.M. Willms and W.D.K. Kernaghan, eds., *Public Administration in Canada: Selected Readings*, p. 216. Toronto: Methuen

Duff, R.A. 1986. *Trials and Punishments*. Cambridge: Cambridge University Press

Duffee, D., and E. McGarrell, eds. 1990. *Community Corrections: A Community Field Approach*. Cincinnati: Anderson

Dumont, L. 1970. 'The Individual as an Impediment to Sociological Comparison and Indian History,' in *Religion, Politics, and History in India: Collected Papers in Indian Sociology*, pp. 133–51. Paris/The Hague: Mouton

– 1985. 'A Modified View of Our Origins: The Christian Beginnings of Modern Individualism,' in M. Carrithers, S. Collins, and S. Lukes, eds., *The Category of the Person*, pp. 93–122. Cambridge: Cambridge University Press

Dussuyer, I. 1979. *Crime News: A Study of 40 Ontario Newspapers*. Toronto: Centre of Criminology, University of Toronto

Economist. 1991. 'Curiouser' (editorial). 3 August, p. 15

Edsall, T.B. 1984. *The New Politics of Inequality*. New York: Norton

Edwards, J. Ll.J. 1964. *Law Officers of the Crown*. London: Sweet and Maxwell
– 1977. 'Emerging Problems in Defining the Modern Role of the Office of Attorney General in Commonwealth Countries.' Paper prepared for the Meeting of Commonwealth Law Ministers, Winnipeg, Manitoba
– 1980. *Ministerial Responsibility for National Security*. Ottawa: Minister of Supply and Services
– 1984. *The Attorney General, Politics, and the Public Interest*. London: Sweet and Maxwell
– 1987. 'The Attorney General and the Charter of Rights,' in R.J. Sharpe, ed., *Charter Litigation*. Toronto: Butterworths
– 1989. *Walking the Tightrope of Justice*. Volume 5 of the final report of the Nova Scotia Royal Commission on the Donald Marshall, Jr., Prosecution. Halifax: Nova Scotia Government Printer
Elkins, C. 1989. 'Corporate Citizenship – Toxic Chemicals, the Right Response.' *New York Times*, 13 November, p. 3
Elliff, J. 1979. *The Reform of FBI Intelligence Operations*. Princeton: Princeton University Press
Emerson, H.G. 1973. 'An Integrated Disclosure System for Ontario Securities Legislation,' in J.S. Ziegel, ed., *Studies in Canadian Company Law*, vol. 2, pp. 400–70. Toronto: Butterworths
Epstein, E. 1974. *News from Nowhere*. New York: Vintage
– 1975. *Between Fact and Fiction*. New York: Vintage
Erber, R., and S.T. Fiske. 1984. 'Outcome Dependency and Attention to Inconsistent Information.' *Journal of Personality and Social Psychology* 47: 709–26
Ericson, R. 1981a. *Making Crime: A Study of Detective Work*. Toronto: Butterworths
– 1981b. 'Rules for Police Deviance,' in C. Shearing, ed., *Organizational Police Deviance*, pp. 83–110. Toronto: Butterworths
– 1982. *Reproducing Order: A Study of Police Patrol Work*. Toronto: University of Toronto Press
– 1989. 'Patrolling the Facts: Secrecy and Publicity in Police Work.' *British Journal of Sociology* 40: 205–26
– 1991. 'Mass Media, Crime, Law, and Justice: An Institutional Approach.' *British Journal of Criminology* 31: 219–49
– 1993. *Making Crime: A Study of Detective Work*, new ed. Toronto: University of Toronto Press
– 1994. 'An Institutional Perspective on News Media Access and Control,' in M. Aldridge and N. Hewitt, eds., *Controlling Broadcasting*, pp. 108–33. Manchester: University of Manchester Press
– and P. Baranek. 1982. *The Ordering of Justice*. Toronto: University of Toronto Press

Ericson, R., P. Baranek, and J. Chan. 1987. *Visualizing Deviance: A Study of News Organization*. Toronto: University of Toronto Press; Milton Keynes: Open University Press

– 1989. *Negotiating Control: A Study of News Sources*. Toronto: University of Toronto Press; Milton Keynes: Open University Press

– 1991. *Representing Order: Crime, Law, and Justice in the News Media*. Toronto: University of Toronto Press; Milton Keynes: Open University Press

Evans, J.M., ed. 1980. *DeSmith's Judicial Review of Administrative Action*, 4th ed. London: Stevens and Sons

Evans, M., and R. Morgan. 1992. 'The European Convention for the Prevention of Torture: Operational Practice.' *International and Comparative Law Quarterly* 41: 590–614

Farson, S. 1991a. 'Criminal Intelligence vs Security Intelligence: A Re-evaluation of the Police Role in the Response to Terrorism,' in D.A. Charters, ed., *Democratic Responses to International Terrorism*, pp. 191–226. Dobbs Ferry, NY: Transnational Books

– 1991b. 'Restructuring Control in Canada: The McDonald Commission of Inquiry and Its Legacy,' in G. Hastedt, ed., *Controlling Intelligence*, pp. 157–88. London: Frank Cass

– and P. Rosen. 1989. 'Efficacy, Propriety, and Balance: An Analysis of the Central Issues before the Special Committee.' Report prepared for the House of Commons Special Committee on the Review of the Canadian Security Intelligence Service Act and the Security Offences Act. Ottawa: House of Commons

'Fauteux Report' – see Canada, Committee to Inquire into the Principles and Procedures ..., 1956

Federal/Provincial Committee of Criminal Justice Officials with Respect to the McDonald Commission. 1983. *Report*. Ottawa: Solicitor General of Canada

Ferguson, G. 1992. 'Judicial Reform of Crown Disclosure.' *Criminal Reports* (4th series) 8: 295–302

Festinger, L., ed. 1964. *Conflict, Decision, and Dissonance*. Stanford: Stanford University Press

Finley, L. 1989. 'Breaking Women's Silence in Law: The Dilemma of the Genderred Nature of Legal Reasoning.' *Notre Dame Law Review* 64: 886–910

Finanne, M. 1990. 'Police Corruption and Police Reform: The Fitzgerald Inquiry in Queensland, Australia.' *Policing and Society* 1: 159–71

Fischhoff, B. 1982. 'Debiasing,' in D. Kahneman, P. Slovic, and A. Tversky, eds., *Judgment under Uncertainty: Heuristic and Biases*, pp. 422–44. New York: Cambridge University Press

Fish, P.G. 1973. *The Politics of Federal Judicial Administration*. Princeton: Princeton University Press

Fishman, M. 1980. *Manufacturing the News*. Austin: University of Texas Press
- 1981. 'Police News: Constructing an Image of Crime.' *Urban Life* 9: 371–94
Fiske, S.T., and S.E. Taylor. 1991. *Social Cognition*. New York: McGraw-Hill
Fitzgerald, R.T.1989. *Report of a Commission of Inquiry Pursuant to Orders in Council*. Brisbane: Queensland Government Printer
Fleming, T. 1983. 'Criminalizing a Marginal Community: The Bawdy House Raids,' in T. Fleming and L. Visano, eds., *Deviant Designations: Crime, Law, and Deviance in Canada*, pp. 37–60. Toronto: Butterworths
Fogelson, R.M. 1977. *Big-city Police*. Cambridge: Harvard University Press
Foucault, M. 1979. *Discipline and Punish: The Birth of the Prison*. New York: Vintage
'Fowler Report' – see United Kingdom, Inquiry into the Cause and Circumstances of the Events at HM Prison Hull, 1977
Fox, F., and B.M. Staw. 1979. 'The Trapped Administrator: The Effects of Job Insecurity and Policy Resistance upon Commitment to a Course of Action.' *Administrative Science Quarterly* 24: 449–71
Fox, L.W. 1952. *The English Prison and Borstal System*. London: Routledge
Frank, N. 1985. *Crimes against Occupational Safety and Health*. New York: Harrow and Heston
Franks, C.E.S. 1979. *Parliament and Security Matters*. Ottawa: Minister of Supply and Services
- 1987. *The Parliament of Canada*. Toronto: University of Toronto Press
- 1989a. 'Accountability of the Canadian Security Intelligence Service,' in P. Hanks and J.D. McCamus, eds., *National Security: Surveillance and Accountability in a Democratic Society*, pp. 19–36. Cowansville: Les Editions Yvon Blais
- ed. 1989b. *Dissent and the State*. Toronto: Oxford University Press
Freckelton, I. 1991. 'Shooting the Messenger: The Trial and Execution of the Victorian Police Complaints Authority,' in A. Goldsmith, ed., *Complaints against the Police: The Trend to External Review*, pp. 63–114. Melbourne: Oxford University Press
Friedrich, R.J. 1980. 'Police Use of Force: Individuals, Situations, and Organizations.' *Annals of the American Academy of Political and Social Science*, November: 80–97
Fyfe, J.J. 1988. 'Police Use of Deadly Force.' *Justice Quarterly* 5: 165–205
Galligan, D.J. 1986. *Discretionary Powers*. Oxford: Oxford University Press
Galnoor, I. 1977. 'What Do We Know about Government Secrecy?' in I. Galnoor, ed., *Government Secrecy in Democracies*, pp. 275–313. New York: New York University Press
Gardbaum, S.A. 1992. 'Law, Politics, and the Claims of Community.' *Michigan Law Review* 90: 685–760

Garland, D. 1990. *Punishment and Modern Society.* Oxford: Oxford University Press

Garofalo, J. 1981. 'Crime and the Mass Media: A Selective Review of Research.' *Journal of Research in Crime and Delinquency* 18: 319–50

Geertz, C. 1983. *Local Knowledge.* New York: Basic Books

Geis, G., and J. DiMento. 1995. 'Is It Sound Policy to Prosecute Corporations Rather than, or in Addition to, Human Malefactors?' in F. Pearce and L. Snider, eds., *Corporate Crime: Contemporary Debates.* Toronto: University of Toronto Press

Genders, E., and E. Player. 1989. *Race Relations in Prison.* Oxford: Clarendon

Ghiz, J., and B. Archibald. 1994. *Independence, Accountability, and Management in the Nova Scotia Public Prosecution Service: A Review and Evaluation.* Halifax, NS: Dalhousie Law School

Giddens, A. 1984. *The Constitution of Society.* Cambridge: Polity Press

Gill, P. 1989a. 'Defining Subversion: The Canadian Experience since 1977.' [1989] *Public Law* 617–36

– 1989b. 'Symbolic or Real? The Impact of the Canadian Security Intelligence Review Committee.' *Intelligence and National Security* 4: 550–75

Gitlin, T. 1980. *The Whole World Is Watching.* Berkeley: University of California Press

Glasbeek, H. 1995. 'Preliminary Observations of Strains of, and Strains in, Corporate Law Scholarship,' in F. Pearce and L. Snider, eds., *Corporate Crime: Contemporary Debates.* Toronto: University of Toronto Press

– and J. Rowland. 1979. 'Are Injury and Killing at Work Crimes?' *Osgoode Hall Law Journal* 17: 507–94

– and E. Tucker. 1992. *Death by Consensus: The Westray Story.* Toronto: Osgoode Hall Law School Occasional Papers

Glasgow University Media Group. 1976. *Bad News.* London: Routledge

– 1980. *More Bad News.* London: Routledge

Globe and Mail. 1980. 'Inspector's Suicide Has Shaken Force.' 7 May, p. 1

– 1981. 'Courts Will Decide What's Legal, PM Says.' 29 August, p. 1

– 1987. 'Detection of Racism a Problem for Lawyers at Marshall Inquiry.' 26 October, p. 7

– (Phillip Day). 1989a. 'Charges Laid in Budget Leak Were Political, Officer Testifies.' 7 November, pp. Al, A2

– (Geoffrey York). 1989b. 'Ending in the Dark Shadow of Death.' 4 November, p. D2

– 1990a. 'Marshall Investigator "Glad" to Be off the Hook.' 27 October, p. A6

– (Graham Fraser). 1990b, 'PMO Didn't Pressure RCMP for Budget Leak Charges, Trial Told.' 13 February, p. A11

– (Associated Press). 1991. 'Workplace Accident Rate Soars.' 21 November, p. B5

Goffman, E. 1961. *Asylums*. New York: Anchor

Goldman, K. 1971. *International Norms and War between States*. Stockholm: Laromedsforlagen

Goldring, J., and R. Wettenhall. 1980. 'Three Perspectives on the Responsibility of Statutory Authorities,' in P. Weller and D. Jaensch, eds., *Responsible Government in Australia*, pp. 136–50. Richmond, Vic.: Drummond

Goldsmith, A.J. 1985. 'Political Policing in Canada: The Report of the McDonald Commission and the Security Intelligence Services Act 1984.' [1985] *Public Law* 39–50

– 1988. 'New Directions in Police Complaints Procedures: Some Conceptual and Comparative Departures. *Police Studies* 11: 60–71

– 1990. 'Taking Police Culture Seriously: Police Discretion and the Limits of Law.' *Policing and Society* 1: 91–114

– 1991a. 'Complaint against the Police: A "Community Policing" Perspective,' in S. McKillop and J. Vernon, eds., *The Police and the Community in the 1990s*, pp. 205–18. Canberra: Australian Institute of Criminology

– 1991b. 'External Review and Self-Regulation: Police Accountability and the Dialectic of Complaints Procedures,' in A. Goldsmith, ed., *Complaints against the Police: The Trend to External Review*, pp. 13–61. Melbourne: Oxford University Press

– ed. 1991c. *Complaints against the Police: The Trend to External Review*. Melbourne: Oxford University Press

– and S. Farson. 1987. 'Complaints against the Police: A New Approach.' [1987] *Criminal Law Review* 615–23

Goldstein, H. 1977. *Policing a Free Society*. Cambridge, Mass.: Ballinger

– 1990. *Problem-oriented Policing*. Philadelphia: Temple University Press

Goode, M. 1991. 'Complaints against the Police in Australia: Where We Are Now and What We Might Learn about the Process of Law Reform, with Some Comments about the Process of Legal Change' in A. Goldsmith, ed., *Complaints against the Police: The Trend to External Review*, pp. 115–52. Melbourne: Oxford University Press

Goodrich, P. 1986. *Reading the Law*. Oxford: Blackwell

Gostin, L., and M. Staunton. 1985. 'The Case for Prison Standards: Conditions of Confinement, Segregation, and Medical Treatment,' in M. Maguire. J. Vagg, and R. Morgan, eds., *Accountability and Prisons: Opening Up a Closed World*, pp. 81–96. London: Tavistock

Gover, B. 1992. 'Stinchcombe: Bad Case, Good Law?' *Criminal Reports* (4th series) 8: 307–15

Graber, D. 1976. *Verbal Behavior and Politics*. Urbana: University of Illinois Press

– 1980. *Crime News and the Public*. New York: Praeger

Graham, M. 1991. 'The Quiet Drug Revolution.' *Atlantic Monthly* 256: 34–40

Gramsci, A. 1971. *Selections from the Prison Notebooks of Antonio Gramsci* (trans. by Q. Hoare and G. Nowell Smith). New York: International Publishers

Gravel, S., and S. Bordelais. 1993. *Le recours aux délateurs dans le contexte de l'administration de la justice québecoise.* Montreal: Centre International de Criminologie Comparée

Greene, I. 1982. 'The Politics of Court Administration in Ontario.' *Windsor Yearbook of Access to Justice* 2: 124

– 1988a. 'The Doctrine of Judicial Independence Developed by the Supreme Court of Canada.' *Osgoode Hall Law Journal* 26: 175–206

– 1988b. 'The Zuber Report and Court Management.' *Windsor Yearbook of Access to Justice* 8: 150–89

Greenless, L. 1991. 'Washington State's Sexually Violent Predators Act: Model or Mistake?' *American Criminal Law Review* 29: 107–132

Greenwald, A.G. 1980. 'The Totalitarian Ego: Fabrication and Revision of Personal History.' *American Psychologist* 35: 603–18

Greenwood, P.W., J.M. Chaiken, and J. Petersilia. 1977. *The Criminal Investigation Process.* Lexington, Mass.: D.C. Heath

Griffin, K. 1981. 'Economic Development in a Changing World.' *World Development* 9: 221–6

Griffith, J.A.G. 1977. *The Politics of the Judiciary.* Glasgow: Fontana/Collins

Griffiths, R. 1981. 'A Background of Risks.' In *Living with Uncertainty: Risks in the Energy Scene.* London: Oyez IBC

Grosman, B.A. 1969. *The Prosecutor – An Inquiry into the Exercise of Discretion.* Toronto: University of Toronto Press

Gunn, J., A. Maden, and M. Swinton. 1991. *Mentally Disordered Prisoners.* London: Institute of Psychiatry

Gunter, B., and M. Wober. 1988. *Violence and Television: What the Viewers Think.* London: Libbey

Gurr, Ted R. 1979. 'A Historical Overview of Violence in Europe and America,' in H.D. Graham and T.R. Gurr, eds., *Violence in America: Historical and Comparative Perspectives*, pp. 353–74. Beverly Hills: Sage

Gusfield, J. 1981. *The Culture of Public Problems.* Chicago: University of Chicago Press

Habermas, J. 1970. 'Towards a Theory of Communiative Competence,' in H. Dreitzel, ed., *Recent Sociology.* New York: Macmillan

– 1975. *Legitimation Crisis.* Boston: Beacon

Hagan, J. 1988. *Structural Criminology.* Cambridge: Polity Press

– J. Hewitt, and D. Alwin. 1979. 'Ceremonial Justice: Crime and Punishment in a Loosely Coupled System.' *Social Forces* 58: 506–27

Hall, J. 1947. *General Principles of Criminal Law*. Indianapolis: Bobbs-Merrill

Hall, S. 1979. 'Culture, the Media, and the "Ideological Effect,"' in J. Curran, M. Gurevitch, and J. Woollacot, eds., *Mass Communication and Society*, pp. 314–48. Beverly Hills: Sage

– C. Critcher, T. Jefferson, J. Clarke, and B. Roberts. 1978. *Policing the Crisis*. London: Macmillan

Halloran, J., P. Elliott, and G. Murdock. 1970. *Demonstrations and Communications: A Case Study*. Harmondsworth: Penguin

Hancher, L., and M. Moran. 1989. 'Organising Regulatory Space,' in L. Hancher and M. Moran, eds., *Capitalism, Culture, and Economic Regulation*, pp. 271–99. Oxford: Clarendon

Hanks, P., and J. McCamus, eds. 1989. *National Security: Surveillance and Accountability in a Democratic Society*. Cowansville: Les Editions Yvon Blais

Hann, R., J. McGinnis, P. Stenning, and S. Farson. 1985. 'Municipal Police Governance and Accountability in Canada: An Empirical Study.' *Canadian Police College Journal* 9: 1–85

Harden, I., and N. Lewis. 1986. *The Noble Lie: The British Constitution and the Rule of Law*. London: Hutchinson

Hare, A.P. 1976. *Handbook of Small Group Research*, 2nd ed. New York: Free Press

Hartley, J. 1982. *Understanding News*. London: Methuen

Harvey, J.H., S.G. Harkins, and D.K. Kagehiro. 1976. 'Cognitive Tuning and the Attribution of Causality.' *Journal of Personality and Social Psychology* 34: 708–15

Heider, F. 1958. *The Psychology of Interpersonal Relations*. New York: Wiley

Herbert, A.P. 1936. *Mild and Bitter*, 2nd ed. London: Methuen

Hirschman, A.O. 1970. *Exit, Voice, and Loyalty*. Cambridge: Harvard University Press

Hogg, P. 1989. *Liability of the Crown*, 2nd ed. Toronto: Carswell

Hogg, R., and M. Findlay. 1988. 'Police and the Community: Some Issues Raised by Recent Overseas Research,' in I. Freckelton and H. Selby, eds., *Police in Our Society*, pp. 44–63. Sydney: Butterworths

Holdaway, S. 1982. 'Police Accountability: A Current Issue.' *Public Administration* 60: 84–91

Honderich, T. 1976. *Punishment: The Supposed Justifications*. Harmondsworth: Penguin

Horowitz, D.L. 1977. *The Courts and Social Policy*. Washington: Brookings Institute

Houston Police Department. 1988. *Developing Neighborhood Oriented Policing*, pp. 71–5. Washington: International Association of Chiefs of Police

'Hugesson Report' – see Canada, Task Force on the Release of Inmates, 1972

Hutchinson, A.C. 1990. 'Mice under a Chair: Democracy, Courts, and the Administrative State.' *University of Toronto Law Journal* 40: 374–404

Investment Dealers Association. 1974. *Submission on Bill 75*. Toronto: Investment Dealers Association

Irwin, A., D. Smith, and R. Griffith. 1982. 'Risk Analysis and Public Policy.' *Physics and Technology* 13

Jacobs, J. 1977. *Stateville – the Penitentiary in Mass Society.* Chicago: University of Chicago Press

Janis, I.L. 1982. *Groupthink*, 2nd ed. Boston: Houghton-Mifflin

– 1989. *Crucial Decisions: Leadership in Policy Making and Crisis Management*. New York: Free Press

– and L. Mann. 1977. *Decision Making: A Psychological Analysis of Conflict, Choice, and Commitment*. New York: Free Press

Janisch, H.N. 1989. 'Reregulating the Regulator: Administrative Structure of Securities Commissions and Ministerial Responsibilities,' in *Securities Law in the Modern Financial Marketplace*. Law Society of Upper Canada Special Lectures, pp. 97–119. Toronto: DeBoo

Jareborg, N. 1989. 'Introductory Report,' in *Disparities in Sentencing: Causes and Solutions*. Reports presented to the 8th Criminological Colloquium (1987). Collected Studies in Criminological Research, vol. 26. Strasbourg: Council of Europe

Jefferson, T., and R. Grimshaw. 1984. *Controlling the Constable: Police Accountability in England and Wales*. London: Muller

Jessop, B. 1982. *The Capitalist State*. Oxford: Martin Robertson

– 1990. *State Theory: Putting the Capitalist State in Its Place*. Cambridge: Polity Press

Johnston, D. 1977. *Canadian Securities Regulation*. Toronto: Butterworths

Johnston, L. 1992. *The Rebirth of Private Policing*. London and New York: Routledge

Jones, E.E. 1979. 'The Rocky Road from Acts to Dispositions.' *American Psychologist* 34: 107–17

– and K.E. Davis. 1965. 'From Acts to Dispositions: The Attribution Process in Person Perception,' in L. Berkowitz, ed., *Advances in Experimental Social Psychology*, vol. 2, pp. 220–66. New York: Academic

– and C. Wortman. 1973. *Ingratiation: An Attributional Approach*. Morristown, NJ: General Learning Press

Jones, H., and R. Morgan. 1990 *Qualified Clerks at Boards of Visitors' Disciplinary Hearings: Report of an Experiment in 13 Prisons*. London: Home Office

Jones, K. 1982. *Law and Economy.* London: Academic

Kagan, R. 1984. 'On Regulatory Inspectorate and Police' in K. Hawkins and J. Thomas, eds., *Enforcing Regulation*, pp. 37–64. Boston: Kluwer-Nijhoff

Kairys, D., ed. 1982. *The Politics of Law.* New York: Pantheon

Kaiser, H. 1990. 'The Aftermath of the Marshall Commission: A Preliminary Opinion.' *Dalhousie Law Journal* 13: 364–75

Kelling, G.L. 1985. 'Order Maintenance, the Quality of Life, and Police: A Line of Argument,' in William A. Geller, ed., *Police Leadership in America: Crisis and Opportunity,* pp. 296–308. Chicago: American Bar Foundation and Praeger

– and M.H. Moore. 1988. *The Evolving Strategy of Policing.* Washington: National Institute of Justice and Harvard University

Kelling, G.L., T. Pate, D. Diekman, and C. Brown. 1974. *The Kansas City Preventive Patrol Experiment: A Summary Report.* Washington: Police Foundation

– and M.A. Wycoff. 1991. 'Implementing Community Policing: The Administrative Problem.' Paper for the Executive Session on Policing, Harvard University, February

Kelman, M. 1987. *A Guide to Critical Legal Studies.* Cambridge: Harvard University Press

Kiesler, A.C. 1971. *The Psychology of Commitment.* New York: Academic Press

King, R., and K. McDermott. 1989. 'British Prisons, 1970–1987: The Ever-Deepening Crisis.' *British Journal of Criminology* 29: 107–28

King, R., and R. Morgan. 1976. *A Taste of Prison: Custodial Conditions for Trial and Remand Prisoners.* London: Routledge

– 1980. *The Future of the Prison System.* Aldershot: Gower

Kitching, G. 1982. *Development and Underdevelopment in Historical Perspective: Populism, Nationalism, and Industrialization.* London: Methuen

Klimoski, R.J. 1971. 'The Effects of Intragroup Forces on Intergroup Conflict Resolution.' *Organizational Behavior and Human Performance* 8: 363–83

Knox, P., and J. Agnew. 1989. *The Geography of the World Economy.* London: Edward Arnold

Kolko, G. 1963. *The Triumph of Conservatism: A Reinterpretation of American History, 1900–1916.* Glencoe: Free Press

Kramer, R. 1984. 'Corporate Criminality: The Development of an Idea,' in E. Hochstedler, ed., *Corporations as Criminals,* pp. 13–40. Beverly Hills: Sage

Kymlicka, W. 1989. *Liberalism, Community, and Culture.* Oxford: Clarendon

La Prairie, C. 1991. *Justice for the Cree: Communities, Crime, and Order.* Quebec: Grand Council of the Crees (Quebec) and Cree Regional Authority

– 1992. *Exploring the Boundaries of Justice: Aboriginal Justice in the Yukon.* Report to Department of Justice, Yukon Territorial Government; First Nations, Yukon Territory; Department of Justice, Ottawa

Labour Research Department. 1989. *The Hazards of Coal Mining.* London: Labour Research Department

Lacey, N., C. Wells, and D. Meure. 1990. *Reconstructing Criminal Law: Critical Perspectives on Crime and the Criminal Process.* London: Weidenfeld and Nicolson

Lane, R. 1980. 'Urban Police and Crime in Nineteenth-Century America, in N. Morris and M. Tonry, eds., *Crime and Justice: A Review of Research*, pp. 1–43. Chicago: University of Chicago Press

Latham, E. 1960. 'The Body Politic of the Corporation,' in E.S. Mason, ed., *The Corporation in Modern Society*, pp. 218–36. Cambridge: Harvard University Press

Law Society of Upper Canada. 1978. *New Securities Legislation*. Lectures/Edited Panel Discussion. Toronto: Law Society of Upper Canada

Law Times (Eduardo Bichon). 1992. 'The Insider.' 3 February

Laws, The Hon. Sir John. 1993. 'Is the High Court the Guardian of Fundamental Constitutional Rights?' [1993] *Public Law* 59–79

Lea, J., and J. Young. 1982. 'The Riots in Britain 1981: Urban Violence and Political Marginalisation,' in D. Cowell, T. Jones, and J. Young, eds., *Policing the Riots*, pp. 5–20. London: Junction Books

– 1984. *What Is to Be Done about Law and Order?* Harmondsworth: Penguin

Le Dain, G. 1973. 'The Role of the Public Inquiry in Our Constitutional System,' in J. Ziegel, ed. *Law and Social Change*, pp. 79–97. Toronto: Osgoode Hall Law School

Leigh, L.H. 1969. *The Criminal Liability of Corporations in English Law*. London: Weidenfeld and Nicolson

Levi, M. 1987. *Regulating Fraud*. London: Tavistock

Lewis, C. 1991. 'Police Complaints in Metropolitan Toronto: Perspectives of the Public Complaints Commissioner,' in A. Goldsmith, ed., *Complaints against the Police: The Trend to External Review*, pp. 153–75. Melbourne: Oxford University Press

– 1992. 'The Exhaustion of Alternative Remedies in Administrative Law.' *Cambridge Law Journal* 51: 138–53

Lewis, E. 1974. *Medieval Political Ideas*. New York: Cooper Square

Linton, R. 1945. *The Cultural Background of Personality*. New York: Appleton-Century Crofts

Lipton, D., R. Martinson, and J. Wilks. 1975. *The Effectiveness of Correctional Treatment*. New York: Praeger

Locke, John. 1690. *The Second Treatise of Government*. (ed. J. Gough). Oxford: Blackwell, 1956

Loftin, C., and D. McDowall. 1982. 'The Police, Crime, and Economic Theory: An Assessment.' *American Sociological Review* 47: 393–401

London Police Strategy Unit. 1987. *Police Accountability and a New Strategic Authority for London* (Police Monitoring and Research Group Briefing Paper No. 2). London: LPSU

Lotz, R. 1991. *Crime and the American Press*. New York: Praeger

Loucks, N. 1993. *Prison Rules: A Working Guide*. London: Prison Reform Trust

Loveday, B. 1985. *The Role and Effectiveness of the Merseyside Police Committee*. Liverpool: Merseyside County Council

– 1987. 'The Joint Boards.' *Policing* 3: 196–213

– 1991. 'The New Police Authorities in the Metropolitan Counties: The Costs and Consequences of Abolition of the Metropolitan County Authorities.' *Policing and Society* 1: 193–212

Lowder, D. 1987/8. 'Obstacles to Holding a Parole Official in Virginia Liable for the Negligent Release or Supervision of a Parolee.' *Richmond Law Review* 22: 83–94

Luban, D. 1988. *Lawyers and Justice: an Ethical Study*. Princeton: Princeton University Press

Lukes, S. 1974. *Power: A Radical View*. London: Macmillan

Lustgarten, L. 1986. *The Governance of Police*. London: Sweet and Maxwell

– and I. Leigh. 1994. *In from the Cold: National Security and Parliamentary Democracy*. Oxford: Oxford University Press

Lyman, S.M., and M.B. Scott. 1968. 'Accounts.' *American Sociological Review* 33: 46–62

Macauley, S. 1987. 'Images of Law in Everyday Life: The Lessons of School, Entertainment, and Spectator Sports.' *Law and Society Review* 21: 185–218

Macdonald, R. 1980. 'Commissions of Inquiry in the Perspective of Administrative Law.' *Alberta Law Review* 18: 366–95

Mackenna, B. 1983. *Justice in Prison: A Report*. London: Justice

Maguire, M. 1985. 'Prisoners' Grievances: The Role of Boards of Visitors,' in M. Maguire, J. Vagg, and R. Morgan, eds., *Accountability and Prisons: Opening Up a Closed World*, pp. 141–56. London: Tavistock

– 1991. 'Complaints against the Police: The British Experience,' in A. Goldsmith, ed., *Complaints against the Police: The Trend to External Review*, pp. 177–209. Melbourne: Oxford University Press

– 1992. 'Parole,' in E. Stockdale and S. Casale, eds., *Criminal Justice under Stress*, pp. 179–209. Oxford: Blackwell

– and C. Corbett. 1991. *A Study of the Police Complaints System*. London: HMSO

– and J. Vagg. 1983. 'Who Are the Prison Watchdogs? The Membership and Appointment of Boards of Visitors.' [1983] *Criminal Law Review* 238–48

– 1984. *The 'Watchdog' Role of Boards of Visitors*. London: Home Office

– and R. Morgan, eds. 1985. *Accountability and Prisons: Opening Up a Closed World*. London/New York: Tavistock

Mahon, R. 1977. 'Canadian Public Policy: The Unequal Structure of Representation,' in L. Panitch, ed., *The Canadian State: Political Economy and Political Power*, pp. 165–98. Toronto: University of Toronto Press

– 1979. 'Regulatory Agencies: Captive Agents or Hegemonic Apparatuses?' *Studies in Political Economy* 1: 165–98

Makens, H.H. 1984. 'Who Speaks for the Investor? An Evaluation of the Assault on Merit Regulation.' *University of Baltimore Law Review* 13: 435–68

Manitoba, Public Inquiry into the Administration of Justice and Aboriginal People ('Aboriginal Justice Inquiry'). 1991a. Volume 1: *The Justice System and Aboriginal People*. Winnipeg: Queen's Printer

– Volume 2: *The Deaths of Helen Betty Osborne and John Joseph Harper*. Winnipeg: Queen's Printer

Manning, P. 1977. *Police Work: The Social Organization of Policing*. Cambridge: MIT Press

– 1980. *The Narc's Game*. Cambridge: MIT Press

Manson, A. 1988. 'Standing in the Public Interest at Coroner's Inquests in Ontario.' *Ottawa Law Review* 20: 637–69

Mark, R. 1977. *Policing a Perplexed Society*. London: Allen and Unwin

– 1978. *In the Office of Constable*. London: Collins

Marr, D. 1984. *The Ivanov Trial*. Melbourne: Nelson

Marsh, H. 1988. 'Crime and the Press: Does Newspaper Crime Coverage Support Myths about Crime and Law Enforcement?' PhD dissertation, Sam Houston State University

Marshall, G. 1965. *Police and Government*. London: Methuen

– 1978. 'Police Accountability Revisited,' in D. Butler and A. Halsey, eds., *Policy and Politics*, pp. 51–65. London: Macmillan

– 1984. *Constitutional Conventions: The Rules and Forms of Political Accountability*. Oxford: Clarendon

Martin, J. 1975. *Boards of Visitors of Penal Institutions*. London: Barry Rose

– 1980. 'Jellicoe and After: Boards of Visitors into the Eighties.' *Howard Journal* 19: 85–101

Marx, G.T. 1981. 'Ironies of Social Control: Authorities as Contributors to Deviance through Escalation, Non-Enforcement, and Covert Facilitation.' *Social Problems* 28: 221–46

– 1988. *Undercover: Police Surveillance in America*. Berkeley: University of California Press

Marx, K. 1965. *Capital*, vol. 1. London: Lawrence and Wishart

Mathiesen, T. 1987. 'The Eagle and the Sun: On Panoptical Systems and Mass Media in Modern Society,' in J. Lowman, R. Menzies, and T. Palys, eds., *Transcarceration: Essays in the Sociology of Social Control*, pp. 59–75. Aldershot: Gower

Matthews, C. 1993. *Accountability in the Administration of Criminal Justice: A Selective Annotated Bibliography*. Toronto: Centre of Criminology, University of Toronto

Matthews, R., ed. 1989. *Privatizing Criminal Justice*. London: Sage

'May Report' – see United Kingdom, Committee of Inquiry into the United Kingdom Prison Services, 1979

McAllister, P.W., T.R. Mitchell, and L.R. Beach. 1979. 'The Contingency Model for the Selection of Decision Strategies: An Empirical Test of the Effects of Significance, Accountability, and Reversibility.' *Organizational Behavior and Human Performance* 24: 228–44

McBarnet, D. 1979. 'Arrest: The Legal Context of Policing,' in S. Holdaway, ed., *The British Police*, pp. 24–40. London: Arnold

– 1981. *Conviction: Law, the State, and the Construction of Justice*. London: Macmillan

– and C. Whelan. 1991. 'The Elusive Spirit of the Law: Formalism and the Struggle for Legal Control.' *Modern Law Review* 54: 848–73

McConville, M., A. Sanders, and R. Leng. 1991. *The Case for the Prosecution*. London: Routledge

McConville, S. 1981. *A History of English Prison Administration*, vol. 1, *1750–1877*. London: Routledge

McCormick, P., and I. Greene. 1990. *Judges and Judging: Inside the Canadian Judicial System*. Toronto: Lorimer

McDermott, K., and R. King. 1989. 'Fresh Start: The Enhancement of Prison Regimes.' *Howard Journal* 28: 161–76

'McDonald Commission' – see Canada, Commission of Inquiry Concerning Certain Activities of the Royal Canadian Mounted Police, 1981a, 1981b

McDonnell, R. 1992. *Justice for the Cree: Customary Beliefs and Practices*. Quebec: Grand Council of the Crees (Quebec) and Cree Regional Authority

McGowan, J. 1991. *Postmodernism and Its Critics*. Ithaca: Cornell University Press

McLaughlin, E. 1990. '*Community, Policing, and Accountability: A Case Study of Manchester 1981–88*.' PhD Thesis, Faculty of Law, University of Sheffield

McMahon, M. 1988. 'Police Accountability: The Situation of Complaints in Toronto.' *Contemporary Crises* 12: 301–27

– and R. Ericson. 1984. *Policing Reform: A Study of the Reform Process and Police Institution in Toronto*. Toronto: Centre of Criminology, University of Toronto

McQuilton, J. 1987. 'Police in Rural Victoria: A Regional Example,' in M. Finnane, ed., *Policing in Australia: Historical Perspectives*. Sydney: University of New South Wales Press

'McRuer Report' – see Ontario, Royal Commission Inquiry into Civil Rights, 1968

Meidner, R. 1978. *Employee Investment Funds: An Approach to Collective Capital Formation*. London: Allen and Unwin

Mendeloff, J. 1979. *Regulating Safety: An Economic and Political Analysis of Occupational Safety and Health Policy*. Cambridge: MIT Press

Mensch, E. 1982. 'The History of Mainstream Legal Thought,' in D. Kairys, ed., *The Politics of Law: A Progressive Critique*, pp. 18–39. New York: Pantheon

Merry, S.E. 1990. *Getting Justice and Getting Even: Legal Consciousness, among Working-Class Americans*. Chicago: University of Chicago Press

Mewett, A. 1981. 'Editorial.' *Criminal Law Quarterly* 24: 1–3

Meyer, J.W., and B. Rowan. 1977. 'Institutionalized Organizations: Formal Structure as Myth and Ceremony.' *American Journal of Sociology* 83: 340–63

Meyer, P.B. 1986. 'The Corporate Person and Social Control: Responding to Deregulation.' *Review of Radical Political Economics* 18: 65–84

Meyrowitz, J. 1985. *No Sense of Place: The Impact of Electronic Media on Social Behavior*. Oxford: Oxford University Press

Mills, C.W. 1940. 'Situated Identities and Vocabularies of Motives.' *American Sociological Review* 5: 904–13

Miyazawa, S. 1992. *Policing in Japan: A Study on Making Crime*. Albany: State University of New York Press

Molotch, H., and M. Lester. 1975. 'Accidental News: The Great Oil Spill.' *American Journal of Sociology* 81: 235–60

Montreal Gazette (Alexander Norris). 1994a. 'Judge Apologizes, Pleads for Job.' 7 January, p. A1

– (Geoff Baker). 1994b. 'Verrault to Face Inquiry.' 17 February, p. A1

Moore, W. 1913. 'Executive Commissions of Inquiry.' *Columbia Law Review* 13: 501–23

Moran, M. 1986. 'Theories of Regulation and Changes in Regulation: The Case of Financial Markets.' *Political Studies* 34: 185–207

Morgan, D.C. 1986. 'Controlling Prosecutorial Powers – Judicial Review, Abuse of Process, and Section 7 of the Charter.' *Criminal Law Quarterly* 29: 15–65

Morgan, R. 1983. 'How Resources Are Used in the Prison System,' in *A Prison System for the '80s and Beyond: The Noel Buxton Lectures, 1982–3*. London: NACRO

– 1985. 'Her Majesty's Inspectorate of Prisons,' in M. Maguire, J. Vagg, and R. Morgan, eds., *Accountability and Prisons: Opening Up a Closed World*, pp. 106–23. London: Tavistock

– 1987. 'Police Accountability: Developing the Local Infrastructure.' *British Journal of Criminology* 27: 87–96

– 1989. 'Policing by Consent: Legitimating the Doctrine,' in R. Morgan and D. Smit, eds., *Coming to Terms with Policing*, pp. 217–34. London: Routledge

– 1991. 'Woolf: In Retrospect and Prospect.' *Modern Law Review* 54: 713–25

– 1993. 'Prisons Accountability Revisited.' [1993] *Public Law* 314–32

– 1994. 'An Awkward Anomaly: Remand Prisoners,' in E. Player and M. Jenkins,

eds., *Prisons after Woolf: Reform through Riot*, pp. 143–160. London: Routledge
– and A. Barclay. 1989. 'Remands in Custody: Problems and Prospects for Change.' The Perrie Lectures 1988. *Prison Service Journal* 74: 13–36
– and M. Evans. 1994. 'Inspecting Prisons: The View from Strasbourg,' in R. King and M. Maguire, eds., *Prisons in Context. British Journal of Criminology*, special issue, 34: 141–59
– and H. Jones. 1991. '"Prison Discipline": The Case for Implementing Woolf.' *British Journal of Criminology* 31: 280–91
– and R. King. 1987. 'Profiting from Prison.' *New Society*, 23 October: 21–2
– and P. Swift. 1987. 'The Future of Police Authorities: Members' Views.' *Public Administration* 65: 259–76
Morris, P., and K. Heal. 1981. *Crime Control and the Police: A Review of Research* (Research Study 67). London: Home Office
Navarro, V. 1983. 'The Determinants of Social Policy, A Case Study: Regulating Health and Safety at the Workplace in Sweden.' *International Journal of Health Services* 13: 517–61
Nisbett, R.E., and L. Ross. 1980. *Human Inference: Strategies and Shortcomings of Social Judgment*. New York: Appleton-Century-Crofts
Nisbett, R.E., H. Zukier, and R. Lemley. 1981. 'The Dilution Effect: Nondiagnostic Information.' *Cognitive Psychology* 13: 248–77
Nixon, S.E. 1963. 'The Preparation of Canadian Corporate Prospectuses.' *Canadian Chartered Accountant* 83: 345
Noble, C. 1986. *Liberalism at Work: The Rise and Fall of OSHA*. Philadelphia: Temple University Press
– 1992. 'Keeping OSHA's Feet to the Fire.' *Technology Review* 95: 42–51
Nova Scotia, Royal Commission on the Donald Marshall, Jr, Prosecution. 1989. *Commissioners' Report: Findings and Recommendations*. Halifax: Nova Scotia Government Printer
Oi, W. 1977. 'On Socially Acceptable Risks,' in J. Phillips, ed., *Safety at Work: Recent Research into the Causes and Prevention of Industrial Accidents*. Oxford: Centre for Socio-Legal Studies
Oliver, I. 1987. *Police, Government, and Accountability*, London: Macmillan
Ontario, Advisory Committee on Charge Sceening, Disclosure, and Resolution Discussions. 1993. (Chairman, The Hon. G. Arthur Martin) *Recommendations and Opinions*. Toronto: Queen's Printer
– Law Reform Commission. 1992. *Report on Public Inquiries*. Toronto: Ontario Law Reform Commission
– Ministry of the Attorney General. 1984. 'Direction re Prosecution of Spouse/ Partner Assault Cases.' Toronto: Ministry of the Attorney General
– 1988. *Crown Policy Manual*. Toronto: Ministry of the Attorney General

- 1991. 'Proposed Code of Professional Standards and Enforcement Procedures.' Unpublished
- 1994. *Crown Policy Manual*, rev. ed. Toronto: Ministry of the Attorney General
Ontario, Race Relations and Policing Task Force. 1989. *Report of the Race Relations and Policing Task Force*. Ontario: Race Relations and Policing Task Force
- Royal Commission Inquiry into Civil Rights. 1968. (Chairman, J.C. McRuer) *Report Number One*, 3 vols. Toronto: Queen's Printer
- Royal Commission to Investigate Trading in the Shares of Windfall Oils and Mines Limited. 1965. *Report*. Toronto: Queen's Printer
- Securities Commission. 1970. *Report of the Committee of the OSC on the Problems of Disclosure Raised for Investors by Business Combinations and Private Placements.* Toronto: Ontario Securities Commission
Optimum. 1993. Volume 24, no. 2. Special issue on independent review and accountability
Owen, T., and S. Livingstone. 1993. *Prison Law: Text and Materials*. Oxford: Clarendon
Pannick, D. 1987. *Judges*. Oxford: Oxford University Press
Paterson, A. 1983. *The Law Lords*. London: Macmillan
Pauktuutit, Inuit Women's Association. 1993. *Inuit Women and the Administration of Justice* (Progress Report No. 1). Ottawa: Inuit Women's Association
Pearce, F. 1985. 'Neo-structuralist Marxism on Crime and Law in Britain.' *Insurgent Sociologist* 12: 123–31
- 1987. 'Corporate Crime: A Review Essay.' *Critical Social Policy* 19: 116–25
- 1990. 'Responsible Corporations and Regulatory Agencies.' *Political Quarterly*, 61: 415–30
- 1992. 'The Contribution of Left Realism to the Study of Commercial Crime,' in J. Lowman and B. Maclean, eds., *Realist Criminology: Crime Control and Policing in the 1990s*, pp. 313–35. Toronto: University of Toronto Press
- 1993. 'Corporate Rationality as Corporate Crime.' *Studies in Political Economy* 40: 145–62
- and L. Snider. 1995. 'Regulating Capitalism,' in F. Pearce and L. Snider, eds., *Corporate Crime: Contemporary Debates*. Toronto: University of Toronto Press
- and S. Tombs. 1989. 'Bhopal, Union Carbide, and the Hubris of a Capitalist Technocracy.' *Social Justice* 16: 116–45
- 1990. 'Ideology, Hegemony, and Empiricism: Compliance Theories of Regulation.' *British Journal of Criminology* 30: 423–43
- 1992. 'Corporate Crime and Realism,' in R. Matthews and J. Young, eds., *Realist Criminology: Theory and Practice*. London: Sage
Pearson, G. 1983. *Hooligan: A History of Respectable Fears*. London: Macmillan

Pells, R. 1985. *The Liberal Mind in a Conservative Age*. New York: Harper and Row

Peltzman, S. 1976. 'Towards a More General Theory of Regulation.' *Journal of Law and Economics* 19: 211–240

'Pepino Report' – see Canada, Board of Investigation, 1988

Petty, R.E., and J.T. Cacioppo. 1986. 'The Elaboration Likelihood Model of Persuasion,' in l. Berkowitz, ed., *Advances in Experimental Social Psychology* 19: 123–205

Pfeffer, J. 1981. 'Management as Symbolic Action: The Creation and Maintenance of Organizational Paradigms,' in L. Cummings and B.M. Staw, eds., *Research in Organizational Behavior*, vol. 3. Greenwich: JAI Press

– and G.R. Salancik. 1978. *The External Control of Organizations: A Resource Dependence Perspective*. New York: Harper and Row

Phillips, K. 1991. *The Politics of Rich and Poor: Wealth and the American Electorate in the Reagan Aftermath*. New York: Harper-Perrenial

Pilkington, M. 1987. 'Monetary Redress for Charter Infringement,' in R. Sharpe, ed., *Charter Litigation*. Toronto: Butterworths

Pocock, J.G.A. 1975. *The Machiavellian Moment: Florentine Political Thought and the Atlantic Republican Tradition*. Princeton: University of Princeton Press

Ponting, J.R., and R. Gibbins. 1986. 'Historical Overview and Background,' in J.R. Ponting, ed., *Arduous Journey: Canadian Indians and Decolonization*, pp. 18–56. Toronto: McClelland and Stewart

Posner, R. 1976. *Antitrust Law*. Chicago: University of Chicago Press

– 1980. 'Optimal Sentences for White-Collar Criminals.' *American Criminal Law Review* 17: 409–18

Powell, W.W. 1990. 'Neither Market nor Hierarchy: Network Forms of Organization,' in B.M. Staw and L.L. Cummings, eds., *Research in Organizational Behavior*, vol. 12, pp. 295–336. Greenwich: JAI Press

Price, D.K. 1965. *The Scientific Estate*. Cambridge: Belknap Press of Harvard University Press

Price, R. 1985. 'Annotation to Nelles v R.' *Criminal Reports (3rd series)* 46: 290–93

'Prior Report' – see United Kingdom, Committee of Inquiry on the Prison Disciplinary System, 1985

Pruitt, D.G. 1981. *Negotiation Behavior*. New York: Academic

– and S.A. Lewis. 1975. 'Development of Integrative Solutions in Bilateral Negotiation.' *Journal of Social Psychology* 31: 621–33

Punch, M. 1985. *Conduct Unbecoming: The Social Construction of Police Deviance and Control*. London: Tavistock

Quebec. 1992. *Rapport du groupe de travail sur l'administration de la justice en matière criminelle*. Quebec: Gouvernement du Québec, Ministère de la Justice et Ministère de la sécurité publique

RCMP, Public Complaints Commission. 1990. *Annual Report 1989–90*. Ottawa: Minister of Supply and Services
– 1991. *Annual Report 1990–91*. Ottawa: Minister of Supply and Services
Radelet, L. 1980. *The Police and the Community,* 3rd ed. New York: Macmillan
Rankin, M. 1986. 'National Security, Information, Accountability, and the Canadian Intelligence Service.' *University of Toronto Law Journal* 36: 249–85
– 1990. 'The Security Intelligence Review Committee: Reconciling National Security with Procedural Fairness.' *Canadian Journal of Administrative Law and Practice* 3: 1732
Rawlings, P. 1991. 'Creeping Privatisation? The Police, the Conservative Government, and Policing in the Late 1980s,' in R. Reiner and M. Cross, eds., *Beyond Law and Order: Criminal Justice Policy and Politics into the 1990s,* pp. 41–58. London: Macmillan
Reiman, J. 1990. *The Rich Get Richer and the Poor Get Prison,* 3rd ed. New York: Macmillan
Reiner, R. 1985. *The Politics of the Police.* New York: St Martin's Press
– 1991. *Chief Constables: Bobbies, Bosses, or Bureaucrats?* Oxford: Oxford University Press
– 1992a. 'Courts, Codes, and Constables: Police Powers since 1984.' *Public Money and Management* 12: 1
– 1992b. *The Politics of the Police,* 2nd ed. Hemel Hempstead: Wheatsheaf/Toronto: University of Toronto Press
– 1994. 'Police and Policing,' in M. Maguire, R. Morgan, and R. Reiner, eds., *The Oxford Handbook of Criminology,* pp. 705–72. Oxford: Oxford University Press
– and L. Leigh. 1994. 'Police Power,' in C. McCrudden and G. Chambers, eds., *Individual Rights and the Law in Britain.* Oxford: Clarendon
– and S. Spencer, eds. 1993. *Accountable Policing: Effectiveness, Empowerment, and Equity.* London: Institute for Public Policy Research
Reiss, Jr., A. 1971. *The Police and the Public.* New Haven: Yale University Press
– 1984a. 'Consequences of Compliance and Deterrence Models of Law Enforcement for the Exercise of Police Discretion.' *Law and Contemporary Problems* 47: 83–122
– 1984b. 'Selecting Strategies of Control over Organizational Life,' in K. Hawkins and J. Thomas, eds., *Enforcing Regulation.* pp. 23–35. Boston: Kluwer-Nijhoff
– 1987. 'The Legitimacy of Intrusion into Private Space,' in C. Shearing and P. Stenning, eds., *Private Policing,* pp. 19–44. Beverly Hills: Sage

Reuss-Ianni, E., and F.A.J. Ianni. 1983. 'Street Cops and Management Cops: The Two Cultures of Policing,' in Maurice Punch, ed., *Control in the Police Organization*, pp. 251–74. Cambridge: MIT Press

Richardson, G. 1985a. 'The Case for Prisoners' Rights,' in M. Maguire, J. Vagg, and R. Morgan, eds., *Accountability and Prisons: Opening Up a Closed World*, pp. 19–28. London: Tavistock

– 1985b. 'Judicial Intervention in Prison Life,' in M. Maguire, J. Vagg, and R. Morgan, eds., *Accountability and Prisons: Opening Up a Closed World*, pp. 46–60. London: Tavistock

– 1993. *Law, Process, and Custody: Prisoners and Patients*. London: Weidenfeld and Nicolson

– 1994. 'From Rights to Expectations,' in E. Player and M. Jenkins, eds., *Prisons after Woolf: Reform through Riot*. London: Routledge

Rideout, G. 1993. 'Parliament and the Subcommittee on Security and Intelligence.' *Optimum* 24: 105–9

Rieselbach, L.N. 1970. *Congressional Reform in the Seventies*. Morristown, NJ: General Learning Press

Roach, K. 1991. 'The Limits of Corrective Justice and the Potential of Equity in Constitutional Remedies.' *Arizona Law Review* 33: 859–905

– 1994a. *Constitutional Remedies in Canada*. Aurora: Canada Law Book

– 1994b. 'Public Inquiries, Prosecutions, or Both?' *University of New Brunswick Law Journal* 43

Robardet, P. 1990. 'Should We Abandon the Adversarial Model in Favour of an Inquisitorial Model in Commissions of Inquiry?' in P. Pross, I. Christie, and J. Yogis, eds., *Commissions of Inquiry*, pp. 111–31. Toronto: Carswell

Roberts, J.V. 1992. 'Public Opinion, Crime, and Criminal Justice,' in M. Tonry, ed., *Crime and Justice: A Review of Research*, vol. 16, pp. 99–180. Chicago: University of Chicago Press

Robertson, J. 1983. 'The Scottish Enlightenment at the Limits of the Civic Tradition,' in I. Hont and M. Ignatieff, eds., *Wealth and Virtue: The Shaping of Political Economy in the Scottish Enlightenment*, pp. 137–78. Cambridge: Cambridge University Press

– and M. Levy. 1986. *The Main Source: Learning from Television News*. Beverly Hills: Sage

Rock, P. 1973. 'News as Eternal Recurrence,' in S. Cohen and J. Young, eds., *The Manufacture of News*, pp. 73–80. London: Constable

Roscho, B. 1975. *Newsmaking*. Chicago: University of Chicago Press

Rose, N., and P. Miller. 1992. 'Political Power Beyond the State: Problematics of Government.' *British Journal of Sociology* 43: 173–205

Roshier, B. 1989. *Controlling Crime: The Classical Perspective in Criminology.* Milton Keynes: Open University Press

Rosner, D., and G. Markowitz. 1989. *Dying for Work: Workers' Safety and Health in Twentieth-Century America.* Bloomington: Indiana University Press

Ross, L. 1977. 'The Intuitive Psychologist and His Shortcomings: Distortions in the Attribution Process,' in L. Berkowitz, ed., *Advances in Experimental Social Psychology,* vol. 10, pp. 173–220

Ross, R. 1993. 'Duelling Paradigms? Western Criminal Justice versus Aboriginal Community Healing.' Unpublished ms. Ottawa: Department of Justice, Aboriginal Justice Directorate

Rossi, P.H., and H.E. Freeman. 1985. *Evaluation: A Systematic Approach,* 3rd ed. Beverly Hills: Sage

Rubinstein, J. 1973. *City Police.* New York: Farrer, Strauss, and Giroux

Ruck, S.K., ed. 1951. *Paterson on Prisons: Being the Collected Papers of Sir Alexander Paterson.* London: Muller

Rumbaut, R., and E. Bittner. 1979. 'Changing Conceptions of the Police Role: A Sociological Review,' in N. Morris and M. Tonry, eds., *Crime and Justice: An Annual Review of Research,* vol. 1, pp. 239–88. Chicago: University of Chicago Press

Russell, P.H. 1987. *The Judiciary in Canada: The Third Branch of Government.* Toronto: McGraw-Hill Ryerson

– R. Knopff, and F.L. Morton, eds., 1989. *Federalism and the Charter: Leading Constitutional Decisions,* 5th ed. Ottawa: Carleton University Press

– and J.S. Ziegel. 1989. 'Federal Judicial Appointments: An Appraisal of the First Mulroney Government's Appointments.' Paper presented to the Annual Meetings of the Canadian Political Science Association and Canadian Law and Society Association

Rutherford, A. 1984. *Prisons and the Process of Justice.* Oxford: Oxford University Press

Ryan, J. 1989. 'The Inspector General of the Canadian Security Intelligence Service.' *Conflict Quarterly* 9: 33–51

Ryan, M., and T. Ward. 1989. *Privatization and the Penal System: The American Experience and the Debate in Britain.* Milton Keynes: Open University Press

Saleilles, R.S.S. 1911. *L'individualisation de la peine: Étude de criminalité sociale.* Paris: Alcan

Salter, L. 1990. 'The Two Contradictions in Public Inquiries,' in P. Pross, I. Christie, and J. Yogis, eds., *Commissions of Inquiry,* pp. 173–95. Toronto: Carswell

Sawatsky, J. 1980. *Men in the Shadows: The RCMP Security Service.* Toronto: Doubleday

Scarman, The Rt. Hon. Lord. 1981. *The Brixton Disorders*. Cmnd. 8427. London: HMSO

– 1983. *The Scarman Report: The Brixton Disorders, 10–12 April 1981*. Harmondsworth: Penguin

Scharf, P., and A. Binder. 1983. *The Badge and the Bullet*. New York: Praeger

Scheppele, K. 1988. *Legal Secrets*. Chicago: University of Chicago Press

Schlenker, B.R. 1982. 'Translating Actions into Attitudes: An Identity-Analytic Approach to the Explanation of Social Conduct,' in L. Berkowitz, ed., *Advances in Experimental Social Psychology*, vol. 15, pp. 193–247

Schlesinger, Jr., A.M. 1974. *The Imperial Presidency*. London: Andre Deutsch

Schroeder, H., M. Driver, and S. Streufert. 1967. *Human Information Processing*. New York: Holt, Rinehart, and Winston

Scott, I.G. 1987. 'The Role of the Attorney General and the Charter of Rights.' *Criminal Law Quarterly* 29: 187–99

Scott, M., and S. Lyman. 1968. 'Accounts.' *American Sociological Review* 33: 46–62

Seaton, J. 1980. 'Politics and Television.' *Economy and Society* 9: 90–107

Semin, G.R., and A.S.R. Manstead. 1983. *The Accountability of Conduct: A Social Psychological Analysis*. London: Academic

Shearing, C.D. 1992a. 'A Constitutive Conception of Regulation.' Paper presented at conference on the Future of Regulatory Enforcement in Australia. Australian Institute of Criminology, Sydney, 3–5 March

– 1992b. 'The Relationship between Public and Private Policing,' in M. Tonry and N. Morris, eds., *Modern Policing*, pp. 399–434. Chicago: University of Chicago Press

– ed. 1981. *Organizational Police Deviance: Its Structure and Control*. Toronto: Butterworths

– and P. Stenning. 1987. *Private Policing*. Beverly Hills: Sage

Sheerman, B. 1991. 'What Labour Wants.' *Policing* 7: 194–203

Shennan, J. 1974. *The Origins of the Modern European State, 1450–1725*. London: Hutchinson

Sherif, M., and H. Cantril. 1947. *The Psychology of Ego-involvements*. New York: Wiley

Sherman, L.W. 1978. *Scandal and Reform: Controlling Police Corruption*. Berkeley: University of California Press

– 1980. 'Causes of Police Behavior: The Current State of Quantitative Research.' *Journal of Research in Crime and Delinquency* 11: 69–100

– 1983. 'Reducing Police Gun Use: Critical Events, Administrative Policy, and Organizational Change,' in M. Punch, ed., *Control in the Police Organization*, pp. 98–123. Cambridge: MIT Press

Sherzer, J. 1987. 'A Diversity of Voices: Men's and Women's Speech in Ethno-graphic Perspective,' in S.U. Philips, S. Steeples, and C. Tanz, eds., *Language, Gender, and Sex in Comparative Perspective*, pp. 95–120. Cambridge: Cambridge University Press

Shetreet, S. 1976. *Judges on Trial*. New York: North-Holland

Shibutani, T. 1966. *Improvised News*. Indianapolis: Bobbs-Merrill

Sibraa, K. 1987. 'Parliamentary Scrutiny of Security and Intelligence Services in Australia.' *Parliamentarian* 68: 120–7

Siebert, J.E. 1974. 'Effects of Decision Importance on Ability to Generate War-ranted Subjective Uncertainty.' *Journal of Personality and Social Psychology* 30: 688–94

Sigal, L. 1973. *Reporters and Officials*. Lexington, Mass.: D.C. Heath

Simmonds, R. 1985. 'Internal Review of the Royal Canadian Mounted Police Investigation of the Hatfield Case.' Ottawa: RCMP

Simon, W.H. 1990. 'Contract versus Politics in Corporate Doctrine,' in D. Kairys, ed., *The Politics of Law: A Progressive Critique*, rev. ed., pp. 387–409. New York: Pantheon

Singer, B. 1986. *Advertising and Society*. Don Mills: Addison-Wesley

Skinner, Q. 1978. *The Foundations of Modern Political Thought*, vol. 1. Cambridge: Cambridge University Press

– 1989. 'The State,' in T. Ball, J. Farr, and R.L. Hanson, eds., *Political Innovation and Conceptual Change*, pp. 90–131. Cambridge: Cambridge University Press

Skolnick, J.H. 1966. *Justice without Trial: Law Enforcement in Democratic Society*. New York: Wiley

– and D.H. Bayley. 1988. *Community Policing: Issues and Practices around the World*. Washington: U.S. Department of Justice

– and J.J. Fyfe. 1993. *Above the Law*. New York: Free Press

– and C. McCoy. 1984. 'Police Accountability and the Media.' *American Bar Foundation Research Journal*, 521–57

Smith, B.L.R. 1971. 'Accountability and Independence in the Contract State,' in B.L.R. Smith and D.C. Hague, eds., *The Dilemma of Accountability in Modern Government: Independence versus Control*, p. 3. London: Macmillan

Smith, D., and J. Gray. 1983. *Police and People in London: The PSI Report*. Aldershot: Gower

Smith, R.S. 1976. *The Occupational Safety and Health Act: Its Goals and Its Achievements*. Washington: American Enterprise Institute for Public Policy Research

– 1979. 'The Impact of OSHA Inspections on Manufacturing Injury Rates.' *Journal of Human Resources* 14: 145–70

– 1982. 'Protecting Workers' Health and Safety,' in R.W. Poole Jr., ed., *Instead of Regulation*, pp. 311–38. Lexington, Mass.: Lexington Books

Snyder, R.C., H.W. Bruck, and B. Sapin, eds. 1962. *Foreign Policy Decision-making.* New York: Free Press

Sopinka, J. 1990. 'Address.' Canadian Institute For the Administration of Justice, 24 August

Sparks, R. 1992. *Television and the Drama of Crime.* Buckingham: Open University Press

– 1994. 'Can Prisons Be Legitimate? Penal Politics, Privatization, and the Timeliness of an Old Ideal,' in R. King and M. Maguire, eds., *Prisons in Context. British Journal of Criminology,* special issue, 34: 14–28

Sparrow, M.K., M.H. Moore, and D.M. Kennedy. 1990. *Beyond 911.* New York: Basic Books

Spelman, W., and D.K. Brown. 1981. *Calling the Police: Citizen Reporting of Serious Crime.* Washington: Police Executive Research Forum

Spencer, S. 1985. *Called to Account: The Case for Police Accountability in England and Wales.* London: National Council on Civil Liberties

Spranca, M., E. Minsk, and J. Baron. 1991. 'Omission and Commission in Judgment and Choice.' *Journal of Experimental Social Psychology* 27: 76–105

Stalans, L.J. 1993. 'Citizens' Crime Stereotypes, Biased Recall, and Punishment Preferences in Abstract Cases.' *Law and Human Behaviour* 17: 451–70

Staw, B.M. 1976. 'Knee-deep in the Big Muddy: A Study of Escalating Commitment to a Chosen Course of Action.' *Organizational Behavior and Human Performance* 16: 27–44

– 1980. 'Rationality and Justification in Organizational Life,' in B.M. Staw and L. Cummings, eds., *Research in Organizational Behavior,* vol. 2. Greenwich: JAI Press

Stellman, J., and S. Daum. 1973. *Work Is Dangerous to Your Health.* New York: Vintage

Stenning, P.C. 1971. 'Observations on the Supreme Court's Decision in R v Osborn.' *Criminal Law Quarterly* 13: 164–83

– 1981a. *The Legal Status of the Police.* Ottawa: Law Reform Commission of Canada

– 1981b. *Police Commissions and Boards in Canada.* Toronto: University of Toronto, Centre of Criminology

– 1981c. 'The Role of Police Boards and Commissions as Institutions of Municipal Police Governance,' in C. Shearing, ed., *Organizational Police Deviance,* pp. 161–208. Toronto: Butterworths

– 1983. 'Trusting the Chief: Legal Aspects of the Status and Political Accountability of the Police in Canada.' Doctor of Juridical Science Thesis, Faculty of Law, University of Toronto

– 1986. *Appearing for the Crown.* Cowansville: Brown Legal Publications

– C.D. Shearing, S.M. Addario, and M.G. Condon. 1990. 'Controlling Interests:

Two Conceptions of Order in Regulating a Financial Market,' in M.L. Friedland, ed., *Securing Compliance*, pp. 88–119. Toronto: University of Toronto Press

Stern, V. 1987. *Bricks of Shame: Britain's Prisons*. Harmondsworth: Penguin

Stewart, R. 1991. 'Opening Statement by Mr R.L. Stewart, Correctional Investigator, Canada, to the Standing Committee on Justice and the Solicitor General, *Bill C-36*,' 2 December. Ottawa: Office of the Correctional Investigator

Stigler, G.J. 1952. *The Theory of Price*, rev. ed. New York: Macmillan

– 1971. 'The Theory of Economic Regulation.' *Bell Journal of Economics and Managerial Science* 2

– 1972. 'The Law and Economics of Public Policy: A Plea to the Scholars.' *Journal of Legal Studies*, 1–12

– 1988. 'The Theory of Economic Regulation,' in G. Stigler, ed., *Chicago Studies in Political Economy*, pp. 209–33. Chicago: University of Chicago Press

Strayer, Barry L. 1983. *The Canadian Constitution and the Courts*, 2nd ed. Toronto: Butterworths

Street, H. 1971. 'Canada's Parole System: A Presentation to the Sub-Committee of the Standing Senate Committee on Legal and Constitutional Affairs.' Unpublished ms.

Stuart, D. 1991. *Charter Justice in Canadian Criminal Law*. Toronto: Carswell

Sunstein, C.R. 1990. *After the Rights Revolution*. Cambridge: Harvard University Press

Sutherland, E.H. 1945. 'Is White-Collar Crime Crime?' *American Sociological Review* 10: 132–9

Szasz, A. 1984. 'Industrial Resistance to Occupational Safety and Health Legislation, 1971–1981.' *Social Problems* 32: 103–16

– 1986. 'The Reversal of Federal Policy towards Worker Safety and Health: A Critical Examination of Alternative Explanations.' *Science and Society* 50: 25–51

Taylor, C. 1979. *Hegel and Modern Society*. Cambridge: Cambridge University Press

– 1989. 'Cross-Purposes: The Liberal–Communitarian Debate,' in N.J. Rosenblum, ed., *Liberalism and the Moral Life*, pp. 159–82. Cambridge: Harvard University Press

Taylor, I. 1986. 'Martyrdom and Surveillance: Ideological and Social Problems of Police in Canada in the 1980s.' *Crime and Justice* 26: 60–74

Taylor, The Rt. Hon. Lord. 1993. 'The Judiciary in the Nineties.' *Commonwealth Law Bulletin* 19: 323–30

Teger, A.I., M. Cary, A. Katcher, and J. Hillis. 1980. *Too Much Invested to Quit*. New York: Pergamon

Terrill, R. 1991. 'Civilian Oversight of the Police Complaints Process,' in A. Goldsmith, ed., *Complaints against the Police: The Trend to External Review*, pp. 291–322. Melbourne: Oxford University Press

Tetlock, P.E. 1983a. 'Accountability and the Complexity of Thought.' *Journal of Personality and Social Psychology* 45: 74–83

– 1983b. 'Accountability and the Perseverance of First Impressions.' *Social Psychology Quarterly* 46: 285–92

– 1985. 'Accountability: A Social Check on the Fundamental Attribution Error.' *Social Psychology Quarterly* 48: 227–36

– and R. Boettger. 1989. 'Accountability: A Social Magnifier of the Dilution Effect.' *Journal of Personality and Social Psychology: Attitudes and Social Cognition* 57: 388–98

– and R. Boettger. 1991. 'Accountability Amplifies the Status Quo Effect When Changes Create Victims.' Unpublished ms.

– and J. Kim. 1987. 'Accountability and Overconfidence in a Personality Prediction Task.' *Journal of Personality and Social Psychology: Attitudes and Social Cognition* 52: 700–9

– and A. Levi. 1982. 'Attribution Bias: On the Inconclusiveness of the Cognition–Motivation Debate.' *Journal of Experimental Social Psychology* 18: 68–88

– and A.S.R. Manstead. 1985. 'Impression Management versus Intrapsychic Explanations in Social Psychology: A Useful Dichotomy?' *Psychological Review* 92: 58–79

– L. Skitka, and R. Boettger. 1989. 'Social and Cognitive Strategies of Coping with Accountability: Conformity, Complexity, and Bolstering.' *Journal of Personality and Social Psychology: Interpersonal Relations and Group Dynamics* 57: 632–41

Thomas, J.E. 1980. 'Managing the Prison Service,' in R. King and R. Morgan, eds., *The Future of the Prison System*, pp. 134–58. Aldershot: Gower

– and R. Pooley. 1980. *The Exploding Prison*. London: Junction

Thompson, J.A. 1988/89. 'A Board Does Not a Bench Make: Denying Quasi-Judicial Immunity to Parole Board Members in Section 1983 Damages Actions.' *Michigan Law Review* 87: 241–75

Thompson, R.S. 1986. 'Judicial Independence, Judicial Accountability, Judicial Elections, and the California Supreme Court: Defining the Terms of Debate.' *South California Law Review* 59: 809–72

Tien, J.M., J. Simon, and R. Larson. 1978. *An Alternative Approach in Police Patrol: The Wilmington Split-Force Experiment*. Washington: U.S. Government Printing Office

Tollefson, C. 1991. 'Ideologies Clashing: Corporations, Criminal Law, and the Regulatory Offence.' *Osgoode Hall Law Journal* 29: 705–45

Tombs, S. 1989. 'Dumb Management or Deviant Workplaces? Understanding and Preventing Accidents in the Chemical Industry.' *Industrial Crisis Quarterly*

Toronto Star. 1983. 'Wrongly Jailed, He Needs $50,000 to Fight City Hall.' 29 December, p. A7
– 1986a. 'How Donald Marshall's Case Unfolded.' 8 June, p. H1
– 1986b. 'The Tangled Trial of Donald Marshall.' 9 June, p. A8
– 1989. 'Killer Looking for New Trial Defies Manitoba Inquiry.' 11 August, p. A3
– 1992. 'Ailing Judge Called Victim of Row over Date-Rape Case.' 4 January, p. A14
Toronto Stock Exchange. 1973. *Submission to the OSC on Bill 154*. Toronto: TSE
– 1974. *Submission to the OSC on Bill 75*. Toronto: TSE
Trachtenberg, A. 1982. *The Incorporation of America: Culture and Society in the Gilded Age*. New York: Hill and Wang
Train, C. 1985. 'Management Accountability in the Prison Service,' in M. Maguire, J. Vagg, and R. Morgan, eds., *Accountability and Prisons: Opening Up a Closed World*, pp. 177–86. London: Tavistock
Trebilcock, M., D. Hartle, J. Prichard, and D. Dewees. 1982. *Choice of Governing Instrument*. Ottawa: Canada Economic Council
Tremblay, P., and C. Rochon. 1991. 'Police Organizations and Their Use of Knowledge: A Grounded Research Agenda.' *Policing and Society* 1: 269–83
Tuchman, G. 1978. *Making News*. New York: Free Press
Tucker, E. 1992. 'Health and Safety Regulation: Dangerous Liaisons.' *Studies in Political Economy*, 37: 95–127
Tumber, H. 1982. *Television and the Riots*. London: Broadcasting Research Unit, British Film Institute
Turpin, C. 1989. 'Ministerial Responsibility: Myth or Reality,' in J. Jowell and D. Oliver, eds., *The Changing Constitution*, 2nd ed., pp. 53–85. Oxford: Clarendon
– 1990. *British Government and the Constitution*, 2nd ed. London: Weidenfeld and Nicolson
Tushnet, M. 1993.'Idols of the Right: The Law-and-Economics Movement.' *Dissent* 40: 475–82
Tversky, A., and D. Kahneman. 1982. 'Judgments of and by Representatives,' in D. Kahneman, P. Slovic, and A. Tversky, eds., *Judgment under Uncertainty: Heuristics and Biases*, pp. 84–100. New York: Cambridge University Press
Uglow, S. 1988. *Policing Liberal Society*. Oxford: Oxford University Press
United Kingdom, Audit Commission. 1990. *Footing the Bill: Financing Provincial Police Forces*. London: HMSO
– Audit Commission. 1991. *Reviewing the Organisation of Provincial Police Forces*. London: HMSO
– Committee of Inquiry into the United Kingdom Prison Services. 1979. (Chairman, May) *Report*. Cm 7673. London: HMSO

– Committee of Inquiry on the Prison Disciplinary System. 1985. (Chairman, D. Prior) *Report*. London: HMSO
– Committee to Review the Parole System in England and Wales. 1988. (Chairman, Carlisle) *The Parole System in England and Wales*. Cm 532. London: HMSO
– Conservative Party. 1979. *Manifesto*. London: Conservative Party
– Her Majesty's Chief Inspector of Prisons. 1982. *Annual Report 1981*. Cm 8532. London: HMSO
– 1984a. *Suicides in Prison*. London: Home Office
– 1984b. *Prison Categorisation Procedures*. London: Home Office
– 1987a. *The Disturbances in Prison Service Establishments in England between 29 April – 2nd May 1986*. HC46. London: HMSO
– 1987b. *A Review of Prisoners' Complaints*. London: Home Office
– 1989. *Prison Sanitation*. London: Home Office
– 1990a. *HM Prison Brixton*. London: Home Office
– 1990b. *HM Prison Leeds*. London: Home Office
– 1990c. *Suicide and Self-harm in Prison Department Establishments in England and Wales*. Cm 1383. London: HMSO
– 1991a. *January 1990 – March 1991*. HC54. London: HMSO
– 1991b. *Inquiry into the Escape of Two Category A Prisoners from HM Prison Brixton on 7 July 1991*. London: HMSO
– 1992. Report of, April 1991 – March 1992. London: HMSO
– 1993a. *HM Prison The Wolds*. London: Home Office
– 1993b. *Doing Time or Using Time*. London: HMSO
– 1993c. *Report of April 1992 – March 1993*. London: HMSO
United Kingdom, Home Office. 1979. *Inquiry into the United Kingdom Prison Services: Evidence by the Home Office, the Scottish Home and Health Department, and the Northern Ireland Office* (vols. 1 and 2) *Evidence by HM Treasury, the Civil Service Department, and the Central Policy Review Staff*, vol. 3. London: HMSO
– 1984. *Managing the Long-Term Prison System: The Report of the Control Review Committee*. London: HMSO
– 1987. *Special Units for Long-Term Prisoners: Regimes, Management, and Research*. London: HMSO
– 1988. *Private Sector Involvement in the Remand System*. Cm 434. London: HMSO
– 1989. *An Improved System of Grievance Procedures for Prisoners' Complaints and Requests: Report of a Working Group*. London: Home Office
– 1990a. *Crime, Justice, and Protecting the Public*. Cm 965. London: HMSO
– 1990b. *The Sentence of the Court: A Handbook for Courts on the Treatment of Offenders*. London: HMSO
– 1990c. *Prison Statistics, England and Wales 1989*. Cm 1221. London: HMSO

- 1990d. *Report on the Work of the Prison Service, April 1989 – March 1990.* Cm 1302. London: HMSO
- 1990e. *Statistics of Offences against Prison Discipline and Punishments, England and Wales 1989.* Cm 1236. London: HMSO
- 1991a. *Custody Care and Justice: The Way Ahead for the Prison Service in England and Wales.* Cm 1647. London: HMSO
- 1991b. *A Digest of Information on the Criminal Justice System.* London: HMSO
- 1991c. *Tender Documents for the Operating Contract of Wolds Remand Prison, Schedule 2 and 3.* London: Prison Service, Home Office
- 1992. *Tender Documents for the Operating Contract of HM Prison Blakenhurst, Schedule 2 and 3a.* London: Prison Service, Home Office
- 1993. *Police Reform: A Police Service for the Twenty-First Century.* (White Paper) Cm 2281. London: HMSO
United Kingdom, House of Commons, Education, Science, and Arts Committee. 1983. *Fifth Report of the Education, Science, and Arts Committee: Prison Education.* London: HMSO
- Expenditure Committee. 1978. 15th Report, *The Reduction of Pressure on the Prison System.* London: HMSO
- Expenditure Committee. 1980. *The Reduction of Pressure on the Prison System: Observations from the Home Affairs Department on the Fifteenth Report.* Cm 7948. London: HMSO
- Home Affairs Committee. 1984. *First Report, Remands in Custody, 1983–4.* HC 252-I. London: HMSO
- Home Affairs Committee. 1987a. *Third Report, State and Use of Prisons, 1986–87.* HC 35. London: HMSO
- Home Affairs Committee. 1987b. *Fourth Report, Contract Provision of Prisons, 1986–7.* HC 291. London: HMSO
- Home Affairs Committee. 1989. *Report on Higher Police Training and the Police Staff College.* London: HMSO
- Social Services Committee. 1986. 3rd Report, *Prison Medical Service, 1985–6.* 72-I, London: HMSO
United Kingdom, Inquiry into the Cause and Circumstances of the Events at HM Prison Hull, 31 August to 3 September 1976. 1977. (Chairman, Lord Fowler) *Report.* London: HMSO
- Inquiry into Police Responsibilities and Rewards (Chairman, Sir Patrick Sheehy). 1993. *Report.* London: HMSO
- Inquiry into Prison Disturbances, April 1990. 1991. *Prison Disturbances, April 1990* (Chairman, Parts I and II, Rt Hon Lord Justice Woolf; with His Honour Judge Stephen Tumim, Part II. Cm 1456. London: HMSO

- Prime Minister. 1984. *Progress in Financial Management in Government Departments*. Cm 9297. London: HMSO
- Prison Service. 1989. *Report of the Working Party on Prisoner Complaints*. London: Prison Department
- 1990. *Evidence to Lord Justice Woolf's Inquiry into Prison Disturbances: Evidence for Phase 2*. London: Prison Department
- 1991. *Model Regime for Local Prisons and Remand Centres*. London: Prison Service
- 1992. *A Code of Standards for the Prison Service: A Discussion Document   Produced by the Code of Standards Steering Group*. London: Prison Service
- 1993a. *Business Plan, 1993–94*. London: Prison Service
- 1993b. *Framework Document*. London: Prison Service

United Kingdom, Royal Commission on Criminal Justice. 1993. (Chairman, Lord Runciman) *Report*. Cm 2263. London: HMSO
- Royal Commission on Criminal Procedure. 1981. (Chairman, Sir Cyril Phillips) *Report*. Cm 8092. London: HMSO

United Kingdom, Royal Commission on the Police. 1962. *Final Report*. Cm 1728. London: HMSO

United States, Department of Justice. 1990. *Sourcebook of Criminal Statistics, 1990*. Washington: U.S. Government Printing Office
- President's Commission on Law Enforcement and the Administration of Justice. 1967. *The Challenge of Crime in a Free Society*. Washington: U.S. Government Printing Office
- Sentencing Commission. 1988. *Guidelines Manual*. Washington: United States Sentencing Commission

University of New Brunswick. 1991. 'Forum on the Canadian Judicial Council's Treatment of the Judges in the Donald Marshall, Jr., Case.' *University of New Brunswick Law Journal* 40: 208–98

University of Puget Sound Law Review. 1991/2. 'Predators and Politics: A Symposium on Washington's Sexually Violent Predators Statute.' 15: 507–877

Vantour, J., ed. 1991. *Our Story: Organizational Renewal in Federal Corrections*. Ottawa: Correctional Services Canada

Van Zyl Smit, D., and F. Dunkel, eds. 1991. *Imprisonment Today and Tomorrow: International Perspectives on Prisoners' Rights and Prison Conditions*. Deventer: Kluwer

Veblen, T. 1889. *The Theory of the Leisure Class*. New York: Macmillan

Viscusi, W.K. 1979. *Employment Hazards: An Investigation of Market Performance*. Cambridge: Harvard University Press
- 1983. *Risk by Choice: Regulating Health and Safety in the Workplace*. Cambridge: Harvard University Press

Vollmer, August. 1936. *The Police and Modern Society.* Montclair, NJ: Patterson Smith, 1972 reprint

von Hirsch, A. 1976. *Doing Justice: The Choice of Punishments: Report of the Committee for the Study of Incarceration.* New York: Hill and Wang

– 1993. *Censure and Sanctions.* Oxford: Clarendon

Waddington, P., and Q. Braddock. 1991. '"Guardians" or "Bullies"?: Perceptions of the Police amongst Adolescent Black, White, and Asian Boys.' *Policing and Society* 2: 31–45

Wagner-Pacifici, R. 1986. *The Moro Morality Play: Terrorism as Social Drama.* Chicago: University of Chicago Press

Walker, C. 1995. 'Worker and State Enforcement of Health, Safety, and Environmental Laws,' in F. Pearce and L. Snider, eds., *Corporate Crime: Contemporary Debates.* Toronto: University of Toronto Press

Walker, S. 1977. *A Critical History of Police Reform.* Lexington, Mass.: D.C. Heath

– 1989. *Sense and Nonsense about Crime*, 2nd ed. Pacific Grove, Calif.: Brooks/Cole

Walzer, M. 1983. *Spheres of Justice: A Defence of Pluralism and Equality.* New York: Basic Books

Waring, M. 1988. *If Women Counted: A New Feminist Perspective.* New York: Harper Collins

Weatheritt, M. 1986. *Innovations in Policing.* London: Croom Helm

Weaver, P. 1978. 'Regulation, Social Policy, and Class Conflict,' in C. Argyris and D.P. Jacobs, eds., *Regulating Business: The Search for an Optimum*, pp. 193–216. San Francisco: Institute for Contemporary Studies

Webb, S., and B. Webb. 1922. *English Prisons under Local Government.* London: Longmans Green

Weber, M. 1964. *From Max Weber* (H. Gerth and C.W. Mills, eds.). New York: Oxford University Press

Weick, K.E. 1979. 'Cognitive Processes in Organizations,' in B.M. Staw, ed., *Research in Organizational Behavior*, vol. 1. Greenwich: JAI Press

Weidenbaum, M., and R. De Fina. 1978. *The Costs of Federal Regulation of Economic Activity.* Reprint No. 88. Washington: American Enterprise Institute of Public Policy

Weinstein, J.B. 1993. 'Memorandum,' reprinted in full in the *Federal Sentencing Reporter* 5: 298–9

Weller, G. 1988. 'Accountability in Canadian Intelligence Services.' *International Journal of Intelligence and Counter Intelligence* 2: 415–41

Wells, C. 1991. 'Inquests, Inquiries, and Indictments: The Official Reception of Death by Disaster.' *Legal Studies* 11: 71–84

Western Australia. Royal Commission into Commercial Activities of Government and Other Matters. 1992. *Report*. Perth: Western Australia Government Printer

Wheeler, G. 1986. 'Reporting Crime: The News Release as Textual Mediator of Police/Media Relations.' MA Dissertation, Centre of Criminology, University of Toronto

Whig-Standard (Kingston, Ont.) (Michael Woloschuk). 1991. 'It's "Open Season" for Campus Rape, Crown Claims.' 21 December, pp. 1, 8

– 1992a. 'Senior Crown Lawyer Won't Fall Discipline.' 24 June

– 1992b. 'Support for Douglas.' 25 January

Whitaker, R. 1991. 'The Politics of Security Intelligence Policy-making in Canada: I, 1970–84.' *Intelligence and National Security* 6: 649–68

– 1992. 'The Politics of Security Intelligence Policy-Making in Canada: II, 1984–91.' *Intelligence and National Security* 7: 53–76

White, S. 1991. *Political Theory and Postmodernism*. Cambridge: Cambridge University Press

Wicklund, R.A., and J.W. Brehm. 1976. *Perspective on Cognitive Dissonance*. Hillsdale, NJ: Erlbaum

Wildsmith, B. 1991. 'Getting at Racism: The Marshall Inquiry.' *Saskatchewan Law Review* 55: 97–126

Wilkins, Jr., Judge W.W. 1990. 'Presentation to the House Subcommittee on Criminal Justice,' quoted in the *Federal Sentencing Reporter* 2: 214

Williams, D. 1986. *Judicial Review of Administrative Actions in the 1980's*. London: Oxford University Press

Williams, R. 1976. *Keywords: A Vocabulary of Culture and Society*. London: Fontana

– 1989. *Raymond Williams on Television*. Toronto: Between the Lines

Williamson, J.P. 1966. *Securities Regulation in Canada Supplement*. Ottawa: Government of Canada

Williamson, O. 1975. *Markets and Hierarchies*. New York: Free Press

– 1985. *The Economic Institutions of Capitalism*. New York: Free Press

Wilson, G.K. 1985. *The Politics of Safety and Health: Occupational Safety and Health in the United States and Britain*. Oxford: Clarendon

Wilson, J.Q. 1969. *Varieties of Police Behavior*. Cambridge: Harvard University Press

– ed. 1980. *The Politics of Regulation*. New York: Basic Books

Wilson, L. 1979. 'The Doctrine of Willful Blindness.' *University of New Brunswick Law Review* 28

Woodiwiss, A. 1991. *Rights v Conspiracy: A Sociological Essay on the History of Labour Law in the United States*. New York: Berg

'Woolf Report' – see United Kingdom, Inquiry into Prison Disturbances, April 1990, 1991

Worsley, P. 1984. *The Three Worlds: Culture and World Development*. London: Weidenfeld and Nicolson

Young, A. 1988. *The Role of an Appellate Court in Developing Sentencing Guidelines*. Research reports prepared for the Canadian Sentencing Commission. Ottawa: Department of Justice

Zajonc, R.B. 1960. 'The Process of Cognitive Tuning in Communications.' *Journal of Abnormal and Social Psychology* 61: 159–67

Zander, M. 1990. *The Police and Criminal Evidence Act 1984*, 2nd ed. London: Sweet and Maxwell

Zeitlin, M. 1989. *The Large Corporation and Contemporary Classes*. New Brunswick: Rutgers University Press

Zellick, G. 1978. 'The Case for Prisoners' Rights,' in J.C. Freeman, ed., *Prisons Past and Future*, pp. 105–21. London: Heinemann

– 1981. 'The Prison Rules and the Courts.' [1981] *Criminal Law Review* 602–16

Zetterberg, H.L. 1957. 'Compliant Actions.' *Acta Sociologica* 2: 188–92

Zuber, The Hon. T.G. 1987. *Report of the Ontario Courts Inquiry*. Toronto: Queen's Printer

Zukier, H. 1982. 'The Dilution Effect: The Role of the Correlation and the Dispersion of Predictor Variables in the Use of Nondiagnostic Information.' *Journal of Personality and Social Psychology* 43: 1163–74

Zussman, D., and J. Jabes. 1989. *The Vertical Solitude: Managing in the Public Sector*. Halifax: Institute for Research on Public Policy